MACMILLAN HISTORY OF LITERATURE
General Editor: A. NORMAN JEFFARES

MACMILLAN HISTORY OF LITERATURE

General Editor: A. Norman Jeffares

Published

OLD ENGLISH LITERATURE
Michael Alexander

ENGLISH GOTHIC LITERATURE
Derek Brewer

SIXTEENTH-CENTURY ENGLISH LITERATURE
Murray Roston

SEVENTEENTH-CENTURY ENGLISH LITERATURE
Bruce King

EIGHTEENTH-CENTURY ENGLISH LITERATURE
Maximillian Novak

NINETEENTH-CENTURY ENGLISH LITERATURE
Margaret Stonyk

TWENTIETH-CENTURY ENGLISH LITERATURE
Harry Blamires

ANGLO-IRISH LITERATURE
A. Norman Jeffares

THE LITERATURE OF THE UNITED STATES
Marshall Walker

THE LITERATURE OF SCOTLAND
Roderick Watson

Forthcoming

A HISTORY OF AUSTRALIAN LITERATURE
Kenneth Goodwin

A HISTORY OF LITERATURE IN THE IRISH
LANGUAGE
Declan Kiberd

COMMONWEALTH LITERATURE
Alastair Niven

MACMILLAN HISTORY OF LITERATURE

THE LITERATURE OF SCOTLAND

Roderick Watson

MACMILLAN

To my mother and father and Olive Mackie

First published 1984

Published by
Higher and Further Education Division
MACMILLAN PUBLISHERS LTD
Houndmills, Basingstoke, Hampshire RG21 2XS
and London
Companies and representatives
throughout the world

Typeset by
Wessex Typesetters Ltd
Frome, Somerset

Printed in Great Britain by
Camelot Press Ltd, Southampton

British Library Cataloguing in Publication Data

Watson, Roderick
The literature of Scotland. – (Macmillan history of literature)
1. English literature – Scottish authors – History and
criticism   2. Scottish literature – History and criticism
I. Title
820.9'9411   PR8511

ISBN 0–333–26923–3
ISBN 0–333–26924–1 Pbk

Contents

List of plates

Editor's preface

THE study of literature requires knowledge of contexts as well as of texts. What kind of person wrote the poem, the play, the novel, the essay? What forces acted upon them as they wrote? What was the historical, the political, the philosophical, the economic, the cultural background? Was the writer accepting or rejecting the literary conventions of the time, or developing them, or creating entirely new kinds of literary expression? Are there interactions between literature and the art, music or architecture of its period? Was the writer affected by contemporaries or isolated?

Such questions stress the need for students to go beyond the reading of set texts, to extend their knowledge by developing a sense of chronology, of action and reaction, and of the varying relationships between writers and society.

Histories of literature can encourage students to make comparisons, can aid in understanding the purposes of individual authors and in assessing the totality of their achievements. Their development can be better understood and appreciated with some knowledge of the background of their time. And histories of literature, apart from their valuable function as reference books, can demonstrate the great wealth of writing in English that there is to be enjoyed. They can guide the reader who wishes to explore it more fully and to gain in the process deeper insights into the rich diversity not only of literature but of human life itself.

A. NORMAN JEFFARES

Preface

IN my researches for this book I owe a debt of gratitude to my colleagues at Stirling University, especially Felicity Riddy and Professor A. N. Jeffares; also Douglas Mack and the Stirling University Library, and Sarah Mahaffy of Macmillan. They were all most patient and helpful. Since many older translations of Gaelic poems adopted a rather tired poetic diction, I have quoted from the most contemporary available English versions whenever possible. In this respect I am indebted to translations made by Iain Crichton Smith, Ian Grimble, and Professor Derick Thomson in his book *An Introduction to Gaelic Poetry* (London: Gollancz, 1974). Finally, my thanks go to my wife Celia for her unfailing support during this project.

Acknowledgements

The author and publishers wish to thank the following who have kindly given permission for the use of copyright material:

Canongate Publishing Ltd, for the poems 'I Do Not See . . .', 'Calvary' and the extract from 'The Cry of Europe' from *Spring Tide and Neap Tide: Selected Poems 1932–72* by Sorley Maclean.

The Executors of the Hugh MacDiarmid Estate, for the poem 'The Eemis Stane'.

Ian Hamilton Finlay, for his poem 'The Cloud's Anchor'.

Macdonald Publishers, for the extract from 'Queer Ongauns' from Robert Garioch's *Collected Poems*; for the extracts from 'Old Woman' and 'What is Wrong' by Iain Crichton Smith from *Selected Poems 1955–1980*, and for the extracts from 'Steel', 'Between Summer and Autumn' and 'Coffins' by Derick Thomson from *Creachadh na Clàrsaich/Plundering the Harp: Collected Poems, 1940–1980*.

The Trustees of the National Library of Scotland, for the extract from 'Song' by William Soutar.

Scotland

Introduction: renewals and revivals

How we see literature, or a continuing cultural tradition, or even our own identity, depends upon an act of perception and hence of selection on our part. Different periods will make different selections from the available evidence according to the spirit of the times. Indeed, the music, literature and arts of the past are truly alive only because our understanding of them *has* to change in this way – from generation to generation, or even during the course of a single life. Literary and cultural history is especially fluid, because persuasive theories, let us say about what 'Scottishness' is, begin to influence how people think of themselves and hence how writers express themselves. Certainly, Scotland has expended enough effort over the centuries defending and defining a sense of national identity which has somehow refused to succumb to political or cultural pressures from her larger and more powerful neighbour to the south. The process started at least as long ago as the wars of independence in the early fourteenth century, and Barbour's *Bruce* and Blind Harry's *Wallace* did much to define the 'idea' of Scotland and to establish an independent-minded and egalitarian outlook as a characteristic part of the Scottish spirit. The fruits of this political identity, its close links with Europe, and the flowering of Scots came to full season in the poetry of Henryson, Dunbar, Douglas and Lindsay. A unique national identity seemed to be assured, not least because it was largely taken for granted.

The next most impressive period in Scottish cultural history was the 'Scottish Enlightenment' of the eighteenth and early nineteenth centuries. It too came from native stock, going back to the best of the Scots Presbyterian intellectual tradition, which had always valued widely available academic teaching and hence the primacy of philosophy, theory and analysis at the heart of education, law and religion. The Enlightenment produced figures of international standing such as David Hume and Adam Smith, and a wealth of talent in engineering and the physical sciences, very often among men who rose from humble backgrounds. Clearly Scotland was flourishing, and yet, paradoxically, the question of national identity arose again, conjured up by the Union of 1707, the economic strength of England and the tendency of educated Scots to look to the metropolitan assumptions and opportunities of London. So the eighteenth century saw a revival of literature in Scots, while Gaelic poetry also came to a new vernacular strength. Antiquarians republished the verse of the great Makars, and they collected and printed Scots songs and ballads from the folk tradition, as a different 'Doric' inheritance just as valuable as the intellectualism of an 'Athenian' Enlightenment. The voice of the common people was heard and in part redefined by the individual genius of Fergusson, Burns, Scott, Rob Donn and Duncan Bàn Macintyre. Yet this mode was liable to decay and by the end of the century its more self-conscious practitioners had slipped into Victorian sentimentality, rural parochialism and tartan stereotypes.

So the 'Scottish Renaissance' happened again in the 1920s, as a political and critical effort to re-establish the native heritage in a country which too many politicians, university professors and popular newspapers were coming to regard as merely 'North Britain'. There was a growing feeling, too, that wider economic forces and the mass media were actually eroding everything that was most distinctive and hence of most value in *all* minority cultures in the modern world. Thus, it was that the twentieth-century Scottish Renaissance contained a new factor, for it realised that the country's Gaelic inheritance was even more seriously in decline than the Scots, and, indeed, it had been neglected and undervalued by the Lowland Scots themselves. By the 1960s, hundreds of young men and women were learning Gaelic and turning out to hear Gaelic poets with all the enthusiasm once shown for Fergusson and Burns and the renewal of the Lowland vernacular over a hundred years before.

As always, this renaissance would have been stillborn

without the talents of great writers such as MacDiarmid and Maclean, Grassic Gibbon and Gunn, but modern literary histories and academics have played a small part too. T. F. Henderson showed the way with his *Scottish Vernacular Literature* (1898), just as the Revd Nigel Macneill had dealt with Gaelic in *The Literature of the Highlanders* (1892) followed by the Revd Magnus Maclean with *The Literature of the Highlands* in 1903, updated in the 1920s. J. H. Millar ignored Gaelic but his exhaustive *Literary History of Scotland* (1903) is still a *magnum opus* on the subject, if very much a product of its time. More recently, in 1977, Maurice Lindsay's *History of Scottish Literature* has taken a similarly all-inclusive approach from a modern point of view. By comparison with Millar's book, Gregory Smith's *Scottish Literature: Character and Influence* (1919), was briefer and more influential. This critical thesis tried to define what might be called a national psychology or at least national habits of expression, as they had appeared in Scottish literature over the centuries. Hugh MacDiarmid was especially impressed and he incorporated many of these ideas in his own poetry and used them as propaganda against the English cultural establishment. Following Gregory Smith, he proposed that the Scottish sensibility was characteristically extreme, containing a combination of opposite tendencies – a 'Caledonian antisyzygy' – which manifests itself in a delight in domestic realism and the accumulation of many small details on the one hand, and a love of excess and wild and uncontrolled flights of fancy on the other. These were 'the polar twins of the Scottish muse', and MacDiarmid welcomed them as allies against the Victorian conception of the Scotsman as a dull, canny, parsimonious peasant. By 1936, Edwin Muir's *Scott and Scotland* was suggesting that the 'Caledonian antisyzygy' was exactly what was *wrong* with the national psyche, for it would swing frantically from one extreme to the other without ever reaching rest or resolution. For better or for worse, Smith's new diagnosis of 'Scottishness' had entered the critical vocabulary and the creative resources of the nation.

The natural inheritor of Gregory Smith's thesis was Kurt Wittig, a German scholar whose work *The Scottish Tradition in Literature* (1958) pursues still further what he takes to be the most unique and persistent features to be found in writing from Scotland. Our contemporary understanding of the Scottish tradition owes much to this and two further books, both from 1961. George Elder Davie's *The Democratic Intellect* stresses the philosophical and egalitarian ideals of traditional Scottish education, and David Craig's *Scottish Literature and the Scottish People 1680–1830* makes a vigorous analysis of the social conditions and assumptions which influenced Scottish writers and readers during a crucial period of their history. David Daiches has also explored the special contradictions of eighteenth-century Scotland in his study *The Paradox of Scottish Culture* (1964). On the Gaelic front most recently, Derick Thomson has offered an invaluable *Introduction to Gaelic Poetry* (1974).

The present volume is not intended to present a selective thesis in the vein of Wittig, Davie, Craig or Daiches; nor can it lay claim to the comprehensiveness of Millar, Lindsay and Thomson. But perhaps there is still a need, as far as the general reader is concerned, for a path somewhere between these two approaches – a straightforward account of the lives, times and major works of Scotland's writers. The brief historical summaries at the start of each chapter have been chosen to reflect those aspects of Scottish history which feature most frequently, or contentiously, in Scottish literature. Whenever appropriate, I have tried to recognise the presence of factors such as the 'Caledonian antisyzygy', or the democratic intellect, or Craig's 'reductive idiom' in the Scottish heritage, without proposing these as necessary, or exclusive proofs of Scottishness. But there are at least two other major contributions to Scottish culture which have only occasionally received a proper recognition – although there are signs that this is changing at last. First, I would point to the *co-presence* of the Gaelic tradition and the mutual interactions between Highland and Lowland society and their conceptions and misconceptions of each other. There are as yet few major scholarly studies in this field. Secondly, it seems that the best of what might be called the Presbyterian intellectual inheritance in Scotland has been undeservedly obscured or denied, because the popular imagination has been so easily distracted (and understandably repelled) by the worst excesses of Calvinism. Thus, many Scots will tell enquiring visitors that the Reformation was the worst thing to happen in Scotland and that John Knox cast a permanent shadow on the Scottish face. This is a misleading myth because it hides the truth about Scots from themselves – for better as well as for worse; and it is just as sentimental in the end as that other mythical Scotland where the wicked English are perpetually chasing Flora MacDonald and Bonnie Prince Charlie across the heather. Yet literature and history make lively and unscholarly bedfellows and some of Scotland's most enduring myths were created by her greatest writers – which brings us back again to the questions of how an author chooses his subject, and why he chooses to see it in a certain light. I hope that this book will help to explain some of these choices and how they came together to make the literature of Scotland.

1

The beginnings of Scotland: two cultures

SCOTLAND is a small place – even today her population is no more than that of Greater London – and she has been part of the United Kingdom for longer than North America has been a nation. But Scotland is a distinctively different country, with a culture, a church, a tradition in education and a legal system of her own. Few visitors can have left the place without being told this and having met a prickly sense of difference in the Scottish people. The national plant is a thistle, after all, whose motto, *Nemo me impune lacessit*, is translated as 'No one touches me with impunity', or, more vigorously, 'Wha daur meddle wi me?' The self-conscious assertion in these words reminds us that, as a small and often embattled country, Scotland has been much exercised over the centuries to protect a sense of identity, and this sense has regularly been stimulated or reflected or redefined and argued about in her literature. The thistle is a harsh talisman, and if it sometimes symbolises the libertarian Scottish ideal (as it does for the modern poet Hugh MacDiarmid), it can also look like a skeleton in an endless history of internal dispute and failure. MacDiarmid is not the first Scottish writer to have felt himself impaled on the national plant.

Many elements go to influence the history and the culture of a people; in Scotland perhaps the single most significant factor has been the geography of the land itself. Scotland is divided by major mountain chains and chopped into odd elbow-shapes by an irregular coastline. Thus isolated areas such as Moray to the north of the Grampians, or Fife between the rivers Tay and Forth, or Dumfries and Galloway between Ayr and the Solway Firth, not to mention the Western Isles, were almost independent little kingdoms of their own for many centuries. The mountains divide the country's resources even more radically. The Lowlands comprise the more open and fertile lands, which follow the southern coasts up to the central belt (where most of the mineral deposits also lie); then they take in Edinburgh, Glasgow, Stirling, Perth and Dundee, and follow the east coast up to Aberdeen and round to the Moray Firth. By comparison the centre of the country is wild and bleak, dominated by the Grampian mountains and the North and West Highlands, which look out to even more remote islands and a rugged western coastline. Many parts of the Highlands were accessible only by sea or by difficult trails until as late as the eighteenth century, when a few strategic military roads were driven into the fastness after the Jacobite rebellions.

Scottish cultural history is equally divided because it has a literary tradition in three languages – Gaelic, Scots and English – and there are a number of modern poets who still use at least two of these tongues to express themselves. Scots and English are cognate languages which belong to the dominant Lowland civilisation, which was agricultural, mercantile, urban, materialistic, literate and eventually industrial. Gaelic, on the other hand, belongs to an older and more warlike tradition of Highland boatmen, small crofters, herdsmen and hunters. These clans held strong family and regional loyalties and prided themselves on who they were, rather than on what they owned, and theirs was a sophisticated oral culture whose songs and poems and tunes were passed on from generation to generation usually without being written down. Not surprisingly, given such widely different values, these two cultures were often in conflict. But the densely populated Lowlands have encroached until Gaelic, once heard throughout the country, is now a minority language confined to the North-West, the Western Isles and the Hebrides, used by about 50,000 native speakers – 1 per cent of the population. Yet everything which the casual visitor most usually associates with Scotland – kilts, bagpipes, mountains and clansmen – stems from this Gaelic minority, even if it is usually promoted by Lowland businessmen. This is not the only paradox which Scotland has to offer and, like the others, it springs directly from the nation's various and changing origins. So, although this literary history will not formally begin until the later fourteenth century, the roots of a Scottish identity take us back much further, at least as far as the Celts and the mysterious Picts.

The Celts

The Celts belonged to a major 'barbarian' culture, the oldest in Europe next to Latin and Greek, whose greatest sphere of influence by the fifth and fourth centuries BC included north-west Germany, France, northern Italy and the Spanish peninsula. Linked by language, culture and custom, these confederated tribes spread from the Danube, and reached their most westerly point in Ireland, Wales and Scotland. The Celtic languages belong to the Indo-European family and are commonly subdivided into two branches – 'Q'-Celts, such as the Irish and Scottish Gaels, who retained the Indo-European 'qu' (later changed to 'c'); and 'P'-Celts, such as the Welsh, the Cornish and the Bretons, whose language changes 'qu' to 'p'. Heraclitus and the classical historians knew the *Keltoi* as tall warriors, fair-skinned, blue-eyed and moustached, who dressed in breeches, tunics and cloaks, wearing gold torcs and armlets with their hair stiffened and swept back like a horse's mane. They grew cereal crops, kept cattle and horses and valued hospitality, music, poetry, and feasts with plenty of fermented liquor to drink. Above all else they took pride in personal courage on the battlefield, where they favoured individual combats before the general mêlée and fought with spears and iron cutting-swords and light chariots. Celtic society was patriarchal, based on tradition and status within the tribe as well as loyalty to the family and its elaborate ties of kinship. All in all, these warrior values are strikingly similar to the ancient heroic mores of Homer's Greece. Songs and epics were composed and recited by privileged tribal bards; a Druid caste carried out the ceremonies of their ritual year; and Celtic artists and craftsmen excelled in fine metalwork and the elaborate decoration of bowls, jewellery, weapons and chariots. Celtic ornamentation is at once organic and abstract, with complex coils of strapwork which often terminate in stylised animal or human heads with fierce or comic little faces. This art is most familiar to us today in its much later Christian manifestation – in the Celtic crosses of Ireland and Scotland, or in the elaborate illuminations on the pages of the Book of Kells or the Lindisfarne Gospels. The Celtic heritage was a strong one, and its influence can still be found in the language, arts and social structures of Wales, Ireland and North-West Scotland. It lasted longest and changed least in these, the most isolated and far-flung outposts, because on the European mainland Celtic tribal culture eventually succumbed to the Roman Empire and evolved in different directions.

The Picts

In almost 400 years of settlement in Britain the Romans rarely penetrated north of the Antonine Wall, which ran from the Clyde to the Forth, nor did they establish their influence in Ireland. Classical writers of the late third century referred to the tribes in the North in only the loosest terms, calling them *Picti*, 'painted men', and in fact, we know very little about them. The Gaels of Ireland called then *Priteni*, 'people of the designs', which may refer to their liking for body-paint or tattoos, and they were most probably descended from a native Bronze Age people who intermarried with later P-Celtic arrivals. Their original tongue may have been non-Indo-European, for some of their inscriptions are in a language unknown to us. Furthermore, this society of tribes and minor kingships seems to have been matrilinear, with precedence given to males descended through the female line, and this, too, may derive from an indigenous Bronze Age population. The Picts and their precursors left vitrified forts (where the stones are fused as if by fire) and distinctive hollow, tower-like brochs all over Scotland, especially in Caithness and the islands. Their skilfully carved symbol stones – many of them in the North-East – testify to their love of animal designs and Celtic-style elaboration. We know little more about the Picts, except that their customs and something of their identity lasted until the ninth century, when they were submerged under pressure from the Norse in the north and the Irish Gaels in the west.

The Gaels

The Gaels arrived from Ireland in the fifth century and established a kingdom of their own, called Dalriada, in Argyllshire and the south-west of Scotland. These Q-Celts – called *Scoti* by the Romans – are the ancestors of the Gaelic-speaking Highland Scots. Christianity also crosses the water from Ireland, and Bede's history tells how St Ninian first showed the way and then how St Columba and his successors brought the Church to Iona in the sixth century and went on to convert more and more of the Picts and the *Scoti*. These early men of God were distinguished by their humble lives and by how humanely they accommodated Celtic mores and Celtic art to their Christian purpose.

Dalriada was not the only other kingdom within the Pictish sphere in the fifth and sixth centuries, for the Welsh-speaking Britons ruled Strathclyde, and Anglo-Saxon Angles from Northumbria held the south-east of Scotland, penetrating at one time as far as the Forth estuary. The epic Welsh (P-Celtic) battle-poem the *Gododdin* tells of a British raid out of Din Eidyn (Edinburgh) against the Angles, whom they fought near Catterick in Yorkshire about the year 600. But the Britons, like the Picts, gradually gave way to a Gaelic culture until the pattern of modern Scotland was finally set between the ascendant Gaels and the Old English-speaking Lowlanders from Northumbria – a minority whose time was yet to come. The Pictish kingdom was eroded still further in the eighth century when Norsemen came to colonise Orkney and Shetland and settled in the Western Isles and the north and west of Scotland.

The supremacy of Gaelic was finally assured in the ninth century when King Kenneth MacAlpin presented a legitimate claim to the Pictish throne and established himself as ruler of both Dalriada and Pictland, a kingdom later to be called Alba. The MacAlpin dynasty lasted almost 200 years, and when Malcolm II died in 1034 his country was called, for the first time, Scotia. There were struggles over the crown of Scotia, not least because MacAlpin's line had tried to favour direct succession instead of the Gaelic tradition of descent through brothers and uncles, or the Pictish preference for a matrilinear inheritance. Shakespeare's Macbeth was one of these claimants

and he ruled for seventeen years before the rise of Malcolm III
– Malcolm Canmore – established a dynasty which lasted for
another two centuries.

A Scottish nation

The new kingdom of Scotland was forged between the presence
of English Norman power to the south and the Norse occupation of the north and the Western Isles. Under the Canmores
the monarchy began to follow Anglo-Norman feudal customs,
for Malcolm's second wife came from the English royal line.
There were bloody wrangles over the disputed south-eastern
parts of Scotland and northern England, and internal disputes,
too, in the clash between Norman and Celtic mores. Still, the
Norman influence gained strength as intermarriage and
periods of peaceful trade consolidated the rule of King David I.
Edinburgh was established as the seat of royal power; Norman
forts, abbeys and monasteries were built throughout the
kingdom and the Church became an increasingly feudal
adjunct to the state. Gaelic Scotland did not succumb easily,
and the intransigently Celtic chiefs of the North-West
reclaimed their territory from the Norsemen and established
themselves as virtually autonomous lords of the isles. The
Anglo-Norman Lothian influence continued to rise, however,
and 'Inglis', the language at court, gradually prevailed over
native Gaelic and spread through the Lowlands and up the
east coast, taking the most fertile land and the most tradewor-
thy settlements into its sphere. Gaelic, the tongue of the original
Scoti, was now called 'Scottis', or 'Ersche' (Irish). The line
between Highland and Lowland Scotland was establishing
itself slowly but surely, although Gaelic did survive in remoter
parts of Galloway into the eighteenth century and in Perthshire
and the north-east almost until modern times.

The reign of Alexander III in the second half of the
thirteenth century was a period of exceptional peace, justice
and prosperity in early Scotland, but this 'golden age' ended
with his death. The succession was not obvious and there
followed a protracted struggle between many contenders, not
least the king's infant granddaughter, known as the Maid of
Norway; two Border lords, John Balliol and Bruce of Annan-
dale; and Edward I of England, who had recently subjugated

Wales and had an old claim of his own to be 'Lord Paramount of Scotland'. It was this claim which persuaded the northern lords to call on Edward to settle what was a very complicated feudal case. They eventually agreed on Balliol, who was crowned in 1292, swore fealty to Edward and promptly became his puppet. In the face of continuing unrest, however, and an alliance contracted between Scotland and France (the original 'Auld Alliance'), Edward reacted violently. He was at war with France, for he had feudal claims there himself, and he could not afford a threat from the north, especially since he was still faced with resistance in Wales. He took his army into Scotland in 1296 and penetrated to Perth, ravaging the Borders and killing thousands along the way. King John, ever since known as Toom Tabard ('empty coat'), ceded his realm to English governors and went south into comfortable captivity. Edward returned to London with much plunder, including the Stone of Destiny – the ancient Celtic throne-stone of Scotland – and the sworn allegiance of 2000 northern landowners. But he had behaved too savagely and it was not long before active revolt broke out and a certain William Wallace, son of a small landowner near Paisley, came to prominence during an uprising in Galloway in 1297. Over eighty years of fighting in what came to be known as the Scottish War of Independence had begun.

The War of Independence

Young William Wallace conducted a brilliant and ruthless guerrilla campaign and managed to join up with De Moray's Highlanders to control most of Scotland north of the river Tay. The great Scottish barons, the ruling Norman-feudal lords of the kingdom, had not as yet committed themselves, but Wallace was not leading a conventional Norman army, with emphasis on heavy troops, cavalry and siege-engines. In fact his forces were largely composed of footsoldiers and spearmen, made up from the Gaelic chiefs and their clansmen, middle-rank Lowland landowners with their followers, and the common people themselves. They could not attack castles, but they could move swiftly and control the countryside. Among men and women such as these a new sense of nationhood was growing – a sense that a country was defined by all those who lived in it and not just by the international family ties of a select few overlords. Wallace's hopes for Scotland were confirmed by a great victory at Stirling Bridge (1297), after which the English forces were driven beyond the Border and several isolated garrisons surrendered. He declared himself Guardian of Scotland on behalf of the exiled King John, but had to forfeit the title within a year when his forces were badly defeated at Falkirk, where they were overtaken by Edward at the head of a seasoned army shortly returned from the French campaign. The guardianship now passed to various members of the conventional nobility, and two in particular who had rival ambitions – John the Red Comyn and young Robert Bruce.

For the first five years of the new century Edward, 'the Hammer of the Scots', led a succession of campaigns across the Border, determined to establish English control by pressing his claim to be feudal overlord to the Scottish barons. Wallace was betrayed in 1305 and taken to London, where his execution provided a ghastly public spectacle. Parts of his body were displayed in Newcastle, Berwick, Perth and Aberdeen, but the example of his short life proved to be more potent than ever. Wallace's and Scotland's cause was taken up early the next year by Robert Bruce, who killed his rival Comyn in a church at Dumfries and had himself crowned king at the traditional site in Scone. Comyn's murder was such an ill-timed and sacrilegious act that it was almost certainly unpremeditated, but the desperation of the moment committed Bruce to the larger challenge of the throne.

Bruce's fortunes did not go well at first, for he had to flee to the Highlands, where he sought support in the west – a perennial haven for disaffected causes. Edward, aging and ill and set on vengeance, led one more army into Scotland, but died by the Solway. His son was less eager to pursue the issue, and Bruce and his brother Edward were granted valuable time to consolidate themselves in fierce internal strife against the Scottish supporters of Balliol and Comyn. Bruce's 'Rape of Buchan' – Comyn country – was particularly terrible; it swept away many of the local Gaelic-speaking lairds, but it secured the North-East for his cause as he gradually established a hold over more and more of Scotland in a campaign based on mobility, ruthlessness and surprise. Perth, Linlithgow and

Edinburgh were reclaimed, but the turning-point came in 1314 in two days at the Bannockburn outside Stirling castle. Here Bruce met a huge English army, brought from the south by Edward II himself, committed to defend his key garrison at Stirling and thereafter to re-establish English power throughout the land. The overwhelming Scottish victory at Bannockburn was the beginning of the end in the struggle for independence, but hostilities were to drag on for many more years.

At last Bruce had gained the support of most of his kingdom, and the Declaration of Arbroath in 1320 made a striking assertion of that nation's rights by appealing to the Pope not to side with the English against Bruce. This declaration, in Latin and signed by numerous earls and barons, is all the more unusual because it places an abstraction such as freedom and the liberty of individuals above the rights of any monarch. The right of subjects to select their king was believed to be part of the Pictish tradition, but this was a new and even a dangerous idea in the feudal world and one that was to endure for a long time in the Scottish people's conception of themselves:

> Yet if he should give up what he has begun, and agree to make us or our kingdom subject to the King of England or the English, we should exert ourselves at once to drive him out as our enemy and a subverter of his own rights and ours, and make some other man who was well able to defend us our King; for, as long as but a hundred of us remain alive, never will we on any conditions be brought under English rule. It is in truth not for glory, nor riches, nor honours that we are fighting, but for freedom – for that alone, which no honest man gives up but with life itself.

The English did not formally recognise Bruce's kingship and the sovereignty of Scotland until a treaty was signed with Edward III in 1328. Worn and sick after years of war, Bruce died the following year, to be succeeded by his five-year-old son David. In no time at all the old Balliol faction had revived – encouraged by Edward, despite his treaty – and a succession of regents and David II himself were once again caught up in internal strife and renewed warfare against the English. By mid century David was held hostage in England and the Black Death had arrived from Europe to ravage a land already laid waste by endless fighting. The absence of the king gave more power to the three Estates of barons, churchmen and burgesses

– the very people who had insisted on their independence at
Arbroath – but the sufferings of the peasants had completely
disaffected them from feudal lords and all their doings. French
knights on Scottish soil were horrified at the 'impudence' of the
common people, who chased them with hoes when they rode
through their crops. Perhaps they had little left to lose, and
perhaps the spirit of that declaration was seeding itself even
among the scorched grass-roots. David returned to his kingdom for the last fourteen years of his reign to be succeeded by
Robert II and Robert III, the 'Stewards' to his kingdom and
the first, if undistinguished, members of a Stewart line which
was to have more than enough problems in the centuries to
come.

The Scots language

In Scotland, as in England and Europe throughout the Middle
Ages, Latin was most commonly used for official purposes
among the educated and governing classes. French was also
used in England, but by the fourteenth century it had fallen out
of use in Scotland and a new literature was growing up with
original works and translations written in 'Inglis' – a version of
Northern English speech which gradually took an even more
distinctive character of its own. Within a hundred years this
tongue was supplanting Gaelic – and came to be called 'Scottis'
in its stead. Although James IV could speak Gaelic himself, the
poet Dunbar at his court could safely taunt his rival Kennedy
for coming from 'inferior' Highland stock and for using 'Irish'.
The kingdom of Dalriada had slipped away.

Inevitably, in 400 years of development, Scots has very many
words in common with English, although some are pronounced
differently. Others come from older Anglo-Saxon forms which
have dropped out of use in the south – words such as *dwine* (to
decay or dwindle), *wersh* (insipid) and *thole* (to endure, suffer).
Alternatively, Scots will take one form of a word from a Latin or
French root when English takes another or leaves it altogether,
as in *dispone* (dispose), or *dominie* (schoolmaster). Even common
English words can be used in un-English ways, as in 'can I *get* to
go' for 'may I go', or 'I *doubt* it's true' to mean 'I'm afraid it *is*
true' – the opposite of what an English-speaker might assume.

Even for Scots themselves the writing, spelling and speaking of their language can provide special problems, not the least of which is the number of apostrophes which are often added, quite wrongly, as if it were simply English with letters missing – thus *a'* for 'all' instead of the more correct *aa*, and *fa'* for *faa*, and so on. The gutteral 'ch' is, of course, well known in Scots words such as *loch*, *licht*, *bricht*, and *nicht* and *heich* ('high'), but the Old English letter 3 (yogh, the name combining its two main sounds) was also retained, although later printers had to use the standard Roman letters 'y', 'g' or even 'z' for it.* Thus Scots words such as *tulzie* (brawl) and especially proper names such as Menzies and Dalziel (and even MacKenzie) are often pronounced with an English 'z' when they should sound like 'toolye', 'Mingis', 'Dalyell' and even 'MacKingie'. By the same – mistaken – token, the unaccented syllables at the end of Scots words such as *pruvit* (proved) and *deavit* (deafened, bored) and *Scottis* itself, are often pronounced especially forcefully by modern readers, when they should be left relatively unstressed.

Some of the most distinctive and tricky features of Scots are to be found among the smallest words in its grammar. Among its pronouns Scots uses *ye* for 'you'; and *yon*, or *thon* as a variant of 'that' with *thae* for 'those'. English 'which' is usually rendered as *that* or *at* and the older form *whilk* (or *quhilk* – same pronunciation) is virtually obsolete. The indefinite article *a* and *an* is the same as English, but a scribal convention often writes them as *ane*, even although they should still be pronounced as usual. So Lindsay's play *Ane Pleasant Satyre of the Thrie Estaits* should simply be called *A Pleasant Satyre*. On the other hand *ane* in Scots is pronounced as it looks when used as an isolated numeral for 'one', as in *ane o them* (consider also *the tane and the tither*, for 'one and the other'); but when joined with a noun the form becomes *ae*, as in *ae weet forenicht* – one wet twilight. Finally, 'one' as an indefinite personal pronoun is not used as such, and the Scots idiom for 'if one thought so' is *gin a body thocht sae* ('if *a person* thought so'), or maybe *gin ye thocht sae*.

Scots had developed differently from English in the pattern of its borrowings from other languages. Thus Gaelic has given many loan words, such as *loch*, *glen*, *ben*, *caber* (originally a

---

* In quotations in this book, such 'z' spellings are avoided. Thus, where a text contained spellings such as *ze*, *zow*, the more familiar *ye*, *yow*, etc., are substituted.

roofbeam), *sonsie* (jolly or plump), *crine* (to shrivel), *partan* (crab) and, of course, *whisky* – *usquebae*, from the Gaelic for 'water of life'. This influence is less than might be supposed, given how widespread Gaelic place-names are throughout the country. Even so, it may well be that Gaelic patterns of expression have entered the speech-habits of Scotsmen, even when they think they are speaking English. Hence 'he's *away to the* fishing' for 'he has gone fishing', and 'Ian can't go to *the* school, he's got *the* measles', which follow Gaelic construction.

Old Norse made a particular contribution to Scots through Old English and its northern dialects, and then from the Viking settlement of the Northern Isles. Many common Scots words come from this source, such as *birk* (birch), *kirk* (church), *breeks* (breeches), and *skreich* (screech), as well as *big* (to build), *frae* (from), *gar* (to make, in the sense of persuade or cause to do), *tyne* (to lose), and so on. The original Anglo-Norman roots of Scots provided the language with a larger number of French-derived words, such as *douce* (quiet or gentle), *ashet* (dinner plate), *aumrie* (cupboard), *tassie* (cup), *houlet* (owl) and *mavis* (thrush), while later trade and the Auld Alliance brought further borrowings, such as *fash* (to bother) and *caddie* (originally *cadet*, a messenger). Finally, from the Netherlands, Scotland's other major source of foreign trade from the late fourteenth century onwards, came words such as *callant* (chap), *mutch* (a woman's cap), *kyte* (belly) and *dowp* (backside).

The literary Scots of the Makars was the dialect of mid-Scotland and this has been the basis of 'standard Scots', which developed as a versatile literary language from the fourteenth to the sixteenth century before meeting a renewed influx of English from south of the Border. By the late seventeenth century the interface with English usage and the availability of old forms, new forms and regional variations made Scots spelling very fluid indeed. The use of Scots itself came under threat when 'educated' people began to eradicate 'Scotticisms' from their writing – even if their accents remained resolutely Caledonian. There were many complicated reasons for this, and of course some shift in practice was inevitable after the two kingdoms were united. Then again, during the Reformation the Scots clergy had used an English translation of the Bible, and so English became associated with high and serious matters while Scots, by the eighteenth century, was linked with colloquial speech, the common folk and rustic life. Ever since then its full literary use has tended to be confined to poetry, for if it appears in prose it is as a 'speaking voice', as with Scott's characters or the 'narrators' of Galt's novels. Robert Burns's 'Lallans' was essentially mid-Scots from Ayrshire, but he introduced words from different dialects (his father came from the North-East, after all), and he also used anglified spellings for words which would still have been pronounced in the Scottish manner (e.g. 'ewes' for *yowes*). The nineteenth century saw a boom in sentimental dialect verses until modern poets in Scots set out to restore serious lyrical and intellectual status to the medium. They recognised that their language was a 'literary' construction to some extent, and MacDiarmid sometimes drew his inspiration from unusual dialect words which had long lain in the dictionary. Sydney Goodsir Smith stayed closer to what the Makars used, while Robert Garioch drew on his North-East roots and his life in Edinburgh in order to stay closer to contemporary spoken language. What exactly comprises 'standard Scots', after the eighteenth century or so, has become a debatable point, although common sense and common practice usually show the way. Scots is still potent in modern poetry, but it is doubtful if the evolution of the language can be reversed in other branches of literature. Its gradual 'vernacularisation' towards the eighteenth century and its literary history since then mean that it will always be associated with verse of colloquial expression. Nor will the formal stateliness of sixteenth-century Scots prose be seen again.

Gaelic literature

From the late twelfth century to the present day Gaelic has enjoyed a strong tradition of poetry, songs and prose tales, but its literature, whether memorised or written down, is most especially rich in poetry. This verse-tradition falls into two main periods. The first stems from the bardic schools, a 'classical' and conservative tradition which followed old Irish models going back to the ninth century. Bardic verse was slow to change, but by the sixteenth century Gaelic songs were flourishing in a more vernacular form of the language, and in the next century poets such as Iain Lom and Mary MacLeod heralded the second great period by beginning to use this language in place of bardic formality. Thus the slow development of a specifically Scottish Gaelic vernacular poetry reached its greatest expression in the eighteenth century among poets such as Rob Donn Mackay, Alexander MacDonald and Duncan Bàn Macintyre. Then the doors of the Gaelic world were flung wider still by such poets as Sorley Maclean, George Campbell Hay, Derick Thomson and Iain Crichton Smith of the twentieth-century Scottish Renaissance. These writers take a specifically modern outlook, yet their work is never far from their heritage. The spirit of Gaelic literature, with its characteristic strengths and subjects, is still remarkably consistent.

Not much survives of early bardic verse in Scotland, and the recitation of genealogies and chronicles is of little specifically literary interest anyway. In fact the classical schools were so stable that Gaelic bardic verse from the fourteenth to the sixteenth centuries can be usefully summarised at this point. The most substantial single source of early Gaelic poetry comes down to us in the Book of the Dean of Lismore, a manuscript from 1512 which was only discovered and published in 1862. The dean collected from oral sources in Argyll, and Perthshire, and these included bardic praise-poems along with much less formal satires, love-lyrics, Christian poems and mildly obscene verses. Most notably the collection includes Ossianic heroic ballads and verses in Irish, which demonstrate Scotland's continuing links with Ireland going back to their common roots. Indeed, one of the very oldest surviving texts to deal with Scotland, the *Duan Albanach* (most probably by an Irish poet at the end of the eleventh century), uses a mixture of legend and oral history to tell how the Irish Gaels first came to settle in the north, and the two countries continued to exchange contacts through bards and poems and patrons into the seventeenth century.

The Gaelic bardic system seems to have been well established by the thirteenth century. At first, this exclusive professional class produced learned and highly wrought verses along classical Irish lines, and bardic colleges were set up to teach the literary conventions, including as many as 300 different and complex metrical schemes. At the highest level these bards were fully literate and could aspire to the status of *filidh*. It is likely, however, that the common folk preferred tales and ballads outwith this antique, formal style and easier for them to understand. The task of the *filidh*, like the slightly less exalted position of bard, was 'eulogy and elegy' – to sing his leader's praises, recite his genealogy, chronicle his times and describe victories in battle. The bard's office was often hereditary, he had considerable prestige and could be a wealthy man in his own right, but he still depended on patronage and a stable aristocratic tradition.

Like all Celtic artists, the bards value impersonality and technical skill for their own sake and their verse is elaborate and conventional in its approach. Perhaps Dunbar's highly wrought aureate verses owe something to this heritage, despite his apparent contempt for things Gaelic. The traditional praise-poem could contain many elements – praise of a horse, a bow, the chief's ancestry, his land, his valour or the beauty of his lady. Other poems strike a more elegiac note with a lament for a leader's death or for the passing of glory. Bardic verses were based on the *rann*, a self-contained four-line stanza made up of two couplets of pre-determined syllabic lengths and a variety of rhetorical devices, including patterns of internal rhyme, assonance and alliteration. *Brosnachadh* poems, or versus as an 'incitement' to war, were also written, and an early example ascribed to Artur Dall MacGurcaigh and dating from about 1310 describes MacSween of Knapdale's fleet in terms which clearly show the parallels between Highland custom and the warriors and longboats of Scandinavia from 400 years before. (Gaelic chiefs from the north often boasted of their descent from Norse fighting-men.) In a later example from 1513, written for the Earl of Argyll before the Battle of Flodden, the unknown poet curses the English and asks the earl to punish their growing spite and power:

> The roots from which they grow, destroy them,
> their increase is too great,
> and leave no Englishman alive after you
> nor Englishwoman there to tell the tale.

> Burn their bad coarse women,
> burn their uncouth offspring,
> and burn their sooty houses,
> and rid us of the reproach of them.

Let their ashes float downstream
after burning their remains
show no mercy to a living Englishman
O chief, deadly slayer of the wounded.

(trs. K. H. Jackson)

Over 200 years later, the same bloodthirsty tradition was called up by Alexander MacDonald (Alasdair MacMhaighstir Alasdair), who wrote many poems in vernacular Gaelic to support the Jacobite rising of 1745.

Not all was war, however, and bardic metres were also used for laments or for gentler, more personal poems, such as the beautiful 'O rosary that recalled my tear' ('A phaidrín do dhúisg mo dhéar'), written in the 1460s by a non-professional poet, Aithbhreac Inghean Corcadail, in mourning for the death of her husband, Niall Og MacNeill:

O rosary that recalled my tear'
dear was the finger in my sight,
that touched you once, beloved the heart
of him who owned you till tonight.

I grieve the death of him whose hand
you did entwine each hour of prayer;
my grief that it is lifeless now
and I no longer see it there.

(trs. D. Thomson)

When the geographical isolation and the autonomy of the clans began to pass during the sixteenth century, the bards passed, too. Nevertheless, later Gaelic poets retained a high prestige, even if they came from humble stock without classical training, and, in fact, aspects of bardic style were to survive in a looser and more vernacular form for centuries to come.

Scots literature in the fourteenth century

After the *brosnachadh* poems of the Gaelic bards, it is appropriate that the first major literary achievement of the emerging Scots tradition should be John Barbour's *The Bruce*, a Lowland poem of war and victory. If Barbour had many predecessors, then they and their works are shrouded by time or hidden in the smoke of scholarly dispute. The oldest surviving fragment may date from the difficult years after 1286 and the end of Alexander III's 'golden age', but it comes to us as transcribed in 1424 by Andrew of Wyntoun from his *Origynale Cronykil of Scotland*:

Quhen Alexander our kynge was dede,	when
That Scotlande lede in lauche and le,	law and peace
Away was sons of alle and brede,	abundance of ale
Off wyne and wax, of gamyn and gle.	mirth
Our golde was changit into lede.	lead
Crist, borne in virgynyte,	
Succoure Scotlande, and ramede,	help
That is stade in perplexite.	beset

Also from Alexander's reign comes a long and relatively unskilled metrical romance called *Sir Tristrem*, often ascribed to Thomas of Ercildoune and later edited by Scott. But this, too, appears only in a fourteenth-century transcription and the authorship is disputed. Ercildoune is better known as 'Thomas the Rhymer' or 'True Thomas', the poet in the later ballads who became the Queen of Elfland's lover and was gifted with prophetic powers.

The Awntyrs of Arthure and *The Pistill of Susan* are two metrical romances, each with rhymed and alliterative thirteen-line stanzas, that survive in English transcriptions from the fifteenth century. The 'adventures' come from the stock of Arthurian tales, although they may be set around the Borders; and the epistle about Susan goes to the Apocrypha of the Bible for the moral tale of Susanna and the Elders. Andrew of Wyntoun ascribed these to someone called 'Huchown off the Awle Ryale' (although he puts 'Gawane' rather than Arthur in the title), and it has been suggested that this Huchown is 'Sir Hew of Eglinton', a Scot whom Dunbar lists among the dead poets of the past in his 'Lament for the Makaris'. ('Awle Ryale' has been rendered as 'the King's palace'.) Whether this connection holds or not, both poems belong to the same literary mode as later Scottish verses such as *Rauf Coilyear* and *Golagros and Gawane*, and these formed part of an 'alliterative revival' in the poetry of the north, even if the names of their authors cannot be convincingly established. 'Huchown' may or may not have been a Scot, but the nationality of John Barbour needs little proving.

John Barbour (1320?–95)

Barbour's famous poem survives in two manuscripts transcribed in the late fifteenth century, and the ubiquitous Wyntoun, a great admirer of *The Bruce*, confirmed its authorship and included 280 lines from it in his *Cronykil*. John Barbour was probably born in Aberdeen, and he is first mentioned in the records as archdeacon there in 1357. In the next eleven years he travelled to study at Oxford and then to Paris on at least two occasions each. Thereafter he was given a post as clerk of audit and was one of the auditors of the Exchequer for Robert II's household. He wrote *The Bruce* during the years 1374–75 and three years later he was granted a royal pension in perpetuity, most probably in recognition of his poem. A larger annual sum was awarded in 1388, and it is the cessation of this payment which marks his death in 1395.

From these slender details it can be seen that Barbour's long historical poem refers to events scarcely sixty years in the past, and it is likely that he had access to oral sources for many of the details in the work. These can be more reliable than might be supposed, although, typically, the odds against the Scots are multiplied for the sake of effect and at one point Bruce and his grandfather are conflated. In the same cause, Barbour's hero king is made of simpler stuff than the original, who suffered such divided Anglo-Norman loyalties and made a succession of broken promises to Edward and Balliol and Comyn. So *The Bruce* portrays an uncomplicated and noble epic from the start, and, although the English are allowed to be brave and chivalrous too, they are never seen as less than prideful and acquisitive enemies. Even so, Barbour's patriotism (and an awareness of his royal patron), does not lead him into mere propaganda or far-fetched romance. In fact *The Bruce* is most striking for its unelaborated narrative: twenty books full of the dispositions of troops, the vagaries of the campaign and the speeches and deeds of individuals, all of which are recounted in forthright style combined with a clerkly eye for the circumstantial details of time and place and equipment:

And went in hy towart the sea;	in haste
Quhar Schir Nele Campbell thaim met	where
Bath with schippis, and with meyte;	meat

Saylys, ayris, and othir thing,   oars
That was spedfull to thar passyng.
                 (v, 570–4)

The same dispassionate and documentary approach even
informs Barbour's account of the notorious 'Douglas larder',
when Bruce's fiercest young lieutenant surprised the occupying
English garrison at worship in the church of his family castle,
and flung their bodies and surplus supplies (and the feast they
had been about to eat) into the wine-cellar:

A foull melle thair can he mak;   mix
For meill, malt, blude, and wyne
Ran all to-gidder in a mellyne.
That wes unsemly for to se;
Tharfor the men of that cuntre,
For sic thingis that mellit were,
Callit it 'the Douglas Lardenere'.
                 (v, 404–10)

Barbour tells us that this master of guerrilla terrorism was
'mcyk and sweyt in cumpany' and spoke with a lisp. Douglas is
a major character in the poem, and the tale ends with his death
in battle against the Saracens twenty-four years later, while
carrying Bruce's heart in a casket on a pilgrimage to the Holy
Land – a journey the king had long promised himself, but did
not live to make.

True stories are a double pleasure, as the author observes in
his preface –

The fyrst plesance is the carpyng,   telling
    And the tothir the suthfastnes,   truthfulness
That schawys the thing rycht as it wes.
                 (I, 6–8)

– and one of the main things for Barbour, 'rycht as it wes', is the
spirit of liberty, famously evoked in the very first book with
lines which add a more than chivalric dimension to the tale:

A! fredome is a noble thing!
Fredome mayss man to haiff liking,   makes; pleasure
Fredome all solace to man giffis: gives
He levys at ess that frely levys.   lives at ease

A noble hart may haiff nane ess,
Na ellys nocht that may him pless,   [if freedom
Gyff fredome failyhe; for fre liking   fail; love of liberty
Is yharnyt our all othir thing.   yearned for over all
Na he, that ay hass levyt fre,
May nocht knaw weill the propyrte,
The anger, na the wrechyt dome,   doom
That is couplyt to foule thyrldome.   thraldom
Bot gyff he had assayit it,   if he had tried it
Than all perquer he suld it wyt;   by heart he should
And suld think fredome mar to pryss   more   [know it
Than all the gold in the warld that is.

(I, 225–40)

The unforced pace of such simple statement in Barbour's
octosyllabic couplets pervades the whole poem as well as the
character of its hero. Most notably, in comparison with Blind
Harry's *Wallace* of a century later, Barbour's work is not
suffused with blind hatred for the English. The same stable and
shrewd virtue is found in the mouths of the common people who
start to side with their king's cause:

He com soyn in the houss, and fand   soon; found
The gud wyf on the bynk sytand.   sitting on the bench
Scho askit him soyn quhat he wes   She; what
And quhyne he com, and quhar he gais.   when; where he
'A travelland man, dame', said he,   goes
'That travalys heir throu the cuntre.'
Scho said, 'All that travaland ere,   formerly
For saik of ane, ar welcom here.'
The King said, 'Gud dame, quhat is he
That garris yow have sic specialte   makes you have
Till men that travalis?' 'Schir, perfay,'   [such special liking
Quod the gud wif, 'I sall yow say;
Gud King Robert the Bruce is he,
That is rycht lord of this cuntre. . . .
'Dame, lufis thou him sa weill?' said he.
'Yea, Schir,' scho said, 'sa God me se.'
'Dame', said he, 'Lo! Him here the by,   he is by you here
For I am he;' – 'Sa ye suthly?'   truly
'Yea, certis, dame;' – 'And quhar ar gane
Your men, quhen ye ar thus allane?'
'At this tyme, dame, I have no ma.'   more
Scho said, 'It may no wiss be swa;   no way be so
I have two sonnys wicht and hardy,   vigorous
Thai sall becum your men in hy.'   in haste

(VII, 237–64)

Not surprisingly, the natural climax of the poem – after the accounts of Bruce's early sufferings – arrives with Bannockburn. Barbour's lengthy description of that two-day battle includes the tactical manoeuvres of the troops, the speeches of the leaders and courageous deeds on both sides; he also tells of the celebrated clash between Bruce and De Bohun, and how the humble camp-followers, determined to fight for Scotland in their own way, formed an army with sheets for banners, and convinced the faltering English that they were new and deadly reinforcements. The sober simplicity of Barbour's verses – and occasional shafts of grim humour – perfectly convey the purpose and the character of the Scottish cause as he sees it. Of course, it is the 'great folk' who stand most in the foreground, but the nobility of plain speech and simple dignity is shared by all. Thus Bruce's chivalric idealism has a sturdily domestic and practical foundation, as he addresses his men before Bannockburn and reminds them that, despite being outnumbered, they have three great advantages:

The first is, that we haf the richt;	
And for the richt ilk man suld ficht.	every man should
The tothir is, thai are cummyn heir,	[fight
For lypnyng in thair gret power,	trusting
To seik us in our awne land,	
And has broucht her, richt till our hand,	brought here
Richness in-to so gret plentee,	
That the pouerest of yow sall be	
Bath rych and mychty thar-with-all,	
Gif that we wyn, as weill may fall.	may happen
The thrid is, that we for our lyvis	
And for our childer and our wifis,	
And for the fredome of our land,	
Ar strenyeit in battale for to stand,	constrained/forced
And thai for thair mycht anerly . . .	only for their might

(XII, 235–49)

Professional knightly pride may have to give way in the face of men who are fighting to survive, but Bruce is king enough to know that the prospect of a little plunder helps, too.

Barbour concludes his account of Bannockburn with the understanding that a king must first earn and then maintain his people's loyalty, and be prays that 'thai that cummynge ar / of [Bruce's] ofspring, maynteyme the land, / And hald the folk . . . As weill as in his tyme did he!' Perhaps the poet had cause to worry, for Robert II was an aging and weak man when he came to the throne, and the Scots barons were, as always, ready to challenge his authority – not least the Douglases, who were fighting what was virtually a private war with England only three years after *The Bruce* had immortalised the loyalty of their most famous ancestor – 'that in his tyme sa worthy was'. The 'suthfast story' of Scotland was as complicated and bloody as ever.

2

The fifteenth century: the flowering

THE national and cultural confidence of Scotland came to fruition in the fifteenth century, but it was neither easy nor peaceful. A succession of Stewart minorities aggravated the power balance between crown and barons and each king had to struggle to establish his rule. The Stewarts made some headway, and yet Douglas and Percy still ruled the Borders, while in the North-West the Clan Donald line claimed and held their own kingly rights as Lords of the Isles. Nevertheless, the royal right of succession gradually became established and accepted by almost all factions in Scotland. It was dearly bought: from James I to James IV no Stewart king lived beyond his prime and all of them died violently. Relationships with England were muted for the most part, but the capture of James I gave early notice that England still nursed hopes of suzerainty. Thus, it was English policy to encourage malcontents in Scotland and particularly to support the ambitions of the Lords of the Isles.

The Scottish connection with France was more cordial and from time to time the Auld Alliance was invoked to enlist Scotland's aid against her southern neighbour. But the end result was usually unhappy, especially when James IV died in an entirely reluctant and futile bid to oblige French expectations by marching on England. Many Scotsmen travelled abroad to enlist as mercenaries in the armies of Europe: some fought for Joan of Arc and two of the elite corps in Charles VII's army were Scottish companies. In her turn, France's contribution was more cultural than military, and Pedro de Ayala noted how many young Scotsmen spoke French and made regular visits to the continent. The Scots pattern of education was based on the curriculum at Paris, and the universities of St Andrew's (1412), Glasgow (1451) and Aberdeen (1495) were all founded along European lines. By the end of the century James IV had established at Aberdeen the first chair of medicine in Britain and had passed an act to require the sons of all barons and landowners to attend school from the age of eight for the study of Latin, law and the arts. In 1507 the same king established Walter Chepman and Andrew Myllar as printers in Edinburgh. They published poetry by Henryson and Dunbar as well as the *Legends of the Saints* and the *Aberdeen Breviary* – a major project by the redoubtable Bishop Elphinstone of Aberdeen, whose intention was to preserve the Scottish form of worship against English influence.

By the second half of the century, in a period of peace with England, the burghs had gained in influence and wealth. Growing numbers of towns began to govern themselves in the pursuit of trade and to defend themselves too. Burgesses were obliged to provide weapons and armour and to turn out for home-guard service if necessary. Royal burghs could send representatives to parliament, and their trading-interests were another factor which maintained cultural links with Europe from Danzig to Spain. These connections and especially the one with France flourished in the architecture of this time. Falkland Palace, Linlithgow, the Border abbeys and the castles at Borthwick and Craigmillar show the full influence of northern 'perpendicular Gothic'. The Renaissance in Scotland could not match the glories of Italy – the national temperament, like the climate, tended to ruggedness rather than grace – but under James IV there was an energy and an excitement in the air.

The second half of the fifteenth century was a time of literary richness – one of the greatest that Scotland has seen. The outstanding poets were Robert Henryson and William Dunbar. Henryson has the finer spirit, but the period is characterised by Dunbar, although his poems actually date from the early 1500s. For this reason he has been included in the present chapter and also because the death of James IV and the psychological impact of his defeat at Flodden in 1513 makes a natural, if sad, conclusion to a century of high literary achievement.

The surface gorgeousness of Dunbar's poems contrasts with

the wilder and more brutal extravagance of his imagination, and these, in turn, play against a darker and more singular spirit of pessimism. Dunbar speaks of the prodigality of court life and he always speaks of himself. Henryson, on the other hand, has a broader and less selfish nature, a mature compassion for the spiritual plight of man and a practical sympathy for the common folk. He commends the values of peace and good order, values that were making difficult but discernible progress during his lifetime, and his poems frequently comment on how the common people are at the mercy of the rapacious and the powerful. There is a sense in which we hear the people in Henryson: a voice that will come to be the characteristic utterance of Scottish literature when the formal and courtly delights of *The Kingis Quair* and 'The Goldyn Targe' have faded. The same voice can be heard in parts of 'Rauf Coilyear' and 'Colkelbie's Sow' and most especially in the rougher folk energy of 'Peblis to the Play' and 'Christis Kirk of the Green'. *The Bruce* and Blind Harry's *Wallace* can be seen as the larger expressions of this force, because they too stem from the sense that a nation is simply its people. Scotland had not yet achieved political stability, and schisms still existed between Lowlands and Highlands; but the prominence of such writers as Henryson and Dunbar, or the distinctively local colouring which was given to traditional European romance subjects, or the technical confidence and verve to be seen in aureate and ballad verse – all these point to what came to be known as the golden age of Scottish poetry.

Inspired by the national spirit of *The Bruce*, **Andrew of Wyntoun** (1350?–1420?), prior to the monastery of Loch Leven, ushered in the new century with a long history of Scotland written in dogged verse couplets. *The Orygynale Chronykil of Scotland* (1424) sets out to establish the heritage of the Scots from 1408 right back to Adam and Eve, and woe betide any English monarch who does not recognise such a proud descent! As a historian Wyntoun is more dependable nearer to his own times, and one of the last events recorded in his book tells how an eleven-year-old boy, newly crowned king of Scotland, fell into English hands.

James I (1394–1437)

Young James I was captured by the English in 1406 while being shipped to France – ironically, for his own safety. He spent the next eighteen years of his life as a political pawn in England, although no doubt his captivity was comfortable enough. He is said to have written *The Kingis Quair* (the King's Book) during the last years of his sojourn, and it seems likely that this ornate allegorical poem does, indeed, describe the circumstances under which he fell in love with his future wife, Joan of Beaufort. There is little reason to suppose, as some scholars have maintained, that James is not the author. Yet the poem was not really 'discovered' until the eighteenth century, and so it had little contemporary influence and James is not one of the poets mentioned in Dunbar's 'Lament for the Makaris'.

The Kingis Quair is an allegorical dream vision framed by the poet's imprisonment and his despair at a 'dedely life full of peyne and penance'. As one might expect from the circumstances, the style is lightly Scotticised and markedly influenced by English models. It uses a seven-line rime-royal stanza similar to that of *Troilus and Criseyde*, and the mixture of realistic description and allegorical abstraction is reminiscent of Lydgate's *Temple of Glas*. The poet sees a beautiful woman outside his window and, rather in the manner of Palamoun in 'The Knight's Tale', he immediately falls in love with her. That night in a dream he presents his case to Venus before an emblematic assembly of all those who have felt the pangs of love. He meditates on free will in the manner of Boethius's *De Consolatione Philosophiae*, but the poem gains most force from its physical descriptions and from the ironies inherent in its theme of love as a kind of captivity which offers escape from literal physical imprisonment. The bright images of birds and the garden of crystal waters and little fish convey the poet's sense of exhilaration, clarity and gratitude when he feels that his fortunes have turned. Although still incarcerated, he begins to feel free. By comparison, although the autobiographical element is openly admitted, his loved one remains a collection of rather abstract virtues. The poet's meditation on Fortune is especially poignant, for James had been hostage to that fickle wheel all his life and yet could win free only by submitting himself once more to her macabre influence. This time she smiles on him, but the king cannot help noticing that her wheel revolves over a hellish pit. In a delightfully original touch he has the goddess give him a tweak on the ear as they part, and this teasing nip wakes him from his dream and serves as a sardonic reminder of Fortune's incorrigible and fatal playfulness. Nevertheless, the poet is now free – at least in spirit – and he can even bless the castle walls that keep him, because they provided the stage for his conversion to love.

It was not long before the king secured his release from Windsor and married Joan Beaufort. By 1424 he was restored to his throne in Scotland, where he determined to reassert his authority. But Fortune's wheel turned again, thirteen years later, when a discontented baron planned his assassination, and the author of *The Kingis Quair* met his death hiding in the privy of the royal bedchambers at Perth.

James's poem introduced the century with an allegorical work in courtly style. The literature which followed was, for the most part, less formal, less in the mode of Chaucer and Lydgate and closer to a more everyday vision of Scottish life. It was once the fashion to define the poets of this century as 'Scottish Chaucerians', but properly speaking only James owes the implied debt. The rest undoubtedly acknowledge Chaucer's greatness, but they draw as much from European and native influences as they do from the old master in England. At least three other poems have been ascribed to James I. 'Good Counsel' is a brief and sententious piece of advice to 'exil al vice and folow trewth alway', modelled after Chaucer's ballad of the same name, and there are few problems in accepting it as the king's work. It is not so, however, with 'Peblis to the Play' and 'Christis Kirk of the Green', and recent critical opinion favours a now unknown author for these pieces, from a time closer to the end of the fifteenth century.

Sir Richard Holland (fl. 1450)

If *The Kingis Quair* operates in the tradition of the dream vision and has moments reminiscent of 'The Knight's Tale', then Sir Richard Holland's *The Buke of the Howlat* (Book of the Owl) is a beast allegory after the fashion of Chaucer's *Parlement of Foules*. Holland's long poem was dedicated to Elizabeth Dunbar, wife

to Archibald Douglas, Earl of Moray, and must have been
written around 1450 to celebrate this powerful family and its
history. The *Howlat* is written in the alliterative stanza used for
'Rauf Coilyear', *Golagros and Gawane* and the English *Awntyrs of
Arthure*, but it is an allegory and an entertaining satire rather
than a romance tale like the others. It is the first substantial
poem of what was to become a Scottish revival of the use of
alliteration in verse.

Holland makes innumerable connections between the world
of birds and the pomp and circumstance of papal and regal
power. Thus the peacock is the pope of birds and the swallow is
his herald, while cranes (cardinals), swans (bishops) and
common sea-birds (monks) throng his holiness's court. In
similar fashion the birds of prey represent temporal power,
with the eagle as emperor and gerfalcons, goshawks and
sparrowhawks as the dukes, captains and knights of his retinue.
In the middle of the poem, while describing the heraldry at the
eagle's court, the poet takes some twenty stanzas to recite the
arms and the prowess of the Douglas family, starting with the
tale of Bruce's heart.

This elaborate poem has a simple moral about the dangers of
pride (Blind Harry's *Wallace* refers to it, to make a timely
warning to Sir William), for the allegory is set in motion by the
owl's desire to be more beautiful. On a traditional May
morning, the poet overhears the howlat's complaint against
Dame Nature, and he follows its course from the papal
congregation of birds to the assembled might of the emperor's
court, where a feast, with juggling and recitations, is being
held. Finally, the company prays for Dame Nature to appear,
and she orders each bird to give one of its feathers to the ugly
howlat. But, as soon as he is arrayed in finery, the owl becomes
insufferably proud ('pomposs, impertinat, and reprovable')
and the other birds waste no time in asking Dame Nature to
return him to his former state – 'hidowis of hair and of hyde'.
This accomplished, they all fly off, leaving the howlat, and the
poet, to contemplate a moral directed at the rich and powerful:

> Now mark yow mirour be me, all maner of man,
> Ye princis, prentis of pryde for penneis and prowe   images; pennies;
> That pullis the pure ay,   exploit [profit
> Ye sall syng as I say,   [the poor
> All your welth will away,
> Thus I warn yow . . . .

The charm of *The Buke of the Howlat* lies in the way it miniaturises human society and dresses it in feathers, for neither the moral nor the celebration of the Douglases survives the test of time. Thus the Rook appears at the banquet as a Gaelic bard speaking gibberish, reciting genealogies, and demanding more food, all at the same time. It is a passage that Dunbar, with his prejudice against 'the ersche' tongue, would certainly have enjoyed:

	[shout and
Sa come the Ruke with a rerd and a rane roch,	a rough rann
A bard out of Irland with 'Banachadee'.	'blessing of God'
Said: 'Gluntow guk dynyd dach hala mischy doch;	('Gaelic' gibberish)
Raike hir a rug of the rost, or scho sall ryme the.	Reach me a chunk
Mich macmory ach mach mometir moch loch;	of the roast or I'll
Set hir dovne, gif hir drink; quhat Dele alis the?'	satirise you (he
O Deremyne, O Donnall, O Dochardy droch;	refers to himself as
Thir ar his Irland kingis of the Irischerye:	'she')
O Knewlyn, O Conochor, O Gregre Makgrane;	
The Schenachy, the Clarschach,	Gaelic bard; harp
The Ben schene, the Ballach,	
The Crekery, the Corach,	
Scho kennis thaim ilkane.	(I) know each one
	[of them

The lapwing and the cuckoo, a pair of clowns, eventually drive off the harsh-voiced rook, but not before he has said his piece: 'Mony lesingis [lies] he maid; wald let for no man / To spek quhill [while] he spokin had, sparit no thingis'.

Although it has a broader and more humorous aspect, the *Howlat*, like *The Kingis Quair*, belongs to the world of formal literary genres. When Henryson uses animals in his versions of Aesop's fables, they are more fully and more humanely characterised and their milieu is recognisably the place of everyday life and common experience, rather than a theatre of courts, castles and enclosed gardens.

Robert Henryson (1425?–1505?)

We know very little about Robert Henryson. If we believe Dunbar's 'Lament for the Makaris' then death must have had his way with the elder poet sometime before 1508. The honorific 'master' says that he was a university man and a graduate, perhaps of an institution in Europe. Among others, the title-page of the Bassandyne printing of *The Morall Fabillis* (done in 1571) refers to the author as a schoolmaster in Dunfermline. There is also evidence to suggest that he trained in law and operated as a notary public, and he does use legal terms and procedures in his poems. Henryson's fame rests on his fables and on *The Testament of Cresseid* – an extraordinary sequel to Chaucer's *Troilus and Criseyde*. Modern readers have come to value him highly and many would place his poetic achievement as second only to Chaucer, whom he acknowledged himself as the 'flower' of poets. Yet, although he shares something of the Englishman's compassion and sweet humour, Henryson has a terseness and sometimes a grimness of outlook that belongs to a harsher northern clime. Dunbar shows this temperament even more clearly and it is worth pointing out that it seems to be a part of the national psyche long before John Knox and Calvinism arrived to give it a doctrinal dimension.

A poem such as 'The Bludy Serk' suggests that the oral tradition was well established in the Scots canon, and this supernatural tale of how a doomed knight rescues a maiden from a giant shows that Henryson could easily match the laconic edge of the ballad style, even if he does add a literary moral which explains that it is an allegory of Christ and man's soul. In similar fashion the poet takes the old French *pastourelle* genre and, with a light touch, creates the rustic dialogue of 'Robene and Makyne', where canny Robene is concerned more with the welfare of his sheep than with Makyne's passion for him. (When he finally does warm to the idea, she has changed her mind.) Thus Henryson almost always works from established models and yet he so consistently transforms and vivifies his material that it seems as though Aesop's fables were always set in Scottish fields, or as though Troy were truly somewhere near Dunfermline. The poet's talent for realistic detail is expressed in succinct and unpretentious utterance – as though we were listening to the man himself speaking. These particular strengths in Henryson and later poets have done much to define the Scottish literary tradition even to the present day.

It is in his commitment to the human and the natural world that Henryson's Catholic faith and his wry and gentle imagination come together. 'Nane suld presume be ressoun naturall / To seirche the secreitis off the Trinitie', he writes in 'The Preiching of the Swallow': 'Yit nevertheles we may haif knawlegeing / Off God Almychtie be his creatouris / That he is gude, fair, wyis and bening.' Thus the separation of the physical from the spiritual seems artificial to Henryson, for in his view the natural world embodies the spirit quite plainly. When winter comes it is the effect on the animals which the poet visualises in his alliterated lines:

Than flouris fair faidit with froist man fall,	must
And birdis blyith changit thair noitis sweit	
In styll murning, neir slane with snaw and sleit.	
Thir dalis deip with dubbis drounit is,	dales; mud
Baith hill and holt heillit with frostis hair;	woods; hoar frosts
All wyld beistis than ffrom the bentis bair	heaths
Drawis ffor dreid unto thair dennis deip,	
Coucheand ffor cauld in coifis thame to keip.	coves/hollows

With the arrival of spring, man's work in the fields is celebrated until the land, the beasts upon it and the labouring folk are all equally present in the poet's eye and in the mind of God:

Sum makand dyke, and sum the pleuch can wynd,	plough
Sum sawand seidis fast ffrome place to place,	
The Harrowis hoppand in the saweris trace:	
It wes grit Joy to him that luifit corne,	
To se thame laubour, baith at evin and morne.	

'The Preiching of the Swallow' is one of thirteen poems in 'Eloquent and Ornate Scottish Meter' later compiled as *The Morall Fabillis of Esope the Phrygian* (most probably written around the 1460s), in which Henryson retells Aesop and other animal tales from popular tradition. He uses rime royal throughout – a seven-line stanza rhyming *ababbcc* with five stresses in each line – and his sense of humour, whether gently mocking, openly satirical or resolutely stern, is never absent. In 'The Taill How the Foxe Maid his Confessioun to Freir Wolf Waitskaith', the fox wants to salve his conscience and so he approaches Friar Wolf with these pious observations:

'Ye ar Mirrour, lanterne, and sicker way,	certain
Suld gyde sic sempill folk as me to grace.	
Your bair feit, and your Russet Coull off gray,	

Your lene cheik, your paill pietious face.
Schawis to me your perfite haliness.'

The wolf does seem surprisingly well versed in scriptural niceties, and for penance he forbids the fox to eat any meat. Temptation overcomes the sinner, however, and to escape the prohibition he catches a kid and 'christens' it a salmon by drowning it in the sea – 'Ga doun, Schir Kid, cum up Schir Salmond agane!' Stuffed with young goat the wily Tod lies dead to the world musing idly in the sun that it only needs an arrow-shaft sticking out of his belly to complete the picture. Whereupon the goatherd comes along and obliges him. The fox has just enough time to give us his last words: 'allace and wellaway! ... Me think na man may speik ane word in play / Bot now on dayis in ernist it is tane.' The moral of the tale is to beware the sudden stroke of death, lest it catch you unaware, but Henryson's wit gives it a crazier twist.

Many critics have commented on the division between the humorous realism of the fables and the formal virtues which are extolled in the concluding morals. It is tempting to enjoy the fable and to dismiss the moral, but it must be stressed that both elements are equally central to Henryson's vision. The *moralitas* may not always convince, but sometimes it can work with striking subtlety to give a broader, rather than a narrower account of the poem's meaning. In 'The Taill of the Cok and the Jasp', for example, *moralitas* and fable produce a kind of stalemate to trap the reader in real moral issues, quite different from simple maxims. A cock finds a precious jewel in the midden, but since he cannot eat it he leaves it there and goes his way:

Thow hes na corne, and thairof haif I neid,
Thy cullour dois bot confort to the sicht,
And that is not aneuch my wame to feid.   enough; belly

In the fable the cock is a realist, yet the moral tells us he is a fool who prizes only his own ignorance, because the jewel symbolises knowledge and prudence – the only really enduring wealth – without which no one 'can Governe ane Realme, Cietie, or hous'. Alas, says the poet, the jewel is lost these days, still lying somewhere on a dunghill of disregard. While this allegory makes sense in its own terms, it does not mesh with the fable. The cock is not a swine who despises pearls because he knows only swill. On the contrary, he is aware of the Jasp's beauty and he recognises that it should be 'Exaltit in worschip and in grit honour' and set, perhaps, in a king's crown: 'Rise, gentill Jasp, of all stanes the flour, / Out of this midding, and pas quhar thow suld be'. But for himself, he observes that 'houngrie men may not leve on lukis'.

The reader is entirely convinced by this level-headed character and can scarcely blame him for leaving the stone, even if it does symbolise 'knowledge'. In fact, there need not be a contradiction between the two elements, and here again Henryson is using the moral to make his case more subtle. The final message which emerges from 'The Cok and the Jasp' is that knowledge and prudence belong in the first place with the king, and he must not expect too much of the common man, who has to struggle to find dry bread for his belly. If prudence is missing at court, why should it be valued in the farmyard? Moral and tale should not, therefore, be separated, for it is only through their conjunction that we reach the fullest insight into the frailties and contradictions of human existence.

In all aspects of his work Henryson's sympathies lie with the common folk. In "The Taill of the Lyoun and the Mous' the king of the beasts spares an importunate mouse, but at a later date it is the tiny mouse and her relatives – the commoners – who gnaw through the nets to let the trapped lion escape. The *moralitas* extols mercy and vigilance in the great, not just as an abstract virtue, but as a matter of political prudence too, because 'Oftymis is sene' how 'ane man of small degre' can have his quittance of a nobleman. The message is clear: the mice may be small, 'wantoun' and 'unwyse', but they would have left the lion to die had he treated them too harshly at their first encounter: 'Bot King and Lord may weill wit quhat I mene'. The reader, too, will remember that the Declaration of Arbroath warned Robert Bruce that his subjects reserved the right to depose him if he betrayed their interests.

'The Wolf and the Lamb' makes the poet's position even more clear. The moral compares the lamb to the poor people and the wolf to those in power who pervert the laws to suit their own ends, particularly those feudal superiors who practice extortion on tenant farmers. Henryson provides details of how this is usually done and cries out at the plain injustice of a social and agricultural system which has the tenant labouring all day only to leave him 'lytill gude to drink or eit, / With his menye at evin quhen he cummis hame'. The abuse of power through the law is directly satirised in 'The Taill of the Scheip and the Doig' in which the poet observes all the technical niceties of legal procedure and places them in the mouths of a wolf as sheriff, a carrion-crow as beadle, a raven as coroner, a fox as clerk and a hawk as advocate. Little wonder, before such a court, that the sheep has to forfeit his fleece. This vivid and comic attack on the vested interests of authority does not hesitate to spell out its links with the human world.

The speech of the country sister in 'The Uponlandis Mous and the Burges Mous' is a model of native canny brevity, as when she is faced with the delicate titbits of her town sister's table and enquires

> '. . . how lang will this lest?'
> 'For evermair, I wait, and langer to.'   know/expect
> 'Giff it be swa, ye ar at eis' (quod scho).   If it be so

Henryson shares her sense of caution as well as a country-man's taste for understatement, and he reminds us, with a straight face, of the part played by Fortune in the affairs of mice – 'Eftir joye oftymes cummis cair' – and then, when the steward discovers the two creatures at their feast in the cupboard, the poet pauses at just the most dramatic moment to comment dryly, 'Thay taryit not to wesche, as I suppose'. The fable's intimate expertise is entirely convincing in the accents of the country mouse – spokesperson for 'blyithnes in hart with small possessioun' – as she cries to her more sophisticated sister,

> 'I had lever thir fourty dayis fast,   rather
> With watter caill, and to gnaw benis or peis,   cold water
> Than all your feist in this dreid and diseis.'

And with this she returns to her own humble home – undoubtedly situated somewhere in the 'kingdom of Fife'.

The same voice gives unique colouring to Henryson's tale of 'Schir Chantecleir and the Foxe'. In 'The Nonne Preestes Tale' Chaucer's narrative style creates a brilliantly extended parody of rhetorical techniques and chivalric virtues, but the Scots poet's version retains the swift colloquial pace of the other fables. The code of *amour courtois* is exploded simply by reporting what the hens say about their fallen lover. At first, Pertok strikes a high-flown note by lamenting 'our dayis darling / Our nichtingall', but Sprutok – a more practical lady – reminds her that 'als gude lufe cummis as gais', and resolves to 'Chant this sang, "wes never wedow sa gay!" ' As soon as Pertok is relieved of the burden of decorum, she too admits that the cock could not satisfy her and resolves to get within the week a fellow who 'suld better claw oure breik'. 'Schir Chantecleir' has been dismissed in three swift stanzas, and the hens' earthy honesty is a more telling judgement on his vanity than the main plot with the fox. Henryson's fables are full of such delights, demonstrating his ability to handle traditional materials as though the stories had never been told before.

Orpheus and Eurydice leaves the warmer world of the fables to make a grim Christian allegory out of that ancient myth, for the poet sees Orpheus's human and fleshly impatience as all too inevitable, despite his inheritance in the arts of celestial harmony and control. Henryson's most famous poem, about Cresseid's downfall, is equally unrelenting, although it shows a stern care too.

The earliest printed version of *The Testament of Cresseid* was added to Chaucer's *Troilus and Criseyde* in a 1532 edition of the English poet's works. While Henryson's poem (also written in rime royal) is, indeed, a sequel to the longer tale, it demonstrates a very different sensibility. Cresseid's failing is clear-cut – she is faithless and her sin is to blaspheme against Venus and Cupid, the fleshly deities to whom she has given her life. She has reason to be bitter in Henryson's version, for, having betrayed Troilus in favour of Diomede, she is herself discarded by her new lover. The Scots poet's view of the affair is sympathetic but clear-eyed and his spare introduction to her plight sets the mood for the whole poem:

> Quhen Diomeid had all his appetyte,
> And mair, fulfillit of this fair Ladie,
> Upon ane uther he set his haill delyte.

Henryson supplements the terse force of that phrase 'and mair' by noting that some men say that Cresseid became a common

prostitute. She pays dearly for this and for her repudiation of
Venus when the planets visit her in a dream trial, and Saturn
and the Moon afflict her with leprosy. Cresseid's complaint is
a passionate lament for the evanescence of wordly beauty and a
warning about the fickleness of Fortune.

'Nocht is your fairnes bot ane faiding flour,	Nothing
Nocht is your famous laud and hie honour	
Bot wind Inflat in uther mennis eiris.	ears
Your roising reid to rotting sall retour:	rosey skin; return
Exampill mak of me in your Memour!	

The medieval *ubi sunt* theme is evoked with a bitter power.
Cresseid's good looks have become abominable and her very
eyesight has been dimmed by disease, but Henryson's relentless and lucid fatalism makes her pay still more. Troilus passes
one day and drops some alms in her leper's cup. He does not
recognise her in her present state, but the pathetic figure
somehow evokes memories of his erstwhile lover and prompts
his charity. The moment is psychologically convincing. When
Cresseid is told who her benefactor was, she finally accepts
responsibility for her own failed honour, commends herself to
chaste Diana and dies: 'O fals Cresseid and trew Knicht
Troilus . . . Nane but my self as now I will accuse.' When he
hears of her fate, Troilus erects a tomb over her grave.

The bare bones of the plot can give only a hint of the
relentless concentration invested in the poem. It has the speed
and the grim concision of a ballad, conveying beauty, terror
and pity with masterly understatement. From the very start the
Testament is unmistakably the product of a northern sensibility.
Thus the opening lines are set in springtime – a traditional
beginning to a tale of love – but this fresh season has been
symbolically countered by harsh and inclement Scottish
weather:

Ane doolie sessoun to ane cairful dyte	A sad season to a
Suld correspond, and be equivalent.	[sorrowful tale
Richt sa it was quhen I began to wryte	
This tragedie, the wedder richt fervent,	
Quhen Aries, in middis of the Lent,	
Schouris of haill can fra the north discend,	
That scantlie fra the cauld I micht defend.	

The poet himself wants to honour the star of Venus that night, hoping that 'My faidit hart of lufe scho wald mak grene', but the cold air drives him indoors to the fire. This wryly informal and domestic note allows Henryson to express his pity for Cresseid, and yet it never loses sight of the fact that she is a pagan character in a book with her fate already long established and inescapable.

I mend the fyre and beikit me about,	wrapped
Than tuik ane drink my spreitis to comfort,	
And armit me weill fra the cauld thairout:	
To cut the winter nicht and mak it schort,	
I tuik ane Quair, and left all uther sport,	book
Written be worthie Chaucer glorious,	
Of fair Cresseid, and worthie Troylus.	

Of his distres me neidis nocht reheirs,
For worthie Chauceir in the samin buik
In gudelie termis and in Joly veirs
Compylit hes his cairis, quha will luik.
To brek my sleip ane uther quair I tuik,
In quihilk I fand the fatall destenie
Of fair Cresseid, that endit wretchitlie

Quha wait gif all that Chauceir wrait was trew?	Who knows if

Henryson sustains his objectivity by admitting that parts of the tale are not clear to him; thus Cresseid's pain is distanced from us and yet, paradoxically, the method actually increases the emotional effect: 'Gif scho in hart was wa [sad] eneuch, God wait!'; and then: '*Sum said* he maid ane Tomb of Merbell gray / And wrait her name. ...' When Calchas sees his daughter's leprosy for the first time his lament is interrupted by the poet's curt comment, 'Thus was thair cair aneuch betwix thame twane'. The same succinct force can be found on Cresseid's lips, too, when she bewails the passing of her old life and realises her fate:

And for they Bed tak now ane bunche of stro,	
For waillit Wyne, and Meitis thou had tho,	choice
Tak mowlit Breid, Peirrie and Ceder sour:	mouldy
Bot cop and Clapper, now is all ago.	Begging cup and [leper's clapper

Chaucer's version of the tale involves itself brilliantly and at length with the sophisticated moods and trials of courtly love; but when Henryson has Troilus reflect on the affair he sums it up with a stunning simplicity: 'Siching [sighing] full sadlie, said, "I can no moir,/Scho was untrew, and wo is me thairfoir."' Such brevity is only the mask of feeling and, indeed, there is a moving tenderness in how the characters treat one another, as when Calchas welcomes his fallen daughter, or when Troilus gives alms, or in how Henryson himself describes the leper folk and how they receive Cresseid with a loving and practical concern:

'Sen thy weiping dowbillis bot thy wo,	Since; doubles
I counsail the mak vertew of ane neid.	
To leir to clap thy Clapper to and fro,	learn
And leve eftir the law of lipper leid.'	leper people

The poet's narrative pace can be fast or lingering to equal effect, as when Cresseid, newly afflicted with her disease, is summoned to dinner by a serving-boy. She notices his good looks.

Quod scho: 'Fair Chyld ga to my Father deir,
And pray him come to speak with me anone'.
And sa he did, and said: 'Douchter quhat cheir?'

At other times the speed of the verse is greatly reduced, as the poet draws on the older alliterative-verse tradition and adds his talent for domestic realism in order to convey the full terror of Saturn's presence:

His face fronsit, his lyre was lyke the Leid.	frozen; skin; lead
His teith chatterit, and cheverit with the Chin,	
His ene drowpit, how sonkin in his heid,	
Out of his Nois the Meldrop fast can rin,	drips
With lippas bla and cheikis leine and thin.	blue

'Robene and Makyne', 'The Bludy Serk' and the *Morall Fabillis* have the same mastery of pace and ballad-like concision, but the humane irony of Henryson's always direct and colloquial presence reach their highest achievement in *The Testament* and have given us some of the finest passages in European literature.

Sum said he maid ane Tomb of Merbell gray,
And wrait hir name and superscriptioun,
And laid it on hir grave quhair that scho lay,
In goldin Letteris, conteining this ressoun:
'Lo, fair Ladyis, Crisseid, of Troyis toun,
Sumtyme countit the flour of Womanheid,
Under this stane lait Lipper lyis deid.'

Henryson has the final word and the last line of the poem
vibrates with his strong and tenderly fatalistic charity: 'Sen
scho is deid, I speik of hir no moir.'

Blind Harry (1450–93)

If Barbour's *Bruce* reads like a historical chronicle and a
consideration of patriotism written by a priest of the Church,
then Blind Harry's *Wallace* is a popular thriller in which the
reader is caught up by the narrative to ask 'what happens next'
through twelve books of verse. The *Wallace* is quite unlike
Golagros and Gawane and other knightly romances of its time –
for in place of tales of chivalry it offers a crude but forceful
character study of its hero, full of circumstantial details and a
heightened and bloody realism. *The Actes and Deidis of the Illustre
and Vallyeant Campioun Schir William Wallace* must have been
written around 1477 – 170 years after the events it describes –
and it is instructive to compare it with the nearly contemporary
Morte d'Arthur. Malory's great prose work looks back to an
imagined world of knights and ladies, and even as he describes
the break-up of the Round Table he enshrines the values of
chivalry and purity symbolised by the quest for the Holy Grail.
Harry's *Wallace* has no such spiritual dimension and little time
for the melancholy nobility of Malory's conclusion. On the
contrary, the Scotsman's many descriptions of split brains and
arms hewn away re-create the details of combat as if from a
footsoldier's point of view. For this reason the poem is much
closer to the truth of warfare and the cruelty of the thirteenth, or
indeed the fifteenth century. It is also closer to what we might
assume to be the popular taste (then as now) for a succession of
gory effects.

We have few details about the author. He seems to have been
a professional poet and it is known that on various occasions he

appeared at court and received money from James IV. He is mentioned in the 'Lament for the Makaris' and probably died about 1492; and, although he is traditionally referred to as 'Blind Harry', it is not certain that he was born blind. At least one scholar has argued that the poet's grasp of military action and his descriptions of the weather and the lie of the landscape suggest that he lost his sight late in life. Harry describes himself as unlearned – 'a burell man' – and late-eighteenth-century critics were keen to support him in the role of rustic Homer – a blind peasant bard. This underestimates the skills available within the oral tradition, nor does it accord with the plain and forceful versifying in Harry's heroic couplets, perhaps the earliest use of this measure in Scotland.

However composed, the *Wallace* became one of the nation's most popular books and, until Burns came on the scene, the most often reprinted. Indeed, the poem virtually 'invented' the heroic figure of William Wallace as it is known today, for, although Harry claimed to be following a Latin original written by Wallace's chaplain, it seems as likely that he compiled the work himself from surviving tales, folk sources and his own imagination. His purpose was unashamedly nationalistic and anti-English. At a time when James III was attempting to make peace with this southern neighbours, Harry speaks for perpetual opposition, for keeping faith with France and for warlike virtues in a leader. Wallace would rather kill Englishmen than ransom them, and this is entirely in keeping with the facts of battle as they have always been for the mere troops. Indeed, this lack of knightly graces probably established him even more securely as a fully fledged folk hero.

The poem is long and in places merely tedious, but gradually a genuinely impressive picture emerges of a martyr swordfighter who will rescue Scotland on three different occasions before going – treacherously betrayed – to his own death. Robert Burns testified to the power of this figure to 'pour a Scottish prejudice' in his veins even in William Hamilton's shortened paraphrased version of the original. From the very start we gain a sense of Harry's Wallace as a fated person, rather like one of Marlowe's granitic heroes. Thus the young man has the misfortune to be bullied by a succession of arrogant (and ill-advised) Englishmen, as when he is fishing peacefully by a river and gets into an argument with five of Percy's men who demand his catch for their lord. The teenage Wallace, armed only with a net on a pole and accompanied by a boy, is prepared to give them some but adds (too familiarly for the Englishmen), 'Gud frend, leiff part and tak nocht all away.' The retainer insists on having the lot and the vivid dialogue takes a more deadly turn:

'We serf a lord. Thir fische sall till him gang'.	
Wallace ansuerd, said, 'Thow art in the wrang.'	
'Quham dowis thow, Scot? In faith thow servis a	Whom do you
blaw.'	[address as 'thou'
Till him he ran and out a swerd can draw.	
Willyham was wa he had na wapynnis thar.	
Bot the poutstaff the quhilk in hand he bar.	netpole
Wallas with it fast on the cheik him tuk	
Wyth so gud will quhill of his feit he schuk.	
The suerd flaw fra him a fut breid on the land.	
Wallas was glaid and hynt it sone in hand,	glad and took it
And with the swerd ane awkwart straik him gawe,	
Wndyr the hat his crage in sondir drawe.	under; neck
Be that the layff lychtyt about Wallas.	the rest set about
He had no helpe only bot goddis grace.	

(I, 397–410)

When two English survivors escape to tell Percy of the fight, the lord laughs at their discomfiture and refuses to pursue the Scot further. All the same, the hero flees the neighbourhood and Harry comments that he never left his sword behind again.

The poem's short sentences, terse dialogue and detailed violence make it particularly active and dramatic. Although larger than life as a warrior, Wallace is not without some human qualities. He has a sense of humour (predictably grim) and his sufferings in battle and in sickness allow us to sympathise with him when his destiny and his own relentless will call him back to the practice of death after an all-too-brief spell of married happiness. At this point, the narrative takes a more tender and musical turn as it slips into ballat royal, an eight-line French stanza-form:

Now leiff thi myrth, now leiff thi haill plesance,	leave
Now leiff this blis, now leiff thi childis age,	
Now leiff thi youth, now folow thi hard chance,	
Now leiff thi lust, now leiff this mariage.	
Now leiff thi luff, for thow sall los a gage	lose a pledge
Quhilk neuir in erd sall be redemyt agayne.	

> Folow fortoun and all hir fers outrage.   fortune
> Go leiff in wer, go leiff in cruell payne,   live
>   (VI, 81–8)

The tale soon returns to heroic couplets, however, as Wallace's
wife is killed and he dedicates himself to further slaughter with
a righteous and savage efficiency. If the tale dwells too much on
killing Englishmen and general mayhem, it draws a veil over
the manner of its hero's actual death, for William Wallace was
hanged, cut down while still alive and disembowelled before his
own eyes. Wallace was a hero and a martyr to his contemporaries, but Blind Harry's poem made him a legend, until
even William Wordsworth intones the name as though it were
talisman for a later revolution, synonymous with freedom itself:

> How Wallace fought for Scotland; left the name
> Of Wallace to be found, like a wild flower,
> All over his dear Country; left the deeds
> Of Wallace, like a family of Ghosts,
> To people the steep rocks and river banks,
> Her natural sanctuaries, with a local soul
> Of independence and stern liberty.
>   (*The Prelude*, I, 213–19)

'Anonymous' poets

If we lack details of Blind Harry, there are poems from the
latter half of the fifteenth century whose authors cannot now be
traced at all. *The Knightly Tale of Golagros and Gawane* might have
been written by Clerk of Tranent, cited in Dunbar's 'Lament'
as the man who 'maid the Anteris of Gawane', but we cannot be
sure. The poem is most likely contemporary with the *Wallace*
but, quite unlike Harry's work, it is a courtly fiction which
belongs to the fabled past with a plot of twelfth-century French
origins in *Le Conte du Graal*. The climax involves a battle
between rival champions Gawaine and Golagros. To save his
opponent's face, and because he cannot bear to kill him
outright, Gawaine pretends to lose the match. In the light of his
gentlemanly discretion the two knights and their factions are
soon reconciled. The poem uses the same thirteen-line stanza-
form as *The Buke of the Howlat* – a favourite for alliterative
romances. The same measure appears in *Rauf Coilyear*, and

other similarities between the two romances suggest that the poet of *Rauf* was at least familiar with the Gawain piece.

Rauf Coilyear goes back to the age of chivalry as well, but it gains a satirical or at least a humorous angle by making its short-tempered hero a charcoal-burner (collier) by trade. Rauf becomes involved with Charlemagne when the king gets lost in a storm while out hunting. The charcoal-burner offers shelter to the stranger but loses his temper with his anonymous guest when the latter's royal manners and polite hesitations make him slow to do his host's bidding. The great king receives buffets and a lecture on manners:

> 'Thow suld be courtes of kynd, and ane cunnand courteir.
> Thocht that I simpill be,
> Do as I bid the,
> The hous is myne pardie,
> And all that is heir.'

The host may be 'thrawin' but his table is generous with much game, taken, he explains, from the king's forest. Charles says he is one Wymond of the queen's wardrobe and they part the next day with an agreement that Rauf will be paid to deliver a load of coal to the court on Christmas Day. The fiery collier is somewhat abashed when he discovers the true identity of his guest, but Charles gives him armour, a retinue and makes him a knight. All the same, he must still win his spurs by combat and this leads to further complications, but the tale ends happily and Rauf is made Marshal of France.

The two parts of Rauf Coilyear's tale almost certainly come from French sources, although stories of incognito kings were common in England, too; but the setting, the weather and the bloody-minded independence of the hero have all been given a distinctively Scottish colouring. What begins as a rather pointed comment on manners, chivalry and the common man ends as an unlikely romance where everyone is rewarded with high office. Nevertheless, we appreciate the peppery Rauf of the earlier passages who proves with his fists the old French proverb that 'Charbonnier est maître chez soi' and who might have been a model for the medieval understanding that to be a Scot was to have *piper in naso*, pepper in your nose.

The world of romance joins with the supernatural in poems such as 'King Berdok', 'The Gyre-Carling' and 'Lord Fergus'

Ghost'. These pieces have an odd flavour, for they read less like magic and more like tall tales, and so they forfeit the sense of mystery and terror that the best of the great ballads have, not to mention that vital intimation of other planes of being. On the other hand, they take a matter-of-fact approach to the everyday and couple it with an unusual sense of the instability of the physical world. It is a grotesque and striking combination. Hence Berdok, king of Babylon, lives in a cabbage-stalk in summer while a cockle-shell keeps him warm in winter, because, as the unknown author patiently explains, 'Kingis usit nocht to weir clayis in tha dayis.' The burlesque is grosser but the dislocating effect is the same in 'The Gyre-Carling', which, among other unlikely things, explains that the distinctive conical shape of the hill known as Berwick Law was produced by a witch who expelled it as a turd in her mirth.

While 'The Gyre-Carling' is outlandish, the scatological anti-Gaelic humour of 'How the First Helandman, of God was Maid', is closer to the realities of social and racial prejudice. (The poem is sometimes attributed to Montgomerie but is most likely to be an earlier production.) The author's position is clear from the start, for the title notes that the hero was made 'of ane horss turd, in Argylle, as is said', and no sooner is he created than he steals God's gully-knife and promises that, for as long as he can get gear thus, he will never work. The whole outrageous slander is expressed in the most good-humoured way, evincing a sturdy Scottish familiarity with the supreme being and his saints:

> God and Sanct Petir was gangand be the way,
> Heiche up in Ardgyle, quhair thair gait lay.
> Sanct Petir said to God in a sport word,
> 'Can ye nocht mak a Helandman of this horss turd?'
> God turned owre the horss turd with his pykit staff,
> And up start a Helandman blak as ony draff.   dregs
> Quod God to the Helandman 'Quhair wilt thow now?'
> 'I will down in the Lawland, Lord, and thair steill a kow.'

The economic foundations for Lowland prejudice could not be more succinctly put.

The failings of the priesthood provided equally popular material for broad comedy in verse, and 'The Freiris of Berwick' is sometimes attributed to Dunbar, although it lacks technical incisiveness and his acerbic spirit. This lively piece tells how two friars outwit the adulterous wife of an innkeeper and enjoy a luxurious meal at her expense. 'Colkelbie's Sow' also mixes the domestic, and the far-fetched (with a rather ponderous sense of humour), by playing on the disparity between its subject and a plot loosely based on the biblical parable of the talents, complete with *sententiae*, a 'prohemium' and apologies for its 'mokking meteris and mad matere'. Its three parts, in rather anglicised Scots, tell what became of the three pennies that Colkelbie got when he sold his pig. The author claims that he learned these tales and their moral implications from his toothless great-grandmother who had many such stories fresh in her mind. The poem's loose structure and its succession of ingenious events are, indeed, very reminiscent of oral fireside tales, although its use of 'literary' apparatus suggests a self-conscious and bookish side to the narrator as well.

A vivid and hilarious sense of country life characterises 'Peblis to the Play' and 'Christis Kirk of the Green', the best of the anonymous poems of this period. They have been ascribed to James I, but a later author is much more likely. Both poems give a light-hearted account of the antics that took place on two holiday occasions. 'Peblis' happens at Beltane (the old Scots fire festival that ushers in the summer), and the description of the 'play' – of the wooing and dancing and drinking and fighting – is undoubtedly true to the life and spirit of that festival. 'Christis Kirk' sets out to cap even Peebles's distinction, with extravagant behaviour described at a local fair-day:

Was never in Scotland heard nor seen
    Sic dauncing nor deray,   disturbance
Neither at Falkland on the green,
    Nor Peblis at the play
As was of wooeris, as I ween,   suitors
    At Christ Kirk on ane day:
There come our kitties washen clean
    In their new kirtillis of grey,
        Full gay,
At Christis Kirk of the green.

Both poems are remarkable for their rollicking rhythms, and this pattern has been much copied, with variations, in later

Scots verse. The stanzas have ten lines each, the first eight of
which rhyme *ababababab* on alternate iambic tetrameter and
trimeter. This provides a 'headlong' pace further emphasised
by alliteration and the recurrence of the rhyme. Then there
comes a 'bob-wheel' line of only two syllables to be clinched by
a six-syllable refrain which is the title of the piece repeated at
this point throughout the poem. The 'bob' line gives a most
distinctive catch at the end of each stanza before precipitating
the reader on to the next. This effect is especially well suited to
recitation or singing and it does much to enhance the broad wit
of the poems and to further their irresistible comic progress.

Fergusson and Burns learned much from these patterns and
both use nine-line versions of them (without the 'bob') for their
own accounts of the people at play: Fergusson in 'Hallow-Fair'
and 'Leith Races' and Burns in 'The Ordination' and 'The
Holy Fair'. What the later poets gain in satirical and social
comment, their unknown predecessor makes up for with a
boisterousness that recalls a Flemish Kermesse by Breughel
full of fierce dancing, willing women, brawling men and some
pretty wild play with bows and arrows:

A yaip young man that stude him neist	keen
Loused off a shot with ire;	
He ettled the bern in at the breist,	aimed at the man's breast
The bolt flew owre the byre;	over the cowshed
And cryit Fy! he had slain a priest	
A mile beyond ane mire;	
Than bow and bag fra him he kest,	cast
And fled as fierce as fire	
Off flint,	
At Christis Kirk of the green.	

'Symmie and his Bruder' is yet another of those popular
verses about merry friars – notable for its use of the 'Christis
Kirk' stanza – but 'The Thrie Tailes of the Thrie Priests of
Peblis' is a longer and more conscientious affair, probably
dating from the 1480s and commenting on the social ills and
political failings in the reign of James III. It is a modest satire
mainly concerned with telling its tales – and stories within the
stories – as recounted by three priests after a particularly
satisfying and worldly supper. Its cheerful vernacular uses
homely couplets based on a pentameter line, and the tales,
borrowed from older models or fablieux, have a simple

domestic realism. It is possible to see an underlying unease in some of them about the growing power of money and the burgess class in the fifteenth century. In the last analysis, however, they remain a series of moral fables, and one has to look to Dunbar for the excitements of witty and acid criticism and to David Lindsay in the next century before social satire becomes a fully sharpened political weapon.

William Dunbar (1460?–1520?)

The fifteenth century ended with a 'second golden age' and a contemporary report from one Don Pedro de Ayala paints a picture of James IV as a gifted Renaissance prince. De Ayala was commissioned to his task because of Spain's eagerness to make an alliance with Scotland, and so in 1498 he sent off a document in cypher which described the king and his country. Doubtless the report is somewhat idealised, but Ayala had no reason to flatter or to lie outright. He tells of a well-read man with several languages, generous, handsome, popular and valiant to the point of recklessness in physical combat. He describes a country which is prosperous but not rich and a people who are extremely hospitable, bold, proud of appearances and quick to take offence. There is a contradictory side to the monarch, however, which de Ayala does not report, although it makes James even more a man of his times – a Renaissance prince whose temperament and whose kingdom, too, still retains something of a darker medieval past. The king was haunted by remorse all his life, perhaps for the part he felt he had played in his father's death, and so he went on religious retreats and was given to bouts of melancholy. He wore an iron chain around his waist in penance and yet he enjoyed an extravagant life, devoted to magnificent pageants, gambling, making love, good clothes and music. He shared these passions with equally strong intellectual pursuits, having an act passed in 1496 to make education compulsory for the offspring of men of substance and sending his own two illegitimate sons to be educated in Italy, where they studied for a while under Erasmus. By the end of his reign the extent of these enthusiasms and his practical excitement with artillery, alchemy, surgery and great warships had left the crown almost bankrupt. He was

considerate and generous to religious orders and equally
open-handed to passing musicians, jugglers and mountebanks.
All his life he hoped to lead a crusade to the Holy Land, but at
home he rewarded the most unsuitable men with powerful
ecclesiastical positions. He was the last Scots ruler to speak
Gaelic and he encouraged the commons to approach him and
give him their opinions freely. In his strengths and failings,
James is not unique among monarchs of his time, but the
generous scope of his involvements and the number of his
contradictions make him an especially colourful, headstrong
and romantic figure – one of Scotland's most popular kings.

William Dunbar is the most significant literary figure of the
late fifteenth and early sixteenth century, a poet whose
technical skill is second to none. He mastered English stanza-
forms from Chaucer and Lydgate and he was equally at home
with French style, especially in the use of refrain. (His
particular forte is to use refrains supported by strong alliteration carried over into two or three lines of the verse.) Despite his
technical brilliance, his humour can be harsh and pessimistic at
times, closer to the late medieval mood than to that of the
Renaissance. And yet, in some of his wilder parodies and in
moments of personal doubt, he seems much more modern – a
spirit from the seventeenth or even the twentieth century.
Because of these contradictions he epitomises more than any
other writer the brilliance, the materialistic confidence and the
spiritual unease of James's court and the stirrings of the
Renaissance in Scotland.

We know little of Dunbar's life except that he was born
around 1460 and educated at St Andrew's University; he may
have become a Franciscan novice and he probably travelled a
fair amount, visiting Paris and Oxford. For the last ten years of
the century he seems to have served James as a notary and an
ambassador, particularly in connection with the king's various
plans for marriage. We know that Dunbar wanted a benefice as
recompense for his services, but he had to settle for a series of
pensions instead, probably given to him for his skill as a poet.
Most of the poems which have survived date between 1490 and
1510 and they give a vivid picture of the court and its doings,
unequalled in their colour and frankness.

Dunbar's commitment as a professional bard can be seen in
formal, ceremonial works such as the poem which has come to

be known as 'The Thistle and the Rose', commemorating the political marriage which James made with Margaret Tudor of England, in 1503. It uses the dream-vision convention to tell how the Thistle is crowned king of plants before celebrating its marriage to the red and white (English) rose. In the same vein, 'Blyth Aberdeane' records the pageants with which this 'beryl of all touns' greeted Queen Margaret when she visited the North-East in 1511. The more ornate alliteration of 'Renounit, ryall, right reverend and serene' is a flattering address to Barnardus Stewart, who arrived at court in 1508 as ambassador from King Louis XII of France: 'B in thi name betaknis batalrus, / A able in field, R right renoune most hie' and so on: a poem doing what is expected of it and no more.

Dunbar admired Chaucer for his 'fresch anamalit termes celicall', but the Scotsman's aureate verse has no equal and his work abounds in brilliant and highly coloured descriptions. He shows us less of the natural sphere than Henryson, whose poems are closer to the world of fields and seasons, but his images have a hard elaborate and jewel-like intensity which has impressed many readers over the centuries. This richness is especially evident in the divine poems, such as the address to the Virgin Mary, 'Hale sterne superne, hale in eterne', where the verse achieves a music-like abstraction wholly given over to bright, clashing metallic effects of alliterative and assonantal virtuosity – the verbal equivalent of a page from the Book of Kells:

Empryce of prys, imperatrice,	Empress
Brycht polist precious stane,	
Victrice of vyce, hie genetrice	
Of Jhesu, lord soverayne:	
Our wys pavys fra enemys	shield
Agane the feyndis trayne,	fiend's followers
Oratrice, mediatrice, salvatrice,	
To God gret suffragane:	
Ave Maria, gracia plena,	
Haile sterne meridiane,	
Spyce, flour delyce of paradys	
That baire the gloryus grayne.	seed

When the poet dreams of Christ's passion on Good Friday ('Amang thir freiris within ane cloister'), it is the physical details of the torment which immediately engage him, and he even imagines that the soldiers let the cross fall deliberately, to hurt the saviour more, before they raise him above Calvary. The poem concludes with abstractions and the dreamer is assailed by personifications such as Compassion, Contrition, Ruth and Remembrance. In another poem it is the Resurrection on Easter Sunday and the harrowing of Hell that stir Dunbar to announce, 'Done is a battell on the dragon blak', where the lines resound like a gong with military triumph as the murk of the pit is suddenly penetrated by crystal-clear light:

> The grit victour agane is rissen on hicht
> That for our querrell to the deth wes woundit;
> The sone that wox all paill now schynis bricht,
> And, dirknes clerit, our fayth is now refoundit:
> The knell of mercy fra the hevin is soundit,
> The Cristin ar deliverit of thair wo,
> The Jowis and thair errour ar confoundit: Jews
> *Surrexit dominus de sepulchro.*
>
> The fo is chasit, the battell is done ceis,
> The presone brokin, the jevellouris fleit and flemit . . .   gaolers
>   [fled and banished

The exalted orchestration of language and sound in these poems leaves little scope for empathy or a more personal approach to God and, despite its great artistic power, this achievement reveals quite a lot about Dunbar's sensibility. Perhaps he did have an affinity with the Celtic love of complex and elaborate organic patterns developed to the point of pure abstraction.

'The Goldyn Targe' demonstrates Dunbar's aureate and emblematic imagination at work in a secular vein. In a dream allegory of a tournament the golden shield of the poet's reason is eventually, inevitably, overcome by a congregation of all the feminine virtues, seasons and goddesses. The players are borrowed from the *Roman de la Rose* and the stanza from Chaucer's 'Compleynt of Faire Anelida'. (The same pattern crops up at the start of Book II of the *Wallace*.) The poem is set traditionally in the month of May. The sunlight becomes 'clear', 'purified', 'crystalline', an effect typical of Dunbar's vision, and reminiscent, too, of parts of *The Kingis Quair*:

The rosis yong, new spreding of thair knopis,	buds
War powderit brycht with hevinly beriall droppis;	beryl
Throu bemes rede birnying as ruby sperkis	
The skyes rang for schoutyng of the larkis;	
The purpur hevyn, ourscailit in silvir sloppis,	overflowing;
Ourgilt the treis, branchis lef, and barkis	gilded over

Henryson's animals and plants have an individual existence as well as a place in the wider domestic ecology; but, for Dunbar, fish, fowl and flowers are turned to enamelled emblems of nature and set in a brilliant and Byzantine mosaic.

In a less elevated mode, the poet's skill with appearances provides a uniquely lively record of domestic behaviour at the court of King James. He describes a dance in the Queen's chamber ('Sir Jhon Sinclair begouthe to dance') and delights in exposing the antics of her retinue. Court physician Robert Shaw staggers like a hobbled cart-horse; Dunbar himself capers like a wanton colt until he loses his slipper; and in the extremity of the jig the Queen's almoner breaks wind 'lyk a stirk stackrand in the ry' [bullock staggering in the rye]. 'A mirrear dance mycht na man se', and Dunbar gleefully exposes the vulgar, mortal clay beneath the rich clothes and the pompous behaviour. From the evidence of such poems it becomes apparent that Dunbar's relationship with the court was at times a mixed and uneasy thing. He reminds the king that he has not yet received his expected advancement and begs him to listen to a petition from the Queen on his behalf ('Schir, for your grace bayth nicht and day'). Or he tells of his ambition to gain a benefice – 'Schir, yit remember as of befoir' – and presents James, and the reader, with a curious amalgam of slyly comic pathos and painful need: 'Jok that wes wont to keip the stirkis / Can now draw him ane cleik of kirkis . . . Worth all my ballatis undir the birkis [birch trees] / Exces of thocht dois me mischief.' With the same wry mixture he portrays himself in another poem as an old grey horse, poorly clad and cast aside without a decent stall to winter in ('Schir lett it nevir in toun be tald'). Yet this is not Dunbar's only persona, and the mask of a faithful old steed is cast aside to reveal sharper teeth and a less venerable nature when he pays off old scores by attacking James Dog, or Doig, the keeper of the queen's wardrobe, who was rash enough to deny him a new doublet. ('The wardraipper of Venus boure' and 'O gracious princes, guid and fair'.)

Flyting and the Gaelic influence

Dunbar's acid and brilliant technique is given traditional scope under the guise of flyting. Literary flyting – 'scolding' – was a popular mode in fifteenth- and sixteenth-century Scotland. It is a disputation in verse between poets, and a licence for inspired and absurd invective. Sheer expressive extravagance and technical ingenuity is the thing, and, like a bout of professional wrestling, the contestants need not actually dislike each other before or even after the exercise. The genre owes much more to oral contests in medieval Gaelic verse than it does to anything in the European canon, and its heavily patterned hyperbolic abuse and its delight in the grotesque show the other side of the bardic praise poems. Indeed, the Gaelic bard's skill with words was truly a weapon in an oral society and he could threaten his enemies or a backsliding benefactor with verses which would confer on them an uncomfortable notoriety. A poet's curse was best avoided, and popular belief held that it could even raise blisters. The Bannatyne Manuscript contains examples of flyting such as 'The Flytting betwix the Sowtar and the Tailyar' – shoemakers and tailors being traditional enemies. In the 1580s Alexander Montgomerie and Sir Patrick Hume of Polwarth produced and delivered between them the 'Polwart and Montgomerie Flytting' and the story is that King James VI pronounced Montgomerie the victor. 'The Flyting of Dunbar and Kennedy' is the earliest surviving example of this genre. The two poets take turns at blast and counterblast, and it is likely that these originally went round the court as manuscripts or they may even have been performed as a verbal duel. Either way, they provide an outlet for the popular delight in grotesquerie already found in 'King Berdok' and 'The Gyre-Carling'.

Walter Kennedy (1460?–1508?), of noble descent, was a contemporary of Dunbar, and in his time he was almost as well known a poet as his adversary. He came from the Carrick district of Ayrshire, and Dunbar takes the opportunity to mock his knowledge of Gaelic and his country manners: 'Thy trechour tung hes ane Heland strynd;/ Ane Lawland erse wald make a bettir noyis'; and 'The gallowis gaipis eftir thy graceless gruntill, [snout]/ As thow wald for an haggeis, hungry gled' [hawk]. Regarding himself as a more sophisticated figure, Dunbar concentrates his attack on Kennedy's personal appearance and on his gaucheness when he appears in the capital: 'Stra wispis hingis owt quhair that the wattis [welts] ar worne . . . Than rynis thow down the gait [street] with gild of boyis, / And all the toun tykis hingand in thy heilis'. The poem gains force like a terrible spell – 'I conjure the, thow hungert heland gaist' – and ends with a veritable snare-drummer's paradiddle of internal rhyme and alliteration:

> Baird rehator, theif of natur, fals tratour,   Bard enemy
>> feyindis gett;
> Filling of tauch, rak sauch, cry crauch, thow art
>> oursett;
> Muttoun dryver, girnall ryver, yadswyvar, fowll fell
>> the;
> Herretyk, lunatyk, purspyk, carlingis pet,
> Rottin crok, dirtin dok, cry cok, or I sall quell
>> the.

Such virtuosity was not limited to flyting, of course, for it appears as a kind of choral music in Dunbar's holy poems, such as 'Hale sterne superne, hale in eterne', and indeed Henryson's 'Prayer for the Pest' concluded with just such a flourish:

> Superne / Lucerne / guberne / this pestilens,
> preserve / and serve / that we not sterve thairin.
> Declyne / that pyne / be they Devyne prudens.

Internal rhyme was a popular device on both sides of the Border in medieval Latin verse and hymns, but its special density in Scottish poetry, especially in the work of Dunbar, and in the later poems of Alexander Scott and Alexander Montgomerie, suggests a particularly northern predilection for such effects. In fact the Gaelic bards delighted in the most complex preset patterns of internal rhymes and alliterations, usually set out in syllabic couplets and four-line stanzas. Whether Dunbar knew Gaelic well or not, it seems very likely that he and his audience responded to such effects, because they were already present as a familir part of Scotland's Celtic heritage. After all, his rival Kennedy and the practice of flyting itself both came from these roots, and we know that James could speak Gaelic and rewarded Gaelic poets for recitals at court. On the other hand, Dunbar's overwhelming use of strong initial stresses, and the harsh and explosive consonants in his lines belong to the Lowland Scots tradition, with its links to Old English and Scandinavian sounds. By comparison, Gaelic verse lays greater emphasis on the softer chiming of assonance among internal vowels.

Despite his Gaelic heritage, Kennedy cannot quite rise to Dunbar's virtuosity in verse; on the other hand, it does lead him to attack his enemy's genealogy by giving his family a long tradition of cowardice and treachery and connivance with the English. He defends Gaelic as 'the gud language of this land' that 'sould be all trew Scottis mennis leid'. Such national feeling is significant, and we remember that Gaelic was still being spoken at this time in Galloway, Perthshire and the North-East, even if it was not the language of Lowland power.

Flyting is a hectic and specialised form, and Dunbar's comic gift is better displayed, at least to modern tastes, in his skill with burlesque and parody. In 'Ane Ballat of the Fenyeit Frier of Tungland' he satirises John Damian, an alchemist and 'sham friar' whom James had made abbot of Tungland in Galloway, much to Dunbar's disgust. Damian literally fell from royal grace, however, when he attempted to fly like Icarus from the battlements of Stirling Castle, only to plummet into a dunghill and break his thigh. In vain did he explain that he only failed because he had glued too many hen feathers among the eagle's plumes on his wings, and that hen feathers 'covet the mydding and not the skyis'. Dunbar tells the tale with undisguised glee, and the same colloquial gusto with which he scolds the merchants of Edinburgh for the noisy, crowded and smelly streets of their city ('Quhy will ye marchantis of renoun'). In other poems he follows French and Latin models by parodying the office of the dead in order to satirise a drunken court physician ('I, Maister Andro Kennedy'), or to persuade the king to stop doing penance with the Franciscans at Stirling, which is 'purgatory' compared to the heavenly delights of holding court in the capital ('We that are heir in hevins glory').

James was a part of this contradictory milieu, surrounded by brilliant men and importuned by place-seekers and charlatans. Dunbar hated the scene and yet he loves to depict it in poems which were written, after all, for the entertainment of the principal players. In 'Schir ye have mony servitouris' he points out that his own work will last as long as anything done by the king's company of diviners, philosophers, shipbuilders and 'uther gudlie wichtis'. Furthermore, he complains that other, much less worthy types seem to thrive at court – the 'fenyeouris, fleichouris, and flatteraris' (pretenders, coaxers and flatterers), the 'fantastik fulis bayth fals and gredy, / Of toung untrew and hand evill diedie', the gossips, spongers, parasites, shovers and pushers, jostlers and thrusters who scurry and crowd in the corridors of power and who respect learning in no man. Here is the darker side of the life described by Don Pedro de Ayala, and in a characteristically devastating use of the catalogue Dunbar assembles it for our delectation and conveys his contempt in a *tour de force* of accumulating alliterative epithets:

Cryaris, craikaris, and clatteraris,	
Soukaris, groukaris, gledaris, gunnaris,	
Monsouris of France, gud claret cunnaris,	
Inopportoun askaris of Yrland kynd,	
And meit revaris lyk out of mynd,	meat rustlers
Scaffaris and scamleris in the nuke,	
And hall huntaris of draik and duik,	
Thrimlaris and thristaris as thay war woid,	
Kokenis, and kennis na man of gude,	rogues
Schulderaris and schowaris that hes no schame,	
And to no cunning than can clame,	knowledge
And can non uthir craft nor curis	
Bot to mak thrang, schir, in your duris,	
And rusche in quhair thay counsale heir,	
And will at na man nurtit leyr	learn

The poet's heart nearly bursts when all these creatures reap favour and he is ignored. He is just at the point of crying 'fy on this fals world', when an outrageous afterthought prompts him to conclude that he might be more patient if he, too, had some reward with the rest:

Had I rewarde among the laif:	others
It wald me sumthing satisfie	
And les of my malancolie,	
And gar me mony falt ouerse	make; overlook
That now is brayd befoir myn e . . .	

The comic effrontery of this offer to write fewer satirical attacks if he is rewarded more is breathtaking, and yet curiously touching as well. We are moved because we sense that he probably means it. Dunbar's eye is unsparing when he regards the court; he mocks, chastises and derides it with all his considerable wit and technical dexterity, but ultimately he needs it, and he belongs to it body and soul.

Perhaps it is his dependence on the court that makes Dunbar's forays against it so successful; but there is a wilder, demonic side to his imagination, and this, too, must play a part in giving his work its special edge. 'The Dance of the Sevin Deidly Synnis' conjures up personifications of Pride, Anger, Envy, and so on, and sets them cavorting to the latest steps from France in a nightmarish version of that dance in the Queen's chamber. The seven sins were a common motif in medieval literature and art, but Dunbar's vision of their awful reel in Hell seems to be an original twist. They are brilliantly and specifically characterised, simultaneously comic and disgusting:

> And first of all in dance wes Pryd,
> With hair wyld bak and bonet on syd . . .
>
> Than Yre come in with sturt and stryfe,
> His hand wes ay upoun his knyfe,
> He brandeist lyk a beir;
> Bostaris, braggaris, and barganeris
> Eftir him passit in to pairis . . . .

Sync Sweirnes, at the secound bidding,	Sloth
Come lyk a sow out of a midding,	
Full slepy wes his grunyie	snout

Each of them leads his human followers in a wretched babble of 'harlottis' and 'prestis', 'druncharts' and 'bakbyttaris in secreit placis', enough to grace the court of any king. The prideful skip in burning fires, the creatures of anger stab and cut each other with knives, the covetous vomit hot molten gold and the lecherous go through the dancing leading each other by the penis.

Than the fowll monstir Glutteny,	
Off wame unsasiable and gredy,	belly
To dance he did him dres;	begin
Him followit mony fowll drunckart	
With can and collep, cop and quart,	flagon
In surffet and excess;	
Full mony a waistles wallydrag	fat weakling

With wamis unweildable did furth wag	unmanageable
In creische that did incres.	fat
'Drynk', ay thay cryit with mony a gaip;	
The feyndis gaif thame hait leid to laip,	hot lead
Thair lovery wes na les.	

The whole terrible carnival continues until the Highlanders arrive, whereupon they take up so much room in Hell and make such a noise with their clatter in 'Ersche' that the Devil smothers the lot with smoke and ends the dance.

The poem has stunning verbal and imaginative force – a wild goliardic drive in the half-way house between horror and farce that is typical of the Scottish sense of humour. The same capacity for eldritch extravagance and all-too-specific physical realism lies at the heart of the sensibility which produced 'Tam O'Shanter' and *A Drunk Man Looks at the Thistle*. It is this precipitous imagination which gives a particularly furious barb to Dunbar's technical virtuosity, whether he is sending up the office for the dead or burlesquing the medieval *débat* on love.

'The Tretis of the Tua Mariit Wemen and the Wedo' begins in high style when the poet overhears three ladies discussing love in a garden on Midsummer Eve. The setting, the aureate terms and the alliterative blank verse all prepare the reader for a courtly poem on a matter of sophisticated interest. It is noticeable, however, that their enjoyment at table as they 'wachtit at the wyne' is just a little heartier than their dainty white fingers might lead one to expect. These suspicions are confirmed and the vision is shattered when they speak. One of the wives wants to be as free as the birds to show herself 'At playis and at preichingis and pilgramages', to move among men and 'cheis and be chosen, and change quhen me lykit'. Like May in Chaucer's 'Merchant's Tale', she is married to a crabbed old man: 'Ane bumbart, [dolt] ane dron bee, ane bag full of flewme, / Ane skabbit skarth [cormorant], ane scorpioun, ane scutarde [shitten] behind'. Unlike Chaucer, however, Dunbar allows no room for compassion at the plight of this 'amyable', so bawdily does she describe the chains of her condition. In response, the widow advocates utter hypocrisy: she has had two husbands and like the Wife of Bath she is a woman of broad experience and appetite. She advises the ladies to keep a lover and to dominate their husbands if they can; but widowhood is best of all – 'My mouth it makis murnyng, and my mynd lauchis'. Like Henryson's Sprutok, she has a lively sexual preference and, as she describes how she comforts and flirts with several men at once, it becomes apparent to the reader that her 'fair calling' is to run a brothel. Yet her speech throughout is larded with the terms of courtly love while she talks of her honour and advocates mercy as a 'meckle vertu' in women, just in case some pining youth should die for want of her. Finally, the poem slips back into its ideal and aureate setting, as Dunbar distances his audience from what the ladies are actually saying and returns to 'silver schouris' and 'the sweit savour of the sward and singing of foulis'. It is a gay and coarse exposure of womankind, very much in the tradition of medieval anti-feminist literature, but without the subtlety and sympathy of the 'marriage cycle' in *The Canterbury Tales*. The Scots poet explodes the romance conventions, but his poem is essentially a cruel laugh at the gullibility of men.

The highly coloured scenes and the sometimes brutally reductive eye at work in Dunbar's poetry have their source in a darker aspect of his vision. He is never far from the 'malancolie' which stems from a strong sense of his own impending dissolution. The shadow provides a contrast which even further heightens the glitter of his wit and the enamelled elaboration of his style. 'Mutability' – the evanescence of man's earthly life – is a constant theme in medieval literature, finding particularly fine expression in Villon's *Testament*, where the general pathos of the refrain from one of the ballades – 'Mais ou sont les neiges d'antan?' (but where are the snows of yester year?) – mingles with Villon's macabre but defiant awareness of the decay of the physical flesh. Dunbar too writes in the vein of *memento mori*, but he is equally prone to moods of highly personal anguish, and these moments of despair give his poems a more modern, even an existential aspect. 'I seik about this warld unstabile' begins by admitting that despite all his wit he has failed to find even one thought that is not ultimately deceitful:

> For yesterday I did declair
> Quhow that the seasoun soft and fair
>   Com in als fresche as pako fedder;   peacock
> This day it stangis lyk ane edder,   adder
> Concluding all in my contrair.

All existence seems to offer him this personal affront, and he judges life to be a violent succession of absolute contrasts: 'Yisterday fair up sprang the flouris, / This day thai are all slane with schouris'. Not even in the closing stanza is there any hint of Christian comfort or eternal assurance.

So nixt to summer winter bein,
Nixt eftir confort cairis kein,
    Nixt dirk mednycht the mirthefull morrow,
    Nixt eftir joye aye cumis sorrow:
So is this warld and ay hes bein.

The masterly use of repetition makes its point and the contrasts are stark and inescapable.

Dunbar's poems in this mood show little of the bitter-sweet pathos of the medieval sense of mutability, nor do they show the compassion for erring man seen in Henryson's 'Preiching of the Swallow'. Instead, his pessimism has a misanthropic and sometimes a curiously triumphant note. His certainty may be unpalatable, but it *is* certainty, and he has found 'ane sentence convenabille' after all. He writes of despair with great intensity, but such moments are almost always prompted by mental or physical weaknesses with little hint of a solely spiritual or moral dimension. He is a materialist and the images he chooses are telling. When his spirit is utterly forlorn and 'no ladeis bewtie' nor 'gold in kist [chest], nor wyne in coup' can help him, it is not because he misses his saviour, but rather it is 'for laik of symmer with his flouris' ('In to thir dirk and drublie dayis'). When he muses on Fortune's wheel and on how we must always be ready to leave this short life ('Full oft I mus'), he concludes that we should enjoy ourselves – 'For to be blyth me think it best' – and yet this last refrain is repeated so often in the poem that it begins to lose all sense of conviction. When Dunbar commends spiritual love over fleshly love in 'Now culit is dame Venus brand', he sees it entirely as a matter of age over youth, made possible only because 'Venus fyre' within him is nowadays 'deid and cauld'. The closing stanzas accept that, left to itself, youth will never consider spiritual matters in the face of 'this fals dissavand warldis blis'. The poet commends Christ's cause, but again he sounds revealingly hesitant about it: 'He suld be luffit agane, think me'. Finally, as an expression of Christian morality, the poem's continuing refrain has an oddly determinist and physiological bias: 'Now cumis aige quhair yewth hes been / And trew lufe rysis fro the splene.' Even if we grant that the theory of humours would seem more apposite in Dunbar's time than it does now, these lines still seem strangely, even grotesquely indecorous, undoubtedly reflecting something of the unease in its author's spirit.

Dunbar's discontent and his materialistic cast of mind have resulted in some poems which seem almost modern, at least to post-Romantic eyes. The poet has suffered a migraine in 'My heid did yak yester nicht'; he can scarcely look on the light and he cannot find words to express his thoughts, trapped somewhere in his memory, 'Dullit in dulnes and distres'. He may rise in the morning but his spirit is still sleeping and it seems that nothing can stir it:

> For mirth, for menstrallie and play,
> For din nor danceing nor deray,
> It will nocht walkin me no wise.

The spirit of this poem is worthy of Coleridge, with its despair at a loss of imaging power, its inability to face the light, source of all illumination, and its failure to 'dyt thought'.

A conventional Christian note is allowed to appear at the very end of the famous poem 'Lament for the Makaris', but it seems like an abrupt and unconvincing afterthought:

> Sen for the deid remeid is none,   Since; death
> Best is that we for dede dispone   prepare
> Eftir our deid that lif may we:
> *Timor mortis conturbat me*.

If this is hope, it is quite outweighed by the force of the previous twenty-four stanzas, not to mention the internal rhyme 're-meid' and the repetition of 'deid' in each of the last three lines. Every stanza ends with that solemn Latin refrain from the Office for the Dead – 'the fear of death disturbs me' – conveying a personal terror which strikes like a funeral bell. By comparison, Henryson's 'Prayer for the Pest' is devoutly Christian, making supplication to God's mercy and power in every stanza. Death by plague was a familiar visitor at the beginning of the fifteenth century, yet Henryson's prayer shows no personal anguish and accepts it utterly in true 'medieval' humility as the justice of God: 'our syn is all the cause of thiss'. In contrast,

Dunbar draws on the medieval *danse macabre* for his poem
(Lydgate before him had used the same Latin line) as well as a
list of type-figures of those who must inevitably come to die:
'Princis, prelotis, and potestatis, / Baithe riche and pur of al
degre' – all are mortal, not forgetting the intellectuals of
James's court, 'Rethoris, logicianis and theologgis, / Thame
helpis no conclusionis sle' [cunning]. Death even takes 'on the
moderis breist sowkand, / The bab full of benignite'. For, with
that thin and relentless "ee' rhyme echoing down the poem,
there can be no suggestion of acceptance. Indeed, from the very
first lines the poem is a personal cry – 'I that in heill wes and
gladnes / Am trublit now with gret seiknes' – and this note is
confirmed when Dunbar begins to name all the other poets who
have played their part in the pageant and gone to the grave.
The toll contains twenty-four makars – a most useful record for
the literary historian, although some remain unknown to us or
only a few lines by them survive. They and their works have,
indeed, been devoured by that 'strang unmerciful tyrand'.

I se that makaris amang the laif	rest
Playis heir ther pageant, syne gois to graif;	grave
Sparit is nocht ther faculte:	
Timor mortis conturbat me.	

He hes done petuously devour
The noble Chaucer of makaris flour,
The Monk of Bery, and Gower, all thre:
   Timor mortis conturbat me.

. . .

In Dunfermelyne he hes done roune	
With Maister Robert Henrysoun.	
Schir Johne the Ros enbrast hes he:	embraced
Timor mortis conturbat me.	

And he hes now tane last of aw	
Gud gentill Stobo and Quintyne Schaw,	
Of quham all wichtis hes pete:	whom; pity
Timor mortis conturbat me.	

Gud Maister Walter Kennedy
In poynt of dede lyis veraly;
Gret reuth it were that so suld be:
   Timor mortis conturbat me.

Sen he hes all my brether tane
He will nocht lat me lif alane;
On forse I man his nyxt pray be: Perforce
    Timor mortis conturbat me.

Sen for the deid remeid is none,
Best is that we for dede dispone
Eftir our deid that lif may we:
    Timor mortis conturbat me.

Starkly and unforgettably, the 'Lament' expresses one of the
great themes of human existence. In this context the capacity to
make poems was all important to Dunbar, for, when it fails, as
in 'My heid did yak yester nicht', or when he foresees his
extinction as a man, he is left with nothing else. Except, of
course, that his work has given him a special kind of life after
death – perhaps the immortality which meant most to him after
all. The darker poems are the antithesis of Dunbar's commitment to the glitter of court life. His technical bravura, his
satirical wit, his worldly cynicism and his inner terror make a
potent and disturbing combination, and perhaps this is why he
speaks so powerfully to modern readers.

   James IV and the brilliance of Scotland's first steps into the
Renaissance were soon to be swept away. The Scottish king had
treaties with both England and France, but Henry VIII's
increasingly hostile acts against France and across the border
finally committed James to the Auld Alliance and led him,
reluctantly, to invade England. The Scots army was defeated at
the Battle of Flodden in 1513, where some 10,000 men were
killed on Branxton hill. James himself died in the thick of the
fighting along with members of his retinue, many nobles and
hundreds of the lesser gentry and yeomanry. The English
retired across the border, the king's infant son succeeded to the
throne for yet another Stewart minority, and a peace was
concluded the following year. The battle had served no military
or political purpose whatsoever, and Scotland was shattered by
the loss of her most popular king. Most households of note
counted one or more members among the dead and Flodden
Field passed into the folk memory, and remains to this day, a
traumatic symbol of failure and grief. Dunbar lived on for
another seven years at least, but we hear nothing more from

him or about him, and we do not even know where he was
buried.

Writing in prose

The works of James I, Henryson, Holland and Dunbar reach a
high order of accomplishment. In fifteenth-century Scotland
such powers of imagination and technique are solely the
province of the poet, and vernacular prose remains in its
infancy. The literature of most countries shows the same
pattern. **Sir Gilbert Hay** (1400?–1499?) provides the earliest
known literary prose in Scots with his translations from French
and Latin originals. Hay is also credited with the *Alexander*, a
lengthy verse translation from the French, and he is mentioned
as a poet in Dunbar's 'Lament'. His career also emphasises the
French connection, because he was at one time Chamberlain to
Charles VII. Back in Scotland in 1456, he made his manuscript
translations at the request of his host, the Earl of Orkney and
Caithness. *The Buke of Armys*, *The Buke of the Order of Knychthood*
and *The Buke of the Governaunce of Princis* all have to do with noble
models of philosophy, behaviour and belief. Caxton was to
publish his own translation of the *Livre de l'Ordre de Chevalrie*
almost thirty years later, so the taste for such topics survived for
quite some time and, of course, long after the chivalric order
itself.

The only other prose-writer of note is **John of Ireland**
(1440?–1496?), who, like Hay, had been to France, spending
thirty years there and ending up as confessor and counsellor to
Charles's successor, Louis XI. He produced an original piece of
Scots prose (again in manuscript only) for the edification of the
nineteen-year-old James IV. *The Meroure of Wysdome* is a rather
tedious treatise on political and personal wisdom, in which the
author is at pains to legitimise his saws by referring to the
authority of holy writ and to the scholarship of Paris. John
reveals something of the status of prose among academics in his
time by being anxious to point out that, for writing, he knows
Latin better than he does the 'commoune langage' of his
country. In fact a considerable tradition in vernacular his-
toriography was soon to evolve in Scotland. The undistinguished verse of Wyntoun's *Orygynale Chronykil* of 1424 was

followed by a number of prose historians in the next era and then by a host of doctrinal historians in the seventeenth century. In the meantime, John of Ireland defends his use of the vernacular, even although he knows that 'mony errouris agane the faith and haly doctrine of iesu and of the kyrk ar writtin in this tounge and in inglis, at a part of the pepil of thi realme ar infekit with it'. It is not too fanciful to detect here already the rumblings of approaching Reformation and the major part that vernacular prose was to play in it.

3

The sixteenth century: John the Commonweill

WHEN the Renaissance came to Scotland it came as a spirit from abroad gradually making itself felt in the harsher climate of a Northern country. The spirit flowered until Flodden left the crown on the head of a two-year-old boy. Then, within only fifteen years, a new factor was added to the perennially shifting balance of power between king and barons. The scale was tipped in 1528 when Patrick Hamilton, a pupil of Erasmus and of Luther, was burned as a heretic at St Andrew's for preaching that man stands alone before God and is justified only by his faith. Hamilton argued that this faith is God's gift only and cannot be earned by good works, or interpreted or ameliorated by the hierarchy of any church. Soon this bare philosophical light, with all the hard clarity of the North, quite outshone the Mediterranean sunshine of that late spring at the court of King James IV. Nor was it simply a matter of religious belief, for kings, too, are only men before their maker, and soon the new church was reminding them of that fact and resisting all attempts at royal control. By the end of the century Andrew Melville was speaking for the very spirit of Scottish Presbyterianism when he reminded his ruler that 'there is twa kings and twa kingdomes in Scotland. Thair is Chryst Jesus the King, and his kingdome the Kirk, whose subject King James the Saxt is, and of whose kingdome nocht a king, nor a laird, nor a heid, bot a member.' This exhilarating and dangerous insight soon overtook the Renaissance in Scotland and absorbed almost all the intellectual and creative energy in the country for the next 200 years. It gave the Reformation a more revolutionary and democratic cast than it had in England, where the monarch remained as head of the Church, yet its fiercer elements would propose a far more total control over the individual spirit than any mere king could hope to achieve.

James V, 'the gudeman of Ballengeich', died in ineffectual despondency, yet at the beginning of his reign he had vigorously advanced the influence of the crown by taxation and military action. He provided funds for the Court of Session, annexed the power of the Lords of the Isles and led expeditions into the Borders to control the reivers there. In those debatable lands the barons still ruled like minor kings, doing nothing to discourage bandit families from raiding property and burning churches in England and Scotland alike. (One of these wild men, Johnny Armstrong, is remembered in tales and ballads; he and forty-eight of his men were hanged in 1530.) When Henry VIII split from Rome he was eager to make an alliance with his Northern neighbour, but James sided instead with Catholic Europe through a French marriage, although his sickly bride died within a year. His second wife was made of stronger stuff, and Mary of Guise, destined to be the mother of Mary Queen of Scots, was an especially staunch supporter of both the old religion and the absolute power of monarchs. This alignment established a tension between Scotland, England and France which was to dominate the century and make it impossible to separate the issues of religion and politics. Thus Protestant reformers would be supported by England against their own sovereign, while Scottish nobles took first one and then the other side according to their conscience and their sense of personal advantage. In such a context there was little hope that more moderate Catholic reformers would prevail, and the fiasco of the battle at Solway Moss further disillusioned both commons and nobles against the notion of military action in the French Catholic cause. 'It cam wi a lass, and it'll pass wi a lass', James is said to have murmured about the Stewart succession when he heard of his daughter's birth as he lay on his death bed.

For the next eighteen years Mary of Guise acted as queen regent. Henry pressed his plans to make an English marriage with the infant Scottish queen and when all else failed he tried brutal persuasion by ordering his armies to make deliberately destructive raids on southern Scotland, 'sparing no creature alyve'. But Henry's 'rough wooing' and his boast that he was the 'very owner of Scotland' only strengthened the Auld Alliance, and the baby Mary remained in France, betrothed to the Dauphin. Meanwhile, the queen regent steadfastly resisted the gathering changes of Reformation. She had a potent ally in Cardinal David Beaton, but he only spurred on the Reformers' cause and ensured his own death when he burned Wishart at St Andrew's, thus launching an aging John Knox into brief exile and a stormy career. Knox returned from Europe inspired with Calvin's doctrinaire vision of a fighting faith. He motivated a Protestant pressure-group among the nobles, calling themselves the Lords of the Congregation of Jesus Christ, and his passionate preaching around the country encouraged his followers to see themselves as the Children of Israel, engaged against an oppressor no less harsh than Pharaoh himself. The country almost came to civil war before the Treaty of Leith and the queen regent's death brought about the first Reformation parliament in 1560, whereupon the Confession of Faith and *The First Book of Discipline* set out the Scottish ideals for a new Protestant kirk. When Mary Queen of Scots landed from France in 1561, she found her mother's religion out of favour and her own priest intimidated at court. The first years of her reign passed off well enough, but hers was a fraught existence, for in the eyes of Catholic Europe she, and not Elizabeth I, was the legitimate heir to the English throne. The young queen was soon submerged in a rising tide of political, religious and sexual intrigue which her own head-strong nature did nothing to quell. After the murder of her favourite, Rizzio, and the assassination of her effete husband Darnley, she allowed herself to be abducted by Bothwell (who was already suspected of complicity in Darnley's death), and then, most ill-advisedly, she married him. In the ensuing uproar Bothwell had to flee the country and Mary was forced to abdicate in favour of her infant son. After a last desperate throw of the dice, she retreated to exile in England, where her cousin Elizabeth kept her in effective captivity for nineteen years before finally resolving the threat of Catholic succession with the edge of the headsman's axe.

James VI's inheritance was not an auspicious one, and his early love of culture and his own pretentions to literature were pursued in an uneasy and isolated context. In the Ruthven raid of 1582 the sixteen-year-old king was actually kidnapped by nobles who feared that his infatuation with the young lord of Aubigny, the Duke of Lennox, would lead to dangerous Catholic influence at court. Lennox fled and James escaped to wage his long but circumspect tug-of-war with Presbyterianism at home, while keeping an eye abroad on his prospects for the throne of England.

After Knox's death it was Andrew Melville who had consolidated Scottish Presbyterianism. The ideals of the Books of Discipline were noble in many ways, although they were never fully realised. The new church was to be based on a democratic hierarchy beginning with each congregation and working up to the General Assembly, a kind of church parliament which was answerable only to God. At the grass roots, ministers had to be elected by their own congregations and no landowner could put his own man in the pulpit. At the same time the clergy were an independent and influential moral authority in the parish and could mete out punishments in public for the social misdemeanours of their flock. The new kirk set great store on the Bible as the full expression of God's will, and so preaching and the education of the masses became a worthy priority. Every householder was to read the Bible to his family; there was to be a schoolmaster skilled in the classics in every parish; bursaries were to be made available for the talented poor, while there were to be colleges in every large town, and divinity was to be taught at the universities along with medicine and law. This practical concern with the status and welfare of the common man, both spiritual and temporal, was radical and humane, yet, as so often happens, the revolutionary ideal contained the seeds of authoritarianism. The Calvinist doctrine of the elect led to exclusiveness, and a narrow literalism in the reading of the Scriptures produced fanaticism and intolerance.

James VI was not slow to see the political implications of such a structure, nor was Melville afraid to point them out, so the king duly noted that 'Presbytery agreeth as well with a monarch as God and the Devil', and gradually set about regaining a degree of royal control. At the end of March in 1603 the news arrived in Edinburgh that Queen Elizabeth had died. A week later, King James set off for the south and the throne of England.

Gavin Douglas (1475?–1522)

In both his work and his life, standing divided between the Renaissance and the late Middle Ages, Gavin Douglas demonstrates something of the contradictions to be found in sixteenth-century Scotland. His greatest achievement was the translation of Virgil's *Aeneid*, and, although it is distinctly medieval in setting and interpretation, its commitment to the classical world and its concern to speak to a broader audience belongs to the new age. Douglas was born into the 'Red Douglases', the earls of Angus, who, with the 'Black Douglases' of Lanarkshire, were among the most powerful and ambitious families in Lowland Scotland, both boasting descent from the line of Robert Bruce's great champion and both with remote claims to the Scottish throne. Gavin, or Gawin, was the third son of the fifth Earl of Angus, Archibald 'Bell the Cat', who earned his nickname when he hanged six of the king's favourites at court. Young Gavin Douglas went to St Andrew's University in 1490 at the usual age of fifteen. He graduated after four years' study (conducted in Latin) of typical subjects such as grammar, rhetoric, Aristotle, mathematics, music and astronomy.

It is likely that he also went to Paris and visited the continent at least once more before settling in his native land. It was during these years that he wrote his poetry, completing the *Eneados* in 1513, scarcely two months before the Battle of Flodden. After the death of James IV all Douglas's energies were directed towards political affairs and to seeking an ecclesiastical appointment commensurate with his family's rank. He was eventually granted a bishopric at Dunkeld, but the French-connected factions of the regent Albany suspected him of political alignment with England. Matters came to a head and the poet had to resort to bribes and threat of arms to retain his place at Dunkeld and his standing in the tangled pattern of influence. But in the end he still had to flee to England, where he spent his days at court trying to arrange his return to the north. He died of the plague in 1522, exiled in London and a victim of the family influence which had promised so much.

Douglas's first poem, 'The Palice of Honour' (1501), is wholeheartedly within the medieval dream-allegory tradition.

The piece follows a French vogue for such subjects and expounds, in three books, the various ways in which honour may be obtained in life. When the poet finally does gain the palace, he is led to a keyhole where he glimpses Honour only to faint before his blinding glory. The style of the poem is aureate and 'enamelled' along the lines of Dunbar's near-contemporary pieces 'The Goldyn Targe' and 'The Thrissil and the Rois'. Thus Douglas delights in using an elaborate polysyllabic diction to 'amplify' or extend his descriptions, and he encourages the formal complexities of his craft by choosing a difficult nine-line stanza that depends on only two rhymes. These factors, and the author's own fluent Latinity, make the poem something of a young man's *tour de force*.

Douglas is often credited with another allegorical poem, called 'King Hart', but some doubt must remain about the attribution since it appears only once, in the Maitland Manuscript, added by a later hand. Such allegories belong to an earlier age, and it is Douglas's translation of the *Aeneid* which kept his name alive in the seventeenth and eighteenth centuries when greater makars were all but forgotten. It also contains, in the form of the prologues to each book, the best of his own original poetry.

Douglas worked on his *Eneados* for a year and half before abandoning literature in favour of his political career. Next to the *Wallace* it was the longest piece of verse yet sustained in Scots. It circulated in various manuscript copies, at least five of which have survived, but it was not published until 1553, thirty-one years after its author's death. (This was in an unsatisfactory edition made in London, anglicised and 'Protestantised'.) Nevertheless, it was common practice at the time for books to be copied by hand, for Chepman and Myllar's press – established in Edinburgh in 1507 – had not yet had time to fulfil the growing demand for Scottish books. Virgil's works were particularly popular throughout Europe, with over a hundred Latin editions printed by the beginning of the century and many others copied by hand. Some classical authors were also being translated and, indeed, in 1509 Octavien de Saint Gelais published an edition of the *Aenid* in French. Whether Douglas saw the French version or not, he felt himself to be in the forefront of the movement to make the classics available to a wider audience, and in the 'Conclusio' to his labours he encouraged fault-finders to do something more useful, like translating Ovid.

Douglas's was the first full-length translation of a major classical text to be made anywhere in Britain and it earns him a deserved place in the cultural history of the northern Renaisance. He was not unaware of the importance of his achievement. Accordingly, he castigates Caxton for inferior passages in his version (1490), which was based on a French paraphrase, and prides himself on keeping close to the 'fixt sentens or mater' of his original, so that 'all thocht my termys be nocht polisht alway, / Hys sentence sall I hald, as that I may'. Nevertheless, the poem is not exactly Virgil's, for the Latin hexameters have been rendered into heroic couplets and the text is expanded and explained in places with the aid of Ascensius's commentary as attached to his Latin edition of Virgil, first published in Paris in 1501. Furthermore, Douglas prefaces the thirteen books (one by Maphaeus Vegius) with original prologues of his own. In six of these (I, III, V, VI, IX and XIII), he gives serious attention to the problems of translation, which he solves by choosing contemporary equivalents in weapons, clothes, ships and manners. He asks for help if he has made errors, and warns against those who would spy out every 'falt and cruyk', even if he admits that he can see very few faults himself; after all, 'the blak craw thinkis hyr awin byrdis quhite'. This running commentary adds great charm to Douglas's version of the classical poem. Indeed his narrative couplets and Scottish settings provide a robust immediacy which may well be better suited to the primitive world of Aeneas than the decorous circumlocutions chosen by Dryden and later neoclassical poets.

Some of Douglas's finest poetry comes from the descriptions of the natural world which introduce Books VII, XII and XIII. These passages have become part of poetic history by anticipating James Thomson's *The Seasons* (1730) and something of what nature was to mean to the English Romantics. The Prologue to Book XII describes dawn on a May morning. Phoebus's chariot appears above the sea, dame Flora scatters flowers and the poet creates a conventional landscape of blossoms, animals and young people in a scene reminiscent of the more formal *Palice of Honour*. Yet there is physical particularity too, as every detail is brilliantly etched in the sun's early light:

Towris, turettis, kyrnellis, pynnaclys hie	battlements
Of kyrkis, castellis and ilke fair cite,	each
Stude payntit, euery fyall and stage,	little tower and
Apon the plane grund, by thar awyn umbrage.	shadow [storey

Plants and flowers are described with botanical specificity. Giddy young lovers pine and tease each other with whispered, oblique phrases:

Smyland says ane, 'I couth in previte	know how
Schaw the a bourd', 'ha, quhat be that?' quod he	jest [to
'Quhat thyng?' 'That most be secrete', said the tother.	

Here and everywhere Douglas catches a sense of movement with telling and realistic detail: 'So dusty pulder upstouris in euery streit, / Quhil corby [crow] gaspit for the fervent heit.' It was just this quality which Thomas Warton admired when he praised the passage for being 'the effusion of a mind not overlaid by the descriptions of other poets, but operating, by its own force and bias, . . . on such objects as really occurred' (*The History of English Poetry*, 1774–81).

If Douglas begins Book XII with a welcome to the May dawn, the Prologue to the following book describes a sunset in June – a luminous northern evening declining slowly into silence and darkness. In the night the poet dreams that Maphaeus Vegius chides him for not having translated his supplement to Virgil. Convinced by the ghost's argument (and the blows it rains on his head) Douglas agrees to satisfy his querulous visitor. Waking in the half-light before dawn he sees the stars quenched one by one – 'That to behald was plesans and half wondir' – until the workaday world gets under way and the spell is broken by a farm steward shouting to his men ' "Awaik! On fut! Go till our husbandry." '

The poet's delight in natural settings, described almost for their own sake, is most striking of all in his account of a northern winter in the Prologue to Book VII. In a scene reminiscent of the opening to *The Testament of Cresseid* we see the translator composing himself for sleep, wrapped in three layers 'fortil expell the peralus persand [piercing] cald', while outside, under the watery light of the moon, he hears 'the geiss claking eik by nyghtis tyde / Atour [around] the cite fleand'. In the morning he peeps from the window at the 'scharp hailstanys

. . . hoppand on the thak [thatch] and on the causay by' before withdrawing to the fireside to take up again the burden of his verses. Outside his window a typically Scottish countryside wrestles in the grip of the 'schort days', ruggedly evoked in harsh alliterative lines:

Thik drumly skuggis dyrknyt so the hevyn,	shadows
Dym skyis oft furth warpit feirful levyn,	hurled; lightning
Flaggis of fire, and mony felloun flaw,	deadly blast
Scharpe soppys of sleit and of the snypand snaw.	biting
The dolly dichis war all donk and wait,	dismal; dank
The law valle flodderit all with spait,	
The plane stretis and euery hie way	
Full of floschis, dubbis, myre and clay.	pools; puddles

Warton was right to find an almost Romantic spirit in such passages, but the poet was still a man of his time, and he was keen to draw acceptably Christian conclusions – 'ful of sentence' – from the 'pagan' world of classical literature.

Douglas distrusts learned Latinate terms, preferring them 'haymly playn' and 'famyliar' without 'facund rethoryk' so that his text will be 'braid and plane, / Kepand na sudron [southern speech] bot our awyn langage, / And spekis as I lernyt quhen I was page'. Indeed, he is the first of the makars to refer to 'Scottis' and 'the langage of Scottis natioun' to describe the tongue which Blind Harry would have called 'Inglis' (to distinguish it from Gaelic, the original 'Scottis'), and, although at times Douglas refers to the limitations of his chosen speech, he is prepared to use some 'bastard Latin', French or English to help out. He is consistently aware of the radical significance of this task and at the close of the thirteenth and final book he expresses the modest desire that his labour shall be a 'neidfull wark', especially 'to thame wald Virgil to childryn expone'. He hopes that the classics will not belong only to 'masteris of grammar sculys . . . techand on . . . benkis and stulys', but that Virgil will now be available to 'euery gentill Scot' – even to those who cannot read: 'And to onletterit folk be red on hight / That erst was bot with clerkis comprehend'. Such an outlook characterises the Renaissance and what was to be the best aspect of the slowly growing spirit of Reformation in Scotland.

Sir David Lindsay (1490–1555)

Like Dunbar and Douglas, but with somewhat more success, David Lindsay spent most of his life at the Scottish court. He was born in 1490, probably on his father's estate in Fife. By the age of twenty-two he was part of the royal household, employed as 'Keeper of the Kingis Grace's Person' – attendant and companion to the infant James V. He tells us in his poems how he used to sing to the royal baby and carry him on his back. In 1522 he married a girl at court, also in royal service. Lindsay's association with the young king was broken for four years when Archibald Douglas, nephew to Gavin and sixth Earl of Angus, became chancellor and assumed total power by holding the twelve-year-old James captive in Edinburgh Castle. In 1528, however, the king escaped to lead an army against his captor, and the Red Douglas had to forfeit his estates and go into exile in England. It is not certain what formal education Lindsay had, but he was undoubtedly an able man and his career prospered. In the 1530s he began to produce poems which presumed to advise the king, making satirical comments on the state of the nation and especially on the failings of the Church. James must have had some sympathy with these views, for he used the first performances of *The Thrie Estaits* as a warning to some of his recalcitrant bishops to reform themselves. Lindsay was made a royal herald and later he was knighted to become Lyon King-at-Arms, responsible for Scottish heraldry and the arranging of pageants, plays and farces for state occasions and the entertainment of the court. Schir Dauid Lyndesay of the Mount, as he was called, also served as an ambassador abroad and may well have visited Italy in his travels.

At home his anti-clerical views inevitably involved him with the cause of reform – he knew John Knox and is said to have encouraged him to take up preaching. In 1546 he acted as intermediary between the king and the group who had killed Cardinal Beaton and taken over St Andrew's Castle. (He called on them to surrender, but they held out until the following year.) 'The Tragedie of the Late Cardinal Beaton' does not leave Lindsay's sympathies in doubt, for the ghost of Beaton effectively condemns himself by describing his own career. The poem is a 'tragedy' only in the old sense that it concerns the fall of a powerful man:

My gret ryches, nor rentis proffitabyll
My Syluer work, Jowellis inestimabyll,
My Papall pompe, of gold my ryche threasure,
My lyfe, and all, I loste in half ane hour.

Lindsay concentrates in some detail on Beaton's great political influence and particularly on the commitments to France and Rome which would not allow him to countenance peace with England despite the high cost to everyone else:

Had we with Ingland kepit our contrackis,
Our nobyll men had leuit in peace and rest,
Our Marchandis had nocht lost so mony packis,
Our commoun peple had nocht bene opprest . . . .

On theological issues Lindsay has the cardinal admit that he did not read the Bible and did not encourage the teaching of it to the common folk, putting to great torment, indeed, the 'fauoraris of the auld and new Testament'. The poet does not mention the fire which consumed Wishart and directly fuelled Beaton's own death, although he does have a line where the ghost confesses to having destroyed many men, 'sum with the fyre'. This may seem a striking omission, but it was probably a well-considered one, for not even the Lord Lyon could challenge the authority of the spiritual arm with impunity. Douglas Hamer has suggested that the printer of 'the Tragedie' had to flee from arrest and that this was the poem of Lindsay's which we know to have been burned by the ecclesiastical authorities in 1549. In fact Lindsay's work does not bear an overtly Protestant doctrine, but it is fired by a hatred of unearned privilege, most especially in the established Church. He seems to have remained a Catholic, albeit a severely critical one who wished to see the Church give up wealth and temporal powers and return to its simple role as teacher of the Testaments to the people.

Beyond all matters of Christian doctrine, Lindsay's morality is founded on his sense of natural justice and his sympathy with the feelings and prejudices of the common people. In the spirit of *Rauf Coilyear* his hatred of oppression, his lurid anticlericalism, and his ribald sense of humour have guaranteed a lasting and general popularity to his work. These forces find early expression in 'The Dreme' and 'The Papyngo' and come to fruition in *Ane Pleasant Satyre of the Thrie Estaits*. It is a measure of Lindsay's influence that he managed to stay at court during these turbulent times, for his views must have made him powerful enemies. Although he continued to write until just before his death at the age of sixty-five, his other work never matched the achievement of *The Thrie Estaits*. His poems were published and republished in subsequent years and a popular collected edition appeared in 1568, but *The Thrie Estaits* itself was not printed until 1602, over sixty years after its first performance.

Lindsay's purpose was clear from the start. 'The Dreme of Schir David Lyndesay' was probably written around 1528, when James V attained the throne. The Prologue describes how the poet used to play the lute and act the fool for his infant sovereign. Then the dream takes him on an elaborate tour of the cosmos from Hell to Heaven and back to Scotland again. 'Why are the people so poor', the poet asks, 'when they live in so pleasant a place?' The answer, of course, is misgovernment, and at this point John the Commonweill arrives in rags to describe how he has fled from oppression in the Borders and Highlands alike, without justice from the king or comfort from the Church. The dreamer awakes to point out the moral to his king.

'The Complaynt of Schir David Lindesay' celebrates James's escape from the bad influence of the Douglas family. It allows the poet to offer yet more advice to his monarch and to remind him along the way that he would appreciate a gift of money, or even a loan – 'Off gold ane thousand pound, or tway'. Clearly the poet enjoyed good relations with the king, and James was not above flyting his old companion in verses of his own, and tolerating a reply too, which warns him explicitly against his sexual adventures ('The Answer to the Kyngis Flyting', 1536). Lindsay wrote a number of other pieces satirising life at court, such as 'In Contemptioun of Syde Taillis' (c.1540) or 'The Confessioun of Bagsche' (c.1534) which has the king's old hound complain about the scuffling for preference, the backbiting and the dogfights which go on in the presence of power. Now that Bagsche is old and despised, he regrets his cruelty when he was on top. 'Belief weill', he reminds the current favourites, 'ye ar bot doggis.' The animal analogy provides Lindsay with further scope for satire in *The Testament and Complaynt of the Papyngo* (1538), in which the king's parrot, wounded by a fall from a tree, makes her last will and testament after setting down two epistles full of advice to the king and her fellow courtiers. The garrulous bird expounds on the follies of climbing too high, on good government, on the fate of the Stewart kings and on the mutability of human affairs – all with awesome fluency. The 'Papyngo' takes its place in what amounts to a Scottish penchant for animal satire, debate or epistle, running from the *Howlat* to Henryson's fables, to Hamilton of Gilbertfield's 'Last Dying Words of Bonny Heck' and Burns's 'Twa Dogs'. Notwithstanding the charms of his preaching parrot, Lindsay's finest satire remains *The Thrie Estaits*.

A short version of this play was performed in 1540 at the palace of Linlithgow on 6 January, the Feast of Epiphany, before James V and the court. Yule at the Scottish court was kept after the French fashion with the election of an 'Abbot of Unreason' to ensure entertainment for all. The ceremonies of Twelfth Night belonged to this tradition, with the choosing of a mock sovereign – the King or Queen of the Bean – to direct dances, games and burlesques. Great licence was allowed on such occasions, and it was in this context that Lindsay's merry exposure of folly and weakness amongst the powerful of this world was first performed. This is not to underestimate the author's seriousness, or his political intention, for when it was next performed, in Fife, at the Castle Hill in Cupar in June 1552, the satirical force had been strengthened and further elements of popular comedy, energetic caricature and vulgar farce were directed towards an audience in which, this time, the commons outnumbered the nobility. The third performance of the *Satyre* was equally public, on the sunny slopes of the Calton Hill in Edinburgh in 1554 in the presence of Mary of Guise, Queen Regent of Scotland. It had been fourteen years since the first performance, during which time James had died shortly after Solway Moss; Wishart and Beaton had both perished in windy St Andrew's and Henry VIII's troops had crossed the Border and even reached Edinburgh in their destructive zeal to persuade Scotland into an English marriage alliance. In this period of reform and counter-reform Lindsay's play must have been a potent instrument, and it was not to be performed again until 1948, when Tyrone Guthrie's memorable production rediscovered Lindsay's dramatic flair and the comic vigour of his verse.

The final version of *The Thrie Estaits* is in two parts separated by an interlude in which the 'rude mechanicals' provide comic relief by making comments on what has gone before. This was a common device between the acts of the early morality plays, and, since the whole performance must have taken many hours, it would have allowed the nobility some leeway to finish lunch and return to the play proper. Here and elsewhere Lindsay displays a shrewd stagecraft, derived no doubt from his experience with pageants and allegorical masques. Thus, when the Estates return to the stage in Part Two, they are led backwards by their ruling vices in a procession; or, at the end, when Falsehood comes to be hanged, his final speech summons all oppressors to follow him into death, until the rope tightens around his neck and a black crow is released to symbolise his soul. There are equally memorable scenes when the Pauper 'invades' the stage from the audience during the interlude and demands that his complaints be heard, despite the efforts of the players to stop him. At every turn, anarchic moments such as this are used, along with what must have been topical local references, to play against the more allegorical set pieces.

Lindsay also manages a number of sophisticated verse-forms and modes of address. The play's formal speeches are made in iambic pentameters with an eight-line stanza and a linking rhyme-scheme, a form used in Latin and French verse and in some early English mystery plays. There are swift-moving passages when single lines rhymed in couplets are exchanged between speakers (stychomythia), and moments when a jogging bob-wheel is used to set a three-stress line against a four-stress norm – a familiar effect and already a favourite with Scots poets:

> I haue sic pleasour at my hart,
> That garris me sing the treble pairt: makes
> Wald sum gude fellow fill the quart
>   It wald my hairt reioyce.
>
> Howbeit my coat be short and nippit,
> Thankis be to God I am weill hippit   padded
> Thocht all my gold may sone be grippit
>   Intill ane pennie pursse.

When John the Commonweill first speaks, his diction is appropriately plain and forceful: 'Out of my gait, for Gods saik let me ga'; and 'Gude maister I wald speir at you ane thing, / Quhair traist ye I sall find yon new cumde King?' But, when he accuses the Estates and their special sins, his couplets ring out in longer and sterner lines: 'And as ye se Temporalitie hes neid of correctioun, / Quhilk hes lang tyme bene led by publick oppressioun'. Such vigour and variety is remarkable for 1540, it is uncommon in contemporary morality plays and predates by at least twenty years the main body of notable pre-Shakespearean plays in England.

Lindsay's drama opens by showing how the young Rex Humanitas, encouraged by his minions, Wantonness, Placebo and Solace, is ensnared by Sensuality, the beautiful natural daughter of Venus. At such a court the aged adviser Good Counsel is ignored, while the vices of Flattery, Falsehood and Deceit dress up as friars and thrive as 'Devotion', 'Sapience' and 'Discretion'. The whole is played out in front of symbolic groups representing the assembled three Estates. Leaders of the Catholic Church, or the 'Spirituality', comprise the first Estate, the second is that of the lords and barons – the 'Temporality' – while the third Estate consists of established burgesses and merchants. Ordinary working folk without property or power have no place in this parliament and they are represented by the Pauper, who 'interrupts' the play, and by John the Commonweill, who comes forward in Part Two and testifies against all three arms of the establishment. Such an abstract gives little impression of the earthy nature of the satire, for the three vices are hilariously and broadly scurrilous and Flattery is a part for a leading comedian, who takes several disguises in the course of the play. Court and Church are his stamping-grounds, while Deceit reigns over merchants, and Falsehood thrives among the craftsmen. The first part of the play follows the promotion of these villains and parallels it with the misfortunes of the two maidens Verity and Chastity, who arrive on the scene only to be spurned by each Estate in turn. (Verity carries the New Testament 'in English toung' and is greeted with horror by the Spirituality and condemned as a heretic and a 'Lutherian'.) Before long, however, Divine Correction arrives to free the maidens from the stocks and assemble a parliament of all the Estates, at which he makes an examination of the condition of the kingdom. Correction strikes an old and familiar Scottish chord by asking 'Quhat is ane King?', and by giving the answer that he is 'nocht bot ane officiar, / To caus his Lieges liue in equitie'. Armed with God's truth, however, there is a new and thrilling resonance to his authority:

I haue power greit Princes to doun thring,	throw down
That liues contrair the Maiestie Divyne:	
Against the treuth quhilk plainlie dois maling	malign
Repent they nocht I put them to ruyne.	

The political and philosophical impact of this insight must have been heady stuff for the commons in the audience, and one notices how often the word 'reformatioun' is repeated in the text.

The interlude provides a vulgar satire on the abuses of mendicant friars and the selling of remissions and relics, made all the more pointed because the audience knows that the corrupt Pardoner is Flattery in disguise. The second movement of the play presents John the Commonweill's case against the three Estates. The barons and the merchants submit to correction without demur, but the Spirituality resists and the parliament turns into a trial against corruption in the Church. Here Lindsay makes a vivid piece of propaganda drama in which many social and ecclesiastical abuses are specifically described, along with their painful effects on the commons and the country in general. The message is driven home at every turn, for the interlude and the epilogue repeat the arguments in burlesque terms; a 'learned Doctor' actually preaches a sermon from the stage, and, towards the end of the play, no less than fifteen acts of proposed reformation are read out formally and at length to the assembled audience. Such complaints are not unfamiliar; Chaucer's Pardoner led the way, after all; but Lindsay's case is outstanding because he links specific suggestions to his talent for drama and comedy.

From the very start *The Thrie Estaits* establishes a stirring and democratic truth about the nature of man, and the audience is brought to realise it on two radically different levels. All men are equal before their appetites; and all men are equal before God. Thus Dame Sensuality speaks to the Estates:

Paipis, Patriarks, or Prelats venerabill,
Common pepill and Princes temporall,
Ar subject all to me Dame Sensuall.

The play's impact depends on us being able to feel the essential
truth of these and the following lines, even while we know that
such feelings are sinful:

Quhat vails your kingdome and your rent,
    And all your great treasure,
Without ye haif ane mirrie lyfe,
And cast asyde all sturt and stryfe . . .
    Fall to and tak your pleasure.

And that pleasure is convincingly portrayed:

Behauld my visage flammand as the fyre.
Behauld my papis of portratour perfyte.
To luke on mee luiffers hes greit delyte.

In just the same way, Lindsay shows that Divine Correction
applies to all classes – 'To rich and puir I beir ane equall hand'
– and that Verity, a simple maid armed only with the New
Testament, can dare to counsel kings.

These recognitions are at the heart of Lindsay's purpose. He
is no puritan (as witness the bawdiness of his verses and
Correction's approval of hunting and lawful merriness), but he
believes in what would now be called public accountability.
Good Counsel points out that, while cobblers and tailors are
skilled workers at their trade, there are bishops and parsons
who can neither read nor preach. Surely the Church should be
no less craftsmanlike than the laity? It should recruit its
members on merit alone: 'Cair thou nocht quhat estait sa ever
he be, / Sa thay can teich and preich the veritie'. But the
Spirituality's only defence is to attack the presumption of its
critics – 'it is heresie, / To speik against our law and libertie' –
until even the merchants see the weakness of such an argument
from those who 'will correct and nocht be correctit'. Good
Counsel, that shrewd courtier, adds that it is only common
sense for a king to look after his humbler subjects, for 'the
husband-men and commons thay war wont, / Go in the battell
formest in the front', while John the Commonweill quotes from

St Paul to make a nobler case for the dignity of 'men that labours with thair hands':

Qui non laborat no manducet.
This is in Inglische toung or leit: language
Quha labouris nocht he sall not eit.

John, Good Counsel, the merchants and the lords all agree that the first duty of churchmen should be to teach the people, and to clarify the Scriptures.

Confronted by Divine Correction and King Humanity, the Spirituality is made to discard its power and its rich robes as Bishop, Abbot, Parson and Prioress all stand nakedly revealed as 'verie fuillis'. They do not leave the stage, however, without a final telling shot – 'We say the Kings war greiter fuillis nor we / That us promovit to sa greit dignitie' – and Lindsay must have counted on these lines to produce a moment of gleeful recognition among the groundlings. John the Commonweill takes his seat in parliament, and in a sequence of light-heartedly brutal vignettes Theft, Deceit and Falsehood make their final speeches and are hanged. Flattery alone survives (by having testified against his fellows) and his escape serves as a reminder that the principle of duplicity and the appetite for fair words will never be extinguished from human society. As though to emphasise the point, the Epilogue reminds us that there is a kind of democracy among dunces, for 'the number of fuillis ar infinite' – and they thrive in every class.

Lindsay's other works are something of an anticlimax, although 'The Historie of Squyer Meldrum' (c.1550) is an enjoyable and rollicking account of the loves and valiant doings of a Fifeshire laird, probably written shortly after the real William Meldrum died. By comparison, *Ane Dialogue betwix Experience and ane Courteour, Off the Miserabyll Estait of the Warld* scarcely moves faster than a crawl. The four books of this poem, also known as *The Monarche*, were probably written between 1548 and 1553, and it seems that in Lindsay's later years his didactic impulse became merely pedantic. With *The Thrie Estaits*, however, he had created a unique form of propaganda drama, fully committed to the public forum, not too extreme in its doctrinal views, acceptably liberal and practical in its proposed reforms, and, above all, brilliantly tailored to influence the audience by the communal delights of laughter, anger and debate.

The theatre in Scotland

It seems very probable that there were precursors to *The Thrie Estaits*: Lindsay's grasp of stagecraft suggests as much; but no dramatic texts or reputations have survived. The Bannatyne Manuscript preserves a fragment from the early part of the century, sometimes attributed to Dunbar, and known as the 'Littil Interlude of the Droichis Part of the Play'. James Wedderburn, one of the brothers responsible for the *Gude and Godlie Ballatis*, is reported to have written comedies and tragedies around 1540, and it is known that the minor poet Robert Sempill had a play performed in 1568. (He also wrote a violently anti-Papist verse attack on the Archbishop of St Andrew's in 1584 – 'The Legend of the Lymmaris Lyfe'.) It seems likely, then, that there was a young dramatic tradition in Scotland and that it was not afraid to comment on the social and religious issues of the day. It is known that John Knox was mentioned in an anti-Catholic piece written by a friar called Kyllour and performed at Stirling in 1535. The older observances of folk festivals, guild processions, clerk plays, passion plays and pageants at court must all have contributed something to the growth of a theatrical understanding. In the course of the Reformation, however, the Kirk sessions came to oppose dramatic performances put on for public entertainment, and, although at first they remained content to ban only clerk plays based on interpretation of the Scriptures, they gradually came to suspect all plays as 'slanderous and undecent'. In 1599 the Kirk attempted to prohibit people from attending a comedy performed in Edinburgh by a group of English players, but James VI stepped in and assured his subjects that they could go to the show.

Even so, James could not make the theatre flourish in the second half of the century. A vernacular play called *Philotus* was published in 1603, but the author is unknown, although Robert Sempill is sometimes suggested. *Philotus* is a comedy after the Italian manner on sexual disguise, mistaken identity and the marriage between age and youth, but the plot moves from comic complexity to sheer confusion. As drama it scarcely compares with Lindsay's play, much less with a contemporary English piece such as *All's Well that Ends Well*. The contentious temper of the times in Scotland was not sympathetic to a theatre still in its infancy, and the success of the *Gude and Godlie Ballatis* speaks for a fairly unsophisticated popular taste. The final factor was that Edinburgh, unlike London, did not support a regular public playhouse nor any settled professional group of actors. Whether this was due to a lack of public interest or to the presence of public 'morals' it is difficult at this distance in time to tell. In either case, the early promise of *The Thrie Estaits* came to nothing. If the theatre never became a popular art in Scotland, the same cannot be said for songs and ballads, however. Of course the great ballads were born out of an oral tradition, as we shall see in the next chapter, and so their creators and the date of their first appearance cannot be identified in the usual way, but they would have been circulating through the sixteenth and seventeenth centuries, and in their own way they brought considerable colour and drama to the folk.

Writing in prose

David Lindsay's hopes that his verse would speak to 'Jok and Thome', like Gavin Douglas's concern for 'onletterit folk', reflect what was to be a growing commitment among prose writers of this period. Latin was still the tongue of learned discourse, and **John Major,** or **Mair** (1467–1550), a school-man of the old order who was educated at Cambridge and Paris, used it for his philosophical commentaries and for his influential *History of Greater Britain both England and Scotland* (1521). Major was distrustful of humanistic culture, but he numbered George Buchanan and John Knox amongst his pupils and something of his scholastic severity in disputation coloured the outlook of both men. Notwithstanding the continued use of Latin at the universities, the spread of printing and the unfolding of the Reformation soon made both Protestant and Catholic writers acutely aware of the public power of their mother tongue. Some, such as Buchanan, retained a strong affinity with Latinate constructions, while others, such as Bellenden or Pitscottie, produced a more natural vernacular style. The most influential example was set by John Knox, who anglicised his Scots prose, with his eye on new readers south of the Border. This tendency was reinforced at the end of the century by James VI's move to London in 1603 and by the literary excellence of English writers such as Francis Bacon and Sir Thomas Browne. Back in Scotland, however, chronicles, pamphlets and theological disputations were more common, and by these means a nation was instructed about its individuality and how that manifested itself geographically, politically and spiritually.

The translation of the Bible into English, linked as it was with the spread of Protestantism, had a profound effect on the development of Scots vernacular prose. Murdoch Nisbet is credited with a Scots version of Wycliffe's fourteenth-century New Testament translation, but the work remained in manuscript and was not printed until 1901, so by far the most potent influence on the northern reformers came from testaments published in English. These began with the work of William Tyndale, undertaken at some personal risk (1525–34); officially tolerated versions followed, with Miles Coverdale's (1535) and the so-called Matthews Bible (1537), which was revised into Cromwell's Great Bible of 1539. The Calvinist Geneva Bible from 1560 came to hold a special place in Scottish hearts, and finally, of course, the Authorised Version appeared in 1611. Thus it was English prose which spoke to Protestant Scotland for the next three centuries, exerting an enormous cultural influence on a people who laid such emphasis on the reading and teaching of Scripture.

It was at James V's request that **John Bellenden** (1495–1550?), the archdeacon of Moray, undertook a free translation of Hector Boece's *Historia gentis Scotorum*, intended, no doubt, for the edification of the king's own barons and courtiers. *The History and Chronicles of Scotland*, in vigorous and straightforward Scots, was completed in 1533 and printed in Edinburgh no fewer than three times within the next fifteen years. Indeed, the current interest in history encouraged one William Stewart in 1535 to versify Boece into Scots. Bellenden also translated the first five books of Livy's *History of Rome* (1532) and prefaced the work with a rhymed prologue of his own.

The Complaynt of Scotland, sometimes ascribed to Robert Wedderburn, was printed and published in 1549 as an account of 'this affligit realme quhilk is my native countre'. The author's patriotism and his anti-English feeling can be explained by remembering that Solway Moss and Henry VIII's 'rough wooing' were still fresh and bitter memories. It is the most colourful early prose in vernacular Scots, and the nearest to imaginative writing in that it follows the allegorical-verse tradition by including a dream vision and using ornate descriptive language. Like Douglas before him, the writer adjusts his mother tongue to meet his needs and asks readers to forgive him if he has, in places, 'myxt oure langage witht part of termis dreuyn fra lateen, be rason that oure scottis tong is nocht sa copeus as is the lateen tong'. He claims that his intention is to speak as plainly as possible:

> For I thocht it nocht necessair til hef fardit ande lardit this tracteit witht exquisite termis, quhilkis are nocht daily usit, bot rather I hef usit domestic Scottis langage, maist intelligibil for the vulgare pepil.

In spite of its distrust of 'exquisite termis' and its purpose as propaganda, *The Complaynt* parades Latinate diction, highbrow prognostication and classical allusions across its pages as if to assure both author and reader of its intellectual respectability. Its main message is conveyed by an extended allegory in which the dire state of the country is explained through Dame Scotia's confrontation with her three errant sons, representing Church, nobles and the common people. This scheme was adapted from the original French prose of Alain Chartier's *Quadrilogue Invectif* (1422) – the most notable of several borrowings in the text – but *The Complaynt* still has a distinctively Scottish flavour of its own. It begins by philosophising on the fate of the nation, the mutability of temporal power and the forthcoming end of the world; then, fatigued by his efforts, the author repairs to the countryside for rest and relaxation. Strictly speaking, this 'Monolog Recreative' has nothing to do with the book's main purpose, but the author launches himself into a descriptive blizzard of detail like some forewarning of Sir Thomas Urquhart's own encyclopaedic muse. At dawn the sounds of the countryside begin to make themselves heard in this manner:

For fyrst furth on the fresche feildis, the nolt [cattle] maid noyis witht mony loud lou. Baytht horse and meyris did fast nee, and the folis nechyr. The bullis began to bullir, quhen the sheip began to blait, be cause the calfis began tyl mo, quhen the doggis berkit. Than the suyne [swine] began to quhryne quhen thai herd the asse rair quhilk gart [made] the hennis kekkyl quhen the cokis creu. The chekyns began to peu quehn the gled [hawk] quhissillit. The fox follouit the fed geise, and gart them cry claik. The gayslingis cryit quhilk, quhilk, and the dukis cryit quaik . . .

When the cacophony is finally documented, the author visits the seashore to witness a complicated naval engagement between two warships; he takes breakfast with a group of shepherds and reports on the joys of pastoral life and its contributions to science and astronomy; when the rustic company turns to recreation, the indefatigable scribe lists by name the forty-seven tales, thirty-eight songs and thirty dances they performed! Having survived this marathon, he wanders among the meadows and eventually falls asleep to have the allegorical dream vision, which is, after all, his main subject – but not before he has made an inventory of all the flowers and herbs and their medicinal properties. Over the centuries this recurring ennumerative exhaustiveness has a mad charm of its own in Scottish literature. But the sheer garrulousness of *The Complaynt* must have been something of a trial for the 'vulgar pepil' who were supposed to be reading it, even if future scholars have cause to bless its documentary zeal.

The most entertaining of the vernacular histories is by **Robert Lindsay of Pitscottie** (1532–90?). His *Historie and Cronikles of Scotland* was completed in the mid 1570s, but not published until 1782, when it went through three more editions at twenty- to thirty-year intervals. Many of the more colourful anecdotes in Scots history – from James II to James VI – come from Pitscottie, for, although his chronology is as uncertain as his sense of relevance, he has a splendid, gossipy journalist's eye for domestic detail, personal dramas and curious events. He knew men who had served at court or gone to war and so it seems likely that their reported experiences are not too far from the truth, even if they gained a little in the telling. Certainly the Scottish tapestry would be paler without the colour of Pitscottie's account of how James II was killed by a bursting gun, or the tragedy at Flodden, or the dying words of Border reiver and Stewart king, or the confusion and panic at the battle of Pinkie

in 1547, or dynastic betrayals and escapes, a ghost at Linlithgow, Siamese twins, strange portents, royal hunting-parties
and all the fascinating details of courtly fashion and behaviour.

By comparison with Pitscottie, **Bishop John Leslie**
(1527–96) is more austere and accurate, but much less
interesting. His ten-volume *History of Scotland* was written in
Latin during the 1570s, published in Rome in 1578, and
translated into Scots by Father James Dalrymple eighteen
years later. Both at home and in France, Leslie remained a
faithful ally to Mary Queen of Scots throughout her life. A more
contentious servant was **George Buchanan** (1506–82), almost
all of whose works were in Latin. In his thirties Buchanan
produced satires against the Franciscans, and, faced with the
charge of heresy, had to flee to Europe, where he spent twenty
years at various universities, including a spell as tutor to
Montaigne at Bordeaux and a scrape with the Inquisition in
Portugal, where he was imprisoned from 1550 to 1552.
Eventually Buchanan returned to Scotland to become an
adviser to Mary, a friend of John Knox's and a severe authority
on education and reformation. It was in this latter role that he
prepared virulent charges against Mary Queen of Scots and,
for the last twelve years of his life, acted as tutor to the young
James VI. Buchanan was famous throughout Europe as
scholar of the new humanism and a Latinist, in which language
he produced, among other pieces, translations from the Greek,
a verse paraphrase of the Psalms, metrical poetry of his own,
biblical and classical masques for the court, and two tragedies
in the Senecan style: *Jephthah* and *John the Baptist*. A lengthy
history of Scotland, *Rerum Scoticarum Historia* (1582), reminded
his royal charge that the people of ancient Gaeldom had had
the right to depose unsatisfactory kings. This was erroneous
but not by any means irrelevant, and *De Jure Regni apud Scotos*
(1579) pursued the same issue in contemporary terms through
seven editions, with translations in English, German and
Dutch, before the king suppressed it in 1586 and produced his
own *Basilikon Doron*, as a counterclaim for the divine right of
monarchs. Buchanan's vernacular prose includes a
propaganda-piece against the Hamiltons, and *The Chamaeleon*
(1570), a short satirical attack on William Maitland of
Lethington, the devious secretary to the queen, who was
accused of changing colours and religions daily. Buchanan's

vernacular prose is impeded rather than helped by his fluency in Latin, and it cannot match the simpler and more forceful style of his contemporary John Knox.

John Knox (1505–72) was born near Haddington, educated at the universities of Glasgow and St Andrew's, ordained as a priest and employed as a notary and tutor in his home district. He was in his forties before he joined himself to the Reformation movement in Scotland. A gradual intellectual commitment was catalysed by his meeting with George Wishart, who returned to Scotland from Switzerland to propose a new church, protected by the state but acknowledging only Christ as its leader. Knox carried a two-handed sword to protect the young preacher, but could not forestall Wishart's trial for heresy, within the year, at St Andrew's, where he was strangled and burned at the stake. Thenceforth Knox was caught up in the conflict. He only began to preach at the insistence of his fellows, and spoke his first sermon to the men who occupied St Andrew's after the revengeful murder of Beaton. When the castle finally surrendered in 1547, Knox was condemned with the other commoners to the French galleys, where he sat at an oar for almost two years before a petition from the English government brought about his release. He served in England as chaplain to Edward VI, but the accession of Mary Tudor in 1553 renewed the persecution of Protestants and Knox planned to go abroad, having married the young woman who was to bear him two sons before her death in 1560. He spent the next four years in Frankfurt and Geneva, where his early thoughts on election were powerfully influenced by Calvin's doctrines. Thus began his politico-religious war on behalf of a revolutionary democratic theocracy, a 'godly discipline' of behaviour to be guided at every turn by reference to the text of the Bible. He toured Scotland briefly in 1555 and savoured the public effectiveness of his preaching. During these years he also produced several pamphlets addressed to the people of Scotland and England, including a violent attack on 'bloody Mary' – *A Faythful Admonition unto the Professours of Goddis Truthe in England* (1554) – which did little to quench the fires of persecution in the South. The famous *First Blast of the Trumpet against the Monstruous Regiment of Women* (1558) had an equally backhanded effect. This treatise is informed with the misogyny of the times and coloured again by Knox's own cantankerous views about the female sex. (These did not stop him from marrying again in 1564 and, at the age of fifty-nine, taking a girl scarcely seventeen years old to be his wife. The disparity in their ages caused some talk, but Knox ignored it and eventually became the father of two daughters.) *The First Blast* turned out to be a rather loud tactical error, for, although it was directed at the political and religious policies of Mary Tudor in England and the queen regent in Scotland, it caused costly offence to Elizabeth I, who was, after all, a champion of Protestantism in her way, and a potential ally.

In 1559 Knox returned to Scotland and made another great preaching-tour – joining in what was now open conflict between the Lords of the Congregation and the forces of Mary of Guise. Each faction sought armed support from outside, the Protestants from England and the Catholics from France. Mobs rioted in Perth for two days after one of Knox's sermons and a situation of virtual civil war was only averted by the military impasse at Leith and by the death of Mary of Guise from dropsy. The spokesman for Christian Reformation hailed her painful end as a judgement from God. After the Treaty of Leith, the Reformation Parliament of 1560 and the Confession of Faith placed religious authority firmly in the hands of the new church and, as author of a treatise on predestination (1560) and as one of the writers of *The First Book of Discipline* (1560), it was John Knox whose vision helped to set the pattern for intellectual, social and religious life in Scotland, an iron mould which endured virtually until modern times. The arrival of Mary Queen of Scots heralded a turbulent seven years, and Knox had several private and public clashes with her, preaching that one Mass was more fearful to him than 10,000 armed enemies landed in the realm to suppress the whole religion. Events and eyewitnesses alike testify to the intemperate power of his rhetoric as he smote the pulpit as though to 'ding it in blads and fly out of it'. All the same, Knox found it prudent to retire from the court for a spell, during which time (1566–7) he completed *The Historie of the Reformation of Religioun within the Realm of Scotland*, published seventy-two years after his death. 'Here lies ane', said Morton at his graveside 'who never feared the face of man.'

It is impossible to warm to Knox's harsh, authoritarian nature, but it is equally difficult not to admit the forcefulness of his prose in *The Historie of the Reformatioun*. The energetic violence of his certainty, his grim sense of humour, his fluency in plain un-Latinate English and Scots colloquial speech, his eye for physical detail and his use of dramatic dialogue – all these testify to what must have been a truly powerful physical and political presence. He is an agitator rather than a philosopher, biased in his judgements and dogmatic in his opinions, yet there is something awesome in his unswerving adherence to what he saw as his duty. 'Madam,' he said to his queen, 'I am not master of myself, but must obey him who commands me to speak plain, and to flatter no flesh upon the face of the earth.' Carlyle saw him as a hero of private judgement, comparing him to some 'Old Hebrew Prophet', with the 'same inflexibility, intolerence, rigid narrow-looking adherence to God's truth, stern rebuke in the name of God to all that foresake truth', and he admired how Knox refused to do reverence to an image of the Virgin Mary when he was a prisoner in the galleys:

> Mother? Mother of God? said Knox, when the turn came to him: This is no Mother of God: this is 'a pented bredd [board] – a piece of wood, I tell you with paint on it! She is fitter for swimming, I think, than for being worshipped, added Knox, and flung the thing into the river. It was not very cheap jesting there: but come of it what might, this thing to Knox was and must continue nothing other than the real truth; it was a *pented bredd*: worship it he would not.
>
> ('The Hero as Priest', *On Heroes and Hero-Worship*, 1841)

Knox's metaphysical audacity and grim-humoured, hard-nosed facticity speak for something in the Scottish spirit, and at least his prose is a stylistic advance on the laboured diction of *The Complaynt*. Here is his account of Cardinal Beaton's end:

> And so he [James Melven] stroke him twyse or thrise trowght with a stog sweard; and so he fell, never word heard out of his mouth, but 'I am a preast; fy, fy: all is gone.'
>
> Whill they war thus occupyed with the Cardinall, the fray rises in the toune. The Provest assembles the communitie, and cumis to the fowseis [moats] syd, crying, 'What have ye done with my Lord Cardinall? Whare is my Lord Cardinall? Have ye slayne my Lord Cardinall? Let us see my Lord Cardinall.' Thei that war within answered gentilye, 'Best it war unto yow to returne to your awin, houssis; for the man ye call the Cardinall has receaved his reward, and in his awin persone will truble the warld no more.' But then more enraigedlye thei cry, 'We shall never departe till that

we see him.' And so was he brought to the East blokhouse head, and schawen dead ower the wall to the faythless multitude, which wold not beleve befoir it saw: How miserably lay David Betoun, cairfull Cardinall. And so thei departed, without *Requiem aeternam* amd *Requiescat in pace*, song for his saule. Now, becaus the wether was hote (for it was in Maij, as ye have heard) and his funerallis could not suddandly be prepared, it was thowght best, to keap him frome styncking, to geve him great salt ynewcht, [enough] a cope of lead, and a nuk in the boddome of the Sea-toore [tower] (a place whare many of Goddis childrene had bein empreasoned befoir) to await what exequeis his brethrene the Bischoppes wold prepare for him.

These thingis we wreat merrelie.

'This is superb,' wrote J. H. Millar drily, 'if not distinctively Christian', and, indeed, John Knox has remained patron saint and domestic demon in the Scottish psyche for 450 years. Knox's 'passion for truth', so admired by Carlyle, was really a passion only for his vision of the truth, with no patience for others or for the balanced judgement of philosopher or scholar. Yet his absoluteness could not have thrived had Scotland not been fertile ground for passionate personal conviction, and a delight in what MacDiarmid has called the 'hard fact', 'the inoppugnable reality'. It is one of history's ironies that equally uncompromising attitudes should be so much a part of left-wing commitment in modern Scotland, and that one of its popular manifestations should be to blame Knox alone for all the puritanical and constricting aspects of the national psyche.

James VI (1566–1625) should be mentioned as a prose-writer, although his work had far less political influence than that of his fiercest preacher. As patron of the poets who came to be known as the 'Castalian band', and at the tender age of seventeen, James produced sonnets of his own prefaced by a short treatise on poetic forms. Three years later he wrote *Daemonologie* as a proof of the dangerous existence of witchcraft. He is no less than a man of his time in this belief, but it is a shameful fact that the persecution and the burning of 'witches' – mostly female commoners – reached appalling heights in post-Reformation Scotland. These epidemics of social hysteria used to break out for a few years at a time, lasting into the mid seventeenth century. In 1588 and 1589 James produced two theological essays – 'meditations' – on verses from the Bible, while the *Basilikon Doron* (1599) was a defence of kingship written for the instruction of prince Henry and informed by James's determination not to allow the Presbyterian Church to dictate to him. About this time, he began to write only in English, as in *A Counterblaste to Tobacco* (1604). A collection of his works was published in London in 1616 and a comparison with earlier texts shows that where possible James replaced Scots words with the English equivalents. This process characterises the development of Scots prose from now on.

Minor poetry of the Reformation

Doctrinal conflict, disputatious pamphleteering, Knox's unyielding personality, the puritanism and religious persecution of subsequent years, all these darken our view of the early Reformation in Scotland. It is easy to miss the revolutionary exhilaration of a new movement which proposed a return to fundamentals, to the philosophical importance of individual judgement and to the surprising, unasked for, unearned, unacquirable descent of God's grace upon the faithful. Something of this Lutheran spirit of celebration is caught in a collection of hymns and lyrics directed to the Protestant cause, mostly collected and composed by **Robert Wedderburn** (1510?–1557) a priest of Dundee, assisted by his older brothers John, also a priest, and James, a merchant. *Ane Compendious Buik of Godlie Psalms and Spirituall Sangs* contains a calendar, the catechism, and metrical psalms and hymns in the Lutheran style, some translated from German. The collection, usually known as the *Gude and Godlie Ballatis*, is mostly notable, however, for the way it rearranges popular and courtly material – 'changeit out of Prophane Sangis in Godlie Sangis, for avoyding of sin and harlotrie'. The lively spirit of many of these pieces, and doubtless their thinly concealed worldliness too, made them a considerable popular success. Editions (also commonly called the *Dundee Psalms*), were published in 1567, 1578, 1600 and 1621. Along with the list of shepherds' songs in *The Complaynt*, they provide useful evidence of a vigorous musical tradition, except that the perennial themes of love, courting and the chase have been assimilated into a spiritual context. The process is not exactly one of bowdlerising or parody, but more like a mimicry of popular airs, especially directed at 'young personis . . . as are not exercisit in the Scriptures':

> Quho is at my windo, quho, quho?
> Go from my window, go, go,
> Quha callis thair so lyke ane stranger?
>   Go from my windo, go.

> Lord I am heir ane wratcheit mortall
> That for thy mercy dois cry and call
> Unto the my Lord Celestiall,
>   Se quho is at my windo, quho.

If these lines look rather thin, it must be remembered that they would have been set and sung to old tunes. A certain parallel suggests itself with Gospel songs or spirituals:

> Downe be yone Riuer I ran,
> Downe be yone Riuer I ran,
>   Thinkand on Christ sa fre,
> That brocht me to libertie,
>   And I ane sinful man.

The practice of 'spiritualising' secular lyrics was not confined to Protestantism, for an earlier Roman Catholic version of the following old love-song also survives, and would have been sung in church on selected occasions.

> My lufe murnis for me, for me,
> My lufe that murnis for me, for me,
> I am not kynde, hes not in mynde
> My lufe that murnis for me.

> Quha is my lufe, bot God abufe,
> Quhilk all this world hes wrocht;
> The King of blis, my lufe he is,
> Full deir he hes me bocht.

Other pieces are considerably less lamb-like, as in this rowdy attack on God's vicar, an original song, if scarcely original in sentiment:

> The Paip, that Pagane full of pryde,
> He hes us blindit lang,
> For quhair the blind the blind dois gyde
> Na wounder baith ga wrang;
> Lyke Prince and King he led the Regne
> Of all iniquitie:
> Hay trix, tryme go trix, under the grene wod tre.

The *Godlie Ballatis* have little in the way of literary merit, but they do convey an often-forgotten side to the Reformation, evoking as they do a hint of the revivalist meeting, with its willing submergence of the self, and perhaps of the critical faculties too, in cheerful congregational singing. Calvin's conception of the elect and his absolutist arrogance have not yet dampened this group celebration.

The rowdier side to the Reformation continued to be expressed in verse, and numerous political and ecclesiastical broadsheets were circulating in the second half of the century, mostly published by Robert Lekpreuik's Press in Edinburgh. The most notable of these satirists is **Robert Sempill** (1530–95), who wrote secular pieces such as 'Margaret Fleming' and 'Johnet Reid', as well as satirical attacks on the Old Church, including a famously abusive diatribe against the Archbishop of St Andrew's: 'The Legend of the Lymmaris Lyfe'.

It is a pleasing paradox that 'godlie' versions may have helped to save 'prophane' originals from oblivion, but two other major verse-collections of the period deliberately set out to record and preserve old Scottish poetry. Without the Bannatyne and Maitland manuscripts, the store of fifteenth- and sixteenth-century Scots verse would be much impoverished, for they contain poems by Henryson, Dunbar and Douglas as well as many anonymous or disputed pieces which would otherwise have been lost. **George Bannatyne** (1545–1608), was an Edinburgh merchant who returned to his home in Forfarshire in 1568 to escape an outbreak of plague in the capital. During his year's sojourn he transcribed many poems from old and tattered copies and prints and even included in the collection some unremarkable verses of his own. Allan Ramsay drew on this source for his *Ever Green* collection in 1724, and editors ever since have had cause to be grateful for the fruits of Bannatyne's enforced retreat. **Sir Richard Maitland of Lethington** (1496–1586), was a legal judge of noble birth and long-standing service who also collected old poems over the years and arranged to have them compiled in two manuscript anthologies. (The next most important manuscript collection in Scottish letters is also from the sixteenth century: the Asloan Manuscript of 1515.) Maitland was himself a poet (a better one than Bannatyne), but he did not start composing until he was in his sixties with failing sight: his verses are seldom cheerful.

Alexander Scott (1525?–1584?) did not share Maitland's personal and political gloom, although his poems date from the 1560s and the turbulent years of the Reformation Parliament and Mary Stewart's reign. Scott's only political poem, 'Ane New Yeir Gift to the Quene Mary quhen scho Come First Hame, 1562', is full of dull advice and reflections, but it includes the worthy wish that the queen will ban all disputations on holy writ by anyone other than qualified scholars, for these days even 'lymmer lawdis and little lassis lo / Will argun bayth with bischop, preist, and freir'. 'The Justing and Debait up at the Drum betwix Wa. Adamsone and Johine Sym' has these two worthy commoners in a burlesque of knightly combat and shares both its earthy vivacity and its metre with the older 'Christis Kirk' and 'Peblis' poems. With the exception of a couple of psalms, the rest of Scott's work (or what was preserved of it in the Bannatyne Manuscript), consists of love lyrics. Some of these follow a medieval ethos by giving a coarse recital of the sexual weaknesses of women ('Ane Ballat Maid to the Derisioun and Scorne of Wantoun Wemen'), while others are more sophisticated in a playfully cynical, Ovidian way, as in 'Of Wemenkynd', where the poet begins by posing himself a problem:

> I muse and mervellis in my mind,
> Quhat way to wryt, or put in vers,
> The quent consaitis of wemenkynd . . . .

Scott's verse is technically various: he can use short, simple lines, rather in the manner of Skelton, or metrical gymnastics reminiscent of Dunbar. The following lines from 'A Rondel of Luve' use the old French rondel form, with an epigrammatic succinctness:

> Lufe is an fervent fyre
> Kendillit without desyre:
> Schort plesour, lang displesour;
> Repentence is the hyre;
> Ane pure tressour without mesour:
> Lufe is an fervent fyre.

In all cases Scott's muse explores the pain of sophisticated love affairs expressed in a worldly, sometimes facile manner, not unlike Wyatt's love poems, but technically more polished. It is physical attraction that Scott pursues, and, if there is little sense of the ideal in his work, he can still rise to an erotic directness.

The 'Castalian band'

The poetry of the sixteenth century closes with the productions of Alexander Montgomerie and James VI's 'Castalian band'. When the boy king escaped from the Protestant nobles who had kidnapped him on the 'Ruthven Raid', he re-established himself at court (in 1583) surrounded by more sympathetic lords. James produced his own poems in *Poetical Exercises* (1591), and the *Essayes of a Prentise in the Divine Art of Poesie* (1584), prefaced by the 'Reulis and Cautelis'. James's pretensions allowed him to style himself as 'Apollo' ruling a court where poetry and song were to prevail. The play *Philotus* was probably a part of the court's entertainment during these years, but the little group could not support a wider theatrical tradition. Among these courtly practitioners of the muse, Alexander Montgomerie is the most distinguished, having taken the king's fancy by challenging another writer – Patrick Hume of Polwarth – to a flyting-match and defeating him in floods of ingenious invective. The other poets remain resolutely minor, including James himself. The king came to call his circle 'brothers of the Castalian band', after the fountain of Castalia, sacred to Apollo and muses. During this special decade of music and poetry, models were sought and works translated from France and Italy, many Petrarchan-style love-sonnets were written in the English manner or after Ronsard, and always the qualities of smoothness and sophisticated lightness were prized.

Although not Castalian 'brothers', Robert Sempill and 'old Alexander Scott' would have visited the court and had a ready audience there, while another poet of the period, **Alexander Hume** (1557–1609) grew tired of seeking royal favour and withdrew to become a minister of the church at Logie, near Stirling. Hume renounced his early secular work in favour of worthier themes and prefaced his collection *Hymns and Sacred*

Songs (1599) with the sour remark that 'In princes' Courts . . .
the chief pastime is to sing prophane sonnets, and vaine ballads
of love.' Despite this moral tone, his best-known poem, 'Of the
Day Estivall', is a beautiful description of a Midsummer's Day,
celebrating domestic, rural observances and every natural
detail bathed in heat and a brilliant light:

> What pleasour were to walke and see
> Endlang a river cleare,
> The perfite forme of everie tree,
> Within the deepe appeare?

> The Salmon out of cruifs and creels
> Up hailed into skowts,   cobles (fishing boats)
> The bells, and circles on the weills,
> throw lowpping of the trouts.   jumping

> O: then it were a seemely thing,
> While all is still and calme,
> The praise of God to play and sing,
> With cornet and with shalme.

Alexander Montgomerie (1545?–1610?) met the favour of his
king – he was a distant blood relation – and came to
prominence in his mid thirties. He had quite a large poetic
output, although much of his work was not published until
relatively modern times. The seventeen-year-old monarch
enjoyed Montgomerie's poetry, hailed him as a master in the
craft and awarded him a pension in 1583 (although it took the
poet some ten years of manoeuvring to collect it). For his part,
Montgomerie took care to admire his royal patron without fear
of excess, even if, at times, he saw quite clearly what life at court
entailed: 'First thou mon preis thy Prince to pleiss, / Thoght
contrare Conscience he commands'. Montgomerie left Scotland in 1586, perhaps on business for James, which took him to
Flanders, France and Spain. He was a Catholic involved with
Catholic interests at court, and this connection may explain his
mission and the fact that he got into unspecified trouble abroad
and was imprisoned there for some years. He returned to
Scotland in 1591, but by this time his fortunes were ebbing, for
he had slipped from James's favour. When he was implicated in
a Catholic plot in 1597 – apparently to do with a Spanish
invasion – he more or less disappeared from public ken.

Montgomerie wrote many love-sonnets without particular distinction, showing the influence of Scott, Ronsard and the English models of Wyatt and Sidney. Although he affects the conventional pose of complaint both as a man of affairs and as a lover, there is at times a genuinely pessimistic and irritable cast to his poems, a note which the affliction of gout and the instability of his financial status probably did nothing to dispel. A coarser and wilder delight, reminiscent of Dunbar's technique, informs the 'Flyting betwixt Montgomerie and Polwart', a sustained and lengthy exercise in the old-fashioned duel of invective 'by ryme' – 'anger to asswage, make melancholy lesse.' Montgomerie begins in relatively mild terms:

> POLWART, yee peip like a mouse amongst thornes;
> Na cunning yee keepe; POLWART, yee peip;
> Ye look like a sheipe an ye had twa hornes:
> POLWART, ye peip like a mouse amongst thornes.

In due course Polwarth replies, and forcefully, too. Enraged that he should be 'bitten' in verse by another, and especially bitten by such 'a duck' as Polwarth, Montgomerie promises to drive him from the 'kings chimney nuike', but not before his adversary delivers a few raspberries more:

> Thou was begotten, some sayes mee,
> Betwixt the devil and a dun kow,
> An night when that the fiend was fow.

Since Montgomerie seems to have spent part of his youth in Argyll, Polwarth chides him for having Highland connections, showing, like Dunbar, a courtier's contempt for life in the west. Tradition has it that James gave the victory to Montgomerie, but it is Polwarth who has the exhaustive last word, sustained for sixty-six lines in lavatorial strain:

> Fond flytter, shit shytter, bacon byther, all defyld!
> Blunt bleittar, paddock pricker, puddin eiter, perverse!
> Hen plucker, closet mucker, house cucker, very vyld!
> Tanny cheeks, I think thou speiks with thy breeks, foul-erse!

In complete contrast to the rude extravagances of the flyting, the aureate lines of 'The Bankis of Helicon' celebrate the beauty of the poet's lady; but they, too, suggest echoes of

Dunbar and really belong to an earlier mode of writing. The same stanza-form (invented by Montgomerie) and the same somewhat antique mode of expression are seen to better effect in *The Cherrie and the Slae*, Montgomerie's longest and most famous work. It was published in 1597 and by the end of the eighteenth century it had gone through twenty-two editions, making it the most widely read Scots poem next to the *Wallace* and the verses of Burns. Allan Ramsay included it in *Ever Green* and copied the form for his own 'The Vision', while Burns later adopted the complex fourteen-line 'quatorzain' stanza for his 'Epistle to Davie' and the recitative parts of the 'The Jolly Beggars'.

The Cherrie and the Slae opens on a May morning whose crystal clear light beams down on a landscape typical of the old dream allegories. Although Montgomerie uses some 'enamelled' terms and peoples the scene with classical references, he also draws on images from nature and manages to imbue the scene with a sense of idyllic freshness. In this setting, the poet accidentally wounds himself with one of Cupid's darts and finds himself possessed not only by Courage, Desire and Hope, but also by their counterparts, Dread, Danger and Despair. Too late he realises that his peace of mind has left him:

> To late I knaw quha hewis too hie
> The spail sall fall into his eie,   chips; eye
>   To late I went to Scuillis:
> To late I heard the swallow preiche,
> To late Experience dois teache,
>   The Skuil-maister of fuillis:
> To late to fynde the nest I seik,
>   Quhen all the birdis are flowin:
> To late the stabill dore I steik,   shut
>   Quhen all the steids are stowin:
>   To lait ay, their stait ay,
>   All fulische folke espye:
>   Behynd so, they fynd so,
>   Remeid and so do I.

Montgomerie's quatorzain is at its best with these wry and *triste* epigrams. In this state of mind the poet comes to a stream before a precipitous crag with a cherry-tree growing at the top, while below, on his side of the water, a bush of sloe-berries offers itself to any passer-by. He is divided between a sweet, impossible ideal, and the humbler, sourer, more attainable fruit of expediency. As a love-allegory the symbols ask him to choose between a high-born lady and a common mistress, and the young lover's divided feelings engage in a symbolic debate before he finally decides to seek the cherries. No sooner has the allegorical company arrived at the unclimbable cherry-tree, than the ripe fruit drops into the poet's hands. When he tastes the cherries he finds himself relieved of every care and offers up praises to God.

The descriptive opening scenes are detailed, charming and in the familiar love-allegory mode, but the debate that follows is lengthy, abstract and rather tedious, despite classical allusions and many familiar proverbs done in telling rhyme. Indeed some critics have maintained that the argument is an addition prompted only by an impulse to moralise. The allegory, too, is undoubtedly odd, for it conveys a fable about erotic experience with all the conventional trappings of the *Roman de la Rose*, and then turns into an extended sermon. Helena Shire explains the predominance of the *débat* by making the convincing case that at one level the choice between cherry-tree and sloe-bush is, for Montgomerie, a choice between the Catholic and the Reformed churches. This fits what we know of the poet's sympathies and it certainly explains why the option is discussed at such length and in such weighty terms. Whatever the complexities of the allegory, the poem most probably earned its wide popularity through the freshness of those opening scenes and because of the epigrammatical impact of dozens of quotable saws, such as 'Quhat can thou losse, quhen honour lyvis?', or 'Brunt bairn with fyre the danger dreidis', or 'als guid drinking out of glas, / As gold in ony wise' and the marvellously 'oratorious' 'Tak time in time or time be tint [lost] / For tyme will not remaine' – worthy of Polonius at his most lugubrious. Montgomerie has been called the 'last of the makars', but, notwithstanding the partial success of *The Cherrie and the Slae*, he cannot really match the earlier work of Henryson, Dunbar, Douglas or Lindsay, and with him the golden age of Scottish poetry undoubtedly declines and comes to a close.

The contest between Montgomerie and Polwarth reminds us that in flyting, at least, Gaelic forms were still present in court life, although it is possible that the wildness of the mode was granted a special tolerance by the sophisticates of the 'Castalian band'. In the oral tradition of Gaeldom at large, bardic measures were still as formal as anything in the classical canon of the Renaissance, but it is not clear if this was ever fully appreciated by that courtly group of musicians and writers with their sights set on England and Europe. In fact the period from the sixteenth to the eighteenth centuries was particularly rich in Gaelic music and songs and the latter introduced a shift towards a more vernacular Gaelic which began to penetrate formal bardic practice later in the following century. A popular tradition in Scots songs and ballads was beginning to stir as well, but it seems appropriate to end this chapter with a closer look at something of the culture which Montgomerie must have left behind him in Argyll.

Gaelic song and music

Gaelic songs derive from the community in the most direct way, and all their values, in both technique and outlook, stem from a conservative society, isolated, clan-based and bound by strong family ties and an enduring sense of place. Thus there are many songs celebrating place – islands, hills and favourite glens, and traditional themes and approaches prevail even in accounts of human relationships. The song-style often uses the first person and offers many striking details and yet it retains an objective and unselfconscious dignity, more elevated than the voice of the Scots ballads but similarly impersonal in its progress, even when involved (as in the Scots tradition too) with songs of betrayal and longing and supernatural encounter.

Many Gaelic songs take a 'functional' context. For instance, the *iorram* or rowing-songs use the rhythms of the oars to deal with battles or laments – for the clans often sailed to war, and a dead chieftain would be carried to burial in his boat. Some of the earliest surviving vernacular songs deal with war, and the Jacobite risings ensured that this particular genre was heard well into the nineteenth century, even if its expression varies from direct incitement to romantic nostalgia. On the distaff side there are innumerable songs connected with the task of reaping, spinning, weaving, waulking and milking, not to mention love-songs, lullabies, and ballads from the point of view of the jealous woman. Early examples of these show all the signs of an oral art by which songs are retained in the memory, performed and transmitted with the help of repetition, traditional images and more or less stock epithets. At the same time, such 'work songs' or songs for particular occasions became a recognised mode within which poets could seek a more literary expression.

The *oran luadhaidh*, or waulking-song, was sung by women, often in a call-and-response pattern, while they 'waulked' lengths of wet cloth by pulling and rubbing on it to thicken the fibres. One such early Gaelic waulking-song, 'Seathan, Son of the King of Ireland' ('Seathan Mac Righ Eireann'), may date from the sixteenth century, and in one version at least, is almost 200 lines long. The singer of 'Seathan' laments the death of her lover in long rhyming paragraphs in which her memories and desires accumulate extraordinary emotional force by way of repetition and a host of details:

> But Seathan is in the lonely chamber,
> without drinking of cups or goblets,
> without drinking of wines from splendid silver tankards,
> without drinking of ale with his cronies and gentlemen,
> without drinking to music, without kiss from seductive woman,
> without music of harp, without listening to melody,
> but strait bands on his shoulders,
> and looped bands on the bier poles.
>
> I am a sister of Aodh and yellow-haired Brian,
> I am a kinswoman of Fionn son of Cumhall,
> I am the wife of brown-haired Seathan, the wanderer,
> but alas! for those who said I was a joyous wife,
> I am a poor, sad, mournful, sorrowful wife,
> ful of anguish and grief and woe. . . .
>
> If Seathan could be but redeemed
> The ransom could be got like rushes,
> silver could be got like ashes,
> gold could be got on the fringe of meadows,
> wine could be got like spring water,
> beer could be got like a cool verdant stream;
> there would not be a goat in the rock or stony upland,
> there would not be a young she-goat in meadow,
> there would not be a sheep on rocky shelf or mountain top,
> there would not be cattle on plain or in fold,
> there would not be pig or cow in pastures;
> the salmon would come from the seas,
> the trout would come from the river-banks,

the geldings would come from the rushes;
there would not be a black or white-shouldered cow
high or low in the fold,
at the edge of the township or in stall,
that I would not send, my love, to redeem thee,
even to my green plaid,
though that should take the one cow from me,
and it was not the one black cow of my fold,
but herds of white-shouldered cattle,
of white-headed, white-backed, red-eared cattle.

But Seathan is to-night in the upper town,
neither gold nor tears will win him,
neither drink nor music . . .
                    (trs. Alexander Carmichael; rev. J. C. Watson, A. Matheson)

(The use of exhaustive catalogues in this way has been a powerful and common device in Gaelic and Irish literature through the ages. The same penchant appears in Scots work such as *The Complaynt of Scotland*, or even Urquhart's *Rabelais*, as well as in the modern world-language poems of MacDiarmid, or in the prose of Irish writers such as James Joyce and Samuel Beckett, who delight in presenting the reader with lengthy and all-inclusive lists.)

The Gaelic song-book has ballads, religious verses, nonsense pieces, drinking-songs and lullabies, but it is especially rich in love-songs and laments – *cumha*. Many love-songs celebrate courting and physical beauty, others have a more melancholy edge of loss or betrayal. The ritual practice of keening over the dead body of a loved one has produced a context for some particularly moving songs, and sometimes chilling images. 'Brown-haired Allan, I would go with you' ('Ailein Duinn, shiubhlainn leat') is a lament from the eighteenth century, composed by Ann Campbell of Scalpay in Harris, and like 'Seathan' it uses long rhymed verse-paragraphs of irregular length. It was made for the death of her fiancé, who was lost at sea on his way to their wedding:

It is a sale tale I have tonight,
not of the death of the cattle in want,
but of the wetness of your shirt,
and of the porpoises tearing at you.

Brown-haired Allan,
I heard that you had been drowned,
would that I were beside you,
on whatever rock or bank you came ashore,
in whatever heap of seaweed the high tide leaves you.
I would drink a drink, whatever my kin say,
not of the red wine of Spain
but of your breast's blood, I would prefer that . . .

(trs. D. Thomson)

If song and music can be said to thrive in Scotland from the sixteenth to the eighteenth centuries, then there is particular genius to be found in the essentially folk-based traditions of Gaelic and the Scots ballads. By comparison, the songs of James VI's Castalian poets belong to a shallower and more urbane genre which looks to European models in form and music and never achieves the penetrating cry of the Gaelic *cumha*, or the grim concision of the Border ballads. And, of course, the full effect of these native songs is not felt until their haunting melodies are heard with all the incisive delivery of the traditional singer, whose sense of timing and use of grace notes far transcend in passion and power the politer classical training of the *salon*.

Gaelic songs can be sung on their own, like the ballads, or they can be accompanied by the little Celtic harp, the *clarsach* – also a solo instrument in its own right for quiet melodies. The *clarsach* goes back to the early society of aristocratic Gaeldom; Highland bards would be sent to Ireland to learn its use, and chiefs of the old style would keep a harper in their entourage, along with a bard, a piper and even a fool. Among the last of these minstrels in Scotland was Roderick Morison – 'the blind harper' – from Lewis, who lived in Lochaber and Skye in the seventeenth century under the protection of the Clan Mac-Leod. Airs to his songs have survived, but little of his purely instrumental work remains. In general the fiddle took over from the harp in succeeding generations, and indeed, some harp tunes were only preserved through fiddle adaptations, until the nineteenth century saw a revival of interest in the *clarsach* as an instrument for ladies in the drawing-room.

As though reflecting the fiercer side of the Highland sensibility, the bagpipe is a more disturbing and warlike instrument. Like the harp, its origins are too ancient to be specifically Scottish, and in the Middle Ages it was widely known throughout Europe. In the isolation of the Highlands, however, pipe-music continued to develop well into the nineteenth century, and thrives today in marches and dances (strathspeys, reels and jigs) as well as the more melodic slow airs. The finest pipe-music is not to be found with the massed bands and tartans of modern times, but with the solo pipes playing *ceòl mór* ('the big music') – unique to Scotland and originally called simply 'pipe-playing' (*piobaireachd*, or, in English, pibroch). This, the 'classical music' of the bagpipe, first states a simple theme as the *urlar*, or ground, and moves to *siubhal*, or variation, the variations increasing in complexity until *crunluath*, the climax, is reached and the progression ends with a return to the bare ground. The rules of construction and variation are highly developed, and pipe-tunes and their proper fingering can be passed on only by personal tuition, so a system of mimetic chanting called *canntaireachd* was evolved as a level of aural notation – although it could also be written down as 'words'. Conventional musical notation only came to be used in the mid nineteenth century and it still cannot give a complete account of the subtleties of the grace notes and how the instrument should be fingered. Like Celtic carving or the art of the Book of Kells, pibroch favours complication and technical virtuosity as the tune is gradually embellished with repetition or variation through the multiplication of notes, all within a fixed framework. Yet the melody too is vital, for these deceptively simple pentatonic lines are the ground or 'floor' upon which everything else is built. Tunes from the pipe-tradition can equal the finest melodies in European music, and it has been suggested that Dvořák first heard the slow movement of the 'New World' symphony in the beautiful air of 'MacIntosh's Lament'. Pibrochs can be stirring war-tunes, or boasts and challenges in the *brosnachadh* vein, but some of the finest tunes of glory have been the laments, poignant and strong, sad and yet somehow exultant.

We know little about early pipe-music except that it existed, and even the development of pibroch is unclear until the sixteenth century, when an almost legendary family called the MacCrimmons appeared as hereditary pipers to the Macleods of Skye, where they are reputed to have run a piping-college at

Boreraig. Some of the finest pibrochs were composed by MacCrimmons during the seventeenth and eighteenth centuries, when pibroch really came into its own, and the same family had pipers in it for another hundred years. Other families made significant contributions too, often beginning with MacCrimmon tuition, and two in particular stand out. The Mackays of Gairloch were descended from Iain Dall MacKay (1656–1754), the blind piper whose masterpiece, 'Lament for Patrick Og MacCrimmon', was composed in honour of his old teacher. The MacKays of Raasay, on the other hand, stem from John MacKay (1767–1845), who mastered about 250 tunes in *canntaireachd* and passed on a large part of the MacCrimmon heritage. In turn his son Angus (1813–58) recorded over 180 tunes in manuscript, to make a link with piping in modern times. Perhaps it is in pibroch, more than in any other art from a relatively remote Highland society, that the autonomy and the sophisticated intensity of Gaelic culture developed to its furthest and purest expression.

4

The seventeenth century: crown and Covenant; the ballads

AFTER the union of the crowns, Scotland was disrupted by conflict for almost ninety years as the struggle between Presbyterians, Episcopalians, Catholics and extreme dissenters continued. For the people in the northern part of the kingdom, the Civil War, the Restoration and the Revolution Settlement were only further episodes in a cause which had started, as far as they were concerned, with the triumph of the Kirk in Mary's reign and the Declaration of Faith in 1560. These disputatious years devoured the intellectual and creative energies of two generations to the exclusion of almost everything else. Among Scottish writers, Drummond and Urquhart are of some note, and of course the oral ballad-tradition must not be forgotten, but, even so, there are no Scots writers to equal Donne, Marvell, Milton and Bunyan. Perhaps the best poetic expression of the turbulent times everywhere in the north came from the biting verses of Iain Lom, who used a more vernacular Gaelic than the old bards had favoured, and whose work looks forward to the flowering of Gaelic verse in the next century.

From the vantage-point of his new throne in London, James VI and I,* began to reconsolidate his authority. He used his powers to restore episcopacy in Scotland, and when Charles I acceded in 1625 he continued his father's policy by reclaiming for the crown all those Church lands which had been redistributed by the Reformation. After the coronation at Edinburgh in 1633, Charles passed acts of parliament to establish

* Henceforth the old line of 'Stewards' were to spell their name 'Stuart'.

Anglican forms of worship – on pain of excommunication. The communion-table was turned back into an altar, confession was restored and a new prayer-book imposed. Popular unrest spread and in 1637 a famous riot broke out in St Giles' Cathedral, when a band of serving-women attacked the priest for following the new ways. At a more responsible level a plebiscite was organised to declare support for the 1560 Confession of Faith. This 'National Covenant' was drawn up at Greyfriars' Churchyard in 1638 and signed by thousands of people from all classes amid scenes of delirious fervour. The Covenant declared loyalty to the king, but requested him to re-establish the goals of Presbyterianism and not to interfere with the proper business of a free parliament and the General Assembly. The next two years saw the spasmodic 'Bishops' Wars' until Montrose's tactics with the volunteer Covenanting armies eventually persuaded Charles to make concessions to the Scots by calling an English parliament – only to have that parliament take away his right to terminate it. (Indeed, the 'Long Parliament' was eventually to depose him.) When the Civil War broke out in the south the Scottish extremists pressed their case and the 'Solemn League and Covenant' was drawn up in 1643 to force the king to stamp out Catholicism and Episcopacy throughout Britain. At this point Montrose's conscience led him to side with Charles, and he was not alone in his belief that the Solemn League had gone too far. The Highlands had never been too enthusiastic, even about the relatively mild National Covenant, and so Montrose found support there to wage a brief and brilliant military campaign. His forces began to dwindle, however, and after defeat at Philiphaugh in 1645 he had to escape into exile. Inspired by their ministers' battle-cry of 'Jesus and no quarter!', the unforgiving Convenanters massacred the beaten clansmen and all their wives and children for days. Despite his defeat, when it finally came at Naseby, Charles still refused to sign the Solemn League and Covenant and by this time the Independents in the New Model Army had become equally uncomfortable with the notion of universal compulsory Presbyterianism. Nevertheless, the Covenanters were still convinced that their faith could be imposed by royal decree, and after Charles's execution in 1649 they took their cause to his nineteen-year-old exiled son. He too refused, and once again Montrose was prevailed upon to take up arms on behalf of kingship and his king, only to be betrayed and captured within a few months. 'Arrayed like a bridegroom' in fine linen and ribbons, he was executed at the Mercat Cross in Edinburgh in 1650 – and only a month later his young Stuart prince signed the Covenant after all. With a bloody reversal only too typical of the times, the Scots Presbyterian forces duly marched south to fight against Cromwell on behalf of what was now the Royalist cause. They were defeated at Worcester in 1651; Charles escaped to France, and Scotland was subdued under English judges and troops commanded by General Monck. Peace prevailed for the next eight years, although after two decades of civil and religious turmoil it had an air of exhaustion about it.

The Restoration in 1660 was welcomed by the Scots – after all, Charles was still a Stuart monarch; but the more radical Presbyterians from the south-west (called 'Whiggamores' during the Civil War) resented the return of bishops, not to mention the king and his favoured lords. Some 300 dissenting ministers left their parishes and held services with their congregations on the open hillsides, despite attempts by troopers to disperse them. It was not long before an armed rising of dissenters from Galloway declared for the Covenant and marched on Edinburgh, only to be routed at Rullion Green in the Pentlands by Sir Thomas Dalyell of the Binns. Many were transported to Barbados and a few were hanged at the gibbet, but the hillside conventicles continued to grow – even after it was made a capital offence to attend them. These were 'the Killing Times', when radical preachers carried weapons and their congregations were harried by the mounted dragoons of Dalyell and John Graham of Claverhouse, who noted that 'there were as many elephants and crocodiles in Galloway as loyal or regular persons'. Walter Scott's novel *Old Mortality* deals with what happened after 1678 when Archbishop Sharp of St Andrew's was brutally murdered by a party of Covenanters who came across his coach outside the city. The dissenters' ambitions were further aroused by a confused engagement at Drumclog, during which an armed conventicle put the dragoons of 'bluidy Clavers' to flight. Flushed with success, but divided by internal disputes, the Covenanters raised an army of 5000 which was eventually defeated by the king's forces at Bothwell Brig. Yet every death was a martyrdom which added to their resolve. Militant working-class groups such as Richard Cameron's 'Society Folk' refused to make allegience to any ruler other than Christ himself, and so they were outlawed and persecuted. Some Cameronians were killed on the spot for refusing to acknowledge the king, and, although such brutal acts were not widespread, they provided powerful moral and political ammunition which the Covenanters were not slow to use in comparing themselves to the Children of Israel under the oppression of a godless Pharaoh.

Paradoxically, the cause of Presbyterianism was best served by James II when he came to the throne in 1685 and proceeded, against advice, to restore Catholics to power throughout the realm. In both England and Scotland this amounted to political suicide, and within three years, faced with widespread revolution, James had to forfeit the crown to his sister Mary and her husband from Protestant Holland, William of Orange. John Graham of Claverhouse ('Bonnie Dundee' to his supporters) came out for James's cause and led some of the clans to victory at Killiecrankie, but he himself was killed on the field. Without his leadership his dispirited forces were finally defeated at Dunkeld at the hands of a Protestant 'Cameronian' regiment who had so recently been outlaws themselves, fleeing from 'Clavers' when he, in his turn, had been the arm of established authority. A similar rising in Ireland was defeated by King William and his army at the Battle of the Boyne, and to this day the date '1690' and the epithet 'King Billy' have been rallying-cries for intransigently anti-Catholic 'Orangemen' in Ulster and Scotland.

The Highland clans were required to sign an oath of fealty to William, and, when the MacDonalds of Glencoe were late to do so in 1692, the Secretary of State in Scotland decided to make an example of them. In due course Campbell soldiers descended on winter-bound Glencoe and sought hospitality from the MacDonalds. After several days of food and shelter, the soldiers turned on their hosts in an act of planned terrorism, killing nearly forty MacDonalds and driving the rest out into the snow. The 'Massacre of Glencoe' outraged public opinion, and, although it encouraged other chiefs to recognise William, they did not forget the matter, nor the treachery of the Campbells. Nor was the Jacobite question resolved, for, when James II died in exile in 1701, his son James (the 'Old

Pretender' and father to 'Bonnie Prince Charlie') was recognised by Louis XIV as the rightful and Catholic heir to the British throne.

The rest of Scotland returned to a semblance of stability, with the wheel of prejudice now turned against the Episcopalians as the General Assembly recovered its influence and restored the heritage of Knox and Melville. In material terms the last twenty years of the century saw a growth in trade and prosperity and Scots capital began to look for investments abroad. Plans were made for expansion to Africa and the East Indies, but, when these were blocked by the influence of the East India Company, Scottish businessmen came up with the optimistic 'Darien Scheme' (1698) to form a trading-company of their own in central America. The chosen site was ridden with fever, however, and when things began to go wrong the English trading-interests in Jamaica refused to help, and even hindered the project. The Darien adventure ended with many deaths, a resounding commercial loss to the country and much bitterness against the English.

The seventeenth century seemed determined to end badly as a series of poor harvests brought poverty and famine to Scotland and most of northern Europe. But Scotland's hardship had been more than material, and, after almost a hundred years of civil, constitutional and religious strife, the cost in psychological and cultural terms can scarcely be calculated. On the one hand the Presbyterian ideal enhanced the status of every individual citizen as he or she stood, literate and alone, before God and the word of God in the Bible. On the other hand, the Kirk could not allow such freedom to lead to licence and unorthodoxy, and so the parish minister and his elders played an influential part in social and moral guidance and control. When narrow Calvinism was in the ascendancy, as it was from 1690 until about 1720, such men had the baleful power of commissars in a one-party state and, indeed, in 1696 an Edinburgh student was actually executed for the crime of blasphemy. In cultural terms the humane spirit and the vigorous language of the makars had all but disappeared. Many Scots intellectuals were turning to London, to English and even to Latin for their models, and gradually Scots was becoming regarded as the vernacular speech of country people. This sad process of 'vernacularisation' continued into the next century, but its results were not entirely negative. If Scots was associated with 'vulgar' directness, then it also spoke with the very voice of the people – vigorous, swift, violent, earthy, realistically in touch with hardship and the seasons and yet capable, too, of romance and a sense of wonder at the supernatural. James's 'Castalian band' had quite lost touch with such forces, but they were burgeoning nevertheless without need of courtly patronage in the great Scottish ballads – some of the finest and most popular examples of the oral tradition to be found anywhere in the world. It was not until the end of the century and the beginning of the next that this colloquial energy was to flourish again in a more peaceful world of books and publishing.

Poets at court

When King James took the road to London in 1603 he retained his role as patron of the muse and was soon joined by a number of Scottish poets. William Alexander and Robert Ayton received knighthoods and positions of favour; Sir David Murray (fl. 1620) later joined the short-lived Prince Henry's retinue, and the sonneteer Robert Kerr (1578–1654) received an earldom from Charles I and became an intimate of the London *literati*. **Sir William Alexander** (1577?–1640) wrote sonnets in the fashion of a gentleman of the day. An admirer of Spenser, he knew Drummond in the north and befriended Michael Drayton in England, but there is little of lasting value in *Aurora*, his collection of sonnets published in 1604. A venture into Jacobean verse drama resulted in four 'Monarchicke Tragedies' (1603–7) outlining the perils of ambition; and a sustained exercise in verse produced over 10,000 moral and unexciting lines in *Doomesday* (1614). Alexander rose to be Secretary of State for Scotland, but he was an unpopular and profit-seeking politician who eventually lost everything and died in poverty.

Sir Robert Ayton (1569–1638) was a better poet with a degree of skill in English verse as well as in Latin, French and Greek. Ayton, from a prosperous Fife family, joined the court shortly after the king's arrival in London, and within eight years he had been knighted and made a member of the royal household. He made friends of Ben Jonson and Hobbes and appears in Aubrey's *Brief Lives*. In common with many of his accomplished contemporaries, however, he was not published in his own lifetime, nor did he consider himself to 'affect the name of a poet'. His best work is probably to be found in songs for the lute rather like Thomas Campion's, and it is possible that he was the author of the original version of the piece which Burns turned into 'Auld Lang Syne'. Only a few of his early poems were in Scots, while almost half his output was in Latin, with verses addressed to the king on all the issues of the day, including some lines on the Gunpowder Plot of 1605.

Many contemporary Scottish writers were similarly fluent in Latin, and they too chose to eschew the vernacular tradition in favour of the scholarly example of George Buchanan. Among these were the gallant James Crichton (1560–83), later hailed by Sir Thomas Urquhart as 'the admirable Crichtoun', and Arthur Johnston (1587–1661) who edited and contributed to an anthology of many other Scottish Latin poets – *Delitiae Poetarum Scotorum* (1637). **James Graham, the Marquis of Montrose** (1612–50), is mainly remembered for the brilliance of his brief military career, but he too produced civilised verses. The best known of these is addressed to his mistress as 'My Dear and Only Love', but four lines from it could well apply to the author's own grim end:

> He either fears his Fate too much,
>   Or his Deserts are small,
> That puts it not unto the Touch,
>   To win or lose it all.

William Drummond of Hawthornden (1585–1649)

Unlike his friend Montrose, William Drummond tried to avoid public life and religious dispute. Educated in Edinburgh and a student of law in France, he inherited his father's estate at Hawthornden near Lasswade, just outside Edinburgh, and decided to settle there at the age of twenty-four on his own terms as a man of letters. He collected books avidly and expanded Hawthornden's already substantial library; he read widely in French and Italian and showed a taste for epigrams, anagrams, ephemera and curiosities of all sorts. Drummond's first poem, 'Teares, on the Death of Moeliades' (1612), was a conventional lament on the death of Prince Henry, James's eldest son, infused with the influence of Sir Philip Sidney. Before long he had compiled a collection of songs and a sequence modelled on *Astrophel and Stella*, with other sonnets translated or adapted from French and Italian, all in a sad neo-Platonic vein. This romantic colouring does seem to have been a genuine part of Drummond's temperament, later reinforced by the early death of his fiancée in 1616. Drummond's collection was first published probably in 1614 and then again in 1616, finely bound and expensively set, just as he insisted all his works should be.

Drummond was especially keen to be appreciated in England, and his manuscripts show his many literary debts and the care he took to excise all Scotticisms of expression and spelling from his verse. Within formal modes his elegant lines aim for a smooth and decorative flow of sound, rather than for the strenuous dialectic of Donne or the wit of Marvell. Nevertheless, Drummond's fellow writers thought highly of his erudition and, like them, we can admire his particular penchant for sweet and sensuously melancholy accounts of loneliness:

> Sound hoarse sad *Lute*, true Witnesse of my Woe,
> And striue no more to ease self-chosen Paine
> With Soule-enchanting Sounds, your Accents straine
> Vnto these Teares vncessantly which flow.
> Shrill Treeble weepe, and you dull Basses show
> Your Masters Sorrow *in a deadly Vaine*,
> Let neuer ioyfull Hand vpon you goe,
> Nor Consort keepe but when you doe complaine.
> Flie Phoebus Rayes, nay, hate the irkesome Light,
> Woods solitaire Shades for thee are best,
> Or the black Horrours of the blackest Night,
> When all the *World* (saue Thou and I) doth rest:
> Then sound sad Lute, and beare a mourning Part,
> Thou *Hell* may'st mooue, though not a Woman's *Heart*.

(Sonnet xxviii of 'The First Part')

Despite his declared preference for Hawthornden, the 'sweet solitarie Place, Where from the vulgare I estranged liue', Drummond was not a complete recluse. He corresponded with Michael Drayton in England and with Alexander and Kerr, his fellow Scots at court in London. Ben Jonson particularly admired Drummond's work, visiting Scotland late in 1618 to stay at Hawthornden for three weeks. The host made notes on his guest's table talk and his *Conversations with Ben Jonson* (1711) have become well known and widely quoted, not least for the portrait they paint of the bibulous playwright as a 'contemner and Scorner of others' and a 'great lover and praiser of himself'.

Drummond developed the melancholy of his earlier poems to produce *Flowres of Sion* (1623), a collection of madrigals, sonnets and hymns all of which reflect on human frailty, on the instability of the world and on the 'contemplation of invisible excellences above by the visible below' (Sonnet xviii).

> O Sunne invisible, that doest abide
> Within thy bright abysmes, most faire, most darke,
> Where with thy proper Rayes thou dost thee hide;
> O euer-shining neuer full seene marke,
>   To guide mee in Lifes Night, thy light mee show,
>   The more I search of thee, the lesse I know.
>
> (Sonnet xvii)

Once again the poet praises the lonely life, but now his sonnets have a more philosophical dimension, named after spiritual solitaries and outcasts – 'For the Prodigal', 'For the Magdalene' and 'For the Baptiste'. Drummond's best poems are in this mode, and if some of them have been translated from other sources then the work has been well and fully assimilated into the poet's own character. In the same volume he developed his theme in prose with *A Cypresse Grove*, a meditation on death derived from Italian models and especially from the French of Montaigne's *Essais*. Written almost twenty years before Sir Thomas Browne's *Religio Medici* was published, *A Cypresse Grove, or Philosophical Reflections Against the Fear of Death* anticipates and matches the latter's achievement with a musical and weighty prose written largely for poetic effect. Perhaps Drummond is the more sober of the two, for he lacks the conjurer's adroitness with which the Norwich man makes to dance the heavy furniture of his style.

Despite *A Cypresse Grove*, 'wormewood' was not Drummond's only food, nor 'Teares his Drinke', and during the course of his life he produced satirical and sexually comic verses as well as various proverbs and epigrams. He is usually credited with a Macaronic jest called 'Polemo-Middinia', where Scots and English words are mixed with dog Latin and given Latin endings to lampoon a countryside quarrel over rights of way on a footpath. He had a mistress and three children and at forty-five he married and fathered another large family. In 1627 he had invented and patented plans for numerous ingenious weapons of war and by 1633 he had become well enough known to be put in charge of the pageant for Charles I's visit to Edinburgh. He found politics uncongenial and had little sympathy with the more extreme Presbyterians, although he had signed the National Covenant in 1638. His pamphlets in favour of peace and toleration on all sides were not published during his lifetime. *Irene, A Remonstrance for Concord, Amitie and Love amongst His Majesties Subjects* (1638) praises Charles I for making concessions to the Covenant and lectures the commoners on the virtues of obedience: 'Good Princes should be obeyed, yea evill Princes should be tollerated . . . they are not to be judged by their Subjectes.'

Perhaps the author's peaceful seclusion on the banks of the North Esk would not have survived the broadcasting of such sentiments; but, in any case, events moved on without Drummond. A lengthy *History of Scotland* covering the period 1423–1542 was published six years after his death and has little to distinguish it. Drummond ended his days at Hawthornden with his wealth greatly reduced, engaged in litigation and embittered by the times in which he lived. He left an unfinished satire about a country 'latlie turned most part Mad' by the worshipping of a golden 'calfe anant' (Covenant) which was really only made of paper after all. His youthful taste for solitude had turned a little sour in the mouth, and, as a conservative who looked back to the Elizabethan England of Sidney and Spenser for his literary values, his isolation in the Scotland of the turbulent 1640s was never more poignantly acute.

Writing in prose

Alas, the music of *A Cypresse Grove* is not typical, and for the most part Scottish prose in the seventeenth century consists of treatises on religious doctrine, church politics, histories, memoirs, letters, or contumacious and wordy mixtures of all these. Whatever their sectarian views, almost everyone followed Knox's example in avoiding overtly Scottish expressions. The historian David Hume (1560–1630) supported the use of Scots but confessed that he too had 'yielded . . . to the tyranny of custom and the times' by 'not seeking curiously for words, but taking them as they came to hand'. His equivocal feelings about Scots may be gathered from the fact that he changed the name of his house from 'Gowkscroft' (Cuckoo farm) to 'Godscroft'. Unlike his namesake (he was no relation), the grammarian Alexander Hume (1558–1631?) did use a diluted Scots to propound his theories on orthography in *Grammatica Nova* (1612); but the title of one of his later pamphlets refers only to 'the Britan Tongue'. Scots was used, again rarely, by Abacuck Bysset (fl. 1610) for a catalogue of ancient historical sites called *The Rolement of Courtis* (1622), in which he defended his 'awin . . . mother tung' as 'pithie and schorte'; although it must be admitted that his own practice does not always attain brevity:

> I haue nocht bene copius in langaig be far drevin, uncouth evill placed termis, and multiplicatioun of wordis be paraphraces of circumlocutioun of speich, silogismes, and refutatioun of argumentis be parablis or comparesonis; nor haue I adhered to auld proverbis or bywordis, fair, flattering, fenzeit [invented], and counterfuit fictionis, uttered be archadicienis, maid up, counterfuit, and phrasing langaige; neither haue I . . . used minzeard [mincing] nor effeminate tantting invective nor skornefull wordis, vane, saterick, or louse wowsting and wanting [boasting and vaunting] speeches; nor haue I . . . .

Most prose at the time was characterised by exactly this tendency to be 'copius'. John Brown (d. 1679), for instance, an exiled Covenanter, could produce a 'pamphlet' of 400 pages on the sufferings of godly ministers in Scotland, while the even more extreme Alexander Shields (d. 1700) produced 700 pages of his *Hind Let Loose* for the Cameronian viewpoint in 1687, including an argument for the assassination of uncovenanted and unrightful authority. On the other hand, **Sir George Mackenzie of Rosehaugh** (1636–91), defended national eloquence in his Preface to *Pleadings* (1673) by claiming that Scots was best suited for arguing in the law court, because 'our pronunciation is like ourselves, fiery, abrupt, sprightly and bold'. As Lord Advocate, Mackenzie founded the Advocates' Library in Edinburgh (now the National Library) and produced several more books on the Law as well as political studies, a novel (*Aretina*, 1660) poems, moral essays and *Religio Stoici* (1663), which contained his reflections on the schisms within the Church. He was a gifted man who abhorred fanaticism and was strongly opposed to the obscene witchcraft trials in his time. He was equally forcefully in favour of the proper authority of the king, and his prosecution of dissenting Covenanters, although legal and humane by his lights, earned him the nickname of 'bluidy Mackenzie'. His *Memoirs of the Affairs of Scotland from the Restoration* was not published until long after his death.

If Mackenzie's legal training made him shun casuistry, the same cannot be said of most of the religious controversialists who took it upon themselves to expound the words of God. Yet there were some divines of great expressive ability and the church-going public relished their demonstrations of dialectical eloquence, whether simple and passionate, or decked in the sesquipedelian flowers of classical rhetoric. Godly debate was as 'forensic' as any lawyer could desire. Men such as Robert Bruce and the unfortunately named Andrew Cant were famous for the power of their preaching, while others were noted more for erudition. Best regarded of all was the extempore composition of complex arguments, redolent with learned references and cunning strophes. Publications in both Latin and English abounded, with titles such as *Instructiones Historico-Theologicae* (1645), by John Forbes, a moderate Episcopalian who was the professor of Divinity at Aberdeen University; *Aaron's Rod Blossoming* (1646), by George Gillespie, a member of the Presbyterian camp; or *Lex Rex* (1644), Samuel Rutherford's case against the king, a work 'stuffed with positions, that in the time of peace and order, would have been judged damnable treasons'. Indeed, seventeen years later, the pamphlet was burned in public by the hangman.

Among the outstanding divines of the day, **Robert Baillie** (1599–1662) was a man of shrewd and moderate temper who possessed a 'golden' Latin style and became known for his intellectual excellence in twelve or thirteen languages. He was a determined Presbyterian, an ecclesiastical diplomat with some service abroad and several publications in defence of his beliefs;

but it is his *Letters and Journals* (1637–62) that provide an invaluable insight into the contemporary world of political and ecclesiastical affairs. They begin in 1637, the year of the riot in St Giles' against the Anglican prayer-book. Baillie was equally opposed to 'Laud's liturgy', but he feared the worst for Scotland:

> What shall be the event, God knows: there was in our Land ever such ane appearance of a sturr; the whole people thinks Poperie at the doores; the scandalous pamphlets which comes daily new from England adde oyl to this flame; no man may speak any thing in publick for the King's part, except he would have himself marked for a sacrifice to be killed one day. I think our people possessed with a bloody devill, farr above any thing that ever I could have imagined. . . . For myself, I think, God, to revenge the crying sinns of all estates and professions . . . is going to execute his long denounced threatnings, and to give us over unto madness, that we may every one shoot our swords in our neighbours hearts.

Within a year the National Covenant was signed to make, in effect, a direct challenge to the power of kings.

A vivid picture of subsequent events can be found in other diaries and memoirs, such as those of Sir John Lauder and Sir James Turner – Presbyterians who gradually came to support the king, or at least the cause of the crown. (Turner was one of the models for Walter Scott's Dugald Dalgetty in *A Legend of Montrose*.) Henry Guthrie (?1600–76), whose opinion of *Lex Rex* has already been heard, was a moderate Episcopalian, and, although he had signed the Covenant, like Montrose he eventually took the king's side. The waters of dissent were certainly muddy enough, and Guthrie maintains that the 'spontaneous' St Giles' riot had actually been planned three months in advance, so that women 'might give the first affront to the book, assuring them that men should afterwards take the business out of their hands'. The diaries of John Nicoll (1590–1667) testify to the confusions of the day in a different sense, for he left blanks in his pages so that he could adjust his views in retrospect and insert 'God save the King!' at appropriately prophetic points! Nicoll's accounts of the passing scene are more reliable, but his belief in witches and his interest in witch trials testify to troubled times and a thoroughly unlikeable character.

History and doctrinal dispute became inseparable, and many chroniclers were intent only on a vindication of their particular church. John Spottiswoode (1565–1639), the Bishop of St Andrew's, had to flee for London when his cause was defeated, but his *History of the Church of Scotland* (1655) shows a relatively generous recognition that 'popular fury once roused can keep no measure, nor do anything with advice and judgment'. The Episcopalian historian Gilbert Burnet (1643–1715) was amazed by another side to the common people when he toured the country in the 1660s to meet

> a poor commonality, so capable of arguing upon points of government, and on the bounds to be set on the power of Princes, in matters of religion: upon all these topics they had texts of scripture at hand; and were ready with their anssers, to anything that was said to them. This measure of knowledge was spread even among the meanest of them, the cottagers and their servants.

David Calderwood (1575–1650) shows a Presbyterian bias, and his *History of the Kirk of Scotland* (1678) is vividly anecdotal, as when he describes how Bishop Spottiswoode (the rival historian) deprived reformer David Dickson of his ministry:

> 'The will of the Lord be done', said Mr David. 'Though you cast me off, yit the Lord will take me up. Send me where ye please. I hope my Master sall goe with me; and as He hath beene with me heirtofore, He will be with me still as with His owne weake servant.'
> 'Sweith away!' said the bishop, as if he had been speaking to a dogge; 'Pack, you swinger!' and crying to the doorekeeper, he sayes, 'Shoote him out!'

It is difficult not to sympathise with the bold Spottiswoode in the face of Dickson's pious complacency, and we shall let him have the last word.

Witchcraft and superstition

It was the Presbyterian extremists who were most committed to the discovery and extirpation of witchcraft, as if the fear of the Lord had turned to a paranoid fear of the Devil as well. Perhaps, too, the Kirk's insistence on rigid paternal authority led to barely submerged resentment against the implications of female sexuality, for witches' covens were widely suspected of the most promiscuous behaviour. James VI's *Daemonologie* had first pursued these various fears in 1597, and towards the end of the seventeenth century two further books on the occult proved to be particularly popular. George Sinclair (1618–87), one-time professor of Philosophy at Glasgow, had already produced studies on engineering and hydrostatics, but in *Satan's Invisible World Discovered* (1685), he set himself equally seriously to the tasks of recounting all the instances he could gather of supernatural events and apparitions, including the evidence heard at contemporary witchcraft trials. *The Secret Commonwealth of Elves, Fauns, and Fairies* (1691), written by **Robert Kirk** (1641–92), is quite another matter, however. Like his father before him, Kirk was a minister at Aberfoyle; he translated the Psalms into Gaelic and in *The Secret Commonwealth* he set about writing a 'natural history' of Celtic fairy lore. The *Sidh* (pronounced 'Shee') are not like the gauzy-winged creatures of Victorian sentiment, but are more likely to appear as full-sized good-looking beings dressed as mortals, though with a preference for green and silver. Nevertheless, they are capricious folk with supernatural powers, so it is not safe to speak ill of them and they are best referred to as 'the good people'.

> [They] are said to be of a midle Nature betwixt man and angel, (as were daemons thought to be of old); of intelligent studious spirits, and light changable bodies, (lik those called astral) . . . they are sometimes heard to bake bread, strike hammers, and to do such like services within the little hillocks where they most haunt. . . . They remove to other Lodgings at the beginning of each quarter of the year. . . . 'Tis one of their tenets that nothing perisheth, but (as the sun and the year) everything goes in a circle, less or greater, and is renewed or refreshed in its revolutions.

James's *Daemonologie* had been less sympathetic to the Sidh, referring to them as 'one of the sortes of illusiones that was rifest in time of *Papistrie*', when the Devil 'illuded the senses of sundry simple creatures, in making them beleeve that they saw and hearde such thinges as were nothing so indeed'. Without doubt, the king regarded himself as the voice of reason in this matter, yet more suffering was caused in James's kingdom by Christian belief in the power of the Devil than can ever be laid at the feet of the fairies.

As a seventh son, Robert Kirk was reputed to have second sight, and, when he collapsed at the age of fifty-one on the Hill of the Fairies in Aberfoyle, the tale went round that he was not really dead, but finally captured by the 'good people'. Walter Scott records how his likeness is reputed to have been seen after the funeral on two occasions. The spiriting away of mortals is the very stuff of the popular supernatural ballads, and these songs of beauty and awe and Kirk's book too, which is a repository of folk belief in itself, make a refreshing change from the blighted fields of dogmatic theology.

Ballads and ballad-collectors

The Scots ballads derive from an oral tradition in narrative songs which flourished during the sixteenth and seventeenth centuries. Since they were not published as 'literature', it is difficult to establish their authorship or when they first appeared, and these matters have led to much speculation ever since. Whatever their origins, the ballads were 'discovered' by antiquarians and literary enthusiasts in the eighteenth century, when many examples were collected and transcribed. In Scotland this appetite for old songs followed the union of parliaments in 1707, and a key part was played by their appearance in Allan Ramsay's *Tea Table Miscellany* anthologies (1724–37). As early as 1711, Joseph Addison had praised 'Chevy Chase' in the *Spectator* for its 'majestic simplicity', while Bishop Thomas Percy's collection, *Reliques of Ancient English Poetry* (1765 *et seq.*) did even more to create the pre-Romantic craze for 'old, unhappy far-off things and battles long ago'. Percy's interest was aroused when he found a manuscript collection of ballads being used by servants to light fires in a friend's house. He saved the sheets and began to gather ballads from enthusiasts around the country, although it can be difficult to distinguish between songs recorded verbatim and pieces 'improved', or patched from older fragments, or specially written for the occasion. Others soon followed. David Herd published *Ancient and Modern Scottish Songs* in 1776, and in the 1780s John Pinkerton produced two collections of old Scottish ballads, although he was not above including forgeries of his own. The irascible Joseph Ritson was a better scholar and his many volumes stressed the importance of recording the melody as well as the words. Sir Walter Scott tells of his excitement at the age of thirteen when he first came across

Percy's *Reliques* and how this youthful delight led him to become a collector himself. The two volumes which he called *Minstrelsy of the Scottish Border* (1802–3) contain some unscholarly editorial improvements which he came to regret in later years (he may even have composed most of 'Kinmont Willie') but nevertheless his work was sympathetic and very influential. Jamieson's *Popular Ballads and Songs* followed in 1806, and Motherwell's *Minstrelsy Ancient and Modern* (1827) took Ritson's line by insisting that collectors should seek authenticity.

The modern study of ballads owes most to the long dedication of an American scholar, Francis J. Child, whose life's work, *The English and Scottish Popular Ballads*, appeared from 1882 to 1898 in five volumes. Alas, Child died before he could produce the critical introduction which was to summarise his findings. Child accumulated and numbered 305 ballads and many variants, which he classified with letters, so that it is now usual, for example, to refer to the twenty-seven different versions of 'The Twa Sisters' as 'Child 10A, B, C', and so on. (In fact there are even more versions of this tale than Child printed.) In Denmark, Grundtvig and Olvik made a similarly extensive gathering of Danish ballads in *Danmarks Gamle Folkeviser* (6 vols, 1853–1920) and the groundwork was laid for what has now become a subject of international expertise drawing on philology, anthropology, comparative literature and folk-life studies. Thus, if doubts exist about the authenticity of 'Edward' as it appeared in the *Reliques*, these can be dispelled by the realisation that the same tale is told in Swedish, Danish and Finnish ballads. The spelling of Percy's version (got from Lord Hailes in Edinburgh) may be contrivedly 'antique', but its narrative patterns clearly belong to authentic tradition. 'Lord Randal' (Child 12), is an equally famous ballad, first collected in Edinburgh in 1710; but versions of it are found in Czechoslovakia, Hungary, Sweden and, a hundred years earlier, in Italy. Thus although there is not enough information to chart when or where the 'Lord Randal' tale first appeared in Scotland, it is clear that the oral tradition can prove to be surprisingly robust and far-travelled. In a more esoteric vein, Stith Thompson has classified the motifs which appear in folk tales from many countries (*Motif-index of Folk Literature*, 6 vols, 1932–6), and it can be shown that many of these motifs are, indeed, international, and that some of them also occur in a few Scottish ballads. Recent theories on the nature of oral composition and transmission have derived from work done by Milman Parry and Albert Lord on Yugoslavian folk epic (Lord, *The Singer of Tales*, 1960), and comparisons have been established between Yugoslavian composition and that of Homer's ancient epic verse. It is also recognised that the ballad-singer is of primary importance in any study of the form, and modern students give full attention to these sources. Thus an early and invaluable contribution to Child's collection was provided by Mrs Anna Brown of Falkland (1747–1810), who came from the North-East and knew thirty-eight ballad stories, no less than one-eighth of all the 'classic' Anglo-Scottish themes ever recorded. Today, the School of Scottish Studies in Edinburgh (founded in 1951) has a huge archive of material gathered from traditional singers over the years, and the advent of the tape-recorder has added a vital dimension to the collection of ballads, songs and tales. The oral tradition still survives in Scotland, especially among the 'travelling people', who lead their itinerant, gipsy-like lives despite society's attempts to make them conform. Some of the finest traditional singers have come from these families, most notably the late Jeannie Robertson (1908–75) a 'sweet and heroic' voice, and her daughter Lizzie Higgins.

Since few ballads were written down or published when they first appeared, problems immediately arise about the date and the 'authenticity' of their eventual texts. In fact the very notion of an 'authentic text' is misguided, and such literary considerations cannot apply to an oral tradition in which the bare bones of the tale remain more or less constant while settings, proper names and other such details vary according to circumstances. The Robin Hood tales come from some of the oldest known ballads, circulating in the fifteenth century, and in this case a link can be made back to the late medieval minstrels who sang and recited the long narrative works so popular in the fourteenth century. Carols, religious lyrics, riddles and folk songs joined the canon and began to disseminate among the people, and it seems likely that the ballad-forms as collected by Child, with their distinctive quatrains and their use of refrain and repetition, had began to appear by the sixteenth century. The author of *The Complaynt of Scotland* (1549) names many tales, dances and old songs as performed by shepherds, and his list includes what must have been versions of 'The Battle of Harlaw' (Child 163), and 'The Battle of Otterburn' (Child 161), and 'The Hunting of the Cheviot' or 'Chevy Chase' (Child 162), which date from at least the beginning of the century and tell about a border conflict which took place as long ago as 1388. Sir Philip Sidney testified to the power of 'Chevy Chase' in 1595, writing in his *Apology for Poetry* that it moved his heart 'moore then with a trumpet: and yet it is sung by some blinde crouder'. *The Complaynt* also mentions the 'dance' called 'Johnne Ermistrang', and, from the 1570s, Pitscottie's *Historie and Chronicles of Scotland* gives an account of that reiver's fate (only forty years before) which uses phrases identical to those found in the ballad of 'Johnie Armstrong' (Child 169) as transcribed in the 1650s. The conclusion to be drawn is that the oral tradition can be remarkably stable, despite our contemporary and literate lack of confidence in the powers of memory and recitation. By the seventeenth century the professional minstrel class was disappearing and ballads had become the property of singers among the common people. At the same time these ballads were beginning to appear more frequently in print and manuscript and, indeed, the old folio which provided Bishop Percy with so many of his 'reliques' was just such a collection, copied out in the 1650s from other written and perhaps some oral sources.

The nature of ballads

If the literary history of the ballads cannot help but be obscure in places, then the question of how they were composed has been a matter of outright disagreement. 'Communalists' held that a ballad is evolved by accretion from tales and the folk consciousness; while 'individualists' made a case for a single 'begetter', at least at first, whose composition might then be gradually disseminated and changed by others as time passes. A version of the latter view has prevailed among modern scholars, although it is not necessary to suppose, as some 'individualists' did, that the process of transmission is always one of decline. On the contrary, it has been held that ballads are sustained by a process of re-creation and not just by simple feats (or lapses) of memory. Thus a singer will reconstruct the song from his or her knowledge of the key moments of the tale, as well as from a deep familiarity with the patterns of ballad expression and their many stock phrases and rhymes. Perhaps that singer's 'best' version of the song would tend to become fixed in his repertoire, but the process of oral re-creation would still play a part between singers, down the generations, or from district to district. Inevitably, some versions are poorer than others and the spread of literacy and printed copies must also be a factor; nevertheless the theory of oral re-creation does help to explain the variations which occur in different versions of a ballad, and how these differences can sometimes be equally effective, sustaining the tale and its artistic impact over the generations. It follows that the 'typical ballad' contains many elements which are of structural help to the singer in remembering and telling the tale effectively, and, by the same token, these features lend themselves to dramatic and poetic results.

The ballad is a song which tells a tale by letting the events and the characters speak for themselves. It focuses on a single crucial dramatic situation; the narrator almost never makes a personal comment, and little time is spent in setting the scene or explaining motives. Even the longest ballad is comparatively brief when compared to verse romance or folk epic, and, of course, it is sung to a distinctive melody. The ballads tell of fated lovers, or battles and blood feuds or visitations from the other world – the very stuff of popular taste; and yet their presentation of this romantic, violent or uncanny material is realistic, objective and concise. In fact it is just this trenchant impersonality which produces effects of great emotional power. Ballad melodies are often appropriately stately and plaintive, repeating themselves hypnotically with each short verse, but they manage to avoid monotony by the singer's use of variations and grace notes at suitably expressive points. A typical stanza uses four lines, with a rhyme scheme such as *abcb*, often alternating between four and three stresses:

> The king sits in Dumfermling toune,
>   Drinking the blude-reid wine:
> 'O whar will I get a guid sailor,
>   To sail this schip of mine?'

('Sir Patrick Spens', Child 58A)

Another common form uses a constant refrain or refrains in lines three and four:

> There was three ladies playd at the ba,
>> *With a hey ho and a lilie gay*
> There cam a knight and played oer them a'.
>> *As the primrose spreads so sweetly.*

('The Cruel Brother', Child 11A)

These opening stanzas from two different ballads show how quickly the songs get to the point as they unfold their tales with a characteristic mixture of immediacy and artful delay, a movement well named 'leaping and lingering'. Here the demands of art and those of oral performance compliment each other most fruitfully, and the ballads are full of stock phrases such as 'then up and spak' or 'loud, loud lauched (or cried) he'; colours come with traditional epithets, such as '*blude*-reid', '*milk*-white' or '*berry*-brown'; and numbers are usually 'magic' quantities such as three and seven. Antithetical sets of questions and answers accumulate in the songs, or whole phrases recur in an incremental repetition which makes the tale 'linger' and yet at the same time produces a sense of steadily advancing inevitability. All these devices bear witness to the ballad's origins, in which an act of oral re-creation meets with an act of memory to recognise the dramatic need for a telling delay before surrendering to sudden and inevitable denouement.

The Scottish ballads

The Scottish ballads are among the finest, for, while the tale may be internationally familiar, the particular form it takes within the genre will be dictated by the cultural and historical forces which shaped the singer. The forces in Scotland up until the sixteenth and seventeenth centuries were particularly well-suited to songs about violent, romantic and eerie encounters, all told with succinct wit and an enduring sense of fatalism. Such qualities were already deep within the Scottish sensibility, from the warlike celebration of Barbour and Blind Harry to the grimly tender understatement of Henryson when he describes how Cresseid's father discovers her leprosy – 'then was thair care enough betwixt them twain'; or, again, to the terrible, witty cruelty of Knox's account of the death of Beaton. The courtly poetry of the early seventeenth century and the studied melancholy of Drummond had completely lost touch with these tough roots, and it is the many anonymous singers of the ballad tradition who carried them over: from the makars to the vernacular revival in the eighteenth century and, ultimately, to Scottish poets of more modern times.

Although the divisions are fluid, the Scottish ballads are concerned with three perennially popular topics – violent history, tragic romance and the supernatural. All of these elements, like the songs themselves, belong in special measure to the Border country – from Edinburgh and Newcastle in the east to Dumfries and Penrith in the west. It is a wild, rolling landscape scattered with old battlefields, castles, towers and fortified houses. Loyalties were fiercely local, and Border barons had long regarded themselves as rulers of their own small kingdoms with no allegiance to politics or boundaries or even the king himself. Equally independent lesser lairds, with notorious family-names such as Armstrong, Ker and Scott, sallied forth as reivers to capture cattle and horses – the wealth of the district – from the English or, with equal facility, from their Scottish neighbours. James V led an expedition against the Borders in 1530 (when he hanged Johnie Armstrong), before having to move north to pacify the equally troublesome clans. It is no accident that the great songs of fighting, loving and terror should have arisen from such conditions: they occur again in the North-East of Scotland, where Lowlands and Highlands met along a different border, but the true crucible of the ballad-tradition lies to the south and particularly towards the centre and west of the country. Here the more open ground of Teviot and Tweed and the route from Berwick to Edinburgh begins to give way to the pass at Carter Bar in the hills above Jedburgh, to the tangled outlawed valleys of the 'debatable lands' at Eskdale and Liddesdale above Carlisle, and to the treacherous boglands of Solway Moss. The 'historical' ballads in particular are full of names, places and events from this part of Scotland.

Tales of violent history

'The Battle of Otterburn' (Child 161) and 'The Hunting of the Cheviot' or 'Chevy Chase' (Child 162), both tell of a raid the Scots made on Northumberland in 1388 and of how the Scotsman Sir Hugh Douglas perished on the sword of Sir Harry Percy, who was in his turn killed or captured by Douglas's nephew Montgomerie. 'Chevy Chase' tells the story from the English point of view, and 'Otterburn' favours the Scots. The latter was sent to Walter Scott by James Hogg, and is best known for the lines in which Douglas has an eerie premonition that the battle will be won only after his own death:

> 'My nephew bauld,' the Douglas said,
>   'What boots the death of ane?
> Last night I dreamed a dreary dream,
>   And I ken the day's thy ain.
>
> I dreamed I saw a battle fought
>   Beyond the isle of Sky,
> When lo, a dead man wan the field,
>   And I thought that man was I.'

(Child 161C)

The Battle of Harlaw was fought north-west of Aberdeen in 1411, between Donald of the Isles and Lowland forces from Angus and the Mearns. The ranting ballad of the same name (Child 163), with its parodies of the Highland accent ('Yes, me cam frae ta Hielans, man'), must date from considerably after the conflict. On the other hand, 'The Battle of Philiphaugh' (Child 202) is probably contemporary with the defeat of Montrose, 'our cruel enemy', outside Selkirk in 1645. 'The Bonny Earl of Murray' (Child 181) laments how, in 1592, James Stewart of Doune was killed by his old enemy the Earl of Huntly, who had been instructed to convey him to the king without harm. As with almost all the ballads, this tale of the doings of great people is seen from the point of view of the common folk. In fact Murray was burned out of his mother's house and killed while trying to escape, but one version of the song has him admit his 'brother' Huntly in a trusting way, only to be stabbed in his bed like King Duncan in *Macbeth*. The

best-known version has a beautiful melody, simultaneously
rousing and tender, which opens with the verses

Ye Highlands, and ye Lawlands,
   Oh where have you been?
They have slain the Earl of Murray,
   And they layd him on the green.

'Now wae be to thee, Huntly!
   And wherefore did you sae?
I bade you bring him wi you,
   But forbade you him to slay.'

He was a braw gallant,
   And he rid at the ring;
And the bonny Earl of Murray,
   Oh he might have been a king.

(Child 181A)

In the ballads, historical accuracy always takes second place
to heroic figures and dramatic events, and so John Armstrong's
deserved execution at the hands of James V is retold as a
treacherous betrayal, and one version (copied, according to
Allan Ramsay from a descendant of Armstrong's) even manages to be patriotic:

John murdered was at Carlinrigg,
   And all his galant companie:
But Scotlands heart was never sae wae,
   To see sae mony brave men die

Because they savd their country deir
   Frae Englishmen; nane were sae bauld,
Whyle Johnie livd on the border-syde,
   Nane of them durst cum neir his hald.

(Child 169C)

Another version ends more convincingly, on a note chillingly
reminiscent of revenge plays by Tourneur or Webster:

O then bespoke his little son,
   As he was set on his nurses knee:
'If ever I live for to be a man,
   My father's blood revenged shall be.'

(Child 169B)

In more recent years an equally unlikely folk hero has been made of a small American murderer called William Bonney, but we still listen to tales of Billy the Kid, and we thrill to Armstrong's grim and cutting retort when his sovereign refused to spare his life:

> To seik het water beneth cauld yce,
>   Surely it is a great folie;
> I haif asked grace at a graceless face,
>   But ther is nane for my men and me.

The memorable history behind 'Mary Hamilton' (Child 173), is equally cloudy when it comes to facts. There are nearly forty variants of the tale, also known as 'The Queen's Marie' and 'The Four Maries', and almost all of them have the poignant lines

> Last nicht there was four Maries,
>   The nicht there'l be but three;
> There was Marie Seton, and Marie Beton,
>   And Marie Carmichael, and me.

> (Child 173A)

The tale has it that Mary Hamilton was executed because she drowned her illegitimate baby, whose father was Darnley, 'the hichest Stewart of a'' and the queen's unworthy husband. Mary Queen of Scots did, indeed, have four Marys attending her, but they were ladies of gentle birth from the families of Seaton, Beaton, Fleming and Livingston. There *was* a scandal at court in 1563, but it involved an apothecary and a French lady of the chamber, with no mention of any Mary Hamilton. In fact, there was a Mary Hamilton who suffered a fate similar to that recounted in the ballad, but she was an attendant to the wife of Peter the Great of Russia at the end of the seventeenth century. All these names and events have merged in the popular imagination to fit a sad and lilting melody full of memorable lines and images. Consider how Mary goes to her death in the following verses, in which the action is typically heightened and delayed by the incremental repetitions of statement and reply, and by the antithesis between laughter and tears:

'O Marie, put on your robes o black,
    Or else your robes o brown,
For ye maun gang wi me the night,
    To see fair Edinboro town.'

'I winna put on my robes o black,
    Nor yet my robes o brown;
But I'll put on my robes o white,
    To shine through Edinboro town.'

When she gaed up the Cannogate,
    She laughd loud laughters three;
But whan she cam doun the Cannogate
    The tear blinded her ee.

When she gaed up the Parliament stair,
    The heel cam aff her shee;   shoe
And lang or she cam doun again
    She was condemned to dee.

Atmosphere, setting, and intense feeling are all conveyed in
these lines, but only through direct speech and direct action.
Her bold decision to wear virginal white, and the ill omen of her
broken heel – these are exactly the kind of details at which the
ballads excel, and they strike the listener with the simple force
of a bolt of electricity.

The creative versatility of oral tradition can be gauged by
comparing what is functionally the same stanza, drawn from
five different versions of the song:

'Last night I washed the queen's feet,
    And gently laid her down;
And a' the thanks I've gotten the nicht
    To be hangd in Edinboro town.'

(Child 173A)

'Yestreen I wush Queen Mary's feet,
    And bore her till her bed;
This day she's given me my reward,
    This gallows-tree to tread.'

(Child 173B)

'Yestreen I mad Queen Mary's bed,
    Kembed doun her yellow hair;
Is this the reward I am to get,
    To tread the gallows-stair.'

(Child 173C)

'Seven years an I made Queen Mary's bed,
    Seven years an I combed her hair,
An a hansome reward noo she's gien to me,
    Gien me the gallows-tow to wear!'

(Child 173N)

'O wha will comb Queen Mary's heed?
    Or wha will brade her hair?
And wha will lace her middle sae jimp,   slender
    Whan I am nae langer there?'

(Child 173W)

It is not possible to advance critical reasons for preferring any one version over the others: they all focus on past services as compared to present fate, and, although the details change, each stanza is effective in its own way.

An equally poetic power, and something of the same historical uncertainty, is at work in 'Sir Patrick Spens' (Child 58). In typical 'leaping and lingering' fashion, the singer goes directly to the beginning and then to the end of the ill-fated voyage, pausing only to record Sir Patrick's reactions, and an old sailor's premonition of disaster:

The first line that Sir Patrick red,
    A loud lauch lauched he;
The next line that Sir Patrick red,
    The teir blinded his ee.

. . .

'Late late yestreen I saw the new moone,
    Wi the auld moone in her arme,
And I feir, I feir, my deir master,
    That we will cum to harme.'

(Child 58A)

When the storm has had its way, the ballad focuses on small details in a series of poignantly understated 'snapshots':

O our Scots nobles wer richt laith
  To weet their cork-heild shoone;
But lang owre a' the play were playd,
  Thair hats they swam aboone.

O lang, lang may their ladies sit,
  Wi thair fans into their hand,
Or eir they se Sir Patrick Spence
  Cum sailing to the land.

O lang, lang may the ladies stand,
  Wi their gold kems in their hair
Waiting for thair ain deir lords,
  For they'll se thame na mair.

Haf owre, haf owre to Aberdour,
  It's fiftie fadom deip,
And thair lies guid Sir Patrick Spence,
  Wi the Scots lords at his feit.　　　　　　　　(Child 58A)

If the functional reason for such repetition in oral art is by now familiar, it still remains to point to the extraordinarily moving symbolic effects which it creates at the same time. Our attention is seized by those fashionably cork-heeled shoes, by the fans and gold combs and all the genteel accoutrements of a privileged class. The physical movement of the ladies, when they switch from sitting to standing, has an equally dramatic eloquence, and this is matched in turn by a contrasting vision of Sir Patrick Spens under fifty fathoms of water with their drowned husbands laid at his feet – like those stone dogs carved on a knight's tomb.

Tales of tragic romance

'Mary Hamilton' and 'Sir Patrick Spens' could almost belong to the 'tragic romance' category of ballads, except that the latter are more fiercely suffused with the passions of love, jealousy or betrayal. 'The Dowie Howms of Yarrow' (Child 214) tells how a Border laird is killed by his brother-in-law after a drunken quarrel, and the first two stanzas, when the tale is 'leaping' at its swiftest, provide an extraordinary example of ballad concision:

> Late at een, drinkin the wine,
>   Or early in a morning,
> They set a combat them between,
>   To fight it in the dawin'.
>
> 'O stay at hame, my noble lord!
>   O stay at hame, my marrow!   partner (spouse)
> My cruel brother will you betray,
>   On the dowie houms o' Yarrow.   dreary low river-banks

(Child 214E)

Jealous brothers, sisters and mothers abound in these tales and, not surprisingly, there are many international variants on the same themes. 'The Twa Sisters' (Child 10) exists in over sixty versions from Scotland, England, Denmark, Norway, Iceland, the Faeroes and Sweden. In most of these versions a musical instrument is made from the bones of the drowned girl, and when it is played it reveals that she was murdered by her sister – clearly a folk tale of wide and enduring force. In another ballad, it is a brother who kills his sister, because, although the rest of the family were consulted, his particular consent to her marriage was not asked. Like so many of its kind, 'The Cruel Brother' (Child 11) ends with a dying person leaving their goods to those around them, until the final bequest is made:

> 'What will you leave to your brother John?'
>   *With a hey ho and a lillie gay.*
> 'The gallows-tree to hang him on!'
>   *As the primrose spreads so sweetly.*

(Child 11A)

The world of the ballads revolves around sudden contrasts between tears and laughter, peace and war, love and hatred, marriage and death; and contrast is found again in the juxtaposition of the dying girl's curse and the sweet refrain which has accompanied the grim narrative from the start. 'Lord Randal' (Child 12) and 'Edward' (Child 13), are among the best-known ballads to use the device of a surprise last bequest, and they too have many international variations. In each case a heavily structured and repetitiously patterned duologue is set up between the hero and another person, until it produces a sense of inevitable process, a painful journey towards death or a final, ghastly revelation. Lord Randal leaves 'hell and fire' to his true love, who has poisoned him, while Edward curses his mother for persuading him to kill his father. Incremental repetition and the melody's slow pace are vital to the overall effect, and in 'Lord Randal' only the first half of the third line in each stanza actually advances the plot, while everything else, rhymes and line-endings included, is said over and over again.

'O where ha you been, Lord Randal, my son?
And where ha you been, my handsome young man?'
'I ha been at the green wood; mother, mak my bed soon,
For I'm wearied wi hunting, an fain wad lie down.'

'An wha met ye there, Lord Randal, my son?
An wha met you there, my handsome young man?'
'O I met wi my true-love; mother, mak my bed soon,
For I'm wearied wi hunting, an fain wad lie down.'

(Child 12A)

In this fashion, the story of how he has been poisoned is haltingly revealed, as though the tale were taking three steps forward in every verse, and two steps back again: 'lingering' has become massively static.

When asked what he will give to his wife and children before he flees into exile, Edward's answer is succinct: 'the warldis room, late them beg thrae life, / For thame nevir mair wil I see O', and his cruel realism is characteristically Scottish. It is instructive to compare 'The Three Ravens', an English ballad, with 'The Twa Corbies' (Child 26), a counterpart from north of the Border. 'The Three Ravens' has a refrain, 'Downe a downe, hay down . . .', and it tells how a slain knight is protected from predators by his faithful hounds and his hawks, until his lady, in the symbolic form of a pregnant fallow doe, comes to bury him and then to join him in death. 'The Twa Corbies' is half the length and much less comforting. The crows have the knight to themselves:

'His hound is to the hunting gane,
His hawk to fetch the wild-fowl hame,
His lady's ta'en another mate,
So we may mak our dinner sweet.

'Ye'll sit on his white hause-bane,
And I'll pike oot his bonny blue een;
Wi ae lock o his gowden hair
We'll theek our nest when it grows bare.

'Mony a one for him maks mane,
But nane sall ken where he is gane;
Oer his white banes, when they are bare,
The wind sall blaw for evermair.'

(Child 26)

The same fatalism reigns with particular force in the ballads of
the supernatural.

Tales of the other world

The 'other world' in Scotland has many of its origins in Celtic
lore, with tales of seal men and kelpies who delight in the
downfall of poor mortals, or of the fairy folk, ruled by a
beautiful queen on a milk-white horse with silver bells in its
mane. The 'good people' live in mounds or under the hills, and
the Eildon Hills are particularly famous as one of the doors to
their kingdom. Mortals enter this realm at their peril, but they
can ensure their return by leaving iron or a dirk at the gate, for
the fairies are afraid of steel. (Another passport to their land is
said to be the branch of an apple-tree, and perhaps there is a
connection here with the apples of the Hesperides, the golden
fruit from the magic West which Hercules had to find in Greek
myth.) The border between the natural and the supernatural is
a misty one, and even the human dead can cross it as revenants
from their home in Tir nan Og – the Isle of the Blest – which is
neither Heaven nor Hell but a pagan Celtic paradise, the land
of the ever-young, somewhere over the western horizon.

When the Queen of Elfland describes her kingdom to
Thomas the Rhymer, it is a middle state where magical awe
meets with sexual danger, quite distinct from the after-worlds
of Christian teaching:

'O see not ye yon narrow road,
  So thick beset wi thorns and briars?
That is the path of righteousness,
  Tho after it but few enquires.

'And see not ye that braid braid road,
  That lies across yon lillie leven?   lea
That is the path of wickedness
  Tho some call it the road to heaven.

'And see not ye that bonny road,
  Which winds about the fernie brae?
That is the road to fair Elfland,
  Where you and I this night maun gae.   must go

'But Thomas ye maun hold your tongue,
  Whatever you may hear or see,
For gin ae word you should chance to speak,   if one
  You will never get back to your ain countrie.'

('Thomas the Rhymer', Child 37A)

Yet there are still some religious elements in the ballad, and
shades of sexual guilt too, for when Thomas first sees her he
mistakes the Elf Queen for the 'Queen of Heaven'. Again,
during their desperate journey to fairyland – 'For forty days
and forty nights,/He wade thro red blude to the knee' –
Thomas is stopped just in time from picking an apple, no less
than the fruit of man's first sin. Thus Christian and Celtic
themes are intermingled along with hints of the romance tales,
for the story of a knight abducted by the Elf Queen also features
in the Arthurian cycle, which, too, contains in its turn echoes
from earlier Celtic sources. Seven years pass before True
Thomas returns to the Eildon Hills, although it seems but a
brief time to him, and he brings back the gift of second sight –
the ability to see aspects of the future. In fact Thomas of
Ercildoune seems to have been a real person, living about 1320,
and various prophecies of his have been preserved, along with
verses from the early fifteenth century which tell of his
adventures in the first person:

Als I me wente this Endres daye,
ffull faste in mynd makand my mone,
In a merry mornynge of Maye,
By Huntle bankkes my selfe allone,

> I herde the jaye, and the throstyll cokke,
> The mawys menyde hir of hir songe,   thrush lamented
> The wodewale beryde als a belle,   woodlark sang like
> That alle the wode abowte me ronge.

The fairies might promise erotic adventure or ambiguous gifts, but it can be fatal to deal too closely with the other world. Clerk Colvill (Child 42) dies because he has made love with a mermaid, while Tam Lin (Child 39) seduces an earthly girl while still himself under the power of the Queen of Fairies. His human lover must reclaim him by pulling him down from his fairy horse at midnight, and by holding him fast, despite the several frightening shapes he will assume. Lady Isabel manages to outwit her eerie seducer by killing him at the last minute ('Lady Isabel and the Elf-Knight', Child 4); but the Daemon Lover (Child 243), is not so easily denied as he lures his former love aboard ship, only to show her 'where the white lilies grow,/ In the bottom o' the sea'.

The finest of the supernatural Scots ballads deal with those moments when the other world and the everyday world come together, if only for a brief time. When the three drowned sons return to their mother in 'The Wife of Usher's Well' (Child 79), their birch-bark hats announce that they have come from the Celtic isle of the dead and, like all ghosts, they cannot stay past the dawn. When the youngest brother says goodbye to home and hearth, the simplicity of his words strikes the listener with the full force of that final, inexorable separation from the common earth and all human warmth:

> The cock he hadna crawd but once,
>   And clapped his wings at a',
> When the youngest to the eldest said,
>   'Brother, we must awa.

> 'The cock doth craw, the day doth daw,
>   The channerin worm doth chide;   whining
> Gin we be mist out o our place,
>   A sair pain we maun bide.

> 'Fare ye weel, my mother dear!
>   Fareweel to barn and byre!
> And fare ye weel, the bonny lass,
>   That kindles my mother's fire!'

> (Child 79A)

The same sweetly painful grief pervades 'The Great Silkie of Sule Skerry' (Child 113), which is known in only one version collected from an old lady in the Shetlands. The 'silkies' are seal folk who can take human shape and earthly lovers, but this tale is especially poignant for its sense of the inevitable parting of all human ties, whether made with the fairy folk or not. The wider symbolic reverberations of this remarkable ballad tell how the saddest thing is not that the heart will eventually stop, but that, sooner than that, it will come to change its affections:

> Now he has ta'en a purse of goud,
>   And he has pat it upo' her knee,
> Saying', 'Gie to me my little young son,
>   An' tak thee up thy nourrice-fee.   nurses fee
>
> 'An' it sall pass on a simmer's day,
>   When the sin shines het on evera stane,
> That I will tak my little young son,
>   An' teach him for to swim his lane.   on his own
>
> 'An' thu sall marry a proud gunner,
>   An' a proud gunner I'm sure he'll be,
> 'An' the very first schot that ere he schoots,
>   He'll schoot baith my young son and me.'

Technical concision and grim realism meet here with insight and tender fatalism, to capture the timelessly popular poetic voice of the Scottish ballads and their many anonymous singers – a timely reminder that great art is not the exclusive property of educated or literary circles.

Robert and Francis Sempill

The energy of the oral tradition in Scots was not entirely lost to written verse, for it makes a brief appearance in the works of **Robert Sempill of Beltrees** (1595?–1665?). Robert's father was Sir James Sempill (1566–1625), the author of several pro-Presbyterian pamphlets and a satirical drama in English called *A Picktooth for the Pope, or the Packman's Paternoster*. (Sir James had been educated with James VI under George Buchanan, and he later served his king as an ambassador in London and Paris.) Robert, laird of Beltrees in Renfrewshire, was a loyalist who fought for Charles I and supported the Restoration. He did not produce much poetry, nor did his son Francis, but the Sempills represent a new class of author, drawn from the educated minor gentry, who were destined to inherit the Scots literary tradition from the clerics, scholars and courtiers who had gone before. At the same time, their resolutely colloquial spirit makes a link between Scots verse in the sixteenth century and the vernacular revival 200 years later. Robert's fame rests on the verse-form which he chose for a naïve elegy called 'The Life and Death of the Piper of Kilbarchan, or the Epitaph of Habbie Simson'.

> At Clark-plays when he wont to come,
> His Pipe played trimly to the Drum
> Like Bikes of Bees he gart it Bum,   made
>   And tun'd his Reed:
> Now all our Pipers may sing dumb,
>   Sen Habbie's dead.
>
> And at Horse Races many a day,
> Before the Black, the Brown, the Gray,
> He gart his Pipe when he did play,
>   Baith Skirl and Skreed,
> Now all such Pastime's quite away
>   Sen Habbie's dead.

Sempill's six-line stanza with its two emphatic short lines produces a notable rhythmic effect. The scene is set and the rhyme sustained by a galloping four-stress rhythm in the opening three lines; then the pace is checked, picked up again and abruptly concluded by a second rhyme appearing in two short lines of only two stresses each. This second rhyme and the entire last line are repeated throughout the poem. The same delight in a lilting metre with its checks and refrains is found in the 'bob and wheel' effects of 'Christis Kirk' and 'Peblis to the Play', and they too seem well suited to the movement of popular dances and reels in celebration of the ordinary domestic scene. Passages with a similar rhythm – also used for satirical effect – appeared in Lindsay's *Thrie Estaits* and in popular airs such as 'Hey Tuttie Taittie' (later sanctified in the *Gude and Godlie Ballatis*). Kurt Wittig has suggested that the pattern may owe something to Gaelic octosyllabic metres, *ochtfhoclach mór*, used for elegies, and *ochtfhoclach beag*, used for verses to dance tunes.

Whatever its precursors, the stanza-form of Sempill's verses became so popular among later Scots poets that it has been known ever since as 'Standard Habbie', or sometimes, slightly varied, as the 'Burns stanza'.

'Habbie Simson' was first published in 1706 in James Watson's *Choice Collection*, and subsequently Allan Ramsay, Robert Fergusson and Burns himself were to make more of its distinctive jig-time measure than ever Sempill achieved with his naïve, but touchingly direct, lament for a dead piper. Fergusson and Burns found 'Habbie' particularly suited to comedy, satire and social comment, for its short lines can produce a variety of ironic, or sly, or sententious effects. Sempill is usually credited with another mock elegy, called 'Epitaph on Sanny Briggs, Nephew to Habbie Simson and Butler to the Laird of Kilbarchan', but it is unlikely that either poem would be remembered had their distinctive pattern not taken fire in the hands of later and better poets.

Francis Sempill (1616?/25?–1682) is said to have shared his father's talent for vernacular verse, and 'Sanny Briggs' is sometimes attributed to him, as well as 'The Banishment of Poverty', a rather contrived account of how the poet was followed everywhere by 'poverty' – like a stray dog at his heels – until he reached the debtor's sanctuary at Holyrood and the Duke of Albany's generosity freed him. The fine song 'Maggie Lauder' is tentatively attributed to Francis, although he may only have reworked it from an earlier popular source. 'The Blythsome Wedding' is an odd and lively piece which juxtaposes a hilarious account of the grotesque guests at a country wedding with an equally extensive list of what there was to eat. The poem's vulgar and encyclopaedic zest belongs to the tradition of 'Christis Kirk' joined to that of *The Complaynt of Scotland*, and the end result is like a peasant feast recorded by Breughel down to the last and grossest detail. If such comprehensive grotesquerie seems to be a Scottish characteristic, it is by no means confined to the peasant world, for Sir Thomas Urquhart, knight and word-spinner extraordinary, must be its undisputed champion.

Sir Thomas Urquhart of Cromarty (1611–60)

The knight of Cromarty was a stout supporter of the Stuart crown, a flamboyant cavalier, a proud and patriotic Scot and the possessor of a uniquely eccentric mind and manner. He began his studies at Aberdeen University at the age of eleven, and, although he left without a degree, he retained fond memories and a taste for esoteric learning. During his travels abroad he describes (typically innocent of modesty) how he gained friends and 'vindicated his native county' by fighting three separate combats of honour in the lists. At home, his father refused to sign the Covenant and Thomas returned to fight for the Royalists. Despite initial successes in the north, the Cavaliers who opposed the Covenanters in the 'Bishops' Wars' were gradually dispersed. Urquhart went to London, was knighted by Charles, and produced an excruciatingly banal book, *Epigrams: Divine and Moral* (1641). His father's lack of business-sense had almost ruined the estate in the far north of Scotland, and when Sir Thomas inherited it in 1642 he was quick to resume his travels. After three years abroad he returned to Cromarty determined to achieve fame as a writer, inventor, scholar and mathematician. Urquhart was an admirer of his countryman John Napier (1550–1617), the inventor of logarithms (whom the famous German astronomer Kepler regarded as the greatest mathematician of his day), and he decided to produce a treatise of his own which would help students to memorise and calculate the theorems of trigonometry. He seems to have known his subject well enough, but *The Trissotetras* (1645) is made almost completely unintelligible by a language crammed with abstract terms and neologisms. The glossary throws even more darkness on the subject: '*Amfractuosities*; are taken here for the cranklings, windings, turnings, and involutions belonging to the equisoleary scheme. . . .'

Immediately after the execution of Charles I, Urquhart took part in an ill-fated Royalist uprising in the north and was declared a traitor – although he was leniently treated by the Covenanters. Within two years he was supporting Charles II's cause (in line with Covenanting policy this time) and marching south with the Scottish army which was eventually defeated by Cromwell at Worcester in 1651. Urquhart travelled with a full wardrobe and writing-desk and many of his manuscripts and papers were looted or lost after the battle, although once more he himself was spared. After a spell in the Tower of London, he was held at Windsor Castle and, to prove his merit to his captors and avoid the confiscation of his estates, he set about the demonstration of his intellectual prowess. *Pantochronochanon* (1652) traces the descent of the Urquharts back to Adam (with Eve, too, on the female side) and promises in a future volume, if the writer is released, to explain why the shire of Cromarty alone in Britain has all its place-names derived from 'pure and perfect Greek'. Equally Greek, if not quite so pure, *Ekskybalauron, or The Discovery of a Most Exquisite Jewel* (1652) attempts to vindicate the honour of Scotland from the canting image given it by the rigid Presbyterian party. Along the way it makes another plea for its author's freedom, as well as a proposal for a universal language which will be easier to learn than any other, despite having eleven genders, ten tenses, and words which can be read just as meaningfully backwards as forwards (This seems to have been a species of code, and not quite as mad as it sounds, although Urquhart never actually perfected it.) The *Jewel* is chiefly notable for its enthusiastic account of many brave and learned Scots, in particular 'the admirable' James Crichtoun (1560–83), soldier, scholar, duellist, polyglot and lover extraordinary – a fitting hero for the knight of Cromarty.

Urquhart was paroled in 1652 and returned to Scotland only to find his creditors awaiting him. The following year saw him back in London, from where he published a many-sided diatribe against those 'stinging wasps' and another proposal for his universal language, *Logopandecteision* (1653). As always, Urquhart's prose is elaborately and relentlessly euphuistic, but it does have a manic energy and, at its best, it is the hilariously inventive and exhaustive text itself which turns out to be the main subject and hero of the piece. Even so, when faced with the cosmic grandeur of his schemes and with a style which occasionally slips into complete gobbledegook, it is difficult not to suspect that the author was a little mad.

Urquhart's peculiar genius found its true *métier* in 1653 with his translation of the first two books of Rabelais's *Gargantua and Pantagruel*. (A third book was published in the edition of 1694, along with Books IV and V as translated by Motteux.) Rabelais is notoriously difficult to translate, because he mixes pompous and learned diction with earthy phrases and accumulates long lists of objects, epithets and synonyms. Such a challenge might have been specially made for Urquhart, and he met it by outdoing the Frenchman, and even himself, with a translation almost twice the length of the original: more compendious in its lists, more outrageous in its vulgarities and more hyperbolic in its hyperboles. When Rabelais notes the animal-noises which spoil the peace of his countryside, he manages to name the calls of dogs, wolves, lions, horses, elephants, snakes, asses, crickets and doves. Urquhart's version contains seventy-one species and their increasingly unlikely cries, including the 'drintling of turkies, coniating of storks, frantling of peacocks . . . rantling of rats, guerieting of apes, snuttering of monkeys, pioling of pelicans', and so on – truly a list worthy of the catalogues to be found in *The Complaynt of Scotland*. Notwithstanding his flamboyant expansions, a good case can be made for Urquhart's essential accuracy, for his version catches the spirit of Rabelais with an immense and greasy gusto:

HOW GARGAMELLE, BEING GREAT WITH GARGANTUA, DID EAT A HUGE DEAL OF TRIPES

The occasion and manner how Gargamelle was brought to bed, and delivered of her child, was thus: and, if you do not believe it, I wish your bum-gut fall out, and make an escapade. Her bum-gut, indeed, or fundament escaped her in an afternoon, on the third day of February, with having eaten at dinner too many godebillios. Godebillios are the fat tripes of coiros. Coiros are beeves fattened at the cratch in ox stalls, or in the fresh guimo meadows. Guimo meadows are those, that for their fruitfulness may be mowed twice a year. Of those fat beeves they had killed three hundred sixty-seven thousand and fourteen, to be salted at Shrove-tide, that in the entering of the spring they might have plenty of powdered beef, wherewith to season their mouths at the beginning of their meals, and to taste their wine the better.

They had abundance of tripes, as you have heard, and they were so delicious, that every one licked his fingers. But the mischief was this, that for all men could do, there was no possibility to keep them long in that relish; for in a very short while they would have stunk, which had been an undecent thing. It was therefore concluded, that they should be all of them gulched up, without losing anything.

Ezra Pound preferred Douglas's *Eneados* to Virgil and many readers have found Urquhart's *Rabelais* equally special: it joins that select company of translations which have achieved their own creative identity, along with Chapman's *Homer*, Fitzgerald's *Omar Khayyam*, some of Pound's Chinese poems, and the Authorised Version itself.

Little is known of Sir Thomas's last years. He is said to have died of a fit of laughing when he heard of the Restoration of Charles II; and, if that is not true, as one writer puts it, then it certainly should be.

Urquhart was not the only distinguished writer to support the Stuart crown, for, of course, the Gaelic Highlands espoused the Catholic cause as well, and the poet Iain Lom (who had been a friend of Montrose's) honed the edge of his Gaelic verse to comment fiercely on the political events of his day.

Gaelic poetry in the late seventeenth century

The second half of the century was a period of transition and renewed activity in Gaelic verse, and, although Iain Lom was probably the most radical and influential poet of the time, there were many others, especially among women, who composed fine songs too. The formal patterns of bardic verse were finally changing, and syllabic metres, high diction and learned historical allusions were giving way to a more colloquial Gaelic with metres based on stress. This had been a gradual change which can be traced to the previous century, and, after all, the modes of eulogy, elegy and bardic satire were to continue unabated into the next. Yet the work of this period stands as a watershed between the bardic schools and what was to become, in effect, modern Gaelic poetry.

Niall MacMhuirich (1637?–1726)

If Iain Lom's verse looks towards modern Gaelic, then Niall stays almost entirely with the old style. This is scarcely surprising, since he and his distinguished predecessor Cathal came from a long line of MacMhuirich bards going back to the thirteenth century, and much of their poetry is in the learned tradition of elegy and panegyric for their patrons in the Clanranald branch of the MacDonalds. Niall was almost the last of the literate bardic school with Irish connections, and his elegy for Donald, son of John of Moidart, who died in the late 1640s, shows his clear and vigorous style and also the extreme formalism of the genre:

> The son of big bodied spirited John of Moidart, the shortness of his life has wounded me sharply; wretched is my state now that this man is dead: that has consumed [as with fire] my flesh and my blood. . . .
>
> He was a lion in the fierceness of his exploits, but would not indulge in anything shameful, a man who was foremost in showing the way to peace, my beloved was he who gave protection to the destitute and to the learned poets.

(trs. D. Thomson)

Niall's verses and his prose history of the Montrose wars were gathered, along with other pieces from the MacMhuirich bards, in a manuscript collection known as the Red Book of Clanranald. Niall wrote very little in vernacular Gaelic, but two poems do survive, both on the death of Allan of Clandranald after the battle of Sherrifmuir in 1715. He laments the passing of the traditional learning of the Gael as if he knew that the aftermath of the Jacobite risings was indeed to change their customs for ever.

Roderick Morison (1656?–1714?)

Known as 'an clàrsair dall' ('the blind harper'), Morison served the MacLeod chiefs at Dunvegan and has often been called (not quite accurately), the last of the old minstrel-class. Tradition has it that he left Lewis to study for the ministry at Inverness, where he caught smallpox and lost his eyesight. He turned to music to survive and visited Ireland to further his craft before roving the Highlands to earn his living. In Edinburgh in 1681 he met Iain Breac MacLeod, who took him under his care at Dunvegan in Skye, although Morison was never the official bard there. Iain Breac was among the last chiefs to keep the old style of establishment, for, as well as his harper, he had a bard and a jester and his piper was the famous Patrick Og MacCrimmon himself, the roar of whose drones, according to blind Roderick, would stir the whole household into cheerful activity every morning. Morison performed the usual eulogies, but in 1688 he fell out of favour at Dunvegan and was 'banished' to Glenelg – perhaps on account of his outspoken Jacobite sympathies at a time when his chief was studiously trying to remain neutral. The harper found another patron at Talisker for a while before returning to his travels and relative obscurity.

When Iain Breac died in 1693 the blind harper composed a unique 'Song to MacLeod of Dunvegan', which begins as a lament for his former patron with a lovingly detailed picture of happy days under his roof. Then the poem turns into a scathing attack on Roderick, the son and heir who went south to live at court, spent money on gambling and clothes and ignored Skye and the old culture. The harper had cause for alarm, for in the six years before he died of consumption the young chief raised loans of £45,000 against an annual income of only £9000 – 'then does the boil fester on the thigh', sings Morison, 'with its pain at the root'. The original uses rhyme in its eight-line stanzas:

He comes out of the shop
with the latest fashion from France,
and the fine clothes worn on his person
yesterday with no little satisfaction
are tossed into a corner –
'The style is unmodish, not worth a plack.
On the security of a townland or two,
take the pen and sign a bond.'

The page will not be regarded
unless his clothes are in the current fashion;
though it should cost a guinea a yard,
that can be got for a mart given in lieu of rent.
As much again in addition
will got to the purchase of a doublet for him,
and breeches of soft velvet
to wrap up gusts at his rear.

(trs. W. Matheson)

A bard's satire could be fearsomely specific, but in this case it was not enough to stop young MacLeod, and many others after him, from breaking the kinship ties and becoming an absentee landlord in Edinburgh or London.

There was another bard with the MacLeods of Skye during

Morison's time, although she was an unlettered and 'unofficial' one.

Mary MacLeod (1615?–1706?)

Mary MacLeod (Màiri Nighean Alasdair Ruaidh) first came from Harris to be a nurse at Dunvegan, and she looked after several members of the family during her long life there. She too fell into disfavour for a while and spent some years in the Hebrides and Mull before being recalled to Skye. This may have been during young Roderick's six years as chief, or perhaps during his father's time, and so it is not certain if Mary ever met with the blind harper in the 'wide mansion' where she spent her last days as an old lady with a taste for whisky and snuff. Mary's laments and eulogies for members of the clan follow the usual bardic form, but she enlivens her verse with freer stress-patterns (often in a three-line stanza) and her vernacular Gaelic is more spontaneous in feeling, music and rhythm than the old schools would have had it.

Much more radical departures were made by our next poet.

John MacDonald ('Iain Lom') (1620?–1707?)

Mary's outlook was limited to Dunvegan and the doings of the family, but Iain Lom lived a more mobile life, with a political eye on the wider world. Descended from the chiefs of Keppoch, Iain was involved in the clan feuds which grew up around Montrose's campaigns. He supported the Royalist cause passionately and was present when the Covenanters and the Campbells were defeated at the battle of Inverlochy in 1645. 'Iain Lom', as the name suggests, was a lean 'bare' man, known for his quick and scathing wit. It is said that the Campbells, all too aware of his talent for invective, offered a reward for his head. Tradition has it that he arrived at Inverary castle to claim the bounty himself and was indeed rewarded for his nerve by being entertained as a guest for a week. The Campbells had cause to fear this bard's tongue, for his account of the battle of Inverlochy shows his impressionistic and ferociously exultant verse in action – a vernacular Gaelic honed to hard, succinct and cruel images all leading to an absolutely merciless conclusion:

Alasdair of sharp, biting blades,
if you had the heroes of Mull with you,
you would have stopped those who got away,
as the dulse-eating rabble took to their heels.

Alasdair, son of handsome Colla,
skilled hand at cleaving castles,
you put to flight the Lowland pale-face:
what kale they had taken came out again.

You remember the place called the Tawny Field?
It got a fine dose of manure;
not the dung of sheep or goats,
but Campbell blood well congealed.

To Hell with you if I care for your plight,
as I listen to your children's distress,
lamenting the band that went to battle,
the howling of the women of Argyll.

(trs. D. Thomson)

An indefatigable Royalist, Iain Lom took Charles II fiercely to task for not claiming his kingdom – 'let not your soft tin sword/be in a fair sheath that is gilded' ('Lament for the Marquis of Huntly'). The king does not seem to have held a grudge, for with the Restoration he made Iain Lom his poet laureate in Scotland and the bard delivered a eulogy for the coronation. The poet was true to his appointment, for, when the Revolution of 1688 arrived, he did not hesitate to denounce William of Orange as a 'borrowed king' and flayed him and his queen in the bitterest possible terms.

Vituperation was not the poet's only voice, and the 'Lament for Montrose' shows a more tender note as he describes his depression at his leader's end; and an early lament for Angus MacRanald Og of Keppoch shows his typically economical images fired with a sense of personal loss. Iain Crichton Smith's translation tries to catch this terse, bright restraint in the rhythms of the Gaelic:

I'm a goose that is plucked
without feather or brood,
or like Ossian condemned by Saint Patrick.

Or a tree that is stripped,
without apple or nut,
the sap and the bark having left it.

That raid to Loch Tay
has darkened my way:
Angus lay dead by its waters.

. . .

What wrung tears from my eyes
was the gap in your side
as you lay in the house of Cor Charmaig.

For I loved your gay face
(branched with blood and with race)
both ruthless and graceful in warfare.

The 'bard of Keppoch' also produced a number of conventional stock elegies, but his most memorable verse deals with his turbulent times and his own incisively 'ruthless and graceful' feelings. Nor did he lose his sharpness in old age, as testified by the bawdy virulence of his 'Song against the Union' ('Oran an Aghaidh an Aonaidh'), on attack on those Lowlanders who promoted the parliamentary union of 1707 for personal gain:

Lord Dupplin, without delay
the vent to your throat opened,
a turbulence rose in your heart
when you heard the gold coming;
you swallowed the hiccoughs of avarice,
your lungs inflated and swelled,
control over your gullet was relaxed,
and the traces of your arse were unloosed.

(trs. D. Thomson)

Iain Lom was far from alone in his distrust of the Commissioners, but Andrew Fletcher, the most outspoken Lowland critic of the Union, would not have welcomed him or his support.

Andrew Fletcher of Saltoun (1655–1716)

As a member of parliament at the beginning of the century, Fletcher is especially remembered for his opposition to the proposed union with Westminster. Scots of all persuasions were equally disturbed. After all, the Highlands still sustained a Jacobite interest, and, as far as the Lowlands were concerned, the failure of the Darien scheme had done little to convince Scottish businessmen of England's good faith. From an English point of view, the union of the parliaments would help to promote much-needed security for the Hanoverian succession after Queen Anne. The 'seven ill years' at the close of the century had left Scotland in terrible straits, with an acute shortage of money and resources and over a quarter of the population dead of hunger and disease. Factions both for and against Union were not slow to make the most of this failure in their arguments. In 1698 Fletcher produced *Two Discourses concerning the Affairs of Scotland*, the second of which contained a passionate denunciation of the state of affairs which had produced a permanent population of some 100,000 vagabonds, 'who have lived without any regard or subjection either to the laws of the land, or even those of God or nature'. The recent famines doubled this number, and, since Fletcher believed in a citizen militia, he condemned the keeping of a standing army when such poverty was rife:

> we had more need to have saved the money to have bought bread, for thousands of our people that were starving afford us the melancholy prospect of dying by shoals in our streets, and have left behind them reigning contagion which hath swept away multitudes more, and God knows where it may end.

Although Fletcher had Highland Jacobite allies in his opposition to Union, as a stout Presbyterian he had little sympathy with their cause or their culture. No Swiss burger could have had a more vehement concern for freedom, peace and healthy trade, and the kin-based, warlike and essentially unmaterialistic nature of clan society was anathema to him. He complained that half of Scotland was occupied 'by a people who are all gentlemen only because they will not work; and who in everything are more contemptible than the vilest slaves, except that they always carry arms, because for the most part they live upon robbery'. Fletcher's patriotism looked back to the great times of the Declaration of Arbroath; and the twelve 'limitations' which he proposed to parliament in 1703 all had to do with making sure that no king could act against the interests, or without the sanction of the Estates of Scotland. He was equally passionately opposed to what he took to be the erosion of wealth and cultural identity, which a parliamentary union with England could only accelerate. To this end he wrote an essay called *An Account of a Conversation concerning a Right Regulation of Governments for the Common Good of Mankind* (1704), which includes his famous saying on nationhood and the ballads. The essay was written in the form of a letter to the marquis of Montrose and other Whig nationalists, and it strikes a surprisingly contemporary note to any reader familiar with the debates on devolution which took place in Scotland in the late 1970s:

> That London should draw the riches and government of the three kingdoms to the south-east corner of this island, is in some degree as unnatural, as for one city to possess the riches and government of the world. . . . And if the other parts of government are not also communicated to every considerable body of men; but that some of them must be forced to depend upon others, and be governed by those who reside far from them, and little value any interest except their own . . . I say, all such governments are violent, unjust and unnatural.

If nothing else, the contemporary recurrence of these opinions suggests that Fletcher's diagnosis of Scotland's condition was more far-sighted than the successful Unionists of 1707 could ever have realised or admitted.

5

The eighteenth century: new Athenians and the Doric

On 28 April 1707 Chancellor Seafield concluded the last meeting of the last Scottish parliament with the words, 'Now there's ane end of ane auld sang', but these were far from the final words on the subject, for Scotland had been so deeply divided over the issue that debates and accusations of bribery and corruption raged for years. Many landowners had been in favour of what they saw as a profitable partnership, and the vested interests of Church and law had been protected by separate acts in both parliaments; but the boroughs feared a reduction in their status and the volatile urban crowds rioted at the prospect of their rulers moving to London, capital of the 'auld enemy'. It was not long before their fears were realised, agreements were broken, and even the Unionists began to have second thoughts as English businessmen denied them the expected benefits in trade and exports. Rises in taxation hit the poorer classes in Scotland much harder than their more comfortable counterparts in the south. The Kirk saw Episcopalian forms return under the new Toleration Act and the principle of lay patronage was introduced contrary to the Acts passed at the Union. Parliamentary action in far-away London was difficult and tedious to implement, and the forty-five new members and the Scottish nobility too found themselves outnumbered and diminished when they moved to the larger stage. For a while these disappointments seemed to have little to do with the Highlanders, who expected to live in their old society much as before. Yet it was only a matter of time before disaffection with the Union and the death of Queen Anne fanned the ashes of Jacobite hopes into a last fitful, destructive flame.

The 1715 rebellion was an abortive campaign despite a fair measure of support with 10,000 men from the clans. At Braemar in September, the Catholic cause of King James VIII was declared by 'Bobbing John', the sixth Earl of Mar, a man who had lost his position as Secretary of State when Queen Anne died. Mar and the clans expected more support from France and the south than they got, for the Hanoverian succession of George I was by no means universally popular and crowds in England had rioted at the prospect. Yet Mar would not commit himself and had to be persuaded to allow 2000 of his men to join English sympathisers on the road to the capital. The Jacobites reached Preston before they were encircled by superior numbers and surrendered. By this time Bobbing John had finally brought himself to Stirling to tackle the Duke of Argyll and his Campbells, who remained loyal to the government although outnumbered two to one. The Battle of Sherrifmuir was confused and indecisive, but in effect it was a defeat for Mar, because he failed to gain access to the south and his Highlanders began to go home. In late December the Old Pretender arrived in Scotland only to return to France in little over a month, leaving money for restitution and a plea for the approaching Argyll to be merciful. In fact the disillusioned rebels were treated relatively mildly, because Scots juries were reluctant to convict Jacobites for anti-Union sentiments. Nevertheless, Lowland Scots and English prejudices against the Highlanders had been reinforced once again, and groups such as the Society for Propagating Christian Knowledge continued to link the spread of schools and Presbyterian Christianity in the north-west with the deliberate extirpation of 'heathenish customs' and the speaking of what they still called 'Irish'. Garrisons were established at Fort William, Fort Augustus and Inverness, and General Wade built a network of roads which finally began to open the Highlands to trade, travel and the military presence of the state. At the same time soldiers were recruited from the north and the Black Watch was formed to deter the clansmen from cattle-raiding and the extortion of 'black mail' – a traditional form of 'protection money'. By 1745 the new Black Watch regiment was in the Netherlands fighting bravely in the service of King George.

Their absence from the home front and the French victory at Fontenoy encouraged Prince Charles Edward Stuart to revive the ambitions of the Stuart dynasty for one last throw of the dice.

The twenty-three-year-old prince was a more daring and attractive personality than his exiled father, but he landed near Arisaig with only a handful of followers and it took all his charm and his assurances to persuade the chiefs to join him – anti-Union sentiment was fading and the last Stuart had left the throne over forty years before. Nevertheless, moved by old loyalties or the threats of their chiefs, encouraged by an early victory at Prestonpans, or by the prospect of settling old scores against the Campbells, or even by a bad harvest at home, the clansmen gradually rallied to the prince's cause, until by November he was on his way south with 5000 men. This time the Jacobites reached Derby and put all London in a panic before their momentum ran out and Charles's advisers persuaded him that their position was too extended and vulnerable. The army returned to Scotland, met a few French reinforcements and won another victory at Falkirk; yet its supplies were dwindling and more and more clansmen were slipping away to spend the worst of the winter at home. Meanwhile the young Duke of Cumberland was pressing north with 9000 men, an army composed of twelve English battalions supported by artillery, horse-troopers and militia, as well as three battalions of Lowland Scots and one from Clan Campbell. On 16 April 1746, and against all advice, Charles insisted on a confrontation at Culloden on the moors outside Inverness. His exhausted and outnumbered troops with their claymores, pistols and shields were torn apart by artillery and decimated again when they finally charged a modern army trained to fire its muskets in alternating volleys. Charles escaped into the west, where he was gallantly (if sometimes reluctantly) hidden from his pursuers until he could set sail for France in September; but the wounded at Culloden were killed on the field where they lay. In the savage aftermath of the battle more than 3000 men, women and children were imprisoned and shipped to the south, where 120 were executed and over a thousand more banished and transported. Even although many were eventually set free, hundreds more died in captivity of hunger, wounds or disease. Meanwhile, as a matter of government policy, 'Butcher' Cumberland began to implement the most brutal repression throughout the Highlands. Clansmen were forbidden to carry arms, to play the pipes, or to wear tartan or the kilt, on pain of death or transportation; their music, their customs and their language were reviled and the glens given over to desultory bouts of terror and killing for over five years. Charles peddled his cause around Europe to increasingly little effect and died forty-two years later, a drunken and disillusioned man whose hopes had ended with the last land battle to be fought on British soil.

In the second half of the century, Scotland began to embark on better times, with a long overdue expansion in agriculture, trade and industry and a powerful and confident middle class. Even the Highlands came to share in this prosperity as rising cattle-prices encouraged clans to keep the peace and to trade with a Lowland society whose growing appetite for fish, timber, wool and latterly kelp, to serve the soap and glass industries, meant still more wealth in the north. Highland regiments became part of the British Army tradition, and men were raised by their clan-chiefs, clad in (legal) tartan and sent out to ply their warlike skills on behalf of a government and culture scarcely less foreign to them than that of the French, Spanish or Americans they were fighting. All these factors resulted in something of a boom for the hitherto underprivileged clans, and when the potato was introduced as a staple crop in times of peace and plenty, the population began to grow dramatically. Trade was accelerated again by the Napoleonic Wars, but it left the Highlands dreadfully vulnerable when peace came in 1815 and prices dropped. Lowland Scotland was less extended: it had coal and industrial resources on the east coast, with the Carron ironworks (which made the famous 'carronade' guns) and linen-manufacture and trade with the Baltic, while, on the west, Glasgow was becoming a major seaport where tobacco and sugar 'barons' made their fortunes from the Americas. It seemed as if the Union was bearing fruit at last and Scotland ready to match the Augustan culture of her new partner to the south.

The 'golden age' of the Scottish Enlightenment began in the 1740s and lasted for a hundred brilliant years, but its origins go back long before the Union, to those more humane aspects of the Reformation which had stressed breadth, accessibility and utility in education. So it was the Kirk's hopes for learning as a route to the word of God which initiated – ironically enough – the flowering of philosophy and the sciences in eighteenth- and nineteenth-century Scotland. Yet the old cultural tensions and insecurities were still there. If Highland mores were being undermined by well-meaning Lowland 'improvers', so the Scots tongue was being increasingly associated with all that was 'characterful' in Scots life – rustic or antique at best, and provincial at worst. The painful ambivalence that had been felt by many over the Union was replayed in cultural terms a generation later. In the 1780s Burns's vernacular muse was ecstatically received by the Edinburgh *literati* – the very people who had made a success of a little guide-book called *Scotticisms*, intended 'to put young writers and speakers on their guard against some of those Scotch idioms', much less broad Scots words, for 'the necessity of avoiding them is obvious'. So it is that there are two contrasting strains in eighteenth-century Scottish letters. The period opened with a marked revival of interest in ballads, songs and the poetry of the makars, and closed with the vernacular genius of Fergusson and Burns. In the mid century, however, the Scottish Enlightenment had also achieved a European scope and a thoroughly Augustan critical stance which led to the major literary periodicals of the 1800s. This extraordinary melting-pot produced Edinburgh as 'the Athens of the North' and it is fitting that the very fabric of the city itself should symbolise the contradictions and the creative vigour of the age, bubbling with the vulgar satirical energy of the 'Doric' and cooled again with hopes for an 'Athenian' clarity and control.

A vivid picture of life in mid-century Scotland can be found in the autobiography of Alexander 'Jupiter' Carlyle (1722–1805), a 'moderate' minister of the Kirk who wrote satirical pamphlets, attended the theatre, and enjoyed dancing and the company of the *literati*. Among the artists of the time, John Kay produced bold likenesses of the many characters to be seen walking in the Edinburgh streets, as did David Allen – 'the Scottish Hogarth', who illustrated 'The Gentle Shepherd' and 'The Cottar's Saturday Night'. Young Allan Ramsay (1713–84), the poet's son, became a well-known painter, a contemporary of Gainsborough and an early influence on Reynolds. He travelled widely, studied in Italy and settled in

London, where he became portrait-painter to George III. By the end of the century Sir Henry Raeburn (1756–1823) was Scotland's best-known portraitist. His most interesting works are divided between studies of Highland chiefs, now become a new class of landowner, clad in romantic tartan and keen to see a grandiose image of themselves in oils, and more sober portraits of his Lowland friends in law, literature, Kirk and sciences.

The boundaries of eighteenth-century Edinburgh were scarcely changed from two hundred years before, and so everyday life was crammed into the high tenement buildings or 'lands' which ran down the Royal Mile from the Castle to Holyrood Palace and spilled over each side of the ridge on the way. These tenements rose ten or twelve storeys high, creating ravine-deep vennels and lanes between them, darkened by overhanging gables and stinking with sewage and slops flung from the windows every evening at ten o'clock. Tenement life had long prevailed in Edinburgh, Stirling and Glasgow, producing a characteristically Scottish mixture of the classes by which elegant apartments were sandwiched among crowded attics, cellars and workshops, all linked by steep and narrow stairs. Advocates, craftsmen, beggars, butchers, porters, churchmen and academics all lived on top of one another in old Edinburgh and continued to do so until the 1780s. At first there was little in the way of formal entertainment, for the Kirk frowned on anything to do with theatre and even the richest apartments were small and cramped, so the life of society, and many professional and business transactions too, took place in the streets and, of course, in innumerable drinking-'howffs'.

A visiting Englishman remarked that Edinburgh streets were as crowded as a perpetual fair – and it was indeed a carnival of vivid contrasts, with St Giles' Cathedral and the town prison facing each other in the High Street, flanked by Parliament House and market-stalls; yet, despite the crowding, burglary, robbery and violent crime were relatively rare events, and the most common misdemeanours were drunkenness and falling into debt. Nevertheless the Edinburgh mob could be a political force to be reckoned with, as in the Porteous riot of 1736, when an army officer of that name opened fire in an attempt to disperse an unruly crowd attending an execution, only to be lynched himself; or when enraged citizens protested against the repeal of the anti-Catholic laws in 1779, by wrecking the house of the Moderator of the General Assembly and burning his library. Walter Scott compared life in these old streets and crowded rooms to 'the under deck of a ship. Sickness had no nook of quiet, affliction no retreat for solitary indulgence.' Yet there was a fierce energy to be found as well (at least for the survivors) in a milieu where everyone knew everyone else's business and where there was no room and little mercy for pretensions or class barriers.

English visitors admired an open-mindedness about Scottish intellectuals and noted that they had a wider range of acquaintances and intimates than was common in 'polite society' and the more rarefied circles of Dr Johnson's London. The talents of mid-eighteenth-century Scotland swung from the abstruse to the intensely practical: from divines, advocates and professors of moral philosophy to no-less-distinguished surgeons, chemists, inventors and civil engineers, many of whom came from humble origins and parish schools. By the 1760s, the School of Medicine at Edinburgh had replaced Leyden as the leading European centre for teaching and research. Glasgow too was an important centre, producing, among others, the famous Hunter brothers, who went to London to revolutionise surgery and anatomy. Chemistry was an equally distinguished field, with William Cullen as one of the great teachers of the subject, as was his successor Joseph Black, who befriended and helped the young James Watt. Black's work on carbon dioxide and latent heat was followed by Rutherford's on nitrogen and Hope's on strontium. The Edinburgh mathematician David Gregory had been friend and colleague to Newton and Halley at the beginning of the century, and James Hutton, who had studied under Gregory's successor, virtually founded modern geology.

These were the days before the need arose for narrow specialisation in the sciences, and in the traditional Scots term such men were all students of 'natural philosophy'. In applied technology James Watt is best known for his invention of the steam condenser. A merchant's son from Greenock, he had an equally learned interest in chemistry, architecture, music, law, metaphysics and language. By the mid seventies he had founded a firm with Boulton in Birmingham to manufacture his new improved steam engines. The next decade saw paddle steamships pioneered by Millar in Dumfriesshire, experiments which bore fruit with Symington's *Charlotte Dundas*, constructed in 1801 to tow barges on the new Forth–Clyde canal – the first practical steam vessel in the world. John Rennie from East Lothian served with Boulton and Watt for a while before becoming the most highly regarded civil engineer in the country, building harbours and canals throughout Britain; while Thomas Telford, a shepherd's son and a parish school-boy from Dumfriesshire, made himself a household name by the end of the century, constructing over a thousand bridges and hundreds of miles of roads and canals, including the Caledonian Canal, a vast system of waterways in Sweden and the Menai suspension bridge. Men such as these founded what was to become a nineteenth-century tradition of Scottish success in engineering and the applied sciences – witness McAdam, who gave his name to an improved road surface; Mackintosh, who waterproofed cloth; and Robert Stevenson, the second in three generations of civil engineers (and the grandfather of Robert Louis Stevenson), who built twenty-three lighthouses round the Scottish coast, including one on the notoriously wave-torn Bell Rock in 1810. Such respect for practical knowledge, and a belief that it should be available to all, was dear to the Presbyterian ethic and the Scots carried it into publishing with the *Encyclopaedia Britannica*, founded in 1771, while in 1810 the *Edinburgh Encyclopaedia* set out to summarise the whole of natural science and technology.

'Auld Reekie' was becoming seriously overcrowded, even by Scottish standards, but the growth in prosperity allowed better-off families to move south to new suburbs and more spacious houses, such as the ones in the homely neoclassical style of George Square. By the 1760s plans were made to expand in the opposite direction across the Nor' Loch (now Princes Street Gardens), and the poet James Thomson's nephew, a young architect called James Craig, won a gold medal for his plan of a 'New Town' to be built in the European neoclassical manner. At last Edinburgh was to have buildings appropriate to the spirit of the Enlightenment, and the old capital, which had been so shaken by the departure of crown and parliament, could express its new-found confidence and ambition in the geometrical symmetries and the grand scale of George Street, flanked by Princes Street and Queen Street and closed by a magnificent square at each end. It did not matter that at first the site was remote and exposed to the notorious Edinburgh winds, for it soon became the most fashionable place to live. Many of the men of the Enlightenment – including David Hume, Lord Kames, Lord Monboddo, Hugh Blair and William Robertson – had been familiar figures in the Canongate, the Lawnmarket and the old High Street, but they all ended their careers in the new and more stately surroundings of 'Georgian' Edinburgh. With buildings such as Register House, designed by Robert Adam, the New Town continued to expand into one of the finest neoclassical cityscapes in the world. If modern literary critics have found the combination of opposites to be a feature of Scottish culture, then no more striking physical example can be found than the two faces of Edinburgh, as clearly defined today as they were in the late eighteenth century, when those spacious Palladian and Grecian symmetries were overlooked by the towering, seething, chaotic tenements and wynds of the vernacular town – new Athens and Auld Reekie, indeed.

By the end of the century egalitarian feeling was afoot once again in Scotland. Stirred by social changes, the American War of Independence and particularly the French Revolution, the newly industrialised working classes and many middle-class liberals sought to extend the franchise to all men over twenty-one. The reform movement was beginning, many 'Societies of Friends of the People' were started, and the Edinburgh mob, never slow to express itself, rioted for three days after the king's birthday in 1792, to cries of 'Liberty, equality and no king!' The notorious Lord Braxfield presided over intolerant trials of freethinkers, sentencing Thomas Muir, a young advocate, to transportation for fourteen years and doing the same for three English delegates who attended a national convention in Edinburgh the following year. Outright republican sentiment gained force in Scotland, to the gradual alarm of liberal sympathisers. Tom Paine's *The Rights of Man* (1790) was especially sought after and even translated into Gaelic. The weavers – the most skilled and educated workers – were particularly active in radical circles and in the proto-revolutionary 'United Scotsmen' movement, whose Calvinist and dissenting roots went back to Rullion Green. However, the terror in France and the eventual rise of Napoleon dampened republican sympathies in the country at large and allowed the government to supress the 'United Scotsmen' by transporting many of them to Botany Bay in His Majesty's newest colony.

'If a man were permitted to make all the ballads,' wrote Fletcher of Saltoun in 1704, 'he need not care who should make the laws of a nation.' When, despite his best efforts, the lawmakers actually went to London, Scotland was left alone with her ballads to test the truth of Fletcher's claim. The result was a revival of interest in the vernacular tongue, especially among the educated middle classes, and literary and creative ambitions began to stir again, despite the Church's puritanical attitude towards 'profane' books and plays. Between 1706 and 1711 an Edinburgh printer and bookseller called James Watson produced three separate anthologies to satisfy the literary nationalism of new readers. The first volume of Watson's *Choice Collection of Comic and Serious Scots Poems both Ancient and Modern* began with a special plea: because the book was 'the first of its nature which has been published in our own native Scots Dialect', the editor hoped that the candid reader may 'give some charitable grains of allowance if the performance come not up to such a point of exactness as may please an over nice palate.' In fact *The Cherry and the Slae* needed no such apology, but for the most part the Scots poems are self-consciously homespun pieces such as 'Habbie Simson', 'Sanny Briggs' and 'The Country Wedding'. A mock elegy by Hamilton of Gilbertfield was especially influential, and when Watson published 'The Last Dying Words of Bonny Heck, A Famous Grey-Hound in the Shire of Fife' it sired an entire menagerie of philosophical talking animals. The convention had come from noble beginnings, and Burns was to rescue it again, but in the meantime the acute social observation of Henryson's animal fables had given way to pastiche and easy pathos:

> 'Alas, alas, 'quo' Bonny Heck,
> 'On Former days when I reflect!
> I was a Dog much in Respect
>   For doughty Deed:
> But now I must hing by the Neck
>   Without Remeed.

William Hamilton of Gilbertfield (1665?–1751) was a retired army lieutenant who assisted Allan Ramsay in compiling and 'improving' songs for his *Tea Table Miscellany*. Ramsay was so impressed by the aptness of standard Habbie in 'Bonny Heck' that he adopted it forthwith and popularised it in many of his own poems, including the 'familiar verse epistles' which the two enthusiasts exchanged, thereby establishing yet another mode which was to catch on widely. It was Hamilton's 1722 edition of Blind Harry's *Wallace* which excited Burns so much with a sense of national pride, and, since the text was abridged and anglicised, the ironic implications of this say a lot about the times. Scots pride was evoked again by Dr George Mackenzie (1669–1725), who produced three volumes of dubious biographies – *The Lives and Characters of the Most Eminent Writers of the Scots Nation*' (1708–22) – while Thomas Ruddiman (1674–1757), a better scholar and a Jacobite sympathiser, produced and glossed an edition of Douglas's *Eneados* in 1710. A developing taste for antiquarian romance was met by Lady Elizabeth Wardlaw (1677–1727), who wrote and published 'Hardyknute' as if it were an old, anonymous ballad 'fragment', and, although her deception did not endure, the poem appeared as such in the *Ever Green* collection. In a more contemporary vein, Lady Grizel Baillie (1665–1746) chose Scots to speak to a polite audience about the love-life of swains – 'Were na my heart licht I wad die'. The romance of 'ancient' poems, national pride, the vernacular comedy of common manners and rustic sentiment – these were the varied and swelling currents upon which a wigmaker in Edinburgh launched what has come to be known as the eighteenth-century revival of Scottish verse.

Allan Ramsay (1685–1758)

Sometime in his middle teens Allan Ramsay left his native Lanarkshire and arrived in Edinburgh to seek his living as a maker of periwigs. In 1710 he became a burgess of the town and two years after that he was married, established as a master wigmaker, and beginning to express an enthusiasm for the world of letters. Brought up on *The Bruce*, *Wallace* and the poems of David Lindsay, he was one of the many Scotsmen of his time who felt indignant at the loss of the Scottish parliament and at what he took to be a subsequent decline in the old capital city. He determined to master English literature and make Edinburgh less provincial. Thus the emblem of his new bookshop at the Luckenbooths in 1726 was a sign with two heads on it – Drummond of Hawthornden for Scotland and Ben Jonson for England. Yet for Ramsay, as for many of his countrymen, England was still the 'auld enemy' in a sentimental sense, even if his Lowland respect for trade and 'the frugal arts of peace' could not envisage reversing the Union. Such contradictions convey the essence of the eighteenth-century Scottish condition, and to some extent they survive in the popular consciousness to the present day. Thus Ramsay and his values play a significant part in the history of Scottish culture, even although he is a much less gifted poet than either Fergusson or Burns.

In 1712 Ramsay helped to found 'the Easy Club' – a group of mild Jacobites dedicated to 'mutual improvement in conversation' and to reading the *Spectator* aloud at each meeting. By 1718 he was calling himself poet and publisher on the strength of a collection of Scots songs and a piece called 'Tartana' – English heroic couplets in praise of the humble plaid. He also published an edition of 'Christis Kirk on the Green' with two extra Scots cantos of his own – added, he said, to show 'the Follies and Mistakes of low life in a just Light, making them appear as ridiculous as they really are.' Ramsay next adopted the form and manner of 'Habbie Simson' for a lively series of Scots poems on the notables of Edinburgh street life. These early 'elegies' celebrated 'Maggie Johnston' and 'Lucky Wood', who kept low alehouses, not to mention 'John Cowper', the Kirk's watchdog on wanton girls and professional ladies. 'Lucky Spence's Last Advice' plays to another convention, with the dying words of one of the city's most famous bawds providing her girls with the benefit of long experience:

O black Ey'd Bess and mim-Mou'd Meg,	affected prim in speech
O'er good to work, or yet to beg;	Too
Lay sunkots up for a sair leg,	something
For whan ye fail,	
Ye'r face will not be worth a feg,	fig
Nor yet ye'r tail.	

. . .

Whan e'er ye meet a fool that's fow, *drunk*
That ye're a maiden gar him trow, *make him believe*
Seem nice, but stick to him like glew;
    And whan set down,
Drive at the jango till he spew, *fornicate*
    Syne he'll sleep soun.

   Whan he's asleep then dive and catch
His ready cash, his rings or watch . . . .

Although the author seems to be in love with his own vulgar daring, there is, at least, plenty of life and good humour in such character-studies. By comparison the invocation to 'Tartana' is impossibly stilted, and, although the *double entendre* in the last line would be worthy of Lucky Spence, the dullness of the rest of the poem suggests that it was an accident only:

Ye Caledonian Beauties, who have long
Been both the Muse, and subject of my song,
Assist your Bard, who in harmonious Lays
Designs the Glory of your Plaid to raise.

By 1719 Ramsay and William Hamilton were exchanging elaborate compliments in the standard Habbie of their 'familiar epistles', reflecting, among other things, that

The chiefs of London, Cam and Ox,
Ha'e rais'd up great poetick stocks
Of *Rapes*, of *Buckets*, *Sarks* and *Locks*,
While we neglect
To shaw their betters . . . .

If there is a hint of insecurity in these lines, then a similar instability marks the 'Pastoral on the Death of Joseph Addison', in which Ramsay constructs a dialogue between 'Richy' and 'Sandy' – none other than 'Sir Richard Steele and Mr Alexander Pope' – discoursing like Lowland shepherds in an excruciating amalgam of broad Scots and Augustan English. Pastoral dialogue in rhyming couplets was used to better effect in 'Patie and Roger', which gains an unforced freshness from Ramsay's vernacular realism:

Last morning I was unco airly out,   very early
Upon a dyke I lean'd and glowr'd about;   wall
I saw my *Meg* come linkan o'er the lee,   tripping
I saw my *Meg*, but Maggie saw na me:
For yet the sun was wadin throw the mist,
And she was closs upon me e'er she wist,
Her coats were kiltit, and did sweetly shaw   petticoats; tucked up
Her straight bare legs, which whiter were than
    snaw . . . .

The popularity of his poems encouraged Ramsay to produce
a proper volume, and this duly appeared in 1721, pretentiously
provided with a portrait of the author, dedications by other
writers, footnotes, a glossary and a preface which defended the
use of Scots in pastoral verse as no less appropriate than the
Doric dialect used by Theocritus. Thus the language of
Henryson and Dunbar was to become increasingly associated
in Ramsay's mind, and in the minds of his readers, with bucolic
simplicity, rustic topics and a dialect of Greek noted for its old,
simple, solemn utterance. This assumption survived up to and
beyond the time of Burns, and, indeed, it complimented the
Edinburgh intelligentsia's picture of themselves as citizens of a
new Athens – urbane and educated and yet conversant, too,
with what they took to be 'Doric' from the countryside beyond.
    The 1721 edition was a success and Ramsay gave up
wigmaking to become a full-time writer and bookseller. He
started his new career by editing 'A Collection of Choice Songs'
(some of them his own) and publishing them as *The Tea Table
Miscellany* in 1724. Ramsay was no scholar, he did not include
the music to the songs and he frequently 'improved' the
originals – 'so that the modest voice and ear of the fair singer
might meet with no affront'. (The first collection of airs for
Scots songs appeared the following year in William Thomson's
Orpheus Caledonius, but the first fully responsible edition of texts
and music was not produced until David Herd's collection of
1769.) The *Miscellany* was popular and influential, eventually
running to four volumes (including English songs) and
twenty-four reprintings in the next eighty years. Ramsay
promptly followed it with two volumes of older Scottish poems
'wrote by the ingenious before 1600' and culled mostly from the
Bannatyne Manuscript. *The Ever Green* (1724) contained
superior ballads and many fine poems by Henryson and

Dunbar, but never achieved anything like the commercial success of the *Miscellany*. Once again Ramsay interfered with the texts, censoring some lines, paraphrasing others and even adding a verse prophecy of his own birth at the end of Dunbar's 'Lament for the Makaris'!

The success of 'Patie and Roger' encouraged Ramsay to produce a sequel in 1723, written from the point of view of the shepherds' girlfriends. The gentle satire of 'Jenny and Meggie' is more pointed than in the earlier piece, perhaps because Jenny's pessimism is closer to the reality of woman's lot:

O! tis a pleasant thing to be a bride;
Syne whindging getts about your ingle-side   whining offspring
Yelping for this or that with fasheous din,   troublesome
To make them brats then ye maun toil and spin.   rags
Ae we'an fa's sick, ane scads itsell wi broe,   scalds; broth
Ane breaks his shin, anither tynes his shoe;
The deel gaes o'er John Wobster, Hame grows
  Hell,
When *Pate* misca's ye war than tongue can tell.

Nevertheless, Patie's girlfriend eventually persuades Jenny to yield to romance by presenting the other side of the old coin:

Yes, 'tis a heartsome thing to be a wife,
When round the ingle-edge young sprouts are rife.
Gif I'm sae happy, I shall have delight,
To hear their little plaints, and keep them right.

These two eclogues gave birth to Ramsay's best-known work and provided him with the first two scenes of *The Gentle Shepherd* (1725) – a dramatic pastoral comedy in five acts. The author was persuaded to add songs in 1728 and to expand it into a ballad opera, whereupon it proved very popular for the next 150 years. The text saw many editions, some of them anglicised, performed by both amateur and professional groups all over Britain, making its author wealthy and famous at last.

The Gentle Shepherd perfectly encapsulates the strengths and weaknesses of Ramsay's muse, and the divided loyalties of his countrymen. The play's rural setting is idealised, but the plain Scots speech of the characters adds a physical conviction to the place and the people in it. Jenny's description of the woes of marriage and poverty is realistic, and yet the plot is an unashamed confection of Arcadian love-matches and hidden blue blood. Patie, the gentle shepherd, turns out to be the son of an exiled Cavalier gentleman, but still he refuses to forsake his milkmaid lover. The conflict between his lineage and his heart need not last long, for Peggy is an aristocratic foundling too, and in next to no time the shepherd and his lass are exchanging Augustan clichés in stilted Anglo-Scots, to the effect that 'Good manners give integrity a bleez [glow] / When native vertues join the Arts to please'. By this stage, not surprisingly, what vitality the play still possesses has passed to the low-life subplot, in which Bauldy seeks witchcraft to make Jenny love him instead of Roger. His energetic descriptions of the uncanny are firmly within a tradition that runs from Dunbar to Burns's 'Tam O' Shanter':

She can o'ercast the night, and cloud the moon,	
And mak the deils obedient to her crune.	devils; croon
At midnight hours, o'er the Kirk-yards she raves,	
And howks unchristen'd we'ans out of their	digs
graves;	
Boils up their livers in a warlock's pow.	skull
Rins wither shins about the hemlock low;	anti-clockwise
And seven times does her prayers backward	
pray,	
Till Plotcock comes with lumps of Lapland clay,	
Mixt with the venom of black taids and	toads
snakes	

(ii. ii)

Notwithstanding the 'black taids', enlightenment prevails, and the poor peasant is disabused with: 'What silly notions crowd the clouded mind, / That is thro' want of Education blind!', and then he is chastised 'because he brak good breeding's laws'. The modern readers will be forgiven for preferring the imaginative force of Bauldy's fantasies to the vapid moralising of Ramsay's gentlefolk, and yet later in the century Adam Smith and Hugh Blair spoke for educated Edinburgh by decrying the passages using a 'homely' style which was 'rustic' and 'not intelligible'. 'It is the duty of a poet', opined Smith, 'to write like a gentleman', and his assumption that this was not possible in Scots was even shared at times by Burns. In this context the wide success of *The Gentle Shepherd* ensured that Scots would continue to present an exclusively bucolic face.

Ramsay moved to new premises at the Luckenbooths – a group of lockable shops near the Mercat Cross and St Giles' – and began the earliest known circulating library in Britain, from which readers could borrow books at twopence a night. The narrow-minded took exception to such pleasures, particularly his interest in the theatre, and on at least two occasions Ramsay's shop was raided by the righteous, who claimed that 'villainous profane and obscene bookes and playes printed at London by Curle and others, are gote downe from London by Allan Ramsey, and lent out, for an easy price, to young boyes, servant weemen of the better sort, and gentlemen, and vice and obscenity dreadfully propagated'. The publisher was not to be deterred from his cultural convictions, and when his teenage son showed a talent for drawing and painting he helped to found the 'Academy of St Luke' (1729) for the graphic arts and the training of students. In due course young Allan continued his studies in Italy and became a famous and respected painter in London.

A new collection of poems appeared in 1728, including 'The Last Speech of a Wretched Miser' in what was now a thriving genre of character monologue. ('Holy Willie's Prayer' owes something to this particular poem.) Ramsay also supported various theatrical ventures in their struggle against Presbyterian prejudice and opened a theatre of his own at Carruber's Close, only to have it threatened in 1737 by those who feared its popularity and invoked the new Licensing Act to try to shut it down. The poet resisted for three years and gave vent to his rage in the (unpublished) 'Epistle to Mr H. S.' (1738):

> Thus whore, and bawd, doctor and pox
> The tavern and a large white ox,
> Are the whole sum for Lord or clown
> Of the diversions of our town,
> Since by a late sour-snouted law
> Which makes great heroes stand in awe
> The morall teachers of broad Truths
> Have golden padlocks on their mouths . . . .

At the age of fifty-five Ramsay withdrew from active business and retired to his fine new house – an octagonal dwelling on

Castle Hill, nicknamed 'the goose pie' by irreverent locals who had to live in the teeming streets below it. Ramsay and his bookshop at the Luckenbooths had been a vital focus for the liberal arts in the early years of the century and the cultural flowering of Edinburgh could no longer be much delayed by frosts from the pulpit. The Licensing Act, for example, was soon countered by the gambit of selling theatre tickets as 'concert' tickets followed by a 'free' play, and numerous Edinburgh lawyers – an influential new audience – supported the deception and enjoyed a night at the theatre.

Pre-Romantics and others

Ramsay had committed himself and the best of his writing to the Edinburgh he loved, but other men looked elsewhere and **James Thomson** (1700–48) left for the south just two months before *The Gentle Shepherd* was completed. The son of a minister in the Borders, Thomson abandoned his career as a divinity student in favour of a literary life in London. He found a job as a tutor, joined circles in which Pope moved, and made an early reputation for himself with four poems begun in 1725 and collected as *The Seasons* in 1730. (They were to be revised quite extensively over the next sixteen years.) Thomson's neoclassical blank verse is conventional enough with poetic diction, personification and echoes of Milton's elevated tone, but a more original note is struck by his painterly eye for the play of weather and light on the landscape and a host of moral, patriotic and scientific observations, all determined to prove that the harmony of God can be shown in the natural world. Such views owe something to the Earl of Shaftesbury's writings at the beginning of the century and were promoted in Scotland by Frances Hutcheson. Thomson's 'philosophy of nature' was an untidy mixture but it proved to be a popular one, and *The Seasons* is often said to anticipate the Romantic 'discovery' of nature. With this, Thomson passes into the history of literature in England, although his descriptions of landscape were also to influence the Gaelic poetry of Alasdair MacMhaighster Alasdair. Of Thomson's later works *The Castle of Indolence* (1748) is a pleasant Spenserian pastiche; *Liberty* (1735–6) is thankfully forgotten; and *The Masque of Alfred* (1740), co-written with Malloch, is remembered only for the words of 'Rule Britannia'.

If the author's Scottish origins can be identified in *The Seasons*, they appear in his didactic Christian rationalism and in a tendency to add more and more examples to his account of the countryside and its weather. 'Winter', published in 1726, was the first of the poems to be completed and it joins a long Scottish line – going back to Henryson and Douglas – in the poetic description of bad weather:

> At last, the muddy deluge pours along,
> Resistless, roaring; dreadful down it comes
> From the chapt mountain, and the mossy wild,
> Tumbling thro' rocks abrupt, and sounding far:
> Then o'er the sanded valley, floating spreads,
> Calm, sluggish, silent; till again constrained,
> Betwixt two meeting hills, it bursts a way,
> Where rocks, and woods o'erhang the turbid stream.
> There gathering triple force, rapid, and deep,
> It boils, and wheels, and foams, and thunders thro'.

(1726 edn)

Thomson's words, punctuated with weighty pauses, establish a chain in the development of the Romantic imagination which stretches from the actuality of the Scottish Borders to Wordsworth's spirit in the Alps and the full-blown symbolism of Coleridge's sacred river.

Another small link in the evolution of the pre-Romantic sensibility was contributed by **Robert Blair** (1700?–46) with the publication of *The Grave* (1743), a blank-verse meditation on mortality. (The 1808 edition was illustrated by Blake.) Blair was a Kirk minister in East Lothian, and, although the pulpit voice can be heard in most of his verse, *The Grave* enjoyed a considerable following. He featured in the so-called 'Graveyard School', along with the Englishman Edward Young, whose *Night Thoughts: On Life, Death and Immortality* (1742–4) influenced the Gaelic poet Duguld Buchanan and catered to a vogue for religiose melancholy. This genre was refined in Gray's 'Elegy' (1751) and popularised by the Gothic novel at the end of the century.

Fourteen years after Thomson, a young surgeon's apprentice called **Tobias Smollett** (1721–71) left Glasgow with a verse tragedy in his luggage, and set out for London to try to get the play performed. He had little luck, and 1741 saw him enlisted in the navy as a surgeon's mate, serving in the West Indies in the war against Spain. Five years later he was back in London with a moneyed wife and a not very successful practice, for surgeons were regarded as the tradesmen of the medical profession in those days. Smollett turned to satirical fiction and achieved success at last with a picaresque semi-autobiographical novel about the travels of a young Scotsman. *The Adventures of Roderick Random* (1748) assured him of an early place in the development of the English novel (*Clarissa* appeared the same year) and Smollett happily joined the *literati* of London to become another of those Scotsmen whose noblest prospect, according to his friend Samuel Johnson, was the high road leading him to England. Yet Smollett did not entirely forget his native country, for he came north on various occasions and was prompted to write an indignant poem against the slaughter at Culloden. His last visit, a trip of some seven months in search of health, provided him with material for the tour undertaken by Matthew Bramble in the final novel, *The Expedition of Humphrey Clinker* (1771).

As editor of the *Critical Review*, Smollett had fallen foul of the Scottish establishment in 1759 by criticising a long Homeric epic which had been produced by **William Wilkie** (1721–72), a Kirk minister from just outside Edinburgh. No less a man than David Hume wrote in defence of the poem, but it must be admitted that his judgement as a critic was unduly influenced by patriotism, friendship and an overdeveloped respect for classical learning done out in English heroic couplets. Nevertheless, Wilkie was a remarkable person: he came from a peasant farming family, and his devotion to learning and his erudition eventually gained him a chair in the sciences at St Andrew's University, even if his eccentric behaviour made him equally notable. He produced fables in verse, including 'The Hare and the Partan' in Scots, but his *magnum opus*, nine books on the siege of Thebes called *The Epigoniad* (1757), remains as dead as the seven heroes who razed that ancient city.

Another of Hume's enthusiasms was a blank-verse tragedy called *Douglas* by his cousin **John Home** (1722–1808) which had scored a notable success on the Edinburgh stage in 1756 before going on to London and Covent Garden. Home was a minister in Berwickshire, a lively, generous, romantic and popular man, remembered with affection by Henry Mackenzie, who wrote a biography of him. Home's next five verse tragedies were not so well received, but his namesake, the famous philosopher, still maintained that *Douglas* was better than Shakespeare and Otway because the Scots play was 'refined from the unhappy barbarism of the one, and the licentiousness of the other'. The tragedy is Romantic in spirit, for it concentrates on evoking wonder at the wild landscape and pity at the plight of the characters; but its structure is essentially neoclassical – elevated, stately and completely static. Notwithstanding its less-than-inflammatory style, there was scandal at the Edinburgh performance when the 'unco guid' heard that some ministers, including the liberal thinker 'Jupiter' Carlyle, had been seen in the theatre. It must be admitted that time has not been kind to the literary judgements of Hume and his educated friends, for most of their favourites are now forgotten, including Professor James Beattie's Spenserian imitation *The Minstrel* (1771–4) and the Augustan verses of blind Dr Thomas Blacklock (1721–91), equally praised by Dr Johnson. But fortunately Hume's taste is not the only yardstick of the man, and a closer look at his milieu and at his contemporaries from the 1720s to the 1770s will show where the real strengths of mid-century Edinburgh were to be found.

The Scottish Enlightenment

Francis Hutcheson (1694–1746) an Irishman who took the chair of moral philosophy at Glasgow in 1729, was the first professor to teach in English instead of Latin. His thinking was developed from Shaftesbury's philosophy, which linked man's moral nature to his aesthetic responses. Hutcheson stressed individual experience and our responses to beauty and happiness, and he believed in a social, caring person whose common humane feelings, rather than any exercise of logic, would encourage them to act for 'the greatest happiness of the greatest number'. (The phrase predates Bentham's more rational utilitarian system by some forty years.) He held that the existence of this moral sense reveals the essence of mankind and the goodness of God. More than an echo of these beliefs can be

heard in Burns's call for 'Ae spark o' Nature's fire, / That's a'
the learning I desire.' Indeed, the primacy of instinctive
sympathetic feeling as a gauge of morality became central to
how northern writers understood themselves, the common
people and the Scottish psyche in general. This tendency
reached a peak of sorts with Mackenzie and degenerated into
sentimentalism by Victorian times, but Burns, Scott, Hogg and
Galt all testify to its healthier influence. Given the holiness of
the heart's affections in their original sense, it follows that
Hutcheson, like Burns, Keats or Shelley for that matter, was
against external authoritarianism, whether on the part of
governments or landowners or even in the family.

Professor Hutcheson was one of the first to contribute to
what became known as the 'Scottish Enlightenment' and to
what was to become a particularly northern exploration of
moral philosophy, the nature of man and the nature of
knowledge itself. Such interests are not entirely divorced from
the intellectual inheritance of Calvinism and the Reformation,
but the new direction was more speculative and humane, being
broadly applied to society at large, and, indeed, Hutcheson was
influential in the growth of a moderate party within the Church
of Scotland itself.

The greatest figure of the time, however, was most certainly
not a Christian moderate, for all that he was a mild and amiable
man with many friends. **David Hume** (1711–76) dismissed all
religion in his works and even struck at the foundations of
reason itself. As a result Presbyterian reaction ensured that he
never did become a university professor, despite at least two
promising opportunities. Hume was the impecunious son of a
small Berwickshire laird. He studied briefly at Edinburgh, but
his enthusiasm for literature overcame his more sober intention
to follow law. He then tried a post as a merchant's clerk in
Bristol before escaping to France, where he stayed for the next
three years. There, still in his middle twenties, he completed his
most important book, three volumes published in London as
The Treatise of Human Nature (1739–40). The work had little
immediate effect, however, and so on returning to his home at
Ninewells in Berwickshire he produced a more accessible series
of essays on moral and political issues. After another two years
abroad he established himself in Edinburgh, became Keeper of
the Advocate's Library and started on his monumental *History*

of Great Britain under the Stuarts (1754–62). The first volume was not well received, partly because his account of the country's religious disputes treated both factions with equal contempt, but eventually the project gained favour not least because of its interest in cultural changes, and it brought him useful income over the years.

Further philosophical works appeared: the *Political Discourses* (1751) prepared the way for Adam Smith's economics, and *An Enquiry Concerning Human Understanding* (1748) and *An Enquiry Concerning the Principles of Morals* (1752) further advanced a radical critique of the age's confidence in reason. Hume's scepticism follows Locke, Shaftesbury and Hutcheson in so far as he too stresses the empirical evidence of our individual experience, but his conclusions take him much further. Thus, for example, in dismissing the possibility of miracles, he undermines religion too by defining the act of Christian faith in an individual as a process 'which subverts all the principles of his understanding, and gives him a determination to believe what is most contrary to custom and experience' (*Enquiry Concerning Human Understanding*). Hume's scepticism is fundamental, for it derives from a radical reassessment of the nature of reason itself. From his earliest work he insists that what we call 'cause and effect' is really only based on our own psychological expectations. Thus, to invent a simplified example, when one billiard ball strikes another it always makes it move, and from repeated observation of the fact we infer certain 'laws' of physics. But Hume says that such 'laws' are only upheld by 'custom' – that is, by our supposition that the future will be conformable to the past. A statistician may assure us that colliding billiard balls have imparted motion in every recorded instance, but the only *cause* he has really identified is the cause of our own *expectations* that such events should always continue to be so. Thus Newton's 'laws of motion' depend on no less than an act of imaginative faith on our part – not so very different, after all, from a belief in miracles. Admittedly this imaginative act does not *feel* the same to us as, say, the idle notion that the billiard balls will turn into hedgehogs when they meet; but the apparent difference between these two expectations is simply a matter of what we used to and not a matter of reason. Therefore, according to Hume, 'logic' itself turns out to be upheld only by reference to what he calls 'custom'.

It is not surprising that such 'notorious' ideas were publicly attacked in 1752 by the General Assembly of the Kirk of Scotland. Nevertheless, Hume was well-enough received in Edinburgh circles, even by some of the more liberal churchmen. By all accounts the philosopher was a calm, genial and sociable man, whose shattering scepticism was not at all dogmatic nor in the least consonant with his comfortable girth and a face, seen in the Allan Ramsay portrait, which was described as that of 'a turtle-eating alderman'; indeed, in the world of practical politics he was a Tory who could see no reason why men could not organise society so that it ran quietly and efficiently. The academic reaction to Hume's books was led by **Thomas Reid** (1710–96), an Aberdeen graduate who succeeded Adam Smith in the chair of moral philosophy at Glasgow. Reid's *Enquiry into the Human Mind, on the Principles of Common Sense* (1764) set out to refute Hume by maintaining that his system (like Bishop Berkeley's) reduces our certitude about the world to a matter of mental sensations and ideas. In place of this Reid invokes 'common sense' to point to the experential difference between the *idea* of touching something and the actual physical act itself – thus Newton's world of actual objects and causal relationships is restored to us. These views were influential in establishing a 'Scottish School' of philosophy which managed to bypass, if not to bridge, the abyss of Hume's scepticism.

In the meantime Hume lived in Paris for two years, where he was lionised by intellectual society and recognised as one of the most trenchant thinkers in Europe. In 1766 he returned to London with Rousseau, whom he befriended until the Frenchman's paranoia led to a parting of the ways. Two years later Hume returned to Edinburgh, where he spent his last eight years and where he died calmly in the sure expectation of eternal extinction. His final demolition of Christian orthodoxy was published posthumously, and the *Dialogues on Natural Religion* (1779) show that the old man kept his wry doubts to the end. Not so the establishment, where the 'common sense' school prevailed, popularised by **James Beattie** (1735–1803), professor of moral philosophy at Aberdeen, minor poet and author of the book against Scotticisms. Beattie's *Essay on Truth* (1770) attacked Hume's 'sophistical arguments' and offered in their place a blindingly inane definition of truth as that 'which the condition of our nature determines us to believe'.

Notwithstanding Beattie's comfortable definition of truth, Hume's clashes with the Kirk, as well as his historical writing and his interests in politics and economics, are characteristic of the Scottish scene at a time when new ideas were afoot and moral philosophy was taken to be central to an understanding of man and society. The Kirk no longer had the monopoly on such issues and was itself divided over matters of internal and external policy and doctrine. Philosophical historians followed, such as **Adam Ferguson** (1723–1816), yet another Edinburgh professor of moral philosophy, who has been called the founder of sociology. His *Essay on the History of Civil Society* (1766) proposed a comparative, almost anthropological, approach to the study of man as a being who creates social structures and moral imperatives for himself – the complete opposite of Rousseau's view of man as an isolated being who is best when least tainted by 'civilisation'. **William Robertson** (1721–93), a minister who became Principal of Edinburgh University and Moderator of the General Assembly, published a successful *History of Scotland* (1759), followed by a *History of the Reign of the Emperor Charles V* (1769) and a *History of America* (1777); next to Gibbon, perhaps, he was the most outstanding historian of his day. Unlike Hume, Robertson could see beyond the excesses of the Scottish Reformation to sympathise with the democratic impulse behind the Presbyterian ideal. He was a sociable and upright character and, although he could be forceful enough in the General Assembly, he employed his eloquence in support of the moderate cause in the Kirk. **Sir David Dalrymple, Lord Hailes** (1726–92) went to original sources to provide his *Annals of Scotland* (1776–9). A Law Lord and an antiquarian, he also collected ballads and edited the Bannatyne Manuscript. A fellow advocate and judge, **Henry Home, Lord Kames** (1696–1782) combined all the interests of philosopher, historian and literary critic. His *Historical Law Tracts* (1758) established a common historical pattern in the links between the evolution of man's institutions and his economic condition. Friend of Hume, Boswell and Benjamin Franklin, patron to Adam Smith and John Millar, Kames took an active and varied part in Edinburgh life, espousing literary criticism, crossing swords with the Kirk and then with Voltaire, publishing tracts on agricultural improvements, and all with equal panache. Kames's engagement is typical of the breadth of interest shown by professional men at the time, and they formed a 'Select Society' to provide an appropriate forum in which the only taboo subjects were religion and Jacobitism. Also in the Select Society was **James Burnett, Lord Monboddo** (1714–99), a famously lively man of the Law, keenly interested in ancient Greek philosophy and the origins of language and primitive societies. His anthropological theories were seriously limited by his dependence on second-hand sources and by his own enthusiastic gullibility, but he is remembered now, as he was ridiculed then, for his theory that the orang-outang is a primitive member of the human species, a form of the noble savage not quite evolved enough for speech.

The philosophical study of society came to fruition in the works of **Adam Smith** (1723–90), who held the chair of logic and then of moral philosophy at Glasgow. In fact it was Smith who founded the Select Society, along with Kames and Hume and Allan Ramsay's son in 1754, as well as contributing to the *Edinburgh Review* in its first short-lived incarnation the following year. The financial success of his *Theory of Moral Sentiments* (1759) allowed him to leave the university to travel in France as tutor and companion to the duke of Buccleuch, who rewarded him with an annuity. In 1766 Smith returned to his birthplace in Kirkcaldy to produce the *Inquiry into the Nature and Causes of the Wealth of Nations* (1776). The modern study of political economy was virtually begun by this book, with its penetrating observation of the conflicts and balances between the individual's urge to accumulate wealth and the wider needs of society, or between the benefits of material prosperity and the needs of workers condemned to labour at monotonous tasks. Smith's prose is succinct and clear-eyed, just as his view of the moral case for social equity is wryly practical:

Is this improvement in the circumstances of the lower ranks of the people to be regarded as an advantage or as an inconveniency to the society? The answer seems at first sight abundantly plain. Servants, labourers and workmen of different kinds, make up the far greater part of every great political society. But what improves the circumstances of the greater part can never be regarded as an inconveniency to the whole. No society can surely be flourishing and happy, of which the greater part of the members are poor and miserable. It is but equity, besides, that they who feed, clothe, and lodge the whole body of the people, should have such a share of the produce of their own labour as to be themselves tolerably well fed, clothed, and lodged.

One of Smith's students at Glasgow went on to make his own study of class-structure in a book called *Observations Concerning the Distinction of Ranks in Society* (1771). **John Millar** (1735–1801), who became professor of civil law at Glasgow, was more radical than many of his fellow intellectuals, for he openly upheld the early egalitarian principles of the French Revolution and joined the Society of the Friends of the People in 1792 at a time when the establishment was bent on their suppression. Millar was a brilliant lecturer and his classes were packed with enthusiastic students.

Romanticism and the cult of feeling

By the 1770s the influence of Rousseau was making itself widely felt in the emergence of the pre-Romantic sensibility. It is ironic that, in using reason to undermine the supremacy of reason itself, even Hume contributed something to a popular interest in personal and passionate experience, uninfluenced by education and society and everything that the Scottish Enlightenment valued so highly. Even Adam Smith seemed to have endorsed the importance of sensibility in an early book, *The Theory of Moral Sentiments* (1759), in which he pleaded for the power of imaginative empathy as a form of moral control. John Home's *Douglas* had invoked the heroic and the pathetic in a wild setting, and Thomas Gray struck another early chord with the Celticism of his poem 'The Bard' (1757). But it was a farmer's son from Inverness who spoke most directly to the new taste, and his 'translations' of Gaelic epic verse entranced the drawing-rooms of Britain and Europe, throwing them open to vistas from another world – Celtic, heroic, ancient and sublime.

James Macpherson (1736–96), encouraged by John Home's support, made his literary reputation in 1760 with a little book called *Fragments of Ancient Poetry Collected in the Highlands of Scotland and Translated from the Gaelic or Erse Language*. These purported to be a few love-poems and battle-verses from the Ossianic tales of the third century, handed down in the Bardic oral tradition, or copied by later scribes and now translated by Macpherson. In an unsigned preface Hugh Blair announced that the young man was keen to translate still more pieces – 'if encouragement were given to such an undertaking'. The *literati* were excited by the evidence of such native genius and encouragement duly came in the form of a subscription. Macpherson, a handsome tutor and schoolteacher in his mid twenties, became a full-time writer and surrendered himself to fame. *Fingal* (1762) was followed by *Temora* and finally in 1765 the *Works of Ossian* were collected in two volumes.

Home and Beattie were enthusiastic and in 1763 Hugh Blair, the professor of rhetoric at Edinburgh, wrote a critical disserta-tion in praise of 'Macpherson's Ossian'. The Germans were even more impressed – an edition appeared in Frankfurt in 1773 – and 'Ossian' joined Rousseau's 'noble savage' as a key figure in the evolution of Romanticism from Goethe to the Gothic novel. Yet, when all is said and done, the poems were neither very good nor very authentic, although some of them were at least based on the Fenian cycle of heroic tales which came to Scotland with the Irish Gaels. As a boy in Inverness when the Forty-five broke out, Macpherson did know some Gaelic and he had contact with the oral tradition, as well as considerable sympathy for Highland culture. But he could never produce the manuscripts he claimed he had seen and the poems remain essentially his own work: a vision of a lost age of gentle and valiant warriors. (He had already tried his hand at sentimental heroism in 1758 with an unsuccessful poem called 'The Highlanders'.) 'Ossian's' style turns out to be a form of neoclassical prose poetry mixing Homeric action with love, noble pathos and a melancholy landscape. Now at last the 'Athens of the North' could lay claim, in Madame de Stael's phrase, to 'l'Homère du Nord':

> By the side of a rock on the hill,
> beneath the aged trees, old Ossian
> sat on the moss; the last of the race
> of Fingal. Sightless are his aged eyes;
> his beard is waving in the wind. Dull
> through the leafless trees he heard
> the voice of the North.

Dr Johnson also heard a voice from the North and he denounced it as a forgery by a man who loved Scotland more than the truth, whereupon Ossian's translator threatened to beat him with a stick if they should meet. But Johnson's judgement could not impede the astonishing success of the poems – Burns, Scott and Byron were all devotees and Napoleon is said to have carried a copy with him everywhere.

Authentic or not, Ossian also spoke to antiquarian interests and was as influential in this as Bishop Percy's *Reliques* (1765 *et seq.*) and Lord Hailes's *Ancient Scottish Poems* (1770). Ironically, nine years before 'Ossian' appeared, the verses of the great Gaelic poet MacMhaighstir Alasdair had been banned in Edinburgh as Jacobite propaganda. The final irony is that Macpherson's popularity created a vogue among lesser Gaelic poets for compositions in its archaic style, and some of his 'fragments' in English were 'retranslated' into Gaelic.

The heart began to claim its own in the second half of the so-called Age of Reason, and by the 1770s the novel-reading public had acquired a powerful appetite for pathos, nobility and sentiment. Richardson's books started the vogue in England. Similar ingredients impressed the Parisians who read Rousseau's novel *Julie, ou la Nouvelle Héloise* (1761) and the genre was brought to new intensities by the first novel of a young Edinburgh lawyer called **Henry Mackenzie** (1745–1831). Mackenzie was a blithe and practical person, a keen sportsman who could remember hunting for hare and ducks on the ground where the New Town had just been built, but he too in his younger years liked to experience the luxury of vicarious feeling. His novel *The Man of Feeling* (published anonymously in 1771) purports to be the biography of a sensitive youth called Harley, except that its 'manuscript' has been broken up and only odd chapters and sections remain. This device gives Mackenzie a certain episodic freedom, for his main intention was to introduce 'a man of sensibility into different scenes where his feelings might be seen in their effects, and his sentiments occasionally delivered without the stiffness of regular deduction.' Indeed the 'sentiments' are regularly delivered in a whole series of affecting scenes as the hero on his first visit to London makes his way among the streets and confidence-tricksters of the metropolis. His adventures include a visit to a madhouse and a brothel, where he saves a young lady by reuniting her with her father. The key term is 'sensibility', for Harley wears his sympathies on his sleeve and Mackenzie's prose invites readers to establish their own emotional credentials by feeling for the sad lives and 'complicated misfortunes' of those he meets on his travels. (The tale is not without satirical irony and echoes of Sterne and Goldsmith.) Harley is absent-minded and more than a little green, yet his generous nature conveys a silent rebuke to his fellow

men, who clothe their selfish interest and self-deceit in what
Harley sees as a 'fabric of folly', as they pursue 'delusive ideas',
which range from sexual seduction to the expansion of the
British Empire. Harley is not made for this world; he retreats to
his father's house, where he pines with unrequited love, catches
a fever and expires with a sigh in the arms of his beloved.
Eschewing 'the intricacies of a novel', the biographer is left to
tell the tale of a 'few incidents in a life undistinguished, except
by some feature of the heart'.

There was a positive fashion for weeping over the sad
passages of *The Man of Feeling*, and Burns had two copies,
calling it 'a book I prize next to the Bible'. In his turn
Mackenzie praised the first collection of Burn's poems in 1786,
marvelling at the 'unimitable delicacy' and the 'rapt and
inspired melancholy' of the 'heaven-taught ploughman, from a
humble and unlettered station'. This gentle creature scarcely
sounds like the Burns we know, but it does testify to the
contemporary propensity for adopting a sentimental attitude to
what Adam Smith called 'the language of nature and simplicity
and so forth' – a process started by Ramsay and equally in line
with the European fashion for the primitive. Mackenzie's next
book, *The Man of the World* (1773), introduced a counterpart to
Harley; a play called *The Prince of Tunis* appeared the same year
and four years later he produced an epistolary novel, *Julia de
Roubigné*. But his best writing is to be found in the later essays
and tales, and his sketches of Scottish life and character
prepared the way for Galt and Scott. Indeed, the latter
dedicated *Waverley* to him as 'the Scottish Addison'. By the late
1780s Mackenzie was a successful lawyer and a well-known
figure in Edinburgh and London. He founded the *Mirror*
(1779–80) and then the *Lounger* (1785–7), both periodicals in
the manner of the *Spectator*, and he became an honoured and
popular elder statesman in the arts, linking the age of Hume
and Smith with that of Burns and Scott – the 'second
generation' of the Enlightenment. As a critic Mackenzie
fostered an interest in Schiller and German literature and was
one of the first to appreciate Byron, Scott and Chatterton. He
welcomed Burns too, mostly for the elements of sentiment in his
work, but his Addisonian bias led him to underestimate the
broader reductive comedy of Fergusson, seeing it as somewhat
tainted by 'blackguardism'. In other respects, too, he demon-

strated a genteel insecurity about the essentially populist spirit of his native city, for he felt that the locals knew the author too well to credit him with wit and confessed that the name of the Canongate seemed to him to lack the sense of 'classic privilege' conveyed by 'the Strand'.

James Boswell (1740–95) is often taken to be the quintessential example of the busy, confident Scot determined to make his name in the Strand and to ingratiate himself with the literary giants of London. Yet this picture does not do justice to a gifted and complicated writer, prey to fits of heavy drinking and plagued by depression. As the son of Lord Auchinleck, a Court of Session judge, Boswell was ordered to become an advocate in Edinburgh, but his heart was given to a life of letters and travel. He had met Johnson in London while still in his twenties, and his appetite for fame and foreign places took him to Europe and to a somewhat contrived acquaintanceship with Rousseau and Voltaire. He produced pamphlets and articles, and a visit to Corsica in 1765 led him to champion the cause of Corsican independence three years later, when General Paoli raised his countrymen against French occupation. The *Account of Corsica* was published in 1768 and brought the young Scot a literary reputation as well as a certain notoriety (partly because of the dress he affected) as 'Corsica Boswell'. In the 1770s he wrote many essays for the *London Magazine* and visited the capital whenever he could, becoming the friend and confidant of Dr Johnson and eventually persuading the old man to undertake their famous trip to Scotland in 1773. The *Journal of the Tour to the Hebrides* (1785) demonstrates Boswell's talent as a gossipy and good-humoured *raconteur* and reveals him, despite the good doctor's frequent discouragements, as a proud Scot eager to show his country in a favourable light. Gradually he gave himself less to Law and more to his biography of Johnson, and four years after the great man died he moved to London to further his researches. Boswell's voluminous letters, notebooks, diaries and journals (many of them available only in this century) testify to an unflagging industry as he documents absolutely everything that caught his fancy. At times he seems breathlessly naïve and tasteless, as when he pestered the dying Hume with questions about his atheism and whether he wanted to change his mind about it in the face of eternity; but his value as a writer also lies in this openness and in his ability to make even the most trivial of encounters vivid, entertaining and revealing. *The Life of Johnson* appeared in 1791 to become the most famous biography ever written, and there is a strong case for saying that the Dr Johnson so popularly known and widely quoted today was actually assembled (if not created) by Boswell's fluent, vain and paradoxically selfless talent.

Gaelic poetry

Bardic verse declined because Highland society was changing, as the blind harper had found when his young chief set out for London. Poets still celebrated clan loyalties of course, and still addressed their work to men who were likely to help them eat, but the old aristocratic tradition was dead, and, when Mac-Donald of Sleat made John MacCodrum his bard in 1763, it was a historical gesture rather than a cultural obligation. The new poets were writing for a more popular audience, and, as ordinary people themselves, were open to new influences and a wider range of subjects than ever before. Alasdair Mac-Mhaighstir Alasdair produced Jacobite poems with all the old warlike swagger, but he was impressed enough by James Thomson's *Seasons* to write poems of natural description as well. Like many of his contemporaries he called his verses 'songs', and specified, like Burns, the airs to which they could be set. From now on the term 'bard' lost its strict technical sense and came to mean simply a composer of poems. Duncan Bàn Macintyre followed Alasdair's lead in nature description; William Ross shows a familiarity with Burns and the Augustan neoclassical tradition, and even Rob Donn, an unlettered man, has echoes of Pope in his poems. Comedy, satire, lampoon, Evangelical religion, everyday community life and love-poems all join the Gaelic canon in the eighteenth century.

   This vernacular Gaelic was much less formal than the bardic syllabic metres with their 'high style' of address, but technique was still valued. The new poems emphasise stressed rhythms – often with four stresses to a line – and internal rhymes, or assonances, are carried over from line to line throughout the verse. A brief example from John MacCodrum's 'Duan na

Bainnse' ('A Wedding Rime') will show how this works, with the different rhyming vowels italicised in the Gaelic text:

> Chaidh mi sìos do Ph*a*ibil
>   Ann am m*a*duinn 's i ro fh*ua*r;
> Chomhdhalaich mo gh*o*istidh mi,
>   E fhéin is L*o*chlann R*ua*dh;
> Ghabh sinn chum na t*u*laich
>   Far 'n robh cr*u*inneachadh math sl*ua*igh:
> Ma rinn iad dearmad b*u*ideil oirnn
>   So m'*u*irsgeul dhuibh g'a l*ua*idh.

> I went down to Paible
>   One morning when 'twas very cold;
> My boon companion met me,
>   He and Lachlan Ruadh;
> We made for the knoll
>   Where there was a goodly gathering of people:
> As they missed us with the bottle
>   Here is my tale to tell of it.

(trs. W. Matheson)

If the internal rhymes are schematised, their pattern makes two quatrains with the 'ua' sound (shown as rhyme *b*) appearing at the end of every second line and the other rhymes distributed as follows:

line 1	$-a-$
line 2	$a-b$
line 3	$-c-$
line 4	$c-b$
line 5	$-d-$
line 6	$d-b$
line 7	$-e-$
line 8	$e-b$

Reputed to be MacCodrum's first effort in verse, this song caused great offence in his small community by lampooning a wedding-party at which the poet got nothing to drink because he turned up as an uninvited guest.

The first-ever publication of contemporary Gaelic verse was

a collection of MacMhaighstir Alasdair's work which he had printed in Edinburgh during a brief visit in 1751. Religious poems by Duguld Buchanan were next to appear in book form in 1767, and in the following year, also in Edinburgh, Duncan Bàn Macintyre's poems were copied out for him (he was unlettered) and published in the city which was now his home. Despite the contemporary enthusiasm for Macpherson's *Ossian*, the authentic genius of these poets passed relatively unnoticed in Lowland literary circles; but, as far as Gaelic speakers were concerned, the availability of work in print was a most welcome affirmation of cultural identity, and this modest growth continued, even after the Forty-five. MacMhaighstir Alasdair had already had a hand in the publication of a Gaelic–English vocabulary in 1741; Duguld Buchanan helped produce a Gaelic New Testament in 1767; Alasdair's son produced an anthology of older Gaelic verse (and some more poems of his father's) in 1776; and Macintosh's collection of Gaelic proverbs appeared in 1785. Gaelic prose, on the other hand, remained scarce and mostly confined to religious tracts, a state of affairs which lasted almost until modern times.

Alexander MacDonald (Alasdair MacMhaighstir Alasdair, 1695?–1770?)

MacMhaighstir Alasdair called his collection of poems *Ais-eiridh na Sean Chánain Albannaich* ('The Resurrection of the Ancient Scottish Language') as a deliberate gesture towards the widening of his art and the promotion of Gaelic. He studied bardic verse, lamenting his lack of 'chiselled stones and polished words', and wrote a praise-poem to vaunt Gaelic as the language of Adam and Eve, no less, which deserved to thrive 'in spite of guile/ and stranger's bitter hate'.

MacMhaighstir Alasdair came from an educated Episcopalian family in Moidart, where his father, 'master Alasdair', was minister. He went to Glasgow University to study for law or the Church, but married young and had to abandon his degree. Little else is known of his early life until 1729, when he appears as a teacher in the Highlands, working at various schools run by the Society for Propagating Christian Knowledge. Alasdair's Gaelic–English word-book was produced for this society, whose aim was to bring literacy, English and the Reformed Church to the North-West. His salary was little more than a pittance, but for the next sixteen years he ran a croft, became an elder of the Kirk, taught the children and composed love-songs, satires and nature-poems.

Alasdair's satires included scurrilous attacks on various local figures and rival bards, and the explicit imagery in these and in some of his love-poems gave such offence to later collectors and editors that even today there is not a complete and unexpurgated edition of his works. Yet the spirit of his famous 'Praise of Morag' ('Moladh Mòraig') is a fine and joyful catalogue of feminine delights, rapidly delivered in an elaborate imitation of pibroch, with 'ground' and 'variation', and making play with *double entendres* drawn from the language of piping itself:

> There's one thing that I'm certain of,
> I'd better not tell Jane of her,
> and how I've fallen headlong,
> and am going at the knees now;
> there isn't enough water
> in Loch Shiel, or snow on Cruachan,
> to cool and heal the raging fire
> that burns away within me.
>
> When I heard the melody
> played on Morag's chanter
> my spirit danced with merriment,
> an answering most joyous:
> the stately ground, most elegant,
> of her tune, with fingers tapping it,
> a music with fine setting,
> the rocks providing bass for it.
> Ah! the chanter with its grace-notes,
> a hard sharp, clean-cut music,
> sedate now, and now quavering,
> or smooth, controlled, soft, tender;
> a steady, stately march then,
> full of vigour, grace and battle-zest,
> a brisk and strutting *crunluath*
> played by sportive swift–soft fingers.

> (trs. D. Thomson)

The poem ends with the bard waking up 'on fire' beside his wife and making love to her. Fantasy or not, his jealous wife is

supposed to have prompted him to write the 'Miomholadh
Mòraig' ('Dispraise of Morag') in which, with equal extravagance, he gives his dream girl red eyes and the face and sexual
habits of a monkey.

If MacMhaighstir Alasdair's Gaelic nationalism was somewhat at odds with his employers' preferences for English, the
bawdy, sly and passionate love-songs were even more unbe-
coming in an elder of the Kirk. The curious tensions and
contradictions of this career came to a head in 1744 when the
SPCK noted that the schoolmaster at Ardnamurchan was 'an
offence to all Sober Well-inclined persons as he wanders thro'
the Country composing Galick songs, stuffed with obscene
language'. In fact Alasdair's son was doing the teaching for him
by this time, and in 1745 the old man, now in his fifties, threw
over his post completely, converted to Catholicism and joined
up as a captain fighting for Clanranald in the Jacobite army.

Almost half of MacMhaighstir Alasdair's poems are dedicated to the Jacobite cause, not just to the prince, although he
wrote many songs to him, but to a vision of resurgent Gaeldom,
free at last from the taint of Lowland manners and values:

> How I welcome the thunder of sweetly-tuned organs,
> And the dazzling bonfires the streets all alighting,
> While the market resounds with 'Great Charles, our own Prince!'
> While each window shines with the light that is streaming
> From high-burning candles fair maidens are tending,
>   Every thing that is fitting to hail him with pomp!
> The cannon all booming and belching their smoke-clouds
> Making each country shake with the dread of the Gaels,
> While we o'er-exultant, lightly, o'er-weening,
> At his heels march in order, embued with such rapture
>   That no one weighs more than three fourths of a pound!
>
> ('Charles Son of James' ['Tearlach Mac Sheumas'], trs. J. L. Campbell)

Alasdair invoked the old incitement-poetry and wrote the most
scathing and bloodthirsty verses against King George and the
Clan Campbell – those perennial enemies of the MacDonalds.
He maintained his fervour even after Culloden, and a piece
such as 'A Waulking Song' ('Oran Luaidh no Fucaidh')
symbolises the exiled prince as a beautiful girl – 'Morag of the
ringlets' – and hopes for her return against the English with
'maidens' (French soldiers) 'to waulk the red cloth firmly'.
Poems such as these renewed for almost the last time the old

vaunting warrior-spirit of the clans, and this was why, no doubt, the unsold copies of his book are said to have been burned as seditious documents by the hangman in Edinburgh in 1752. By comparison, John Roy Stewart (1700–52) has a quieter voice as a Jacobite bard, and his two fine songs on Culloden are eloquent with pain and the sorrow of defeat.

From bardic praise-poems to the 'songs' of the eighteenth-century revival, the spirit of Gaelic poetry is objective, detailed and descriptive. It responds to the physical world with such a disinterested but passionate observation of the surface of things that it positively discourages subjectivity or the symbols and philosophical reflections so favoured by the English Romantic poets. Prompted by James Thomson's *Seasons*, it was Mac-Mhaighstir Alasdair who brought this Gaelic love of passionate catalogue to bear for the first time on poems of natural description, until he, and Duncan Bàn Macintyre after him, created some of the finest and most influential poems in the whole body of Gaelic verse.

Poems such as Alasdair's 'Song to Summer' ('Oran an t-Samhraidh'), 'Song to Winter' ('Oran a'Gheamhraidh') and 'Sugar Brook' ('Allt an t-Siùcair'), were most probably written around the early 1740s, and, although they follow Thomson's descriptive lead, they do not share his sentimental and didactic bias. Instead the Gaelic displays intellectual precision and a characteristically crystalline excitement:

> The lithe brisk fresh-water salmon,
> lively, leaping the stones;
> bunched, white-bellied, scaly,
> fin-tail-flashing, red-spot;
> speckled skin's brilliant hue
> lit with flashes of silver;
> with curved gob at the ready
> catching insects with guile.
>
> May, with soft showers and sunshine,
> meadows, grass-fields I love,
> milky, whey-white and creamy,
> frothing, whisked up in pails,
> time for crowdie and milk-curds,
> time for firkins and kits,
> lambs, goat-kids and roe-deer,
> bucks – a rich time for flocks.

('Song to Summer', trs. D. Thomson)

The descriptive detail of nature-pieces such as these, and the fierce spirit of the later Jacobite songs come together in *Birlinn Chlann Raghnaill* ('Clanranald's Galley'), which was probably written after 1751. As MacMhaighstir Alasdair's most famous poem (and one of the longest in modern Gaelic), it is a *tour de force* among oar-songs. Attentive to the individual tasks of the crew, and all the lengthy preparations needed for a voyage to Ireland, the poem is filled with exact technical detail and inspired by the rhythms of the sea in both storm and calm. This is how the storm begins in Hugh MacDiarmid's translation of the poem, in which he attempts to convey something of the original metre and the impacted energy of the verse:

Now they hoisted the speckled sails
  Peaked and close-wrought,
And stretched out the stubborn shrouds
  Tough and taut
To the long resin-red shafts
  Of the mast.
With adroit and firm-drawn knotting
  These were made fast
Through the eyes of the hooks and rings;
  Swiftly and expertly
Each rope put right of the rigging;
  And orderly
The men took up their set stations
  And were ready.
Then opened the windows of the sky
  Pied, grey-blue,
To the lowering wind's blowing,
  A morose brew,
The sea pulled on his grim rugging   tugging (Scots)
  Slashed with sore rents,
That rough-napped mantle, a weaving
  Of loathsome torrents.
The shape-ever-changing surges
  Swelled up in hills
And roared down into valleys
  In appalling spills.
The water yawned in great craters,
  Slavering mouths agape
Snatching and snarling at each other
  In rabid shape.

If heroism still thrives in MacMhaighstir Alasdair's verse,

his contemporaries John MacCodrum and Rob Donn Mackay look more to the everyday life of small communities.

John MacCodrum (Iain Mhic Fhearchair, 1693?–1779)

John MacCodrum was married three times in the course of a long and quiet life on North Uist. His many songs make a wry commentary on domestic themes and local personalities – from his own problems with eager widows, to grasping tacksmen and landlords, to his last wife, who did not look after him as well as she should – at least, according to 'A Complaint about his Wife' ('Gearan air a Mhnaoi'):

> 'Tis no small cause of displeasure,
> When I am not short of sheep,
> To be buying cloth,
>   Though my wife is alive;
> And though it is not much to say,
> I am ashamed at times
> To be reduced to thigging sewing thread,
>   Though my wife is alive.

(trs. W. Matheson)

MacCodrum was famous for the sharpness of his wit and the refrain of his complaint becomes more pointed with every repetition. Most of his poems were composed when he was in his fifties or older, and, although he was not a literate man, he belonged to an oral tradition which was capable of remarkable feats of memory. When James Macpherson arrived in Uist in 1760, MacCodrum was recommended to him as a man who could recite at length from the old Ossianic cycle, but the visitor's bad Gaelic and his bad manners evinced only a dry evasion from the bard. MacCodrum's own verses, so often based on village events, are far from Macpherson's notion of the antique sublime, as witness the descriptive comedy of such pieces as 'Macaskill's Wedding' ('Banais Mhicasgaill'), or a rhymed debate on the delights and pitfalls of drinking, 'The Friend and Foe of Whisky' ('Caraid agus Namhaid an Uisge-bheatha'), or 'A Song to Fever' ('Orain do 'n Teasaich') in which he characterises fever as the *cailleach* – an old crone:

She planted confusion in my head;
a host of men, both alive and dead,
like those whom the Trojan Hector led,
and Roman warriors, thronged my bed;
   that dismal, dark and hunch-backed crone,
   to scandal and lying tales too prone,
   reduced my speech to delirious moan
   and left me stripped of sense, alone.

. . .

Your coat has grown too big, and throws
into relief your wrinkled hose,
your splayed, pathetic ankle shows,
long as a wild-cat's the nails of your toes.

(trs. D. Thomson)

The poet's classical references, and his remarks on European politics in other poems, remind us that an oral culture need not be a parochial one; nor are Gaelic poets unaware of each other's work, whatever their geographical isolation. MacMhaighstir Alasdair visited MacCodrum on at least two occasions, and his poem 'The Mavis of Clanranald' was very probably composed in emulation of the Uistman's famous 'Mavis of Clan Donald'. The tradition was swift and fluid, for MacCodrum's 'Dispraise of Donald Bàn's Pipes' ('Diomoladh Pioba Dhomnaill Bhain') was his reply to another poet's extravagant praise of an inferior piper. Such interchanges were common when poems were recited and their composers valued as a part of communal experience. A skilled bard could memorise a song after only one hearing, and, indeed, MacMhaighstir Alasdair recalled two of MacCodrum's songs well enough to print them complete and without acknowledgement in his own book. Then again, Rob Donn, another unlettered poet, had such a grasp of Mac-Mhaighstir Alasdair's 'Song to Summer', that he could produce a complex parallel to it in line after line of his own 'Song to Winter', entirely composed in his head. The tale of how MacCodrum came to be bard to the MacDonalds of Sleat also testifies to the potency of verse in an oral culture.

Tradition has it that MacCodrum satirised the itinerant tailors of Uist for being unwilling to travel to his remote house; and when they heard his lampoon ('Aoir nan Tailleirean') they retaliated by swearing to boycott him for ever more. The bard's ragged condition subsequently attracted the attention of Sir James MacDonald, who was on a visit from Skye, and when he heard the reason (and the poem) he gave MacCodrum a pension and made him his bard on Uist. The old man duly produced many praise-poems and elegies on behalf of Sir James and the heroes of Clan Donald – that 'death-dealing bright company of keen blades'. But the clan-system had been irrevocably damaged at Culloden, and its close ties of kinship were breaking down at all levels.

In the 1770s the more prosperous farmers and tacksmen began to emigrate, many of them choosing to go to South Carolina. (Tacksmen used to be responsible to the chief for raising so many armed men, and they sublet their holdings to clansmen lower down the hierarchy.) When they left, their places at home were taken by strangers who did not hesitate to raise the rents until the poorer subtenants were forced to leave their crofts in turn. Thousands departed the western Highlands during these years and MacCodrum's late poem 'Song to the Fugitives' ('Oran do na Fogarraich') lamented what was happening:

'Tis a sad matter to consider,
The land is being made dearer;
Our people have swiftly left,
    And sheep have come in their place:
A weak host they and ineffective
At going into quarrel and strife,
Full of braxy and leanness,
    At the mercy of a guileful fox;
Smearing will not save you
In presence of battle on a field,
Nor will the moorland shepherd's whistle
    Change your misfortune a whit;
And though you were to gather
Fifty wedders and hornless rams,
Never would one of them lift up
    An edged sword of steel.

(trs. W. Matheson)

In fact the 'edged sword of steel' was to be lifted again, but this time the Highland regiments were fighting for a British cause. Among the first of them were MacDonald troops from Skye raised by Sir James's successor to fight the American 'rebellion' in 1776.

Robert Mackay (Rob Donn MacAoidh, 1714–78)

Rob Donn lived in Sutherland on the far north coast of Scotland, remote from the traumas of Culloden. He came from a humble Presbyterian family (the Reformed Church was well established in the north), and like John MacCodrum, he was not literate. Rooted in his home community, he occasionally drove cattle to Falkirk or Carlisle, and a brief spell as a regimental bard took him to most Scottish cities in the early 1760s. As a boy Rob Donn ('Brown Robert') had a precocious gift for rhyming, encouraged by John Mackay of Musal, who took him under his care and gave him his first job as a herdsman. An early failure in love is remembered with bawdy sweetness in 'The Shieling Song' ('Is Trom Leam an Airigh'):

> Fair Anna, daughter of Donald,
>   If you only knew my condition,
> It is unanswered love,
>   That took away my reason:
> It's alive in me yet
>   As if you were here.
> It teases and squeezes
>   In my heart like a spear
>   All though the day
>   It's an uproar for me
>   Trying to quell it
>   While it grows like a tree.

(after a translation by I. Grimble)

The shieling was a hut in the high pastures where village boys and girls would take the cattle for summer grazing. Many would associate the first pangs of adolescent love with their long days at the shieling.

Rob Donn's heart survived to write other love-poems, as well as verses on his passionate fondness for hunting deer, but most of his poems reflect on the events and personalities around him. He celebrated his native glen in verses which had young Isabel

Mackay defend the delights of Strathmore against the attrac-
tions of Thurso, where her sister had been sent to school. When
Isabel was married in 1747, her mother slighted the bard by not
inviting him to the wedding. He turned up anyway with a
light-heartedly bawdy lampoon on the family and their guests in
which he puzzled over the fate of a supposedly missing pair of
trousers. The bride's mother makes her appearance in the
fourth 'verse of 'MacRory's Trousers' ('Briogais Mhic
Ruairidh'):

> Catherine, William's daughter,
> Make some trousers for the lad
> And don't take a penny
>   In payment for them.
> Who knows but it was your father
> Who took them to wear?
> He needed as much
>   And time was when he would have done it.

(trs. I. Grimble)

No doubt the community enjoyed such pieces immensely, but
Rob Donn also took a more general view of character, morality
and politics, as with his long poem against the government ban
on the wearing of the kilt. John MacCodrum's piece on the
same theme had simply complained about the discomfort of
trousers, and called up the old vision of a warrior in a plaid –
and 'not a Saxon in the world but will blench at the sight of
him'; but Rob Donn's 'The Black Cassocks' ('Na Casagan
Dubha') takes a more astute and dangerous line:

> So, so King George!
> What a mockery of your good faith
> To make new laws
> That double the bondage.
> But since they are fellows without honour
> It would be better to strike than spare,
> And there will be fewer to support you
> When the same thing happens again.
>
> If your enemy and your friend
> Receive the same punishment in Scotland,
> Those who rose against you
> Made the better choice. . . .

(trs. I. Grimble)

This was so pointed that he was called to task before the sheriff and the (Hanoverian) chief of the Mackays.

Rob Donn's verse can rise to virtuoso effects, as in 'Song to Summer' ('Oran an t-Samhraidh') or the pibroch poem to young Isabel Mackay, both of which follow the technical dazzle of MacMhaighstir Alasdair. But for the most part his muse speaks more plainly on his own and his neighbours' foibles. There is a grave, reflective quality in many of his commentaries which has been likened to the balance in Pope's couplets. In fact we know that Rob was familiar with the English poet's work through his local minister's habit of translating it into Gaelic and quoting it in his sermons. When the minister died in 1763, Rob Donn's 'Elegy to Master Murdoch Macdonald' ('Marbhrann do Mhaighstir Murchadh Macdhomhnaill'), made a truly Augustan homage to the old man, if tempered with an appropriately Calvinist sternness:

> What has grieved me in spirit
> And those who loved and followed you
> Is the magnitude of your labour before you left us
> And the scantiness of its traces that remain after you.
> Some profitable lessons will flow
> From the fringes of your grace,
> That fools did not heed
> By listening to your teaching. . . .
> You made the reluctant willing
> And the ignorant wise,
> And the absolute joy of your life
> Was in imparting more light to them.
> You were gentle to those in need,
> You were generous with reasonable people,
> You were shrewd of aspect, hard
> As stone towards the miscreant,
> You were bountiful in giving,
> You were a diligent preacher,
> You gave timely advice
> And even your hostility turned to love in the end.

(trs. I. Grimble)

Like the poet, Macdonald enjoyed the unaccompanied singing of metrical psalms in church. These 'long tunes' are a kind of Gaelic Presbyterian plainsong, with each line chanted by the precentor and then sung at length and freely embellished by the congregation. The effect is one of wild and chilling grandeur.

The Presbyterian tradition was strong in the poet's community and in his own outlook. His verse did not hesitate to reproach Lady Reay (wife of the fifth Lord) when she tried to secure his silence over a marriage of convenience which she had forced upon two of her servants:

> With sharp command and counsel
> There was placed in my mouth a gag like a skewer
> Concerning the incident to be spoken of,
> Which did not resemble a love-affair so much as a hunt,
> Indeed I am sorry for the pair of them. . . .

('Lady Reay and her maid': 'Ged a thuit mi' n car iomraill . . .', trs. I Grimble)

He took morality seriously, but Ron Donn was no prude. His wry sense of humour had enjoyed singing the praises of Sally Grant – the darling of his Sutherland regiment – and his satires and lampoons were bluntly spoken and reinforced with a typically Gaelic awareness of family-history:

> Your grandmother was lustful
> And bore children to twelve men,
> And your mother did not refuse
> One single man apart from her husband
>
> . . .
>
> Your mother was illegitimate
> And a great strumpet of a wench
> And she bore you a bastard
> To a lout of a fellow.
> Many a lamentable day
> They punished her on the stool of penitence,
> And you yourself got a yelping little creature
> In the usual way before you were married.

('Barbara Miller': 'Tapadh leat a Bharb'ra . . .', trs. I. Grimble)

Perhaps Rob Donn's most powerful poetry lies in his elegies – which were as likely to be for ordinary men as for chiefs. His wry 'Lament for Ewan' ('Marbhrann Eoghainn') compares the approaching end of an old man in a remote cottage with the reported death of a head of state – only to have the ancient revive at the last gasp in a rage at the poet for his presumption. 'The Rispond Misers' ('Marbhrann, do Thriuir Sheann

Fhleasgach') uses its subjects to reflect on the uselessness of hoarding gold. In poems such as these, and in the verses to the fourth Lord Reay, Murdoch Macdonald and his old friend John Mackay (Iain Mac Eachainn), Rob Donn reshaped the Gaelic tradition of almost uncritical lament, in order to make his own more sombre commentary on men and the times.

Duguld Buchanan (Dùghall Bochanan, 1716–68)

Born and brought up in Strathyre, near the Trossachs in Perthshire, Duguld Buchanan, like Rob Donn, also came from a Presbyterian family. His mother's excessive devoutness, however, gave him morbid religious fears as a boy, and these visions marked his nature and his poetry for the rest of his life. He completed his education at Stirling and Edinburgh and spent some restless years as an apprentice carpenter for various masters. He moved from job to job as he alternated between wild escapades and the acute religious depressions which he described in his diary. He worked as an itinerant teacher before settling as schoolmaster at Kinloch Rannoch, where the General Assembly recognised his religious fervour by confirming him as a lay preacher and catechist. A later move to have him appointed as minister was frustrated by his lack of university qualifications, and by fears that his style was too inflammatory. The poems which he was beginning to write were disturbing enough – replete with images from the Book of Revelation and racked by a morbid empathy with suffering and damnation. His most famous poem, 'The Day of Judgement' ('Là a 'Bhreitheanais'), is over 500 lines long. It describes the sublime and terrible descent of Christ on the last day, and the doom that all the sinners of history have to endure:

> On fiery chariot he sits
> with roars and thunder all around,
> calling to Heaven's outmost bounds,
> and ripping clouds tempestuously.
>
> From out his chariot's wheels there comes
> a stream of fire aflame with wrath,
> and that flood spreads on every side,
> until the world is flaming red.

The elements all melt with heat,
just as a fire can melt down wax;
the hills and moors are all aflame,
and all the oceans boil and seethe.

(trs. D. Thomson)

No doubt Dante, and Robert Blair's 'graveyard school' or Young's *Night Thoughts* were influences on Buchanan. By the same token his poem in forty-four stanzas 'The Skull' ('An Claigeann') most likely borrowed its outlook from Hamlet's speech on Yorick. Nevertheless, Buchanan's terse Gaelic and his visionary imagination create a special intensity.

Towards the end of his life Buchanan studied in Edinburgh, where he met David Hume and compared notes with him on the sublime. He helped the Revd James Stewart produce the New Testament in Gaelic for the SPCK, and published a small collection of his own poems, *Spiritual Songs* (1767). These had a wide influence within the Evangelical movement, and many other minor Gaelic writers were to produce hymns and religious poems over the next hundred years.

William Ross (Uilleam Ros, 1762–90)

Towards the end of the century William Ross produced a number of wryly personal and elegaic love-poems. This was a new departure for the Gaelic muse, and perhaps it owes something to Ross's education in the classics and his familiarity with the poems of Burns. He was born in Skye and spent his boyhood in Strath Suardal between Broadford and Torrin, where, indeed, Dr Johnson and Boswell had stayed during their tour of the Hebrides in 1773. Ross's poem on whisky 'The Son of Malt' ('Mac-na-Bracha') pays testimony to its effect on the good doctor, who was for once in his life 'tongue-tied', despite his English 'and his Latin and Greek speech beside'. William was sent to the grammar-school in Forres on the mainland, where he excelled as a scholar. Then the family moved to Gairloch and the young man accompanied his father as travelling pedlar, carrying a pack of sundry goods throughout Scotland and recording his travels in verse. After some years at this trade he returned to Gairloch to settle as the schoolmaster there. He became a popular member of the community, but died of tuberculosis at the age of twenty-eight.

Ross was more than familiar with the Gaelic tradition in poetry and some of his own pieces follow the pattern of praise-poems – to his native glen, a Highland maiden, or to whisky, not to mention the by now almost obligatory 'Song to Summer' and an 'Elegy for Prince Charlie'. His Lowland education appears in the classical allusions which he makes in comparing his beloved to Venus or Diana, or in his references to Cupid as 'the Black Laddie' in a lightweight piece ('Oran air Cupid') which has a priest smitten with love for a pretty cowherd. It may be that he had found something of this spirit in Burns, and certainly his 'Toothache Reprimanded' ('Achmha-san an Deideidh') looks familiar; but at the same time it is likely that vernacular Gaelic was evolving the personal lyric in its own right. (And of course Burns and Ross could draw on the folk-song tradition in each of their cultures.) Whatever their antecedents, it is Ross's love-songs which are best remembered, along with the romance which grew up around his unrequited affair with a girl called Marion Ross.

The poet must have met Mòr Ros in Stornoway during his youthful travels. He fell in love with her but she married a sea captain in 1782 and went to live with him in Liverpool. Tradition has it that she was unhappy and sent for the poet in later years. He got as far as Stirling before deciding that the affair was hopeless, and turned back only to catch the chill which killed him. His best poems do deal with this girl, and her image crops up indirectly in other verses. 'Love Song' ('Oran Gaoil') – also called 'Monday Evening' ('Feasgar Luain') – is the poet's recollection of seeing Marion at a ball in Stornoway. The formality of the occasion is matched by the verse with its classical allusions and rather highly wrought compliments. 'Song of Lament' ('Oran Cumhaidh') involves oblique references to a traditional tale of Cormac – an Irish harper who cured his love-pains with his own music. But Ross has no such consolation:

> Why was I not born sightless,
> dumb, without power to see,
> before I saw your modest face
> that dimmed a hundred's light;

since first I ever saw you
your virtues were renowned,
and death to me were easier
than to live now you are gone.

(trs. D. Thomson)

This poem was followed by 'Another Song on the Same Theme'
('Oran Eile, air an Aobhar Cheudna'), an even barer expression of personal anguish. The Gaelic tradition had seldom
attempted such confessional force, although of course the
impersonal lament was well established. The verse begins with
the shocking image of a maggot hatching in the poet's chest:

I am lonely here and depressed
No more can I drink and be gay.
The worm that feeds on my breast
is giving my secret away.
Nor do I see, walking past,
the girl of the tenderest gaze.
It is this which has brought me to waste
like the leaf in the autumn days.

Iain Crichton Smith's verse translation catches Ross's sense of
desperate vulnerability very well, especially in the closing
stanzas:

Ill-wishers who hear of my plight
call me a coward and worse.
They say that I'm only a poet
whose fate is as dead as my verse.
(His father's a packman. You know it.
His father, in turn, couldn't boast.)
They'd take a good field and plough it.
I cut better poems than most.

My spirit is dulled by your loss,
the song of my mouth is dumb.
I moan with the sea's distress
when the mist lies over the foam.
It's the lack of your talk and your grace
which has clouded the sun from my eyes
and has sunk it deep in the place
from which light will never arise.

I shall never praise beauty again.
I shall never design a song.
I shall never take pleasure in tune,
nor hear the clear laugh of the young.
I shall never climb hill with the vain
youthful arrogant joy that I had.
But I'll sleep in a hall of stone
With the great bards who are dead.

The oblique and brooding pain in William Ross's love-poetry was to be recalled in modern times by Sorley Maclean's *Songs to Eimhir*. By comparison the last great Gaelic poet of the century composed hardly any love-poems, for his work returned to the older descriptive tradition and shows no trace of introspection or personal unhappiness.

Duncan Bàn Macintyre (Donnchadh Bàn Mac an t-Saoir, 1724–1812)

Duncan Bàn Macintyre lived half his life in Edinburgh, and he and his family are buried in Old Greyfriars' churchyard, but he is remembered above all Gaelic poets as a composer of songs about the remote hills and the running deer. His poems were more popular than any others and his printed collection went through two editions in his own day and three more in the following century.

Born and brought up in Glen Orchy, Duncan Bàn was unlettered and without formal education, but he could recite his own work by heart and much more again from the older Gaelic tradition. He served reluctantly in the Forty-five, for the Argyll Militia on the government side, and from 1746 to 1766 he worked as a gamekeeper for the Earl of Breadalbane and then the Duke of Argyll, walking the hills and forests of Glen Lochay, Ben Dorain and Glen Etive. His great descriptive verses were composed in these years, as well as dutiful praise-poems to various members of the Glen Orchy Campbells.

Duncan Bàn wrote few love-poems, but his marriage to 'fair-haired young Mary' prompted a long praise-poem called 'Song to his Bride' ('Oran d'a Cheile Nuadh-Phosda'), as a fine and elaborately courtly compliment to Màiri Bàn Òg. Macintyre's strength as a poet lies in his observation of nature, so, while a reference to Cupid in his poem remains pretty stock stuff, some of his other similes are truly fresh and unexpected. He compares his bride's skin to white quartz, or her soft body to moor cotton-grass, or he thinks of her like a slender tree:

> I went to the wood where grew trees and saplings
>   that were radiant to view all around;
> my eyes' desire was a branch outstanding
>   in the dense growth of twigs overhead –
> a bough from top to base in blossom,
>   which I tenderly bent down:
> 'twere hard for others ever to cut it,
>   as this shoot I was destined to pluck.

(trs. A. MacLeod)

The other side of this coin can be found in the relentless flyting against Donald MacNaughton, a tailor who had dared to lampoon the bard – 'Song to the Tailor' ('Oran do 'n Tàillear'). The poor man paid a high price for his presumption, measured in long lines of frightful attributes, worthy of Dunbar's satire or a warlock's curse. The image of the tree is used again:

> Thou art the rotten tree, withered,
> full of decay and microbes,
> grown scraggy and stunted,
> short, hump-backed, distorted;
> a stump bound for the embers art thou,
> who didst deserve to be burned as sacrifice:
>   thou hast grossly neglected the gospel,
>   thou hast grossly neglected the gospel.

(trs. A. MacLeod)

Much of Duncan Bàn's output, especially in later years, is cheerfully occasional. He loved deer-hunting and he sang about what he knew and saw around him – Glen Orchy, a gift sheep, a favourite gun, an unsuccessful hunt, or, in mock elegy, a cockerel that was shot by mistake. He was an uncomplicated extrovert, unlike the fiercely touchy MacMhaighstir Alasdair; nor did he share Rob Donn's moral nature or the capacity for pain to be found in the works of Buchanan and William Ross. Nevertheless, it is with Macintyre that the Gaelic passion for objective observation reaches its highest point.

'Song to Summer' ('Oran an t-Samhraidh') is an overly formal and elaborately crafted attempt to match MacMhaigh-stir Alasdair, but with 'Song to Misty Corrie' ('Oran Coire a' Cheathaich') and 'Praise of Ben Dorain' ('Moladh Beinn Dòbhrain'), Macintyre is – literally – on his home ground and he charts it with loving detail. Verse after verse of 'Misty Corrie' moves to a measured pace, reading like some lyrically precise botanical catalogue, bringing together the life of plants and then fish, birds and deer:

> Thy genial braes, abounding in blaeberries and cowberries,
>   are studded with cloudberries of the round, red head,
> with garlic forming pads in the angles of ledges,
>   and fringed rock stacks, not a few;
> the dandelion and penny-royal,
>   soft, white cotton sedge, and sweet grass are there
> in every part of it, from the lowest hill foot
>   to the crested regions of the highest reach.
>
> . . .
>
> Around each spring that is in the region
>   is a sombre brow of green water-cress;
> at the base of boulders is a clump of sorrel,
>   and sandy gravel, ground fine and white;
> splashing gurgles, seething, not heated,
>   but eddying from the depth of smooth cascades,
> each splendid rill is a blue-tressed plait,
>   running in torrent and spiral swirls.
>
> In that rugged gully is a white-bellied salmon
>   that cometh from the ocean of stormy wave,
> catching midges with lively vigour
>   unerringly, in his arched bent beak. . . .

(trs. A. MacLeod)

Such intensely focused observation is a kind of sublime passion, and it clearly influenced Hugh MacDiarmid who from the 1940s came to see his later English work as a scientifically based 'poetry of fact' dedicated simply and entirely to the material world for its own sake. The 'Song to Misty Corrie' is 'nature-poetry' of the purest sort, entirely free of personal or symbolic reflection; perhaps some of John Clare's verses come close, but there is nothing else in the English tradition quite like it. The clarity of Macintyre's eye belongs to what Kenneth Jackson has called 'the high sunlight of the Celtic vision', and it is deeply ironic that within the next century the Gaelic muse would be associated – as far as Lowland culture was concerned – with glamorous shadows in a Celtic twilight.

'Praise of Ben Dorain' is based on a pipe-tune, and like MacMhaighstir Alasdair's 'Praise of Morag' its light and lively rhythms imitate the pibroch changes between theme and variation (*urlar* and *siubhal*). In over 500 lines Duncan Bàn is attentive to the minutiae of grasses and streams on Ben Dorain's slopes; but the poem is particularly dedicated to the herds of deer which he had watched and hunted there for years. He is no sentimentalist, for, if he admires their delicate movements, he also takes delight in describing the intricacy of the flintlock on the gun which will kill them. The poem ends, moreover, with dogs pulling the deer down to die in moorland pools, and these last scenes are described by means of unstressed extra syllables in imitation of *crunluath*, the most complex movement in pibroch which marks the climax of the tune. Iain Crichton Smith's English catches something of the Gaelic's hectic excitement, and also the way the poem suddenly stops just like a pipe-tune. Perhaps, like pibroch again, the effect is to bring us back to the beginning in an endless cycle:

Erratic was the veering then
and rapid in its motion
when they would go sheering on
short cuts with exertion.

Tumultuous the baying and
echo of the crying as
the hairy-coated violent
dogs would show their paces.

Driving them from summits to
lakes that are unplumbable
bleeding dying swimming and
floundering in water.

Hounds hanging to their quarries while
they sway and toss and rock and kill –
their jaws will never let them feel
their haughty style again.

The little that I've sung of them
is not enough to tell of them
O you'd need a tongue for them
of a most complex kind.

The bloody water where the deer met their end comes from the
same fresh springs praised earlier in the poem, in the quieter
pace of *urlar*:

Transparent springs that nurse
the modest water cress –
no foreign wines surpass
these as drink for her.

. . .

The spotted water-cress
with forked and spiky gloss;
water where it grows
so abundantly

This is the good food
that animates their blood
and circulates as bread
in hard famine-time.

That would fatten their
bodies to a clear
shimmer, rich and rare,
without clumsiness.

It is characteristic of Duncan Bàn's muse that he should
celebrate the deer's diet with such tenderness and expertise.
More than anything else, however, his poem is full of the
movement of these graceful animals, with what Crichton Smith
has called a pagan spirit which is absolutely free from any
moral dimension. Here the movement is the quicker *siubhal*:

The hind that's sharp-headed
is fierce in its speeding:
how delicate, rapid,
its nostrils, wind-reading!
Light-hooved and quick limbèd,
she runs on the summit,
from that uppermost limit
no gun will remove her.
You'll not see her winded,
that elegant mover.

Her forebears were healthy.
When she stopped to take breath then,
how I loved the pure wraith-like
sound of her calling,
she seeking her sweetheart
in the lust of the morning.

By 1768 other men were employed on Duncan Bàn's favourite estates and he found himself and his family in Edinburgh. With the help of his former captain in the Argylls he joined the City Guard – a local police-force largely composed of Highlanders. As a member of what Fergusson called 'the black banditti' he wrote songs in praise of his halberd, his musket and whisky and brandy – those indispensable items of company equipment. A volume of his poems was published by subscription and sold well, but he had already done his best work. In the 1780s he composed a series of prize-winning poems on pibroch and Gaelic – to be recited at an annual piping-competition in Falkirk as organised by the London Highland Society. The same society gave him a modest grant in recognition of his status as a poet. In preparation for a second subscription volume, Duncan Bàn and his wife spent a couple of years, sometime after 1786, touring the Highlands and islands. Dressed in the plaid with a sword and a fox-skin cap, the bard was widely welcomed. He left the City Guard in 1793 and served as a soldier for six years with the Breadalbane Fencibles, although exactly what duties were asked of a man in his seventies is not clear. His last poems, musing on death and advancing age, adopt an untypically moralistic tone; but a livelier note in the old vein is struck by his 'Song to the Foxes' ('Oran nam Balgairean'), which praises them for killing the sheep that were taking over the hillsides from his beloved deer. His lines stand for the experience of many at the beginning of the nineteenth century, puzzled by social changes beyond their control as an old, old way of life finally found itself in the modern world:

The villages and shielings
where warmth and cheer were found,

have no houses save the ruins,
and no tillage in the fields.

Every practice that prevailed
in Gaeldom has been altered,

and become so unnatural
in the places that were hospitable.

(trs. A. MacLeod)

Even so, some of these changes had produced the culture's finest achievements in Gaelic verse, and in the second half of the eighteenth century Lowland Scotland too was about to enjoy a vernacular revival.

Robert Fergusson (1750–74)

If Mackenzie and his respectable friends had doubts about the 'classic' status of the Canongate, they were never shared by young Robert Fergusson, whose poems immortalised the vulgar intimacy of the streets in his native 'Auld Reekie'. Fergusson's parents came to Edinburgh from Aberdeenshire and 'The Farner's Ingle' shows his familiarity with North-East Scots. As the fourth in a family of five, young Robert went to St Andrew's University at the close of 1764 and enjoyed a lively undergraduate life despite poor health. While at university he wrote two acts of a tragedy on Wallace and then abandoned it because he felt it was not original enough. Fergusson's sympathies were patriotically Scottish, even Jacobite, and his ambitions were set on a literary career, but the sudden death of his father meant that he had to leave St Andrews in 1768 and find work to support the family. He ended up as a copying-clerk – a dull-enough job, but one which kept him in Edinburgh and gave him some freedom to write for himself. He soon made friends in theatrical and musical circles by producing English words to Scots tunes, and these pieces were included in two operas performed at the Theatre Royal in 1769. In 1771 the *Weekly Magazine or Edinburgh Amusement* began to publish Fergusson's English poems, which were pastorals, mock heroics and complaints in the prevailingly genteel Augustan manner. Fergusson continued to produce such verses for the rest of his life, but his energetic genius was only to be realised in Scots when 'The Daft Days' appeared in January 1772. This seasonal piece heralded an extraordinary two years during which Fergusson produced poem after poem in the *Weekly Magazine* – almost his entire output before he collapsed and died at the age of twenty-four. The magazine's owner, Walter Ruddiman, continued to promote his poet over the next twelve years by publishing no fewer than three editions of the collected works.

'The Daft Days' hailed the Scottish custom of celebrating the New Year with drinking and dancing. Other poems soon followed in the same vein – lamenting the decline of Scots music, laughing at the noise made by 'The Tron-kirk Bell', or praising the virtues of 'Caller Oysters' and 'Braid Claith' – all expressed in vigorous Scots and standard Habbie. These verses offered a vision of Edinburgh street-life that had not been matched since Allan Ramsay or Dunbar. It was a world of lawyers, farmers, Highland porters, change-house keepers, magistrates, stall-owners, police, maids, whores, servants, men of fashion and the ubiquitous cadies (guides and errand boys), who were intimates to the whole town. The citizens were delighted to find themselves and their activities so hilariously and irreverently reflected:

On Sabbath-days the barber spark,	
Whan he has done wi' scrapin wark,	
Wi' siller broachie in his sark,	shirt
Gangs trigly, faith!	finely dressed
Or to the Meadow, or the Park,	
In gude Braid Claith.	
Weel might ye trow, to see them there,	believe
That they to shave your haffits bare,	cheeks
Or curl an' sleek a pickle hair,	
Wou'd be right laith,	reluctant
Whan pacing wi' a gawsy air	stately
In gude Braid Claith.	

. . .

Braid Claith lends fock an unco heese,	folk; considerable help
Makes mony kail-worms butter-flies,	caterpillars
Gies mony a doctor his degrees	
For little skaith:	expense
In short, you may be what you please	
Wi' gude Braid Claith.	

Readers from Edinburgh, the Borders and Fife wrote letters to Ruddiman in praise of Fergusson's 'auld words' in a 'sonsy canty strain' and he became a well-known figure, greeted as the 'new Ramsay'. He joined the Cape Club, one of the wilder of the many drinking- and debating-clubs which were so popular at all levels of society. Fellow-member David Herd must have encouraged his love of Scots songs, and Fergusson (unlike Burns) was known for his good voice. (Later members of the Cape included the painter Henry Raeburn and William Brodie, a respectable deacon by day and a robber by night who was eventually hanged in 1788.) Fergusson became the very patron poet of Edinburgh tavern-life:

When big as burns the gutters rin,
Gin ye hae catcht a droukit skin,   If; soaked
To *Luckie Middlemist's* loup in,   Mistress/Goodwife; jump
    And sit fu snug
Oe'r oysters and a dram o' gin,
    Or haddock lug.   ear

When auld Sanct Giles, at aught o' clock,
Gars merchant lowns their chopies lock,   blokes; shops
There we adjourn wi' hearty fock   folk
    To birle our bodles,   ring our copper coins
And get wharewi' to crack our joke,
    And clear our noddles.   heads

('Caller Oysters')

No doubt the poet's rowdy pranks led him to fall foul of the City Guard, for he never misses an opportunity in his verses to satirise the 'black banditti' and their Highland accents.

Ruddiman published a collection of Fergusson's poems in 1773 and it sold moderately well, but polite literary taste had been otherwise engaged for the past fifty years and the established critics were slow to report on the work. 'Auld Reikie', which appeared separately the same year, was greeted with a similar silence, and perhaps this is why Fergusson never developed it beyond 'Canto I'. Then again, the young poet had parodied the melodrama of Henry Mackenzie's *The Prince of Tunis* by putting a highly rhetorical lament, full of 'sensibility', into the mouth of an English-speaking and neoclassically inclined pig. 'The Sow of Feeling', as he called it, would scarcely have endeared him to Mackenzie, and that influential literary figure could see little but 'coarse dissipation' in such a bohemian muse. In fact the poet's health was beginning to collapse under the pressures of late nights and heavy drinking, and his wild behaviour and unkempt appearance became ever more conspicuous. He gave up his job at the end of 1773 because of increasing physical illness and bouts of religious melancholia. It is possible that he was suffering from syphilis, and, although he made a brief recovery in the summer of 1774, a fall in which he struck his head broke his health completely and plunged him into morbid fears and virtual insanity. In the end he had to be taken from his mother's home and lodged in the Bedlam next to the Edinburgh poorhouse, where he died in a straw-littered cell in October 1774. He was buried in Canongate churchyard in an unmarked grave.

Fergusson's life was short and his poetic output relatively small, but he had considerable literary influence, not least on his successor, Robert Burns. The Ayrshire man's direct debt can be established in various specific poems, but his true inheritance comes from the integrated comic spirit of the younger writer, whose vigorous and racy tongue expressed a complete personality enlivened by an ironic eye for the pretensions of his fellow citizens. Fergusson's range is limited by the topics he chooses, but never by literary or class-conscious preconceptions, for he is not concerned with appearing genteel nor with making points about 'simple' life and pastimes. Thus Fergusson's 'dialogue' poems, such as 'Mutual Complaint of Plainstanes and Causey' and 'A Drink Eclogue', are used to make satirical reflections on the world in general, and, although the debates are personified and the 'road' and the 'pavement' or 'brandy' and 'whisky' are revealed in speech as the broadest of Scottish characters, this alone is not Fergusson's subject. Poems such as 'Hallow Fair' and 'Leith Races' have a more local focus and they are certainly satirical and even downright impudent, but they are never condescending. In this vein Fergusson's masterpiece is 'Auld Reikie', a poem of over 300 lines in octosyllabic couplets in which he conjures up the institutions and the lively folk and the crowded, odiferous streets of his native city:

Now some to Porter, some to Punch,
Some to their Wife, and some their Wench,
Retire, while noisy Ten-hours Drum
Gars a' your Trades gae dandring Hame.   makes
Now mony a Club, jocose and free,
Gie a' to Merriment and Glee,
Wi' Sang and Glass, they fley the Pow'r
O' Care that wad harrass the Hour:
For Wine and Bacchus still bear down
Our thrawart Fortunes wildest Frown: obstinate
It maks you stark, and bauld and brave,
Ev'n whan descending to the Grave.

Fergusson's spirit is bold, ribald, cheerful or stark, but
never in the least 'polite'. He lived the life he wrote about, even
if 'Wine and Bacchus' did serve him sadly in that last descent.

Robert Burns (1759–96)

Thirteen years after Fergusson's death, Robert Burns commissioned a headstone in memory of a poet whom he generously acknowledged as his 'elder brother in misfortune, by far
my elder brother in the muse'. At this time (February 1787) the
twenty-eight-year-old Burns was newly famous after a winter
season in Edinburgh literary society. The Kilmarnock edition
of his poems had appeared the previous year and Henry
Mackenzie in the *Lounger*, the blind poet Dr Blacklock, Hugh
Blair, Professor Duguld Stewart and even 'plough boys and
maid-servants' were all 'delighted, agitated, transported' by
what the *Edinburgh Magazine* saw as 'a striking example of
native genius bursting through the obscurity of poverty and the
obstructions of laborious life'. The critics underestimated
Burns's education, but they were not wrong about his poverty
at the time. Indeed, he had prepared the Kilmarnock collection
under the most pressing need for money and, until the volume's
success, had planned to emigrate to Jamaica. Things were not
going well at home: he already had an illegitimate daughter by
a servant girl and now his mistress Jean Armour was pregnant.
Jean's father was determined that they should not marry (and
she seems to have agreed with him at the time), because, with
the death of his father in 1784, the poet was having to support
his mother, three brothers and three sisters and his farm at

Mossgiel was failing. Burns and Jean had made public repentance in church according to Kirk law and her father was seeking support for what turned out to be twins. To cap it all, in the aftermath of Jean's rejection Burns seems to have become involved with a Highland girl called Mary Campbell, who features in some of his tenderest poems and songs but who died of a fever (perhaps in child-birth) later in 1786. The details of the 'Highland Mary' affair remain conjectural, for Burns was understandably reticent about a painful memory. Along with the other pressures upon him it may explain a letter written at the height of his literary fame in Edinburgh in which he confessed to 'secret wretchedness':

> The pang of disappointment, the sting of pride, with some wandering stabs of remorse, which never fail to settle on my vitals like vultures, when attention is not called away by the calls of society or the vagaries of the Muse. Even in the hour of social mirth my gaiety is the madness of an intoxicated criminal under the hands of the executioner.

The 'heaven-taught ploughman' was a more dynamic and complicated personality than Mackenzie's epithet implies, or than the *literati* realised in their eagerness to see Burns as the gifted offspring of Rousseau's savage and the Gentle Shepherd. Yet the time was right for Burns's success and there is no doubt that he was aware of his role as a 'rustic bard': after all, the Preface to his poems craved the reader's indulgence by assuming just such a persona. But literary and critical fashions cannot detract from his exciting debut, and the Kilmarnock edition and the 1787 Edinburgh edition which followed it reveal a young writer leaping straight to the height of his powers with astonishing assurance. Almost all of his most famous poems appeared in these collections (the exceptions are 'Holy Willie's Prayer', which was omitted; 'The Jolly Begars' which Hugh Blair persuaded him to leave out; and 'Tam o' Shanter', which was yet to be written).

Burns's book revitalised the Scots language as a medium for verse – it had not been so potent since the days of Lindsay and Montgomerie – but at the same time its success virtually 'type-cast' poetry in Scots until modern times. His was the genius which crowned and concluded the domestic, 'Doric' vein to be found in the works of the Sempills, Hamilton, Ramsay and even in such a city poet as Fergusson. For the next hundred years and more 'poetry in Scots' meant 'poetry like Burns's', and as late as the 1920s Hugh MacDiarmid could curse the influence of a writer whose brilliance set the mould for so many inferior imitations.

Burns's background was genuinely close to the spirit of 'Christis Kirk on the Green', and in this sense his convivial muse belongs to the world of small farms and market towns with their local gossip and a tradition of occasional verse. On the other hand, he had also read the makars, and his vernacular approaches a standard literary Lowland Scots – he called it 'Lallans' – for he used Scots words from dialects other than his own. In 'The Vision' Burns uses an eloquent Scots, well worthy of the makars, to set the scene and to talk of his own sombre feelings. But, when his muse appears as an idealised girl, it is, significantly, English which both she and her bard adopt as the most appropriate language in which to discuss 'the dignity of Man'. Like most educated men of his day, Burns was inclined to abandon his mother-tongue when he sought what he took to be a sophisticated or 'literary' voice.

Robert Burns was born the first of seven children on 25 January 1759 at Alloway in Ayrshire. His father, William Burns or Burnes, married a local girl after coming south from Kincardineshire in search of work. But the land at Mount Oliphant farm was unproductive and at forty-four Burns found himself bound to a life of lonely toil until his health was damaged by the effort. By the age of fifteen Robert too was labouring in the fields, and despite his natural sturdiness he contracted a rheumatic heart-condition that eventually killed him. Even in hardship, Burns wanted a good education for his two eldest boys and so he and four of his neighbours arranged for a young tutor called Murdoch to teach their children. These arrangements were known as 'adventure schools' and meant that in areas where parish schooling was not practicable most of Scotland's rural population could still read and write. Thus Robert was introduced to English literature in selections from Shakespeare, Milton, Dryden, Addison, Thomson, Gray and Shenstone.

During the summers when he could be spared from the farm, Burns was sent away to continue his studies, and at Kirkoswald near the coast he met Douglas Graham of Shanter farm, said to be a model for Tam o' Shanter, and 'Soutar Johnnie', who was the local cobbler. He made a start at Latin, trigonometry and French, and took pride in the letters which he sent home. His commonplace book records his early rhymes and the first stirrings of what was to be a lifetime's infatuation with girls. The lease at Mount Oliphant expired when Burns was eighteen, and the family moved some ten miles to Lochlie farm in the parish of Tarbolton. Here Robert befriended the apothecary John Wilson, an innocent model for the fatal 'Dr Hornbook', as well as John Rankine and 'brother poet' David Sillar, who were to feature in his later epistle poems. In the company of such lively young men Burns became first president of the 'Bachelor's Club' – a debating-society dedicated to the fair sex and 'honest-hearted' male friendship. The farm was failing, however. William Burns's goods were impounded to pay for back rent, and only his death in 1784 saved him from being arrested for debt. It is not difficult to explain the poet's lifelong hatred of landlords and the kind of factor who 'thinks to knit himsel the faster/ In favour wi' some gentle Master' by seeing that 'decent, honest, fawsont [seemly] folk,/ Are riven out baith root an' branch,/ Some rascal's pridefu' greed to quench' ('The Twa Dogs'). Robert and Gilbert leased a farm less than three miles away at Mossgiel and they took the rest of the family there in 1784. This time their landlord, Gavin Hamilton, proved to be a good friend and Burns dedicated the Kilmarnock edition to him.

Now in his early twenties, Robert was set on a literary career. By this time he had read and admired *The Man of Feeling*, as well as Thomson, Sterne, Macpherson's *Ossian* and Hume and Locke. Moreover, he had discovered an enthusiasm for old Scots songs and for the works of Ramsay and Fergusson. It was the latter's 'Scotch poems' in particular which encouraged him to persevere with his own verse and to 'string anew', as he put it later, his 'wildly-sounding, rustic lyre, with emulating vigour'. Accordingly, the next two years were extraordinarily full as Burns produced poem after poem and made several songs to traditional airs. No doubt the setting of words to old tunes (as well as his delight in dancing) helped to develop an early facility with strong rhythms and internal rhymes, for Burns's verse is characterised by such qualities, and the onward, reel-like thrusting of standard Habbie became such a favourite of his that it is also known as 'the Burns stanza'. The poet's energies were more than fully engaged, for he committed himself to farming and flouted his shaky health by adopting an equally hectic social life. With his talent for friendship he was not slow in becoming well known and liked in the nearby village of Mauchline, where his landlord Gavin Hamilton worked as a lawyer and where he met Jean Armour and began an affair with her. Mauchline people went straight into his poems, and, when Hamilton's free behaviour was reprimanded by the local Kirk, Burns took his side and claimed that he would rather be damned in his friend's company than saved among such 'canting wretches'. One of the 'wretches' was an elder called William Fisher, whose vindictive hypocrisy is immortalised in 'Holy Willie's Prayer'. When Hamilton came before the presbytery at Ayr it was 'glib tongued' Robert Aiken who demolished Holy Willie's case, and this distinguished senior lawyer became the poet's close friend and something of a patron in influential circles. (Burns dedicated 'The Cottar's Saturday Night' to him.)

In this most creative period the poet's emotional life was complicated; furthermore, the family depended on him, but Mossgiel was not flourishing and he needed money badly. Hamilton, Aiken and others helped to collect subscriptions for a volume called *Poems, Chiefly in the Scottish Dialect*, which was published at Kilmarnock in July 1786, and the immediate success of this book catapulted him into fame and allowed him to give funds at last to Gilbert and the family. That winter Burns went to meet his reputation in Edinburgh, where plans were immediately made for an expanded 'Edinburgh' edition, which appeared in April 1787. This volume contained extra poems, including more work in English, but, if his Augustan verses pleased his new literary friends, they seem merely imitative and conventional today. The most significant additions are poems such as 'The Ordination', 'The Calf' and the 'Address to the Unco Guid', which give openly satirical accounts of the Kirk and its doings. More personal attacks such as 'The Holy Tulzie' or 'The Twa Herds' were left in manuscript circulation only, and, indeed, 'Holy Willie's Prayer' did not see print until 1801.

In Burns's time it was not possible in a small community (as Gavin Hamilton found out) to ignore the church's mandates on everyday social behaviour. Yet the Kirk was divided on several doctrinal matters, including lay patronage. The 'Moderates' were in favour of tolerating other creeds and of accepting the law which allowed the local landowner to propose a minister for the parish. However, the minority 'Popular party', or 'Evangelicals', took a harder line and were becoming more influential in country districts. Some seceded to form a separate presbytery, and before long the seceders split and split again, reviving all the fanaticism of the old Covenanters. The history of these changing alliances, of Burghers and anti-Burghers, 'Auld Lichts' and 'New Lichts', serves to demonstrate once again the Scottish preference for theoretical or organisational disputes over what should be spiritual issues. Burns and his friends in Edinburgh regarded themselves as liberal Christians, and scoffed at the 'three mile prayers and hauf-mile graces' of the extreme faction; yet they still had to accept the Kirk's authority in a society where elders could act like moral policemen with the right of access to people's houses to ensure that the Sabbath was being kept. As a fallible lover of women, Burns had little sympathy with the 'unco guid', nor was he slow to draw attention to their hypocrisies and excesses. Thus 'The Holy Fair' satirises the annual Communion at Mauchline, a custom common in rural parishes where, in what usually became a tent show and a rowdy picnic, hundreds gathered once a year in the open air to hear the preaching, to drink ale and see the sights, and – officially – to prepare for Communion:

> Here, some are thinking on their sins,
>   An' some upo' their claes;   clothes
> Ane curses feet that fyled his shins,
>   Anither sighs an' prays:
> On this hand sits a Chosen swatch,   sample
>   Wi' screw'd up grace-proud faces;
> On that, a set o' chaps, at watch,
>   Thrang winkan on the lasses   busy
>   To chairs that day.

This easy, loping verse was borrowed from Fergusson, who cast a similarly genial eye on public holidays in 'Hallow-Fair' and 'Leith Races'. The Breughelian spirit goes back to 'Christis Kirk' and 'Peblis to the Play', but Burns's more modern eye is quicker to note the contradictions of the scene and to use the antitheses towards a wider and wittier satirical end:

How monie hearts this day converts,
  O' Sinners and o' Lasses!
Their hearts o' stane, gin nicht are gane   at nightfall
  As saft as ony flesh is.
There's some are fou o' love divine;   full
  There's some are fou o' brandy;   drunk
An' mony jobs that day begin,
  May end in Houghmagandie   fornication
    Some ither day.

The barbed subtlety of Burns's educated punning can be more fully appreciated if the original passage from Ezekiel 36:26 is recalled: 'A new heart also will I give you, and a new spirit will I put within you: and I will take away the stony heart out of your flesh, and I will give you an heart of flesh.'

Burns's knowledge of the Bible and his familiarity with the language of God's Presbyterian spokesmen makes 'Holy Willie's Prayer' particularly potent. Here the high-flown diction of Evangelical fervour bumps and tangles with standard Habbie and parochial Scots to lay bare the unctious vindictiveness of the speaker.

Lord, mind Gau'n Hamilton's deserts!
He drinks, an' swears, an' plays at cartes,   cards
Yet has sae mony taking arts
    Wi' great and sma',
Frae God's ain Priest the people's hearts
    He steals awa.

And when we chasten'd him therefore,
Thou kens how he bred sic a splore,   quarrel
And set the warld in a roar
    O' laughin at us:
Curse Thou his basket and his store,
    Kail an' potatoes!   cabbage

The poet dons the flesh of his enemy to explode him from within, and Willie's rolling syntax falters only when he has to confess his own failings, even if his complacency remains unmoved:

But yet – O Lord – confess I must –
At times I'm fashed wi fleshly lust; . . .   troubled
O Lord – yestreen – Thou kens – wi' Meg –
Thy pardon I sincerely beg! . . .

1. Carved Pictish cross at Aberlemno, 12 miles east of Montrose. The cross is filled with an intricate interlacing, while the surrounding symbols (some of them similar to those in the Lindisfarne Gospels) show horses, hounds and a deer to convey a delight in hunting. The other side of the slab has a battle scene.

2. Craigievar Castle, Aberdeenshire, 5 miles south of Alford, a 'Scots Baronial' fortified house from the 1620s. The great fireplace has an inscription: 'Doe not vaiken sleeping dogs'.

3. A street in old Edinburgh. The scene would not have been much different from the seventeenth to the nineteenth century when this was painted by Henry Duguid.

4. *The Black Stool*, by David Allan, 1784. An unwed mother takes the 'cutty stool' in the foreground, while the minister rebukes her lover in a crowded and noisy kirk.

5. The General Assembly of the Kirk of Scotland (1783) is a more sober body of men, but David Allan still notices plenty of fringe activity.

6. The 'lands' of James' Court, a typical Scots tenement at the Lawnmarket above the Mound in early nineteenth-century Edinburgh, painted by Henry Duguid.

7. Ainslie Place in the 'Athenian' New Town of Edinburgh in the early nineteenth century, painted by Thomas H. Shepherd.

8. Country life at 'Pitlessie Fair', by Sir David Wilkie (*detail*).

9. The Revd Robert Walker skating on Duddingston Loch, by Sir Henry Raeburn (1784).

10. Crofter's house (1889).

11. Planting potatoes (1890) with the help of the *cas-chrom* ('crooked spade'), a kind of foot-plough.

12. Herring gutters at Ullapool. The Scottish fleets followed the herring from the east to the west coast and then to the Shetlands and East Anglia.

ROBERT BURNS

13. David Hume, by Allan Ramsay, the poet's son.
14. Robert Burns, from the 1787 Edinburgh edition and considered a good likeness by the poet himself.

15. Sir Walter Scott, by Andrew Geddes (1823).

16. James Hogg, by William Bewick.

17. Thomas Carlyle.

18. Robert Louis Stevenson.

19. *Left to right:* Norman MacCaig, Sorley Maclean, Hugh MacDiarmid and Sydney Goodsir Smith in Edinburgh (1972). The portrait of MacDiarmid on the wall is by R. H. Westwater.

Besides, I further maun avow   must
Wi' Leezie's lass, three times – I trow –
But Lord, that friday I was fou   drunk
        When I cam near her!

The characterisation is repulsively convincing, but Burns's
satire expands to attack the whole system of Calvinist belief
which allows such a self-styled elect to set themselves apart
from the majority of folk, who will be damned no matter how
they behave:

O Thou that in the Heavens does dwell,
Wha, as it pleases best Thysel,
Sends ane to Heaven an' ten to Hell
        A' for Thy glory,
And no for ony guid or ill
        They've done before Thee!

I bless and praise Thy matchless might,
When thousands Thou hast left in night,
That I am here before Thy sight,
        For gifts an' grace
A burning and a shining light
        To a' this place.

Burns satirised the Auld Lichts again in 'The Ordination', and
in a letter of 1788 expressed his opposition to the Calvinist
doctrine that we are born 'wholly inclined' to evil. He believed
instead that we come into the world 'with a heart and a
disposition to do good for it', and this conviction explains his
affinity with Rousseau's ideals and his lifelong preference for
'the social, friendly, honest man / Whate'er he be' ('Second
Epistle to J. Lapraik').

On a broader note, Burns enjoyed hearty companionship,
like Fergusson before him, and in Edinburgh he joined a
drinking-club called the 'Crochallan Fencibles'. He goes
further than his 'elder brother', however, by celebrating a
Blakean faith in energy as eternal delight. The fullest expression of this anarchic, disreputable but always gloriously alive
spirit comes in 'Love and Liberty – A Cantata', more familiarly
known as 'The Jolly Beggars'. This sequence of poems and
songs seems to have been a little too potent for his intellectual
friends in Edinburgh, and Hugh Blair persuaded him to leave it
out of the 1787 collection. Like 'Holy Willie's Prayer', the piece

was never published in Burns's lifetime, and in fact the version that has survived may be incomplete. As so often in his work, Burns owed the initial conception to an already-established genre, for a song-sequence called 'The Happy Beggars' was featured in the *Tea Table Miscellany* and John Gay had drawn on the romance of thieves and vagabonds with his *Beggar's Opera* in 1728. Burns went further to produce an anti-pastoral (the very reverse of *The Gentle Shepherd*) which Matthew Arnold later hailed as a world of 'hideousness and squalor' and yet a 'superb poetic success' with a 'breadth, truth and power . . . only matched by Shakespeare and Aristophanes'.

Arnold's analogy with drama is appropriate, because Burns enters into the lives and voices of others as he describes a wild autumn night of merriment and song amongst a gang of wandering beggars and their doxies in Poosie Nansie's tavern. The effect of the whole is greater than any one section, for the 'Cantata' alternates between narrative passages to set the scene, and songs in which the various characters lay bare their lives and loves in a variety of stanza forms and traditional airs. The poem's diction keeps changing, too, as Burns swings from rich Scots to a cooler English and back again, so that the juxtapositions heighten the effectiveness and expand the field of his satire. The beggars, raddled, drunk, noisy and boastful, dance and fight and sing in a greasy dive; yet their antics also cast wild and telling shadows which ape the wider world outside, the world of social pretension and sexual gallantry, of political expediency, business-affairs and wars. An old soldier and his lover pledge themselves to drink and fornication, and their songs tell how he has lost an arm and a leg, while she has been through the regiment from drummer boy to chaplain; a tiny fiddler and a tinker fight over a raw-boned widow who earns her living as a pickpocket – the caird wins but the musician soon consoles himself with another lady:

> The Caird prevail'd – th'unblushing fair   tinker
>   In his embraces sunk;
> Partly wi' LOVE o'ercame sae sair,
>   An' partly she was drunk:
> Sir VIOLINO with an air,
>   That show'd a man o' spunk,   spirit
> Wish'd UNISON between the PAIR,
>   An' made the bottle clunk
>   To their health that night.

But hurchin Cupid shot a shaft,
  That play'd a DAME a shavie –   trick
The Fiddler RAK'D her, FORE and AFT,
  Behint the Chicken cavie.   coop

Burns's diction switches contexts with a speed and irreverence
which anticipates Byron's *Don Juan*. A positively Augustan
epithet such as 'th' unblushing fair' is matched with abstractions such as 'LOVE' and 'UNISON' and other elements from
Cupid's vocabulary. These phrases are almost serviceable, if
slightly shop-soiled (entirely appropriate to the would-be
sophistication of 'Sir VIOLINO'), but Burns dynamites them and
all their romantic conventions with the brutality of an ugly
rhyme ('drunk' / 'spunk' / 'clunk') and the outrageousness of
the shaft and the shavie played out behind a hen-house.
    The little fiddler's *amour* is one of three ladies in tow with a
'bard of no regard', and it is this night-town version of Burns
himself who sings a closing song which shakes the rafters of
Poosie Nansie's and strikes at the foundations of the establishment's respect for property, religion and order itself;

Here's to Budgets, Bags and Wallets!
  Here's to all the wandering train!
Here's our ragged Brats and Callets!   children and wenches
  One and all cry out, Amen!

CHORUS
A fig for those by Law protected,
  Liberty's a glorious feast!
Courts for cowards were erected,
  Churches built to please the Priest.

The political implications of these lines are reinforced because
the song and chorus are written almost entirely in English – as if
the poet means to generalise. Burns's sympathies are not just
fashionably radical; they are fundamental to his background,
to his optimistic and humanitarian nature and to that sense of
dour pride and self-respect so important to his class. This
attitude appears repeatedly in those letters and poems where he
protests his independence and the honesty of his feelings with a
telling and even excessive emphasis. 'The Twa Dogs' comments pointedly on the superficiality of rank in human society
just as the early 'Epistle to Davie' predicted another kind of

democracy by insisting on the primacy of the heart and its affections.

> It's no in titles nor in rank;
> It's no in wealth like Lon'on Bank,
>   To purchase peace and rest;
> It's no in makin muckle, mair: much, more
> It's no in books; it's no in lear,   learning
>   To make us truly blest:
> If Happiness hae not her seat
>   And centre in the breast,
> We may be wise, or rich, or great,
>   But never can be blest.

The terms may be hedonistic but the spirit of these lines is not far removed from that of Presbyterian dissent (substitute 'Grace' for 'Happiness' in the seventh line); and Burns is certainly speaking from a tradition of sturdy independence within his own milieu of crofters, tenant farmers and 'bonnet lairds'. The same dignity is at the heart of the song 'Is there for honest poverty', and it is the source of Burns's sympathies with the American fight for independence and, later, with the early stages of the French Revolution:

> What though on hamely fare we dine,
>   Wear hodden grey, and a' that.
> Gie fools their silks, and knaves their wine,
>   A Man's a Man for a' that.
> For a' that, and a' that,
>   Their tinsel show an' a' that;
> The honest man, though e'er sae poor,
>   Is king o' men for a' that.

The popular success of Burns's work, with its many expressions of universal brotherhood speaks volumes for the change in outlook, both political and personal, which was to accompany the Romantic movement in literature. By 1795, however, the Reign of Terror, the threat of invasion and perhaps his new responsibilities as an excise-officer combined to put revolution in a different light for the poet, and, like Wordsworth and many others, he became disillusioned with the French experiment. He helped to organise the Dumfries volunteers and even wrote a song for them which rather

uneasily combines his distaste for authoritarian rule, whatever
its origins, with a jingoistic British patriotism:

> The wretch that would a Tyrant own,
>   And the wretch, his true-sworn brother,
> Who'd set the mob above the Throne,
>   May they be damned together.

As far as his celebrity in Edinburgh was concerned, the poet
remained the 'man of independent mind' who refused to have
his head turned by the admiring salons. He took pleasure in
meeting and corresponding with influential friends but he
foresaw the day when he would return to his 'rural shades',
recognising that at least part of his fame came from what he
called the 'novelty of his character' among learned and polite
people. As 'To a Louse' and 'The Twa Dogs' testify, Burns was
too sensitively aware of social pretentiousness and class-
differences to be blind to these currents at work in the tide of his
own reputation:

> O wad some Pow'r the giftie gie us
> To see oursels as ithers see us!
> It wad frae mony a blunder free us
>   An foolish notion.

('To a Louse')

In 'The Twa Dogs' the poet's sympathies are openly with the
labouring classes, and although he does not underestimate
their hardships he allows them the satisfaction of stout hearts
and simple pleasures and feels, too, that it is their toil which
supports the restless hypochondria and the corrupt activities of
their idle masters. Neither Luath, the poor man's collie, nor
Caesar, the rich man's Newfoundland, has a complete picture
of the human world, but it is not long before one emerges from
their conversation. Caesar gives a hilarious version of the
propertied classes at play abroad: but Burns has not forgotten
how his father died trying to pay rent and feed his family.

> At Opera an' Plays parading,
> Mortgaging, gambling, masquerading:
> Or maybe in a frolic daft,
> To Hague or Calais takes a waft,
> To make a tour an' take a whirl,
> To learn *bon ton* an' see the worl'.

There, at Vienna or Versailles,
He rives his father's auld entails;   grabs/robs; mortgages
Or by Madrid he takes the rout,
To thrum guittares an fecht wi' nowt;   cattle (bullfights)
Or down Italian Vista startles,
Whore-hunting amang groves o' myrtles:
Then bowses drumlie German-water,   drinks muddy
To make himsel look fair an' fatter,
An' clear the consequential sorrows,
Love-gifts of Carnival Signioras.

The poet's gaiety never curdles and yet at times its ferocious intensity hints at the pain of injustice and the pressures and resentments felt by the labouring poor. The coarser pleasures of Poosie Nansie's and the groaning excesses of Evangelical fervour both bear witness to how these pressures were so often sublimated in small Scottish communities. There are hints of a similar strain behind the male vaunting with which Burns so often declares his passion for the 'lasses'. Thus in 'Epistle to James Smith' the poet makes a fine allegiance with the 'hare-brained sentimental' 'ramstam boys' and scoffs at 'douse [prudent] folk that live by rule,/ Grave, tideless-blooded, calm and cool', whose hearts 'are just a standing pool'. But it is less easy to admire the 'Epistle to John Rankine', a favourite poem of his, in which he tells how he was fined for 'poaching' Elizabeth Paton like a partridge, leaving her pregnant because 'ae night lately, in my fun,/ I gaed a rovin wi' the gun':

The poor wee thing was little hurt;
I straiket it a wee for sport,
Ne'er thinkan they wad fash me for't . . .   bother

As soon's the clockin-time is by,   hatching
An' the wee pouts begun to cry,   young partridges
Lord, I'se hae sportin by an by,
      For my gowd guinea . . .

In contrast to his coarser moments, Burns's taste for sentiment was understandably popular in Henry Mackenzie's sophisticated circle. 'The Cottar's Saturday Night' was praised by contemporaries for giving Augustan dignity and 'the true flavour of natural tenderness' to rustic life; but modern readers often find the poem too condescending and prone to moralise, as well as marred by an uneasy mixture of Scots and English.

Burns wanted to depict the virtues of artless, common folk and to this end his descriptive passages are more successful than has sometimes been allowed, but the barer, sterner language of Wordsworth's 'Michael' (1800) succumbs less to the cult of feeling and makes a better job of the same subject. The Scot achieved an even-toned and successful combination of natural tenderness and moral reflection with 'To a Mouse'; but the very similar 'To a Mountain Daisy' contains a hint of self-pity, easy sentiment and that use of the Scots diminutive that was to multiply like frogspawn in so many luckless imitations. Nevertheless, the poem was highly regarded, not least by Mackenzie and the poet himself. A more robust comic talent finds expression in 'To a Haggis' and especially in 'Address to the Deil', where Milton's fallen archangel has to endure Burns's cheery familiarity and sceptical good wishes. Satan seems to have been something of a cronie of Scottish poets since at least Dunbar's time, and Calvinist Hell-fire has obviously done nothing to curb their presumptions:

> An' now, auld Cloots, I ken ye're thinkan,
> A certain Bardie's rantin, drinkin,
> Some luckless hour will send him linkan,   tripping along
>   To your black pit;
> But faith! he'll turn a corner jinkan,   dodging
>   An' cheat you yet.

The same irreverent spirit is directed at Death in 'Death and Dr Hornbook' and finds its high point in 'Tam o' Shanter', written three years later.

Burns's life was unsettled after the triumph of his first winter in Edinburgh. He left two lovers behind him and returned to Mauchline a hero; there was a reconciliation with the Armours and Jean became pregnant again, although he still did not want to marry her (he was nursing an affection for Peggy Chalmers, another new friend in Edinburgh, but she married someone else the next year). The 'Edinburgh edition' appeared in April 1787 and thereafter Burns took various tours through Scotland, being awarded the freedom of Dumfries and visiting relatives in the North-East. Creech, his Edinburgh publisher, was always slow in paying royalties, but the prospects were good and the poet arranged for half the profits to go to Gilbert and the family. Still, he was not sure how he should live and that winter saw him back in the city again. His arrival was not the social sensation it had been in 1786. He found himself involved with the beautiful Nancy M'Lehose, a married lady separated from her husband, and they conducted an impassioned and sentimentally spiritual affair, mostly through their many letters to each other as 'Sylvander and Clarinda'. Burns's major literary commitment was now entirely given to songs, for he had begun to help James Johnson with *The Scots Musical Museum*, which appeared in six volumes from 1787 to 1803. Burns became the literary editor of most of these books, although he refused payment for the work, collecting and altering old songs and writing completely new ones to old airs and fiddle-tunes. He was very enthusiastic about the task and before his death he had created over 200 songs of his own.

Leaving Edinburgh in the spring of 1788, Burns returned once more to Mauchline. Jean had borne him twins for the second time but the two little girls died within weeks. The poet arranged to lease a new farm at Ellisland and finally married the girl who had endured more from him and for him than ever Clarinda had, but it was never to be a marriage of minds and he had other affairs, including one with Anne Park, who bore him a child. Jean produced a second and then a third son and Burns was given a post at last with the Excise. He did well in the service but the long miles he had to ride did not help his health. His last literary poem was 'Tam o' Shanter', written in the winter of 1790. It is a brilliant and corruscating summation of all the vigour, local comedy, satirical irreverence and the driving technical virtuosity which he had inherited from the tradition and made his own. The poem incorporates the mock heroic, the bawdy and the tender; it relishes a local ghost story well told and presents a 'proper' eighteenth-century moral conclusion with a poker face; it focuses on domestic rural life with convincing realism only to leap to the grotesquerie of a hallucinatory encounter with sexuality and diabolism. 'Tam o' Shanter' is a unique poem in European culture, for it straddles literary and cultural gulfs by combining an earthy peasant *joie de vivre* with the more rarefied possibility of individual imaginative transport: in it 'The Miller's Tale' meets the world of 'Kubla Khan'.

When Ellisland eventually failed at the end of 1791 (not through lack of effort on Burns's part) the poet fell back on his

Excise appointment and moved to Dumfries with his family. Jean gave him a daughter and he brought Anne Park's little girl into the household as his own. Here, despite uncertain health and official suspicion about his liberal views, he found the energy to continue his commitment to old songs and song-writing. The popular appetite for songs, whetted by Ramsay's *Tea Table Miscellany*, had been fed by many writers. Among the best known were two men from Aberdeenshire, Alexander Ross (1699–1784), a schoolmaster who produced lively pieces such as 'The Rock and the Wee Pickle Tow' and 'Woo'd and Married an' A''; and John Skinner (1721–1807), an Epis-copalian minister whose racy, reeling 'Tullochgorum' was held by Burns to be 'the best Scotch song ever Scotland saw'. Burns's own editorial work for *The Scots Musical Museum* was not unscholarly, but David Herd (1732–1810) was more exacting and published fragments without embellishment. Herd's *Ancient and Modern Scots Songs* (1769; 1776) includes some of the first printings of the old ballads, and, although Burns had copies of the book, the ballads rarely influenced him in his own songs, which concentrate on tender love-lyrics, drinking-verses such as 'O Willie Brew'd a Peck o' Maut', and sturdy airs such as 'Scots Wha Hae', 'Is there for honest poverty' and (refined from several originals) 'Auld Lang Syne'.

The love-songs and their beautiful tunes are particularly memorable. 'The Lea Rig' and 'Corn Rigs are Bonie' celebrate the bitter-sweetness of first assignations and the joys of sexual meeting, while 'Mary Morison', 'Ae Fond Kiss' and 'Highland Mary' are songs of parting and death suffused with the poet's sense of mortality. These intimations of inevitable ending invade love-lyrics such as 'A Red, Red Rose' and 'O wert thou in the cauld blast', while others (such as 'Whistle O'er the Lave o't') take a bolder, gayer note, and an old and bawdy complaint about fading potency was rewritten as an expression of simple companionship between ageing lovers – 'John Anderson my Jo'. Even with optimistic words, the plangent tunes chosen by Burns give the force of a lament to songs such as 'The Young Highland Rover' and 'Where braving angry winter's storms'. The latter was set to a fiddle-tune by Neil Gow and so, like several of Burns's airs, it provides the singer with a fairly severe challenge to his or her vocal range. The poet's affinity with the age's taste for honest sentiment is seen at its clearest in these songs and Burns was by no means the only writer to work in the genre. As a popular art-form it is closer to pastoral in its moods and expression than it is to the oral traditions of the folk tale and the ballads. Lady Grizel Baillie pointed the way at the beginning of the century and she was followed by other educated women who wrote and adapted material to their view of humble life. These include Jean Elliott (1727–1805) and her 'The Flowers o' the Forest'; Lady Anne Lindsay (1750–1825), 'Auld Robin Gray'; Joanna Baillie (1762–1851), 'Tam o' the Lin'; and, in the next century, Lady Nairne's 'The Land o' the Leal'. Such pieces were usually touching, sometimes comic and always decorous. Later writers, such as Scott and Stevenson, felt that Burns's songs were a lesser achievement than his early poems, but modern critics have come to emphasise the high level of their musical success. Indeed, his best Scots poems were never far removed from the rhythms of popular dancing and the traditions of sentiment and humour in song.

By 1793 Creech's second 'Edinburgh' edition – with some additional poems – was published, and on top of his contributions to the *Musical Museum* Burns was sending songs to George Thomson's *Select Scottish Airs*. (The poet's private collection of Rabelaisian verses, later known as *The Merry Muses of Caledonia*, was never intended for publication.) Burns kept up his editorial tasks until a few weeks before his death at the age of only thirty-seven. He could not have foretold the international fame which was to come, nor the ambiguous influence which his work was to have on Scottish life and culture for the next hundred years.

6

The nineteenth century: history, industry, sentiment

In Scottish cultural history the writers of the late eighteenth and early nineteenth century contribute to a single period of change and unusually creative activity. Walter Scott made Scotland and its past famous throughout Europe, periodical literature flourished in the capital, and there was a massive expansion of cities and industry. The population of Edinburgh doubled, with a powerful middle class to confirm its supremacy in law, medicine, the Church, banking, brewing and publishing. Farming and fishing were equally well established, on the east coast, along with heavier industries in coal, textiles, paper and especially the manufacture of linen. Great streets and houses in London were built with Aberdeen granite, and the finest American clippers were matched by sailing-ships from yards in the North-East.

The north's most significant export was people, and the economic and cultural life of the area was dominated by emigration to Canada and America. Estate-owners and clan-chiefs had been enclosing the land from the 1770s, and the ancient runrig style of strip cultivation, with its emphasis on subsistence farming shared by the community, had finally begun to disappear. Sheep-farming made a profitable appearance in the South-West, where there was plenty of grazing and urban markets close to hand, but in the Highlands, where the poorer land could no longer support an expanding population, the arrival of sheep only added to their problems. Landowners in search of grazing encouraged tenants to leave their crofts by offering them new jobs or assisted passage and emigration. In the second decade of the century the vast Sutherland estate set about 'improvement' in this manner, planning to resettle families on the coast, where the herring industry was enjoying a boom. (Neil Gunn's novel *The Silver Darlings* is set in this period.) The Countess of Sutherland intended these developments for the best, but old customs and loyalties could not be uprooted without pain. The evictions carried out by her agents, and the particular cruelty of Patrick Sellar in the small glen of Strathnaver made the Sutherland 'Clearances' and Sellar's name notorious. Many Gaelic poems were written about the pains of eviction, and the small crofters conceived a hatred of sheep and the English language alike:

> Not sweet the sound that waked me from slumber,
> coming down to me from the mountain tops:
> the Lowland shepherd whose tongue displeases,
> Shouting there at his lazy dog.

(Iain MacLachlainn, 'Alas my State' ['Och, och mar tha mi'],
trs. D. Thomson)

The use of Gaelic in Highland schools was officially permitted, but, in practice, the Education Act of 1872 set up a system of national control and inspection which inevitably favoured English. For the most part the Highlanders offered only passive resistance to changes forced upon them; but there were outbursts from time to time between evicted crofters and the police, the militia and even the army. Women often joined in these skirmishes, and their leading part in the famous 'Battle of Braes' in Skye in 1882 gained the support of public opinion and helped to bring about the Crofters' Act, which finally offered secure tenure and controlled rents. Not the least effective in this campaign were the songs and poems of Mary Macpherson of Skye, who spoke out fearlessly on behalf of the old culture and land-reform.

For the first half of the century, however, the poorer parts of the North-West Highlands had no protection from the demands of capital and the burgeoning of market-forces elsewhere. When wool-prices declined, or when the demand for kelp collapsed in the face of cheaper imports and chemical substitutes, many old families went bankrupt and landowner-ship fell into new, perhaps less caring, hands. The pattern of clan obligations had not survived the aftermath of the 1745 rising, and many chieftains now regarded themselves as landowners in the capitalist mould, spending their time and their money elsewhere. When the potato-crop failed in 1846 there was no government relief for famine in the north, and thousands of impoverished Highlanders went abroad or came in search of work, like their Irish fellows, to the Lowland cities of Scotland. Little wonder that many Gaelic verses of the period, composed in Glasgow or in the settlements of Nova Scotia, are steeped in nostalgia for the communities, customs and girls left behind in the 'homeland'. Yet it is difficult to imagine how even the most enlightened of policies could have solved all the problems of the Highlands, in the face of their limited resources and a growing population.

If the brash and confident heart of the industrial nineteenth century belongs to any one area of Scotland, it belongs to Paisley, Greenock, Glasgow and the South-West. The groundwork was done by many small merchants who had invested in the weaving of cotton imported from the Americas. Their business had begun as a scattered rural industry with hand-looms for linen and cotton; next it developed with water-powered mills until, finally, steam-driven factories with large work-forces were concentrated near the cities. This led to an increased demand for coal, more industrialisation and higher wages for the miners, who had only recently been emancipated from virtual slavery on the estates of mine-owners. Iron foundries began to produce steam engines to pump the mines and power the mills. Chemical works developed new techniques in bleaching and dyeing for the textile-trade, and the production of coal-tar and gas brought advanced lighting to many factories and towns. The Industrial Revolution saw Glasgow's population increasing faster than that of any other town in Britain. Thousands of labourers arrived from Ireland and the Highlands, and under such pressure the old fabric of the city could not cope. By the 1850s half the children born in Glasgow died before the age of five, and there were outbreaks of cholera until the new Loch Katrine water-supply was brought into service ten years later. The Scottish Act of the great Reform Bill of 1832 was welcomed by everyone, but gradually it became apparent to the new labourers that their lot had hardly improved at all. The Chartist movement's demand for universal male suffrage found ready support in industrial Scotland,

and its struggles in the 1840s confirmed a radical sensibility in the South-West and a sense of solidarity among the working class. But early attempts to gain better wages when times were hard had failed. In later years unions such as the Coal Miners' Association did better for their members, but it was 1867 before most workers got the vote and the Factory Act afforded some protection and a limit to the hours worked by women and children.

After the expansion of the railways in order to transport coal and then manufactured goods and passengers, the second half of the century saw an astonishing growth in heavy industry. Blast furnaces, fuelled by cheap coal and ore, supplied the raw material for engineering and ship-building. For twenty years after 1850 nearly three-quarters of all the iron vessels launched in Britain came from Clydeside, and the developing British Empire ensured that these ships, locomotives, boilers, pumps, marine engines and the engineers themselves went into service all around the world. 'Clyde-built' became synonymous with advanced technology and durability. Glasgow was called the 'second city of the Empire', middle-class ironmasters and ship-building families made their fortunes and beautiful new terraces and parks were created in the city. But a shortage of housing for the proletariat meant that social problems got worse and worse. In 1880 a quarter of the city's families lived in one-room apartments, and many took lodgers as well. New tenements in the Scottish style were erected, and life in these crowded buildings had a special sense of community; but they were also subject to overcrowding and decay, until by the end of the century the slums of Glasgow were among the worst in Europe, breeding-grounds of violence, drunkenness and vice. Yet the booming city bred a native resilience in its people, and, if the influx of families from Ireland led to religious prejudices between Protestants and Catholics, it also contributed a unique humour and vitality to the working population, not to mention a healthy scepticism about the British establishment.

As far as the Kirk was concerned, the old Presbyterian principles were once again in arms against centralised government control and patronage by landowners, while fundamentalist Evangelical preachers were coming to the fore, especially in the crowded cities, where there was a fear of Catholic emancipation. Ten years of wrangling between the state and various Church factions came to a head at the General Assembly of 1843, when nearly 40 per cent of the establishment broke away from the 'Auld Kirk' on a matter of principle and formed the Free Church, claiming to represent the true values of Presbyterianism. The 'Disruption' caused considerable hardship to the rebel congregations and their ministers, for in the early days they were harried by their landlords and forced to worship on the open hillside. They survived, however, to form a General Assembly and a parallel organisation of their own, even down to schools and overseas missions. The Free Kirk was particularly successful in the Highlands, much to the dismay of the landowners, and its radical tendency immediately made itself felt in votes for the Liberal Party which unseated many established Tory members. In other respects, however, the Protestant ethic was entirely in tune with the pursuit of profit and the age's materialistic belief that every man should make his way by dint of personal initiative, 'respectability' and hard work. Thousands of Scots took this course by leaving home, and skilled, unskilled, Highland and Lowland alike, they spread throughout the British Empire to become a byword – both loved and hated for their ambition, hardiness and ingenuity.

By the 1880s Scotland was indisputably part of British Victorian industrial society, yet the Scots' own sense of their cultural differences from England had not died out. Thus, when the country's prosperity was most fully centred on heavy industry in the urban areas, there grew up a vogue for 'cabbage-patch' literature – backward-looking and sentimentally rustic tales extolling simple 'Scotch' folk, pawky humour and 'honest' feeling. When Queen Victoria built Balmoral in 1855, it confirmed an English vogue for tourism, tartan and turrets in the north, and 'Scottish baronial' architecture in the same style appeared throughout the country in a rash of railway-stations and hotels. A monument to Wallace towered over the plain at Stirling; the new railway-station at Edinburgh was called 'Waverley', and the Scott monument commanded Princes Street like a mislocated cathedral spire. Burns had his monument in Auld Reekie too, and Burns Associations were formed throughout the world to promulgate his works and to consume a ritual supper each year on the anniversary of his birth. The typical 'canny Scotsman' began to appear in the press with a famous *Punch* cartoon in 1860 along the lines of 'I hadna been in London mair than half-an-hour, when bang! went saxpence!' This northern counterpart to John Bull – staid, bewhiskered and famously cautious with his money – has more in common with his *petit bourgeois* Victorian inventors than he has with an older, prouder and more volatile Scottish spirit.

Not all was tartan ribbons and bardolatry, however, and national feeling took a political dimension too, for the Association for the Vindication of Scottish Rights was formed in 1853, and, of course, the Disruption of the Kirk had already served to remind folk of old Scottish values. When those crofters on Skye resisted eviction by physical force, they were aware that similar action had made nationalism a potent political issue in Ireland, and so the Highland Land League was formed along Irish lines to press for reform. In the face of the 'Irish question' to the west and the so-called 'Crofters' War' to the north, the Liberal government was pleased to make concessions by passing the Crofters' Act. When the government fell after the failure of the Irish Home Rule Bill in 1886, Liberal and nationalist opinion in Scotland was further stimulated and an all-party Home Rule Association was formed to promote political independence. Their case did not have the urgency or the violence of the Irish movement, but it contained a separatist and a nationalist feeling which has played a part in Scottish politics ever since.

Although the century began in Scotland with Walter Scott's verse romances, there was no poet to match the achievement of Burns, nor was there any Scottish equivalent to the English Romantic poets, unless, of course, **George Gordon, the sixth Lord Byron** (1788–1824) is seen as a Scottish writer. This claim is not as eccentric as it may seem, for Byron's early childhood was spent in Scotland – he attended Aberdeen Grammar School and his mother was Elizabeth Gordon of Gight, an unstable member of an unstable family from Donside. He himself claimed to be 'half a Scot by birth and bred / A whole one' (*Don Juan*), and T. S. Eliot believed there was a particularly Calvinist element in his delight in posing as a damned creature. Gregory Smith identified Byron's mercurial temperament with the 'clean contrair' spirit of the Scottish sensibility, and it must be admitted that the poet's swift transitions from pathos to mockery, or from moral satire to self-deflating parody, scarcely correspond to an English conception of literary decorum. The case can be developed at greater length, but for present purposes Byron's career must be left to the realm of English letters, where he came to prominence with *Childe Harold's Pilgrimage* in 1812 to join Walter Scott as one of the most famous writers in Europe.

Notwithstanding Byron's fame and Scott's early success in verse, the medium of the age in Scotland was undoubtedly prose, and the spread of literacy, of circulating libraries and the book-buying habit created an enormous appetite for books and periodicals of all sorts. Writers came to depend on the periodical scene to make their living, and, of course, many novels appeared there in serial form. Edinburgh became a most influential publishing-centre, largely due to Archibald Constable and William Blackwood, whose presses, along with the *Edinburgh Review* and *Blackwood's Magazine*, made them household names throughout the kingdom. The phenomenal popularity of Scott's fiction was intimately bound up with Constable's firm and it exactly matches the expansion of what was coming to be known as 'the reading public' – a new critical conception and a new market.

Scott, Hogg, Galt, Ferrier, Lockhart and Moir were all writing at the same time, and this talented '*Blackwood's*' group played a large part in the growing status of prose fiction throughout urban Britain. Yet their work is curiously divided, not least because they rarely deal with city life. Scott and Hogg look to an earlier and still potent Romantic tradition; while Galt, Moir and Ferrier, with their novels of small town or rural society, foreshadow the *petit-bourgeois* provincialism of late-Victorian Scottish culture. In fact the essence of this latter vision had first appeared as early as 1806 in the work of the painter David Wilkie (1785–1841). In that year Wilkie, a son of the manse from Fifeshire, made his reputation at the Royal Academy in London with a picture called 'Village Politicians'. He produced genre paintings in similar vein for the next two decades – all distinguished by a novelistic desire to imply a story and to portray humour, pathos and sturdy 'Scottish' character-types, rather in the style of 'The Cottar's Saturday Night' or Wordsworth's poems about Cumbrian folk. When Galt and Moir wrote for *Blackwood's* they confirmed a whole country's view of its own nature in terms which were not essentially different from Wilkie's genre painting. This is not to undervalue Galt's keen documentary eye and his sense of comedy, character and irony, but in the hands of lesser men and women the inheritance became 'provincial' in the worst sense of the word, leading to the 'Kailyard' at the end of the century, with its vision of Scotland as a charming rustic backwater.

Unaware of these future developments, Scott's contemporaries felt themselves to belong to the 'second generation' of the Scottish Enlightenment. John Pinkerton (1758–1826) had tried to repair the public neglect of poets such as Barbour and Dunbar with his collection of *Ancient Scotish Poetry* (1786), and the Revd Dr John Jamieson (1759–1838) produced his *Etymological Dictionary of the Scottish Language* (1808, 1825) a work which remained a substantial scholarly reference until modern times. As antiquarians, Sibbald, Irving and Laing wrote biographies and literary histories, and Scott founded the Bannatyne Club in 1823 to publish rare historical texts. In the field of moral philosophy, Duguld Stewart (1753–1828) succeeded Adam Ferguson as professor at Edinburgh, and, while Stewart was not an original thinker, being content to follow Thomas Reid's 'common sense' school, his personality, eloquence and liberal views influenced a whole generation. Most prominent among his peers were Henry Thomas Cockburn (1779–1854), and his friend Francis Jeffrey (1773–1850), two middle-class lawyers who played a part in establishing the Reform Bill and went on to become Whig law lords. Cockburn's *Life of Jeffrey* (1852) and his own various memoirs, published posthumously, give an attractive account of his life and times. Francis Jeffrey started the *Edinburgh Review* in 1802 with the support of Henry Brougham and the English clergyman and wit Sydney Smith – former pupils of Duguld Stewart – and the new quarterly immediately made a name for itself. Within ten years the *Review* had a circulation of over 13,000 and its publisher Constable could attract the best writers in the country with astonishing fees of up to 20 guineas a sheet for anonymous reviews and £1000 or more for a single poem or article. Cockburn wrote on matters of law, and during the twenties and thirties Macaulay and Carlyle contributed regularly with some of their most famous essays.

The *Edinburgh Review* was never more successful than during its early years. Jeffrey was sympathetic to the literature of feeling, but it had to be supported by formal style and moral content, so that Burns, for example, was criticised for espousing 'vehement sensibility' without 'decency and regularity'. In this sense Jeffrey's values are neoclassical and it is not surprising that he began a famous review of Wordsworth's *The Excursion* on a typically proscriptive note – 'This will never do.' The *Review* was celebrated for the scathing and superior tone of its criticism, and, while it allowed Wordsworth and the English 'Lake School' to have 'a great deal of genius and of laudable feeling', it did not hesitate to chastise the poets for 'perverseness and bad taste'. Scott's *Marmion* was pruned with equal rigour, as if the task were an irksome duty – 'because we cannot help considering it as the foundation of a new school, which may hereafter occasion no little annoyance both to us and to the public'. Little wonder that Byron satirised Jeffrey and his 'critic clan' in *English Bards and Scotch Reviewers* by referring to them as the 'bloodhounds of Arthur's Seat'!

It was not long before Scottish Tories lost patience with the dominance of the *Review* and its Whiggish politics. Walter Scott helped to found the (London) *Quarterly Review* in 1809, but Jeffrey's periodical did not meet its match until 1817, when William Blackwood, Constable's rival in publishing, produced the *Edinburgh Monthly Magazine*, which was soon changed to *Blackwood's Edinburgh Magazine*. The revised 'Maga' or 'Ebony', as it came to be known, was edited by John Gibson Lockhart and John Wilson, two young lawyers determined to make their mark on the cultural scene. This they did without delay, helped by James Hogg, in a mock biblical 'Translation from an Ancient Chaldee Manuscript', which satirised the 'war' between Constable and Blackwood and provided malicious caricatures of their Whig enemies and literary rivals. There was an immediate scandal, the October issue sold out, new readers were left panting for more, and the (anonymous) authors found it expedient to leave town. Over the next two years the publisher had to pay out £1000 in damages, but he stood by his 'wild fellows' and *Blackwood's* flourished, to be published without a break until 1980. Under Wilson and Lockhart, and an Irishman William Maginn, 'Maga' continued to make a stir, particularly in its wholehearted opposition to the poetry of Leigh Hunt, Shelley and Keats, motivated, perhaps, by the fact that Francis Jeffrey had greatly praised Keats in the *Edinburgh*

Review. Whatever the reason, *Blackwood's* roasted 'the Cock-
neys' with a vituperative glee virtually indistinguishable from
snobbish and personal spite. Of course, Keats's fiery mind was
not 'snuffed out' by any such 'article', as Byron has it in *Don
Juan*, nor was he the only writer to suffer from the critical
hostilities declared between Constable and Blackwood. Wilson
and Lockhart were not above petty lies and libels and political
prejudices and old scores were settled forcefully on all sides.

John Wilson (1785–1854) continued as contributing editor
to *Blackwood's*, and as 'Christopher North' he produced many of
the 'Noctes Ambrosianae' (1822–35), a long-running series of
essays in the form of conversations or monologues supposedly
overheard by the scribe. (They were published in four volumes
in 1885.) These often featured a version of his friend James
Hogg somewhat broadly sketched as the 'Shepherd', a bibulous
and loquacious countryman, spokesperson for common sense,
but given to tall tales or sudden flights of philosophising:

> *Tickler*: James, would you seriously have North to write dramas about the
> loves of the lower orders – men in corduroy breeches, and women in
> linsey-woollen petticoats –
>
> *Shepherd*: Wha are ye, sir, to speak o' the lower orders? Look up to the sky,
> sir, on a starry nicht, and, puir, ignorant, thochtless, upsettin' cretur you'll
> be, gin you dinna feel far within, and deep down your ain sowl, that you are,
> in good truth, ane o' the lower orders – no, perhaps, o' men, but o'
> intelligences! and that it requires some dreadfu' mystery, far beyond your
> comprehension, to mak' you worthy o' ever in after life becoming a dweller
> in those celestial mansions. Yet think ye, sir, that thousan's, and tens o'
> thousan's o' millions, since the time when first God's wrath smote the
> earth's soil with the curse o' barrenness, and human creatures had to earn
> their bread wi' sweat and dust, haena lived and toiled, and laughed and
> sighed, and groaned and grat, *o' the lower orders*, that are noo in eternal bliss,
> and shall sit above you and Mr. North, and ithers o' the best o' the clan, in
> the realms o' heaven!
>
> *Tickler*: 'Pon my soul, James, I said nothing to justify this tirade.

The 'Noctes' proved very popular, and other writers, most
notably Lockhart and Hogg, contributed, while De Quincey
featured as a character in them and wrote for *Blackwood's* in his
own right. (Wilson had befriended him and Wordsworth
during a stay in the Lake District in his earlier years.)

Sir Walter Scott (1771–1832)

Scott's career belongs to the nineteenth century but his links are with the earlier Edinburgh of Burns and Mackenzie, and it was his interest in ballads and Romantically 'medieval' adventure-poems which led him to prose fiction and the virtual invention of the 'historical novel'. He was born in a house in College Wynd among the crowded, disease-ridden streets of Old Edinburgh, where only six of his parents' twelve children survived infancy. Walter was the third of three healthy boys, but at eighteen months a bout of infantile paralysis left him weak with his right leg permanently lamed. His next eight years were spent at his grandfather's farm in the Borders, where he regained his health and acquired a taste for tales and ballads and stories of the Jacobite rebellion. He never did lose his lameness, but he thrived among doting elders, turning into a robust lad, forthright and full of confidence.

Back with the family at a new house in George Square, he attended the old High School in Edinburgh and read Shakespeare, Macpherson's *Ossian*, Pope's Homer, Ramsay's *Ever Green* and Spenser, all of which developed his appetite for 'the wonderful and the terrible', as he put it – 'the common taste of children . . . in which I have remained a child even unto this day'. Little wonder that he came to admire the Stuart cause, with the Cavaliers and Montrose and his Highlanders, and yet his private tutor was a Whig and a Presbyterian and so their amicable wrangles ensured that Scott also heard about the history of the Kirk and the sufferings of the Covenanters. Summer holidays were still spent in the Borders, where he discovered Bishop Percy's *Reliques* and the 'historical incidents and traditional legends' associated with the ruins of castles and abbeys all around.

Apprenticed as a copy-clerk to his father's law-practice in 1786, he learned to produce hundreds of pages of legible manuscripts to short order, and business travels to Perth and the Trossachs (once with an escort of armed soldiers) gave him tales and settings enough for his later fiction. The young clerk attended the theatre and mixed with literary people, leaving a memorable description of Robert Burns, whom he met briefly in the home of Professor Adam Ferguson. But it was decided that Walter should follow his father's profession, so he graduated as a qualified advocate in 1792, although his studies did not preclude him from the city's convivial drinking-habits, nor from joining various clubs and debating-societies. Despite his withered leg, Scott had matured into a strong, raw-boned man who could ride, walk or drink with the hardiest farmer or sportsman. When French invasion threatened in 1797, he joined the Royal Edinburgh Volunteer Light Dragoons, delighting in the uniform and the dashing practice with horse and sabre on the sands of Portobello.

A predilection for boisterous, manly company was characteristic of his class and countrymen, and Scott was equally typical in his more sentimental longings. For five years in the early 1790s he had nursed passionate feelings for Williamina Stuart-Belsches of Fettercairn, a young and beautiful heiress whom he called the 'lady of the green mantle' – the model for a character of the same name in *Redgauntlet* and for several more of his gentle and rather pallid heroines. Williamina married someone else in 1797, but within the year Scott had met Charlotte Margaret Charpentier, of French extraction, who became his loyal and affectionate wife until her death in 1826.

The young advocate harboured literary ambitions and under the spur of the Romantic Gothic craze he translated Gottfried Bürger's 'Lenore' and 'Der Wilde Jäger'. In fact the German poet had already been influenced by ballads in Percy's *Reliques*, and so Scott's versions brought the wheel of fashionable influence full circle. A meeting with 'Monk' Lewis led to a translation of Goethe's *Götz von Berlichingen* – the essence of Romantic medievalism – and a visit to London to see the volume published in 1799. Scott's links with the Borders were renewed when he was appointed Sheriff-depute of Selkirkshire, shortly after his father's death in 1799, and he needed no further encouragement to roam among the hills and rivers of Ettrick, Tweed and Yarrow. In a sense he had been preparing all his life for such a collection as *The Minstrelsy of the Scottish Border* (3 vols, 1802–3), and it seems equally inevitable that he should have followed its success by writing poems of his own, suffused with the romance of antique battles in a benevolent wilderness.

As an editor Scott was inclined to collate what he regarded as the 'best' text from different versions, but he also collected from oral sources and sought the help of better scholars and local people too, including the redoubtable James Hogg, whom he met in the summer of 1802. The *Border Minstrelsy* was an immediate success, beautifully printed by his old friend James Ballantyne, with an enthusiastic introduction and footnotes full of history and quaint details. A third volume was projected for the following year and the work was reprinted several times thereafter, to become a milestone in the Scottish literary world's rediscovery of its own past.

Scott contributed to the newly founded *Edinburgh Review*, encouraged Hogg in his hopes of being published and received William and Dorothy Wordsworth on their Scottish tour. He persuaded James Ballantyne to move to Edinburgh and entered into a secret partnership which ensured that Ballantyne got plenty of printing-commissions, including legal work, Scott's own books and other antiquarian projects from various different publishing-houses. Scott lent money, took a share of the profits and thought it a good scheme, although it put him in an ambiguous position sometimes, and eventually went badly wrong. At first, however, business thrived and Archibald Constable took a commercial interest as well. Preferring to leave the Bar, Scott managed to get appointed as one of the clerks of Session who sit below the judge in the High Court at Edinburgh. His duties as Sheriff of Selkirkshire encouraged him in 1804 to set up a house at Ashestiel in that county, and henceforth he spent half the year sitting at the Court of Session and the rest of the time in travel, or living happily by the Tweed as a 'rattle skulled half-lawyer, half-sportsman' surrounded by his children, his dogs and various family retainers.

Prompted by the Countess of Dalkeith's enthusiasm for a local story of supernatural mischief, *The Lay of the Last Minstrel* was originally intended as an imitation ballad for the third volume of the *Minstrelsy*. It grew considerably, however, under Scott's compulsion to spin a tale of love, magic and chivalry, with English and Scottish armies in conflict, and many descriptions of Border lore and 'scenery and manners'. Whatever he learned from the ballads, it was not concision, and the poem is a typically Romantic confection of that glamorous 'medieval' world already familiar from the poems of Spenser, Chatterton and Coleridge. (Scott acknowledged a metrical debt to 'Christabel' and used much the same pattern of octosyllabic iambic couplets for his other long poems.) *The Lay* was an unprecedented popular success throughout Britain in 1805, with several editions and over 21,000 sales in the first four years, rising to almost 44,000 copies by the time the collected poems appeared in 1830. Francis Jeffrey gave it an enthusiastic review, although he felt that it was too 'local', and opined that 'Mr Scott must either sacrifice his Border prejudices, or offend his readers in the other parts of the empire' – a revealing point of view from the leading critic in 'the Athens of the North', and completely blind to what made Scott's poem special. The author's literary ambitions were thoroughly aroused and he started on a novel which was to deal with Highland life of sixty years earlier. But public acclaim demanded another metrical romance, and so Scott put away prose fiction and set to work on *Marmion*, which was promptly purchased by Constable – unseen and still unfinished – for 1000 guineas.

The Lay was essentially an old legend, but *Marmion* is closer to a novel in conception. Set in 1513 as 'a tale of Flodden field', it visualises the melancholy end of James IV and his army in rather the same spirit as Malory describes the fate of Arthur's Round Table. Marmion is an English knight, an anti-hero with a complicated and treacherous love life. His peace-mission to the Scottish court fails just as his private affairs catch up with him disastrously, and he dies on the battlefield with 'repentance and reviving love'. The melodrama is relieved by a wealth of geographical and historical detail, drawn from Scott's own youthful memories and his reading of the chronicles of Froissart and Pitscottie. He never did take Jeffrey's advice to eschew the 'local', and there are striking set descriptions of the abbey at Lindesfarne, or the battle at Flodden, or Marmion's first sight of Edinburgh. It was another huge success, and after his work on Dryden Scott accepted a further contract with Constable to produce an edition of Swift which was to take him six years to complete. He was unpretentious enough to compare such editorial work to a good cash crop of 'turnips and peas', but a growing dissatisfaction with the Whig politics of the *Edinburgh Review* led to a split with Constable. Scott had Ballantyne form his own publishing-house under the name of his younger brother John, an entertaining but somewhat dilettante character, who was also to act as Scott's agent. The rival business did not last much beyond 1813, for the principals were not good enough judges of what would sell, but it did produce Scott's best and most popular poem.

The Lady of the Lake (1810) takes place in the reign of James V, some twenty-five years after Flodden, and it turns on the king's habit of travelling incognito among his people. (Popular legend refers to him as 'the Gaberlunzie man' – a travelling beggar.) Here the Gothic furniture of knightly chivalry is abandoned in favour of the excitements of stag-hunting, and the real romance of the tale lies with the beauty of the wild countryside around Loch Katrine and 'the ancient manners, habits and customs' of the Highlanders. Scott was sensitive to trends in popular taste and he knew that Anne Grant's *Highland Memoirs* (1806) and *The Cottagers of Glenburnie* (1808), a novel by Elizabeth Hamilton, had already stirred an urban interest in Highland life. He was no expert in Gaelic culture, however, despite a liking for talking to old Jacobites, and it is an oddly bitter reflection that when he was visiting the country around Loch Katrine, convinced that 'the old Scottish Gael' was a subject 'highly adapted for poetical composition', Duncan Bàn Macintyre, one of the greatest Gaelic poets of the eighteenth century, was far from his beloved Ben Dorain and passing the last years of his life virtually unknown to polite Edinburgh as a retired member of the City Guard in the narrow streets of the old town. Yet Scott's 'discovery' of the 'aboriginal race by whom the Highlands of Scotland were inhabited' took lowland Britain and Europe by storm. In fact his romantic and selective view of the clansmen as a warrior-class, volatile, proud, loyal to their own and cruel to others, still prevails in the popular consciousness. In a confrontation between Roderick Dhu and the disguised King James, Scott has the Highlander justify his clansmen's raids in exactly the same terms as a North American Indian chief might have used when speaking to the white man. (Fenimore Cooper came to be known as 'the American Scott' fifteen years later, for his leatherstocking novels proposed a very similar vision of native Americans living in the wilderness.)

> These fertile plains, that soften'd vale,
> Were once the birthright of the Gael;
> The stranger came with iron hand,
> And from our fathers reft the land.

Where dwell we now? See, rudely swell
Crag over crag, and fell o'er fell. . . .
Pent in this fortress of the North,
Think'st thou we will not sally forth,
To spoil the spoiler as we may,
And from the robber rend the prey?
Ay, by my soul! While on yon plain
The Saxon rears one shock of grain,
While of ten thousand herds there strays
But one along yon river's maze,
The Gael of plain and river heir,
Shall with strong hand redeem his share.

(v. vii)

In another striking scene, 'Black Roderick' only has to give a whistle and the bare hillside comes alive with armed men, springing up like Satan's minions in *Paradise Lost*:

And every tuft of broom gives life
To plaided warrior arm'd for strife. . . .
As if the yawning hill to heaven
A subterranean host had given.
Watching their leader's beck and will,
All silent there they stood, and still.
Like the loose crags, whose threatening mass
Lay tottering o'er the hollow pass.

(v. ix)

These are not the only Miltonic aspects which Scott ascribes to James's fierce antagonist, for earlier in the poem the 'waving of his tartans broad' and his 'darken'd brow' had, indeed, made him seem like the 'ill Demon of the night', and even on his death-bed he is described with an epic simile worthy of the fallen angel:

As the tall ship, whose lofty prore
Shall never stem the billows more,
Deserted by her gallant band,
Amid the breakers lies astrand
So, on his couch, lay Roderick Dhu!

(vi. xiii)

Thus the chieftain is revealed as a Romantic anti-hero in the

Satanic/Byronic mould – arrogant, intractible and yet honourable according to his own lights. Nevertheless, Roderick must
die to leave the way clear for a bitter-sweet reconciliation
between *Lowland* lords – the exiled Douglas, whose daughter
Ellen is the 'Lady of the Lake' herself, and the stag-hunting
'Fitzjames', now revealed as an enlightened and forgiving
monarch. The future is clearly theirs.

The poem concludes somewhat in the spirit of *A Winter's Tale*
as identities are revealed and the opposing values of country
and court set aside (if not reconciled) with the promise of a
noble marriage and a happy ending. Another Shakespearean
analogy is suggested by the way Scott intersperses ballads and
songs throughout the poem – a device he was to use to even
greater effect in the novels. Scott's octosyllabic measure is not
markedly better than in his previous verses, but for once the
plot avoids Gothic elaboration, and so the hunt-scenes and the
beautiful landscapes are given room to stand forth as swiftly
paced and effectively unified symbols of freedom and daring, to
convey a strikingly ritualised, almost balletic, vision of heroic
conflict: as if war, too, were sport on the shores of Loch Katrine
– a remote Arden in the north.

The Lady of the Lake was Scott's greatest success to date. A few
critics, and Coleridge in particular, continued to dislike his
loping couplets ('prose in polysyllables'), but the public had no
doubts and bought over 20,000 copies within the year. Even
Jeffrey changed his tune about 'local subjects' and hoped in the
Edinburgh Review that the poet would turn to 'a true Celtic
story':

There are few persons, we believe, of any degree of poetical susceptibility,
who have wandered among the secluded valleys of the Highlands, and
contemplated the singular people by whom they are still tenanted – with
their love of music and of song – their hardy and irregular life, so unlike the
unvarying toils of the Saxon mechanic – their devotion to their chiefs – their
wild and lofty traditions – their national enthusiasm – the melancholy
grandeur of the scenes they inhabit – and the multiplied superstitions
which still linger among them – without feeling that there is no existing
people so well adapted for the purposes of poetry, or so capable of
furnishing the occasions of new and striking inventions.

We are persuaded, that if Mr Scott's powerful and creative genius were
to be turned in good earnest to such a subject, something might be
produced still more impressive and original than even this age has yet
witnessed.

Scott's poem and Jeffery's new-found enthusiasm show how strongly a Highland version of 'Scottishness' seized the popular imagination. Here at last was the formula for a national identity uncomplicated by the rigours and the old pains of Presbyterianism, and most gratifyingly separated from the everyday political and commercial facts of the Union. At last 'Scottishness' could be glamorous and noble and fashionable – and 'safe'. Before the publication of *The Lady of the Lake*, Loch Katrine and surrounding hills were little known and virtually inaccessible. After 1810, thousands of visitors flocked to the Trossachs to see the place for themselves, and innkeepers and pony-hirers never knew such trade. As if inspired by his own subject, the author himself set out on a trip through the Hebrides to collect more old customs and 'legends of war and wonder'.

Scott felt that he could now afford a home of his own in the Borders, and so he bought a little farmhouse called Cartley Hole situated on the Tweed between Melrose and Galashiels, builders were engaged to add to it, and the famous poet and his family, his horses, dogs and fishing-rods, arrived in the summer of 1812. He called it Abbotsford and spent the next twelve years buying property, planting trees and developing the building until it grew into a huge mansion – a maze of wings and towers filled with antiques, ancient arms and armour. In order to finance these baronial ambitions, Scott took on heavier and heavier commitments, borrowing, mortgaging and spending advances on books not yet written. The laird of Abbotsford was not ashamed of financial success – indeed, he saw it as a merit – yet, when the Waverley novels first appeared, he kept his authorship secret, and, although it was a well-known secret for years, he did not publicly acknowledge them until 1826. Scott's sense of honour and his material ambitions brought him much heartache in the end, but his generous temperament remained unspoiled. In the early hours of every morning he worked hard at his desk – scorning 'artistic' affectations and taking pride in his capacity for workmanlike, profitable toil. Later in the day he was an outgoing host to many friends and famous visitors – the very image of a sporting country laird and a spokesperson for the culture of romantic Scotland.

Rokeby, a poem of the Civil War, appeared at the beginning of 1813 but it could not match the economy and force of *The Lady of the Lake*. Besides, Byron had burst on the scene with the first two cantos of *Childe Harold's Pilgrimage* – a publishing-sensation scarcely less glamorous than its young creator. The elder poet recognised *Childe Harold* as 'a piece of most extraordinary power', and he and Byron entered into an amicable and respectful correspondence, despite the public's desire to see them as bitter rivals. They met each other frequently in London during two months in 1815 and parted good friends. Byron's romances, such as *The Giaour* (1813), *The Bride of Abydos* (1813) and *The Corsair* (1814), owe something to the genre created by Scott, but his settings were even more wildly exotic, and the modern misanthropical psychology of Childe Harold quite overtook the antiquarian romance and the chivalric code of the 'last minstrel'.

Scott recognised that his vogue was over, and later romances – *The Bridal of Triermain* (1813), *Harold the Dauntless* (1817) and *The Lord of the Isles* (1815) – were never to recapture his early triumphs. 'Well, well, James, so be it', he remarked to Ballantyne with typically pragmatic modesty; 'but you know we must not droop, for we can't afford to give over. Since one line has failed, we must just stick to something else.' 'Something else' was prose fiction, with the resumption of *Waverley*, the novel he had conceived in 1805 and never finished. At the age of forty-three Scott embarked on an entirely new creative career.

In a 'postscript which should have been a preface' the author of *Waverley* explained his point of view, giving notice, in effect, of the themes which were to inspire and guide him in all the later novels. He felt that the most extreme historical and social changes had taken place in the Highlands and Lowlands during the last two generations, as if the sixteenth century had led straight to the nineteenth century, so that 'the present people of Scotland [are] a class of beings as different from their grandfathers as the existing English are from those of Queen Elizabeth's time'. Scott thought that he had come to terms with these changes, but his feelings were crucially ambivalent. As a Lowland Tory and a Unionist, he was half in love with a warlike Stuart cause. As a man of aristocratic prejudices, and a lifelong opponent of the Reform Bill, he delighted in the oral tradition and the sturdy independence of common Scots folk. These are the conflicting claims at the heart of his novels, in which he places ordinary people at a time of violent change. His young heroes, whose inheritance is progress and the United Kingdom, learn to accept what Scott calls 'the prose of real life', but it seems colourless by comparison with the old ways and the 'poetry' of a lost Scotland.

Conflicts between 'emotional' and 'rational' responses to the Union had been manifest in Ramsay's time; but their sublimation in Scott's novels raised what might otherwise have been adventure-fiction to a penetrating exploration of loyalty and historical change. It is as if the author's own contradictory feelings were being replayed through his account of the characters and events of the past, and the difficulties of his position may well be reflected in the nature of his young protagonists. Thus it is that a typical Scott hero seems rather passive: he is often cast as a stranger and an observer from 'outside' who is caught up in events, so that the scenes and actions of the novel are introduced to the readers in just the same way as they are introduced to him. This allows the author to describe at length the landscape and manners of his native country in what amounts to an act of recognition, translation and explanation – not just for his readers, but for himself too. Edward Waverley in the novel of that name is a young Englishman whose father is a Whig interested in commercial and political advancement in the city of London, but whose uncle is a Tory cavalier of the old aristocratic school. Young Captain Waverley despises his father's values, and when he is posted to Scotland and visits Baron Bradwardine he becomes involved in the freebooting life of the Highlands, falls in love with a Highland girl, is cashiered from the army and ultimately joins the Jacobite rising of the Forty-five. (He returns to the fold in the end, however, and is granted a pardon.) In Waverley's case it is psychologically convincing that his sentimental and romantic nature should have been stirred by the charm of Charles Edward Stuart and his cause, just as he was fascinated (like his creator) with the clansmen, so strange and fierce in their loyalties and wild as the countryside they inhabit.

Of course, Scott's glamorous settings are part of the popular Romantic taste for the 'picturesque', but they also touch on the wellsprings of his inspiration, for he frequently makes his landscapes play a part in the workings of plot and denouement, and they relate to his understanding of mood and character too. A chapter from *Waverley*, 'The Hold of a Highland Robber', perfectly displays the author's talent for combining the awesomely picturesque with detailed observation and a lively sense of contrast:

> The party preserved silence, interrupted only by the monotonous and murmured chant of a Gaelic song, sung in a kind of low recitative by the steersman, and by the dash of the oars, which the notes seemed to regulate, as they dipped to them in cadence. The light, which they now approached more nearly, assumed a broader, redder, and more irregular splendour. . . . As he saw it, the red glaring orb seemed to rest on the very surface of the lake itself, and resembled the fiery vehicle in which the Evil Genius of an Oriental tale traverses land and sea. They approached nearer, and the fire sufficed to show that it was kindled at the bottom of a huge dark crag or rock, rising abruptly from the very edge of the water; its front, changed by the reflection to dusky red, formed a strange and even awful contrast to the banks around, which were from time to time faintly and partially illuminated by pallid moonlight. . . .
>
> The principal inhabitant of this singular mansion . . . came forward to meet his guest, totally different in appearance and manner from what his imagination had anticipated. . . . Waverley prepared himself to meet a stern, gigantic, ferocious figure, such as Salvator would have chosen to be the central object of a group of banditti.
>
> Donald Bean Lean was the very reverse of all these. He was thin in person and low in stature, with light sandy-coloured hair, and small pale features, from which he derived his agnomen of *Bean*, or white. . . . He had served in some inferior capacity in the French army, and in order to receive his English visitor in great form, and probably meaning, in his way, to pay him a compliment, he had laid aside the Highland dress for the time, to put on an old blue and red uniform, and a feathered hat, in which he was far from showing to advantage, and indeed looked so incongruous, compared with all around him, that Waverley would have been tempted to laugh, had laughter been either civil or safe.

Waverley, or 'Tis Sixty Years Since (1814) was an immediate success and it remains one of Scott's best novels. Critics and readers admired the colourful minor characters and enthused about the use of 'Daft Davy Gellatly' as a kind of Shakespearean fool. They expressed enlightened relief that the pains of discord and civil war were now in the past, and the author (often surmised as Scott) was congratulated on his portrayal of a northern race which was assumed without question to have 'vanished from the face of their native land . . . within these few years'. Here and in succeeding novels the reading public found action, adventure and morality tied to outdoor places and 'real' historical events – a great relief from the contrived settings and overheated horrors of the prevailing Gothic school. Maria

Edgeworth's Irish novels, such as *Castle Rackrent* (1800), had pioneered the use of regional settings, and Scott acknowledged their influence on him, but his version of the Highlands was even more intriguing for a growing urban readership. On top of this, his many colourful secondary characters provide a comedy of manners less fine than Jane Austen's, but broader and more various, for Scott delights in robust contrasts between Highlanders and Lowlanders, Englishmen and Scotsmen, young and old, rich and poor, noble and devious, all to great effect. By comparison, the love-interest in these novels is a more conventional thing and his heroes and heroines are not without a flavour of the juvenile lead. Even so, the 'passive hero' so familiar in Scott's fiction does allow him to concentrate on the pressure of events and on how social, political or religious influences manifest themselves. In the last analysis these influences, and Scott's evocation of travel, landscape and local history all drive the novels along just as effectively as any more unique or dominant hero could. Indeed, the reader may find it easier to empathise with a protagonist who is caught up in events in the same way that he, or she, is caught up in reading the book. This sort of empathy is common to many popular novels, then as now, and no doubt it was yet another factor in the extraordinarily wide appeal of the 'wizard of the North'. *Waverley* went through four editions in as many months and sold 40,000 over again when the complete 'Waverley Novels' edition appeared with notes in 1829. Scott returned from a tour of the Northern Isles to find himself famously suspected of being 'the Great Unknown', and he gave himself up to fiction with a complete concentration of his remarkable energies.

Constable published *Guy Mannering* in 1815 and *The Antiquary* in 1816, both 'by the author of Waverley', as well as *Paul's Letters to his Kinsfolk* (1816), which appeared under Scott's own name as an account of his visit to Europe and the battlefield of Waterloo. In the same year two more novels, called *The Black Dwarf* and *Old Mortality*, from a series to be called 'Tales of my Landlord' were published by Blackwood as apparently collected and retold by an old schoolmaster named Jedediah Cleishbotham. It seems to have been John Ballantyne who persuaded Scott to go to another publisher with this scheme. In the face of this prolific output Scott explained how the first three Waverley novels were to fit together:

The present Work completes a series of fictitious narratives, intended to illustrate the manners of Scotland at three different periods. *Waverley* embraced the age of our fathers, *Guy Mannering* that of our youth, and *The Antiquary* refers to the last ten years of the eighteenth century.

(Introduction to *The Antiquary*)

Compared to *Waverley*, *Guy Mannering or the Astrologer* is something of a disappointment to the modern reader; being closer to a conventional romance of its day, it lent itself well to stage-adaptation, with a lost heir, supernatural agencies and a happy ending. Yet the novel still gains from its setting and its evocation of country life in the Borders, and characters such as the lawyer Pleydell, Dandie Dinmont and the wild old crone Meg Merrilies – a fated instrument of fate herself – give it life and charm. *The Antiquary*, more nearly contemporary, is Scott's best comedy of manners. It involves a melodrama – also about a lost heir – but the elaborations of this plot about unsung noble birth and its eventual discovery are the least important elements in a novel rich with sympathetic humour and charged with topographical, psychological and social details. As with many of Scott's novels, it is possible to trace originals for some of the more entertaining characters: Jonathon Oldbuck, the eccentrically enthusiastic 'antiquary', owes something to old George Constable, a friend from the author's boyhood, and Edie Ochiltree the travelling beggarman had a real counterpart too. These figures are not isolated creations, however, for they fit into a wider portrait of a small Scots coastal community of fishermen, modest gentlemen and landed aristocrats, and Scott drew on his own upbringing to show that the spirit of such a place belongs most enduringly with the common folk. They are the ones who transmit the tales and legends from old times; they meet poverty and bereavement with strength and dignity and their opinions, prejudices and sufferings are a sturdy yardstick against which we measure the unlikely Gothic entanglements of the better-born, or the enthusiasms and hobby-horses of the better-educated. Among his many novels it was Scott's own favourite.

While such figures as Edie Ochiltree are drawn with a generosity which rescues them from caricature, Scott is not, on the whole, a novelist who explores the psychological depths of motivation and introspection; nor do his characters evolve much or stray from their original casting in the course of his books. Yet, if he does not seek a directly analytical depth, he still achieves subtlety by the telling juxtaposition of events, scenes and characters. When the Earl of Glenallan, for example, has to face error, cruelty and shame in his own past, he hears of it in a fisherman's cottage from the mouth of old Elspeth, a singer of ballads and one time lady's maid to his mother. She spins a complicated tale of hatred, intrigue, suicide and a posthumous baby heir since lost. Glenallan is plunged into frozen gloom. By direct and deliberate contrast, the fisher family has just lost its eldest boy to the sea, and old Saunders Mucklebackit, stiff and grim with grief, stands on the beach repairing the shattered boat that drowned his son – even as Glenalmond hears how his own mother arranged to kill the baby daughter he never knew he had. The sentimental Gothicism of these tangled webs is highly contrived, to say the least, but Scott manages it by having it told by a storyteller who is herself implicated in guilt and half-crazed with age, and it is distanced again by comparison with the silent, clumsy pain of Saunders as he fumbles blindly with his repairs:

> 'And what would ye have me to do,' answered the fisher gruffly, 'unless I wanted to see four children starve, because ane is drowned? It's weel wi' you gentles, that can sit in the house wi' handkerchers at your een when ye lose a friend; but the like o' us maun to our wark again, if our hearts were beating as hard as my hammer.'

Scott has a dramatist's grasp of how to use such juxtapositions to sustain powerful effects in pathos and in comedy too, and he may well have learned it from his early love of Shakespeare. Indeed, Edie Ochiltree, the garrulous and dignified old beggar who links the various strands of the plot together, is a truly Shakespearean creation. Licensed by his age and humble station, he moves between cottage and manor like some unlikely, interfering Prospero whose native wit, tricks and compassion are all mobilised to help the other characters, and the author himself, to achieve a proper resolution:

> '. . . what wad a' the country about do for want o' auld Edie Ochiltree, that brings news and country cracks fae ae farm-steading to anither, and gingerbread to the lasses, and helps the lads to mend their fiddles, and the gudewives to clout their pans, and plaits rush-swords and grenadier caps for the weans, and busks [dresses] the laird's flees [fishing flies], and has skill o' cow-ills and horse-ills, and kens mair auld sangs and tales than a'

the barony besides, and gars ilka body laugh wherever he comes? Troth, my leddy, I canna lay down my vocation; it would be a public loss.'

The final factor in Scott's realisation of comedy and drama is to be found in his selective use of the spoken vernacular. This sinewy and lively idiom (never too dense for the average reader) varies the narrative and illuminates character and society with such impact that the author hardly needs to comment more. For thousands of delighted readers, it was Scott rather than Wordsworth who revealed the democracy of plain values and common sense among humble folk, and reaffirmed, not least in Scotland itself, a sense of native character with all its strengths and its terrible blind spots too.

For the theme of *Old Mortality* (1816) Scott returned to civil strife, this time between Cavalier and Covenanter in the late seventeenth century. The novel, from the 'Tales of my Land-lord' series, is a much plainer and grimmer work than *The Antiquary* and it was Scott's first attempt to re-create an historical past quite beyond living memory and his own boyhood roots. True to his muse, he seizes on the voices and features of the commons to measure his vision of the divided times, so that it is the old widow Mause Headrigg, expelled from her house and out on the hillside with the open-air conventicles, who speaks for the pride of ordinary folk, keeping to the harsher demands of their faith despite all consequences. Her son Cuddie is less convinced, however, and his hopes for a comfortable life are constantly and comically frustrated by his mother's insatiable need to testify, at the drop of a Bible, against 'popery, prelacy, antinomianism, erastianism, lap-sarianism, sublapsarianism, and the sins and snares of the times'. 'Hout tout, mither', he complains as he drags her away from yet another confrontation, 'ye preached us out o' our canny free house and gude kale-yard . . . sae ye may haud sae for ae wee while, without preaching me up a ladder and down a tow.' We enjoy the exchange and yet in this novel it is likely that Scott's tendency to equate passionate principles with comic or grotesque characters goes some way towards defusing and disguising the fundamental divisions which caused so much unhappiness in seventeenth-century Scotland.

Old Mortality works well enough as a warning against extremism, or as an adventure among the Covenanters, but, despite Scott's researches in the writing of it, its historical and philosophical insight is very limited. Undoubtedly he intended to make a case for moderate Presbyterianism, for his hero Henry Morton comes from dissenting stock and when circumstances make him a leader in the Covenanters' camp he stands by the cause, even when his sympathies are divided because his sweetheart, Edith Bellenden, and some of his friends are Royalists from old families. He retains his humanity and disowns the men of perpetual violence, such as the daemonic Balfour of Burley, one of the murderers of the archbishop of St Andrew's. Yet Morton remains unconvincing because he never expresses intellectual conviction about his religious or political principles, and Scott surrounds him instead with a host of wild and curious figures with such names as Habakkuk Mucklewrath – a fanatical madman – or Poundtext, Kettledrummle and Macbriar, all of whom are satirical figures who expatiate on their cause in endlessly pedantic or comic fashion. Like Waverley before him, Morton is pardoned for his beliefs and reconciled with conventional authority in the end. He marries Edith Bellenden and the book ends happily, even if the more truly revolutionary issues of these times were never to be so easily reconciled or dismissed.

Scott's next novel, *Rob Roy*, published in December 1817, returned to the Highlands. It is not particularly well constructed but Scott compensated by creating some memorable characters, most especially Baillie Nicol Jarvie, that most pragmatic of Glasgow traders, who within a year became the star of a stage-adaptation which was packing theatres in Edinburgh and Glasgow. Six months after *Rob Roy*, despite severe stomach pains from gallstones, Scott completed the book which many critics hold to be best of all his novels.

The Heart of Midlothian (1818) is set in the Edinburgh of 1736, the year of the Porteous riots, and its central theme is the moral and physical journey which Jeanie Deans undertakes to save her pretty young half-sister from the death penalty. Eighteen-year-old Effie is accused of murdering her illegitimate baby – it has, indeed, disappeared – and in the absence of an infant body the complicated case against her depends on the fact that she kept her pregnancy secret from everyone because her lover, implicated in the killing of Captain Porteous, has had to flee and leave her unsupported. She does not know it, but she is innocent of the child's death, for it was stolen away from her while she was in a fever. Even so, she would probably be acquitted if only her sister Jeanie would testify that she had told her she was pregnant, for this is the key point in a law intended to stop heartless infanticides. But Jeanie, the daughter of 'Douce David Deans', a stern and moral old Covenanter, cannot tell a saving lie, despite the agony it brings to them all. It is a classical conflict between two kinds of good – the inviolable nature of truth as opposed to family love and natural justice. In this case stern Kirk morality and the unshakable strictness of the letter of the law are shown to be equally absolute and inescapable imperatives – a very Scottish pairing. The truth prevails and Effie is condemned to death. Jeanie sets out on an epic walk to London and has to experience several adventures and setbacks along the way before she succeeds in winning clemency for her sister at the court of Queen Caroline.

Jeanie Deans is quintessentially Scottish but there is no trace of the colourful 'Scotch character' about her, and at last Scott has created a positive hero, central to the novel, who makes things happen and takes responsibility firmly into her own hands. Indeed, Jeanie and her father embody the Presbyterian strengths and the moral seriousness which Scott had failed to evoke in Henry Morton and the Covenanters of *Old Mortality*. The central debate between law and conscience is pursued and renewed at many levels, not least in setting it against the Porteous riots and the Tolbooth prison – the so-called 'Heart of Midlothian' itself. The issues are discussed again at a comic level in the inspired gobbledegook of Bartoline Saddletree, a harness-maker with legal pretensions, while the novelist's talent for wild and touching scenes creates Madge Wildfire, a demented creature who dies singing 'Proud Maisie' and acts as an instrument of fate in the same mould as old Elspeth or Meg Merrilies. Madge too is caught up in the theme of guilt and compassion, for the poor creature is accused of witchcraft and subjected to the 'justice' of a mob near Carlisle.

Scott continues the tale of Effie and her lover beyond the more obvious conclusion which would seem to have arrived with her pardon. The unhappy pair are eventually reunited and return to high society as 'Sir George and Lady Staunton'. Sir George meets a violent end at the hands of a wilful young bandit whom he comes upon by accident in the Highlands, without ever knowing that he is Effie's lost child and the son he has, himself, so long sought. This latter part of the book is often criticised for slipping into melodrama and it is usually accepted that Scott was under pressure to make the novel long enough for four volumes. This is not the whole story, however, for the conclusion does try to continue the unifying theme of guilt, mercy and justice, a topic which Scott pursues far more consistently in this book than any other theme in his other novels. He was not often so single-minded and was given to dismissing the extent of his labours and the importance of unity in them. 'I am sensible', he wrote in his journal, 'that if there be anything good about my poetry or my prose either, it is a hurried frankness of composition, which pleases soldiers, sailors and young people of bold and active dispositions.' Beneath his bluff disclaimers he was genuinely clear-sighted about the strengths and weaknesses of his art. He could make complicated plans for the structure and evolution of his novels, but characters and incidents seemed to lead him astray of their own accord:

> When I light on such a character as Bailie Jarvie, or Dalgetty, my imagination brightens, and my conception becomes clearer at every step which I make in his company, although it leads me many a weary mile away from the regular road, and forces me to leap hedge and ditch to get back into the route again. If I resist the temptation, as you advise me, my thoughts become prosy, flat, and dull; I write painfully to myself, and under a consciousness of flagging which makes me flag still more; the sunshine with which fancy had invested the incidents, departs from them, and leaves everything dull and gloomy. I am no more the same author, than the dog in a wheel, condemned to go round and round for hours, is like the same dog merrily chasing his own tail, and gambolling in all the frolic of unrestrained freedom.
>
> (Introductory Epistle, *The Fortunes of Nigel*)

Scott was to provide plenty more sunshine in his novels, but the image of that dog condemned to toil for hours was to become all too grimly apposite of his later creative life. In the meantime he continued to be extraordinarily productive and, despite a severe illness which only slowly retreated, he turned out two and sometimes three multi-volume novels a year. The manuscripts show virtually no signs of revision or hesitation, and in 1819 the most part of *The Legend of Montrose*, *The Bride of Lammermoor* and *Ivanhoe* were actually dictated during convalescence. Thus he managed, once more, to pay various debts and bonds, even if the expenses of Abbotsford more than kept pace with his considerable earnings. He wrote essays and reviews and took part in the launching of *Blackwood's*, through which he made friends with John Wilson and John Gibson Lockhart, his future biographer and son-in-law. He was made a baronet in 1818 and his place in established society was confirmed when he was asked to organise King George IV's visit to Scotland in 1822. Still Scott poured out books – 'let us stick to him', wrote Constable's partner, 'let us dig on and dig on at that extraordinary quarry'. For southern readers *Ivanhoe* (1819) was the greatest success yet, and although its history is faulty it opened a whole new seam of picturesque romance in a 'medieval' English setting. *The Monastery* and *The Abbot* (both 1820) returned to sixteenth-century Scotland, while *The Pirate* (1821) drew on earlier visits to the Shetlands, and *Kenilworth*, from the same year, took readers to the English court of Queen Elizabeth. Scott's daughter Sophia had married Lockhart in 1820, and, when young Walter married five years later, his father made a will which settled the whole of Abbotsford on his favourite son and his bride. These were happy and varied years for 'the Great Unknown', now in his fifties and recovering something of his former strength. He had become the most celebrated writer in Britain and a famously generous host at Abbotsford, where he entertained guests in a setting which brought Gothic interiors together with the most modern of gadgets, including pneumatic bells and gas lighting.

The Fortunes of Nigel (1822) was followed a year later by *Peveril of the Peak*, *Quentin Durward*, set in fifteenth-century France, and *St Ronan's Well*. Jacobite themes returned with *Redgauntlet* (1824) – a fine novel made even more memorable by 'Wandering Willie's Tale', a *tour de force* of the supernatural told in broad Scots and often published as if it were a separate short story. The Middle Ages featured once again in lesser novels called *The Betrothed* and *The Talisman* (1825), and Scott also began a lengthy nine-volume *Life of Napoleon Bonaparte* not published until 1827. Despite his industry, however, his financial affairs were finally and disastrously overextended. For years now, Constable the publisher, Ballantyne the printer and Scott, that 'extraordinary quarry', had erected an ever-more-complex tower of mutually supportive credit and bills of exchange. In the meantime Constable's London agent had been speculating on the volatile money-market of the day, and when he was finally swept away the financial backwash brought down the Edinburgh partners as well. Scott was faced with private debts of £30,000 and a further call for over £96,000 owed through Ballantyne, Constable and various other parties. Not even his closest friends knew of his financial involvement with these businesses, and so the news of his ruin at the beginning of 1826 fell on Edinburgh, in Cockburn's words, like a thunderbolt: 'if an earthquake had swallowed half the town, it would not have produced greater astonishment, sorrow and dismay. . . . How humbled we felt when we saw him – the pride of us all, dashed from his honourable and lofty station, and all the fruits of his well-worked talents gone.' Even so, Scott refused to accept bankruptcy, just as he resisted various subscriptions which were proposed to help him. A trust was formed for his creditors, he took lodgings and sold his Edinburgh house, but was allowed to live at Abbotsford rent-free, despite the fact that he had only recently mortgaged the estate for a further £10,000 in a futile attempt to help Constable just before the crash.

So Scott, bound by his sense of honour in the matter, set about the massive task of clearing his debts by the further labours of his pen. At first his spirits were stimulated by the immediate controversy which surrounded his *Letters of Malachi Malagrowther* (1826), a lively pamphlet in opposition to the government's plan to do away with the distinctive paper currency of the Scottish banks. Such emblems of national identity were important to him, and he felt equally strongly about threats to the unique character of Scots law, just as he had revered the old Scottish regalia when they were discovered in 1818. The Malagrowther letters carried the day, but Scott was becoming increasingly isolated. The splendid years were over and the establishment at Abbotsford much reduced. Lady Scott died in the early summer of 1826, leaving her husband shaken with grief and melancholy. He had just begun a private journal and this intimate work provides a unique record of his last years. Bothered with rheumatism and palpitations of the heart, he seemed almost to welcome the routine of endless writing. He completed *Woodstock* in 1826 and the next year produced his *Life of Napoleon*, a set of short novels called 'Chronicles of the Canongate', and the first series of *Tales of a*

Grandfather – a retelling of Scottish history for children, written for his frail grandson, who had only four more years to live. Three further volumes in this series appeared between 1828 and 1830, along with *The Fair Maid of Perth* (another of the 'Chronicles'), and what he called his 'Opus Magnum', a complete new edition of the Waverley novels furnished with introductions and notes. After *Anne of Geierstein* (1829) a serious stroke finally broke his strength. He retired as clerk of the Court of Session, but refused to give up writing, although he was sorely extended by his *Letters on Demonology and Witchcraft* (1830), and two further short novels (*Count Robert* and *Castle Dangerous* from 1831) show only a failing hand. His all-too-limited energies were further expended by more Malachi letters against the various Reform Bills which were dividing parliament and country in those years. The redistribution of political seats and the extension of franchise were long overdue, but Scott could only see anarchy and an end to the values he loved, and even his more conservative friends thought his views were intemperate. They persuaded him to burn the Malachi manuscript, but they could not stop him from speaking for the Tory candidate at an election in Jedburgh, where he was shouted down and his carriage stoned.

By now Scott was markedly frail and prematurely old. Ironically, perhaps, it was a Whig government which helped the novelist to escape from a Scottish winter, by arranging for a frigate to take him to Malta and Naples. He saw the sights and struggled with another novel, to be called *The Siege of Malta*, as if the old dog could not give up the wheel to which he had been bound so long. But his mind was fading and his main anxiety was to reach Abbotsford before the end. Another stroke threw him into a coma, but he gained a few days of clarity by Tweedside in the early autumn, before dying at the age of sixty-one on 21 September 1832. He is buried among cloisters in the ruins of Dryburgh Abbey.

The 'wizard of the North' was one of the best-loved and most famous writers in Europe and America – a figure along with Goethe and Byron who dominated the literary scene of his day, moving and influencing thousands of readers and dozens of writers who were to be famous in their turn. Yet the years to come belong to Dickens, Balzac, Flaubert, Tolstoy or Dostoevsky, for Scott strikes an older balance between the robust and rational world of the Enlightenment and a Romantic love for the fabric of Scotland and her people. Conservative, nationalistic, antiquarian, sentimental and yet down to earth, his spirit, and the contradictions within it, belongs to the Edinburgh of the late eighteenth century – divided as always between a United Kingdom and the call of an 'auld sang'.

Scott's own life became part of the song too, largely owing to Lockhart's massive biography (1837–8), a long and entertaining study which made full use of his journals and thousands of letters, thus earning a place in all subsequent studies despite an account of Hogg which was coloured by personal dislike. Educated at Glasgow and Oxford, **John Gibson Lockhart** (1794–1854) was another of those advocates who took to literature in Edinburgh. He wrote a somewhat genteel life of Burns in 1828 and so the book on Scott was not his first biography. After the scandal of the 'Chaldee Manuscript' in his youth, *Peter's Letters to his Kinsfolk* (1819) was a much more illuminating, although still scathing, series of sketches on the intelligentsia and Scottish manners. Lockhart's contributions to 'Maga' included many poems, and in the early 1820s he began writing novels. *Valerius* and *Reginald Dalton* have less to commend them than *Adam Blair* (1822) and *Matthew Wald* (1824), which manage to hint at darker psychological tensions in northern society. Adam Blair is a Presbyterian minister who eventually makes love to a married cousin, a girl who enters his life after his wife's death. Blair is tormented by what they never doubt to be a sin, most especially against the cloth, and he can find peace again only through public atonement and long suffering. *Matthew Wald* is a less satisfactory novel, but a similar involvement with crime and the Presbyterian conscience reminds us that Hogg's *Justified Sinner* was not the only book to explore this aspect of the country's psyche. Lockhart's early success with *Blackwood's* in Edinburgh was followed by his editorship of the Tory *Quarterly Review*, a post he held in London from 1825 until the year before his death.

The best of the women novelists whose works appeared during Scott's reign is **Susan Ferrier** (1782–1854), who looks to the novel of manners in the vein of Jane Austen or Maria Edgeworth. Earlier writers such as Anne Grant and Elizabeth Hamilton brought social life in the Highlands to the public eye, and **Mary Brunton** (1778–1818) chose the same setting for her second novel, *Discipline* (1814). These writers intended to instruct and 'improve' their readers, and Susan Ferrier shares something of this aim – her last work was called *Destiny* (1831), and it too was set in the north with a Highland heroine. Nevertheless she writes with more humour and penetration than her predecessors. Her themes were established from the first in *Marriage* (1818), probably her best novel, in which social observation and comedy are used to explore the condition of young women in contemporary society. In her books (*The Inheritance* followed in 1824) she sets the fashionable world of London or Bath against the provincial life of Scotland, where her heroines find the virtues of peace, piety and common sense, even if the accents and the behaviour of the Scots – well caught in her prose – are finally judged to be uncultivated. After *Destiny* she wrote no more novels and in later years her religious convictions led her to disapprove of her early work. No such polite qualms ever occurred to James Hogg, her fellow *Blackwood's* writer, whose roots were inextricably bound to the vernacular tradition.

James Hogg (1770–1835)

When Hogg's father's sheep-farm failed, his seven-year-old son was obliged to leave school and go to work. As a shepherd in his teens the boy taught himself to play the fiddle and laboured to develop his rudimentary grasp of reading and writing. One employer, a Mr Laidlaw of Blackhouse, gave Hogg access to his library, and the shepherd stayed with him for ten years, befriending his son William, who was later to be steward of Scott's estate at Abbotsford. At the age of twenty-seven, 'ravished', as he put it, by 'Tam o' Shanter', Hogg resolved to be a poet like Burns, and before long his 'Donald MacDonald', a war song against Napoleon, became well known throughout the country. His *Scottish Pastorals* appeared in 1801 – a small collection of songs and poems in the style of Ramsay's *Gentle Shepherd* – 'sad stuff, although I judged them to be exceedingly good'. In 1802 Scott's *Border Minstrelsy* inspired Hogg to set old tales into rhyme, and his friend William Laidlaw was instrumental in introducing Hogg's mother to Scott as a source of further traditional material. The 'Ettrick Shepherd' and the Sheriff of Selkirkshire became friends.

Hogg was never to be a successful farmer, and when a plan to run sheep on Harris came to nothing he lost his savings and had to turn again to shepherding in the Borders. His ballad-imitations were published as *The Mountain Bard* (1807), prefaced by a romantic account of his humble origins, but a treatise on the diseases of sheep proved more profitable. By 1810 he was finally out of work and came to Edinburgh to try his luck as a writer. Constable was persuaded to publish *The Forest Minstrel* (1810), an unsuccessful anthology – 'but the worst of them are all mine', as Hogg reflected later. He started a weekly paper called the *Spy*, mostly written by himself, which lasted for a year before closing. Disappointed at his inability to emulate Burns's success, Hogg used the last issue of his paper to publish a 'Memoir of the Author's Life' which deliberately encouraged the popular image of the 'Ettrick Shepherd' as some illiterate native genius who 'ran away from his master' to seek his fortune in the arts. He lived to regret this role, but for the moment he was at the mercy of his insecurity, and his responses to the educated society which he longed to join could be naïve, vain or aggressive by turns.

The popularity of Scott's narrative verse was at its height and Hogg determined to try a long poem in the same style, choosing a framework which allowed him to offer several different poems as 'recited' by bards in a competition before Mary Queen of Scots. *The Queen's Wake* finally appeared in 1813 and it was successful enough for Blackwood to take it onto his lists. Two of the best and most popular 'songs' were 'The Witch of Fife' a Scots ballad full of grotesque misadventures, somewhat in the spirit of 'The Gyre-Carling'; and 'Kilmeny', a supernatural lay in antique Scots, later anglified. Both poems are enlivened by Hogg's familiarity with folk tales and the uncanny, but 'Kilmeny' makes something more original and disturbing out of its account of how a young virgin is spirited away, perhaps to Heaven, by the fairies and given an allegorical vision of the future. Hogg's unsophisticated taste adds a chaste eroticism and a spiritual idealism to the bare bones of the ballad, and the result, with echoes from Ramsay's 'The Vision', is prophetic of the mystical other realms in George MacDonald's books

'O, bonny Kilmeny! free frae stain,
If ever you seek the world again,
That world of sin, or sorrow and fear,
O, tell of the joys that are waiting here;
And tell of the signs you shall shortly see;
Of the times that are now and the times that shall be.'

They lifted Kilmeny, they led her away,
And she walked in the light of a sunless day:
The sky was a dome of crystal bright,
The fountain of vision, and fountain of light:
The emerald fields were of dazzling glow,
And the flowers of everlasting blow.
Then deep in the stream her body they laid,
That her youth and beauty never might fade;
And they smiled on heaven, when they saw her lie
In the stream of life that wandered bye.

The narrative links in *The Queen's Wake* are weak, and Hogg was
satisfied in later years to acknowledge Scott's supremacy in 'the
school o' chivalry'. But he would not relinquish his own claim
to be 'the king o' the mountain an' fairy school', and his poem
'Superstition' (1814) testifies to the impact of folk lore on his
young imagination.

At last the poet had 'arrived', and the Duke of Buccleuch was
so impressed that he gave Hogg Altrive Lake Farm, rent-free
for the rest of his life. He was introduced to Wordsworth in
Edinburgh and toured with him in the Borders before visiting
Rydal Mount to join John Wilson, and De Quincey too. The
little gathering was not without its tricky moments, as Hogg
later recalled in typical style. The party was viewing a meteor
in the night sky when Hogg ventured a pretty remark to
Dorothy:

'Hout, me'm! it is neither mair nor less than joost a treeumphal airch,
raised in honour of the meeting of the poets.'
'That's not amiss. – Eh? Eh – that's very good', said the Professor
[Wilson], laughing. But Wordsworth, who had De Quincey's arm, gave a
grunt and turned on his heel, and leading the little opium-chewer aside, he
addressed him in these disdainful and venomous words: – 'Poets? Poets? –
What does the fellow mean? – Where are they?'

Hogg produced further long poems in English over the next two
years, but they offered only derivative romance or contrived
philosophising. *The Poetic Mirror*, however (1816), did show his

considerable talent for imitating his famous contemporaries, including Scott, Byron, Coleridge and – sweet revenge – Wordsworth, whom he hilariously parodied.

These volumes had a mixed reception, but the 'Ettrick Shepherd' was established as a kenspeckle figure, even if it is difficult not to suspect a certain condescension among his friends when they refer to their 'good honest shepherd' and his 'quaint originality of manners'. The *Blackwood's* connection encouraged Hogg to return to prose with essays and tales for this and other periodicals. He needed the money, for his verse was flagging and *Dramatic Tales* (1817) for the stage had been a failure. Accordingly *The Brownie of Bodsbeck* appeared in 1818, a rather long-winded novel, yet a book which touches the tap-roots of Hogg's imagination by linking folk superstitions with tales of the Covenanters. As a stout Presbyterian, brought up on the sufferings of the just under 'bloody Clavers', Hogg was bound to differ from Scott's more gentlemanly preferences in *Old Mortality*. The Shepherd claimed that his manuscript predated Scott's novel (published at the end of 1816) and defended it against the great man's displeasure. Hogg was no liberal – 'the great majority o' shepherds are Conservatives', according to his *alter ego* in 'Noctes', 'no to be ta'en in by the nostrums o' every reformer'. But on the issue of religion, his sympathies belonged with the common people and the folk-history of their persecution by the establishment – a theme he was to return to in later stories such as 'The Edinburgh Baillie', 'A Tale of Pentland' and 'A Tale of the Martyrs'. *The Brownie of Bodsbeck* is set after the Battle of Bothwell Brig, telling how a shepherd is arrested for secretly helping Covenanters to escape from Claverhouse, and how his daughter, suspected of conniving with evil spirits, is denounced by the local curate, who has his own designs upon her. Even the father himself comes to fear that his Katherine is in league with the shambling 'Brownie' before it is revealed that the 'spirit' is really an injured Covenanter and that the odd happenings have been owing to her tending the wounded at night. Yet Hogg's evocation of the uncanny has been so successful that the possibility of magic survives his realistic 'explanation'. He was to use this double vision again.

Hogg married in 1820 and took a nearby farm at Mount Benger for nine years until the lease expired and his finances failed again. In the meantime he edited collections of his own and other stories and worked on his most ambitious novel yet, *The Three Perils of Man: War, Women and Witchcraft* (1822). The subtitle does indeed set the main topics for this ramshackle, picaresque book, mobilising allegory, fantasy, historical romance, coarse comedy and mock epic in a series of adventures in which knights and border reivers rub shoulders and tangle with wizards, magic and old-fashioned skulduggery. It includes a set of tales told by characters within the tale – each in an appropriate style – and it is all set against Robert II's determination to besiege the English in Roxburgh castle in the fourteenth century. The book is lively, savage and longwinded by turns, and its anachronistic history owes more to ballads and the oral tradition than to any notion of scholarship. Pressed by Scott to try for 'a little more refinement, care and patience' in his work, Hogg admitted that he was inclined to let his imagination sail on 'without star or compass'. The *Blackwood's* circle did not appreciate the wild vigour of his inspiration, and in the face of such gentility, Hogg's next book, *The Three Perils of Women, or Love, Leasing and Jealousy* (1823), rashly attempted the novel of manners and emotional entanglement. Written 'as if in desperation', it was roundly condemned by the critics – not least by Christopher North, whose 'Noctes Ambrosianae' had just begun to fix Hogg in the role of an aboriginal worthy, to the delight of thousands of *Blackwood's* readers. There is a telling irony in the fact that a man on the point of writing one of European literature's earliest masterpieces of the divided psyche should have been so caught up in the doings and sayings of 'the Shepherd', or 'the Caledonian Boar' – his own familiar, vulgar and profitable *Doppelganger*. The tensions in Scottish cultural identity, already felt by Ramsay and Scott, were about to take a stranger, darker twist.

The Private Memoirs and Confessions of a Justified Sinner (1824) was published anonymously because its author was particularly concerned that his identity be kept from his friends at the 'Maga'. He need scarcely have worried, for it made very little critical impact and the *Westminster Review* took him to task for 'uselessly and disgustingly abusing his imagination'. Yet it is a novel of extraordinary force, economically written and darkly modern in its psychological insights, so that some critics, more familiar with the 'Noctes', perhaps, have wondered whether

Hogg actually wrote it at all, as if the Shepherd were suddenly revealed as a Raskolnikov. Yet the book contains so many thematic and stylistic elements already used in Hogg's earlier work – however imperfectly – that his authorship is not in serious doubt, even if it does stem from the tradition of Hoffmann or from Lockhart's novels of religious anguish. Louis Simpson has also noted a possible documentary seed in the real confessions of a religious-minded murderer called Nicol Muschet, which were published in Edinburgh in 1818.

The *Justified Sinner* is told in three parts: the 'editor's' narrative; the sinner's confession; and finally a brief account of how the editor and his friends had a hand in recovering the middle part of the tale from the sinner's grave. The book opens as a story of rival brothers in the early eighteenth century. Their parents are mismatched, for the father is an easy-going sensualist and his wife is a narrow-minded Presbyterian, much under the influence of the Revd Robert Wringhim, a fanatically Calvinist minister. The elder son is called George Colwan, but his father disowns the younger boy, Robert, because he suspects him to be the natural son of Wringhim. Cut off from his inheritance, Robert is brought up by the minister and even baptised as a Wringhim. He is more intelligent and intense than George, whom he hardly ever sees, but his mother and the minister educate him to hate his father and his brother, and they fill him with extreme antinomian doctrines. This creed takes Calvinist predestination a step further by arguing that, since good works and faith alone are not enough to get to Heaven (for that would be like purchasing salvation), then good works may not even be *necessary* for the 'justified' – like Burns's Holy Willie – who are already chosen for heaven. Still more startling is the possibility that sins committed by the justified may not be sins at all, but merely a part of God's higher plan.

Fired by a mission to chastise the unbelievers, young Robert begins to haunt his brother like a dark counterpart to George's cheerful, generous and athletic nature –a political counterpart too, for, whereas Wringhim looks to the Covenanters, old Colwan is a Tory MP given to sentiments in favour of the Cavaliers. The turning-point between the two brothers comes early one morning on the hill known as Arthur's Seat which overlooks Edinburgh. George has gone for a walk on the cliffs and is admiring the brilliant morning when a huge threatening shadow appears in the mist. He turns away in panic only to stumble into Robert, who is right behind him, and George strikes him in the ensuing confusion. Robert soon recovers his usual disdainful composure and prosecutes George for attempted fratricide, but he loses the case when his habit of following George everywhere is revealed in court. George goes off to celebrate with his boisterous friends, but quarrels with a Highlander called Drummond, and is found stabbed later that night. Drummond flees. The bad news kills George's father and Robert inherits everything. The first half of the novel ends when eyewitnesses to George's death are tracked down and persuaded to tell how it was Robert who stabbed him in the back while his brother was duelling with another figure, who only resembled Drummond. The Highlander's name is cleared, but now Robert cannot be found.

The second part of the novel is Robert's 'confession', recovered from his grave, in which the events already described are told all over again to show him in a noble and righteous light. The unbalanced intensity of this narrative inspires the novel and draws the reader into another world, utterly alien to the comfortable and shallow assumptions of young bloods such as George and his companions. We discover that Robert has a friend and religious mentor called Gil-Martin – a 'brother' in the revealed truth – who haunts him just as he himself has pursued George. Gil-Martin instructs him in godly doctrine at every step and it is he who encourages and aids Robert in seeking justified vengeance on sinners and on George in particular. The reader soon suspects that Gil-Martin is the Devil. On the other hand, Robert's state seems strangely alienated, and in a fit of illness he feels himself to be two people, Gil-Martin and his brother, between whom he has somehow lost himself. The extreme subjectivity of Robert's tale would certainly suggest that he is deluded, except that Hogg produces independent witnesses to testify to Gil-Martin's actual physical presence at crucial times. Robert may profit through his shadowy companion, but his mental state deteriorates. He conceives a mortal fear of Gil-Martin, until, alcoholic, amnesiac and still raving in his belief that he is one of the elect, he publishes his confession as a moral pamphlet and ends it with a promise to take his own life.

The novel concludes with how the editor tracked down the author's grave from an essay published in *Blackwood's* in which James Hogg (no less) had given an account of an unknown suicide and strange events associated with his burial site in the country. The editorial party seeks the aid of the Shepherd himself, but he proves unhelpful and too busy to 'houk up hunder-year-auld banes'. It is left to the editor to exhume the text and to republish *The Private Memoirs and Confessions*. He explains it as an 'allegory', born out of 'dreaming or madness', in which the unfortunate author came to believe that he was his own fictional character. This is the final sophisticated twist to the novel's capacity to set tales within tales, as different narrators come up with different explanations for the same events.

Hogg's discovery of the mirror mazes of subjectivity takes him beyond these merely relative differences, however, and his use of 'the double' anticipated Dostoevsky's Golyadkin by more than twenty years to give dramatic and psychological depth to a study of obsession and madness. On the other hand, Gil-Martin's role as the Devil suggests an unearthly rather than a psychological explanation, and it is not easy to choose between them, for the book provides evidence for both points of view, allowing Hogg to reconcile his domestic realism with a penchant for the supernatural and the grotesque. This combination becomes especially potent given the Presbyterian Church's historical obsession with witchcraft and demonology and the paradox that puritanism has always been prone to imagining the personifications of temptation and evil. In this case the 'shadow' may throw light on the 'substance' of all such religious convictions based on fear. Yet there are no easy answers, for in the face of such mysteries George's complacent Tory rationality is almost as unattractive as Robert's fanaticism and both are bound together in a complicity of unhappiness. The novel can be called a moral and cultural allegory as well as a supernatural tale or a study of psychotic delusion, for it offers a searching analysis of the nature of the Scottish psyche as it engages with its own religious history, divided loyalties and lost inheritance. Hogg's book goes far deeper into such matters than the author of *Old Mortality* could comprehend. He was never to achieve its like again, however, and, as far as literary Edinburgh was concerned, he returned to his role as 'Maga's' favourite Shepherd.

When the poem *Queen Hynde* eventually appeared in 1825 it was found to be a lengthy failure and Hogg settled for tales and sketches, including the notable 'Brownie of the Black Haggs' (1829). He visited London for three months in 1832 and was a considerable social success while organising a collected edition to be called *Altrive Tales*, only one volume of which ever appeared. Two years later he produced essays on good manners and *The Familiar Anecdotes of Sir Walter Scott*, which Lockhart found so very offensive because Hogg dared to recall his old friend's undignified end, and remarked on Scott's 'too strong leaning to the old aristocracy of the county' – namely those families descended from 'old Border Barbarians'. 'In Wilson's hands the Shepherd will always be delightful', wrote Lockhart, putting the Chaldee manuscript and his old collaborator firmly behind him, 'but of the fellow himself I can scarcely express my contemptuous pity'. Undaunted by the quarrel, Hogg continued to select and revise his prose, and a three-volume collection of previously unpublished stories appeared as *Tales of the Wars of Montrose* in the spring of 1835. That November he died of a liver-disease at the age of sixty-five. The *Tales and Sketches of the Ettrick Shepherd* were published two years later, but Hogg had abridged the *Justified Sinner* to 'The Confessions of a Fanatic' and his greatest novel was not printed again until 1895, nor appreciated by literary critics until at least the 1920s. The French novelist André Gide set the book in a European perspective with an enthusiastic preface to the edition of 1947.

John Galt (1779–1839)

Although it was *Blackwood's Magazine* which serialised his early novels, John Galt did not seek out or belong to the Edinburgh milieu of Scott, Hogg and Ferrier. He was born in Irvine on the coast of Ayrshire and brought up in Greenock, the seaport to the west of Glasgow where his father was a shipmaster to the West Indies. Galt left for London when he was twenty-five, but by 1809 his business-plans in the capital had foundered and he took a two-year tour through the Mediterranean and the Near East, befriending the young Lord Byron along the way (and eventually publishing a biography of him in 1830). Back in London he wrote about his travels and produced a biography of Cardinal Wolsey and a volume of five tragedies. He turned to writing full-time after his marriage in 1813, and offered Constable a book looking back to an old-fashioned Scotland to be called *Annals of the Parish*. The publisher turned it down as too local and too Scottish, but the success of *Waverley* was soon to change such assumptions. Galt drew on his voyages again for a book of poems and an equally unsuccessful novel called *The Majolo* (1816), and he persevered with a variety of articles and projects, including text-books, further biographies and two more novels. But these were dull, hard years and critical success eluded him until he entered his forties and *Blackwood's* began to serialise *The Ayrshire Legatees* in 1820. Galt may have taken his pattern from Lockhart's *Peter's Letters to his Kinsfolk*, or from Smollett's *Humphrey Clinker*, for the work comprises a series of letters in which an Ayrshire family tell their friends at home all about their visit to London. The exchanges are full of topical details, and the Scots family – naïve and level-headed by turns – is used as an affectionately comic and ironic touchstone for the sophistication of London. This anonymous series proved very popular; William Blackwood made it a book in 1821 and asked Galt for more. The author sent him *Annals of the Parish* and this time it was published straightaway.

Galt did not consider these books to be true novels, preferring to call them sketches, observations or 'theoretical histories' which outlined the manners and the changes in provincial society, often through the voice of a single character. The *Annals* purports to be the chronicles of the country parish of Dalmailing from 1760 to 1810 as recorded in the Revd Micah Balwhidder's journal. Its companion volume *The Provost* (1822) reminisces about small-town politics and public events over the same period, all recounted in the revealingly opportunistic and blithely unself-conscious tones of Provost James Pawkie. ('Pawkie' in Scots means artful, with suggestions of country cunning.) These ironic 'autobiographies' owe their success to Galt's capacity for sympathy with his narrators, even while he uses their voices to cast indirect reflections on their own failings. 'What happened in my parish was but a type and index to the world', Balwhidder assures us serenely, and no doubt Galt's urban readers allowed themselves a smile at his parish-pump priorities:

> The Ann. Dom. 1763, was, in many a respect, a memorable year, both in public and in private. The king granted peace to the French, and Charlie Malcolm, that went to sea in the *Tobacco* trader, came home to see his mother.

Yet Galt has the eye of a social historian, and these amusing chronicles accumulate a host of minor but significant details in fashion, economics, manners and politics as the old ways of speaking and living gradually changed during the second half of the eighteenth century. Galt's intention was to chart the recent past just as Scott claimed to have done with *Waverley*, *Guy Mannering* and *The Antiquary*, and it can be argued that his diaristic approach allowed him to do a better job.

The autobiographical style suited Galt's strengths as a writer because it allowed him to use the distinctive rhythms of Lowland speech (in Scots or English) as his central narrative medium, with plenty of scope for broad Scots and proverbial expression. He uses a denser dialect than Scott allowed himself – amounting to a *tour de force* in the case of Lady Grippy in *The Entail* – and this oral flow, with its encapsulation of regional and national attitudes, lies at the ironic heart of Galt's understanding of how 'voice' reveals character, and how that 'local' voice can be used to make double-edged social comments on the wider world of his more sophisticated readers.

The Entail (1832) completes Galt's sequence of major Scottish books and it is closer to a conventional novel in that it abandons the autobiographical mask and follows the fortunes of a single family over three generations and a forty-year period. As a study of the ties of property, avarice and affection in the rise and fall of a self-made man, and in the legal disputes within the family after his death, *The Entail* has been seen as a forerunner in the line of Balzac, Dickens, Zola, Hardy and Galsworthy. It has a claim to be Galt's most powerful novel, if less fully realised than *Annals*; yet, while Scott, Byron, Coleridge and Jeffrey had all admired the Scottish series, there were also complaints about the latest book's 'sordidness' and its impenetrable dialect. It was not reprinted in the author's lifetime. Galt stepped up his output of fiction with four more novels using Scottish settings and three historical novels all within four years of 1822, but, not surprisingly, these works seem hastily written and were less successful than their precursors.

Ringan Gilhaize (1823), however, is notable as another imaginative autobiography, this time in a grim and tragic mode. It was written to vindicate the Covenanting spirit, 'hugely provoked', in Galt's words, by *Old Mortality* and by what he felt to be Scott's ridicule of the defenders of the Presbyterian Church and their sufferings over more than three generations. This time Galt immersed himself totally in the mind and voice of his narrator – full of long phrases, ringing with biblical rhythms and echoes, as he asserts, 'I have not taken up the avenging pen of history, and dipped it in the blood of martyrs, to record only my own particular woes and wrong.' There is no hint of comic or ironic distance in Ringan's savage experiences and in his ultimately successful quest to shoot Claverhouse down. Galt's achievement is to let that iron-hard, obsessive nature speak for itself, without apology and without entirely forfeiting the reader's sympathy. He was particularly proud of this technique of imaginative 'transfusion', but it was not fully understood by readers and the novel got little credit for a serious attempt to come to terms with some of the most painful themes in the Scottish inheritance.

Galt's success was on the wane and his best books were behind him. Between 1825 and 1829 he worked in Ontario as superintendent for the Canada Company, but his health was poor and problems with the board of directors led to resignation, bankruptcy, and a spell in debtors' prison in London. He continued to write, but a series of strokes in his mid fifties left him an invalid, and in 1834 he returned to Greenock, where he died five years later.

Perhaps the popularity of Galt's early Scottish novels obscured the subtleties of his approach to imaginative biography, and the importance of sympathy in the ironic distances which he established between author, 'narrator' and reader. His successors settled for much broader effects, almost exclusively in the vein of domestic comedy. The first step in this direction was taken by **David Macbeth Moir** (1798–1851), a friend and biographer of Galt's and a doctor in Musselburgh near Edinburgh. Moir contributed regularly to *Blackwood's* with both prose and poetry under the *nom de plume* of 'Delta', or Δ. His best-known book, *The Life of Mansie Wauch, Tailor of Dalkeith*, 'written by himself', began as a series for the magazine in 1824 and was published as a book four years later. These small-town 'memoirs' were dedicated to Galt, but they lack the older man's sense of perspective and social irony. The result is genre literature, and the pattern was set for the 'Kailyard' and a Victorian vogue in Scottish 'worthies'.

Sentimentalists and Spasmodics

By the 1850s nationalism had become a revolutionary force in Europe, but Lowland Scottish culture was to remain remarkably complacent for the rest of the century. Of course, the patriotic appeal of Scott's novels had always been romantic and conservative. On the other hand, Patrick Fraser Tytler's *History of Scotland* (1823–43) gave scholarly support to a popular understanding of how the nation had evolved and defended its frontiers, while the Disruption had done much the same for the old values of the Kirk, and movements such as the Association for the Vindication of Scottish Rights were formed to attack the centralisation of government around Westminster interests. Yet somehow these scholarly, religious and political stirrings never came together to achieve any truly effective cultural or political expression. With poetry in particular, the distinctively Scottish tradition seems to have completely lost its way.

Carolina Oliphant, Lady Nairne (1766–1845), disguised as 'Mrs Bogan of Bogan', had written and adapted many Scots songs for *The Scottish Minstrel* in the early 1820s. Her work is genteel and pastoral or suffused with the nostalgic parlour Jacobitism which Hugh Millar characterised as 'a sort of laughing gas' agreeably exciting to the feelings. 'Will ye no' come back again?', 'Caller Herrin'', 'The Hundred Pipers' and 'The Land o' the Leal' are still sung today. The various *Whistle-Binkie* anthologies from 1832 to 1890, subtitled 'A Collection of Songs for the Social Circle' have lasted less well (with the possible exception of 'Wee Willie Winkie') and the title has provided a generic label for all such milk-and-water vernacular verse, in a sentimental, complacent and utterly trivialised notion of what poetry might be. On the other hand, the only alternative seemed to be the sub-Miltonic rhetoric of epics such as *A Life-Drama*, which appeared in 1851. Its author, **Alexander Smith** (1830–67), a working-class lace-pattern-maker from Kilmarnock, was immediately hailed by the critics for the portentous ambition of his English verse, although he was accused of plagiarising from Tennyson after his second collection, *City Poems*, appeared in 1857. Smith also wrote essays and a novel, but he died young and neglected. His vein of extravagant Byronic expression had a certain vogue, however, even if it did keep dropping into flat and turgid lines. This was a failing shared by his English contemporaries, Philip Bailey and Sydney Dobell, so that they all came to be known as the 'Spasmodic school'.

The 'Spasmodics' were christened and parodied by **W. E. Aytoun** (1813–65), yet another Tory Edinburgh lawyer, son-in-law to John Wilson and a contributor to 'Maga'. Aytoun became professor of Rhetoric at Edinburgh in 1845, he supported the Scottish Rights Association and wrote solemn poems on national topics such as 'Edinburgh after Flodden' and 'The Execution of Montrose'. He is best remembered for humorous short stories and his satirical verse parodies. The mock-tragical *Firmilian* (1854) tells us enough about the Spasmodics to justify their oblivion, and the *Bon Gaultier Ballads* (1855), a collaboration with Theodore Martin, show a good critical ear at work, closer to burlesque than to any more pointed satire. There is one indisputably great writer of this period, however, who would have nothing to do with parody, rustic sentiment or the likes of Mansie Wauch, and he came from a small village in Dumfries whose name might have been invented on the pages of *Whistle-Binkie*.

Thomas Carlyle (1795–1881)

Born in Ecclefechan, about ten miles from the Border, Carlyle came from a strongly Presbyterian family, and this early theological discipline, along with his philosophical disposition and an intense romantic idealism combined to make him one of the most complicated and intransigent thinkers and cultural critics in Victorian Britain. Carlyle lived and worked in

London after the age of thirty-nine, yet his roots were deeply Scottish; he kept in touch with family and home through regular visits and correspondence, and before he died in February 1881 he declined a place in Westminster Abbey and asked that his body be returned to Ecclefechan in the plainest of coffins.

Carlyle's father was a stonemason–builder, a grim and taciturn man who was largely self-educated. He and his family belonged to the 'Burghers', a branch of the secession Church which had condemned the Church of Scotland for lax doctrine, and so his son grew up with a creed which stressed the power of preaching and solemn exposition, and the importance of individual acts of will and judgement in the face of eternity. Inevitably destined for the Church, Carlyle set off for Edinburgh University in 1809. He was excited by science and mathematics, but become disillusioned with university life just as his faith in the religious doctrine of his childhood began to falter, along with his health. He supported himself by working as a tutor and teacher – which he hated – and made abortive plans to study law. He learned German, undertook translations and reviews and corresponded with Goethe. The German Romantics made a deep impression on his idealistic, mandarin and uncouth temperament. Dyspeptic, sleepless and prone to depression, he seems to have undergone something of an existential crisis at this time – later described in *Sartor Resartus* as a sense of the 'Everlasting NO':

> To me the Universe was all void of Life, of Purpose, of Volition, even of Hostility: it was one huge, dead, immeasurable Steam-engine, rolling on, in its dead indifference, to grind me limb from limb.

He was not the only Victorian to be so haunted.

By the mid 1820s translations and his life of Schiller were gaining Carlyle a place in the world of letters, and he had met, and clumsily wooed, a doctor's daughter called Jane Welsh, a witty and beautiful middle-class girl who became his lifelong companion. Jane's *Letters and Memorials* (1883) provide a fascinating insight on their liaison. The couple married in 1826 and had two happy years in Edinburgh before financial constraints took them to remote Dumfriesshire. Their life was isolated at Craigenputtock and Jane had to cope with Carlyle's intense, restless and hypochondriac nature, which required absolute silence as he struggled with his thoughts, his journal and his highly-wrought prose style. Among the essays of this period, 'Signs of the Times', which appeared in the *Edinburgh Review* in 1829, launched a prophetic attack on the evils of Victorian materialism and the cool calculation inherent in Utilitarian ideas. In the 1830s Carlyle continued to develop a complex and transcendental analysis of his own relationship with the world in what was to be his first major work.

The extraordinary, nearly unreadable prose of *Sartor Resartus* was serialised in 1833, but it did not appear as a book until an American publisher took the risk in 1836, and it was a further two years before it was published in London. The title – literally, 'The Tailor Retailored' – refers to an elaborate disquisition on the philosophy of clothes, or of 'appearances', supposedly edited from the life and writings of 'Herr Teufels-dröckh' ('Devil's cast-off') a fictional German philosopher and mystic. 'Rightly viewed,' he tells us (in a sentence which sums up his creator's hopes for cultural criticism), 'no meanest object is insignificant; all objects are as windows, through which the philosophic eye looks into Infinitude itself.' The alter ego of Teufelsdröckh, and his peculiar brand of pedantic whimsy (as much a Scottish failing as a German one), allows Carlyle to air his transcendental views in an unashamedly prophetic style. Yet his account of the 'Everlasting NO' is conveyed with passionately autobiographical force. (His black depression was eventually dispelled by 'the Everlasting YEA', a dynamic, if unclear, revelation of hope in man's urge always to seek light in the beauty and mystery of the universe.)

The couple moved to London in 1834 and set up house in Chelsea. Carlyle wrote with difficulty, and his sentences are highly crafted and rugged at the same time, full of biblical echoes, repetitions, allusions and antitheses. At his best this method of address is bold, jagged and direct as he seeks to persuade the reader by the very passion of his own conviction, using tones of intimacy, irony or open scorn as he seeks to achieve rapport, agreement or downright surrender. Here is his lively defence of the transcendental, but it is not an argument in any sense of the word at all:

Thou wilt have no mystery or mysticism; wilt live in the daylight (rushlight?) of truth, and see the world and understand it? Nay, thou wilt laugh at all that believe in a mystery; to whom the universe is an oracle and temple, as well as a kitchen and cattle stall? *Armer Teufel!* Doth not thy cow calve, doth not thy bull gender? Nay, peradventure, doest not thou thyself gender? Explain me that, or do one of two things: retire into private places with thy foolish cackle; or, what were better, give it up and weep, not that the world is mean and disenchanted and prosaic, but that thou are vain and blind.

Is anything more wonderful than another, if you consider it maturely? I have seen no men rise from the dead; I have seen some thousands rise from nothing. I have not force to fly into the sun, but I have force to lift my hand, which is equally strange.

(Early Life, II, 1830)

And no Scottish Presbyterian Whig divine could be firmer than Carlyle in his praise of the humble labourer (such as his own father), or more convinced of the power of work as an existential act of faith: 'Whatsoever thy hand findeth to do, do it with thy whole might. Work while it is called Today; for Night cometh, wherein no man can work' (cf. Ecclesiastes 9: 10).

Carlyle's historical writing is haunted by that 'Night' – a poignant sense of the 'pastness' of the past – and a furious sympathy for the unsung plight of the common people who remain in the shadows while the same few aristocrats strut in the limelight of posterity's attention: figures such as 'Mary Stuart, a Beauty, but over light-headed; and Henry Darnley, a Booby who had fine legs'. Like his contemporary Macaulay, a fellow contributor to the *Edinburgh Review* and equally fierce in his opinions, Carlyle preferred what would now be called social history and he looked for moments of what he took to be evolutionary change in the spirit of the times. The Reformation was such a moment, when 'all Scotland is awakened to a second, higher life . . . convulsed, fermenting, struggling to body itself forth anew'; or the turmoil in France, which threw new ideals and a new fanaticism into the world. For the writing of *The French Revolution* (1837) Carlyle's research drew on the memoirs of other men, but it is supremely his own imagination and his rhetorical use of the present tense which transforms his material to the atmospheric immediacy of an eye-witness account. 'History, after all, is the true Poetry', he had proposed in 1832. 'Reality, if rightly interpreted is grander than Fiction; nay, that even in the right interpretation of Reality and History does genuine Poetry consist'. Some critics were puzzled by the style of *The French Revolution*, but for most it established Carlyle as a major writer and historian, one of the most sought-after intellectual figures in London. As 'the sage of Chelsea', he became friends with J. S. Mill, Emerson, Browning, Arnold, Tennyson and Dickens. Mill called *The French Revolution* the 'truest of histories . . . not so much a history as an epic poem', and its author was pleased to concur.

With *Chartism* in 1839, and in *Past and Present* (1843), Carlyle once more brooded angrily on *laissez-faire* economics and the plight of the poor and the working classes; and showed bitter contempt, too, at the inadequacies of Reform, which could only tinker with a rotten system. Yet sympathy for the oppressed did not make Carlyle a democrat. He mistrusted the emancipated masses and, when he extolled new directions and a new humanity in the evolving spirit of the times, he looked for them to be manifested in 'heroic' individuals. These thoughts were taken further with *On Heroes and Hero Worship* (1841), which began as a set among his many public lectures. The 'forerunners of history', according to Carlyle, included Odin, Mahomet and Napoleon; and his Scottish bias appears in his choice of Burns and Rousseau and in his respect for the authority of Luther, Knox and Cromwell. Such heroes, like the Calvinist elect, were chosen above others to lead or to show the way.

As he grew older, however, Carlyle's bracing prophesies of needful transformation and turmoil gave way to fears of anarchy and led him to equate heroic authority with control as a bulwark against change. He spent the latter part of his life working on an exhaustive and sterile act of homage with a *History of Frederick the Great* (1858–65), and the gross insistence of such pieces as *The Nigger Question* (1853) caused controversy and offence by maintaining that slaves (in the spiritual as well as the literal sense) are deemed slaves by the 'Supreme Powers' and should remain so. The harsh prophetic urgency of his early voice had become strained, hysterical and intolerant of all but its own views. Like the pattern of the Reformation in his native land, it is as if Carlyle's philosophy moved from an iconoclastic striving of the highest spirit, to a death grip of the most rigid and gloomy sort.

Hugh Millar (1802–56)

Hugh Millar never aspired to Carlyle's stature, but he came from a similar background and was an influential figure, by precept and example, in his own right. Essayist, journalist and geologist, he embodies the independence and the didacticism of the Scottish dissenting tradition. A self-educated stonemason from Cromarty, near Inverness, he became a local journalist and entered the national lists with a pamphlet letter against Church patronage. On the strength of this he was brought to Edinburgh to edit the *Witness*, the newspaper which became the voice of the Free Church after the Disruption. Millar was a moderate in Free Kirk circles and played a worthy part in their concern to bring education, self-advancement and self-expression to the labouring classes. He and his newspaper roundly condemned the clearances in Sutherland, for example, and protested against landowners who would not allow the Free Kirk – with its radical overtones – to build on their land. Atheist John Maclean and the Independent Labour Party workers of the next century were to lay similar emphasis on the education of the working classes as the route to social justice, but Millar's sturdy Presbyterian respectability was never revolutionary. He opposed Chartism and the formation of unions as too violent a step for the times, even although his own lungs had been damaged by stone-workers' silicosis in his youth. In the end his health did collapse, and exhausted and depressed, he took his own life with a gun. Among his books, the succinct prose of *The Old Red Sandstone* (1841) is something of a geologist's classic, even if he did try to reconcile the biblical account of creation with his scientific observations in a later work called *Footprints of the Creator* (1849). *Scenes and Legends of the North of Scotland* (1835) and an autobiography called *My Schools and Schoolmasters* (1854) testify to the life of the times and his constant interest in the landscape around him. Carlyle commended Millar as a genial fire 'tempered down into peaceful radical heat' and described the natural stateliness of his prose as 'luminous, memorable, all wholesome, strong and breezy' – an image of the man himself that outlasted his poor end.

William Alexander (1826–94)

The Disruption was a major historical and personal event in the life of Millar and thousands like him in parishes throughout the country. It revived communal ideals and redefined, if only through opposition, the traditional centres of authority in village life balanced as they were between minister, school-teacher and laird. The dialect novel *Johnny Gibb of Gushetneuk* (1871) describes just such a community. Its author, William Alexander, worked on farms in Aberdeenshire until an accident in his twenties cost him one of his legs and he turned to journalism as a career. He became editor of the *Aberdeen Free Press* and published his memoirs and the collection *Sketches of Life among my Ain Folk* (1875), both dedicated, like his novel, to preserving a record of the life, manners and speech in the countryside of his birth. Then, as now, he spoke to a potent sense of pride and regional identity in his North-East readers. Alexander uses formal English for passages of objective narrative and comment, and this tends to distance him from his creation, but the true life of the novel comes from the density of its dialect speech – a repository of wit, scorn, gossip and common wisdom. This oral inheritance is the social and moral focus of the book – weighty, considered and drily alert to pretension, it is the voice by which a community knows and guides itself.

Alexander's tendency to explain his characters at every turn was part of his documentary intention, for he was looking back some thirty years and his little community already seems frozen in time. Of course, change did not come quickly to the remoter parts of Scotland, and, even when it did, few writers seemed able to manage more than nostalgia at the prospect. This was particularly evident in the Highlands, where continuing and considerable changes failed to produce literature that was equal to the occasion, although some poets did manage political commitment and a fine rage in their verse. Perhaps new forms were needed to respond to the times, and most Gaelic poets were still loyal to the old communities and the old ways of looking at the world.

Gaelic literature

In search of opportunity, faced with rising rents, or simply cleared off their lands, thousands of Highlanders set sail for America in the opening years of the century. The oral treasury of Gaelic verse, music and tale-telling went with them and the old propensity for elegy and lament found new scope in their leavetaking. The homeland verses from the Gaelic-speaking settlements of Nova Scotia, South Carolina or the cities of Lowland Scotland all speak of exile, parting lovers, childhood and a simplified past. Popular songs poured out on these themes – typified by the 'Canadian Boat Song' in a translation sent back to *Blackwood's Magazine* by John Galt in 1829:

> From the lone shieling of the misty island
>   Mountains divide us and the waste of seas;
> Yet still the blood is strong, the heart is Highland,
>   And we in dreams behold the Hebrides.
>
> CHORUS
> Fair these broad meads – these hoary woods are grand;
> But we are exiles from our fathers' land.

There were many competent voices singing in these nostalgic pastures, but they did not produce any poets to equal those of the previous century.

In the very years when so many Gaels were leaving for America, tartan was breaking out like a rash, thanks to the 'wizard of the North', all over Britain and France. Fashionable society endured a craze for extravagantly formal 'Highland dress', and McIan's still popular clan prints or the formal, plaid-ridden portraits of Raeburn all testify to the glamour of the kilt. The uniform dress of the Highland regiments was gradually adapted to civilian purposes and mill-owners and chieftains got together to define 'recognised' clan tartans and to associate them with Lowland families so that any Scot with any surname could be told to which clan he or she 'belonged'. The respectability of the kilt and all things tartan was finally assured when Queen Victoria sojourned at Balmoral and Prince Albert, that worthy Hanoverian, bared his knees and appeared in public as a Jacobite pretender.

In the meantime native Gaelic-speakers were coming to terms with life in modern urban society. The Free Church, the

Society for Propagating Christian Knowledge, and the rise of Evangelical Christianity all played a part in promoting literacy and the publishing of hymns and religious verses in Gaelic as well as homilies and sermons in prose. Yet the true fluency and power of Gaelic prose was largely unrecorded, for it came from the extempore oral tradition of the Free Church pulpit, and the passionate address of these sermons was to influence later Gaelic poets even if they were not church-goers or Christians. Prose fiction, on the other hand, remained almost unknown, and the market had little chance of developing for as long as Gaelic speakers lacked the leisure, the spending-power or the literacy to read novels in their own language. Songs and poems were published successfully, however, because they had the strength of the oral tradition behind them, and for the same reason folk stories and proverbs were collected in books such as John F. Campbell's four-volume *West Highland Tales* (1860–2). Gaelic periodicals were established to speak to the growing Highland communities in Glasgow and the west of Scotland. **The Revd Norman Macleod** (1783–1862), called 'the friend of the Gael', was an influential editor and contributor to these magazines. He worked on a Gaelic dictionary (1831) and composed the beautiful song 'Farewell to Fiunary'; his short essays and dialogues were particularly widely appreciated and were collected posthumously in a volume called after him – *Caraid nan Gaidheal* (1867). His pieces such as 'The Emigrant Ship' ('Long mhór nan Eilthireach') extracted the maximum pathos from the leave-taking of the young who crossed the Atlantic and the grief of the elderly left behind. Such tales of piety and sentiment were equally popular in the Lowland Scots 'Kailyard' school, most of whose authors reached a large urban readership through the Revd William Robertson Nicoll's Evangelical *British Weekly*.

By the end of the century anthologies and collections of Gaelic poems were being published, popularised and trans-lated by journalists such as Henry Whyte ('Fionn', 1852–1914) who was particularly keen on the song tradition. From 1909 into the 1920s Marjory Kennedy-Fraser produced *The Songs of the Hebrides* in several volumes, although she was inclined to 'improve' her folk sources to meet what she felt to be more refined standards of taste. Alexander Carmichael spent the last forty years of the century collecting the vast storehouse of anonymous Gaelic tales, songs, hymns and incantations which was finally published in six invaluable volumes as *Carmina Gadelica* (1900–69). Highland societies flourished in Glasgow and Inverness, while Gaelic churches, ceilidhs, concerts and shinty-matches all established themselves as part of Scottish city life. Under the same stimulus amateur dramatic societies performed short Gaelic plays, and An Comunn Gaidhealach was formed to promote Highland culture and music. The first National Mod was held in 1893, and before long regular competitions were arranged, with Gaelic choirs assembled and an official 'bard' crowned as if to bring concert-hall status to the informality of the old oral ways.

Gaelic literature was not entirely given over to sentiment and respectability. **William Livingstone (Uilleam MacDhun-léibhe,** 1808–70) looked back to a heroic past and wrote battle-poems dramatising old conflicts against the Norse or the wars of independence against England. A self-educated man with a fierce hatred for everything English, he brought his rage to bear on the problem of depopulation in the Highlands. In 'A Message to the Bard' ('Fios thun a'Bhàird') he paints a loving picture of his native Islay and then upsets the convention by crying out against the absence of people in the scene. His refrain 'carry this clear message / as I see it, to the Bard' comes to seem increasingly bitter as the poem progresses.

John Smith (Iain Mac a' Ghobhainn, 1848–81) composed lampoons and humorous verses about village life in Lewis, but his best poems are directly political. 'Song for Sportsmen' ('Oran Luchd an Spòrs') attacks the Scots themselves for allowing their lands and their heritage to fall into the hands of sportsmen and industrialists, and its scathingly radical outlook is prophetic of Hugh MacDiarmid's disgust for the 'pickle makers' who now 'own' the hills.

> Some of them trafficed in opium,
> they gathered a great deal of riches,
> their vice made the Chinamen suffer,
> their people destroyed by the poison;
> men without kindness or mercy,
> who were hard to prick in the conscience;
> in payment for all of their plunder
> they deserved to be stabbed with a whinger.   short sword

(trs. D. Thomson)

Smith was thinking of James Matheson, a native of Sutherland who had made his fortune in the disgraceful opium-trade with China and purchased the whole island of Lewis in 1844. He and his factors were not popular, most especially Donald Munro, whose autocratic rule – he held almost every official post on the island – earned him the title of 'the Shah'. The poet recognised that the poor man can be arrogant, too, and he mocks the unco guid of the Free Church in 'The Spirit of Pride' ('Spiorad an Uamhir'). But his finest rage is reserved for the world of social injustice and misused privilege. Among other lines in favour of *caritas*, 'The Spirit of Kindness' ('Spiorad a' Charthannais') speaks on behalf of the Highland regiments at Waterloo to make a complaint which Scotland, and Lewis in particular, was to hear again at the end of the First World War:

> What solace had the fathers
> of the heroes who won fame?
> Their houses, warm with kindliness,
> were in ruins around their ears;
> their sons were on the battlefield
> saving a rueless land,
> their mothers' state was piteous
> with their houses burnt like coal.

> While Britain was rejoicing
> they spent their time in grief.
> In the country that had reared them,
> no shelter from the wind;
> the grey strands of their hair were tossed
> by the cold breeze of the glen,
> there were tears upon their cheeks
> and cold dew on their heads.

Smith reminds his oppressors that death is a landlord who comes to us all, and he saves his most vehement hatred for the factor Munro:

> The wriggling worm will praise you then
> for your flesh's enticing taste,
> when it finds you placed before it
> on its table, silent now,
> saying 'This one's juicy flesh
> is good for earthy worms,
> since he made many hundreds thin
> to feed himself for me.'
>
> (trs. D. Thomson)

Smith's images are strong, concrete and uncomfortably savage, with something of the spirit of Iain Lom in place of the nostalgia which prevails in so many of the 'homeland' verses.

The struggle for land-reform in Skye in the 1880s motivated many of the poems of **Mary Macpherson** (**Màiri Nic a' Phearsain**, 1821–98). Màiri Mhór lived latterly in Inverness and Glasgow, and some of her songs, such as 'Farewell to the New Christmas' ('Soraidh leis an Nollaig ùir'), for instance, evoke longing for the island of her youth; but her popular songs in support of land-reform made her something of a legend, and she became known for her outspoken and earthy expression, made doubly impressive by her energy and her huge size. Imprisoned at Inverness on what she insisted was a false charge of shoplifting, she explained in 'The Oppression I Suffered' ('Na dh'fhuiling mi de dh'fhòirneart') that the injustice of the experience was what turned her talents to verse. In the cause of land-reform she composed 'Incitement of the Gaels' ('Bronsnachadh nan Gaidheal') and listed the movement's heroes in 'Song of Ben Lee' ('Oran Beinn-Lì'). It is entirely fitting that 'Big Mary of the songs' should have become one of the heroes herself, for it was, after all, the crofting womenfolk who had driven off the police in the 'battle of Braes'.

Margaret Oliphant (1828–97)

In complete contrast to Mary Macpherson, the many books of Margaret Oliphant returns us to the Lowlands and to a politer provincial scene. Born near Edinburgh and brought to Liverpool as a girl, Mrs Oliphant's sympathies remained with small dissenting communities and her northern origins. The heroine of her first novel, *Margaret Maitland* (1849), encapsulates all the Scottish Victorian spinsterly virtues of piety, good sense, reticence and industry. The author herself had to draw on these strengths soon enough, for she was widowed while scarcely in her thirties and had to turn to writing to support herself, her family and an alcoholic brother, too. Her career in England spans forty-five years of extraordinary industry during which time she produced innumerable articles and reviews for 'Maga' as well as biographies, criticism, literary histories, an autobiography, a history of *Blackwood's* and over sixty two- and three-volume novels. She prided herself on being a *Blackwood's* author, as well she might, but her life's work did not make her particularly rich or famous.

Margaret Oliphant wrote several Scottish novels, including *Merkland* (1851), *Katie Stewart* (1853) – an historical piece – and *Kirsteen: A Story of a Scottish Family Seventy Years Ago* (1890). In some other novels and short stories she focuses on supernatural or theosophical intimations of a realm of spirits beyond death – a growing Victorian obsession; but the bulk of her work concerns itself with the more mundane tribulations of provincial life and manners. Q. D. Leavis has cited these novels as a useful link between the worlds of Jane Austen and George Eliot, and indeed Oliphant's *Miss Marjoribanks* (1866) may have been a direct influence on *Middlemarch* (1871–2). (George Eliot was suspected of being the author of *Miss Marjoribanks* because it was serialised in *Blackwood's*, where her own *Scenes of Clerical Life* had first appeared.) *Miss Marjoribanks* belongs to a series of novels and stories set in England which were collected as 'The Chronicles of Carlingford' (1863–6) after the style of Trollope's 'Barchester' books and Mrs Gaskell's 'Cranford' sketches. By the end of the sixties, however, Mrs Oliphant had to support another of her brothers and his family, and her increased literary output led to a decline in quality for the rest of her life as a professional author. Even so, she was a respected friend of Carlyle's, and Barrie and Henry James admired her best work for the potential they saw in it, just as they acknowledged her good humour and her indomitable spirit.

James Thomson (1834–82)

Among the other Scots working in London at this time, James Thomson was to make a grimmer indictment of late-Victorian life and belief than even Carlyle had attempted. Thomson's father was a merchant seaman in Port Glasgow until a stroke paralysed him when James was six. The family moved to London, but Thomson's mother died within two years and he went to an asylum for the children of poor Scottish servicemen. With his limited means he joined up as an army schoolmaster, but after eight years his drinking led to dismissal and in 1862 he found himself back in London looking for a new livelihood. He turned to literature and journalism, having published some poems and articles while he was still in the army, and eventually gained a post with the *National Reformer* – a periodical directed at freethinkers who wanted to keep up with the views of Darwin, Spencer and Huxley.

Thomson's mother had been an Irvingite and no doubt he assimilated some of her passionate Christianity along with a youthful enthusiasm for Shelley and Novalis – the late-eighteenth-century German Romantic poet. (Thomson used 'BV' – Bysshe Vanolis – as a pseudonym for his verses.) Early poems and articles suggest a struggle between idealistic and mystical beliefs and a conviction that the profit-motive and the old ways of worship have corrupted and enslaved mankind. He attacked Christianity for ignoring the vital present in favour of rewards and punishments in an afterlife, and proposed a kind of pantheism in which each man's duty is to realise the true freedom of his spirit before it returns to the infinite, impersonal evolutionary flow of matter. Thomson gradually came to atheism and a philosophical pessimism which recognised the disparity between human hope and man's imperfectibility, and he published these views in the *National Reformer*. He also produced a memoir of the Italian pessimist Giacomo Leopardi and translated his dialogues and discourses.

Thomson's drive to show 'the bitter, old, and wrinkled truth, stripped naked' culminates in *The City of Dreadful Night*, published in parts during 1874 and as a book in 1880. The poem is often cited as a 'modern' vision of the city as nightmare, but it is essentially a Dantesque allegory, a symbolic rather than a realistic visit to a cold Inferno of streets, squares and graveyards. (In fact earlier poems such as 'Sunday up the River' and 'Sunday at Hampstead', from 1865, are markedly more 'realistic' and more modern in their use of colloquial English. They also show London in a cheerful and sunny mood, to remind us that Thomson was not entirely given over to gloom.) Even so, *The City of Dreadful Night* does look forward to T. S. Eliot's vision of London as a wasteland, and Thomson's empty squares have a strange and menacing calm, which seems to anticipate surrealism and the modern paintings of De Chirico. For the most part, however, the echoes are of Dürer and Shelley, and the poet's atheism is suffused with a

melancholy which might have been drawn from Fitzgerald or
even Drummond of Hawthornden:

> And now at last authentic word I bring,
> Witnessed by every dead and living thing;
>   Good tidings of great joy for you, for all:
> There is no God; no Fiend with names divine
> Made us and tortures us; if we must pine,
>   It is to satiate no Being's gall.
>
> . . .
>
> This little life is all we must endure,
> The grave's most holy place is ever sure,
>   We fall asleep and never wake again;
> Nothing is of us but the mouldering flesh,
> Whose elements dissolve and merge afresh
>   In earth, air, water, planets, and other men.

Even the readers of the *National Reformer* were startled by the
sustained threnody of Thomson's 'comfort', and, although he
received encouraging letters from George Eliot and Meredith,
most reviewers accused the poem of insincerity or heresy or
both, and they preferred the other pieces in the 1880 collection.
Thomson despaired of finding favour with the prestigious
literary periodicals, and a break with his editor saw him
reduced to writing reviews and biographical essays for *Cope's
Tobacco Plant* – a journal subsidised by a Liverpool tobacco firm.

Increasingly given to bouts of excessive drinking, the poet's
health and morale declined until a particularly destructive
episode killed him in June 1882. He had achieved a modest
reputation, but *The City of Dreadful Night* spoke more clearly to a
later generation. If its images of despair look rather romantic to
readers used to Eliot and Kafka, we can still sympathise with
his courageous attempt to face the indifference of the universe
without flinching. At least he felt that poetry should tackle
serious philosophical issues, and in this he shared his idealism,
and a preference for evolutionism too, with John Davidson.
Hugh MacDiarmid's later poetry can also be seen to have a
place in this company, going back to Carlyle himself, in what
amounts to a school of Scottish writers who have followed a
'metaphysical' direction with polemical urgency.

By comparison, the desperate plight of poetry in Scotland
may be judged by the continuing success of the *Whistle-Binkie*

anthologies and the vogue which grew up for the verse of
William McGonagall (1825?–1902), 'poet', 'tragedian' and
public performer from Dundee. McGonagall himself was
sincere (or deluded) in his ambitions to be a great poet, but his
audiences came mostly to laugh. His naïve verses on all the
issues of the day – preferably 'tragedies' such as the Tay Bridge
disaster in 1879 – do have a kind of genius for the banal, stuffed
with prosaic details and hilariously contrived rhymes.
McGonagall undertook poetry-readings throughout Scotland
(in a variety of striking costumes) and even visited London and
New York. His *Poetic Gems* (1890) have seldom been out of print
– a reflection that would have given poor Thomson little
comfort.

Robert Louis Stevenson (1850–94)

Thomson's confrontation with the problems of modernity –
urban despair and scientific materialism – scarcely features
in the fiction of Robert Louis Stevenson, whose best-known
books belong to an extrovert tale-telling tradition which looks
back to Scott. He was not alone, and for the rest of the century
the preferred modes of Scottish novelists will be Stevensonian
romance, symbolic fantasy, or nostalgic rusticism. While these
forms undoubtedly represent a reaction to the materialistic face
of the contemporary world, they cannot be said to deal with it
directly. It would be wrong to accuse Stevenson of escapism,
however, for his mercurial personality had a most complicated
relationship with Scotland and his own Scottishness. Critical
and nostalgic by turns, he wrote about his homeland from exile
in the South Seas, seeking to express a vision shaped by the
rigours of Calvinism and yet self-consciously dedicated to the
free life of art and the imagination. Such internal divisions fuel
the best of Stevenson's fiction, as if he were replaying in
psychologically ambiguous terms Walter Scott's own conflict
between Unionist stability and Jacobite romance. He had
scarcely begun to fulfil his deepening grasp of these old themes
when a brain haemorrhage ended his life at the age of
forty-four.

Stevenson's health was perpetually at the mercy of acute
lung-troubles and tuberculosis, and the damp and windy

climate of Edinburgh plagued his boyhood with coughs and chills which put him to bed for weeks of fever and sleepless nights. As an only child, he would not have survived if he had not come from a well-off and caring family, for his father was a harbour engineer and lighthouse-builder, like his grandfather, who had constructed the 'impossible' light on Bell Rock. Stevenson senior was a devout and conservative man, whose sense of duty had led him in his father's footsteps to be a civil engineer, despite his own rather intense and imaginative nature. He was fond and affectionate with his son and encouraged his youthful writing. So often confined to bed, the boy thrived on escapist tales and delighted to create plots with cut-out figures from his toy theatre – a pastime he recalled in his essay 'A Penny Plain and Two Pence Coloured' (1883). Many of his poems in *A Child's Garden of Verses* (1885) – assembled while he was convalescing as an adult – relate to this imaginative life of bedside dreams and games on the counter-pane, and he dedicated the collection to Alison Cunningham, the devoted young nurse of his childhood whom he never forgot as 'My second Mother, my first Wife'. 'Cummie' came from strict Presbyterian stock and, although she disapproved of plays and novels, she still fired her charge's imagination with stories of the Covenanters and tales of righteousness.

Stevenson entered Edinburgh University at the age of seventeen, but his studies in civil engineering (to please his father) took second place to new friends, new books and the. bohemian life. He declared a romantic preference for the low life of Edinburgh – 'the lighted streets and the swinging gait of harlots' – so excitingly different from a New Town background in middle-class bourgeois respectability. When engineering failed to enthuse him he attempted law, but growing differences with his father came to a head over his professed agnosticism and his bohemian friends – notably his lively cousin Bob Stevenson. Louis's parents (his name was pronounced 'Lewis') were disproportionately frightened and dismayed by their son's loss of grace and he was made to feel extremely guilty. Life at home became tense, and a very early story only recently published – 'The Edifying Letters of the Rutherford Family' – deals with this crisis. The young man found relief in letters to Mrs Francis Sitwell, an older woman whom he had met at a cousin's house in Suffolk. She believed in his talent, and she and

Sidney Colvin – later her husband – helped him to make London contracts in journalism and publishing. The following year saw something of a reconciliation with the family, who never ceased to support him financially, and he was back in Edinburgh studying Scots law again. His father gave him £1000 when he finally became an advocate in 1875, but had to accept that his son's career was henceforth to be a literary one. Stevenson began his peripatetic adult life with regular visits to London and the continent, especially to the forest of Fontainebleau, where his cousin Bob spent the summers painting in congenial artistic company, away from the cold winds and the sterner expectations of the North.

A few essays and book-reviews had already appeared under Stevenson's name, including a piece on what he took to be John Knox's two-faced attitude to women. At Edinburgh Infirmary he met the English poet W. E. Henley, who had come to have the tubercular bones of his foot treated by Joseph Lister. Stevenson based Long John Silver's better qualities on his rumbustious friend, and they wrote four plays together in the 1880s, without much stage success. The two writers remained close for thirteen years until a quarrel over a slight to Stevenson's wife parted them. Neither gave in to their ailments, and both seemed determined to pursue an actively physical life. Indeed, Louis's first book – *An Inland Voyage* (1878) – describes a canoe holiday he took through the canals of Belgium in the summer of 1876. Later that year at a hotel in Fontainebleau he met the woman he was to marry.

Fanny Osbourne was an American in Europe with her children, where she intended to study painting and make a break from her husband. Stevenson was struck by this resourceful and intelligent lady – ten years his senior – and she was intrigued by his physical frailty combined with an extraordinarily vital and volatile personality. They became lovers, but Fanny's money finally ran out and she had to return to America. That autumn Stevenson set out on a twelve-day mountain-walking tour in the south of France, travelling alone with his pack, his notebook, a revolver and a donkey called Modestine. By now his delight in France and the free life had produced a study of François Villon and a short story featuring him – 'A Lodging for the Night' (1877) – as well as 'The Sire de Malétroit's Door' (1878). He had made friends with Andrew

Lang and Edmund Gosse and produced a number of essays for Henley's *London*, later collected in *Virginibus Puerisque* (1881). In the winter he completed *Edinburgh: Picturesque Notes*, and in June 1879 *Travels with a Donkey in the Cévennes* became a minor classic among travel-books. His literary career was under way at last.

Then Stevenson received a cable from Fanny Osbourne in California, and, to the absolute consternation of friends and family, he decided to go to Monterey to join her, though she was not yet divorced. Excited by the prospect of America, he expected to meet the energy and optimism which he had found in the works of Walt Whitman; but the rigours of the journey and the strain of his arrival nearly killed him. *Across the Plains* (1892) and *The Amateur Emigrant* (1895) give a rawly realistic account of the sufferings he shared with his fellow voyagers, but neither piece appeared in his lifetime. Louis's fiction was more successful, and 'The Pavilion on the Links' (1880) was published as an atmospheric short story set on the bleak sands of the Scottish east coast – full of convincing detail, mysterious doings at night and the lore of tides and winds. His youthful visits to lighthouses with his father had not been forgotten, and many later works show the same delight in shores, islands, harbours and coastal inns.

Louis and Fanny were married in May 1880. With limited means, but tough and resourceful in her own way, Fanny took her husband into the mountains for the sake of his health, and their experiences in an abandoned shack at an old silver-mine produced *The Silverado Squatters* (1883). Fences were mended with Edinburgh and by August the new couple and twelve-year-old stepson Lloyd Osbourne were in Heriot Row, where Fanny succeeded in befriending Louis's parents and friends. As ever, the approach of a Scottish winter drove them abroad, but the following summer saw them back in Pitlochry and Braemar, and Stevenson began to write again, using Scots for the first time as a major narrative voice. 'Thrawn Janet' (1881) is a gripping account of supernatural possession with its roots in the oral tradition – not unlike Scott's 'Wandering Willie's Tale'. It tells how the Revd Murdoch Soulis is forced to recognise the power of the Devil, although as a college-educated and liberal young minister he used to scoff at such superstition and to chide the locals for their cruelty to Janet, the local witch. The community's beliefs are vindicated when Janet is found to be a reanimated corpse and, on the imaginative level at least, Stevenson joins Hogg in accepting the intimate proximity of the Devil and all his works. Fired by his theme and its native setting, Louis followed it with 'The Body Snatcher' and then 'The Merry Men' (1882) as a tale of Cameronian piety and guilt among the shipwrecks on an elemental Scottish coast in the eighteenth century. Not far from the spirit of Hawthorne and Poe (whom he had read and admired), 'The Merry Men' is made surprisingly subtle by Stevenson's mastery of atmospheric description. The same expertise, and memories of the California coast, came to fruition when he began to write *Treasure Island*.

Conceived in Braemar and finished in Switzerland, where they wintered again, 'The Sea Cook' began as a tale around a map drawn for young Lloyd's amusement. It followed a genre already established by Captain Marryat (1792–1848) and popularised by a fellow Edinburgh writer, **R. M. Ballantyne** (1825–94), whose dozens of books include *Martin Rattler*, *The Coral Island* (both 1858) and *The Gorilla Hunters* (1861). Yet *Treasure Island* (1883) was more than another adventure serial in *Young Folks*, for Stevenson had uncovered a theme which spoke to his life-experience and his imagination with equal force. Indeed, its psychological and moral patterns were to reappear in all his mature works. The typical Stevenson hero is an untried young man faced with formative experience: Jim Hawkins is a teenager, while the protagonist of 'The Merry Men' and David Balfour of *Kidnapped* are scarcely older – lads of university age at a time when studies started young. Archie Weir also fits this pattern, although he is less typical in other respects. On leaving home, or travelling, these young heroes are freed from the security of convention and routine, much as the author himself threw over Heriot Row in favour of Fontainebleau and Silverado. Impressions of the world are heightened in such new surroundings – an effect which the readers share – and the protagonists have to make judgements on people and events entirely from their own resources. Having lost their fathers (a motif of interest to the psychoanalytical critic, perhaps) the heroes look to friends for guidance instead, or to charismatic strangers or distant uncles, only to be shocked by what they find. The world of their elders, like the elders themselves, is not what it seemed to be from the security of childhood. Nevertheless, when Jim Hawkins finally realises that Silver is a lot less than the 'best of shipmates', he still cannot condemn him. Dr Livesy, Squire Trelawney and Captain Smollett belong to the world of gentlemen – the world Jim will enter after these rites of passage – but it is Silver who strikes a strange note of sympathy and complicity with the boy, and it is Silver, like a dangerous mixture of Iago and Falstaff, who dominates the stage with his power to charm. Thus Jim and Long John, like David Balfour and Alan Breck, or the two Duries in *The Master of Ballantrae*, or the two sides of Dr Jekyll, represent opposed tendencies in a shifting balance between stability and adventure, or social responsibility and individual freedom. If Walter Scott proposed a similar polarity, he always ended with the *status quo*, but for Louis the condition is psychological and less easily resolved – a struggle within the hearts and minds of his heroes, who are still haunted by the booming surf, or by nights on the bare hillside, even after they have accepted a settled future. In this way Stevenson transcends the adventure novel by using its uncomplicated lines to say some rather complicated things about the tensions between imagination and convention, and the changes which take place, for better and for worse, between youth and maturity.

When Stevenson chooses the past – and almost all his stories do – it is imaginative freedom which he is choosing – as if the past were another kind of exotic location, more appropriate for such deeds and dilemmas than late-Victorian Edinburgh. A moment's comparison with Dostoevsky or James will show his limitations in this respect, yet the landscapes of *Treasure Island* or *Kidnapped* are so vividly realised, and the reader is so involved with the physical immediacy of vicarious experience, that all is made contemporary again. Despite his favourite eighteenth-century settings, Stevenson is not a historical novelist at all, certainly not in the style of Scott or Galt, who were so keen to explore the differences between 'then' and 'now'. Nevertheless, Louis was sensitive about his standing as a conscious and serious artist. He explained his theories about fiction and defended prose romance in an essay called 'Gossip on Romance' (1882), and again in 'A Humble Remonstrance' (1884), which was offered as a reply to Henry James's essay

'The Art of Fiction'. The Scot maintained that truth to life was not enough in fiction, for life is inchoate, while the novelist's job is to construct order by subsuming character, setting and incident to an overriding creative conception. At the same time he must meet the challenge to convey a sense of 'real' and dazzling experience in his prose. This concern with style and the writer's craft gave him common ground with James, and the two men met and corresponded and became admirers of each other's work.

Further collections of essays and short stories and the book-publication of *Treasure Island* brought critical status and much-needed royalties; but Stevenson's health forced him abroad again, where he completed a lesser romance, *Prince Otto* (1805), and began *The Black Arrow* (1888). After a year, the family returned to Britain for the last time, settling in Bournemouth at 'Skerryvore', where Stevenson wrote 'Markheim' and the novels *Kidnapped* and *Jekyll and Hyde*, both of which appeared in 1886.

As a novel of travel and the Scottish landscape *Kidnapped* has few equals, yet its fascination comes as much from character as from action, although its main protagonists need to be considered together to realise the author's theme in this respect. David Balfour is the canny heir to Walter Scott's Lowland, Presbyterian, Unionist world, while Alan Breck Stewart epitomises the wilful courage and Jacobite romance of the Highlands – still potent five years after Culloden. Yet, even although David is carried along by events, rather like a Scott hero, Breck's loyal, vain and dangerous spirit seems to echo something within himself. When their escapade is over, Alan Breck must go into exile in France and David must turn to the gentlemanly responsibilities of his inheritance. This is symbolised by his passing through the doors of the British Linen Bank at the end of the adventure, and all the time 'there was a cold gnawing in my inside like a remorse for something wrong'. The remorse is not unlike J. M. Barrie's regret for the loss of boyhood – Peter Pan's kingdom of ruthless innocence and amoral imaginative freedom. Peter Pan crows like a cock at the defeat of his enemies, with just the same untrammelled spirit as Alan Breck does when he claims staid and earnest Balfour for his own:

> He came up to me with open arms. 'Come to my arms!' he cried, and
> embraced and kissed me hard upon both cheeks. 'David,' said he, 'I love
> you like a brother. And O, man,' he cried in a kind of ecstasy, 'am I no' a
> bonny fighter?'
>
> Thereupon he turned to the four enemies, passed his sword clean
> through each of them, and tumbled them out of doors one after the other.
> As he did so, he kept humming, and singing, and whistling to himself . . .

Such is the 'brother' David must learn to leave behind, but his
call is felt from within and it cannot be denied without that
feeling of 'remorse for something wrong'.

Stevenson had already realised that duality was the true
and underlying theme of his fiction, for he had just given an
overtly psychological focus to it in *The Strange Case of Dr Jekyll
and Mr Hyde* (1886). Its origins as a Gothic 'shilling shocker' are
obvious and Louis had already written a play about the good
Deacon Brodie's secret career of crime in Edinburgh. But this
novel's interest in the unconscious and interior nature of good
and evil give it a more serious moral dimension, just as it also
symbolises a social truth about Victorian society and the
anonymity of its great cities, where depravity and respectability rub shoulders. Although the tale is set in London, it has
deeply Scottish roots, and true to the ethos of the *Justified Sinner*
it shows the principle of evil as a kind of double which threatens
the upright personality from within. Jekyll's experiments were
originally intended to remove this unworthy self, but they
released him instead, and it is the experience of pleasure which
subverts the doctor's Calvinist ideal of 'a life of effort, virtue
and control'. At first he rejoices in his new ability to slip off
'genial respectability', as he puts it, like a schoolboy who sheds
his clothes to 'spring headlong into the sea of liberty'. But he
discovers that he cannot escape from his freer and darker side
without killing himself.

Stevenson's long and complicated relationship with his
father – resentful, affectionate and dependent by turns – finally
came to an end when the old man died, and the writer decided
to leave Britain once and for all with his mother, Fanny and
Lloyd in 1887. They went to the Adirondacks near the
Canadian border, where he could attend a TB clinic. His
American royalties alleviated his perpetual money-problems at
last, until wanderlust and a longing for the sun took them all to
California, where they chartered a schooner for an extended

cruise in the South Seas. *The Master of Ballantrae* (1889) was completed in Hawaii, shortly after the new year.

This time Stevenson symbolised the divisions of eighteenth-century Scotland in the lifelong struggle between two brothers. Staid and worthy Henry Durie is briefed to support the Hanoverian cause, while his younger brother James – a charming and amoral character – becomes a Jacobite adventurer. Their father's plan is that the house should survive, whatever the outcome of the rising. Here the differences between a Balfour type and a Breck type are exacerbated by rivalry in love, moral obsession and fraternal betrayal. At first our judgement of the two brothers is biased because the most part of the tale is told by Ephraim Mackellar, an educated and dogmatic servant, jealous on behalf of his 'Mr Henry' and prone to see things from his point of view. Mackellar is a limited narrator worthy of Galt, and the quality of the novel flags without his distinctive voice. Thus we only slowly come to realise that young James is neither a Byronic chevalier in exile, nor the Devil incarnate, although the Durie family casts him in both roles. The rather colourless and pious Henry is obsessed with his 'Satanic' brother, but it is his own sense of grievance, justification and wounded pride which takes over his sanity and ruins him. In the end, the old religious fears and the old Stuart romances have killed them both, and Stevenson's novel has made a more subtle point about Scottish character and history than its melodramatic moments might suggest.

The Stevenson family found itself on another sea trip, on a trading-schooner through the Gilbert Islands, and these voyages on the fringes of respectable commerce provided the material for the author's best South Sea stories. In his fortieth year he was making a growing commitment to life in the Pacific, and when they came to Samoa again they bought a large estate at Upolu and built a house there. Thinking to visit Britain just one more time, they travelled to Sydney in 1890, but Louis's health collapsed, and collapsed again even after another convalescence. The little party returned to Vailima, where they remained for the last four years of Louis's life. Slowly the estate established itself, and Stevenson became a respected figure in the community as a champion of native rights and a 'Tusitala' – a storyteller.

Louis's thoughts turned to Scotland, which he never

expected to see again. He corresponded with J. M. Barrie and invited him to Samoa, longing to talk to a fellow Scot; and he began *Weir of Hermiston*. Faced with more immediate demands for money, he fell back on David Balfour and wrote *Catriona* (1893) as a sequel to *Kidnapped*, substituting moral complications and a love interest for the topographical brilliance of the earlier book. Further adventure stories were in order, so he worked on *St Ives* (finished by Quiller-Couch in 1897) and started books on the Covenanters and Prince Charlie. In the meantime, the South Seas featured in a collaboration with his stepson, while *Island Night's Entertainments* (1893) included 'The Beach at Falesa', perhaps his plainest and finest South Sea story. *The Ebb Tide* followed in 1894 as a picture of moral decay and the seamy side of island existence. It is ironic that Stevenson was so resolutely unromantic about his exotic surroundings while the Kailyard school was reinventing Scotland as a homespun Eden. At the end of 1894 Louis was working once more on *Weir of Hermiston*, excited by its exploration of the doomed relationship between an overbearing father and his sensitive son. It was his practice to read passages aloud to the family at the end of each day, but on 3 December he suffered a sudden cerebral stroke and died in the evening with the story unfinished.

Weir of Hermiston (1896) might have been Stevenson's greatest work, or it might have turned to melodrama in its closing stages like *The Master of Ballantrae*. What survives is a magnificent beginning in which the author's fascination with the duality of Scottish character and the mysterious influences of inheritance and history, are expressed as a conflict between father and son, with the very spirit of Calvinist authority set against the frailer virtues of imagination and empathy. Loosely based on the real Lord Braxfield, judge Adam Weir is an unforgettable fictional creation. A brutally plain-spoken Lord Advocate of the early nineteenth century, he faces harsh truths about the world with a cruel relish for absolute exposure. He cares for his son Archie, but is suspicious of his own tenderness as if it were a weakness to be despised. Yet Stevenson manages to make us thrill to the savage flair and the awkward, granite integrity of his crushing and grim humour: ' "Weel it's something of the suddenest" ', he comments when he hears of his ineffectual wife's unexpected death, ' "But she was a

dwaibly body from the first. . . . It was a daftlike marriage."
And then, with a most unusual gentleness of tone, "Puir bitch,"
said he, "puir bitch!" '

Weir fears that his son will take after his weak mother, and
certainly the young man's excitable, imaginative and sentimental nature is as yet unformed and untried. Stevenson was
setting a green version of his own impulsive sensibility against
archetypal Scottish mores, whose fascination and whose kinship he could not deny, even from the distance of Samoa. Could
these two elements ever be at peace with each other, or within
one nature? The stage is set for a terrible confrontation, which
will come about when the son has to be sentenced by his own
father for the murder of the man who betrayed him with his girl.
The psychological drama of the Weirs, father and son, is set
against the remoter backdrop of oral tradition associated with
the Weaver's Stone – where the lovers meet, where a Covenanter was once brutally murdered and where murder will be
done again. This ballad-like sense of community history and
fate is emphasised by Stevenson's narrative distance and the
ironic compassion with which he treats the sweetly foolish
love-games of the young people. Archie and Christina are
infatuated with the idea of being in love, and Frank Innes, the
rival suitor, toys with their affections and his own impulses like
a cruel boy. Their sentimental idyll at Archie's country home
will come to a bad end, and Archie will soon have to face his
father in a suddenly and tragically adult world.

The violent folk-history of the Borders and a symbolic model
of Scottish society are brought together in the four 'black
Elliott' brothers – a businessman, an improving farmer, a
radical weaver and a poet – who rode down the robbers who
killed their father in years past. It is likely that Stevenson would
have had them ride again to free Archie for the sake of their
niece, but we cannot tell whether this would have led to a
melodramatic rescue or a more mature and less predictable
outcome. Stevenson was not immune to the dangers of
romance, but the ironic 'folk-historical' distance of his narrative style in *Weir of Hermiston* suggests a new control in his
treatment of it. If the novel had come to show the limitations of
swashbuckling solutions, it would, indeed, have been his
greatest work.

Stevenson's talent for telling a tale gained him a considerable popular audience, and in this respect his skills were shared by his compatriot **Arthur Conan Doyle** (1859–1930). Both writers, incidentally, admired the stories of Émile Gaboriau, the inventor of the French detective-novel in the 1860s. Conan Doyle, who was born in Edinburgh nine years after Stevenson, took a medical degree in 1881 and turned to writing to help his finances as a struggling doctor in Portsmouth. Sherlock Holmes was introduced to the world in *A Study in Scarlet* (1887) and thereafter on the pages of *Strand Magazine* throughout the nineties. (His deductive talents were based on those of Dr Joseph Bell, one of Doyle's teachers at Edinburgh and a pioneer of forensic medicine.) Historical adventure-novels, the Professor Challenger stories and books on the Boer War, the First World War and, latterly, on spiritualism, all added to Conan Doyle's reputation, but Holmes and Watson remain his best-loved and best known creations, forever associated with the atmospheric streets of late Victorian London.

Conan Doyle's interest in spiritualism was not unconnected with the death of his son in the First World War, but the late Victorian age had already seen many such responses to a prevailing sense that established religion had somehow failed to give comfort in the face of scientific materialism, industrialisation, and the anonymity of the great cities. This urge to restore the primacy of the imagination and the spirit manifested itself in the Oxford Movement or in the Evangelical fervour of the 'Irvingites', who encouraged 'speaking in tongues' at their meetings. There was a wide interest in theosophy, while William Morris's fantasy novels and the Pre-Raphaelite artists all speak to the public's longing for other realms and modes of being. One of the most striking literary exponents of this tendency was a large dandified Scot with a black beard, whose mythopoeic novels and fairy stories prompted G. K. Chesterton to declare him the most original writer of his age.

George MacDonald (1824–1905)

Brought up on an Aberdeenshire farm, MacDonald went to his home university, where he studied German and graduated with an MA in 1845. Unable to afford a medical career, he worked in

London as a tutor for three years, until, encouraged by his future wife, he became a minister of the Congregational Church – a moderately Calvinist dissenting body, more numerous in England than in the north. He was invited to take the pulpit at Arundel in 1850 and married in the spring of the following year, despite a severe lung-haemorrhage. MacDonald was to be haunted by the spectre of tuberculosis all his life: it had killed his beloved mother when he was eight, his father lost a leg to it, his brother and a half-sister died young and his wife shared the condition too. Not surprisingly, perhaps, he conceived an early interest in Novalis, who had died of TB at twenty-nine and held a mystical conception of death as the doorway to another existence – a doorway his fifteen-year-old fiancée had already passed through. Before long, MacDonald's unorthodox views in this regard forced him to resign from the ministry, and he set about establishing himself in the world of journalism and letters. He became a popular lecturer in the Manchester area, and a rather 'spasmodic' blank-verse drama achieved a modest success. A collection of poems was completed in 1857 after a winter in Algiers for the sake of his health, and the following year saw the publication of his first novel – 'a faerie romance for men and women'.

The hero of *Phantastes* (1858) is called Anodos ('pathless'), and the book follows his dream-fantasy journey into fairyland. MacDonald's imagination shows the influence of Novalis, Hoffman, Dante, Spenserian allegory, Celtic lore and Victorian sentiment, but in the end this eclectic realm is a place of his own devising. The book is suffused with a search for maternal love along with an almost erotic surrender to death, and, in a startlingly Freudian world of dream-like transformations, mysterious prohibitions and stifled sexual longings, it is difficult to be sure that the author is in full control of his imagination. Yet later readers have praised MacDonald's intuitive grasp of the inner logic of dreams, and this aspect of his work has taken his reputation into the twentieth century, with a direct influence on such writers as C. S. Lewis, Charles Williams and David Lindsay.

Still much in demand on the popular lecturing-circuit, MacDonald moved to London in 1859 to take up a professorship of English at Bedford College. He made friends with many writers and started another novel and several fairy stories.

David Elginbrod (1863) was the first of three novels to be set in the author's native Aberdeenshire. Poorly constructed and inclined to preach, it has many faults, but MacDonald used it to reassess his own background and to argue for the need for every man to rediscover human and divine love, free from false sophistication and free from the strictures of Calvinism. MacDonald himself had been persuaded of this by F. D. Maurice – a controversially popular Christian socialist – and had joined the Church of England. The same search occupies *Alec Forbes of Howglen* (1865), perhaps his best book on this theme and his most consistent picture of regional life. The third novel in the series, *Robert Falconer* (1868), is less unified and more didactic.

MacDonald continued to publish fairy-stories during the 1860s – 'Works of Fancy and Imagination', which were collected in ten volumes in 1871. One story in particular, 'The Golden Key' (1867), has a rare imaginative power. Much more coherent than *Phantastes*, it is probably MacDonald's best work, with disturbing images of search and fulfilment through death in some other world. *The Princess and the Goblin* (1872) and its sequel *The Princess and Curdie* (1883) are still popular with young readers, while *At the Back of the North Wind* (1871) was an even more successful children's novel about the 'land of everlasting dream' once visited, as the boy hero discovers, by James Hogg's fated girl Kilmeny. MacDonald balanced these mystical experiences with social realism and a concern for reform, a cause close to his heart and fuelled by vicarious descriptions of the sufferings of poor children. This very Victorian taste for a mild sentimental sadism can be disturbing to the modern reader, and episodes of abasement and whipping feature rather too vividly in some of MacDonald's later adult novels. It is difficult not to suspect several such unhealthy tensions in Victorian fantasy literature in general, and MacDonald's Scottish inheritance left him uneasily balanced between senti-mental realism and mystical idealism, always with the harsher shadows of Calvinist authority in the background.

By the late sixties MacDonald had become a well-known figure in nonconformist and spiritualist circles and he was the friend and confidant of Ruskin, Arnold, Carlyle, Browning, Tennyson, Kingsley and Lewis Carroll. He made a lecture tour of America in 1872 and dazzled his audiences with charismatic eloquence and a taste for cloaks, white suits, or the kilt and plaid – not exactly the expected dress for a farm boy from Aberdeen. His American friends included Emerson and Mark Twain. During the rest of his career MacDonald produced a further eighteen novels – ten of them with Scottish settings – but they tend to cover already-established themes and he admitted that he saw them as a popular substitute for preaching. His last book, however, is notable because it returns once more to the mode of dream fantasy.

   Lilith (1895) offers a strange other-dimensional world which is grimmer and more frightening than his earlier versions of fairyland. This realm, a place without tears or rain, lies beyond a looking-glass in the house of 'Mr Vane' and he visits it several times in the attempt to understand why skeletons slowly regrow their flesh there, or why lost babies turn into rapacious giants. The land is terrorised by Lilith, a beautiful vampire demon princess who kills children and assumes the shape of a spotted leopardess. MacDonald's metaphoric images are strange and cruel, or sweet and sickly sentimental – for example, the lisping baby-talk of 'the little ones' – and the author's mystical optimism is juxtaposed with morbid visions of horror and pain. MacDonald was never afraid to give his imagination free reign, and perhaps in this book above all it took its colouring from a life experience in which tuberculosis had now killed his favourite grandchild and five of his own children. His own disease was arrested, but that was little consolation. The last eight years of his life were spent in virtual silence, waiting for the death he had thought to welcome in his younger days.

The Celtic twilight

MacDonald was not alone in his hatred of industrial capitalism. Matthew Arnold proposed 'culture' as a weapon against the spiritual sterility of the times, and in the 1860s he had identified a 'Celtic' spirit as the antithesis of narrow materialism. William Morris and Ruskin advocated a new art and utopian socialism in the 1870s, while the more aesthetic bias of the 1890s, with Dowson, Lionel Johnson, Symons and Yeats, looked to French Symbolism or the hermeticism of the 'Golden Dawn' as some sort of alternative to materialism. The

Irish Celtic revival sought a renewal of poetic force and imagination in myth and legend, and, from a more conventional academic direction, two Scots scholars did much to further this new interest in mythology and primitive societies. J. G. Frazer (1854–1941), a Glasgow man who became a fellow in classics at Cambridge, began his monumental study *The Golden Bough* in the 1890s; while Andrew Lang (1844–1912), from Selkirk and St Andrew's University, and a classics don at Oxford, had been one of anthropology's pioneers in the eighties with his own studies of myth and comparative religion. Lang also worked at poetry, fiction, history, biography and literary journalism, and his *Fairy Books*, published under various colours, are still enjoyed by children today.

There was a vogue for Celticism in Scotland, with a self-conscious preference for France rather than England, and an interest in Breton and Belgian cultural minorities. This outward-looking nationalism was supported by Patrick Geddes (1854–1932) a polymath biologist and architect who established the Outlook Tower in Edinburgh in 1892, as a focus for his new ideas in sociology, ecology, and environmental planning. His views brought him fame abroad, but they never flowered in his native country. Geddes and his friends wanted to publish 'Celtic' work, and so they established a periodical and a Celtic library series in an attempt to match the Irish revival. The 1890s saw a new outburst of 'Ossianism' which influenced craft and design, with art-nouveau style and organic abstractions of a decoratively 'Celtic' sort being produced in Glasgow by the Macdonald sisters, Herbert MacNair and the brilliant young architect and designer Charles Rennie Mackintosh (1868–1928).

Scottish Celticism never produced a writer to compare with Yeats, but its best exponent was **William Sharp** (1855–1914), whose self-consciously musical prose is not unlike the cadences of Synge in *Riders to the Sea*. Sharp was born in Paisley and cut short a degree in Glasgow University to go to London to work as a journalist, biographer, art-critic and essayist. His dashing bohemian looks and nervous intensity gained him admission to the Rossetti circle, where he espoused the Pre-Raphaelite cause and met most of the writers of the day, including Walter Pater, who impressed him greatly, and the young Yeats, with whom he shared an interest in spiritualism and the occult. He was informed about the art and literature of many countries and travelled widely all his life, spending short spells in Europe, the Middle East and America. As a cosmopolitan journalist and a lively, dandyish figure, Sharp had a curious relationship with his own identity, for he came to perceive a sensitive, secret and feminine side to his personality, coloured by hints of a mystical Catholicism quite different from his Presbyterian roots in Paisley. He associated this side of his nature with visits to the Highlands and psychic experiences from childhood, and he identified his sense of passive poetic fatedness with what he took to be the Celtic inheritance. Eventually this *persona* entered his writing under the name of 'Fiona Macleod', whom he pretended was a cousin of his and something of a recluse. *Pharais* ('Paradise') appeared in 1894, the *Mountain Lovers* and *The Watcher of the Ford* in the following year. These books dealt with timeless and archetypal patterns of love and death in remote Highland settings. They sold well, and further novels, essays and short stories appeared in the next ten years as 'Fiona Macleod' gradually took over literary production from William Sharp. This was more than a successful pseudonym, and Sharp took elaborate steps to maintain the fiction of Fiona's existence and dreaded exposure and the disillusionment of his readers.

Sharp's Celticism lacked the linguistic, political and nationalistic direction which fuelled the Irish movement. His ideal was to seek a mystical expression of the eternal feminine which would add a much needed leaven to Anglo-Saxon pragmatism and the Presbyterian work-ethic. But he belongs to the 'Celtic twilight' because his world of hills and islands is sentimentally charged by the conviction that it is already passed or doomed to pass. He paints a 'golden age' that never existed in Gaelic culture, and its popular appeal depended on the fact that it was far from industrialisation and the gaslights and tenements of Glasgow streets. Even so, a similar belief in archetypal values is very marked in the work of Edwin Muir, Lewis Grassic Gibbon, Neil Gunn and George Mackay Brown, and all these writers from the next century could be said to form a distinctively Scottish school of 'mythopoeic realism' whose origins go back to these earlier movements in anthropology and the 'Celtic' ideal.

Apart from Stevensonian romance or symbolic fantasy, Scottish fiction ended the century with a vision of itself which was parochial, sentimental and almost entirely given over to nostalgia. Late-Victorian readers seem to have refused to countenance the industrial and urban growth around them, and, although the prolifically popular novelist 'Sarah Tytler' (Henrietta Keddie, 1827–1914) touched on the poverty and disease of Glasgow in *St Mungo's City* (1884), the theme was not central to her tale of a self-made businessman who learns charity and recovers his holdings. For most other novelists the honourable tradition of domestic realism had not advanced beyond the hearthside piety of 'The Cottar's Saturday Night'. Fiction in just this vein by J. M. Barrie, S. R. Crockett and Ian Maclaren achieved widespread success in the 1890s, as if Lowland Scots were longing, like their Gaelic-speaking compatriots, for their own 'homeland' literature of childhood memories and maternal security.

The Kailyard

The term comes from the verse epigraph to a collection of tales published by Ian Maclaren in 1894:

> There grows a bonnie briar bush in our kail-yard,
> And white are the blossoms on't in our kail-yard.

Within a year W. E. Henley's *New Review* attacked the genre as cabbage-patch – 'kailyard' – writing, and J. H. Millar, the critic in question, renewed the assault in 1903 in his *History of Scottish Literature*. Perhaps the most scathing comments over the years have been made by other creative writers, such as the novelist George Blake, who contributed *Barrie and the Kailyard School* in 1951. Critics have found it difficult ever since to say anything positive about these tales, for their vogue, like the Victorian appetite for tearful death-scenes, has undoubtedly passed away. Yet the case of the Kailyard reveals much about the complicated nature of Scottish cultural identity, going back at least as far as the genteel insecurities of Alan Ramsay.

The best works of Scott, Hogg, Galt and Stevenson were derived from the passions of the past, the difficulties of change, or from their authors' grasp of psychological or moral tensions. But the Kailyard is against change, and when it looks to the past – usually one generation back – it describes a timeless stasis of isolated rural communities whose dramas revolve around the doings of the minister or the dominie – arrivals, departures, weddings, funerals and the pitfalls of petty presumption. It must be admitted that these themes belong within the Scottish tradition of feeling and domestic realism, but it has sadly dwindled to a sentimentalised subgenre.

As *Blackwood's* was the forum for so many influential writers earlier in the century, so the *British Weekly* and a number of liberal Presbyterian ministers were the patrons of the Kailyard. This Evangelical periodical was edited in London by **the Revd William Robertson Nicoll** (1851–1923). Born and educated in the North-East, Nicoll trained as a Free Church minister like his father before him, and from him he inherited a vast library and a voracious appetite for books. He served as a minister for twelve years before moving to London to establish a career in journalism with Hodder and Stoughton, one of the Kailyard's principal publishers. He founded the *British Weekly* in 1896, aimed at a nonconformist market where Christian doctrine was leavened by humorous sketches and articles on moral issues such as the 'temptations of London'. On literary subjects *The Bookman* followed in 1891 and *Woman at Home* (1893) spoke to married women with fashion-notes, advice and popular fiction-serials. Nicoll championed the young J. M. Barrie and persuaded Ian Maclaren to take up writing. Anne S. Swan (1859–1943), the redoubtable creator of innumerable romantic stories, was an early contributor and became the mainstay of *Woman at Home*, subtitled 'Annie S. Swan's Magazine'. The *British Weekly* and the *Christian Leader* – a Baptist weekly from Glasgow – were particularly responsive to Kailyard fiction, in which sentimental piety was so conveniently packaged. On the strength of this market Ian Maclaren toured America with lectures and sermons in 1896, followed by Nicoll and **J. M. Barrie** (1860–1937) who were well received in their turn by large audiences in Boston and New York.

Only the initial stages of Barrie's career properly belong to the Kailyard school, but his sketches of village life in 'Thrums', most of which appeared in the *St James's Gazette* and the *British Weekly* were among the earliest and most successful publications in the genre. Barrie came from a large working-class family in Kirriemuir, where his father was a linen-weaver, working the loom from his own home. The children – five daughters and three sons – (two more died as infants) were all brought up in the Free Kirk, although their mother Margaret Ogilvy came from a more puritanical sect called the 'Auld Lichts', who objected to hymns, religious music and even to written prayers and sermons. True to type, the family was determined that the boys should gain advancement through education, so the eldest son became a teacher and David, Mrs Barrie's favourite, was destined for the ministry. But David was killed in a skating-accident at the age of thirteen and his mother fell into an obsessive grief which at first entirely excluded her youngest son. Wracked with jealousy, sympathy and guilt, James Matthew Barrie, scarcely seven years old, tried very hard to take David's place in his mother's heart. He spent long afternoons with her, telling stories and listening to tales and memories from her own childhood, and the pair grew very close. When eventually she died Barrie was compelled to relive their intimacy publicly in a loving memoir called *Margaret Ogilvy and her Son* (1896). His complicated feelings for this emotionally smothering and puritanical little woman almost certainly led to the failure of his marriage, and it is tempting to find the roots of his affection for children, his fear of ageing and his fascination with death in the overwhelming nature of this early relationship.

Barrie graduated with an MA from Edinburgh in 1882 and set his mind on a literary career. He reviewed plays and worked as a journalist in Nottingham for two years before moving to London, where he placed articles with the *St James's Gazette* and various other periodicals (sometimes using the name 'Gavin Ogilvy') and made friends with W. E. Henley and Robertson Nicoll. A light novel called *Better Dead* was published at his own expense in 1886, but his sketches of 'Scotch' life for the magazines were so popular that he was encouraged to assemble them in book form. *Auld Licht Idylls* appeared in 1888 and *A Window in Thrums* was ready the following year. Both derive from his mother's recollections of an isolated community of farmers and nonconformist weavers, a world of parish-pump politics, proud, pious and obsessed with keeping up appearances. Barrie's descriptive prose is well realised and his observant and cutting humour can rise to bleak irony, for he remembered enough about Kirriemuir to know that 'Thrums' was not entirely idyllic. Yet he 'miniaturises' its society in a way that Scott or Galt would not have done, and in place of a changing social scene he writes a series of brief vignettes and invites us to eavesdrop upon them. As vignettes do, these depend on single moments of pathos or comic discomfiture, and the result is static, knowing and patronising.

If these sketches have any wider scope, it comes from Barrie's awareness of change and mortality – we have already been told that such communities died away in the last fifty years – and the opening piece of *A Window in Thrums* evokes Jess McQumpha's cottage, now empty and fallen into disrepair. Hers is the window where she sat 'for twenty years or more looking at the world as through a telescope'. In the narrator's reminiscences we share this window with Jess, but the telescope is the wrong way round, and what we really see is Barrie's sense of his own lost childhood – suspended in time, and ever so far away. Thrums exists like Shangri-La in a charmed circle and Barrie is overcome by pathos whenever characters have to leave it, for, in this nostalgic light, death or a departure for London seem equally final; and any hint of the outside world would certainly be fatal.

The Thrums books were popular and even Stevenson admired them (although the folk at Kirriemuir were not so sure), but Barrie's greatest success in the mode came with two later novels. *The Little Minister* (1891) was originally serialised in the *British Weekly* as the improbable tale of a minister's love for a gipsy girl; and *Sentimental Tommy* (1896) draws on Barrie's childhood with rather more insight to describe how his character's intensely sensitive and imaginative inner life fits him for artistic creativity and prevents him from achieving maturity. The theme became still more pointed in *Tommy and Grizel* (1900), which raised the question of marriage. By this time the author had been married for six years, but he found it easier to work in his study for hours, or to visit his club, than to share his thoughts or his physical affections with his beautiful actress wife. His chronic shyness, the emotional tensions of his childhood and his elegiac sense of Thrums as a place one cannot return to were all to achieve their fullest expression in the disturbing network of symbols behind *Peter Pan*.

'Thrums' renewed a vogue for pawky Scotchness and what *The Times* admired as 'unstrained pathos'. **The Revd John**

Watson ('Ian Maclaren', 1850–1907), was a Free Kirk minister who was persuaded to recount his experiences of Perthshire for Robertson Nicoll's magazine. Henceforth the collections *Beside the Bonnie Briar Bush* (1894) and *The Days of Auld Lang Syne* (1895), the village of 'Drumtochty' and the name Ian Maclaren all became widely known. Watson was a minister in Liverpool when he began writing and produced as many religious works as fiction. He also helped to found the University of Liverpool and Westminster College, Cambridge, and was much in demand as a public speaker and preacher. A Drumtochty novel called *Kate Carnegie and those Ministers* appeared in 1896, and other collections followed in the next six years, including the sketches in *St Jude's* (1907), set in the Glasgow where he had preached for three years before 1880.

The Drumtochty tales came from three happy years at a church in Glen Almond, and they are suffused with longing for a country life left behind. Not surprisingly, perhaps, the narratives revolve around the kirk and many of the stories focus on either man's chief end (to glorify God) or man's mortal end:

> 'Ye can hae little rael pleesure in a merrige,' explained our gravedigger, in whom the serious side had been perhaps abnormally developed, 'for ye never ken hoo it will end; but there's nae risk about a "beerial".'

In this, and indeed in general, the author shares the views of the community, for, unlike Barrie, Maclaren writes from within its values and does not erect the former's affectionately satirical and ultimately condescending distance between his creatures and himself. On the other hand, his prose is often weak and sentimental and his piety has an untried, naïve air, especially when it is exercised over the frequent deaths which occur in the tales. Like most Kailyard fiction, it is as if all the more profane human passions which Presbyterianism was so intent on stifling could be rechannelled and respectably expressed only through vicarious grief at one fictional death after another. Such green pathos cannot appeal to modern readers, but in its day the evocation of Drumtochty as another lost Eden proved to be extraordinarily popular – especially in the United States, where over 500,000 copies were sold in the first few years. Maclaren died in America during his third tour of readings and lectures.

S. R. Crockett (1860–1914) was yet another Free Church minister, although he gave up his charge in 1895 once his success seemed assured and became a productive best-seller with over forty novels and adventure romances in the mode of Stevenson. The Kailyard sketches from his native Galloway first appeared in the *Christian Leader* and were collected in 1893 as *The Stickit Minister*. Crockett's descriptive style is ambitious in its evocation of place and atmosphere, and at their best the energy of stories such as 'The Lammas Preaching' makes the 'idylls' of Drumtochty seem naïve in execution. But most of Crockett's tales are too obviously designed to move his readers to laughter, or pity and horror, although they always manage to come to a comforting conclusion. To this end he mobilises sentimentality with ruthless insistence. In 'The Tragedy of Duncan Duncanson', a drunken schoolmaster, once a minister himself, strikes one of his pupils with a poker – quite forgetting that he had it in his hand. But the wounded boy protects him, for love of his young daughter, and swears that he hurt himself in a fall. 'Oh, Flora but yer e'en are terrible bonny!' the lad whispers as he regains consciousness. In another tale an old spinster who aspires to be a poet dies with tears of happiness in her eyes just as she sees her work mentioned in the newspaper. She does not know that the review was a savage one concocted by a smart young reporter. 'God is more merciful than man', intones Crockett at the end of 'The Heather Lintie'. Such is his preferred method – to evoke pain and then to 'kiss it away' with anodyne conclusions. The device is especially noticeable in *Cleg Kelly, Arab of the City* (1896), which does at least recognise the harshness of Victorian Edinburgh, but an insistently idyllic sentimentality entirely overwhelms the love story behind *The Lilac Sunbonnet* (1894). Crockett's talent for vigorous description does better with his later historical romances such as *The Raiders* (1894) and *The Men of the Moss Haggs* (1895), but they lack the psychological tensions of Stevenson's work and remain popular adventure fiction.

John Davidson (1857–1909)

If the Kailyard failed to acknowledge the modern world altogether, the same cannot be said of the poetry of John

Davidson, and it is fitting that this chapter should end with the only Scottish writer of his generation who tried to find a voice for the coming century. Davidson was a contemporary of William Sharp, and, although the two Scots were very different in outlook, they both came to prominence in the London of the nineties. Davidson contributed early lyrics to the *Yellow Book*, mixed with the Rhymers' Club at the Cheshire Cheese and had some of his novels illustrated by Beardsley. He made friends with Max Beerbohm, Richard Le Gallienne and Edmund Gosse, and he crossed swords with Yeats on one occasion. As a writer, however, he did not really belong to their circle. Outwardly conservative in appearance and manners, he was often contemptuous of his bohemian friends, preferring to see himself as a more truly intellectual rebel.

As the son of an Evangelical minister, Davidson was brought up in Glasgow and Greenock. He was an enthusiastic reader and soon tried his hand at poetry, but had to leave school early to earn a living, first as a laboratory assistant and then as a pupil teacher. He went to Edinburgh University in 1876, but his student career, or his money, or perhaps his patience, lasted only a year. He returned to teaching, with a post in Glasgow where he met John Nichol, professor of English at the university, a friend of Swinburne's and a freethinker. Davidson's absolutist nature and his impatience with his father's creed responded to the Carlylean fervour of Nichol's mind, and his literary ambitions must have been greatly stimulated when Swinburne admired his youthful verses and pronounced him poet. After getting married in 1884 he worked for a while as a clerk, but soon found himself teaching again, although he did not enjoy it. During these years in Glasgow, Perth and Crieff, his output of prose, verse and drama received very little recognition, but he nevertheless decided to commit himself to journalism and set out for London in 1888 with his young son and his pregnant wife.

His first collection of poems, *In a Music Hall* (1891), made little impact, but the next two, *Fleet Street Eclogues* (1893) and *Ballads and Songs* (1894), were rather well received. Sadly, he was never to regain this early success, although he produced further collections of eclogues and ballads in the next five years. His impressionistic poetic sketches of cityscape and country scenes are not untypical of their time, with Kiplingesque ballads and 'ninetyish' mood pieces with titles such as 'Nocturne'. Yet some of the ballads strike a new note of barely-suppressed rage at the futility and humiliations of daily urban life as suffered by Britain's equivalent of Gogol's clerks and the 'superfluous persons' of Russian fiction. 'In a Music Hall' reflects his own experiences as a clerk in Perth and it catches the fevered and sleazy excitements of popular entertainment as seen from both sides of the footlights. 'Thirty Bob a Week' is equally animated by a ferociously ironic spirit raging at the material difficulties of making ends meet on a pittance. Yet these poems are not merely 'social realism', for they offer a vision of the individual spirit – a spirit capable of a metaphysical destiny – somehow trapped and sullied in the ordinary world. The effect is startling – as if Kipling were suddenly to speak like Shelley, or Carlyle.

During the early nineties Davidson wrote several light novels somewhat in the manner of Beerbohm or Chesterton. *Baptist Lake* (1894), for example, lampooned the pretensions of aristocrats and aesthetes alike and there are moments in some of his books when the writer's humour can seem disconcertingly sadistic or ironically wild, rather like the later satire of Huxley or Wyndham Lewis. Since he always wrote slowly and with difficulty, Davidson found the demands of journalism particularly exhausting. Yet he needed the work, for he had to support his mother in Edinburgh as well as his wife, children and a younger brother too, whose alcoholism and irrational violence had brought him to an asylum. Towards the end of the century he tried his luck with adaptations and plays for the London theatre, with only short-lived success. His *New Ballads* (1897) were given bad reviews in the *Athenaeum*, and his spirits and general health – he suffered from chronic bronchitis – began to decline. He particularly resented his lack of poetic success, yet the rough-hewn and ambitious scope of a poetry so full of abstruse ideas could never have appealed to popular taste and his critics began to call it chopped-up journalistic prose. Even so, despite their imperfections, these verses were his most original achievement.

Davidson was beginning to evolve a vitalist philosophy of how the universe and consciousness emerge out of matter as if driven by an evolutionary will. He linked a growing fascination with scientific materialism with the romantic spirit of assertion to be found in Carlyle and especially in Nietzsche. This was his answer to the Victorian crisis of faith and his own bouts of terrible depression. Thus he celebrates the crystalline structure and the 'purpose' of a snow-flake – which is to achieve form for its own sake ('Snow'); or he commands his soul to do the same by casting-off bourgeois values and conventional notions of good and bad in favour of being 'haughty, hard, / Misunderstood' ('The Outcast'). There can be harsh inconsistencies in voice and craft in some of Davidson's verses, but an awkwardly powerful and original poetry does emerge from the assertive violence and confusion of his metaphysics. In the last ten years of his life he pursued this vision into longer and longer blank-verse poems, knotted with argument and ideas, increasingly idiosyncratic, increasingly unsuccessful with the public.

'The Crystal Palace' (1908), one of Davidson's last poems, was constructed – like several others – from an article he had already written in prose. It is a long, low-key, Browningesque monologue on the urban crowd as it throngs through the Victorian age's most famous monument to modernity. The juxtaposition it makes between aristocratic cultural values and vulgar entertainment anticipates something of the spirit of Pound and Eliot:

> A dense throng in the central transept, wedged
> So tightly they can neither clap nor stamp,
> Shouting applause at something, goad themselves
> In sheer despair to think it rather fine:
> 'We came here to enjoy ourselves. Bravo,
> Then! Are we not?' Courageous folk beneath
> The brows of Michael Angelo's Moses dance
> A cake-walk in the dim Renascence Court.

T. S. Eliot admitted to being influenced by 'Thirty Bob a Week' as well as by the poet's eye for 'dingy urban images', for Davidson was one of the few poets of his generation (along with Thomson, whose work he admired) to portray the squalor, despair and grim beauty of the modern city:

> Now wheel and hoof and horn
> In every street
> Stunned to its chimney-tops,
> In every murky street –
> Each lamp-lit gorge by traffic rent
> Asunder,

Ravines of serried shops
By business tempests torn –
In every echoing street,
From early morn
Till jaded night falls dead,
Wheel, hoof and horn
Tumultuous thunder
Beat
Under
A noteless firmament
Of lead.

('Yuletide', 1905)

The Scot also wanted poetry to 'certify the semi-certitudes of science', and he brought the very stuff of the sciences into his verse. The result was not always successful but there are original and striking passages too:

The other atoms, as the planets cooled,
Became; and all the elements, how much
So ever differing in appearance, weight,
Amount, condition, function, volume (gold
From iodine, argon from iron) wrought
Of the purest ether, in electrons sprang
As lightning from the tension filling space.
Forms of the ether, primal hydrogen,
Azote and oxygen, unstable shapes,
With carbon, most perdurable of all
The elements, forthwith were sifted out
To be the diverse warp and woof of life,
The lowest and the highest, louse and man.

(*The Testament of John Davidson*, 1908)

Hugh MacDiarmid also acknowledged a debt to this aspect of Davidson's vision, and his own later world-language poems are equally laden with esoteric scientific ideas. Davidson's long monologues and dialogues, darkly Spasmodic poetic tragedies and his polemic testaments – there were five of them – were his last achievements. They can be disturbingly desperate: *The Testament of a Vivisector* (1901), for example, revels in images of sado-masochistic pain, and yet manages to convey, too, the author's sensitive anguish at the material plight of our bodies. Uneven as they are, passages from Davidson's later works did genuinely enlarge the subject-matter of poetry, and Davidson certainly pushed his vision and his grasp well beyond the comfortable and accepted limits of his day.

The poet's sense of isolation was not helped by a move to Penzance in 1907. When *The Testament of John Davidson* appeared the following year, he became angry and depressed at the incomprehension and hostility of the critics, and in the belief that he had contracted cancer he took a revolver and disappeared from home in March 1909. His body was recovered from the sea after six months.

7

The twentieth century: the Scottish Renaissance

WHEN the French critic and philosopher Denis Saurat wrote an influential essay on the 'Scottish Renaissance' in 1924, he was thinking mainly of the writers associated with Hugh Mac-Diarmid's *Northern Numbers* anthologies and his magazine the *Scottish Chapbook*, started two years earlier. Yet the notion of a renaissance was not a new one, and signs of a revival in culture and politics can be traced to the beginning of the century. Of course, MacDiarmid's creative example, not to mention his nationalism and his indefatigable propaganda, soon became the heart of the matter, just as the insistence on a European outlook and his satirical attacks on his own countrymen gave the movement a necessary international and critical dimension. Today 'the Scottish Renaissance' is used more generally to describe the remarkable outpouring of cultural activity which has gone towards making this the third major period of literary achievement in Scotland's history. It has become convenient to refer to a 'second wave' in the Renaissance to describe those writers who came to prominence in the forties and fifties, and after that we can talk of a third generation as well, even if some of the younger writers discussed briefly at the end of this chapter would deny any direct literary debt to MacDiarmid, Gibbon, Gunn, Muir or Maclean, or, indeed, any connection with each other. Thus, while some of the sixties' writers looked to Europe or America or England for their models, others, especially in Glasgow and the west, turned to a lively appreciation of working-class Scottish speech and topics. These three 'waves' of literary activity can also be found in the country's periodicals, with MacDiarmid's *Chapbook* leading the way from

1922. In the thirties and forties J. H. Whyte's *Modern Scot* and Maurice Lindsay's *Poetry Scotland* were among the more influential publications, with the *Saltire Review* and then the *New Saltire* taking over between 1954 and 1964. (Among the little magazines *Lines Review*, which started in 1952, Duncan Glen's *Akros*, David Morrison's *Scotia Review* and *Chapman* have all been particularly constructive.) Finally, the 'third generation' was heralded by the publication of magazines such as Bob Tait's *Scottish International* (1968–74), the *New Edinburgh Review* from the same year, and *Cencrastus* from 1979.

The century began with the popular success of Charles Murray's vernacular verse in *Hamewith*, while Professor H. J. C. Grierson had begun to teach Scots literature and language at the University of Aberdeen. Literary histories by Millar and Henderson followed in the next ten years, while Gregory Smith's *Scottish Literature, Character and Influence* (1919) provided MacDiarmid with just the argument he needed to propose a dynamic and contradictory spirit in the Scottish sensibility – a psychology worthy of Dostoevsky himself – and utterly opposed to the sentimental dilutions of the Kailyard. MacDiarmid tried to align even the vernacular tradition with the swift collisions of imagery in modernist verse, or claimed that Scots was well suited to the spirit of D. H. Lawrence's prose. The Irish literary revival had impressed Scotsmen at the turn of the century, and by the 1920s James Joyce was being cited as a figure who could achieve international status and universal significance for books which were still deeply rooted in his native Dublin. The local need not be parochial, and MacDiarmid stressed the point by insisting that true internationalism could not even exist without small nations. The unique identity of such countries and the need to resist their slide into the anonymity of larger political and economic bodies became an early concern of Scottish nationalism and was to be revived in the seventies, after the spirit of E. F. Schumacher's *Small is Beautiful* (1973) – a 'study of economics as if people mattered'. The First World War had played a part in this understanding, for it was fought – so the population was told – 'to preserve the right of small nations', and yet many servicemen returned to a Scotland whose cultural and economic identity seemed to be at a very low ebb indeed. MacDiarmid and Saurat were not slow to adopt the motto of the Belgian literary revival – 'Soyons nous mêmes'

– although, surprisingly, the Irish example was seldom used. For the 'Renaissance group' at least, cultural and political identity were inseparable.

In fact political nationalism and the demand for 'Home Rule' go back to Liberal politics of the previous century, and also featured in the thinking of the Scottish Left in the Independent Labour Party and the trade-unions. Labour-tensions had come to a head in Clydeside during and immediately after the war – under the influence of internationally minded socialists on the shop-floor, and the ordinary worker's recognition that the ailing heavy industries of the central belt had been ruthlessly expanded to meet the war-effort only to face decline again in the years of peace. The anti-war speeches of John Maclean, strikes, mass meetings, and his imprisonment with James Maxton on charges of sedition all led to real fears of revolution and 'Red Clydeside' on the part of the establishment, especially during the famous mass strike for a forty-hour week in 1919, when armoured cars and troops policed the streets of Glasgow. Maclean's hopes for a form of Scottish republican communism (free of Moscow) were not to be realised, but his many trials and his early death in 1923 made him a martyr for the cause and a potent symbol of it ever since. Sorley Maclean, MacDiarmid, Edwin Morgan, Hamish Henderson and Sydney Goodsir Smith were all to write verses about him, for the old Covenanting spirit had not lost its power to move – most especially as reflected in the secular but evangelical intensities of Sorley Maclean's political poems.

After the initial euphoria at the coming of peace, the post-war slump took hold with particular force in the heavy industries and coal-mines of Scotland, Tyneside and south Wales, and these areas suffered disproportionate hardships in the Depression years to come. By 1922 the Left and the ILP had made major advances in Scotland, sending twenty-nine Labour MPs to Westminster, with ten 'Red Clydesiders' headed by John Wheatley and including Maxton, Mannie Shinwell, Tom Johnston and one Communist – Willie Gallacher. The Labour movement continued to grow during the years around the General Strike in 1926, and many figures from Scotland's radical tradition played leading parts on the national stage. After all, social conditions in the post-Victorian Scottish cities and especially in the industrial west were truly appalling. Yet internal strife, dispute between the ILP and the Labour Party, widespread fears of communism, and simple dread at the prospect of the Depression getting worse, all helped to put Ramsay MacDonald's essentially conservative National Government into power in the 1930s. The radical 'Red Clyde' entered the realms of legend, although Glasgow and the west continue to be a heartland of left-wing politics in Britain.

Meanwhile a more culturally centred drive for nationalism had led to the foundation of the National Party of Scotland at Stirling in 1928, with R. E. Muirhead and John MacCormick as chairman and secretary (both from the ILP), and a spectrum of support from workers, liberals, students and radical intellectuals such as MacDiarmid and their president, Cunninghame Graham. In the 1930s the National Party amalgamated with the more liberal Scottish Party to form the Scottish National Party, and the movement began to gain strength during and after the Second World War, when the tendency once again had been to submerge Scotland's economic and social problems for the sake of Britain as a whole. It was popularly believed that, for as long as power was centralised in Westminster and in the massive population of the Home Counties, government would never come to grips with matters in Scotland and the north of England, which continued to suffer from unemployment, industrial decline, inadequate housing and high emigration. By the more prosperous sixties the case for 'devolution' had attracted widespread interest, and after the winning of Hamilton by Winnie Ewing in 1967 the SNP began to influence Westminster, if only because its presence as an electoral threat stimulated both Labour and Conservative parties to accommodate themselves to Scottish needs. (The Liberal Party had continued to support decentralisation but made less of a threat to the *status quo* in parliament.)

The discovery of oil in the North Sea heralded a boom for the SNP as well, typified by the opportunistic slogan 'It's Scotland's Oil'. The widespread success of John McGrath's play *The Cheviot, the Stag and the Black, Black Oil* in 1973 had as much to do with sentimental nationalism as it had with his own brand of republican socialism, but, even so, it seemed that a devolved socialist Scotland was just around the corner. Had not Scotland voted Labour since the war? Was there not a bill before parliament for moderate devolution? The bill passed at the close of 1976 only to die the death of a thousand cuts in committee-stage. Then Westminster decreed that the referendum result could not be valid unless 40 per cent of all registered Scottish voters voted 'yes', which meant that none of the parties could agree on how to interpret the result in 1979, when only 33 per cent of the total electorate voted 'yes' to Scottish devolution, with a majority of 80,000. In any case the bill died, and in the face of world economic recession the political popularity of devolution or separation died as well. These matters from the twenties and the seventies are worth recounting at length, for to many it seemed as if the 'auld sang' had been heard again – in two different keys – only to be lost again, twice in one century.

If MacDiarmid's hopes for a Scottish republic never bore fruit, his vision of a broader cultural revival fared better. His own poems were set to music by his friends F. G. Scott (1880–1958) and Ronald Stevenson (b. 1928), both of whom played leading parts in the Renaissance by developing modern music from aspects of traditional Scottish sources. At a less academic level – although MacDiarmid himself hated 'folk music' – there has been a notable revival in traditional playing, singing and song-writing, while the School of Scottish Studies, since 1951, has developed the field of folk-life studies and promoted a new and wider appreciation of traditional and oral culture. Of course, institutions do not make art, but the foundation of the two major Scottish-language dictionaries and the Scottish Gaelic Text Society in the years between 1929 and 1937 helped to make up for the past neglect. The publications of the Porpoise Press and William Maclellan and then, in the sixties, the popularity of public poetry-reading, the rise of small presses, the growth of interest in Gaelic and the availability of the Traverse Theatre in Edinburgh and the Third Eye Centre in Glasgow have all helped to bring new Scottish creative work to a wider audience.

Among painters the 'Scottish Colourists' at the beginning of the century had looked to Europe and the 'Fauves', most notably J. D. Fergusson (1874–1961), who had lived abroad until the outbreak of the Second World War. The 'Edinburgh School' also remained true to the expressive and poetic use of colour and pattern – from its formation in 1922, with William Gillies (1898–1973) and William MacTaggart (b. 1903), into the post-war years, and the appearance of Anne Redpath (1895–1965), John Maxwell (1905–62) and Robin Philipson (b. 1916). These painters represent what was to be the mainstream of Scottish art in the mid-century period, as opposed to the more surreal and abstract works of James Cowie (1886–1956) and William Johnstone (b. 1897). The brilliant work of Joan Eardley (1921–63) combined an eye for colour, landscape and abstract textures with an equal commitment to the social surface of the cities. Elizabeth Blackadder (b. 1931), James Morrison (b. 1932), John Knox (b. 1936) and Willie Rodger (b. 1930) all have established reputations, as have John Bellany (b. 1942), whose sparse realism contrasts with the primitive naturalism of Alexander Moffat (b. 1943), who has painted many portraits of Scottish writers – in complete contrast to the photographically realised but brooding and dreamlike images of Neil Dallas Brown (b. 1938).

If a Renaissance exists at all, however, its most developed expression has been achieved in the literature of the last eighty years as writers have sought to express themselves in a modern Scotland where more than ever before they have felt the need to evaluate and to remake an understanding of their own present nature and past history. No two writers have taken the same route, but the polarity between MacDiarmid and Muir is suggestive of two broadly different responses, in which the materialist and extrovert energy of the one contrasts with the more inward and mythopoeic response to life from the other. The same distinction can be seen between the poetry of Edwin Morgan and that of George Mackay Brown; while Neil Gunn, Sorley Maclean, Iain Crichton Smith and most especially Lewis Grassic Gibbon tried to bring both modes together with varying degrees of success. Their work, however, speaks best for itself. The modern period really begins with a young journalist who wrote one good novel before he died; but first we must pick up the later career of J. M. Barrie, by far the most famous and successful Scottish writer of his day.

J. M. Barrie (1860–1937): later career

Following the success of the Thrums stories and *Margaret Ogilvie*, Barrie made a triumphal visit to America with

Robertson Nicoll. In 1897 he adapted his Kailyard novel *The Little Minister* for the stage and it was such a hit on both sides of the Atlantic that he turned all his considerable energies to the theatre, producing twenty-nine more plays in the next two dozen years. These brought him a knighthood, wealth and public status, yet he was a complicated and withdrawn personality, reclusive, hard-working, small of stature and intensely shy. Barrie had made friends with Shaw – a vigorous supporter of Ibsen and 'Ibsenism' at the time – but the Scotsman's social comedies rarely attempted Shaw's didactic wit, and they settled, like *The Admirable Crichton* (1902), for comfortable endings within the *status quo*. Thus *What Every Woman Knows* (1908) proposed that a briskly competent wife – his ideal woman – is the real power behind a successful man; but the point is painlessly made and in flattering both sexes the play entertained large audiences who were not quite ready for *A Doll's House*.

Barrie never allowed his own wife to share his inner life or his physical attentions and she left him for a more generous man in 1909. He was still in emotional bondage to memories of his boyhood and his mother. Plays such as *Dear Brutus* (1917) and *Mary Rose* (1920) are full of hints of death, eternal childhood, and the poignant divisions between inevitable age (or maturity) and carefree youth. Innocent of Freud, and without the capacity for sophisticated self-analysis, Barrie, like George MacDonald, can still create moments of disturbing symbolic power, and perhaps this innocence makes their work even more startling for the modern reader. Barrie's first and most enduring achievement in this vein was, of course, *Peter Pan, or The Boy Who Never Grew Up* (1904).

The play sprang from a friendship which he had formed with the neighbouring Llewelyn Davies family and their three (later five) sons. It was as if this famous writer, with his gruff manner and an unpreposessing pale face, had adopted another man's family – somewhat to the consternation of his own wife, not to mention Arthur Llewelyn Davies. The stories in *The Little White Bird* (1902) grew from the fairy-tales he began to spin about Kensington Gardens, and *Peter Pan* soon followed. No one was really sure at first if it was a play for adults or one for children, but it was a huge success in any case, going on to become a family Christmas treat for year after year. Even so, its dreamlike evocation of flight, the plight of the lost boys, the motherly comfort offered by a child, and paternal authority burlesqued as 'Captain Hook' seem like hints of a fable from the unconscious. Most memorable of all is the relationship between Peter and Wendy, in which her motherly, fussy and yet loving character hopes for some deeper bond only to be betrayed in the end by the innocently cruel forgetfulness of Peter's eternally immature nature. Barrie's earlier novels *Sentimental Tommy* and *Tommy and Grizel* had shown that he understood something of this betrayal in his own innermost being.

The playwright's relationship with the Llewelyn Davies family was deepened when Arthur died in 1907, and became closer still when Barrie's marriage broke up. Within three years Sylvia Llewelyn Davies died as well and Barrie became guardian and unofficial father to 'my boys', paying for their education at Eton and taking a great interest in their careers. Nevertheless, he could not avoid Wendy's fate, for the Davies boys, and then other young friends, inevitably matured and left him behind. Viewed in this light Sir J. M. Barrie seems a rather lonely figure, and, although he continued to write successful plays for years, few of these later works have been worth reviving. He died in 1937, but developments in Scottish literature had long left him behind – almost from the moment of his early theatrical success in London. Indeed, the first expression of the new spirit in the north had been a howl of anger at the sentimentality of Thrums and all its Kailyard imitators.

George Douglas Brown (1869–1902)

George Douglas Brown is remembered on the strength of only one novel – his second attempt at the form – and he died of pneumonia at the age of thirty-three within a year of its publication. *The House with the Green Shutters* (1901) was greeted by many critics and readers as a savage attack on the Kailyard, and Brown agreed but also maintained that he had wanted to picture small-town Scottish life accurately, and then to 'get inside the heads' of old John Gourlay and his son. The book does show a community undergoing social and economic changes – quite unlike the static nostalgia of Thrums and

Drumtochty, and in this, as with his desire to catch the humour and strength of Scots speech, Brown follows his admired John Galt. Yet he also explores several personally sensitive and autobiographical themes.

Brown must have known small communities well enough, not to mention their propensity for gossip, for he was born as an illegitimate child in the little village of Ochiltree – in the heart of Burns and Galt country near Mauchline in Ayrshire. His mother was the unlettered daughter of an Irish labourer, and his father, a local farmer renowned for his dour independence and his colourful Scots speech, never did marry her. Young George moved from the village school to Ayr Academy – with the help of the rector there – and William Maybin's confidence in his new pupil was rewarded when the boy excelled in English and Classics and won a bursary entrance to Glasgow University, where he became a favourite student, and later the assistant, of young Professor Gilbert Murray. Brown's mixed feelings about his father appear in the matriculation forms from these days, in which he sometimes listed him as a farmer and at other times claimed he was dead. Artistic rather than scholarly, Brown's temperament was given to bursts of energy and vivid intuitive insights, but he graduated with first-class honours and won the Snell Exhibition Scholarship, which took him to Balliol College, Oxford. Brown's years as a student in the south were fruitful, and he took a lively part in college life, but his studies were erratic with periods of intensive activity followed by spells of depression and poor health – a familiar pattern in his later life. He read Balzac, Tolstoy and Dostoevsky – without liking the Russian giants – and began to think of writing a novel which would say something about his own background and the Scottish character. Perhaps such themes were in his mind because he had finally confronted his father before leaving for England, only to find a tired and peppery old man in place of the hard-hearted creature he must have imagined in his youth. Whatever the reasons, Brown's classical studies began to suffer, and when his mother's health collapsed – she had been ill for years – he returned home to nurse her. She died in 1895 and he graduated later in the year with a third-class degree and a certain sense of failure, despite his recognition that such matters were no longer so important to him. He was later to modify these experiences in his portrait of young John Gourlay as a boy who finds himself out of his depth at university – a disappointment to a domineering father and his dying mother.

Set on a literary career, Brown took up freelance journalism in London, using the pen-names 'William Douglas' and 'Kennedy King' for short stories and a boy's adventure novel called *Love and Sword* (1899). He became involved in a small publishing-scheme with friends and continued to produce what he regarded as hack work. He was more serious, however, about a long story written in June 1900 which features a powerful character named Gourlay in a village to be called Barbie. His friends encouraged him to develop the theme, so at the end of the year he retreated to a cottage in Haslemere, bought a supply of exercise books and began to write his novel.

The House with the Green Shutters, by 'George Douglas', appeared in October 1901 and was widely and well reviewed. Andrew Lang – himself a distinguished Snell Scholarship man before Brown's time – likened Gourlay to Weir of Hermiston and compared Brown to a Scottish Balzac or Flaubert 'with a bitter sense of humour'. Other reviews invoked Galt and the power of Greek tragedy, and indeed Brown had drawn on his classical education for the 'bodies' – the common folk of Barbie, whose gossip responds like a Greek chorus to the doings and the sufferings of the Gourlay family. Most of the gossip is malicious, and the grimness of Brown's picture of village life derives from the fact that the few decent voices are seldom heard against the spiteful and cowardly backbiting of the majority, led in specially loathsome fashion by the lisping hypocrite Deacon Allardyce. Compared to these uncharitable nonentities, John Gourlay – the self-made carter – stubborn, brutal and tyrannical though he is, strides like a tiger among worms. Like Stevenson's Adam Weir, old Gourlay is imbued with all the absolutist paternal authority of Calvinism, although he is a more limited and stupid man than the judge. Thus Brown's study of a mother's son in conflict with such a father follows the psychological symbolism of Stevenson's novel, as if the Scottish sensibility were torn between broadly feminine and masculine outlooks, between what it owes to the muse and what to Jehovah. Stevenson, Brown and Lewis Grassic Gibbon all make use of the struggle between fathers and sons (or a daughter, in the case of Chris Guthrie) and the same late Victorian battle with puritanical authority motivated

Edmund Gosse's powerful study *Father and Son* (1907). Brown's sympathies are not easily given, however, for, although he paints Barbie and Gourlay in hellish colours, young John is little better – ending up as a weakling and a drunk.

Old Gourlay, like the house of which he is so proud, dominates the little town on the brae below, but times are changing because of the railway and the coal-mines nearby, and he begins to lose commercial supremacy to a wilier businessman called Wilson who diversifies from a general store to take over Gourlay's monopoly as a goods-carrier – the only trade the older man knows. Like his business, Gourlay's personality is monolithic and inflexible, and when his rival's son is sent to university he insists that young John should go as well – as a 'lad o' pairts' whose success will reflect credit on his father. But John's weak and sensitive character cannot cope, and he fails, just as his father's business is failing, and returns home to sulk in disgrace. He takes to drink, kills his father in a drunken fit and then commits suicide, only to be followed into death by his tubercular sister and his mother – an abused creature who has nursed a fear of Gourlay all her life just as she nurses the secret cancer gnawing at her breast. Before they take poison, Mrs Gourlay and her daughter turn to the Bible and read the famous passage on charity from 1 Corinthians.

The conclusion is excessively unrelenting – not formal enough for Greek tragedy and too melodramatic for realism. Yet the earlier parts of the novel are well controlled, with a forensic detachment in the narrative style, in effective contrast to descriptive passages which might have been written with the nervous excitation of young John Gourlay himself. Brown's prose is frequently criticised for a tendency to analyse his creatures, pontificating on them and on Scottish failings in general; but this is a deliberate device against the cosy familiarity of Scots speech and the Kailyard setting. Contemporary readers familiar with post-modernist fiction may find this authorial position less intrusive than did earlier critics:

When we think of what Gourlay did that day, we must remember that he was soaked in alcohol – not merely with his morning's potation, but with the dregs of previous carousals. And the dregs of drink, a thorough toper will tell you, never leave him. He is drunk on Monday with his Saturday's debauch. As 'Drucken Wabster' of Barbie put it once, 'When a body's hard up, h:s braith's a consolation.' If that be so – and Wabster, remember, was

an expert whose opinion on this matter is entitled to the highest credence –
if that be so, it proves the strength and persistence of a thorough alcoholic
impregnation, or, as Wabster called it, of 'a good soak'. In young Gourlay's
case, at any rate, the impregnation was enduring and complete. He was like
a rag steeped in fusel oil.

Brown defended such ironic objectivity in his notes for *The
Novelist* – a study he never completed – and in the 'Rules for
Writing' collected during 1901, in which he described the artist
as an 'Observer of Humanity *from the outside*'. Thus he aspired to
be philosophically aloof, as if *sub specie aeternitatis*, and even
'callous', for ''tis the weakling-artist who invites his lachrymose
readers to a petty whine over the merited sorrows of the human
race'. If there is a young man's arrogance to such a programme,
it is not so very different from Stephen Dedalus's theory that the
writer should be like God – indifferent and beyond his
handiwork. The device is not always successful, but it was an
original effort to bring a crystal-clear, hard-edged definition to
the flattering mists of 'Scotch' setting and sentiment. It is
especially fitting that his forensic tones – reminiscent of a
pedantically precise Scots advocate – should be used to
reinforce an equally Scottish taste for Old Testament retribu-
tion as it came to be visited on the Gourlays at the end. Without
Brown's ironically inhumane distance, *The House with the Green
Shutters* would be a more predictable book, and certainly less
disturbing in its effect – at least until he relaxes his steely grip
and melodrama takes over in the final scenes.

At the age of thirty-three George Douglas Brown was
delighted with the success of his first serious novel. He visited
friends in Ayrshire, assembled notes on his theories of writing
and contemplated another novel, to be called 'The Incompat-
ibles'. But pneumonia, left untreated for too long, killed him in
August 1902. His novel became a special milestone in Scottish
letters because it used the Kailyard's own ingredients to blight
the bonnie briar-bush itself. Hay's *Gillespie* followed in 1914,
but it was overtaken by the Great War and, despite enthusiastic
reviews, it never became as well known as *The House with the
Green Shutters* and it was 1963 before it was published again.

John MacDougall Hay (1881–1919)

Hay was born and brought up in Tarbert at the mouth of Loch Fyne to the west of Glasgow. It was a community with Highland roots, but he did not speak Gaelic. He graduated with an ordinary MA at Glasgow University, where he had begun, even as student, to write creatively and to earn money as a freelance journalist. He worked as a teacher in the west until a severe attack of rheumatic fever changed his plans and he determined to train as a minister for the Church of Scotland, returning to university in 1905 and graduating five years later. He supported himself during this time and kept up his writing with a succession of reviews and articles for various Glasgow newspapers and London magazines. He made friends with Neil Munro, already an established novelist, and he started to think of the book that was to become *Gillespie*. In 1909, after a probationary period, Hay became minister at Elderslie, a largely urban parish on the outskirts of Glasgow, between Paisley and Johnstone. He married and settled down to a reticent life as minister and author, working late into the night on his bulky and intractable manuscript.

Hay had few pastimes, beyond reading and fishing, but his imaginative life must have been dramatic enough, for he said in a later interview that the intense sensations experienced by his character young Eoghan were based on his own visions and on memories of childhood. Certainly *Gillespie* is remarkable for the hallucinatory richness of its style, and it caused a sensation when it appeared in 1914, being highly praised by Hardy and particularly well received by American critics. A second novel, *Barnacles*, followed in 1916 and a collection of free verse called *Their Dead Sons* was published in 1918, but neither volume recaptured the impact of the first book, and *Gillespie*'s unrelenting grimness must have seemed less and less palatable after the war. Hay's health had never been very strong since his early illness, and he succumbed to TB in the winter of 1919. His son is the Gaelic poet George Campbell Hay.

There are obvious similarities between the stories of Gillespie Strang and John Gourlay. Both novels paint a savage picture of Scots community life and Hay's Brieston is also based on his home town – namely Tarbert. Both books have a tyrannical father who dominates all those around him, includ-

ing his suffering wife and a fey and sensitive son. Both end with
death and destruction. Clearly Hay had read Brown, but his
literary tastes owe nothing to his predecessor, nor does he
attempt the embryo modernism of a detached prose style. In
this respect it is significant that Hay liked Dostoevsky – a writer
Brown considered exaggerated and obscure. There is an
extravagant symbolic richness to Hay's outlook and on every
page he elevates the Scottish penchant for descriptive detail to
overpowering heights – like a development of Mannerism in
prose. Consider this description of herring-gutters at work:

> Those beautiful fish, silk-shot with a greenish-blue through the scales, are
> the strongest hostages against penury. From the cold deep they have come
> to brighten the hearth; fashioned in silver in the dark, as diamonds in the
> bowels of the earth. The burnishing of knives was a labour of love in the
> Back Street. What a sight it was to see again the big fishing-boats laced
> with scales and the shining pile in the Square. The women sat on empty
> herring boxes by the pile, their arms bared and dappled with blood. . . .
> When the dusk came the work was continued within the store, whose
> interior, lit with torches, presented a weird spectacle. Beneath the glare of
> the torches mingled with smoke, the gutters with blood-stained hands sat
> around, their faces starting out of the reek in the murky light and falling
> again into shadow. The pile of herring smouldered in pools of dull gold. . . .
> The big guttings of former days were recalled when the splendid fishing
> lured gutters from Stornoway and Peterhead to Brieston. Old times were
> restored; the old dead were resurrected; the aged were seen as young.
>   'Many's the guttin' ye hae sang at noo, Flory'; and as the torches flicker
> and the knives grow idle, and the weary hands are at rest a moment, a sweet
> treble voice sings the Scottish ballad:
>
>> 'Last night there were four Maries,
>> To-night they'll be but three',
>
> and fifty women take up the haunting air, making it swell beyond the
> rafters and the roof to the night and the stars. In that song the hungry days
> are ended, and the sorrows of the sea.

Scene after scene is illuminated in this portentous light, rising
to moments of apocalyptic intensity, for Hay's outlook is
genuinely metaphysical or theological, and he conceives Gillespie Strang as a demonic force whose very birth was heralded,
in unashamedly Shakespearean fashion, by evil omens. Gillespie's soul is like an iceberg, and yet he wears the outward guise
of a hearty self-made businessman. Unlike John Gourlay,
Hay's clever protagonist turns the law, technical progress and

other people's cupidity all to his own advantage, destroying everything around him (and finally himself) in the successfully calculated pursuit of profit and self-interest. Hay reported that his target was the growing spirit of materialism in Scotland, and in true Evangelical fashion he gave its spokesman a Mephistophelian stature, a capitalist convinced that 'the stars were fighting for him in their courses', a figure who even seems to have chance and natural disaster on his side. Overcharged with physical detail and portents, Gillespie looks back to the Gothic Romanticism and the folk energy of Hogg's visions of evil and uses this spirit to give an eldritch animation to the nineteenth-century world of commerce and bourgeois materialism.

Neil Munro (1864–1930)

Like his young friend Hay, Neil Munro came from the Central Highlands lying to the west of Glasgow. Following a spell in a lawyer's office he turned to journalism and for two years after the First World War he was editor of the *Glasgow Evening Times*, where George Blake also came to know him. Although Gaelic was in decline in Inverary, where Munro was born, his own familiarity with the language and its speech-patterns is clearly reflected in the spare English prose of his early stories. In a sense the bitter-sweet short stories of *The Lost Pibroch* (1896) belong with the Celtic twilight, except that Munro regards Highland culture and the destructively romantic pull of its old loyalties with gentle irony. Beyond the Stevensonian romance of his historical novels, Munro shows an ironic fatalism which recognises that the love of 'romance' is dangerous, just as the melancholy narrator of *John Splendid* (1898) looks back to the tragic futility of Montrose's bitter campaign in Argyll, and recalls how he was caught up in it by an adventurer in the mould of Alan Breck. *Doom Castle* (1901) is an ironically Gothic tale set in the years after the Forty-five, while Munro's excellent sense of landscape and the excitements of eighteenth-century travel make *The New Road* (1914) an adventure in the footsteps of *Kidnapped*. The young hero is harried across Scotland only to discover that the story of his father's distant death in the

Jacobite cause is a lie – a lie concocted to conceal a sordid murder for simple gain at home.

As a journalist Munro wrote short stories and newspaper sketches calling himself 'Hugh Foulis', and it was under this name that he created the droll characters 'Archie' and 'Jimmy Swann'; but his most famous comic achievement was 'Para Handy', the skipper of a puffer called *Vital Spark*. The 'puffers' were tiny tramp steamers – like sea-going trucks – which used to operate out of the Clyde estuary, and the adventures of Para Handy and his eccentric crew are full of sly humour and delight in the manners and affairs of small townships up and down the west coast. Munro was reluctant to own up to these tales, but their popularity has quite overshadowed his more serious ambitions as a poet and they inspired a television comedy series in the 1970s.

John Buchan (1875–1940)

If Munro's historical fiction followed Stevenson's example, then the novels of John Buchan brought the same approach to contemporary settings. Buchan spent his teenage years in Glasgow, where his father – a Free Kirk minister – had his parish in the Gorbals. From Glasgow University Buchan won a classical scholarship to Oxford, where he arrived just as George Douglas Brown left for London. By the end of his student days he had produced a first-class degree, two historical novels and three other volumes, making a splash, too, as a Union president who made contributions to *The Yellow Book*. *John Burnet of Barns* (1898) looks to Covenanting times with lovingly detailed descriptions of Buchan's favourite Tweedside, where the holidays of his youth were spent, and this use of landscape set the pattern for most of his later fiction. After Oxford, Buchan turned to law in London and managed another couple of novels before going to South Africa for two years to work for the British High Commission at the end of the Boer War. He returned to London and the Law in 1903, accepted the post of literary adviser to Nelson's publishing-house and eventually became a director in 1915.

The novelist drew on his African experience for *Prester John* (1910) – a boys' adventure which begins on the Fife coast and takes its protagonist to a veritable heart of darkness where warring tribesmen follow a charismatic black leader who speaks with all the old passion of the Covenanters – the distorted religious inheritance of 'Prester John'. Buchan's enthusiasm for the original ideals of Presbyterianism and his hatred of its latent fanaticism illuminates his study of *The Marquis of Montrose* (1913), a subject he returned to with *Montrose* in 1928. The marquis's lightning campaigns over wild country particularly appealed to him and confirmed his belief that every man should be prepared to support his convictions or his social privileges by direct action. A simplified version of this creed motivated the exploits of Richard Hannay, who first appeared in 1915 with *The Thirty-nine Steps*. Indeed, Buchan's 'shockers', as he called them, show a strongly Calvinist sense of the presence of evil and savagery just beneath the 'civilised' surface of the everyday world, and they are equally alert to the dangers of fanaticism – just as extreme Calvinism was prone to what he saw as 'dark and vehement emotions'. Against such forces Buchan, like his heroes, values success born of hard effort, a simple clarity of purpose and a stubborn unwillingness to give up, rather than subtlety of insight or any more profound philosophical motivation. Such was the Presbyterian work-ethic of a Scottish gentleman conservative and, no doubt, there were thousands like him in the colonial service. If these values seem naïve in the face of the terrible sophistication of contemporary dilemmas, at least they made for grand adventure tales, as another Scot, Ian Fleming, was to discover – although his James Bond is a more cynical creation reflecting the consumerism of the sixties.

By the early twenties Buchan was living in Oxford and commuting to London to work for Reuters and Nelson, for whom he had written a huge history of the war. He took an interest, too, in the new stirrings in Scottish poetry and contributed to Grieve's *Northern Numbers*. Although Buchan's own verse rarely strays from the ordinary, his taste was sound, and in 1924 he compiled an excellent anthology of old and new Scots poems which he called *The Northern Muse*, prefaced with an essay on how Scots vernacular literature had sunk to a provincial genre. Fond of walking and fishing, Buchan took regular holidays in Scotland and these settings feature in many of the thrillers he produced – one a year – between 1922 and

1936. The last five years of his life were spent as Governor General of Canada – with the title of Baron Tweedsmuir. As a confidant of Franklin D. Roosevelt, Buchan tried to mobilise American opinion to support Britain against Hitler and hence to forestall the outbreak of war. He failed, and in 1940 he died of a cerebral stroke. During the course of his life he had produced over a hundred books.

As far as his 'shockers' were concerned, Buchan was content to entertain, and, although they lack the historical or psychological depth of Scott and Stevenson, their approach, like Buchan's own craft, is honourably descended from that line. The historical novel itself, with the glamour of Scottish history and landscape, has continued to thrive. Its later exponents include Nigel Tranter (b. 1909), a professional writer for most of his life who has used his enthusiasm for Scottish history and architecture to give authentic detail to his fictionalised biographies, scholarly publications and local guides. By comparison Dorothy Dunnett (b. 1923) has developed character and atmosphere in a sequence of six books beginning with *The Game of Kings* (1961), featuring a charismatically Byronic Scottish soldier of fortune called Francis Crawford of Lymond. These long novels use the most densely realised dialogue and settings to evoke the cruel and glittering brilliance of sixteenth-century Europe and the north.

R. B. Cunninghame Graham (1852–1936)

Among the remaining prose writers from the first twenty years of the century, the fiery, dandyish and Quixotic Graham might have been invented in some unlikely collusion between Oscar Wilde, John Buchan and Hugh MacDiarmid. With Spanish blood on his mother's side and remote connections with Robert the Bruce, Graham came from a privileged background and got an early taste for foreign parts by going to Argentina at the age of eighteen to spend most of the next seven years living as a rancher, dressed like a gaucho and known as 'Don Roberto'. He returned to London, eloped with a Chilean girl whom he met in Paris, and roamed around Texas and Mexico before returning to Scotland to become a radical Liberal MP. This did not prevent him from being imprisoned after the riots in Trafalgar

Square in 1887 and suspended from Parliament more than once for his support of nationalisation, socialism or communism on a platform which demanded free education, a better deal for women, stronger trade-unions and more wages for a shorter day's work. A friend of Keir Hardie, Graham became first president of the Scottish Labour Party when it was founded in 1888. During the 1890s he began to write and came to know literary figures such as Conrad – whom he helped with *Nostromo* – Edward Garnett, Henry James, Oscar Wilde, Masefield, Hardy and Shaw. (He was the model for Saranoff in *Arms and the Man*, although Shaw felt that he was so much larger than life that a full account would never be believed on stage.) Don Roberto cultivated his own piratical and idealistic personality to an unusual degree. His South American background and fresh adventures as a latter-day explorer and gold-prospector in Morocco and Spain gave him material for his first travel books in the 1890s and then in the 1920s and 1930s he published biographies and historical studies of the conquistadores.

Several of Graham's first short stories and sketches were set in Scotland, for he was proud of his nationality but contemptuous of the vogue for Kailyard parochialism: 'Today a Scotsman stands confessed a sentimental fool . . .', he wrote in *The Ipané* (1899), 'oppressed with the tremendous difficulties of the jargon he is bound to speak, and above all weighed down with the responsibility of being Scotch.' Never afraid to put his spurs to sacred cows, Graham was equally scathing about the Kirk and all its doings. English imperialism fared little better, for he had a natural sympathy with foreign peoples, however distant their mores were from his own. His prose is succinctly and vigorously set down with telling and original details. Often hovering somewhere between sketch, free reminiscence and fiction, it is usually controlled by his own alert and astringent sense of irony – a style admired by many of his more famous writer friends. Further stories were collected in *Faith* (1909), *Hope* (1910), *Charity* (1912) and *Scottish Stories* (1914). In the post-war years Graham became critical of the Labour Party and renounced his socialism to campaign as a Liberal. He became president of the National Party in 1928 and of the Scottish National Party when it was brought together in 1934. In these circles he met with Hugh MacDiarmid, who criticised his retreat from the radical Left but shared his delight in slashing artistic mediocrity and bourgeois values whenever possible.

Norman Douglas (1868–1952)

As a cultivator of personality, a 'writer's writer' and an iconoclast in his own way, Douglas was as cosmopolitan as Graham. He became famous for his loving evocation of the southern tip of Italy in *Old Calabria* (1915) and for the sardonic zest of his first novel, *South Wind* (1917), which is replete with the hedonistic spirit of Capri – fictionalised as 'Nepenthe' – and full of the author's favourite topics and disquisitions. Douglas's family came from Tilquhillie Castle to the west of Aberdeen, but his father managed cotton-mills in Austria and Norman was born there with German as his first language. Young Douglas disliked the damp castle on Deeside and hated his English public school even more, regarding himself as a sophisticated European. At the age of twenty-eight he abandoned his short-lived career in the Foreign Service and settled in Italy as an amateur enthusiast – producing short stories with his wife before their marriage broke up. He had early fallen in love with Capri and the civilised ease of the Mediterranean, where he felt that his classical hedonism, and a cheerfully pagan interest in adolescent boys, was validated by past cultural history and the unsentimental brilliance of the light – all very far away from the puritanism of the North or the stuffiness of English society. Douglas became a professional writer relatively late in life, and was forty-eight before *South Wind* brought him fame by speaking for wit and sophisticated freedoms against the greyness that was post-war Europe. Two further books of fiction – both fantasies – appeared during the twenties, but Douglas's real talent was for the evocation of place in the celebration of a sun-drenched world and his own spiky nature – defined again in *Alone* (1921), *Together* (1923) and *Looking Back* (1933).

Urban writing in the early twentieth century

Nothing could be further from the spirit of Cunninghame Graham or Douglas's Mediterranean than the popular literature which still prevailed on the home front in Scotland. George Douglas Brown's savage detachment may have shaken the Kailyard's more serious pretensions, but he did not dent the market for parochial light comedy – the literary equivalent, as MacDiarmid put it, of cold haggis and ginger beer. Neil Munro's friend J. J. Bell (1871–1934) was among the best of these pawky humorists and his work is not without charm. His *enfant terrible* 'Wee Macgreegor' made his debut in the *Glasgow Evening Times* at the beginning of the century, but Bell mined the same vein of working-class character comedy for over thirty years. This 'urban kailyard' lived on through the forties and fifties, with Helen W. Pryde's 'McFlannels' series on Scottish Radio, and D. C. Thomson of Dundee had already founded a considerable publishing-empire on dozens of periodicals aimed at a working-class and lower-middle-class market for conservative values, sentiment, piety, true-love romances and droll Scots humour. MacDiarmid and other writers of the early Renaissance came to regard the comedian Harry Lauder as the patron saint of this version of Scottishness – a music-hall figure of fun, swathed in surrealistic tartans, sporting bare knees and a knobbly walking stick. Yet Lauder and the other 'Scotch comics' were undeniably popular with their audiences, representing an absurd stereotype that had come to be loved for its own sake.

Some writers, however, particularly in Glasgow, did attempt a more realistic picture of Scottish city life. John Blair gave an unusually direct account of the life of a factory girl in *Jean* (1906); while twin novels by Patrick MacGill (1890–1963), called *Children of the Dead End* (1914) and *The Rat-pit* (1915), spoke of the Irish immigrant experience in Scotland and Glasgow, with grim details of life in the slums and lodging-houses of the city. As the son of a Glasgow manufacturer, **Frederick Niven** (1878–1944) turned to writing, and, after early ambitions to become a painter, he led a restless life between Scotland, Canada and London before finally settling in British Columbia shortly after the First World War. Several of his many novels – most notably *The Justice of the Peace* (1914) and *The Staff at*

Simson's (1937) – give a detailed account of bourgeois and commercial Glasgow society in the first years of the century. Not surprisingly the first stirrings of urban realism in this 'Glasgow school' were confined to prose, and it was to be many years before Scottish poetry could turn to city life, and even longer before it took a distinctively Glaswegian accent.

The Renaissance of poetry in Scots: MacDiarmid's precursors

As far as poetry in Scots was concerned, the Kailyard strain went back at least as far as the *Whistle-Binkie* anthologies, fifty years before the new century. Stevenson's Scots poems were better, but linked the language with nostalgia or bairn rhymes. As for the rest, the sentimental rustification of Scots had left it frozen in time and place as a language apparently reserved for the 'poetry corners' of local newspapers and hundreds of talentless imitators of Burns. Even James Logie Robertson (1846–1922), who had edited many valuable popular collections of the works of Ramsay, Scott, Dunbar and Burns, could produce little more than pastoral pastiche when he wrote as 'Hugh Haliburton', with titles such as *Horace in Hamespun* (1882) and *Ochil Idylls* (1891). The language seemed lost to serious use. Yet it did retain some credibility in the hands of authentic dialect poets, and in this respect it was Charles Murray, Violet Jacob and several other North-East poets who showed what could be done in Scots a significant number of years before MacDiarmid took up Lallans for himself.

Born in Alford, trained as an engineer in Aberdeen, and working in South Africa for most of his life, **Charles Murray** (1864–1941) was completely at home with North-East speech and his poems move with the easy flow of oral expression – often as dramatic monologues. His taste for pithy epigrams, like his eye for landscape, weather and the trappings of country life, all stem from a folk tradition which had remained particularly rich in Aberdeenshire and Angus. Alexander's *Johnny Gibb of Gushetneuk* was first published as a serial in the Aberdeen newspaper, and Gavin Greig (1856–1914), with the help of the Revd J. B. Duncan, had spent the last ten years of his life making a monumental collection of oral lore and ballads from the region. To this day North-East Scots has retained an unforced linguistic confidence. *Hamewith* (1900) made Murray's reputation, and it was enlarged, reprinted three times and then collated with two later collections to make the complete works of 1927. After a distinguished career in South Africa the poet returned home to a considerable degree of local fame. 'Gin I were God' and 'The Whistle' ('He cut a sappy sooker from a muckle rodden tree') are widely anthologised, but poems such as 'Dockens afore his Peers', 'The Three Craws' and 'A Green Yule' give a better sense of his sardonic wit, while the lyrical conclusion to the last-named poem goes beyond dialect verse to the voice of the ballads infused with the grim weight of Dunbar:

Bring them alang, the young, the strang,	
The weary an' the auld;	
Feed as they will on haugh or hill,	low meadow
This is the only fauld.	fold
Dibble them doon, the laird, the loon,	Plant; boy
King an' the cadgin' caird,	travelling tinker
The lady fine beside the queyn,	girl
A' in the same kirkyard	

Violet Jacob (1863–1946), came from the Kennedy-Erskine family, who had held the lands near Montrose since the fifteenth century. Her first books (1902 and 1904) were historical novels, and she went on to write short stories and three main collections of poems – *Songs of Angus* (1915), *Bonnie Joann* (1921) and *Northern Lights* (1927). She is more prone to sentimentality than Murray, partly because her focus is on the pains of love, the fears of children, or the onset of old age. Even so, her Scots is rarely coy and her sense of muted sexual shame, like her sympathy with landscape or the supernatural, is often illuminated by particularly effective small-scale images – a broken stone and black nettles ('The Jaud') or brambles and toadstools among dark fir-trees ('Craigo Woods') or a thistle going to seed on a river-bank ('The End o' t'). Jacob contributed to MacDiarmid's *Northern Numbers* anthologies at a time when he himself was still writing in English, and she was generously represented in Buchan's *Northern Muse*.

Marion Angus (1866–1946) and **Helen Cruickshank** (1886–1975) also had their roots in the North-East, and, although most of their poems were not published until after

MacDiarmid had shown what the Scots lyric could achieve, they qualify as forerunners along with Violet Jacob. Cruickshank also appeared in *Northern Numbers*, and Angus's *The Lilt and Other Poems* dates from 1922, followed by *The Tinker's Road* (1924) and four further collections during the twenties and thirties. Within her chosen range Marion Angus is technically the most accomplished of her generation, and a later English piece on Mary Stuart – 'Alas! Poor Queen' – might have been constructed by a young Ezra Pound. She also learned from the ballads, and, although the lilting sadness of her lines can become excessively fey, her best lyrics are terser and genuinely disquieting – 'The Can'el', 'Ann Gilchrist' and 'The Blue Jacket'. Angus lived most of her life in Aberdeen, away from the storms of literary Edinburgh. Helen Cruickshank's poems, by comparison, are nearer once more to a vernacular muse with its interest in landscape and reminiscence, although she uses this to make political points, too. She succeeded MacDiarmid as secretary of the Scottish PEN Club and proved to be a loyal supporter of most of the younger Renaissance poets and a particularly good friend to MacDiarmid and his family during their difficult years in the thirties.

The North-East connection was continued with Mary Symon (1863–1938) from Banffshire, another contributor to *Northern Numbers*, who published her work in *Deveron Days* (1933) and with **Pittendrigh MacGillivray** (1856–1938), the sculptor who made the statues of John Knox in St Giles' and Byron at Aberdeen Grammar School. Born near Inverurie, MacGillivray was an enthusiast for eighteenth-century Scots verse, but for the most part it is his own native voice which controls poems such as 'Observances' – drawing on folk-customs for greeting a new baby – or 'Mercy o' Gode', a finely sardonic account of two old men sitting in a churchyard. His first publication was *Pro Patria* (1915), but his best Scots work appeared in *Bog Myrtle and Peat Reek* (1922) – a privately produced and expensive little book. **Alexander Gray** (1882–1968) was born in Dundee and worked for the Civil Service before becoming professor of political economy in Aberdeen and Edinburgh. He too drew on North-East Scots for his poems, and used a modified version of it to translate pieces from Danish and German, including *Songs and Ballads Chiefly from Heine* (1920) and German ballads and folk-songs done into an efficient Scots verse for *Arrows* (1932). **Lewis Spence** (1874–1955) came from Dundee, working for the *Scotsman* and the *British Weekly* before becoming a full-time writer. In forty years he produced almost as many books, on legends and mythology from the Celts to the civilisations of Mexico, South America and 'Atlantis'. Spence championed the cause of new writing in Scots and, although most of his own poems use a rather poetical diction in English, he chose an archaic Scots for some of them. 'The Queen's Bath-house, Holyrood', 'The Prows o' Reekie' and 'The Firth' catch the dour strength he was seeking, even if they are mainly descriptive and backward-looking.

Most of the above-mentioned poets using Scots were featured in three anthologies called *Northern Numbers*, which appeared between 1920 and 1922. Edited by a writer in his late twenties called C. M. Grieve, these planned to do for contemporary Scottish poets what Edward Marsh's *Georgian Poetry* collections had already achieved in England. Indeed, these little books from Montrose do mark the first stirrings of what was to be a renaissance in Scottish poetry, as well as the first significant appearance of its most energetic proponent. At this stage, however, Grieve's own poems were all in English and for his part he doubted if Scots would ever be an effective medium for modern poetry. 'Hugh MacDiarmid' was soon to change all that.

Christopher Murray Grieve ('Hugh MacDiarmid', 1892–1978)

C. M. Grieve launched *Northern Numbers* when he was twenty-eight years old – married and recently demobilised from the Army Medical Corps, he was a self-confessed 'late ripener'. Now that he was working as a journalist in Montrose he set about taking the first serious steps towards a literary career planned during the long watches as a quartermaster sergeant in military hospitals in Salonika and near Marseilles. He had shown creative promise from the start, and throughout the war and after he kept up a correspondence with George Ogilvie, his English-master from Broughton Student Centre in Edinburgh, pouring out his doubts and ambitions and sending him examples of the many sonnets which he was writing at the time. These poems in English tended to deal with death, eternity and God in a rather studiously crystalline poetic diction

Grieve was working in prose too, and since 1919 he had been assembling material written or planned during the war, to be called *Annals of the Five Senses* – a series of psychological studies or sketches, each of them laying bare, under various personae, the author's sense of his own enthusiastic mental life. The collection was ready by 1921, but could not be published until 1923, and, although it is not about the war, *Annals* does relate to some of Grieve's experiences in Greece and France. He contracted cerebral malaria in Salonika and had been invalided home as a chronic case in 1918 (it was during this leave that he married Margaret – Peggy – Skinner) and it is possible that the positively feverish intensity of the consciousness described in *Annals* stems at least in part from this illness. Every character in each of the six stories has a 'brain like a hall of mirrors in which he caught countless reflections of every theme in as many shapes and sizes', and those themes are evoked in long and lovingly elaborated lists of the most esoteric details culled from his own sensations or the world of books and newspapers to make 'a swift, beautiful catalogue of the most delightful and unexpected of interests'. (Grieve had been a compulsively omnivorous reader since his early boyhood, when the family lived in rooms beneath the Langholm public library, where his mother worked as a caretaker.) The *Annals* stories mix a furious sense of physical detail with unacknowledged quotations from dozens of writers and a tendency to abstruse or metaphysical speculation – a striking combination, even when the young man's prose style cannot quite support the strain. Nevertheless, in view of the poems which he was to write in the late thirties, these first studies are of great interest.

The Montrose years were among the most productive in Grieve's life, despite his commitments to many other fields as well. Apart from working for the *Montrose Review*, he sat on the town council as an Independent Socialist, becoming a parish councillor as well and, in 1926, a justice of the peace. After *Northern Numbers* his next project was to found a literary monthly called the *Scottish Chapbook*, which appeared in August 1922 and managed fourteen issues before the end of 1923. By then he was also publishing and editing the *Scottish Nation*, a weekly dedicated to Scottish nationalism, and the *Northern Review*, which appeared for four months in the summer of 1924. These short-lived periodicals mark the beginning of the 'Scottish Renaissance' as a defined modern literary movement, and for the next twenty years Grieve promoted the cause of literary and political self-awareness with a constant stream of newspaper-articles, books, reviews, essays, letters and public speeches, all of which made him one of the most vociferous and best-known cultural figures in Scotland. Some of his more influential and contentious essays, from a regular series in the *Scottish Educational Journal*, were collected as *Contemporary Scottish Studies* in 1926, to be followed by *Albyn, or Scotland and the Future* in 1927.

The first *Chapbook* contained a playscript by Grieve and a visionary poem called 'A Moment in Eternity' dedicated to George Ogilvie. Subsequent numbers embarked on 'A Theory of Scots Letters', which developed Gregory Smith's definition of 'antisyzygy' to show what Scots could offer to the modern poet – especially in its 'reconciliation of the base and the beautiful' and in its potential for creating images drawn from physical and psychological states no longer available, so Grieve claimed, to an urbane and oversophisticated English tradition. He found these strengths particularly evident in Jamieson's *Scottish Dictionary* and used many words and phrases from its pages to make his point. Grieve cited the works of Dostoevsky, Lawrence and Joyce as writers who had felt the need to overthrow the old modes in order to express their vision, and for him Scots should be equally capable of contributing to the modernist movement. He had no time, therefore, for Scots as an exercise in nostalgia, nor for the Victorian stereotype of Scottish 'dourness', and he redefined the 'true Scot' as a figure possessed by Gregory Smith's combination of opposites – 'dominated by the conception of infinity, of the unattainable, and hence ever questioning, never satisfied, rationalistic in religion and politics, romantic in art and literature' – a figure not unlike 'Hugh MacDiarmid', in other words. Grieve's desire to follow Pound and to 'make it new' is central to his conception of the Renaissance, and from the start his periodicals and essays looked outwards to Europe and beyond. The *Chapbook*'s motto was 'Not Traditions – Precedents' and, if its editor cried 'Back to Dunbar!', it was because he hoped that Dunbar's complex spirit and technique would be a salutary antidote to the bucolic sentimentality of the post-Burns tradition. Yet all this activity would have come to nothing from a literary point of view were it not for the poems which Grieve produced in four extraordinary years from 1922 to 1926.

Grieve published his first poems in Scots in the *Dunfermline Press* in September 1922, but he pretended that they were written by a friend – later named as 'Hugh M'Diarmid'. He now admitted an interest in the poetic potential of 'obsolete' or 'distinctively local' words and opined that his friend's verses had a 'descriptive potency otherwise unobtainable'. One of the poems was 'The Watergaw' and Grieve was right. It was as if the vocabulary and idiom of Scots with its long tradition of colloquial utterance and domestic detail added a special and much needed physical body to the metaphysical inspiration of his early work. This was a voice which could express both the sublime and the vulgar, moving from one to the other with speed, wit and the appearance of ease. Gregory Smith had described this 'medieval . . . freedom in passing from one mood to another', and it turned out to be exactly right for the author of *Annals of the Five Senses* and his volatile sensibility, so wildly idealistic and materialistic by turns. Struck by this insight, Grieve immediately explained it in his 'Theory of Scots Letters', and acknowledged the debt by adopting the name Hugh MacDiarmid for all his poems thereafter.

MacDiarmid's first two collections of Scots poems were called *Sangschaw* (1925) and *Penny Wheep* (1926) and both were enthusiastically received. Edwin Muir admired 'a crazy economy' in the language, 'which has the effect of humour and yet conveys a kind of horror', and he saw this as 'truly Scottish' and as distinct from the English ethos as was the prose of George Douglas Brown or Carlyle. The reviewer for *The Times Literary Supplement* praised 'an unusual sense of the movement and changing aspects of the earth in its diurnal round', and Professor Denis Saurat of the University of Bordeaux, who had taken such an early critical interest in the Scots revival, translated many of them into French. Danish versions were made, and the poet's former schoolteacher from Langholm, a composer called Francis George Scott (1880–1958), set several of the lyrics, and ultimately about seventy of MacDiarmid's poems, to music. *La Renaissance ecossaise* was off to a properly international start. Scott and MacDiarmid renewed their old acquaintance and became close friends, for 'F. G.' helped the poet assemble the long sequence which became *A Drunk Man Looks at the Thistle* and the book was dedicated to him.

Some of the early lyrics use a vernacular voice – 'Crowdie-knowe' and 'Focherty', for example, might have been conceived by Charles Murray – but for the rest the domestic realism of the Scots is astonishingly transformed, as if their landscapes have become charged with a strange energy – like Expressionist paintings by Munch or Soutine. MacDiarmid creates a world of vivid contrasts, of 'Cloudburst and Soarin' Mune', or of wind and light where the trees fatten and thin themselves like turkeys screaming ('Sunny Gale'). Even the filthy gutter in the cowshed is transmuted – 'The aidle-pool is a glory o' gowd' – and we seem to cling to the surface of the planet with an exhilarating sense of the vastness of time and infinite distance:

> The moonbeams kelter i' the lift,   waver in the sky
> An' Earth, the bare auld stane,
> Glitters beneath the seas o' Space,
> White as a mammoth's bane.

> ('Au Clair de la Lune')

Other poems in this vein include 'Ex Vermibus', 'Country Life' and 'Farmer's Death', and their hallucinatory intensity is charged again by MacDiarmid's choice of not-quite-familiar Scots words or by the succinct and subtle breaks which he makes from what would otherwise be fairly predictable ballad-like stresses. (In this respect his handling of rhythm is reminiscent of Wordsworth's 'Lucy' poems, or some of Hardy's pieces on his wife.) A sense of cosmic scale characterises also 'Au Clair de la Lune', 'The Innumerable Christ', 'Servant Girl's Bed' and 'Empty Vessel'. 'The Eemis Stane' is rightly famous:

> I' the how-dumb-deid o' the cauld hairst night   harvest
> The warl' like an eemis stane   insecure, wobbling
> Wags i' the lift;   sky   [stone
> An' my eerie memories fa'
> Like a yowdendrift.   blizzard with snow
> [rising from ground

Like a yowdendrift so's I couldna read	
The words cut oot i' the stane	
Had the fug o' fame	moss
An' history's hazelraw	lichen
No' yirdit thaim.	buried

The specific earthiness of Scots words such as 'fug' and 'hazelraw' contrasts with the more English abstractions 'fame' and 'history', while the planet teeters like a rocking boulder in the sky. If there is some primal message or meaning to be found there, the poet cannot read it, because it has been hidden by his own memories and by all the experience of the world itself – like moss and lichen on the surface of a gravestone.

These poems, and others such as 'Moonstruck', 'The Watergaw', and 'The Bonnie Broukit Bairn', reach a truly extraordinary imaginative compression of image, language and ideation. They meet the requirements of Imagist verse more effectively than any of the poems written by Pound, HD, or T. E. Hulme, and in this respect MacDiarmid took the Scots tradition to a new and truly modern expression. Even so, the poet's mercurial sensibility, his polemical humour and his enthusiasm for metaphysical flights, had further to go and he turned his energies to a much more ambitious project.

A Drunk Man Looks at the Thistle (1926) is MacDiarmid's single most famous book and one of the great poems of modernist literature – a testament to creative energy and optimism at a time when Yeats, Pound and Eliot could see only cultural decline and spiritual failure all around them. The poem's setting is simple enough – a drunk man lies gazing at a thistle on a moonlit hillside. His intoxicated state and the fickle and deceptive light of the moon send him on an imaginative odyssey as strange as any undertaken by Tam o' Shanter or Thomas the Rhymer. Operating somewhere between dramatic monologue and stream of consciousness, the poem's technique is fairly conventional – he uses simple ballad-like rhyme-schemes and the language is a lightly colloquial Scots. Yet this familiarity is deceptive, for MacDiarmid creates and juxta-poses so many startling images, and makes so many swift changes of pace and tone – from broad satire to tender lyrics to ribaldry, metaphysical anguish and back again – that the poem is electric with energy and exhilaration. The drunk man finds that the world around him and his own thoughts seem to mix and change with alarming fluidity, and the whole universe is destabilised by whisky, moonlight and his own overheated cerebration.

The poem has little formal structure beyond its individual rhyme-schemes and it can be bewilderingly garrulous and repetitious, but particular images do recur to give it a certain thematic coherence. Most notably the thistle is a deeply ambivalent symbol – representing some ideal beauty or fulfilment by its purple flower (the thistle's 'rose') but conjuring up sterility, failure and pain in its ugly stalks and spikes. It seems that we are fated always to be caught between the two: 'Man torn in twa / And glorious in the lift and grisly on the sod'. The drunk man finds this division within himself, his country (it is the national plant, after all) and the fate of all humankind. He is obsessed with it, just as Ahab was obsessed with the mystery and menace of Moby Dick, and the thistle takes a dozen different shapes throughout the poem – comic, vulgar or terrifying – as he wrestles with its personal, social and philosophical implications:

> A black leaf owre a white leaf twirls,
> A grey leaf flauchters in atween,   flutters
> Sae ply my thochts aboot the stem
> O' loppert slime frae which they spring.   clotted
> The thistle like a snawstorm drives,
> Or like a flicht o' swallows lifts,
> Or like a swarm o' midges hings,
> A plague o' moths, a starry sky,
> But's naething but a thistle yet,
> And still the puzzle stands unsolved.
> Beauty and ugliness alike,
> And life and daith and God and man,
> Are aspects o't but nane can tell
> The secret that I'd fain find oot
> O' this bricht hive, this sorry weed,
> The tree that fills the universe,   (Yggdrasil, the tree of life)
> Or like a reistit herrin' crines.   dried herring shrivels

In the course of this Dionysian exploration, the broadest satirical attacks are delivered on Burns Clubs, Harry Lauder and all the conventional trappings of bourgeois 'Scottishness'. MacDiarmid also created hundreds of the most startling poetic images, where the abstractions of his theme are embodied in the concrete particularities of Scots speech: 'nocht but a chowed core's left whaur Jerusalem lay / Like aipples in a heap!' If Grierson and Eliot admired a quality of 'felt thought' in the poetry of John Donne and the Metaphysicals, this is no less than MacDiarmid achieves in almost every page of his long poem:

I tae ha'e heard Eternity drip water
(Aye water, water!), drap by drap
On the a'e nerve, like lichtnin', I've become,
And heard God passin' wi' a bobby's feet   policeman's
Ootby in the lang coffin o' the street
– Seen stang by chitterin' knottit stang loup oot   paroxysm;
Uncrushed by th'echoes o' the thunderin' boot,   [shivering
Till a' the dizzy lint-white lines o' torture made   flax-white
A monstrous thistle in the space aboot me,
A symbol o' the puzzle o' man's soul.

These lines make broad comedy collide with the most intense spiritual longing, as if Fergusson and Shelley were united in profound grotesquerie – a new category of literary taste.

Unlike Yeats and Eliot, MacDiarmid welcomes the insignificance of man and the vastness of the universe, just as he welcomes the myriad conflicting sensations and impulses within himself. In this he is a truly post-Romantic modernist with absolutely no hankering for the balance or the certitudes of some idealised classical past:

I'll hae nae hauf-way hoose, but aye be whaur
Extremes meet – it's the only way I ken
To dodge the curst conceit o' bein' richt
That damns the vast majority o' men.

Thus he gives himself up to change, fluidity and perpetual opposition, and embraces – rather like Walt Whitman – the *élan vital* of the universe itself.

If *A Drunk Man* rings with MacDiarmid's special brand of optimistic modernism, fuelled by his interests in materialism, socialism and Scottish nationhood, it also has moments of visionary intensity when he glimpses some spiritual or neo-platonic ideal of peace and enlightenment beyond the endless whirl of the world or his own introspection.

And O! I canna thole	endure
Aye yabblin' o' my soul,	gabbling
And fain I wad be free	
O' my eternal me.	

This ideal is symbolised by the bride carrying a bunch of thistles, or by the 'silken leddy' who drifts into a crowded and noisy tavern to create a moment of stillness and insight. For the drunk man the mystery of existence and the challenge 'to be yersel's – and to mak' that worth bein'', is an imperative that goes beyond Scottish national identity (although that is the first step), for he believes that human consciousness is an integrated part of universal evolution and that an outstanding effort must be made to *realise* it – in every sense of the word. This is what he refers to as the 'seamless garment' or the 'diamond body' in later poems. For the moment, however, the drunk man can solve nothing in a world where the only constant seems to be eternal change. But at least for one glorious, intoxicated night he has given himself up to the flux of the universe and joined the dance in his own wild and fantastical imagination. If he comes to silence in the closing lines of the poem, it is the silence of human experience, or repletion, or even exhaustion, but never the stillness of extinction, blind faith, acquiescence or despair – those common ailments of the modern spirit.

MacDiarmid's drunk caused a critical sensation in Scotland – at last a fully modern poem in Scots had appeared, bursting on the nation with all the force, in one incomparable phrase, of a childbirth in church. Yet already some readers were regretting his move away from the lyric. The poet remained in Montrose for the next three years, as prolific as ever with reviews and innumerable articles on Scotland and all things Scottish. He worked on another long poem, to be called *To Circumjack Cencrastus* (1930), in which the puzzle of the thistle is pursued yet again in the form of 'Cencrastus', which Mac-Diarmid associated with the Celtic curly snake with its tail in its mouth – a symbol of eternity – and with the mythological serpent whose coils surround the world. But the mode had been better realised in *A Drunk Man*, and, although the theme is central to MacDiarmid's poetry, the new book had passages where he seems bitterly dissatisfied with his life and his job as an underpaid journalist in Montrose. By the 1930s the poet was looking for a new direction and for a way of more overtly expressing his socialist principles in verse.

When Compton Mackenzie suggested that he edit *Vox*, a recently founded arts magazine for the radio, MacDiarmid seized the chance and moved to London with his wife and two children late in 1929. But London proved to be an unhappy experience. Towards the end of the year he fell from a bus and suffered severe concussion – experiencing headaches for some years afterwards – and *Vox* had died before he recovered. The poet's marriage was under strain and, when he eventually found a job as a publicity officer in Liverpool, Peggy refused to go with him and they agreed to separate. The Liverpool appointment did not last long and MacDiarmid found himself back in London. *First Hymn to Lenin and Other Poems* appeared in 1931 with an introduction and a portrait of the author by 'AE', but it was limited to only 500 copies. Many of the poems looked back to his roots in Langholm as if seeking a new stability there. He was drinking heavily and estranged from his wife, for she had found someone else, and in the middle of an economic depression he had no job and no savings at all. (The couple were finally divorced at the beginning of 1932.) 'My story', he was to write later, 'is the story of an absolutist whose absolutes came to grief in his private life.' The one good thing that happened to him at this time was his meeting with a Cornishwoman called Valda Trevlyn, a creative lady in her own right, who became his wife and an unfailing source of support and courage for the rest of his life. They lived in a cottage in Sussex and then moved back to Scotland with a new baby, Michael, who had been born in the summer.

When *Scots Unbound and Other Poems* appeared in 1932, MacDiarmid explained that it was to join *First Hymn to Lenin and Other Poems* as part of an extended sequence in five books to be called 'Clann Albann' – 'the children of Scotland'. The first book, 'The Muckle Toon', would consider his years in Langholm and the influence of parents, childhood, socialism and the Church on his growing sensibility. The project was never realised, but most of the poems and some short stories of the period do, indeed, relate to autobiographical themes. He chose a light colloquial Scots, for pieces such as 'At my Father's Grave', 'Charisma and my Relatives', and 'Kinsfolk'; and his home town and the surrounding country feature in poems such as 'Whuchulls' and 'Tarras'. Langholm is a place where three rivers meet, and MacDiarmid's fascination with water in all its changes appears as a symbol of life itself in 'Prayer for a Second Flood', 'Water of Life', 'Excelsior' and 'The Oon Olympian', reaching a climax with 'Water Music', a Joycean extravaganza which uses a plethora of the most obscure Scots words to imitate the sound and the movements of his favourite rivers.

Socialism was a further theme in MacDiarmid's poems of the early thirties, and in this, of course, he was in line with most other left-wing writers of the day. Yet his polemical roots are deeper and narrower than those of Auden, Spender, MacNeice and Day Lewis, and his idealism is more far reaching. His father was a country postman and a socialist (as well as an elder in the United Free Kirk) and MacDiarmid had joined the Fabian Society and the ILP when he was sixteen. As a young journalist in South Wales in 1911 he had worked for a miners' newspaper, witnessed police baton charges, and made speeches in support of the Labour cause. Thus in later years he took a hardliner's delight in opposing 'bourgeois liberalism', and his overtly political poems often adopt a harshly polemical stance. The three 'Hymns to Lenin' celebrate Lenin's heroic ruthlessness, as if he were one of Carlyle's heroes who represents 'the flower and iron of the truth' and has the courage to stand apart from 'the majority will that accepts the result'. Even so, MacDiarmid's brand of millennial socialism has little to do with 'bread and butter problems', for he regards all political goals and structures as merely the first steps towards a far more radical – evolutionary – reorganisation of man's physical and spiritual resources. 'The Seamless Garment', set in a Langholm woollen-mill, makes just this point in a good-humoured way, using a low-key colloquial Scots to explain it to a 'cousin' who works there:

The haill shop's dumfoonderin'
 To a stranger like me.
Second nature to you; you're perfectly able
 To think, speak and see
Apairt frae the looms, tho' to some
That doesna sae easily come.

Lenin was like that wi' workin' class life,
    At hame wi't a'.
His fause movements couldna been fewer,
    The best weaver Earth ever saw.
A' *he'd* to dae wi' moved intact
    Clean, clear, and exact.

A poet like Rilke did the same
    In a different sphere,
Made a single reality – a' a'e 'oo' –   all one wool
    O' his love and pity and fear;
A seamless garment o' music and thought
But you're ower thrang wi' puirer to tak' tent o't.   too caught up with
                                                       [poverty to heed it
What's life or God or what you may ca't
    But something at ane like this?

In Christian doctrine the seamless garment represents the
unity between Christ's life and his divine being, but 'Second
Hymn to Lenin' recognises the practical difficulties of reaching
that state ourselves without being 'Unremittin', relentless, / Organised to the last degree'. Thus he extols the ruthless
concentration of Lenin's vision – those 'lizard eyes' – and the
cold and granite-hard creed which will be necessary to realise
'The Skeleton of the Future'. In the meantime the poet could
not earn enough to support his family and they were practically
destitute until friends rallied to their support in the spring of
1933 and found them a cottage in the Shetlands. At last
MacDiarmid had made a break with his problems in Scotland
and London, and for the next nine years he committed himself
to living and writing on the remote island of Whalsay.

MacDiarmid was stunned by the Shetlands. His health was
poor and they were living at little more than subsistence level,
but the remote beauty of this treeless landscape, caught
between the sea and the vast northern skies, offered an austere
peace and a return to fundamentals. Letters to William Soutar
and Neil Gunn, and a chapter in *The Islands of Scotland* (1939) all
testify to this new inspiration:

the vivifying element of water breaking up the land everywhere, and the
strange glories of the displays of the Aurora Borealis; and beautiful when
these are absent, in an awe-inspiring way, like a foreglimpse of the end of
the world! – bedrock indeed! – Earth's final state to which all else has been
tending under all the veils of Maya – a world of stone, water, and light. . . .

The family ate seagull-eggs and mackerel, cut peat for their fire, and MacDiarmid began to write longer poems, 'valuable new departures' he thought, in a cool and icily controlled English diction. He undertook prose too, in order to earn a living, and in 1934 his essays appeared in *At the Sign of the Thistle* (1934), while a collaboration with Lewis Grassic Gibbon resulted in an irreverent and entertaining book called *Scottish Scene or The Intelligent Man's Guide to Albyn*. In 1938 he founded the *Voice of Scotland*, a quarterly dedicated to 'Scottish Workers' Republicanism *à la* John Maclean', which published work by several of the younger poets – the 'second wave' of the Renaissance – including Norman MacCaig, George Bruce, Sorley Maclean and George Campbell Hay. The magazine reached five issues before the outbreak of war stopped it.

Stony Limits and Other Poems (1934) was the poet's most substantial and challenging collection for years. It contained fine work in Scots, including a set of 'Shetland Lyrics', 'Harry Semen' and 'Ode to All Rebels', but he was using English for political poems such as 'The Belly Grip' and 'John Maclean', and most especially for those 'new departures'. These turned out to be long meditations on scientific, geological and philosophical themes, full of obscure technical terms and a deliberately intellectualised diction – verses as austere and hard as the Shetland coast itself. There are poems in memory of Rilke and Charles Doughty (of *Arabia Deserta*), whose visions had also taken them into remote and desert landscapes of the spirit; and in the same vein 'Lament for the Great Music' welcomes pibroch as the sternest and loveliest art of all – 'like the metaphysics of light . . . in the grey life of these islands.' The most outstanding of these productions is 'On a Raised Beach', a meditation on death, truth and the 'bedrock' of the world, and one of the finest existential poems in modern literature.

If one can compare MacDiarmid's career with that of T. S. Eliot, then the energy of *A Drunk Man* would correspond to *The Waste Land*, and the philosophical restraint of 'On a Raised Beach' would stand on equal terms with *Four Quartets*, except that the Scot, unlike Eliot, gives himself up to the absolute and unrelenting materiality of the world:

What happens to us
Is irrelevant to the world's geology
But what happens to the world's geology
Is not irrelevant to us.
We must reconcile ourselves to the stones,
Not the stones to us.
Here a man must shed the encumbrances that muffle
Contact with elemental things, the subtleties
That seem inseparable from a humane life, and go
    apart
Into a simpler and sterner, more beautiful and
    oppressive world,
Austerely intoxicating; the first draught is
    over-powering;
Few survive it . . . .

The 'raised beach' in question is an ancient shoreline left far
from the movements of any contemporary tide, and the
'otherness' of this strange world is literally conjured up in the
poem's opening lines with an incantation of magically unap-
proachable words – 'Deep conviction or preference can seldom / Find direct terms in which to express itself':

All is lithogenesis – or lochia,
Carpolite fruit of the forbidden tree,
Stones blacker than any in the Caaba,
Cream-coloured caen-stone, chatoyant pieces,
Celadon and corbeau, bistre and beige,
Glaucous, hoar, enfouldered, cyathiform,
Making mere faculae of the sun and moon,
I study you glout and gloss . . . .

'These stones are one with the stars' writes the poet, with the
same imaginative leap from domestic to cosmic which characterised the early lyrics. He insists too that 'This is no heap of
broken images', and, if the phrase reminds us of *The Waste
Land*'s spiritual despair, it serves to emphasise MacDiarmid's
refusal to submit to the comfort of organised religion – 'Let men
find the faith that builds mountains / Before they seek the faith
that moves them'. In place of faith the poet asks only that we
'Be ourselves without interruption / Adamantine and inexorable', although the task may well require that men become like
stones themselves by some 'immense exercise of will, / Incon-
ceivable discipline, courage, and endurance, / Self purification

and anti-humanity'. MacDiarmid celebrates the 'deadly clarity' of this materialism throughout, even if his tone is unmistakably reminiscent of Knox and the rock-hard inheritance of Scottish Calvinism: 'Listen to me – Truth is not crushed; / It crushes, gorgonises all else into itself. . . . Do not argue with me. Argue with these stones.' The poem ends with a call to 'participate' in material life – which 'is nearest of all and easiest to grasp'; except that man may have to come face to face with the inevitability of his own death before he sees that 'barren but beautiful reality' clearly enough: 'I lift a stone; it is the meaning of life I clasp / Which is death . . . .'

It seems likely that his philosophical confrontation with a universe of stones, not to mention years of strain and the hardships of life on the island, took a considerable toll on MacDiarmid's health, and he suffered a complete nervous and physical collapse in the summer of 1935. His condition was serious and friends arranged for him to enter hospital in Perth, where he spent seven weeks in care. Recovery was slow and a photograph of the time shows an emaciated and exhausted figure, like a prisoner of war who has just been released from some frightful camp. Back on Whalsay, he soon picked up the threads of his indefatigable correspondence and renewed contacts with the outside world. But he had not lost his sense of literary and political isolation, and his contentious absolutism, which had an air of desperation about it, led him to break with many old friends and fellow writers. Edwin Muir had been a friend since the twenties, when they both contributed to the *New Age*, but now that Muir had come to live in St Andrew's he was reassessing his views on the future of literature in Scots. Despite his early enthusiasm for the language (and a few ballad-like poems of his own), he had come to believe that the use of Scots only encouraged a split between thinking and feeling, and offered no hope for a national literature for as long as English prevailed as well. He thought that Scots poets would do better to use English, and worse still, from the point of view of MacDiarmid's hopes for creative contradiction, he held that the 'Caledonian antisyzygy' could only result in a sterile cultural impasse. When Muir expressed these views in *Scott and Scotland* (1936), MacDiarmid felt betrayed and launched a bitter personal attack which ended their friendship and emphasised his own isolation as a John Maclean socialist at odds with what he took to be liberal or reactionary tendencies in Scottish culture and politics. On these grounds too he parted company with Neil Gunn, whose success as a novelist was about to be confirmed with *Highland River*.

More prose projects were planned, and although some fell by the wayside others, such as *Scottish Eccentrics* (1936) and *The Islands of Scotland* (1939), brought in much-needed royalties. He also wrote *Lucky Poet. A Self-Study in Literature and Political Ideas* (1943), in which he set out to explain himself by way of an infuriating and entertainingly wayward chronicle of his multitudinous interests and opinions. The book also contained passages from unpublished long poems and a new assessment of the Gaelic spirit. MacDiarmid had already produced 'Lament for the Great Music', and a translation of MacMhaighstir Alasdair's *Birlinn Chlann Raghnaill* had followed from his meeting with Sorley Maclean in 1934; now the 'Gaelic Muse' and three 'Dìreadh' poems appeared in *Lucky Poet*. In these and other verses, MacDiarmid invoked the Celtic spirit, and an 'East–West synthesis' with Russia, as necessary opposition to what he saw as the commercial values and the cultural imperialism of an English-speaking ascendancy in the Western world. The same resistance to received values and literary modes inspired his plans for an epic poetry which would cast off the 'irresponsible lyricism in which sense impressions/ Are employed to substitute ecstasy for information' ('The Kind of Poetry I Want'). In the cause of that 'information' MacDiarmid redefined Celtic complexity and developed Duncan Bàn Macintyre's penchant for lengthy objective description, until his own verses became vast extended catalogues, full of borrowings from a host of unacknowledged prose sources, as if he were determined to list everything that interested him in the material universe. MacDiarmid spent the rest of his life working over these epic poems from the late thirties and early forties. They were supposed to come together in a *magnum opus* to be called 'Mature Art', only sections of which – such as *In Memoriam James Joyce* (1955) – have ever appeared.

Even if 'Mature Art' did not materialise, the poems that were written under its influence offer an extraordinary 'vision of world language', as if the poet has decided to relinquish his creative and image-making power in favour of merely listening to the details of the world as it 'speaks' itself, choosing only to select examples, perhaps, from that fascinating monologue:

> They are not endless these variations of form
> Though it is perhaps impossible to see them all.
> It is certainly impossible to conceive one that doesn't
>   exist.
> But I keep trying in our forest to do both of these . . . .
>
> ('In Memoriam James Joyce'; also 'In the Caledonian
>   Forest', from *Stony Limits*)

The principle behind these catalogue poems was anticipated by one of the characters in *Annals of the Five Senses*, who observed that, 'if every opinion is equally insignificant in itself, humanity's bewilderment of thought is a mighty net which somehow holds the whole truth'. The 'world language' poems were MacDiarmid's mightiest 'net' ever in the attempt to match the thistle, to capture Cencrastus, or to achieve 'the diamond body'. Scientific detail and detachment has not dimmed the poet's sense of sudden wonder at the unity of all things when 'time whuds like a flee' and microcosm and macrocosm come together before his eyes:

> What after all do we know of this terrible 'matter',
> Save as a name for the unknown and hypothetical
>   cause
> Of states of our own consciousness? There are not two
>   worlds,
> A world of nature, and a world of human
>   consciousness,
> Standing over against one another, but one world of
>   nature
> Whereof human consciousness is an evolution,
> I reminded myself again as I caught that sudden
>   breathless glimpse,
> Under my microscope, of unexpected beauty and
>   dynamic living
> In the world of life on a sliver of kelp
> Quite as much as the harpooning of a forty-two foot
>   whale shark.
>
> ('Diamond Body', 1939)

MacDiarmid called such works a 'poetry of fact'. Truly he had abandoned 'lyricism' in favour of 'information', often culled from other sources, and perhaps he had abandoned poetry altogether. The literary status of these works still provokes controversy, and analogies might be made with Ezra Pound, who devoted the latter half of his life to the *Cantos* only to question their worth in the end. MacDiarmid managed to sustain faith in his project, but it did get increasingly unrealisable and perhaps more and more unreadable as the years went by.

The Second World War imposed its own priorities on the poet and MacDiarmid was conscripted in 1941, leaving Whalsay to become a fitter in a munitions-factory in Glasgow, later transferring to work as first engineer on a Norwegian vessel servicing ships in the Clyde estuary. When the war ended, MacDiarmid found himself, at the age of fifty-three, without regular work and with poems too long and too abstruse for easy publication. Undaunted, he threw himself back into public life by standing as an independent Nationalist candidate for Kelvingrove during the 1945 general election. He lost his deposit and parted company once again with the SNP. Few political parties could satisfy or tolerate his contentious, contradictory and idealistic nature for long. He himself saw no necessary conflict between his communism and his Scottish nationalism, but neither of the two parties concerned was very happy about his affiliations with the other and he continued to fluctuate between them.

MacDiarmid revived the *Voice of Scotland* and renewed his friendship with the younger writers on the literary scene. In 1950 he was awarded a Civil List pension and visited Russia – the first of several visits to Eastern European countries, where his status was high. In 1951 a small farm cottage became available at Brownsbank, near Biggar, some twenty-six miles from Edinburgh, and the Grieve family moved in. Edinburgh University students helped to modernise it and Valda Grieve still lives in this comfortable little house, which is lined with books and portraits of the poet.

As the last of the early modern giants in the generation of Eliot, Pound, Yeats and Joyce, MacDiarmid enjoyed the stimulation of controversy to the end, and his spirit, intellect and courage were unimpaired until in September 1978 cancer killed him at the age of eighty-six. He is buried on a hillside cemetery above Langholm. He was the first Scottish poet for generations to draw on the full canon of his country's literary tradition and to add a substantial contribution of his own. Thus his poetry embraces lyrical subtlety and the simple force of the ballads, the goliardic glee of Dunbar and the bitter polemic of Iain Lom. He unites Duncan Bàn's loving catalogue of the familiar landscapes of Scotland with John Davidson's scientific and philosophical abstractions, just as his poetic voice moves from colloquial Scots to the elitist and passionate tones of Carlyle. Whatever the outward style, his work shows a Blakean delight in the movement of the spirit and a materialistic delight in the physical universe, as he tries to show us 'the fundamental similarity of all activities', or the mystery to be found in the chemistry of water – 'aye, and ilka drap a world / Bigger than a' Mankind has yet unfurled'.

Edwin Muir (1887–1959)

As if to satisfy the principle of 'Caledonian antisyzygy', MacDiarmid's position as the major poet of the Renaissance movement is balanced by the life and work of Edwin Muir, a quiet, shy man five years his senior, who came from the Orkney Isles. For a time, in fact, Muir was better known to English and American readers than his friend from the Borders. MacDiarmid's rejection of him in the 1930s had to do with Muir's political and cultural opinions, but the two men always did possess radically different poetic sensibilities. MacDiarmid's work is charged with lyrical, linguistic, intellectual or polemical energy, while Muir adopts an English verse of calm and neutral tone to meditate on time and the timeless by way of classical allusions or images drawn from the realms of childhood, mythology or dreams.

Muir's first book of poetry appeared in the same year as *Sangschaw*. He was living in London at the time and had already made a small reputation as a journalist and literary critic, writing as 'Edward Moore', for Orage's *New Age* – an idiosyncratically radical journal which numbered Pound and MacDiarmid among its contributors. Muir had come to the capital in 1919 with his new wife, a Shetland girl called Willa

Anderson (1890–1970) who was to become a novelist in her own right with *Imagined Corners* (1931) and *Mrs Ritchie* (1933). The couple worked together in translating German literature, and are particularly remembered for their versions of Kafka. At first Muir was oppressed by London, and his already insecure psychological state was made worse by the size and anonymity of the city. His marriage was a happy one, however; he made friends and began to adjust; and Orage encouraged him to undertake Jungian analysis. This experience led to the unlocking of his creative capacity, as he kept a dream diary and began to reconstruct the meaning of his life with the help of images and archetypes from his subconscious. Such insights were to become central to his poetry, with its neo-Platonic sense of some timeless pattern beyond the contingent everyday. The couple moved to Europe in 1921 and lived and travelled there for three years before returning to England. Muir remembered Prague, Italy and Austria with gratitude – 'everyone should live his life twice', he wrote, and indeed he went over his old life and exorcised old griefs during that happy time abroad. Free at last, he began to write poetry at the age of thirty-five.

First Poems (1925) shows the influence of the Scots ballads and Heine, with the adoption of ballad stanzas (he experimented with Scots only briefly) to convey a childlike sense of simplicity and suspended wonder. Time seems to stand still and the world shrinks to a toy in 'Childhood':

> Grey tiny rocks slept round him where he lay,
>   Moveless as they, more still as evening came,
> The grasses threw straight shadows far away,
>   And from the house his mother called his name.

The mood is characteristic, and further insight can be gained into Muir's mature work from his account of how the 'Ballad of Hector in Hades' came to him:

> I must have been influenced by something, since we all are, but when I try to find out what it was that influenced me, I can only think of the years of childhood. . . . These years had come alive, after being forgotten for so long, and when I wrote about horses they were my father's plough horses as I saw them when I was four or five, and a poem on Achilles pursuing Hector round the walls of Troy was really a resuscitation of the afternoon when I ran away, in real terror, from another boy as I returned from school. The bare landscape of the little island became, without my knowing it, a

universal landscape over which Abraham and Moses and Achilles and Ulysses and Tristram and all sorts of pilgrims passed; and Troy was associated with the Castle, a mere green mound, near my father's house.   (*An Autobiography*, 1954)

It is not difficult to understand the origins of Muir's unhappiness as a young man, nor the sense of mythopoeic timelessness which haunts his verse. They both go back to his childhood on Orkney, and in a sense all his poems, although they never speak directly about himself, stem from a single biographical and metaphysical insight which he rediscovered there. As the youngest of six children, the poet was raised in the loving shelter of his father's farm on Orkney, and from his sixth to his eighth year the family lived on the little island of Wyre. He never forgot this idyllic experience of freedom and innocence, and in later life he came to see his childhood as a dream of Eden itself. The dream was all the more vivid when it stopped, for his father was evicted when Muir was fourteen and the family had to move to Glasgow in 1901.

It was as if they had travelled forward in time from a place whose seasonal and communal pattern of life went back to earliest days. Muir used to say that he was born 250 years ago, and when he finally met the industrial and urban age it came as a grim shock. Within four years both his parents died and two of his brothers as well, from consumption and a tumour in the brain. Muir was on his own at the age of nineteen. He earned his living as a clerk in a variety of offices, and in his own time he taught himself German, read Nietzsche, joined the ILP and educated himself as best he could. Latterly he spent two years in the office of a factory at Fairport where rotting bones were rendered down to make charcoal and fat. Already nervous and in poor health, he conceived a lasting dread of the place, and it seemed the very image of his unhappiness. Things improved towards the end of the war when he began to write for the *New Age*, and in Glasgow he made friends with Denis Saurat and the musician F. G. Scott. Then he met and married Willa – 'the most fortunate event in my life' – and the pair of them set off for London. He did exorcise the bone factory in the end, for he used his poetry as a means of personal reintegration: to discover a glimpse of Eden beyond the stench, and the stray dogs fighting over railway trucks of rancid bones.

In the late twenties the Muirs translated Kafka's *The Castle* and began to write novels for themselves. Edwin produced *The Marionette* (1927), a historical piece called *The Three Brothers* (1931) and *Poor Tom* (1932), which was closely based on his grim years in Glasgow and Greenock. A rather diffuse poem-sequence called *Variations on a Time Theme* (1934) did not escape echoes of T. S. Eliot's style. By 1935 the Muirs and their son were in St Andrew's, and Edwin made a sympathetic but curiously detached analysis of his country in *Scottish Journey* (1935) and then offered his controversial reassessment of its culture in *Scott and Scotland* (1936). He diagnosed something like Eliot's 'dissociation of sensibility' in which the Scots had long been divided between Lallans and English without a 'homogenous language' to convey thought as well as feeling. He admired MacDiarmid as an exception to this rule, but his general opinion was that Scots writers should settle for English. The fact that MacDiarmid was beginning to write in English himself at just this time did not save Muir from his fury.

The poet was fifty years old when his second collection, *Journeys and Places* (1937), developed its imagery of time and fate as a 'stationary journey' endlessly repeated by poets, heroes, lovers or Trojan slaves. These poems reflect the distinction which he liked to make between the 'story' and the 'fable' (this was to be the title of his autobiographical study in 1940) to show how the archetypal pattern of a fable can be discerned within the everyday, historical details of the 'story'. So his symbols become emblems, or heraldic devices on a shield – one of his favourite images – and 'Merlin' and 'The Enchanted Knight' share the same road with 'Ibsen' and 'Mary Stuart', all somehow on the way back in search of some 'Solitary' or 'Unattained' or 'Dreamt of Place' before, or beyond, man's fall from grace. Muir uses simple ballad-forms and a dispassionately plain diction for this elusive metaphysical theme and a lightly and skilfully measured lyricism:

> There is a road that turning always
>   Cuts off the country of Again,
> Archers stand there on every side
>   And as it runs time's deer is slain,
>   And lies where it has lain.

('The Road')

In St Andrew's the poet felt frustrated and isolated and began once again to review his life, having come to realise that his creative vision was essentially religious. When war broke out, he and Willa made ends meet as best they could until 1942, when Edwin was offered a post in Edinburgh with the British Council. In 1946 he went to Prague for three years as Director of the British Institute, but post-war Czechoslovakia was an unhappy place in the throes of a Communist take-over, and Muir felt that one kind of oppression had merely been supplanted by another. The couple were glad to return to London and take another British Council post in Rome, where Edwin found himself deeply moved by the Catholic Church's emphasis on incarnation and mystery. Muir's *Essays on Literature and Society* (1949) confirmed his reputation as a literary theorist and critic, and in 1950 he returned to Scotland to become the much-admired warden of Newbattle, an unconventionally creative college for adult education just outside Edinburgh.

The three volumes of poems from these years – and especially *The Labyrinth* (1949) – contain most of Muir's finest work, and his last collection, called *One Foot in Eden*, followed in 1956. The inwardly metaphysical themes of 'The Journey Back' – age, guilt, redemption, mystery and sweetness – are still pursued, but the grimmer historical experience of the forties, and his own frustrations with Scotland, gave a needed edge to other poems. 'Scotland 1941' rises to rage at what he saw as the pernicious influence of Knox and Presbyterianism on his country and its long history of futile internal strife – 'Such wasted bravery idle as a song, / Such hard-won ill . . . .' (He had taken a similar line in the study of Knox which he wrote in 1929.) 'The Incarnate One' and 'Scotland's Winter', from the last collection, offer a vision of his homeland crippled by 'the fleshless word' where 'all the kings before / This land was kingless, / And all the singers before / This land was songless' lie locked under ice 'content / With their poor frozen life and shallow banishment'. Muir also drew on his post-war European experience in poems such as 'The Refugees', 'The Good Town' and 'The Interrogation', and gains a typically understated power – not unlike the spirit of Kafka in places – by refusing to be specifically biographical or documentary:

My old friends
(Friends ere these great disasters) are dispersed
In parties, armies, camps, conspiracies.
We avoid each other. If you see a man
Who smiles good-day or waves a lordly greeting
Be sure he's a policeman or a spy.
We know them by their free and candid air.

('The Good Town')

Stranger images of dread, confusion or loss appear in 'The Combat', which was directly based on a dream, or 'The Horses', which describes the symbolic return of the old ways after some future holocaust, or 'The Return', which develops his understanding of our life as if it were a strange journey back to reconsider childhood. Muir's vision reached one of its most evocatively mysterious expressions in 'The Labyrinth', in which his theme is mirrored by the Kafkaesque and labyrinthine extension of his syntax in an opening sentence which unwinds for thirty-five lines without a break. Theseus seems to have emerged from the Minotaur's maze, but nothing is certain, and he still sees the mark of the labyrinth in the landscape all around:

all the roads
That run through the noisy world, deceiving streets
That meet and part and meet, and rooms that open
Into each other – and never a final room –
Stairways and corridors and antechambers
That vacantly wait for some great audience,
The smooth sea-tracks that open and close again,
Tracks undiscoverable, indecipherable,
Paths on the earth and tunnels underground,
And bird-tracks in the air – all seemed a part
Of the great labyrinth.

He is haunted by a vision of a perfect, toy-like world, or perhaps it was the truly real world – a Platonic ideal beyond the shadows of the cave – but, then again, nothing is certain. The difficult double negatives of lines such as 'I could not live if this were not illusion', and the poem's brooding last lines, epitomise the tale which precedes them (and the experience of trying to read it) so that by implying a familiar context which we cannot place, they throw everything into doubt again:

Oh these deceits are strong almost as life.
Last night I dreamt I was in the labyrinth,
And woke far on. I did not know the place.

After a year as Norton Professor at Harvard in 1955, Muir retired to Swaffham Prior near Cambridge, where he died in the first week of 1959. *An Autobiography* (1954) gives a memorably sensitive and unegocentric account of the poet's travels and his absorption with his inner vision, and Willa Muir's memoir *Belonging* (1968) adds further details of their life together.

Muir's concern to find the 'fable' as a state of grace beyond the circumstance of history is absolutely contrary to MacDiarmid's furious dedication to the specific material details of the world. Yet the Orcadian does have affinities with other Scottish writers, and most notably with the mythopoeic patterns which Grassic Gibbon and Neil Gunn sought to establish in their novels during the thirties. Perhaps the impulse to seek a place outside time has been an attempt to escape the pressure of past history on the Scottish psyche, or to evade the problems of present politics; or perhaps it has been an attempt to reassess that history and to align it towards more creative developments in the future. Gibbon and Gunn were the most outstanding novelists of the Scottish Renaissance, the two figures whose books most surely complement the poetic achievements of MacDiarmid, Muir and Sorley Maclean, and yet, of course, they were not alone.

Compton Mackenzie (1883–1974)

Among the first to support the new political feeling in the north was Compton Mackenzie, who moved from London to Barra in 1928. Born in England and educated at London and Oxford, Mackenzie abandoned his studies in law to write for the stage – his father was an actor and his sister Fay Compton was a star in Barrie's plays in the 1920s. Mackenzie's youthful milieu was Edwardian literary London, in which he cultivated a romantic and dashing personality. Success did not come, however, until he turned to prose fiction and embarked on a long and prolific career. Life behind the scenes of a variety theatre provided him with the best-selling material for *Carnival* (1912), followed by *Sinister Street* (1913), which was particularly admired by Henry James and Ford Madox Ford. The book is a lengthy semi-autobiographical 'development novel' which tells of Michael Fane's growth to maturity from childhood to Oxford, and from there to London and experiences in the shadier parts of society. It is a long novel with atmospheric settings, and its approach to sexual frankness made it something of a *cause célèbre* when circulating-libraries tried to restrict access to it. Mackenzie developed the scenario by carrying characters over into four further books.

The First World War took Mackenzie – now in his thirties – to the campaign in the Dardanelles (*Gallipoli Memories*, 1928) and thence to a leading role in British Intelligence in Greece and the Aegean, recounted in *Extremes Meet* (1928). He delighted in the Mediterranean and continued to produce novels after the war, visiting Norman Douglas at Capri, where he renewed a friendly acquaintance with D. H. Lawrence. The Englishman could not quite approve of Mackenzie's theatrical manner, and satirised him later in 'The Man who Loved Islands'. Certainly the Scot was a flamboyant and patrician figure, and it was typical of his romantic nature that he should express his commitment to Scotland in the post-war years by setting up home in the remote island of Barra. He was a founder member of the National Party, and in those early years Mackenzie, MacDiarmid and the party's first president, Cunninghame Graham, made a formidably eclectic trio on political platforms throughout the country. Mackenzie remained an enthusiastic nationalist to the end of his life, but up to this point he had not dealt with questions of Scottish character or politics in any of his novels. These issues finally appear, if indirectly, in *The Four Winds of Love*, a series of six volumes published between 1937 and 1945.

With a truly Scottish didactic exhaustiveness, Mackenzie's *magnum opus* is a lengthy romance of travel, ideas and, once again, semi-autobiographical character-development. The hero of the sequence is Juan Pendarves Ogilvie – public-schoolboy, playwright, traveller, lover, philosopher, politician and pedagogue – and each book adds a few more years to his odyssey, from the beginning of the century to the outbreak of the Second World War. Mackenzie explained that his plan was to equate the four winds with 'four love stories and four philosophies of love and four decades of a man's life', and he associated different seasons, political motifs and different countries from his own travels with each 'wind' in turn. The action starts with early life and love in England from 1900 to 1911 and moves to Poland (*The East Wind of Love*); then it shifts to love and war under the South Wind of the Mediterranean from 1912 to 1917; thence to the post-war years in America and the plight of Ireland and Ogilvie's hopes for nationalism in the rise of Mussolini (*The West Wind of Love* and *West to North*); finally the sequence comes round to the North Wind, with Ogilvie's home on a Hebridean island and his (and Mackenzie's) hopes for a Catholic Christian confederation of small Celtic nations. The hero renews his travels in Europe until Hitler's increasingly grandiose vision of Nordic nationalism makes him flee from the coming of a new winter to seek the sunshine of the Greek isles. *The Four Winds of Love* offers over three thousand pages of travel, complicated love-affairs and political, personal and philosophical discourse, and in the end the tireless eloquence of its hero–spokesman may overwhelm all but the most dedicated reader.

After the 1940s, Mackenzie became best known and loved for a light-hearted series of Highland farces, featuring a cantankerous, English-educated laird called 'Ben Nevis' (*The Monarch of the Glen*, 1941), or the natives of the island of 'Todday', most famous in *Whisky Galore* (1947). The author was knighted in 1952, an honour entirely in keeping with his colourful role as a literary personality, dividing his time between Edinburgh and the south of France. *Thin Ice* (1956), his last serious novel, was a sympathetic treatment of public scandal in the life of a homosexual. In later years Mackenzie dedicated himself to ten volumes ('Octaves') of exhaustively detailed personal reminiscence in *My Life and Times* (1963–71).

Eric Linklater (1899–1974)

Less directly involved with Scottish nationalism, Eric Linklater still shared Mackenzie's view that democracy and culture were best served by preserving the identity of small nations in the face of larger and more anonymous forces. He outlined these theories, very much in the spirit of the times, in *The Lion and The Unicorn* (1935) and Mackenzie dedicated the first volume of the *Four Winds* sequence to Linklater as his 'junior contemporary'. Linklater's father was a master mariner, and the novelist was actually born in Wales, but they were an Orkney family and he spent his childhood in the islands and later returned to live there for a number of years, before settling in the North East. Educated at Aberdeen Grammar School, Linklater joined the Black Watch in the last years of the First World War to serve as a private soldier in the trenches of France, where he nearly died from a bullet wound in the head. He went on to take a degree at Aberdeen University, changing from medicine to English literature, before going to Bombay for two years as a journalist on *The Times of India*. 1927 saw him back in the granite city as an English assistant at the university, where he began his first novel and gained a Commonwealth Fellowship which allowed him to travel through America from 1928 to 1930.

White-Maa's Saga, published in 1929, drew on the author's own background in Aberdeen and Orkney to tell of his student hero's growth to maturity and love, while *Poet's Pub* (1929), a light comedy in Chestertonian vein, was conceived as 'sheer . . . invention', an exercise in the craft of fiction. With its acceptance Linklater determined to earn his living as a writer, and his presence in America had already given him the material for what was to be his most successful and possibly his best book. He later describd *Juan in America* (1931) as a 'historical novel' about the United States during Prohibition – 'a country and a society which were vanishing even as I left them'. Juan Motley, descended from Byron's Don Juan, is Linklater's picaresque foil for a series of grotesque and hilarious adventures through the length and breadth of a nation apparently given over to college football, gangsterdom, bootlegging, movie-making and West Coast cults. Everywhere he goes Juan creates disorder, like a Byronically amorous but still innocent Candide. Linklater moves with linguistic precision from an ironically classical detachment, through straight-faced lampoon, to episodes of wild, chaotic farce, and this preference for absurdity and irreverent laughter was to become essential to his conception of satire.

Linklater took pride in his professional ability to suit style to subject-matter, and his next book was radically different, for

The Men of Ness (1932) adopted a stripped and austere prose as the most appropriate voice for the epic Norse past and a bare saga of Viking fate – although it is significant that it is the 'little man', Gauk, who survives when grim heroes die at the end. The author returned to live in Scotland, and a short-lived involvement with the National Party saw him adopted as their candidate for an East Fife by-election in 1933. He was 'resoundingly defeated' and *Magnus Merriman* (1934) gives a satirical account of the affair from the point of view of its hero. Magnus is a sexual and political adventurer who moves from the ambitious social circles of London to end up as an inefficient crofter on his native Orkney, where he is trapped in marriage by the shy guiles of a young, beautiful and pragmatically unimaginative farm girl. She may represent his punishment or the making of him, but it is difficult to tell, for he is a romantic chameleon who changes his stripes to suit his situation whatever it may be – city sophisticate or island poet. Linklater himself seems unsure, as if he were divided between his plain love of Orkney and a delight in travel and smart company. In later years he liked to describe himself as a 'peasant with a pen', but his sharp talent for society farce is very far from the worlds of Grassic Gibbon or George Mackay Brown. In this sense the impasse of Magnus Merriman's fate may be revealingly honest about Linklater's position in Scotland, and even his own careless brush with politics. Given the satirical portraits in his novel, it is not surprising that he soon broke with the Nationalists, although MacDiarmid remained delighted with his incarnation as 'Hugh Skene' and liked to quote it with approval.

More novels followed, including an exuberant comedy of upper-class manners exploded by gross farce in *Ripeness is All* (1935), and *Juan in China* (1937), which did not match the success of his American adventures, despite Linklater's actual visit to China. Long aware of the brutality of fascism in Germany, Linklater's liberal imperialism was equally critical of communist ideology, and his essays and novels from the late thirties and early forties reflect a concern to oppose oppression and find values worth fighting for. The outbreak of war found him in uniform again, helping to establish land defences for the fleet at Scapa Flow. He renewed his regard for what he saw as the simple decency of ordinary men in the ranks and helped to run a service newspaper for the Orkneys. Later he travelled widely as a freelance correspondent for the War Office, ending up with the campaign in Italy for which he wrote the official history. Among his autobiographical books *The Man on my Back* (1941) records his early life as a writer, and the travails of two wars are described in *Fanfare for a Tin Hat* (1970).

Linklater's Italian experiences produced *Private Angelo* (1946) in celebration of a peasant soldier's good sense in knowing when to run away. This is his most gently controlled statement in favour of the fallible individual, innocent of ideology and the 'serious' abstractions by which large organisations seek to control him. The novelist shows compassion for those who are fated to be maimed by life, and Angelo has to lose a hand before the war is done with him. 'Without irony history would be intolerable', a character remarks in a later novel, and to some extent Linklater's stance does depend on a rather precarious balancing-act between grotesque farce and melodrama, and sometimes his irony seems to slip into a rather heartless and mechanical process without final commitment. His later works include *Laxdale Hall* (1951), *The House of Gair* (1953) and *The Dark of Summer* (1956); he considered *Position at Noon* (1958) to be his wittiest novel and certainly, along with *A Man Over Forty* (1963), it recovers the wilder satirical exuberance of his earlier work.

By comparison with Linklater and Mackenzie, who wrote many entertaining best-sellers, the few works of David Lindsay and Fionn MacColla take a darker and more metaphysical twist. Lindsay's fantasy novels have affinities with the painful world of John Davidson or the strange landscapes of George MacDonald; while Fionn MacColla's angry muse has a vision of Scotland inherited from Douglas Brown or John Mac-Dougall Hay.

David Lindsay (1878–1945)

David Lindsay is best known for *A Voyage to Arcturus*, a philosophical fantasy novel of considerable power, yet his writing-career ended in obscurity and for years he enjoyed only an 'underground' reputation. Born in London, Lindsay lived most of his life in the south but took regular holidays with his father's relatives near Jedburgh, for it pleased him to maintain the connection despite the fact that his Scottish father had abandoned his wife and children without support, thus forcing his youngest son to give up hopes of university in order to earn a living as an insurance-broker. Lindsay became a shy and puritanical person, deeply interested in music and philosophy but largely self-educated in these fields. It is difficult not to identify the marks of this early history in his mature work and thought, with its almost Calvinistic distrust of pleasure and its urge to confront the face of God, and then to unmask and go beyond that ultimate figure of paternal authority. Lindsay's books are haunted by the need to identify a reality beyond reality, and the metaphysical fantasies of George MacDonald were a potent early influence on him. His rather unbending and cerebral nature responded equally to the writings of Schopenhauer and Nietzsche, who seemed to support his convictions about the importance of will in the universe, and of the need for the individual to adopt a lonely and prophetic stance in his quest for a truth beyond the mob. In this respect his affinities also lie with the unhappy spirits of James Thomson and John Davidson.

Lindsay led a life of bachelor routine in his his city office for over twenty years. When he was finally conscripted to help the war-effort, at the age of thirty-eight, he managed to find an administrative post with his regiment in yet another London office. The move led to a meeting with a vivacious eighteen-year-old, and within two months they were married. Spurred by his bride's enthusiasm, Lindsay determined to take up full-time writing. The couple found a house in Cornwall and by 1919 Lindsay had embarked on his first novel – derived from the notes and reflections of many years. His practical inexperience as a writer betrays itself in a clumsy pedantic prose, and he never did perfect his style or the ability to handle plot and character smoothly. Nevertheless, *A Voyage to Arcturus* (1920) is a work of such conceptual originality that it was accepted by the first publisher to read it.

Usually referred to as a fantasy, and sometimes mistaken for crude science-fiction, Lindsay's book is more properly an allegory of spiritual and philosophical search. The opening chapters depend on contrivances to do with a seance in Hampstead, and a crystal torpedo which takes off from a tower

on the North-East of Scotland to fly its passengers to the planet
Tormance under the double star of Arcturus. Once there, the
protagonist Maskull begins his quest to confront the nature of
the universe. He has already received premonitions of his fate
back on earth, where he knew Nightspore, who will later be
revealed as the *alter ego* of his spirit, and Krag, their mysterious
guide on the voyage. After landing, Maskull is separated from
his friends and sets out to look for them, like Bunyan's pilgrim
in some nightmarishly precise but undecipherable allegory. He
finds new colours on Tormance and grows extra organs for his
senses. He meets people whose names – Joiwind, Crimtyphon,
Panawe and Spadevil – might have come from one of Blake's
more obscure prophetic books. Nothing will turn out to be quite
what it seems in this world under a double star – the very image
of duality. Tormance is a stark place of strange sexuality bound
up with kindness, pain, nameless sensations, beauty, shame,
terror and successive deaths. Its ultimate nature is only
gradually and indirectly revealed to the reader as Maskull
journeys through grim landscapes and makes ambiguous
encounters with various semi-human creatures. When Maskull
finally arrives at the end of his quest it is only to meet death to
the sound of the eerie drumbeats, or heartbeats, which he had
first heard on the Scottish coast before parting. Yet through
death he rejoins his 'double', Nightspore, and moves to a
confrontation with Muspel, the source of all light. He finds that
Muspel is locked in Manichean conflict – like some eternal
symbiosis – with Crystalman, the shaping-force of worlds,
whose advocacy of pleasure, art and beauty turns out to be a
deceitful masquerade covering a shameful, vulgar, leering grin.
This, the true aspect of the material universe, has haunted the
novel from the start, for it has appeared on the face of every
creature in the moment after death. When Nightspore realises
this, he almost despairs, but Krag is there to assure him that
they will continue the moral combat, and that Crystalman will
not prevail. Maskull's journey is over. Nightspore's has only
begun. The book ends at this point, and Krag reveals that his
true name on Earth is 'pain'.

C. S. Lewis acknowledged the influence of *Arcturus* on his own
Perelandra novels, and successive readers and critics have
testified to the disturbing power of Lindsay's universe, suffused
as it is with symbols of music, repressed sexuality, shape-

changing, death, pain and moral effort. Against such a vision even his awkward prose comes to seem curiously effective. It is Lindsay's finest book and, although reviews were mixed and sales small, it achieved a serious critical reputation. Lindsay was encouraged and in the next three years he produced two further metaphysical fantasies, this time set in the contemporary everyday world. *The Haunted Woman* (1922) evokes the proximity of other times and realms of being with some brilliantly memorable and ambiguous images; *The Sphinx* (1923) is less effective, however, and neither book did very well. Lindsay immediately wrote *The Adventures of M. de Mailly* as a historical-romance potboiler, but it was not published until 1926. For the next five years he struggled with the drafts and revisions of his next novel, *Devil's Tor* (1932), but most readers found it humourless and wordy. The family moved to Sussex and eventually to Hove, near Brighton, where Mrs Lindsay ran a boarding-house to help support them. Her husband persevered with his writing and his philosophical notes, but his publishing-career was over and he died in 1945, in great pain from an abscess in the jaw for which he refused treatment. *The Violet Apple* (1976) did not find a publisher in Lindsay's lifetime, and his last book, *The Witch* (1976), was left unfinished. In the light of more recent studies, however, the later books still offer valuable insights into the unique and underrated imagination which produced *A Voyage to Arcturus*.

Tom Macdonald ('Fionn MacColla', 1906–75)

Tom Macdonald had only a little more luck with publishers during his career, and he shares something of Lindasy's austere and philosophical bias. A native of Montrose, Macdonald trained and worked as a teacher in the North-East before going to Palestine to teach in a Church of Scotland college at Safed. He had a happy childhood brought up as a member of the Plymouth Brethren – an extremely severe Presbyterian sect – but he later came to reject everything to do with the Reformed Church and eventually joined the Catholic faith. His critique of Protestantism is one of the themes of his first novel, *The Albannach* ('The Highlander'), which he began when he returned to Scotland in 1929. The condition of his country at the height of the Depression made him an active member of the National Party, and he went to Glasgow University to study Gaelic. Henceforth 'Fionn MacColla' dedicated himself to a vision of a transcendent Highland culture, which would be utterly opposed to the Kirk and the bourgeois interests of Scottish establishment and English imperialism alike. He defined Protestantism as the historical expression of a desire to control mankind by negating individuality and creativity, and hence he saw Knox as the first in a line of dictators leading to Lenin and Hitler. For Macdonald, history was the by-product of malign or benevolent forces in the human spirit, and as an imaginative writer he possessed a powerfully empathetic understanding of the negative pleasures to be gained from the Calvinistic exercise of the will.

The Albannach (1932) describes how Murdo Anderson grows away from the repressive faith of his home, only to be recalled from Glasgow University when his father dies. Returned to the narrow confines of life in a Highland village, he succumbs to an unwise marriage and comes close to alcoholism and suicide before he learns compassion and rediscovers his creative balance and a place in the community, too, by way of crofting, piping and traditional poetry. In typical style, Macdonald's prose adopts Murdo's point of view, and the physical details of local places and faces are brilliantly charged with his subjective intensity. The same effect characterises *And the Cock Crew* (1945), a novel of the Clearances whose central scene is a long debate between an old Gaelic bard and the local minister, Zachary Wiseman. 'Maighstir Sachairi' is the protagonist who first defends and then betrays his parishioners by encouraging them to submit to the most brutal of evictions as 'the will of God'. (The novel's title refers to Peter's betrayal of Christ.) The minister's tortured moments of certainty and doubt and his melodramatic death dominate the tale; and, although the quieter tones of the poet Fearchar imply a kinder vision, there is no sign of it at the end. If Gunn's *Butcher's Broom* was a poetically controlled protest against the Clearances, *And the Cock Crew* is a Gothic cry of philosophical anger.

The descriptive intensities of Macdonald's prose, and his occasional melodrama, recall aspects of *Gillespie* and *The House with the Green Shutters*, and his fiction gains further force through his fascinated and polemical hatred of Protestantism as part of a more universal 'nay-saying'. In this sense Macdonald's case against the Presbyterian conscience goes further than Hogg did, or Lockhart's *Adam Blair*. His theories were published in *At the Sign of the Clenched Fist* (1967), and a short autobiography, *Too Long in this Condition*, appeared posthumously in 1975. Macdonald worked as a head teacher in the Highlands in later years, but came to believe bitterly that fate, critics and other writers had been less than kind to his creative development, especially during his hard times in the thirties. His case is complex, for he was a flamboyant and unhappy personality whose real gift for vivid writing was fuelled and ultimately overwhelmed by his own philosophical obsessions. *Scottish Noël* (1958) and the debate *Ane Tryall of Heretiks* (1962) were potent fragments from what was to be a larger historical novel. After his death several other unpublished manuscripts were found among his papers, including a novel from the late fifties, *The Ministers* (1979).

Lindsay and Macdonald had a long struggle to find an audience for a few brilliantly flawed books, but the single most sustained and innovative achievement in modern Scottish fiction was made by a man who died when he was thirty-four, after only seven years as a serious writer.

James Leslie Mitchell ('Lewis Grassic Gibbon', 1901–35)

The three books in *A Scots Quair* were Mitchell's last and finest work. They give a powerful account of history and social change in Scotland between 1911 and 1932, and at the same time they explore the fate of a particular spirit, ancient, free and intuitive, in the face of the modern world. Mitchell found this spirit in the enduringly feminine psyche of his heroine Chris Guthrie, as she grows up in the rural North-East, and he associated it with his own mythopoeic vision of Scotland's past. Neil Gunn and Edwin Muir shared a similar understanding of how timeless values were to be found within the tradition – for Gunn they were Celtic, because he himself came from the Highlands, while Muir looked to the Eden of his childhood in Orkney. Mitchell is unique, however, in bringing his poetic vision into contact with life in the modern city and in confronting it with his own fiercely socialist principles – a conflict which led to difficult tensions which made the elegiac note of his art all the more poignant.

The author's sense of place could not have been more authentic, for *A Scots Quair* sprang from his own upbringing on crofts in the Howe of the Mearns, especially at Bloomfield above Inverbervie, later fictionalised as 'Blawearie' in the parish of 'Kinraddie'. Here is the heart of the rich farming-land which lies to the south of Stonehaven between the Grampians and the coast. The author liked to recall that he was 'of peasant rearing and peasant stock', and expressed pride 'that the land was so closely and intimately mine (my mother used to hap me in a plaid in harvest time and leave me in the lee of a stock while she harvested)'. Yet he was not fitted for farm work, and grew to be a sensitive and bookish boy, interested in archaeology and astronomy, with thoughts of becoming a journalist or an editor. Mitchell's village schoolmaster – a friend in later years – preserved his brightest pupil's early compositions and encouraged him to take secondary education at Mackie Academy in Stonehaven. But he was not to be a 'lad o' pairts', for Mitchell's teenage years were disturbed and unhappy and he walked out of school at the age of sixteen, to work as a junior reporter for the *Aberdeen Journal*. Stirred by the promise of the Russian Revolution in 1917 he became an enthusiastic communist; and when he went to work for the *Scottish Farmer* in Glasgow in 1919 his experiences of the unrest on Clydeside, and the terrible urban poverty which he found there, reinforced his commitment to revolutionary socialism. His career in journalism was cut short, however, when a minor scandal over the padding of expenses led to his dismissal without references. Greatly disturbed by the experience, he made a clumsy attempt at suicide and had to return home – under something of a cloud – to recover his bearings.

All too aware that his parents could not support him, and driven by the need to escape from his home background, he decided to join the army. He enlisted in August 1919 and spent the next three and a half years working for the Service Corps in Persia, India and Egypt; and his letters to Rebecca Middleton – who came from the croft next to Bloomfield – are full of a young man's enthusiasm for the romance of these distant countries and their ancient ruins. When Mitchell left the army in 1923,

Hugh MacDiarmid had just started his own literary campaign from Montrose, but they were not to meet until later and the younger man's own efforts brought him no success at all. After six months during which he 'nearly starved to death', Mitchell settled once again for the security of enlistment, joining the Royal Air Force this time, in which he served as a clerk on various stations in England until 1929. He tried his hand at poetry without finding a publisher, but one of his short stories won a magazine competition and, although it was to be another four years before he saw himself in print again, Mitchell was duly encouraged. He renewed contact with Rebecca Middleton – she was a civil servant in London – and the couple took a holiday together in the Mearns and married in the summer of 1925. Rebecca, or Ray as he called her, had to leave her job and times were hard for them during the next few years.

Mitchell persevered with more stories, planned a book on exploration, and worked on a novel to be called *Stained Radiance*, closely based on his ideas and experiences. Its heroine fore-shadows the later Chris Guthrie and his own ambivalent feelings of pride in and distaste for peasant life in Scotland, but is is an ironic and often an angry work, and many publishers rejected it. He continued to work at the manuscript while pursuing his interests in archaeology, anthropology and the culture of the Mayans and the Incas in America. He was particularly keen on 'Diffusionism', a theory which held that civilisation began with the discovery of agriculture in ancient Egypt and spread throughout the world, sweeping away a 'golden age' of primitive nomadic hunters in the process and bringing all the ills of property, nationalism and the slavery of labour in its place. The theory appealed to Mitchell's communist ideals and he associated the golden age in Scotland with the lost era of the aboriginal and matriarchal Picts, whose remote descendants were still, he felt sure, to be found among the peasants of his native North-East – far from the slums and factories of 'progress'. (He summarised this idiosyncratic account of prehistory and Scottish culture – including his regard for the Reformation as a people's cause – in a later essay called 'The Antique Scene' written for *Scottish Scene* in 1934.)

Mitchell's fortunes began to change when his speculative book *Hanno, or the Future of Exploration* was published in 1928. Early next year another of his Middle East stories was accepted for *Cornhill Magazine* – after the recommendation of H. G. Wells – and this led to the publication of twelve more in a cycle of tales later collected as *The Calends of Cairo* (1931). Mitchell could now leave the RAF with some hopes at last for his future as a writer. Articles on the Mayans had appeared in *Antiquity* and he already had a small reputation in this field. *Stained Radiance* came out in 1930, and Jarrold's, who were to publish nearly all his work, accepted his next novel too. *The Thirteenth Disciple* is another thinly disguised autobiographical book, filled with his interest in Diffusionism and particularly frank about his unhappy schooldays and his troubles in Glasgow. A daughter, Rhea, was born to the couple, and in 1931 they all moved to Welwyn Garden City, a genteel new town outside London. Leslie Mitchell poured his energies into more and more work, composing straight onto the typewriter, as was his habit, with few revisions. Within a year he produced two novels on the romance of Diffusionism – *Three Go Back* (1932), which was a time-travel fantasy about Atlantis, and *The Lost Trumpet* (1932). Both were well received by writers such as Compton Mackenzie and H. G. Wells, one of Mitchell's boyhood heroes. But Leslie's thoughts had already turned back to his native Mearns, enhanced by a sense of perspective gained in the south, and encouraged, perhaps, by the critical success being accorded at home to Neil Gunn's *Morning Tide* (1930).

Mitchell wrote *Sunset Song* (1932) in a single and remarkably sustained creative effort which lasted less than two months. It was published under his mother's name as the first in a planned trilogy of novels on the life of a girl called Chris Guthrie. These books were to give the definitive account of the land he loved and hated, with Chris as its spokesperson and the vessel for his own imaginative spirit. The second volume, *Cloud Howe*, appeared in 1933 and the series ended with *Grey Granite* in 1934. Early in the following year Mitchell suffered a perforated ulcer, and after an emergency operation he died on 7 February. He was a man of vivacious and unusually intense energy, but not even he could sustain the pressure of work to which he had committed himself at the end. In those last two years he produced seven more books, including a fine historical novel, *Spartacus* (1933), which shows his sympathy for the oppressed and the exploited. Then in 1934 there appeared a life of Mungo Park; *The Conquest of the Maya*; another time-travel adventure,

Gay Hunter; the collaboration (as Grassic Gibbon) with Hugh MacDiarmid in *Scottish Scene*; and, finally, nine short biographies of famous explorers published as *Nine against the Unknown*. Part of a further novel on North-East life was left unfinished when he died, and this was published in 1982 as *The Speak of the Mearns*. The trilogy remains his finest achievement, widely popular among Scottish readers and televised as three major serials.

The voice and personality of Chris Guthrie lies at the heart of all three books in *A Scots Quair*, but it is felt most strongly in *Sunset Song*, which deals with her upbringing and young womanhood. For all its failings and the occasional brutality of country folk, her home parish of Kinraddie still offers the security of an extended family circle. It stands for 'the Scots countryside itself', as the minister remarks wryly, 'fathered between a kailyard and a bonny briar bush in the lee of a house with green shutters', but the spell of the sunset will not last and all the kailyard securities will be swept away. In fact Gibbon had few illusions about country life: Chris's mother commits suicide, worn out by childbirth and terrified of another pregnancy, while her father, brutalised by toil and made still more severe by his religion, drives his son to emigrate and eventually suffers a paralysing stroke which leaves his daughter to struggle with the farm and to ward off his delirious sexual advances. In such circumstances Chris comes to physical and intellectual maturity, determined to be her own woman, divided between the two Chrisses 'that fought for her heart and tormented her':

> You hated the land and the coarse speak of the folk and learning was brave and fine one day and the next you'd waken with the peewits crying across the hills, deep and deep, crying in the heart of you and the smell of the earth in your face, almost you'd cry for that, the beauty of it and the sweetness of the Scottish land and skies.

This passage is typical of Gibbon's internalised colloquial narrative method, in which the impersonal but familiar 'you' encloses Chris, the community and the reader in an easy assumption of shared experience. To the same end, the novelist italicises speech and includes it in the narrative without breaking the flow of description or reported thought. In this way the whole book is integrated within Chris's sensibility as she recalls the key events of what passed before, advancing the story chapter by chapter, like a retrospective diary which returns to the 'present' at the end of each section. Chris carries out these acts of recollection while resting among standing stones beside a loch on the hill above her home. As her favourite private spot, this place sets her experiences against the passage of epochs, and allows Gibbon to express his Diffusionist feelings for the timeless value and innocence that once prevailed when the world was young. She has an affinity with these mysterious perspectives, and is haunted, in all three novels, by a sense that nothing endures but change itself, and beyond it all, the land which made her:

> The wet fields squelched below her feet, oozing up their smell of red clay from under the sodden grasses, and up in the hills she saw the trail of the mist, great sailing shapes of it, going south on the wind into Forfar, past Laurencekirk they would sail, down the wide Howe with its sheltered glens and its late, drenched harvests, past Brechin smoking against its hill, with its ancient tower that the Pictish folk had reared, out of the Mearns, sailing and passing, sailing and passing, she minded Greek words of forgotten lessons, Παντα῾ρει *Nothing Endures.*
>
> And then a queer thought came to her there in the drooked fields, that nothing endured at all, nothing but the land she passed across, tossed and turned and perpetually changed below the hands of the crofter folk since the oldest of them had set the Standing Stones by the loch of Blawearie and climbed there on their holy days and saw their terraced crops ride brave in the wind and sun. Sea and sky and the folk who wrote and fought and were learnéd, teaching and saying and praying, they lasted but as a breath, a mist of fog in the hills, but the land was forever, it moved and changed below you, but was forever, you were close to it and it to you, not at a bleak remove it held you and hurted you. And she had thought to leave it all!

Not surprisingly, the land and its elegiac and seductive voice features most strongly in *Sunset Song*, for the novel deals, after all, with Chris's sexual growth from girlhood to maturity and with her decision to stay at home to work the croft with her new husband Ewan Tavendale – a boy of Highland descent with a darker and more fragile temperament than her own. In this respect the book is indeed a 'song' which combines Hardy's sense of season, place and rural custom with a Lawrentian insight into the sexual and psychological intensities between two young people making a life together. But the novel has a social dimension as well, for modern transport and city life are making their presence felt, and finally the Great War – at first so little heeded by Kinraddie – marks or destroys everyone in the little community. All the trees in the neighbourhood are felled for timber, and larger and more commercial farming takes over until the old peasant crofter-class finally passes away. Ewan is brutalised by barrack-room life long before he is shot for desertion at the Front, and the fighting kills kindly Chae Strachan and even Long Rob of the Mill, who finally enlisted, despite his socialism and the objections of his conscience.

Chris herself heralds a more peaceful social change, for Long Rob was one of the few people in Kinraddie who was her intellectual equal (he was modelled on Ray Mitchell's father), and she is distinguished by her determination to remain spiritually and mentally her own person in the face of a community which offers only the narrowest and most domestic of roles to women. But her pride and her poetic sense of change make her a solitary figure too, and she finds another love, and a father for her young son Ewan, in the new minister of the parish, an idealistic young man called Robert Colquhoun. Chris cannot promise him her old self – for that belongs to her first husband – but she offers him 'maybe the second Chris, maybe the third'. The novel ends with Colquhoun's sermon at the dedication of a memorial to those who died in the war. Set among the standing stones, and followed by the playing of 'Flowers of the Forest' on the pipes, this scene serves to recall once again, older perspectives on mutability and human loss.

Sunset Song is not without its sentimental side, but Gibbon shows that subtle and mature art can be achieved beyond the Kailyard genre. In setting and development it has several striking similarities with a German novel called *Jörn Uhl* (1901) by Gustav Frenssen, and Gibbon may have read it in earlier years, although some similarities are inevitable in so far as both books deal with a common fund of peasant experience. Nevertheless, Gibbon's voice and his wider use of symbolism is decidedly his own, and his prose style is redolent of North-East Scots, for, although relatively few dialect words are used, his narrative rhythms remain distinctively local. Yet *Sunset Song* has no difficulty in communicating with its readers, and its evocation of the seasons and rural life has made it by far the most popular of the three novels, even in America, where it was widely praised. But the full scope of Gibbon's complex and disturbing vision is lost if the novel is studied on its own, for Chris will not find happiness in the end, and the world beyond Blawearie will offer little comfort. (Gibbon followed the success of his novel with three stories in the same vein for the *Scots Magazine*, and 'Smeddum' and 'Clay' were published again, along with 'Greenden' and two others, as part of the author's contribution to *Scottish Scene*.)

Appropriately enough, perhaps, since she has left the scenes of her childhood, Chris's sensibility is less central to the town of Segget, where her husband takes her in *Cloud Howe*. The doings and the gossip of the place, and the strike among the linen-spinners there, give a more social and political focus to their life together as the new minister and his wife, and the voice of the community can be heard more often as it joins Chris's voice in the narrative flow – not unlike the spiteful reports from the 'bodies' of Barbie.

Colquhoun calls his wife 'Chris Caledonia', observing wryly that he has 'married a nation', and indeed she does have a symbolic part to play in her progress from the setting sun of Kinraddie to the township of Segget and eventually – in *Grey Granite* – to the industrial city of 'Duncairn' at the height of the Depression, where her son will become a communist organiser. This movement towards a more immediate historical awareness is foreshadowed by her fascination with the Kaimes and the ruined castle there, which replaces the standing stones as her favourite vantage-point, evoking years of bloodshed, fallen barons and the sufferings of the Covenanters. Robert Colquhoun is an idealistic liberal socialist who preaches about the thousands of Christs who died in the war, supports the miners in the General Strike of 1926, and tries to assuage the cynicism and the political violence of the linen-workers. These spinners have always been an exploited class, for they were cannon-fodder in the war and are little more than that now to the owners of the mills. They are equally despised by the petty bourgeoisie, for Segget has lost men such as Long Rob and Chae – if it ever had them – and it is a community largely without wisdom, conscience or charity. Colquhoun starts well, but the struggle is too great for him. The General Strike fails and Chris's new baby dies at birth. She recovers, but her husband suffers a crisis of personal faith and terror – haunted by a vision of Christ and by the memory of an evicted worker's baby which was gnawed by rats. Finally his health collapses, for his lungs were gassed in the war, and when he dies Chris finds herself alone once again at the end of a grimmer book than *Sunset Song*.

She will survive, for beyond the social surface of the novel Gibbon shows us a woman grappling with her identity as if she were a succession of different Chrisses, each reacting to different men in her past and yet always remaining herself and, in some vital sense, untouched. This ancient spirit stands aloof from politics or her husband's religion, symbolised by the 'clouds' whose various formations are used to name the chapters of the book, just as the chapters of *Sunset Song* used the farming-seasons. Ewan and Chris's father were men of the earth, but Colquhoun's idealism has taken her beyond those fertile cycles to a more elevated and abstract point of view. Yet she cannot find substance in any of the doctrines of men, and, for her, even love itself is only another mirage from their busy world:

> Once Chris and Robert came to a place, out in the open, here the wind blew and the ground was thick with the droppings of sheep, where a line of the ancient stones stood ringed, as they stood in Kinraddie far west and below, left by the men of antique time, memorial these of a dream long lost, and hopes and fears of fantastic eld.
>
> Robert said that they came from the East, those fears, long ago, ere Pytheas came sailing the sounding coasts to Thule. Before that the hunters had roamed these hills, naked and bright, in a Golden Age, without fear or hope or hate or love, living high in the race of the wind and the race of life, mating as simple as beasts or birds, dying with a like keen simpleness, the hunting weapons of those ancient folk Ewan would find in his search of the moors. . . .
>
> And she thought then, looking on the shadowed Howe with its stratus mists and its pillars of spume, driving west by the Leachie bents, that men had followed these pillars of cloud like lost men lost in the high, dreich hills, they followed and fought and toiled in the wake of each whirling pillar that rose from the heights, clouds by day to darken men's minds – loyalty and fealty, patriotism, love, the mumbling chants of the dead old gods that once were worshipped in the circles of stones, christianity, socialism, national-ism – all – Clouds that swept through the Howe of the world, with men that took them for gods: just clouds, they passed and finished, dissolved and were done, nothing endured but the Seeker himself, him and the everlasting Hills.

The chapters of *Grey Granite* are named after the silicates and crystals to be found in that durable rock, reflecting the hardships of the Depression years in Duncairn, a big city on the east coast, modelled on the granite of Aberdeen with aspects of Dundee and Glasgow. Gibbon may not have been entirely at ease with an urban setting, and certainly the book, like *Cloud Howe* in places, bears the evidence of hasty work, for it came from that last and most desperate year of writing. It is a harsh and unsettling novel and many readers have found it difficult after the lyricism of the first volume. Yet it was clearly Gibbon's intention to disturb us in this way, for the granite imagery also charts young Ewan's commitment to communism as he comes to develop the same flinty dedication which MacDiarmid had admired in his hymns to Lenin. In fact, the book was dedicated to MacDiarmid, and Gibbon shared the poet's convictions, but his picture of Ewan has a darker side, for he appears to be an activist who will sacrifice his girl, his friends, and the truth itself to the cause of revolution. Ewan loses his idealism when he is physically beaten by the police for his part in a labour demonstration. He experiences a vivid identification with all suffering humanity, and from then on he has stone in his soul and the quiet and precocious child who collected flint arrow-heads in the hills around Segget has died within him. The passage is disturbing, masochistic and suffused with hatred:

> He was one with them all, a long wail of sobbing mouths and wrung flesh, tortured and tormented by the world's Masters while those Masters lied about Progress through Peace, Democracy, Justice, the Heritage of Culture. . . .
> And a kind of stinging bliss came over him, knowledge that he was that army itself – that army of pain and blood and torment that was yet but the raggedest van of the hordes of the last of the Classes, the ancient Lowly, trampling the ways behind it unstayable: up and up, a dark sea of faces, banners red in the blood from the prisons, torn entrails of tortured workers their banners, the enslavement and oppression of six thousand years a cry and a singing that echoes to the stars. No retreat, no safety, no escape for them, no reward, thrust up by the black, blind tide to take the first brunt of impact, first glory, first death, first life as it never yet had been lived –. . . .

Grey Granite offers no deliverance, nor could its author see an easy conclusion to the work. The city of factories, owners, shopkeepers, workers and sheer drudgery is seen through Chris's eyes as she helps to keep Ma Cleghorn's boarding-house, but the narrative is shared with Ewan and one of his worker friends, and, when the voices of various characters in the boarding-house are heard as well, the result is a comic and sometimes savage satire; but it means that the warmth of Chris's sensibility no longer infuses and controls the book. She marries again, but her husband, Ake Ogilvie – an old acquaintance from Segget – realises that he does not have her true self, and he grants her freedom by emigrating to Canada. Chris is finally alone and wholly given over to her vision of changeless change and independence in 'a world without hope or temptation, without hate or love, at last, at long last'. She moves to another cottage, in the countryside where her family lived before they moved to Blawearie, and she finds another vantage-point on the site of an ancient Pictish fort on the Hill of Fare. Here she reflects on the journey of her life and on the role of change as 'Deliverer, Destroyer and Friend in one', and she seems to die away in the closing sentence of the trilogy.

It is difficult not to feel that Chris has been somehow defeated – she is only in her forties and yet her life seems over. Ewan is left planning a workers' hunger march on London and his story is still to be decided. Perhaps Gibbon could see no further, for the novel ends in virtually contemporary times, with all the issues of the thirties necessarily unresolved and a heroine already much older in experience than he was himself. On the other hand, Chris's end returns us to a vision of the land in which she is the harbinger of a fundamentally feminine and disinterested faith in existence, simply for its own sake. The vision grew from Gibbon's poignant sense of his own lost past, and it sustains the trilogy at a poetic level, more moving, profound and problematical than any of his more 'masculine' and intellectual allegiances to Diffusionism or communism. Yet Chris simply drops out of history, and, although the future must belong with Ewan, Gibbon's heart seems to stay behind with the rain and the lapwings and the eternal stasis of Scotland's empty spaces. Thus *A Scots Quair* belongs with the several great books in Scottish literature which have dealt with the theme of the divided self and the spiritual antithesis between 'masculine' authority and 'feminine' sensitivity. Most of these novels forced a confrontation and ended tragically, but Gibbon's gift seems to be suspended between the two, although it is possible that Chris's early death tells us that it is time to leave the enduring power of 'Kinraddie' and all its sister villages in the heartland of Scottish letters.

The genre survives, however, for it is derived from common Scottish experience, and, like Chris Guthrie herself, it has great strength. It appears without ambiguity in the work of Fred Urquhart (b. 1912), whose first and autobiographical novel, *Time Will Knit* (1938), showed his interest in the stream-of-consciousness technique. His short stories contain strong Scots speech and a particularly realistic evocation of rural life – collected in *The Dying Stallion* (1967) and *The Ploughing Match* (1968). Vivid sentimental realism thrives in the work of Jessie Kesson (b. 1916), who re-creates a past North-East town and country scene in *The White Bird Passes* (1958) and *Glitter of Mica* (1963), while the stories and novels of John Reid, ('David Toulmin', b. 1913), a farm worker from the same region, revive the world of Grassic Gibbon in more melodramatic and emotive terms – *Hard, Shining Corn* (1972), *Blown Seed* (1976). Further novels of growth and development in the same vein include *The Taste of Too Much* (1960) by Cliff Hanley (b. 1922) and *The Magic Glass* (1981) by Anne Smith.

If Mitchell's fiction looks through Chris's spirit to find a golden age of free hunters long ago, Neil Gunn's origins offered him a similar ideal rather closer to home, and he was to develop this single vision of Highland landscape and culture through a long and productive literary career.

Neil M. Gunn (1891–1973)

Gunn grew up as a fisherman's son, the fifth of seven boys in a family of nine, living in Dunbeath near Helmsdale on the far north-east coast of Caithness, and, although he was not a native Gaelic speaker, he was always very aware of the Gaelic, Norse and Pictish influences in the region. He valued a Celtic inheritance in the face of the modern world and his first short stories were in the style of 'Fiona Macleod' and Neil Munro. He soon threw over their twilight fatalism, however, and his best work has a clarity of style and focus which relates to the Gaelic delight in the actuality of things, and then points to universals beyond them. This tendency is also evident in his treatment of character and of women in particular. The result might be called 'Celtic Platonism' if it were a philosophy, and 'symbolic realism', or even allegory at times, in fiction. Gunn shares this mythopoeic tendency with Grassic Gibbon, but the two writers arrive at radically different conclusions. Hence Chris and Ewan represent an impasse of irreconcilable spiritual and political values at the end of *A Scots Quair*, while Gunn's intention was to try to restore completeness to the individual and to offer Scottish culture at least the possibility of regeneration from within.

This search for self-development and wholeness motivates most of the characters in Gunn's books, and, like Wordsworth, he feels that the philosophical implications of this quest can be found in the journey to maturity from the landscapes and exploits of childhood. He was an athletic and adventurous boy who loved to go exploring, fishing and poaching in the sheltered strath of Dunbeath water. The central symbols in his later fiction come from these years when he watched the men go to sea in their little boats while the women waited at home, and he saw a wider meaning in the search for herring – 'the silver darlings' – or in clandestine expeditions after salmon – that ancient Celtic symbol of wisdom, now reserved for the gentry and protected by gamekeepers. Like Wordsworth, too, Gunn made a creative act of recollection at the end of his life in an autobiography called *The Atom of Delight* (1956), and in a key passage he remembers cracking hazelnuts as a boy, and how a sudden moment of insight and unity gave him the ideal which he sought so long in later adult experience:

> I can't remember now how I got on to the boulder in the river but I was there. It was a large flattish boulder and I was sitting on it with my legs stuck out in front at the angle which is wide enough both to give complete comfort and to crack nuts within it. I had picked a stone from the bed of the stream and was using it as a cracking hammer. . . .
>
> The shallow river flowed around and past with its variety of lulling monotonous sounds; a soft wind, warmed by the sun, came upstream and murmured in my ears as it continuously slipped from my face. As I say, how I got there I do not remember. . . .
>
> Then the next thing happened, so far as I can remember, for the first time. I have tried hard but can find no simpler way of expressing what happened than by saying: *I came upon myself sitting there.*
>
> Within the mood of content, as I have tried to recreate it, was this self and the self was me.
>
> The state of content deepened wonderfully and everything around was embraced in it.
>
> There was no 'losing' of the self in the sense that there was a blank from which I awoke or came to. The self may have thinned away – it did – but so

delightfully that it also remained at the centre in a continuous and perfectly natural way. And then within this amplitude the self as it were became aware of seeing itself, not as an 'I' or an 'ego' but rather as a stranger it had come upon and was even a little shy of.

Transitory, evanescent – no doubt, but the scene comes back across half a century, vivid to the crack in the boulder that held the nut.

This passage is typical of how Gunn approaches the world as a writer, for he insists on a local and scrupulous clarity and on the difficulty of describing inner experience in words. Yet in Scottish folk lore hazelnuts are associated with the putting-on of wisdom or prophetic ability, and so the little scene is also invested with intimations of magical or symbolic power. Gunn's fondness for such archetypes tends to place his vision outside history and politics, just as Chris's standing stones are remote from the injustices of the factory floor which Ewan had to face. Yet Gunn would claim that his espousal of wholeness, traditional wisdom, communal care, courage and loyalty is exactly what is needed to redeem the sad vacuum of modern life, even if Gibbon would have felt that such gains were meaningless without an economic revolution too. In either case, these two novelists tackle universal questions about man's spirit, just as they draw on a poetic sense of the past to confront the central issues of modern alienation. In their books the regional setting of the 'Scottish novel' is redeemed, and Caithness and the Mearns, like Auchtermuchty in MacDiarmid's *Drunk Man*, become part of a continuing concern with the 'timeless flame'.

At Dunbeath the fishing-industry was in decline and times were hard; so Gunn left home when he was twelve, to stay with his married sister in Dalry. At fifteen he went to London and worked as a bank clerk for a couple of years before coming to Edinburgh to prepare for a career as a Customs and Excise officer. He passed his Civil Service exams in 1911 and was posted to Inverness, from where he travelled as an 'unattached' junior to a variety of offices and distilleries all round the north. Gunn spent the war-years working with shipping from Kinlochleven and was just about to be called up when the conflict ended. This was a considerable relief to his mother (his father had died in 1916), for, among her sons, Ben had been killed on the barbed wire, John was badly gassed (their stories are used in *Highland River*) and the twins who had gone to Canada also lost their lives as a result of their army service. Prompted by a posting to the south, Neil married his Dingwall girlfriend Daisy Frew in 1921 and the couple set up house in Wigan. During a year there Gunn had to assess pension-claims on behalf of miners who were suffering the worst of poverty as a result of wage-cuts and lockouts by the owners – for the coal mines had been returned to private hands after the war. Such experience, so close to the sacrifices of the Front, marked him deeply and confirmed his socialist sympathies. He was glad to return to Lybster and then to Inverness, for, even if the Highland economy was in ruins too, there was always the familiar countryside and a sense of surviving community life. He settled in a permanent post as Excise officer for the Glen Mhor distillery and began to write seriously.

Gunn corresponded with MacDiarmid in Montrose and soon placed short stories in the *Scottish Chapbook* and other periodicals. The best of these pieces suggest a darker version of the Celtic twilight or hint at themes to come, and a collection, *Hidden Doors*, appeared in 1929 from the Porpoise Press in Edinburgh – a new Scottish Renaissance publisher which was to produce most of his books in the thirties until Faber and Faber took over. Grieve was enthusiastic about Gunn's talent, and, although he criticised a predictable 'anti-Kailyard' impulse in parts of the first novel, he detected the arrival of an original vision and 'a purely Scottish use of English'. The two men became close friends. *The Grey Coast* (1926) is an account of rivalry in love set against Highland life in a small fishing- and crofting-community. Coloured 'grey' indeed by Gunn's hatred of poverty, avarice and lust, it offers a bitter and gloomy account of the fate of the Gael in the generations after the Clearances. He developed the same theme more melodramatically in his next work, *The Lost Glen* (serialised in the *Scots Magazine* in 1928, but not published in book-form until 1932), in which a failed university student returns home – a disgrace to his family – to work as a gillie and to see his people as a depressed peasant-class, slyly subservient to southern incomers with superior airs. Depressed by this bleak book, and by his inability to find a publisher for it, Gunn turned to drama for a spell, with the help of John Brandane and James Bridie. But the three-act symbolic drama *The Ancient Fire* was not well received and he settled for a lasting friendship with Bridie and a return to prose. His hopes were greatly rekindled by the success of his third book.

Morning Tide (1930) is a happier thing than its predecessors. Prompted by the recollections of his brother John, Gunn turned back to the scenes of his childhood in Dunbeath – as if to recover optimism by means of the story of a growing boy, Hugh, and how he comes to terms with his parents, his sisters and the dangers of the sea. It is the first of four notable novels in Gunn's output (*Highland River*, *The Silver Darlings* and *Young Art and Old Hector* are the other three) which deal with the growth of a boy's mind, looking to childhood as an age of primitive and intuitive truths. When *Morning Tide* was selected as a Book Society choice, Gunn followed it with a revision of *The Lost Glen*, whose grimmer theme was less popular, and then plunged into a more symbolic and philosophical vision of the ancient past with *Sun Circle* (1933). Here another young protagonist, Aniel, has to learn about Viking power and the 'civilising' influence of Christianity, both of which will sweep away his ancient Pictish–Celtic world; and yet its spirit will survive in the Highlands beyond the reach of history and change – in the imaginative wholeness and timeless affirmation symbolised by the sun circle:

> As the Sun puts a circle round the earth and all that it contained, so a man by his vision put a circle round himself. At the centre of this circle his spirit sat, and at the centre of his spirit was a serenity for ever watchful.

The next book turned to more immediate history, and *Butcher's Broom* (1934) describes how the values of Highland life – personified by the healer Dark Mairi – were betrayed by the Clearances at the beginning of the nineteenth century. The Strathnaver events were still a matter of bitter folk-memory in Gunn's Caithness, and English-speaking 'improvers', such as the factor 'Heller' (Patrick Sellars) can see nothing but poverty and 'gibberish' in the community, because the Gaelic tongue is not available to them. In fact Gaelic's graceful sensitivity to minute discriminations (paralleled by Gunn's talent for subtle detail and inner states in prose) is the real cultural and philosophical wealth of the place – uncountable, of course, by those who can think only in material terms. *Butcher's Broom* spoke directly to the political and nationalist issues of Scotland in the thirties, and Gunn himself was active for the Scottish National Party behind the scenes in Inverness. The book was a great success and Grassic Gibbon wrote to marvel at how Gunn had managed to control his rage at the fate of 'those people of yours'. Faber and Faber were interested in Gunn, and T. S. Eliot and the American publisher Alfred Harcourt came north to visit him at home. Up in Shetland, however, Neil's old friend MacDiarmid was becoming rather cool, and naming Fionn MacColla as the true Gaelic novelist of the future. Gunn's next book was one of his finest.

Highland River (1937) returns once more to Dunbeath and the river strath where the author spent his childhood – a simple landscape in which a boy's struggle to land a poached salmon with his bare hands becomes an initiation into life's mystery, wisdom, fear and secret delight. Gunn dedicated the book to his brother John, for it encapsulated their youthful adventures together, and his hero, Kenn, becomes a scientist as John had done and shares his experiences of gas and a brother's death at the Front. Gunn found unexpectedly deep resonances in this book, and his imagination was profoundly stirred. The story is told in a series of overlapping presents which annihilate the apparent passage of time, so that Kenn's childhood and his wartime and adult experiences coexist and reflect on each other through a series of witty and moving associative links. Finally, he revisits the river of his boyhood in order to trace it, and the nature of his own being, back to the source. The river-mouth and its shallows are associated with infancy, just as it was the middle reaches which he frequented as an older boy; but he never did find the source before he left home and, indeed, he could not truly have attained it or understood its nature until the end of the book, when he returns as a mature and solitary man. The theme is very evocative, with traditional overtones of the 'river' of life and time; and yet its style imitates the scientific precision of Kenn's trained intellect, and this dispassionate and analytical enquiry is very different from the poetic surrender to mood and the flow of dialect which Gibbon chose to use for his Chris:

> The heath fire and the primrose: the two scents were jotted down by Kenn as simple facts of experience, without any idea of a relationship between them.

And then suddenly, while the mind was lifting to the cold bright light of spring, to the blue of birds' eggs and the silver of the first salmon run, there came out of the tangle in a soft waft of air the scent of primroses.

An instant, and it was gone, leaving a restlessness in the breast, an urgency that defeats itself, an apprehension, almost agonising, of the ineffectiveness of the recording machine. Finally nothing is jotted down and the mind is left exhausted. . . .

But the grown Kenn knows quite exactly one quality in the scent of the primrose for which he has an adjective. The adjective is innocent. The innocency of dawn on a strath on a far back morning of creation. The freshness of dawn wind down a green glen where no human foot has trod. If the words sound vague, the pictures they conjure up for Kenn's inner eye are quite vivid. The grasses and green leaves in the clear morning light have a quality of alertness like pointed ears. And they sway alive and dancing-cool and deliciously happy.

As a scientist, Kenn – whose name suggests the act of knowing – also finds this elusive delight in art and good action. It is the very spirit of Duncan Bàn's 'Ben Dorain' – a pagan realism quite removed from the strictures of organised religion or politics or official dogma of any kind. He remembers when he first found it in science, too, in an exam question on how 'the principal forms of energy are traceable to the sun':

Forests of dead trees turn into coal. . . . Sun takes up water into clouds; clouds fall and form rivers and waterfalls; falling water directly used for making electricity. . . . The cycles of action were cosmic wheels, opening fanlike, each spoke glittering in Kenn's mind. The excitement of apprehension made his brain extraordinarily clear; his sentences were factual and precisely written.

The 'sun circle' has been rescued from the Celtic twilight to be redefined as the 'energy cycle' with a scientific clarity which actually enhances its symbolic force. The 'salmon of knowledge' and this 'excitement of apprehension' (in both senses of the word) lie at the heart of Gunn's novels, and Kenn emerges into the sunlight as a new kind of sensibility – a solitary atheist, ready for laughter at the unexpectedness of the universe, and yet coolly detached, too, for his war-experiences have marked him with a ferocious sense of irony:

The blowing of gaps in the advancing Germans on that early morning towards the end of 1917 on the Somme was coarse unskilled work, though its sheer devastating efficacy had its fascination, because – apart from the joyous potting of church steeples and such – even observers saw little of the actual results of the gun-teams' labours. On this particular morning, however, precision in its trigonometrical sense was almost entirely confined to the exquisite narrowness of the shaves by which death passed them by or the instant and annihilating manner in which it got them. Escape was a matter of pure chance.

After his brush with death and a near blinding by gas, Kenn goes back to memories of the river, and eventually, years later, at the age of thirty-seven, he reaches the source and comes to understand the humour and the beautiful indifference of being:

> Bow to it, giving nothing away, and pass on the moor like sunlight, like shadow, with thoughts hesitant and swift as a herd of hinds. In this way one is undefeatable – until death comes. And as death is inevitable, its victory is no great triumph.

Yet beyond the watershed he sees a mountain; and, beyond that, 'the grey planetary light that reveals the earth as a ball turning slowly in the immense chasm of space'. In the end, there is no end and no goal – only the quality of the moment.

Gunn's prose achieves a memorably cool expression of the elusive, considering nature of the human mind, where symbolic insights meet the Gaelic poetic genius for impersonal and detailed actuality. This is a Scottish novel which is entirely free from 'Celtic' twilight, not to mention the old penchant for rural sentiment. *Highland River* has a claim to be Gunn's finest book: it was awarded the James Tait Black Memorial Prize for 1937, widely acclaimed and frequently reprinted; and as a novel of individual development it bears comparison with Joyce's *Portrait of the Artist.* Encouraged by Eliot and the directors of Faber, Gunn committed himself to full-time writing by resigning from his job at the age of forty-six and taking his wife to live at Braefarm House near Dingwall, to the north of Inverness. *Off in a Boat* (1938) gives an autobiographical account of that summer of freedom. Essays, plays and two more novels followed in the next two years, but they seem to be marking time somewhat before the appearance of his most popular book.

The Silver Darlings (1941) links the theme of personal development in *Highland River* with an account of the growth of the herring-industry after the Highland Clearances in the early nineteenth century. It is Gunn's most fully researched histori-

cal novel. Based on his own Dunbeath, now fictionalised as
'Dunster', it is founded on two generations of economic and
social change and filled with fine descriptions of local character, landscape and the thrill and danger of the sea. Against this
densely realised setting, Gunn relates the inner odyssey of the
boy Finn, growing up without a father, coming to terms with
his mother's affection for another man, finding a girlfriend
himself and eventually a boat of his own and a place in the
working community of men. These simple themes are filtered
through the Lawrentian intensity of young Finn's pride and
innocence, but the book begins with his mother Catrine, who
was forced to the shore by the Clearances. Her inexperienced
young husband is press-ganged by the navy while he is fishing
in his little boat, and eventually he dies abroad. In later years
Catrine's suitor Roddy is one of the most successful skippers on
this dangerous coast, but she fears and hates the sea, to which
he, with now her son, is so inevitably drawn. Thus Finn comes
to realise that his home embraces polarities beyond the obvious
truths of everyday, just as Gunn himself describes his own
background as 'the boy' in *The Atom of Delight*:

> As his existence had two parents, so it had the earth and the sea. If his
> mother was the earth, his father was the sea. In fact he could hardly think of
> his father without thinking of the sea. Out of the sea came the livelihood of
> the household. They depended on the sea, and of all the elements in nature
> it was the least dependable. You could never be sure of it as you could be
> sure of the earth.

Here the presence and authority of all those Scottish fathers –
Weir, Gillespie or Gourlay – has come down to its most
elemental role. Yet, despite the terrors of the waves, a man at
peace with himself can approach them and work in harmony,
although he must never take anything for granted. On the other
hand, the land is always there, comforting, stable and feminine.
In figurative terms, Finn's achievement is to reach maturity by
bridging the gap between the empathetic and land-oriented
spirit of Chris Guthrie and the unrelentingly harsh universe of
Adam Weir, symbolised by the capricious sea. More conventionally, Gunn likens the sea to a mistress and the land to a wife,
and Finn has to learn to share the sea, and his mother too, with
Roddy, whom he greets at first with jealousy and suspicion.
Finn's rite of passage is made during a voyage to Stornoway

when the crew of Roddy's boat comes close to shipwreck and starvation until the boy makes a courageous ascent of an impossible cliff to fetch water and raw food to sustain them all. When the tale is retold it is as if it has become a part of folk history, linking Finn with Finn MacCoul, his heroic namesake in an epic past; but Finn's real victory comes later in the book, in the quiet moment when he finds peace within the circle of his own heart and a place within the circle of the community. Only now can he enter the bustle of history, and the book ends by recognising that Finn is at last truly ready to begin: a properly whole person with a part to play in the world and plans for a family of his own. The novel's closing words are 'Life had come for him', and the optimism of this conclusion makes a marked contrast with the melancholy diffusion which overtakes Chris Guthrie at the end of *Grey Granite*.

The popularity of *The Silver Darlings* is not unrelated to its foundation in social history and realistic detail, but later novels would seek an increasingly symbolic exploration of his favourite themes. At first *The Serpent* (1943) marked time with another plea for the whole individual in the face of a narrow-minded, Kirk-ridden village, but Gunn's new direction is particularly clear in the development from *Young Art and Old Hector* (1942) to *The Green Isle of the Great Deep* (1944). These are two separate but linked narratives which move from the gently light-hearted and instructive vignettes of the first to an anti-utopian fantasy novel which casts reflections on the nature of totalitarian rule. As a wilful eight-year-old, young Art gains 'instruction' and exasperation in the company of Hector, an old poacher with his best years behind him but still wise in the insights of folk lore and tradition. Their first book together has a grave whimsy which can stray dangerously close to sentimental 'philosophy'. Naomi Mitchison suggested as much in a letter to the author which initiated a friendly debate over the years, in which Gunn stubbornly defended his case for simplicity and individual self-realisation in the face of her more conventionally socialist enthusiasm for concerted action and political involvement. The indirect result of their wrangle was *The Green Isle of the Great Deep* – a different kind of book altogether, in which Art and Hector fall into a salmon-pool and find themselves in a version of Tir nan Og which is run like an enlightened totalitarian state. An early reference to Nazi concentration-camps reminds us of the date when the two protagonists 'drown', but the main target of this anti-utopian allegory is the rational arrogance of faceless 'scientific' authority, which presumes to know best and attempts to tranquillise and control us for our own good. Gunn had read Koestler's *Darkness at Noon* (1940) and been dismayed by recent reports of 'brainwashing' in Stalin's Russia. At an imaginative level he saw the materialistic assumptions of corporate decision-makers as a more real menace for the future than the Gothic horror of Nazi fascism, currently approaching its end in the ruins of Europe. The question was, how would the quiet, interior wisdom of his two unlikely Highland heroes fare against these 'Administrators'? The answer is worked out through humour, surprise and Art's anarchic boyish spirit, which his captors seem to be incapable of suppressing or trapping. He becomes a 'legend', until God returns to investigate and put things right in the domain he left long ago. In the end it is Art's understanding that beyond 'knowledge' there is 'wisdom', and beyond that 'magic', which returns them to the real and imperfect world where they are fished out of the salmon-pool, dripping wet and alive. It may be debatable whether 'magic' is enough in the face of the power of the corporate state, but Gunn's defence of what MacDiarmid called 'the shy spirit that like a laich wind moves' would be to say, as anarchists do, that, if every individual had such quality within them, then external coercion would indeed wither away.

In the last six years of his writing-career, Gunn's novels tried to realise the quest for intuitive wholeness in more contemporary settings, for he was determined to avoid a return to the 'chronicle novel' and he could do little more with the overt allegory of *The Green Isle*. Besides, he was sensitive to accusations that his spiritual outlook was mystical or escapist. Thus in a realistic setting the symbolism of *The Drinking Well* (1947) relates to earlier work, looking back to the paternal conflicts in *The Serpent* and *The Lost Glen*, as does the more melodramatic psychological thriller *The Key of the Chest* (1945).

The post-war years were difficult ones in Gunn's personal life, and, like many of his friends, he had become increasingly pessimistic about the future of socialism in the light of Stalin's tyranny. The novels of this period – *The Shadow* (1948), *The Lost Chart* (1949) and *Bloodhunt* (1952) – take a darker look at the split between the rational intellect and the wholeness of feeling, with symbols which often relate to the intuitive power women as opposed to the reductive habits of the masculine mind, and images which conjure up the atavistic thrills of violence and the hunt. A lighter-hearted book, *The Silver Bough* (1948), had been well received – Edwin Muir particularly admired it – but Gunn had not recaptured his earlier sucesses and he began to feel a sense of literary and geographical isolation in his beloved north. He was fifty-nine years old and his career as a writer was nearly at an end; yet, if his last novels relate to themes and books which had gone before, they were still to be transmuted in significant ways.

The Well at the World's End (1951) follows the spirit of *The Silver Bough* to make a triumphant return to the archetypal innocence and humour of the world of *Highland River*, but this time it is experienced by a middle-aged academic, a man who already knows the wider world and the horrors of history. He comes to moments of comedy, mystery and near death in the course of a picaresque camping-holiday in the everyday Highlands, and the world is renewed by his experience of delight and laughter, even laughter at himself, just as his own inner being and his relationship with his wife is refreshed. The protagonists are not unlike Gunn and Daisy themselves, and the novel is the sweetest of the late works, for it manages to catch the ineffable 'nothingness' of interior insight – clear as water in a well, transparent as the Caithness light itself. There is a stranger humour and affirmation too in *The Other Landscape* (1954), in which an anthropologist narrator struggles to understand the archetypally mischievous nature of existence in the vision of a gifted and eccentric musician who has lived as a recluse ever since his wife died in childbirth, cut off from help. This novel, as 'metaphysical' as any by David Lindsay, was followed by Gunn's autobiography – his last book.

The Atom of Delight (1956) is the author's defence of a lifelong preference for personal unity and insight in the face of fashionable pessimism, collectivism and the aesthetic and political violences of the 'modern' world. In retrospect he found affinities between the pagan spirit of freedom in his boyhood and the irreverent teachings of the Zen masters who demonstrate a letting-go of self in moments of intuitively integrated action. This was the single vision which Gunn had pursued in various forms through all his novels:

Without consciously thinking or striving, 'It' is achieved, spontaneity comes into its own, the arrow lands in the bull. Musical composers, scientists, painters, writers, know how in the midst of their striving 'It' takes charge, strife ceases, and the 'marked passage' is born. In that moment of delight freedom is known; as, not to be high falutin, its rare moment is known in archery, cricket and putting the shot, not to mention the way a rosebush looked at the boy when he had landed his fish.

The future remains open to this kind of freedom.

Neil Gunn lived for another seventeen years, actively engaged in local affairs, literary magazines and broadcasting, until he died after a short illness in January 1973. The Neil Gunn International Fellowship has since been awarded to many distinguished overseas novelists, including Heinrich Böll, Chinua Achebe and Saul Bellow.

Other novelists of the early twentieth century

Among the other novelists who were prominent in the 1930s, **Naomi Mitchison** (b. 1897) heralded a wave of interest in the myths and rituals of primitive societies, especially with *The Conquered* (1923) and her twelfth book, *The Corn King and the Spring Queen* (1931). Following her own interests in ancient history and anthropology after the manner of J. G. Frazer, the later novel revolves around the rituals of kingship and fertility in the ancient world of Scythia and the Mediterranean. Linklater's *Men of Ness* and Gunn's *Sun Circle* followed within two years. Closer to home, *The Bull Calves* (1947) drew on her family-history – she was a member of the distinguished Haldanes – to tell a tale set in Perthshire after the Forty-five. She has played a leading part in left-wing politics and women's rights and has travelled widely and written many novels. **Ian Macpherson** (1905–44) anticipated aspects of *Sunset Song* in his first novel, *Shepherd's Calendar* (1931), based on his own youth and education in the rural North-East. Occasionally overwritten, the book charts an adolescent's painful farewell to the farm he loves in order to satisfy his mother's desire to see him 'succeed' at university. Macpherson's next two novels took the Clearances for their theme, but his last and best work, *Wild Harbour* (1936), was a more original tale about a young married couple trying to live in the Highlands away from the universal future war which has broken out in '1944'. Their love for each other, the summer wilderness of remote Speyside, and the skills of stalking and lonely survival are all economically recounted before the anarchic world catches up with their idyll and sweeps them to random and meaningless deaths. The author himself was killed in a motorcycle accident in 1944.

A. J. Cronin (1896–1981) began a long career as a popular author with *Hatter's Castle* (1931), re-creating some of the themes of *The House with the Green Shutters* in a vein of sentimental realism. His own medical expertise and his interest in politics and social problems enlivened several of his books and made *The Citadel* (1937) a best-seller. Based on his own experiences as a doctor in the mining-towns of Wales, it was successfully translated into a TV serial, like the adaptations which went to make the series *Dr Finlay's Casebook*.

Other novelists at this time looked to modern city life for their material, in what might be called a 'Glasgow school'; and, although there was no formal movement as such, their devotion to urban realism in the west of Scotland makes a significant counterbalance to the symbolism of Gibbon and Gunn. In the later 1920s, Dot Allan had placed several stories of family life in a Glasgow setting from the First World War or during the Depression, and a later novel called *Hunger March* (1934) dealt with the plight of the city's unemployed workers. Chief among these writers was **George Blake** (1893–1961), a Law graduate who turned to journalism after the war, becoming a colleague of Neil Munro at the *Glasgow Evening News* and later the editor of *Strand Magazine* in London. He returned to Scotland in the 1930s to join George Malcolm Thomson at the Porpoise Press when it amalgamated with Faber. Throughout his career, Blake made a sustained effort to write about Scotland's mercantile and working classes in the face of industrial decline in the Clyde and Greenock from the 1920s to the Second World War. His first book, *Mince Collop Close* (1925), was a melodramatic tale about a female gang-leader in the slums, but *The Wild Men* (1925) and *Young Malcolm* (1926) – dealing with revolutionary politics and the education of a young man – were less sensational, if still inclined to sentimental realism. Blake is best known for *The Shipbuilders* (1935), a major attempt to evoke Glasgow during the Depression by following the problems, the family-ties and the different fortunes of two men who formed a friendship during the Great War. Ex-soldier and officer's batman Danny Shields is now a riveter at Pagan's shipyard, working for his admired 'Major' – the owner's son and manager, Leslie Pagan. But the yard has taken its last order. Pagan bows to economic forces, although he keeps his wealth, and before he leaves for England he offers the riveter a job on his estate there. Danny's proud nature decides to 'stick to his trade' and seek work among the other yards on the Clyde. He does not know it, but his skills are already made obsolete by the new electric welding.

The Shipbuilders is notable for its evocation of a grimy and beloved city, with its lively culture of tenements and trams, street gangs, pubs and football-matches. But Danny is sentimentalised as a loyal and stalwart type-figure, as if the author himself saw the workers from the point of view of Pagan's officer-class. The human interest of the friendship with Pagan, like the latter's fatalism, is neither developed nor shaken by circumstances, and this draws the centre of the novel well away from any more crucial psychological, political or economic understanding. Even so, Blake handles the urban scene well. *David and Joanna* (1936) and *Late Harvest* (1938) developed his understanding of the strength and the plight of women tied to frailer menfolk, and the resignations of life in a declining industrial town. The latter book painted a particularly detailed picture of shabby respectable existence in a fictionalised Greenock, and this paved the way for a series of later works set in 'Garvel'. These include *The Constant Star* (1945) and *The Westering Sun* (1946), which follow the dynastic history of the shipbuilding Oliphant family, from the early nineteenth century to the fate of the last daughter of the line, who struggles through the Depression in Glasgow to die in a wartime air raid. Blake's personal commitment to the history of his home region led him to produce several books on ships, shipbuilding and the lighthouses of the Clyde – a fascination which also featured in his autobiographical study *Down to the Sea* (1937).

Edwin Muir's unhappy years in Glasgow are reflected in his third and last novel, *Poor Tom* (1932), in which the painful relationship between alcoholic Tom, who is dying of a brain tumour, and his brother Mansie, is used to convey all Muir's distaste for the slums and the cultural and political shallowness of lower-middle-class life in the city. Among the novels of

James Barke (1905–58) *The Land of the Leal* (1939) tells the epic story of a peasant family's progress through various jobs in nineteenth-century rural Scotland, to finish in Glasgow during the Depression. The book draws on Barke's own background and socialist sympathies to make popular fiction out of social history – full of humour, dialect, and admiration for the indomitable strength of his heroine, Jean Ramsay. His play *Major Operation* (1936) explored the dialectics of labour and capital by placing a union-organiser and a businessman in the same hospital-ward. Barke also edited the poems of Burns, and from the late forties he produced five novels based on the life of the poet. Alexander McArthur and H. Kingsley Long became famous for their collaboration on *No Mean City* (1935), a lurid semi-documentary novel on slum life and gang-warfare in the Gorbals of the 1920s. **Edward Gaitens** (1897–1966) was born in that once-notorious district and with the support of James Bridie he sought publication for stories based on his life there before the First World War. Some of these were collected as *Growing Up and Other Stories* (1942), and six of them appeared again as chapters of a novel called *Dance of the Apprentices* (1948). These books are notable for handling domestic realism and working-class vitality without the usual pitfalls of melodrama or sentimentality. By comparison the novels of **Guy McCrone** (1898–1977) belong to a popular mode of domestic history and family romance. His second novel introduced readers to a middle-class family in Victorian Glasgow, and their saga was completed as the *Wax Fruit* trilogy in 1947, and then extended by two further sequels. McCrone was deeply interested in opera and singing, and as a cousin of James Bridie he also became involved with the Glasgow Citizens' Theatre, which was to play such an influential part in modern Scottish drama.

Theatre, plays and playwrights

Barrie's successes on the London stage offered little support to the idea of a literary renaissance in the north, nor were there to be any truly outstanding Scottish playwrights in the modern period. Nevertheless, new growth did appear in a field which had lain fallow for a very long time. Paradoxically, it is this lack of a theatrical tradition which may explain why most Scottish writers have been content to work within already-established genres and conventions. Even in the 1970s – a boom-time for Scottish plays – the prevailing and most popular mode was a proletarian social realism which had done well in the twenties, and a stagecraft which Ibsen would have found loose and predictable. On the other hand, it could be argued that dramatic naturalism has now *become* the tradition.

It was the example of the Irish National Theatre which stirred theatre lovers north of the Border. If the Abbey Theatre in Dublin had managed to nurture a native Irish drama, might not the same be accomplished in Scotland? The formation of the Glasgow Repertory Theatre in 1909 marked one of the first steps, and, if it lacked a fully Scottish programme, at least it provided a stage for northern actors which lasted until the outbreak of war. In the 1920s **Dr John McIntyre ('John Brandane'**, 1869–1947) started the Scottish National Players and wrote their first production, which was a piece called *Glenforsa* (1921), set on a Hebridean island and suffused, rather like Synge's plays, with the rhythms of Gaelic speech. The Scottish National Theatre Society followed and for the next twenty-five years the National Players provided a forum for a succession of writers, including George Blake, George Reston Malloch, Donald Carswell and the plays of Robert Kemp. 'If anything becomes of the Scottish Drama,' wrote Bridie, 'John Brandane is its begetter. He spent more time . . . on raw young dramatists than he spent on work that might have made him famous.' Brandane's best-known play was *The Glen Is Mine* (1923), set once again in the Hebrides, where the old ways have to meet with the new – not without sentiment – while his one-act comedy *Rory Aforesaid* (1928) is still a regular favourite with amateur companies. Yorkshire-born Dr Gordon Bottomley (1874–1976) was equally committed to theatre in Scotland and became a leading light in the Community Drama Association which started in the thirties. His rather antique verse play *Gruach* – a prelude to *Macbeth*, no less – made a hit in 1923 and shared the bill with *The Glen Is Mine*. In complete contrast, the plays of **Joe Corrie** (1894–1968) introduced urban domestic realism and political issues to the National Players' repertoire. Corrie was a coal-miner who gradually turned to full-time writing, and his best play, *In Time of Strife* (1929), deals with the fate of a mining-family during the General Strike. He wrote poems too, and dozens of one-act plays for amateur productions. Corrie's stylised working-class speech was a brave new experience on stage in the 1920s, although it can seem rather stilted when asked to bear the full literary burden of dramatic description and evocation.

O. H. Mavor ('**James Bridie**', 1888–1951) was a young friend of Brandane's and a fellow doctor, who joined the board of the Scottish National Theatre Society in 1923 and played a generous role himself in helping young playwrights, including Neil Gunn. Mavor's interest in writing went back to his student days at Glasgow, for he had enjoyed them enormously and taken a long time to graduate. He served in the Royal Army Medical Corps (as he did in the Second World War) and when he returned to general practice and hospital work he resumed his enthusiasm for the stage as well. Brandane and a brilliant young producer called Tyrone Guthrie helped Mavor with *The Sunlight Sonata* (written by 'Mary Henderson') at the Lyric Theatre, Glasgow, in 1928. This was the first of over forty plays by Mavor, who became much better known as 'James Bridie' and gave up practising medicine in 1938. He was a popular and witty character with a droll sense of humour, who liked to conceal considerable energy and commitment behind a pretence of laziness and irreverent frivolity. One of the best early plays and his first London success was *The Anatomist* (1930), a study of the egocentric Dr Knox's involvement with the Burke and Hare body-snatching scandal in Edinburgh. In *Tobias and the Angel* (1930) Bridie's use of colloquial speech and his experience of the Middle East during the First World War help to transform the story in the Apocrypha of an archangel's visitation into a lively comedy of modern attitudes. *A Sleeping Clergyman* (1933) was a more innovative play: it follows the sorry family history of a medical researcher back through three generations in order to refute the suggestion that we are slaves to heredity. The tale is told by means of 'flashbacks' from a chat between medical men in a respectable Glasgow Club in the 1930s, but the clergyman of the title – like God, perhaps, in the modern world – sleeps throughout the whole play.

Bridie has a very Shavian delight in the excitement of debate, and his talent for this and for novel conceptions and confrontations on stage helps to make up for the structural imbalances in many pieces. Thus *Mr Bolfry* (1943) – one of his wittiest works –

draws on the Scottish penchant for religious dualism and diabolerie to conjure up the Devil on a dull Sunday evening in a Free Kirk manse in the contemporary Highlands. When 'Mr Bolfry' appears, he is dressed like the minister himself and the two engage in a ferocious debate, before the man of God finally suspects that he is confronting an aspect of himself and learns to find strength in simple faith rather than disputation. Bridie's plays were regularly produced in the West End but he kept in touch with the arts in Scotland, helping to establish the Glasgow Citizens' Theatre in 1943 and involving himself with the Edinburgh International Festival, and in particular with the Robert Kemp and Tyrone Guthrie production of Lindsay's *Satire of the Three Estates* in 1948. In 1950, the year before he died, he helped to establish a College of Drama at the Academy of Music in Edinburgh.

Bridie's best later plays include a telling study of the hopes and despairs of a middle-aged teacher (*Mr Gillie*, 1950), while *The Queen's Comedy*, from the same year, is set among the gods and mortals assembled around Troy. It is given a modern bias, however, and its satire on war and power is contemporary enough. The author called *The Baikie Charivari* (1952) a 'miracle play', mixing together fantasy and symbolism, with the stories of Punch and Judy and Pontius Pilate in a contemporary setting, to make his most experimental work.

Although Bridie was the most notable and successful playwright of his day, there have been no successors to his style. It can be argued that the formation of a Glasgow branch of the Unity Theatre in 1946 was more influential while it lasted, because its working-class socialist dramas, such as George Munro's *Gold in his Boots* (1947) look forward to the 1970s and the plays of Bill Bryden and Roddy McMillan (who began his acting career with Unity). Bridie's achievement is equally isolated from the other main tendency in Scottish theatre, which has been to produce dramas in broad Scots, and here the most prominent names from the 'second wave' of the Renaissance are Robert McLellan and Alexander Reid.

Not surprisingly, historical themes prevail in broad Scots drama, and the reductive spirit of the language delights in bringing great men and great events down to earth. **Robert McLellan** (b. 1907) grew up among Scots-speaking farm people in Lanarkshire, and his book *Linmill and Other Stories*

(1977) evokes that milieu with considerable linguistic and personal sensitivity. His first play, the one-acter *Jeddart Justice* (1934), was a comedy based on Border feuds in the sixteenth century, as were *The Changeling* (1935) and his first full-length play, *Toom Byres* (1936). His best and most popular work was the 'historical comedy' *Jamie the Saxt* (1937), distinguished by the pace and humour with which it recounts the struggle between the scheming Earl of Bothwell and King James, 'the wisest fool in Christendom' – harried on all sides, weak, wily and finally triumphant. McLellan's Scots is vividly concrete in its idioms, colloquial, versatile and unstrained – the perfect vehicle for a comedy of character and deflation. Such free and vernacular skill is more than a pasing delight in McLellan's plays, for it encapsulates a literary tradition and a habit of mind which in itself makes an indirect critique of affairs of state and fallible human beings, however lordly their dress. Other plays followed, including *Torwatletie* (1946) and *The Flouers o Edinburgh* (1947), which are set in the eighteenth century. McLellan has three volumes of collected plays to his credit, but he stopped writing for the stage in the 1950s. Given the fluency of his Scots and the importance of its spirit to his meaning, he became understandably depressed at the difficulties which arose in finding enough native actors who could speak it well. *Jamie the Saxt*, however, has enjoyed frequent revivals, and the late Duncan Macrae is particularly remembered for his brilliance in the leading role.

The two Scots comedies of **Alexander Reid** (1914–82) placed legendary medieval figures in humble settings among the common folk of the Borders. *The Lass wi' the Muckle Mou'* (1950) features Thomas the Rhymer returned from fairyland, while *The Warld's Wonder* (1953) became another hilarious vehicle for Duncan Macrae, as the wizard Michael Scott. It was the skill of actors such as Andrew Keir and Roddy McMillan at the Glasgow Citizens' which first inspired Reid to write in Scots, and he made a sturdy defence of it in the Foreword to the 1958 edition of his plays. Yet, to meet a wider audience, he anglicized the texts of that edition and sadly diluted the spirit of his work. Sydney Goodsir Smith used an entirely stiff and rhetorical language for *The Wallace* (1960), which is more of a political pageant than a play. Robert Kemp (1908–67) also used Scots for his stage and radio drama, while the poet

Alexander Scott followed his flair for the language in three rumbustuous verse plays in the 1950s. In more recent years, however, broad Scots has declined in favour of the wit and violence of colloquial urban speech in a notable resurgence of proletarian drama.

The link with earlier days at the Glasgow Citizens' is provided by Roddy McMillan (1923–79), whose first play in a naturalistic mode, *All in Good Faith*, was a success there in 1954. Stewart Conn (b. 1936), poet and radio-producer for the BBC, wrote *I Didn't Always Live Here* (1967), evoking the humour and harshness of Glasgow life and speech from the Depression to the post-war years through a series of flashbacks from its two female protagonists. Then **Bill Bryden** (b. 1942) came to the Edinburgh Lyceum, where he assembled an extremely talented company of Scottish actors, many of whom were already stars. With such a cast, *Willie Rough* (1972) was an enormous success. Set in Bryden's native Greenock, it follows the political education of a moderate shop-steward on 'Red Clydeside', whose increasingly radical commitment costs him his freedom and his job, but not his spirit. It is a story of working-class life and sentiment with a naturalistic succession of scenes from 1914 to 1916. Bryden is a skilful and successful director, but the limitations of his writing became clearer with *Benny Lynch* (1974) and clearer still with *Civilians* (1981). Nevertheless, *Willie Rough* was the vanguard of a revival in urban realism and a new popular interest in the Scottish stage.

The very name of the 7:84 Company proclaims the political purpose of its founder, John McGrath, who came north in 1973 to start a Scottish branch of the theatre company he had first conceived in London. (The numbers claim that 7 per cent of the population owns 84 per cent of Britain's wealth.) McGrath developed a style of Brechtian propaganda drama which mixed together documentary material, music-hall routines, folk-song, jokes and satirical ditties to make fast moving and hilarious shows, full of melodrama, pathos and didacticism. The actors were encouraged to help to construct the play, and audiences were encouraged to sing along with them on the stage. The company's Scottish debut was *The Cheviot, the Stag and the Black, Black Oil* (1973), which argues for Scottish republicanism against English and American influences from the time of the Clearances to the present day. It arrived at just the moment when devolution and North Sea oil were the hottest topics in the country, and the play was taken on tour to community centres and remote town halls before it ever saw the major theatres. Visibly fuelled by the talent and conviction of the actors themselves, *The Cheviot* was an enormous popular and critical success, with a tour of Ireland and two appearances on national television. Subsequent plays adapted different themes and different social problems to the same political end, and perhaps inevitably the message became predictable, despite individually brilliant actors and the high energy of the group's demotic style. Nevertheless, a vital new contribution to theatrical experience and community involvement had been made, linking a long standing polemical tradition in Scotland to the popular arts of variety theatre, folk-song and protest-songs.

Looking back to the more conventional drama of the Citizens' Theatre, Roddy McMillan's second play, *The Bevellers* (1973), is a sympathetic study of an apprentice's initiation into life on the shop-floor of a glass-bevelling works where the language is anything but polished, and Hector MacMillan (b. 1929) used a similar freedom in exploring the internal horrors of Protestant bigotry in Glasgow with *The Sash* (1973). In 1976 the Traverse Theatre presented *The Jesuit* by the poet Donald Campbell (b. 1940), set in the seventeenth century at the trial of Catholic martyr John Ogilvie. Like much of Campbell's work, the play focuses on an historical moment of personal crisis, but the modern style of the common soldiers' speech gives it a place in what was fast becoming a vogue in Scottish plays for colloquial coarseness and 'hard man' attitudes. Thus a play called *The Hard Man* (1977) by Glasgow writer Tom McGrath (b. 1940) was based on the life and times of his collaborator Jimmy Boyle to paint a grim picture of street violence and prison oppression.

It is difficult to deny the immediate impact of such plays, although it can be argued that some of them create a new Kailyard sentimentality out of urban deprivation, or that they use sensationally brutal speech and action merely as a substitute for dramatic force. Nevertheless, they also brought the demotic immediacy of Scots street speech to the stage, and to thousands of playgoers it seemed like a breath of salty air. John Byrne (b. 1940), from the 7:84 Company, rose to the occasion with the banter of *The Slab Boys* (1978), set in a carpet-factory in Paisley. Here 'patter' reigns supreme, appropriately enough for teenagers in the 1950s, and Byrne was encouraged to produce a sequel about the staff dance called *The Loveliest Night of the Year* (1979). A grimmer mixture of comedy and violence in speech and action, and the same depressed urban setting in the west of Scotland, characterised several gripping television plays by Peter Macdougall while on the wider screen this new Scottish confidence had already made its mark with the pioneering 'My Childhood' trilogy – an austere set of films by Bill Douglas, later followed by the gently humane comedy of Bill Forsyth, whose films *That Sinking Feeling*, *Gregory's Girl* and *Local Hero* have become internationally famous. On an equally popular note the gritty Chandleresque anti-romance of Edward Boyd (b. 1916) created entertaining Glasgow thrillers and serials for radio and television – a line also followed in Hugh C. Rae's fiction and William McIlvanney's 'Laidlaw' books – while the nationwide success of Billy Connolly the comedian brought the creative wit and the broad irreverence of Glasgow humour to a wider audience than ever before.

More experimental drama has yet to gain wide recognition in Scotland, but the roots are there in plays by Cecil Taylor (1929–81), Tom Gallacher (b. 1934), Stanley Eveling (a Newcastle man who lives and works in Edinburgh) and Tom McGrath, whose play *Animal* (1982) depends largely on brilliant mime. There is promise too in the fact that younger poets than the more established figures of Stewart Conn, George Mackay Brown and Donald Campbell have found it possible to write for the theatre, and Liz Lochhead, Alan Spence and Catherine Lucy Czerkawaska have all had work produced in close co-operation with director and players.

The 'second wave' of the Scottish Renaissance

It remains now to turn back to those writers after MacDiarmid, Gibbon and Gunn who made up the 'second wave' of the Renaissance. One man in particular – the Gaelic poet Sorley Maclean – might be ranked with the first generation, but his poetry did not reach a wider audience until relatively late in his lifetime and so he joins the many fine poets in Scots, English and Gaelic who came to prominence between 1940 and 1960. Quite apart from MacDiarmid's propaganda for a renaissance, the number of writers who achieved a high literary standard in this period speaks for itself.

Poetry in Scots

Poets were not slow to follow the example of MacDiarmid's early lyrics, as Albert D. Mackie (b. 1904) acknowledged in *Poems in Two Tongues* (1928). Even **William Soutar** (1898–1943), whose first three collections were all in English and who was not to return to Scots until the 1930s, sent four 'Triolets in the Doric' to be published in *Scottish Chapbook* in 1923. Soutar's health had started to deteriorate during his service in the navy, and when he graduated after the war he had to live at home in Perth because of recurring pain in his feet, legs and back. He turned to private study and writing poetry, influenced by Romantic and Georgian models. Initially opposed to MacDiarmid's polyglot energy (he produced a satire called 'The Thistle Looks at a Drunk Man'), Soutar's nationalist sympathies were aroused and he began to formulate his own theories about making Scots available to children. By 1928 he was writing 'bairn rhymes' for Evelyn, the little girl his parents had adopted, for he was more or less housebound and much in her company. He had contracted a progressive disease of the spine and by 1930 he found himself confined to bed in a ground-floor room which he was not to leave for the rest of his life. His journals and dream-books are a testament to the courage with which he faced a painful fate. Resettling his life around books and visits from friends and fellow writers, he developed an eye for detail and a love of nature from what he could see of the world beyond his window, and a selection from his journals was published as *Diaries of a Dying Man* (1954). Four further collections of his English poems were published in his lifetime, and his socialist and pacifist beliefs illuminate verses such as 'Beyond Country', 'The Children' and 'The Permanence of the Young Men'. But Soutar is chiefly remembered as a poet in Scots, for he found a colloquial ease, humour and pathos there which escaped the precision of his English work. The first Scots poems were for children, and *Seeds in the*

Wind (1933) was dedicated to young Evelyn. 'If the Doric is to
come back alive,' he wrote to MacDiarmid, 'it will come back
on a cock horse', and he based the rhythms of his animal fables
and rhymes on playground chants and dance games. He had
discovered the ballads, too, and learned a lot from them, as in
'The Whale', which spins a fantastic tale in ballad stanzas, or
'The Lanely Mune', which catches a moment of uncanny
simplicity in only six lines.

Soutar came to believe that it was in the ballads 'that we hear
the voice of Scotland most distinctly' and he hoped for a 'new
age in which the people shall regain their articulateness and art
has an anonymous character'. At times his own ballad poems
can seem rather too 'anonymous', but the best of them
rediscover the true eerie note, and then add a powerful sense of
anguish that never states its personal origin. 'Song' and 'The
Tryst' from his second collection of *Poems in Scots* (1935) are
rightly famous:

> Whaur yon broken brig hings owre;
> Whaur yon water maks nae soun';
> Babylon blaws by in stour: dust
> Gang doun wi' a sang, gang doun . . . .

('Song')

A collection of riddles followed in 1937, but the rest of Soutar's
work in Scots comes from manuscripts which were first
published posthumously in an otherwise unsatisfactory *Collected Poems*, edited by MacDiarmid in 1948. The poems in
'Theme and Variation' move away from bairn rhymes to offer
a sequence of variations and imitations of English poems
and translations from European literature, while the
'Whigmaleeries' contain some of his most humorous verses,
such as 'Ae Nicht at Amulree' and 'The Philosophic Taed' –
deceptively small pieces infused with an irreverent philosophical glee that refused to submit to his illness.

Soutar's example lived after him in the work of J. K. Annand
(b. 1908), a teacher whose delightful bairn rhymes are widely
used in Scottish schools. *Sing it Aince for Pleisure* first appeared in
1965; two further collections followed suit; and *Poems and
Translations* (1975) covers the work of nearly fifty years, going
back to his early contacts with MacDiarmid. The Scots of the

next poet, however, is far removed from the simpler tongue of Annand and Soutar, or the more colloquial language of his other contemporaries.

Sydney Goodsir Smith (1915–75)

Born in New Zealand of a Scottish mother, Smith did not arrive in Edinburgh – where his father had been appointed professor of Forensic Medicine – until his late teens. After an unsuccessful start as a medical student, he completed his education at Oxford before returning to Auld Reekie, the city he loved and was to celebrate for the rest of his life. *Skail Wind* (1941) contains poems in English and his first awkward verses in Scots, but by the time his third book appeared – *The Deevil's Waltz* (1946) – he had attained a characteristic literary voice. Indeed, he launched himself into the world of the middle-Scots makars as if he had found his own spirit and enthusiastic appetites reflected there. Beginning with obvious debts to Dunbar, Montgomerie and Douglas, Smith created a modern poetry of his own, just as Pound had done with the echoes from his interest in Provençal, Old English and Chinese poets. Smith's vocabulary and his cultural references can be arcane enough, but the energy of his expression becomes increasingly colloquial as the years go by. *The Deevil's Waltz* placed poems to John Maclean alongside a hymn to Venus, while its allusions link Prometheus, Beethoven, Pompeii, Tchaikovsky, Delacroix and the Declaration of Arbroath to the fall of Warsaw and the struggle at El Alamein. The whole war-torn world has become a Devil's waltz in the poet's eyes.

Most of Smith's best poetry was written in the post-war period, although his main collections did not appear until the fifties, with *So Late into the Night* (1952) and *Figs and Thistles* (1959). At the heart of his work at this time there are two outstanding books. The first is *Carotid Cornucopius* (1947), a prose extravaganza that reads as if Sir Thomas Urquhart had got Rabelais to describe the joys of drink and fornication in Edinburgh after the style of *Finnegans Wake*. Begun in 1945 – 'Anno Dambomini' – it is an ultimately exhausting *tour de force* of scatological and creative etymology with the author himself –

known as 'the Auk' to his friends – as the thinly disguised hero
of the title page:

> Caird of the Cannon Gait and Voyeur of the Outlook Touer, his splores,
> cantraips, wisdoms, houghmagandies, peribibulatiouns and all kinna
> abstrapulous junketings and ongoings abowt the high toun of Edenberg,
> capitule of Boney Scotland.
>   A drammantick, backside, bogbide, bedride or badside buik . . . .

Smith's undoubted masterpiece, however, is *Under the Eildon
Tree* (1948), a linked series of twenty-four love-poems, meditations, satires and elegies, and the only other long Scots poem of
the period to match *A Drunk Man*. By now his poetry, and his
life too, had come to celebrate a Villonesque vision of man's
fate, with himself cast as a bard at the mercy of love and drink,
swinging between exaltation and fornication as if to drive home
the glorious fallibility of a human condition utterly opposed to
Presbyterian respectability, material possession and industrial
progress. His setting was Auld Reekie in the spirit of Fergusson,
except that for Smith it becomes a timeless place where Diana
and Eurydice haunt the streets along with Bothwell and Huntly
and 'fair Montrose and a the lave / Wi silken leddies doun til the
grave' – not to forget sixteen-year-old 'Sandra', picked up in a
pub, 'drinkan like a bluidie whaul' with her 'wee paps, round
and ticht and fou / Like sweet Pomona in the oranger grove'
(XIII: 'The Black Bull o Norroway').
    This ribald, goliardic spirit is constantly qualified by the
poet's sense of that moment when all the merry music 'turns to
sleep' and 'The endmaist ultimate white silence faas / Frae
whilk for bards is nae retour' (I: 'Bards Hae Sung'). In the
meantime, as he sees it, there is only love, whose spiritual or
carnal delights bind us to our physical natures and undermine
the 'serious' world of politics and public affairs. Yet, even so, in
post-coital sadness or romantic partings the ties of love bring us
to a sense of death again. Hence the title of the poem refers to
Thomas the Rhymer's eerie encounter with the Queen of
Elfland, and Smith's elegies reflect on the unhappy fates of
'Highland Mary', Orpheus, Cuchulainn, Dido, Tristram and
Antony. Elegy XII from Orpheus is a particularly fine example
of the poet's capacity to move between mockery, pain, rage and
tenderness in the space of a few lines. Such pace is reminiscent
of the 'jostling of contraries' in MacDiarmid's *Drunk Man*, but

Smith has more confidence in handling free verse in Scots and a
Poundian breadth of reference:

– Euridicie stummelt.	stumbled
(*Lauchter cracked abune, Jupiter leuch*;	above; laughed
– And richtlie sae!	
Och, gie the gods their due,	
They ken what they're about.	
– The sleekans!)	crafty ones

She stummelt. I heard her cry. And hert ruled heid
again.
– What hert could eer refuse, then, siccan a plea?   such a
    I turned –
          And wi neer a word,
               In silence,
Her een aye bricht wi the joy o' resurrectioun,
She soomed awa afore my een intil a skimmeran wraith
And for a second and last time was tint for aye   lost
Amang the gloams and haars o Hell   shadows
      – Throu my ain twafauld treacherie!   [and mist

      '*Quhar art thou gane, my luf Euridices!*'

        iv

Sinsyne I haena plucked a note   Since then
    Nor made a word o a sang . . . .

The same dramatic and technical confidence appeared in
Figs and Thistles in the unlikely form of a poem written 'To Li Po
. . . *in memoriam* Robert Fergusson', and in 'The Twal', which is
the liveliest available translation of Alexander Blok's long
visionary poem in which the dispossessed of the earth drive
towards revolution through the snowstorm of history with
Christ in the lead. The play *The Wallace*, however, was less
successful and *Kynd Kittock's Land* (1965), written for television,
and *Gowdspink in Reekie* (1974) were longer poems which
covered already familiar ground without refreshing it. Smith
also wrote for radio and edited a number of Scottish literary
texts. Among his last poems there are several fine lyrics as well as
'Three', 'The Riggins of Chelsea' and 'Spring in the Botanic
Gardens', which recaptured the ironical swagger and the brave

melancholy of a generous, comic and genuinely anarchic spirit who lived like some reincarnation from the vulgar and scholarly howffs of eighteenth-century Edinburgh.

More scholarly still, and almost as unconventional, **Douglas Young** (1913–73) was one of several of the new makars (including Smith) who met in Edinburgh in 1947 to formulate rules for the spelling of modern literary Scots. (They were well intended, but poets soon went their own way again.) A polyglot enthusiast and Oxford scholar, Young taught classics at the universities of Aberdeen and St Andrew's before accepting a chair in North America. Over six feet tall, with a large black beard, he was a notably extrovert figure in Scottish Nationalist circles, and during the war he refused conscription on a point of politics and served a term in prison. He produced two volumes of his own poems in the mid forties and, although his Scots is not always smooth, it included verses taken from Russian, German, French, Italian and Latin originals, as well as translations of Gaelic poems by Maclean and Hay. His *Selected Poems* appeared in 1950 with *The Puddocks* (1957) and *The Burdies* (1959) as Scots versions of the comedies by Aristophanes.

Robert Garioch (1909–81)

A quieter and more retiring personality than his friend the Auk, **Robert Garioch Sutherland** (1909–81) graduated from the University of Edinburgh with a degree in English and spent the next thirty years as a schoolteacher – rather unhappy with the drudgery of the task and with the necessity for keeping discipline. He first appeared on the literary scene in 1933, with a column in the *Scots Observer* and 'The Masque of Edinburgh' – a satirical scenario of life in his native city, complete with famous figures from past and present. (An expanded version was published in 1954). Garioch (he rarely used his last name) committed himself to his main subject and to what he called 'artisan Scots' from the very start, and declared in 'The Masque' that 'a man who'd write in Edinboro / maun seek his language in a pub'. It was to be many years, however, before he found a publisher for his work, and his first two slim pamphlets were printed by himself. During the war Garioch was captured in North Africa in 1942, and *Two Men and a Blanket* (1975) gives an anti-heroic account of his time as a prisoner of war in Italy and Germany, bored and obsessed with food, like all the other prisoners. When peace came, he lived in London for thirteen years before returning to Edinburgh. Thenceforth Garioch adopted the position of a sceptical bystander in all his poetry. He felt a strong affinity with Robert Fergusson's outcast fate, making his own tribute to him in the fine sonnet 'At Robert Fergusson's Grave' and imitating his manner in a light-hearted satire on the Edinburgh Festival, called 'Embro to the Ploy'.

Garioch had a scholarly grasp of literature, for he translated George Buchanan's *Jephthah* and *The Baptist* from Latin into Scots in 1959, as well as poems from Apollinaire and many sonnets from the nineteenth-century Roman dialect of Giuseppe Belli. Nevertheless, the most frequent voice in his own poetry is that of the disaffected common man. Thus a brilliant sequence of 'Saxteen Edinburgh Sonnets' deflates the Athens of the North and its International Festival by describing it from the sidelines:

Some dignitaries in the cawrs, gey posh	cars
in queer, auld-farrant uniforms, were haean	old-fashioned; having
a rare auld time, it looked a lot of tosh	
to me, a beadle of some sort displayin	
frae ilk front sait a muckle siller cosh:	each; seat; great silver
shame on them aa, whativer they were daean!	doing

('Queer Ongauns')

If the speaker in 'Heard in the Gairdens' is newly unemployed, he is also free at last, for 'nae gaffer, boss nor beak / can touch me ferder . . . And nou I drop my guaird, / bide still in my ain neuk, lift up my heid'. The poet's own experience as a schoolteacher is never very far away in these and other pieces, and the comedy of 'Sisyphus' shows the teacher as a man who actually chooses the pointless labour of heaving boulders endlessly up a hill, simply for the sake of job security – 'shair of his cheque at the month's end'. 'Repone til George Buchanan' warns any would-be poets to avoid a profession in which 'ilka weekend, month and year / his life is tined [lost] in endless steir, / grindan awa in second gear'. At such moments there is a hint of rage and pain beyond the light comedy, and, if a belief in God, work and education lies at the heart of the Scottish Presbyterian ethos, then many of Garioch's verses are subtly subversive. 'A! Fredome is a noble thing!', cries 'The Canny Hen', but then she adds 'and kinna scarce, to tell the truth, / for naebody has muckle rowth [much to spare] / of fredome gin [if] he warks for wages'. Another thoughtful bird, 'The Percipient Swan', has 'ideas and notions and aĩbstract conceptions', but is still condemned to swim round and round in its pond because its wings have been clipped 'to keep me good':

> soumin roun
> like a mous in a well,
> glowred at by ratepeyers
> bored like masel.   myself

Henryson's beast fables and the romantic debasement of Baudelaire's 'Le Cygne' have been redefined in typical Garioch fashion. Yet even while going through the motions 'laid doun for me / by the Parks Committee', the bird plans a 'swan-song' that 'sall rhyme the end / of your hale stupid faction'. 'Brither Worm' describes the stone slabs of the New Town, whose neoclassical squares and crescents are the epitome of property and propriety; yet here the poet finds a worm, like a messenger of lowly life from another world:

> I was abaysit wi thochts of what was gaun-on ablow my feet,
> that the feued and rented grund was the soil of the naitural Drumsheuch
>   Forest,
> and that life gaed on thair in yon soil, and had sent out a spy . . . .

The realisation brings him to the wonders of Nature and 'the deeps of the soil, deeper nor the sea' until the mood is broken by the arrival of a rat – 'he leukit at me, and wes gane'.

Robert Garioch was very popular in public readings on the strength of his gently comic personality, and so the subversive nature of his humour and the darker vision which lies beneath it has sometimes been underestimated by his many admirers. 'The Wire' offers a nightmare allegory of entrapment and death on some vast moor, perhaps a Scottish grouse moor, where the heather, blaeberries and gossamer spider webs are overtaken by barbed wire and guard towers – images from his own imprisonment during the war, and more clearly universal ever since. 'The Muir' is a more ambitious attempt to write a discursive verse in Scots which can describe relativity, atomic physics, gravity and light, but Garioch's final mastery of free verse in Scots came with the longer poems from slightly later in his career. Verses such as his translations from Apollinaire, or 'Lesson' or 'The Big Music', are effectively weighty but still colloquial, with his own unique voice balanced between sober judgement and a kind of sadness at the small limitations of life and art:

> The piobaireachd comes til an end, gin we my cry it
>   end,
> the grund naukit again, as tho it had aye been sae.   naked
> Gin it werenae a competition, wi international rules,
> there seems nae reason why it sudnae stert owre again,
> gin the piper has braith eneuch, and there's nae dout
>   about that,
> but he neatly thraws the thrapple of the deil in his   rings the
>   pipes,   [throat
> that dees decently, wi nae unseemly scrauch.
> He taks leave of us wi dignity, turns, and is gane.
> The judges rate him heich, but no in the first three.

                              ('The Big Music)

The poetry of **Alexander Scott** (b. 1920) is equally collo- quial – he grew up speaking Scots in his native Aberdeen – but his own bold and vigorous nature, and a preference for alliterative effects, gives his work a rough-hewn formality – a paradoxical combination which suits his resolutely physical and anti-sentimental stance. This began with an early transla- tion of the Anglo-Saxon 'Seafarer' and it characterises poems such as 'Haar in Princes Street' and 'Heart of Stone', a notable long poem on his native city. Scott has championed Lallans and the teaching of Scots throughout his long career at the Department of Scottish Literature at Glasgow University, and as a well-known critic and editor his opinions are as forthright as his verse. His own writing in both English and Scots has remained consistent ever since *The Latest in Elegies* appeared in 1949, but his best work is in Scots. Poems such as 'Dear Deid Dancer' and 'To Mourn Jayne Mansfield', from *Cantrips* (1968), show his extrovert and sometimes cruelly sardonic outlook – 'Cauld is thon corp that fleered sae muckle heat, / Thae Babylon breists . . . .' Yet he shows a kind of brutal sympathy for the fate of such 'beautiful people', as if his real topic were to rage against mortality itself – a theme first raised in 'Coronach', a fine poem for the dead of the Gordon Highlanders with whom he served in the war.

The earliest poems of **Tom Scott** (b. 1918) were in English after the style of the New Apocalypse. He came to write Scots while he was a research student in the fifties, and his work reflects his scholarly involvement with the European cultural world of Villon, Dante and especially Dunbar – the subject of a book by him. Scott's *Seevin Poems o Maister Francis Villon* (1953) manage an effective balance between the colloquial and a sense of the originals' medieval nature. In *The Ship and Ither Poems* (1963) he produced verses on Ahab, Orpheus, Adam and Ulysses ('Ithaka'), all of which pursued the theme of freedom and renewal through pain and worldly experience. As a poet and an 'old fashioned utopian socialist' Scott deplored the egocentricity of modern 'confessional' verse and argued for the older and more culturally stable literary forms of allegory and epic. Thus 'The Ship' is a long symbolic piece on the plight of our materialistic culture, using the *Titanic* as the model for a modern ship of fools. His didactic impulse and the poetic problems of describing actions and speech eventually overburden the poem, but Scott has persevered with what he describes as 'symphonic verse' in *The Tree* (1977). The moments of excitement in this massive verse meditation on evolution do not offset dull pages of scientific and moral philosophising in English, but Scott has determined to follow the example of the later poems of MacDiarmid and Davidson with a lonely and acerbic integrity rather similar to that of his friend Fionn MacColla. Most critics have preferred the colloquial Scots in 'Brand the Builder', from a series of St Andrew's studies which he began in the fifties.

The publication of *Clytach* (1972) and *Back-Green Odyssey* (1980) came relatively late in life for **Alastair Mackie** (b. 1925) but they show a sensitive use of conversationally unforced Scots in his wry and humane reflections on family history, the nature of parenthood and middle age, or nostalgia for boyhood in Aberdeen. Mackie makes the ordinary world new again with a plain dignity and a growing craft free from sentiment or bombast. **Duncan Glen** (b. 1933) seeks a similar end with a low-key Scots in deliberately prosaic and transparent lines, at its best in the poems of personal recollection from *In Appearances* (1971) and *Realities* (1980). Glen founded and edited the poetry-magazine *Akros* from 1965 to 1983, and through many books from the Akros Press and his extensive work on Hugh MacDiarmid he has made a valuable contribution to Scottish letters for the last twenty years. From the younger generation a rougher urban Scots can be found in the work of Donald Campbell (b. 1940) – well suited to express the life of the streets in Edinburgh, where he lives, and this gift for dramatic speech has led him to work increasingly for the theatre. In the west of Scotland Stephen Mulrine (b. 1938), Tom McGrath (b. 1940), Alan Spence (b. 1947) and most notably Tom Leonard (b. 1944) have used the idiosyncratic aspects of Glasgow speech (and spelling) for their poetry, and although it may not be a purist's definition of literary Scots there is no doubt that they are writing succinct and witty poems in a valid colloquial idiom, in a movement whose work stems from the same upsurge of cultural confidence which characterised the Glasgow novel of the sixties and the new wave of proletarian plays ten years later.

Poetry in English

The works of Linklater, Gunn, Muir, Goodsir Smith and Sorley Maclean all testify to the fact that the 1940s were a productive period, despite the exigencies of war, and many new poets writing in English made their mark during these years. Figures such as J. F. Hendry, Maurice Lindsay, G. S. Fraser and Norman MacCaig had all had early contacts with the 'New Apocalypse' movement in the south, while William Soutar, MacDiarmid, Muir, Maclean, Alexander Scott, George Bruce and Douglas Young also featured with them in *Poetry Scotland* – an influential set of four magazine-format anthologies founded and edited by Maurice Lindsay between 1943 and 1949. R. Crombie Saunders and the artist J. D. Fergusson followed suit with five issues of *Scottish Art and Letters* from 1945 to 1950. Both these annuals were published by William Maclellan, whose fine press produced some of the best poetry-books of the period.

Among the poets whose works appeared in these volumes were William Jeffrey (1896–1946) and R. Crombie Saunders (b. 1914), both of whom wrote in Scots as well; and Joseph Macleod ('Adam Drinan', 1903–84), who worked in theatre and wrote poems for broadcasting before retiring to live in Florence. Ruthven Todd (b. 1914) was educated in Scotland and spent the war years in London before returning to his native America. Many of his verses reflect toughly or tenderly on his own northern inheritance and the Scottish landscape. Like Todd and Macleod, William Montgomerie (b. 1904) has spent many years abroad, and he and his wife also followed Soutar's lead by collecting and editing Scottish nursery-rhymes. Norman Cameron (1905–53) lived mostly abroad and in London, and he is especially remembered for his poems on the war in the desert.

The same campaign gave **Hamish Henderson** (b. 1919) his one, most remarkable book of verse – *Elegies for the Dead in Cyrenaica* (1948), based on his service there with the Highland Division. As an intelligence officer he played a role in the invasion of Italy, and his love for the country and his socialist convictions led him to translate Antonio Gramsci's *Letters from Prison*. The *Elegies* offer an effective documentary, sometimes rhetorical, picture of the desert war, but Henderson takes in a larger perspective too. In his Foreword he noted how frequently vehicles would change hands in the 'deceptive distances' of the desert, and how the landscape and dust seemed to turn their enemies into mirror images of themselves. Thus he sees the ordinary soldiers of both sides united in death, and united against death – a metaphysical and egalitarian theme for which he uses colloquial slang as well as more austere passages coloured by Gaelic speech-patterns:

> There were our own, there were the others.
> Therefore, minding the great word of Glencoe's
> son, that we should not disfigure ourselves
> with villainy of hatred; and seeing that all
> have gone down like curs into anonymous silence,
> I will bear witness for I knew the others.
> Seeing that littoral and interior are alike indifferent
> and the birds are drawn again to our welcoming north
> why should I not sing *them*, the dead, the innocent?

> (First Elegy, 'End of a Campaign')

Henderson joined the School of Scottish Studies in 1951 and is widely known and respected among traditional musicians, not least for his own songs, such as 'The Banks o Sicily', 'The Freedom Come All Ye', 'The John Maclean March' and 'Free Mandela'. Morris Blythman ('Thurso Berwick', 1919–82) belongs to the same radical tradition, with songs such as 'The Scottish Breakaway', but his roots as a writer go back to the socialism of Glasgow in the thirties.

The short-lived Apocalypse movement reacted against overtly political commitment by following a programme of much more inward-looking, symbolic or surrealistic verse. One of the leading lights of this movement, along with Henry Treece and G. S. Fraser (their theorist) was **J. F. Hendry** (b. 1912), who coedited all three Apocalypse anthologies. His novel *Fernie Brae* (1947) describes life in Glasgow and the west from his own childhood, but his verse has a much more abstract and intellectual style, with staccato lines and a crystalline coolness, especially in the visionary title-poem, called a 'polar sonata', in *Marimarusa* (1978). **G. S. Fraser** (1915–80) was born in Glasgow and educated in Aberdeen, but after the war he spent most of his time in England working as a freelance journalist, a critic and then a lecturer at Leicester. His own verse had never been truly Apocalyptic and, indeed, he became an influential figure with the 'Movement' poets in London in the fifties. Some of his best early poems took the form of 'letters home' during the war, which he spent in the Middle East ('A Winter Letter'), and this mode continued to suit his relaxed, civilised and wryly self-deprecating verse. He admired the selfless mildness of Edwin Muir's poetry, but mental tensions of his own gave new urgency to the work of the late sixties – 'Speech of a Sufferer', 'The Insane Philosophers'. Fraser never truly lost his gently sceptical neoclassical balance, however, as can be seen in *Poems of G. S. Fraser* (1981), which reprints all four of his earlier collections.

Norman MacCaig (b. 1910)

Although this poet wrote his first two collections in the Apocalyptic vein, he has taken care to disown them in later years, having come to value clarity, compassion and a certain humane elegance of the mind above all else – fitting qualities for a classics graduate of Edinburgh University. MacCaig returned to schoolteaching after the war – his abhorrence of killing made him a conscientious objector – and he has lived in Edinburgh ever since. He was the first 'writer in residence' at the university there in 1967, and three years later he joined the English Department at the University of Stirling, subsequently becoming Reader in Poetry until his retirement in 1978. He was a friend of Goodsir Smith's and had a close relationship with Hugh MacDiarmid in the poet's later years. Greatly in demand at public poetry-readings, MacCaig has produced a book every one or two years since *Riding Lights* in 1955. The most recent selection of his work is *Old Maps and New* (1978), and a *Collected Poems* will appear in 1985.

Despite his long career in Edinburgh, the spiritual fulcrum of MacCaig's work is to be found nearer to Lochinver, where he retreats from the city every summer. 'Return to Scalpay' – the island where his Gaelic-speaking mother was born – affirms his love for the people and the landscapes of the North-West, from which he derives the gaiety, the penetrating understatement and the wry modesty which characterise him. MacCaig's poetry grows from the delight with which he greets the world, but the images which he creates to describe people, animals and landscapes also reflect back on language and his own observing mind. So MacCaig is never simply a 'nature' poet, and his preference for linking precise observation with creative wit can be seen in an early poem, 'Summer Farm': 'A hen stares at nothing with one eye, / Then picks it up'. He recognises that this is a perception which depends on his own eye, as if he could lift the farm 'like a lid and see / Farm within farm, and in the centre, me'. MacCaig's work came to full maturity of expression and technique with his move to free verse in the mid sixties, and in a succession of poems over the years he has delighted readers with his deftness in creating likenesses which seem so just, but were never there before – frogs die on the roads 'with arms across their chests . . . like Italian tenors' ('Frogs'), or a toad is told to 'stop looking like a purse' ('Toad'). In such a world the poet has cultivated his capacity for surprise ('Country Dance') or even sudden terror ('Basking Shark'), while a quiet rage at the fact of human suffering is found in 'Assisi'. Nevertheless, the reflective–reflexive habit of mind is not an unmixed blessing, and in other poems MacCaig has explored the more awkward implications of the relationship betwen himself, language and other people. 'A Man in My Position' and 'Private' recognise that there is a 'comfortable MacCaig whose / small predictions were predictable', while 'Equilibrist' tells how the radio can be switched from tortures in foreign prisons 'to a sonata of Schubert (that foreigner)'. He draws his own conclusions from the juxtaposition with typical reserve: 'Noticing you can do nothing about. / It's the balancing that shakes my mind'. Since he does not accede to Christian or political dogma of any kind, he has to achieve that balance on his own, just as he had to reconcile himself to the death of MacDiarmid and to that of a close friend in Inverkirkaig. That effort led to a collection called *The Equal Skies* (1980), which contains some of his most moving and finely controlled poems.

A more theoretical involvement with the problems of creative language can be found in the poetry of **W. S. Graham** (b. 1948), a Greenock man who has lived in Cornwall for many years. As a friend of Dylan Thomas and George Barker, Graham showed affinities with the Apocalyptic writers in his early work, although verses such as 'The Children of Greenock' were more autobiographical. He became well known with *The Nightfishing* (1955), a long poem which makes fishing and the sea (which features in much of his work) a symbol for the creative process. The making of poetry and the nature of language itself have been consistent themes in Graham's work ever since. Thus the cerebral wit of 'Malcolm Mooney's Land' associated the awful spaces of arctic exploration with the terrifying whiteness (for a writer) of blank paper, and 'The Dark Dialogues' brought this more abstract concern with the place 'where I am, between / This word and the next' into closer touch with his childhood in Greenock. This welcome biographical directness returns in such fine poems as 'Loch Thom' and 'To Alexander Graham', from *Implements in their Places* (1977). In the same collection 'Joachim Quantz's Five Lessons' uses a well-realised historical setting to consider the disciplines of art, and he reintroduces 'Malcolm Mooney' to ask 'What is the Language Using Us For?', in a witty sequence on the elusive, illusive, nature of syntax and sentences.

Graham's more speculative poems show that he has long recognised what contemporary critics have had to say about the artificial status of the word. On the other hand, the bare and telling verses of **George Bruce** (b. 1909) see the word and the world as inescapable verities. He grew up in the fishing town of Fraserburgh to the north of Aberdeen, and the stern religious faith of the place, its clear light and its harsh coast are all reflected in the linguistic austerity which he chose for his first collection, *Sea Talk* (1944). 'Inheritance' maintains that 'This which I write now / Was written years ago. . . . It was stamped / In the rock formations / West of my home town'. The longer lines of the title-poem describe the culture of the place, using the sand-blown fields, the boney-faced fishermen and a beach of stones, crabs, bones and splinters of shell for his images and setting them against the terrors of the sea and the shapelessness of salt fog. Bruce has written fine occasional poems on the social scene and political events, but his best later work has always seemed to come from the originally stark themes of *Sea Talk*. 'A Man of Inconsequent Build' remembers his father as cooper in Fraserburgh, while a set of four poems on 'Tom' mixes the pathos of childhood with more chilly premonitions of the future – 'We hold out our hands to History / Then ask not to be taken'.

George Bruce's *Collected Poems* appeared in 1970, the year he retired from a long career as talks-producer for the BBC, during which time he did much to encourage younger authors. Since retiring he has been even more active as a visiting writer in Scotland, America and Australia. **Sidney Tremayne** (b. 1912) also worked in the media, as a journalist, but has taken little active part in literary circles. His *Selected and New Poems* (1973) shows how he achieves an unselfish descriptive purity which grows from his observational delight in the countryside with its animals and the weather in all its moods. His is a genuine 'nature poetry', thoughtful, but without the metaphysical stress which Bruce finds in his landscapes.

All the foregoing poets appeared in *Poetry Scotland* during the forties. It is appropriate to close that particular group with the work of **Maurice Lindsay** (b. 1918), who had so much to do with the series and who has continued an active career as journalist, editor, critic and literary historian ever since. He became director of the Scottish Civic Trust in 1967 and his contacts with television have kept him in the public eye. His early experiments with Scots (*Hurlygush*, 1948) did not master the medium, but by the 1960s his own polished and urbane responses to the social scene had come into their own. His essentially conservative nature has more in common with Philip Larkin, perhaps, than with many of his Scottish contemporaries, and, if he lacks Larkin's capacity for flashes of sudden rage or despair, he has a more companionable enjoyment of the world. No slave to fashion, and certainly not a modernist, Lindsay explains in the Preface to his *Collected Poems* (1979) that he has been glad to write as 'an enjoyable poet'. This stance was further celebrated in a long autobiographical poem in *ottava rima* called *A Net to Catch the Winds* (1981).

The last four figures to be considered in the 'second wave' of poets who used English could not be more different from each other. They come from the four corners of the country and embrace literary and philosophical views almost equally far apart.

George Mackay Brown (b. 1921)

Born in Orkney, Brown worked as a local journalist until he was in his thirties, before becoming one of Edwin Muir's mature students at Newbattle College. It was through Muir's direct encouragement that his first major collection, *Loaves and Fishes*, was published in 1959. Brown suffered badly from tuberculosis, which was to interrupt and curtail his studies more than once; nevertheless he persevered and graduated from Edinburgh in 1960, continuing with research for a couple of years before returning to Orkney, where he has lived ever since. From the very first, Brown's poems have presented a consistent vision of Orkney life in a style derived from the sagas and reduced to its archetypal essentials, so that the little community of 'fishermen with ploughs' becomes a model for all life, and especially of the 'good life' which he prizes. He is deeply opposed to the values of industrial materialism, which he sees as an inheritance from the Reformation, being influenced in these views by Muir's autobiography and the friendship he formed with the older poet. Mackay Brown goes much further than Grassic Gibbon and Gunn as a writer who seeks to evoke timeless values and mythopoeic patterns in his work, and, like Muir and Fionn MacColla, he found these qualities in Catholicism and joined the Church in 1961. The very title of *Loaves and Fishes* relates to the sacramental symbols in his ideal vision of life on Orkney, while a poem such as 'Our Lady of the Waves', from his next collection, uses the simple ritual of labour among the brothers at Eynhallow in order to reflect all experience:

> Queen of Heaven, this good day
> There is a new cradle at Quoys.
> It rocks on the blue floor.
> And there is a new coffin at Hamnavoe.
> Arnor the poet lies there
> Tired of words and wounds.
> In between, what is man?
> *A head bent over fish and bread and ale.*
> *Outside, the long furrow.*
> *Through a door, a board with a shape on it.*
>
> Guard the plough and the nets.
>
> Star of the sea shine for us.

Such pure images and terse lines are typical of Mackay Brown's lucid, gentle inspiration, and his feeling for reverence and ritual in the humble acts of life has produced memorable work. His best and most innovative poems appear in *Fishermen with Ploughs* (1971), a linked 'poem cycle' which records, very obliquely, the rise and fall of the community of Rackwick on Hoy. Different sections take it through the ages from the epic days of its foundation to modern decline, and then on to a resettlement which is described in prose journals after some unknown future cataclysm. It is characteristic of Brown's historical position that he should explain that 'the same people appear and reappear through many generations . . . all are caught up in "the wheel of bread" that is at once brutal and holy'. This is not to say that he does not have a dry sense of humour in some of these verses, as also in, for example, the 'Tea Poems' from *Winterfold* (1971). Even so, after several collections, the poet's cyclical themes do tend to lead always to the 'same people', until the timeless is in danger of becoming merely static.

Brown's short stories bring him back into contact with the world, and they may yet be judged to be his finest achievement.

The title-story from *A Calendar of Love* (1967) takes place in modern times, but the author calls on episodic cycles of fertility, birth, shame and forgiveness, to set the stage for a succession of such tales from different eras. He is closest to contemporary life in *A Time to Keep* (1969), and his studies of alcoholism and loneliness in 'Celia' and 'The Eye of the Hurricane', and of the cruelty of fate in 'A Time to Keep', show that his prose can rise to an outstanding tact and sensitivity. 'Celia' was made into a memorable television production and Brown has written many other plays and radio plays, not least through his association with the composer Peter Maxwell Davies and their work together for the Orkney Festival. His book *Magnus* (1973) establishes a pared-down, epic quality to the life and martyrdom of St Magnus, operating somewhere between a saga and a devotional mediation. Brown's prose is effective, but the work is not a novel in the conventional sense, unlike its predecessor, *Greenvoe* (1972), which describes the end of an island community on 'Hellya' in the 1960s.

Greenvoe is taken over by an unspecified military-research or defence project called 'Black Star'. Brown assembles a picture of the community by revealing the foibles of its various inhabitants from different points of view, but the reader may be forgiven for feeling that it is rather close to the Kailyard, despite the author's obvious affection for it. Hellya is no sooner cleared of its inhabitants than the project closes down, although in the larger perspective of history and with the survival of the old rituals of the 'Lord of the Harvest' the saga continues. Brown could be describing several such military and industrial projects in modern Scotland, but the author's mythic and fatalistic habit of mind will not let his theme develop to tragedy or anger, nor does it always do justice to the tensions and complexities inherent in the contemporary world.

Iain Crichton Smith (Iain Mac a'Ghobhainn, b. 1928)

In a different sense, Crichton Smith is equally at the mercy of a metaphysical point of view, for his upbringing on Lewis brought him into contact with the absolutism of the Free Kirk and his poetry has reflected that meeting ever since. Caught between discipline and freedom, or 'Thistles and Roses', or

'The Law and the Grace' (the titles of his first two collections), Smith is divided again between Gaelic and English, for he has written poetry and prose in his mother tongue, and translated some of it into what he has called a 'foreign language'. Nevertheless, it was as an English teacher that he worked in Oban for twenty-two years. A complex, sensitive and intelligent poet, Smith is a compulsive and sometimes too prolific writer, with over eighteen volumes of verse to his name, as well as plays, short stories and several novels.

MacDiarmid saw excitement in the thrilling clash of contraries, but Smith finds it a more personal and painful thing, closer, perhaps, to Edwin Muir's diagnosis of a Scottish division between the head and the heart – 'I am tied to the Highlands', he wrote in the Gaelic poem 'Eight Songs for a New Ceilidh', 'that is where I learnt my wound'; and, again, 'it was the fine bareness of Lewis that made the work of my mind'. If he paraphrases Sidney's advice to poets to ' "Look in your own heart and write" ', then his heart is a divided place. Translations of his two main Gaelic collections can be found in *The Permanent Island*, 1975. They are *Biobuill is Sanasan Reice* ('Bibles and Advertisements'), 1965; and *Eadar Fealla-dha is Glaschu* ('Between Comedy and Glasgow'), 1969. Smith seems able to speak more directly in his Gaelic verse, and many poems in the 1965 collection offer invaluable insights into his work as a whole – from his love of the stark landscapes of his native island and his desire for the 'bareness of the knife's blade' to the sense of desolation which he finds there, too, and an awareness of Nagasaki, Hiroshima and Belsen set against the standing stones of Callanish. He writes of division in his relationship with language, seeing himself 'In the dress of the fool, the two colours that have tormented me – English and Gaelic, black and red, the court of injustice, the reason for my anger': 'The Fool' ('An t-Amadan'), and he concludes that the result is a motley 'so odd that the King himself will not understand my conversation'.

Crichton Smith is a poet haunted by images, sometimes almost beyond his capacity to comprehend them; thus, in the Gaelic poem 'What is Wrong' ('Dé tha Ceàrr'), he feels once again divided between head and heart, until a characteristic moment of insight occurs:

> But one day I saw a black pit in green earth, a gardener kissing flowers, an old woman squeaking in her loneliness, and a house sailing on the water.

I don't know whether there is a language for that, or, if there is, whether I
would be any better breaking my imagination into a thousand pieces. . . .

His many volumes of poetry in both Gaelic and English
describe a continuing search to find 'a language for that' and,
sometimes too, the breaking of his imagination into a thousand
pieces. Thus the sequence 'Am Faigh a' Ghaidlig Bas?' ('Shall
Gaelic Die?', 1969), links a passionate concern with the future
of his native tongue with a more philosophical understanding of
the nature of all language-systems as limited conventions
standing between the real and the abstract – and yet they still
encapsulate untranslatable subtleties.

The bareness of Lewis and the starkness of Calvinism come
together in Smith's early work to make a complicated weave of
love and hate – 'Here they have no time for the fine graces of
poetry', he wrote in 'Poem of Lewis', from his first collection in
1955. His admiration for the stoic strength of such an
inheritance and his equal alarm at its grim narrowness feature
in his many poems about old women, who become symbols of
mortality for him, as well as key figures in the daily life between
hearth and Kirk. He can describe the 'thorned back' and the
'set mouth' of righteousness which 'forgives no-one, not even
God's justice / perpetually drowning law with grace' ('Old
Woman'); yet at the same time he understands this spirit and
shares its delight in hard certainties. 'There is no metaphor', he
concludes in *Deer on the High Hills* (1962); 'The stone is
stony. / The deer step out in isolated air. . . . Winter is wintry,
lonely is your journey.' The deer are symbols for the spirit
which moves him in this long poem, because 'A deer looks
through you to the other side, / and what it is and sees is an
inhuman pride'. He knows compassion too, and the importance of dignity in the face of death, and 'Old Woman', from
Thistles and Roses (1961), is one of the finest and most lyrically
moving studies of old age in modern literature:

And she being old, fed from a mashed plate
as an old mare might droop across a fence
to the dull pastures of its ignorance.
Her husband held her upright while he prayed

to God who is all-forgiving to send down
some angel somewhere who might land perhaps

in his foreign wings among the gradual crops.
She munched, half dead, blindly searching the spoon.

Outside, the grass was raging. There I sat
imprisoned in my pity and my shame
that men and women having suffered time
should sit in such a place, in such a state

and wished to be away. . . .

Crichton Smith chose an old woman as the protagonist of his
first novel, *Consider the Lilies* (1969), giving a grim account of the
Clearances through her consciousness. His memories of his
mother – he lived with her for many years and married
relatively late – add to his insight into such themes, and he has
reflected on the harshness of her youth as a fish-gutter following
the herring fleet around Britain, compared to his own sheltered
education at Aberdeen University (*Love Poems and Elegies*,
1972). In other poems his compassion for young girls may well
grow from his awareness of the hardships which the world will
probably bring to them.

While many of Smith's poems respond to the physical beauty
of the hills and the islands, other verses, in *From Bourgeois Land*
(1968) and in sequences such as 'By the Sea' and 'The White
Air of March', convey his scathing impatience with much of
Lowland Scottish life – stifled by respectability, given over to
third-rate jokes and music, or cluttered with souvenirs for the
tourist trade. His novels produce a similarly critical, but less
savage, account of bourgeois life and the limitations of a timidly
intellectual middle class – especially schoolteachers. *My Last
Duchess* (1971) and *An End to Autumn* (1978) make their points
by exteriorising the inward states of such characters, rather
than through any broader social analysis. Despite the rather
grey world of these books, it would be wrong to suppose that
Crichton Smith lacks humour, for his dry wit can be found in
English and Gaelic alike, most notably in the poems of *Eadar
Fealla-dha is Glaschu*, an entertaining series of epigrams, 'Gaelic
stories' and 'haikus' in affectionate mockery of his own
background. In prose, too, *Murdo and Other Stories* (1981)
expresses a wilder and hilariously absurd side to his nature,
which was always there, along with an elusive and fey quality,

among the darker intensities of his work in both the languages
of his inheritance.

Edwin Morgan (b. 1920)

Edwin Morgan might be said to epitomise MacDiarmid's
hopes for a cosmopolitan and outward-looking culture in
post-Renaissance Scotland. As an academic and poet, his
interests range widely, turning more often to Europe and
America than they do to London and the south, and he has
translated verse by Mayakovsky, Montale, Voznesensky,
Quasimodo, Brecht, Neruda, Weöres, Juhasz and many
others. His own poetry is equally varied, for he is a man whose
essentially private and optimistic nature is attuned to the face
of the contemporary world, very often as it comes to us by way
of newspapers and television. Where other writers see only
confusion, decay or empty technology, Morgan discovers
growth, change, flux and delight. He uses his poetry to report
back on these discoveries or to push our imaginations a little
further beyond them. With over 400 pages (excluding his books
of translations), Morgan's *Poems of Thirty Years* (1982) testifies
to his witty engagement with science fiction, sound poetry and
concrete verse, and his grasp of dramatic and imaginative
narrative verse. Among more than twenty books and pamphlets the major collections have been *The Second Life* (1968),
From Glasgow to Saturn (1973) and *The New Divan* (1977).

As a lecturer and then a professor of English at the
University of Glasgow, Morgan has spent his working life in the
city of his birth, and it features in many of his poems. 'King
Billy', 'Death in Duke Street', 'Glasgow Green' and a sequence
of ten 'Glasgow Sonnets', describe a grim and sordid world of
urban decay, old age, religious bigotry, and muttered threats of
violence or desire, all very much in the popular image of 'No
Mean City'. Yet 'King Billy' ends with an admonition to
'Deplore what is to be deplored,/ and then find out the rest',
and 'Glasgow Green' comes to sympathise with the hunter and
the hunted and the violent demands of the flesh 'as it
trembles/ like driftwood through the dark'. Morgan can find
compassion and a kind of beauty in his city, for he sees energy

and a superb carelessness in the drunks of 'Saturday Night', or he celebrates the 'happy demolition men' in 'For Bonfires', who tear down an old slum 'stacking and building/their rubbish into a total bonfire . . . they all stand round,/and cheer the tenement to smoke'. Anonymous encounters in the city can lead to fear or the thrill of sexual danger ('The Suspect', 'Christmas Eve'), but there is redemption too, in the ordinary charity of people ('Trio'), or in the almost unbearable, dull courage of a blind hunchback ('In the Snack-Bar'), just as there is beauty in a Joan Eardley painting of decayed shop-fronts and city urchins – 'Such rags and streaks that master us!' ('To Joan Eardley'). Morgan's Glasgow poems do try to 'find out the rest', and his unsentimental eye for beauty and compassion in the grimy streets makes him unique among British poets of his generation.

If the tenements and the 'rags and streaks' are transformed into smoke – or poetry – in the Glasgow verses, then Morgan's many sound-poems and 'computer' poems also have to do with transmutation, especially as it occurs when information is transmitted. 'Message Clear' and 'The Computer's First Christmas Card' act out a painful progress towards some final statement – a telling theme for any poet to choose. Thus a succession of broken lines are slowly reconstructed from scattered letters down the page to end with 'I am the resurrection and the life' ('Message Clear') or a manic ticker-tape of worthy attempts is churned out only to fail at the last line, by wishing the programmer

```
m e r r y C h r i s
a m m e r r y a s a
C h r i s m e r r y
a s M E R R Y C H R
Y S A N T H E M U M
```

Morgan has written many poems around similar effects, including sound-poems such as 'The Shaker Shaken', in which a stanza of nonsense syllables is repeated five times – each time with a few more real words substituted until the listener begins to experience a poem with strangely beautiful surreal images as it emerges from the abstract rhythmical noise. Morgan called his early ventures in such modes 'Emergent Poems', and the same process features in many of his 'science fiction' pieces. 'In

Sobieksi's Shield', 'The Gourds', 'Memories of Earth' and the hilarious 'The First Men on Mercury' all deal with confusions, transmissions or transmutations when the world of matter and of words is suddenly seen to be mutable, frightening, beautiful or insecure. This understanding lies at the core of all Morgan's art, and it links the Glasgow poems to the science-fiction verses, just as it runs through the computer and the concrete poems to go back to language itself and the world that language creates, whether it be on Glasgow, Saturn or the printed page. Morgan's fine talent for the evocative and elusive image transcends all categories, especially in the exotic and opaquely personal meditations in the sequence of 'The New Divan' – 'Let matter/envy you the metamorphoses a/dancer steals and cannot stay'.

Ian Hamilton Finlay (b. 1925)

Finlay is a writer who has gone beyond the page to become known as one of Europe's leading concrete poets. His work began with short stories, a radio-play and a collection of more or less conventional poems, *The Dancers Inherit the Party* (1960), although their odd humour and deliberately small scale was already rather original. A set of animal haikus followed in urban patois, but after *Glasgow Beasts, and a Burd . . .* (1961), Finlay became involved with the international movement known as 'concrete poetry'. There are many kinds of concrete verse, but essentially it is a move away from egocentrically romantic self-expression towards a poetry which concentrates on the import, or even the shape, of individual words and how they are spaced out on the page. Edwin Morgan's concrete verse often plays on witty shapes, puns and acrostics: for instance, his poem to Isambard Kingdom Brunel is shaped like a bridge made out of lines which ring the changes on his name – 'I am bard/I am Isobar/I am Iron Bar', etc. By comparison Finlay has taken a quieter and more classical line towards his declared goal of 'lucidity, clarity, resolved complexity'. *Poems to Hear and See* (1971) uses coloured inks and graphic effects, such as the word 'a c r o b a t s' printed over and over to fill the page as if the letters are standing on each others' shoulders. Alternatively the word 'STAR' is repeated in a wavering column down the page until it suddenly becomes 'STEER' at the last line. In these examples the conceptual implications within and beyond what the words mean have been explored in an engagingly unpretentious way. He also wrote 'one-word' poems which operate rather like the Japanese haiku in that they depend on an imaginative leap between the title and the verse. Thus the poem called 'The Cloud's Anchor' consists of a single word – 'swallow'.

In 1969 Finlay and his wife settled in a remote farmhouse, 'Stonypath' at Dunsyre, to set up a small press and produce dozens of booklets and over 200 cards and poem-prints in this vein. He uses favourite images of fishing-boats, nets, waves, canals, sailing-ships, stars, sundials and the seasons, and his poems and constructions share a simple and beautiful integrity – a welcome alternative to the then prevailing vogue for agonisingly 'confessional' verse. Finlay's work has continued to evolve and much of it is now realised in stone, wood and glass constructed to his designs by different artists and craftsmen. His work has been more widely exhibited and commissioned in Europe than in Britain, and the carefully landscaped garden which he has created around his house has become another kind of artistic statement, expressed through plants, sundials and inscribed stones. The link with eighteenth-century landscape gardening is not accidental, for Finlay takes a learned and resolutely classical approach to his art, enlivened by his fondness for apparently iconoclastic, but ultimately satisfying, images – such as a nuclear submarine's sail (conning-tower) in black slate, which serves as a worldless *memento mori* at the edge of an ornamental pond. In this at least, Hamilton Finlay has passed beyond the conventional definition of 'poetry', although he has never lost touch with its essence in surprise, illumination and delight.

Poetry in Gaelic

Although MacDiarmid's programme for the Renaissance began with Lowland Scots, it was not long before he included Gaelic in his vision of how a truly distinct Scottish culture should develop. By 1930 specifically Gaelic references were appearing in his work, and major poetic statements such as

'Lament for the Great Music' and 'Island Funeral' soon followed. Nevertheless, it was the poetry of Sorley Maclean which most truly brought the Gaelic tradition into the twentieth century, and in this respect he has been as vital an example to his fellow writers as ever MacDiarmid was to poets in Scots and English. As with the Kailyard, comic Gaelic verses and sentimental 'homeland' themes had persisted into the new century, while other poets were content to stay within the traditional modes – as, for example, the Skye man Angus Robertson (Aonghas MacDhonnchaidh, 1870–1948), who also wrote a novel (*An t-Ogha Mor*, 1913) set between the Jacobite risings. All this changed when Maclean's first collection of poems appeared in 1943.

Sorley Maclean (Somhairle MacGill-Eain, b. 1911)

Maclean was born on the island of Raasay, between Skye and the mainland, coming from a family with strong roots in the tales, music, songs and poems of the Gaelic tradition. Studying for a degree in English at the University of Edinburgh in the 1930s, the young man came into contact with the poems of Eliot, Pound and the seventeenth-century metaphysicals. In his final year he came across MacDiarmid's lyrics and the *Drunk Man*, and they left a lasting impression on him, crystallising many of his feelings about Scottish culture and how a poet could encompass both intellect and passion in his work. By 1934 Maclean had met the older poet and was helping him with his translations of MacMhaighstir Alasdair's *Birlinn Chlann Raghnaill* and Duncan Bàn Macintyre's 'Moladh Beinn Dòbhrain'. Maclean's pursuit of what he called 'the lyric cry' in verse took him in a completely different direction from MacDiarmid, and he was never a fully convinced Scottish nationalist; nevertheless, the two men found much in common – they were both committed socialists, after all – and they remained close friends for many years.

Maclean was one among many writers in the thirties to be deeply concerned by the rise of fascism and the outbreak of the Spanish Civil War. Social justice at home seemed equally important, and the poem 'Calvary' ('Calbharaigh') from his student years reflects his outrage at the slums of the Depression:*

> My eye is not on Calvary
> nor on Bethlehem the Blessed,
> but on a foul-smelling backland in Glasgow,
> where life rots as it grows;
> and on a room in Edinburgh,
> a room of poverty and pain,
> where the diseased infant
> writhes and wallows till death.

Employment as a schoolteacher took the poet to Mull for two years, where he saw the effects of cultural decline and the Clearances on every beautiful and barren hillside. This experience led him to compose more poems and to seek publication for them. The bitterness of 'A Highland Woman' ('Ban-Ghàidheal') belongs to this period: 'Hast Thou seen her, great Jew,/who art called the One Son of God?' Then, in the later thirties, Maclean underwent an extremely intense and tortured love-affair, and the pressure of events in the world at large joined with his own heightened emotional state to produce the creative outpouring of the poems to 'Eimhir' and other works, in his first and most famous collection. (He had already shared a little booklet with Robert Garioch – *17 Poems for 6d*, 1940.) The new manuscript was complete by 1941, when Maclean left Scotland to serve in the desert campaign in North Africa, but the problems of wartime publishing were such that the book did not appear until 1943, by which time its author was in an English hospital, convalescing from serious wounds suffered at the battle of El Alamein. The publication of *Dain do Eimhir agus Dain Eile* (*Poems to Eimhir and Other Poems*, 1943) was a milestone in modern Gaelic poetry, assuring Maclean of a lasting reputation, even although it was to be twenty-seven years before his next book was published.

Among the 'other poems' in the collection there are pieces, such as 'Glen Eyre' ('Gleann Aoighre') and 'The Island' ('An t-Eìlean'), which celebrate his own family history and the beloved landscapes of Skye; others focus on his political convictions. 'Cornford' is an agonised lament on the Spanish

---

* All the modern Gaelic poems in this chapter have been translated by the poets themselves – usually in their own dual text editions.

Civil War, in which John Cornford, Julian Bell and Garcia Lorca died, and the poet feels that he should himself have made some more active commitment. The heart of the book, however, is to be found in the forty-eight lyrics to 'Eimhir', although they are not conventional love-poems at all. It is as if Maclean's mixed feeling about the affair, his thoughts on his Gaelic heritage, his political awareness of the agony of Europe and a passionately spiritual idealism have all been heated and brought to almost unbearable intensities by the catalyst of love. Poem IV, 'The Cry of Europe' ('Gaoir na h-Eorpa'), is terribly divided between personal desire and a more general awareness:

> Girl of the yellow, heavy-yellow, gold-yellow hair,
> the song of your mouth and Europe's shivering cry,
> fair, heavy-haired, spirited, beautiful girl,
> the disgrace of our day would not be bitter in your kiss.
>
> Would your song and splendid beauty take
> from me the dead loathsomeness of these ways,
> the brute and the brigand at the head of Europe
> and your mouth red and proud with the old song?

In poem XLIII, 'The Blue Rampart' ('Am Mùr Gorm'), she becomes 'my reason and the likeness of a star', or he celebrates her as a 'dawn on the Cuillin' (LIV: 'Camhanaich') or he muses on the pointlessness of writing anything at all:

> I do not see the sense of my toil
> putting thoughts in a dying tongue
> now when the whoredom of Europe
> is murder erect and agony;
> but we have been given the million years,
> a fragment of a sad growing portion,
> the heroism and patience of hundreds
> and the miracle of a beautiful face.
>
> (LV: 'I Do Not See . . .': 'Chan Fhaic Mi . . .')

Maclean creates an extraordinary tension in these poems, and, although they are still based on traditional Gaelic metres and modes of expression (he admired William Ross and Mary Macpherson), he brings many other elements from beyond the native canon. Thus he has been influenced by his reading of Yeats and the Metaphysicals, there are echoes of Sidney's plight in *Astrophel and Stella*, and he uses musical and opaque images in the manner of European Symbolism. Driven by his own urgent socialism, mixed with feelings of desire and guilt, Maclean's verse is haunted by images of hurt and desolation, as when the 'knife' of his brain 'made incision, my dear, on the stone of my love,/ and its blade examined every segment' (xLV: 'The Knife': 'An Sgian'); or his unwritten love-poems come to seem like dogs and wolves with the spoor of their paws dappling the snows of eternity, 'their baying yell shrieking / across the hard bareness of the terrible times' (xxIX: 'Dogs and Wolves': 'Coin is Madaidhean-Allaidh'). In the end Eimhir becomes a symbol of beauty and pain, as if the poet were struggling to reach an aspect of his own ideal spirit against the world itself and the inevitability of defeat and loss. This metaphysical dimension also appears in 'The Woods of Raasay' ('Coilltean Ratharsair'), and, although it is not one of the love-lyrics, this long celebration of the woods shifts from the detailed descriptive tradition of Gaelic praise-poems to a more complex and symbolic meditation on the tangles of love and idealism, concluding,

There is no knowledge of the course
    of the crooked veering of the heart,
    and there is no knowledge of the damage
    to which its aim unwittingly comes.

There is no knowledge, no knowledge,
    of the final end of each pursuit,
    nor of the subtlety of the bends
    with which it loses its course.

After the war Maclean returned to teaching in Edinburgh, and from 1956 until he retired he was headmaster at the school in Plockton on the mainland to the east of Skye. He published fine poems in *Poetry Scotland* and other periodicals from time to time, but the emotional storm of *Dain do Eimhir* had passed, and it was 1970 before a substantial selection of his work appeared again. His *Selected Poems* from 1932–72 were published in two languages as *Reothairt is Contraigh / Spring Tide and Neap Tide* (1977). The poet's war experiences in the desert feature in poems such as 'Heroes' ('Curaidhean'), 'An Autumn Day' ('Latha Foghair') and 'Death Valley' ('Glac a Bhàis'), but there are no polemics against fascism here, rather a resigned wisdom and compassion for the living and the dead of either side. From such experience, perhaps, Maclean's socialism has not retained the bitter certainties of his youth, and in this respect he makes better poems from the modulated and complex insights of 'At Yeats's Grave' ('Aig Uaigh Yeats'), 'Palach', and 'The National Museum of Ireland' ('Ard-Mhusaeum na h-Eireann'). In 1939 he abandoned 'The Cuillin', a long symbolic poem as a meditation on communism and only sections of it have been published since.

Maclean's later work has come to have the power of a threnody or incantation sustained through a web of historical, cultural and family references within which traditional metaphors and his own singular and haunting images take their place. The elegy for his brother Calum Maclean takes a modern form to raise the old tradition of lament (*cumha*), while 'Hallaig' invokes an eerie beauty in a long deserted township on Raasay where his own ancestors lived before the place was cleared to make a sheep-farm in the 1850s. In this outstanding poem the trees become like girls in some vision of the past and its verses end with the symbolic death of Time, like a deer in the woods.

and when the sun goes down behind Dun Cana
a vehement bullet will come from the gun of Love;

and will strike the deer that goes dizzily,
sniffing at the grass-grown ruined homes;
his eye will freeze in the wood,
his blood will not be traced while I live.

As the son of the author of *Gillespie*, **George Campbell Hay** (**Deòrsa MacIain Deòrsa**, 1915–84), taught himself to speak Gaelic and wrote in English and Scots as well, which is a relatively unusual combination, although William Neill (b. 1922), was to take a similar route in the late sixties. Not surprisingly, given his scholarly nature and his nationalistic convictions, Hay's poems in Scots and Gaelic show interest in traditional modes, metrical structure and rhymes. Many of them celebrate the natural world, as in 'To a Bonny Birch Tree' 'Do Bheithe Boidheach' or 'Song' ('Oran'), and especially the sea in all its moods ('Pleasure and Courage'). Hay also follows classical themes with a ballad-like narrative approach in 'The Return of Ulysses' ('Tilleadh Uiliseis'), or a supernatural tale of shipwreck in the Scots poem 'The Three Brothers'. This delight in formal pattern, and his patriotic care for Scotland, is evident in 'The Four Winds of Scotland' ('Ceithir Gaothan na h-Albann'), while his feeling for weather and landscape features in 'An Ciùran Ceòban Ceò', for which he also has a most musical version in Scots – 'The Smoky Smirr o Rain':

> A misty mornin' doon the shore wi a hushed an' caller   fresh
>   air,
> an' ne'er a breath frae East or West tae sway the rashes
>   there,
> a sweet, sweet scent frae Laggan's birks gaed breathin'
>   on its ain,
> their branches hingin' beaded in the smoky smirr o
>   rain.
>
> The hills aroon war silent wi the mist alang the braes.
> The woods war derk an' quiet wi dewey, glintin'
>   sprays.
> The thrushes didna raise for me, as I gaed by alane,
> but a wee, wee cheep at passin' in the smoky smirr o
>   rain.

(Other Gaelic poems of Hay's were translated into Scots by his friend Douglas Young.) A much more agonised vision of the world, however, characterises 'Bisearta', based on his unhappy experiences during the war, when he saw Bizerta in flames in the distance while he stood night guard:

> What is their name tonight,
> the poor streets where every window spews
> its flame and smoke,
> its sparks and the screaming of its inmates,
> while house upon house is rent
> and collapses in a gust of smoke?
> And who tonight are beseeching
> Death to come quickly in all their tongues,
> or are struggling among stones and beams,
> crying in frenzy for help, and are not heard?
> Who tonight is paying
> the old accustomed tax of common blood?

A similarly impassioned empathy for the underdog informs 'Atman', a poem on behalf of an Arab convicted for theft by a well-fed judge, and he developed this concern in a distinguished long poem *Mochtar and Dougal* (*Mochtàr is Dùghall*), which was not published until 1982. Hay's peace of mind was damaged by the war, and he wrote at infrequent intervals, but recent work showed no diminution of his powers.

Derick Thomson (Ruaridh MacThómais, b. 1921)

As critic, scholar, and founder-editor of the quarterly *Gairm* since 1952, Derick Thomson has played a leading part in Scottish Gaelic studies, and most of his own poems from previous collections can be found in *Creachadh na Clàrsaich / Plundering the Harp* (1982). His language is more colloquial than Maclean's and he uses freer verse-forms, although of course he still draws on Gaelic's capacity to use subtle rhymes and assonances in the vowels within a sequence of words. Over the years his work has shown a sustained engagement with his origins in Lewis in relation to the wider world beyond. As an academic educated at Aberdeen and Cambridge, and after years as a professor of Celtic at Glasgow University, Thomson cannot look back on the distant island of his boyhood without recognising that there is no longer a working-place for him in it. The poem 'Coffins' ('Cisteachan-laighe'), from his second collection, describes what has happened to him and others like him by remembering his grandfather as a carpenter making coffins. He associates the process with his own education, in which English was compulsory, and, indeed, until a generation ago Gaelic children were actively dissuaded from speaking Gaelic in the classroom at any time:

> And in the other school also,
> where the joiners of the mind were planing,
> I never noticed the coffins,
> though they were sitting all around me;
> I did not recognise the English braid,
> the Lowland varnish being applied to the wood,
> I did not read the words on the brass,
> I did not understand that my race was dying.
> Until the cold wind of this Spring came
> to plane the heart;
> Until I felt the nails piercing me,
> and neither tea nor talk will help the pain.

The same sad recognition informs the plaintive cadences of 'When This Fine Snow is Falling' ('Triomh Uinneig a' Chithe'), but there is a sharper edge to poems such as 'Steel?' ('Cruaidh?') and 'Strathnaver' ('Srath Nabhair'), which manage a bitter wit at the recollection of the Clearances:

> And throw away soft words,
> for soon you will have no words left;
> The *Tuatha De Danann* are underground,
> the Land of the Ever-young is in France,
> and when you reach the Promised Land,
> unless you are on your toes,
> a bland Englishman will meet you,
> and say to you that God, his uncle, has given him a title to the land.

('Steel')

(The Tuatha De Danann are a supernatural race in Ireland, sometimes said to be progenitors of the fairies.) 'Donegal' and 'Budapest' extend this wry rage beyond Scotland's borders, while the fine movement of 'Between Summer and Autumn' ('Eadar Samradh is Foghar') shows the music of Thomson's Gaelic in a quieter mood:

> Up from the sea, in a lonely hollow
> is a patch of grass where the shoots were bruised,
> on a summer's day I can never forget;
> but when I garner both grass and corn,
> autumn stays not for me in the stacks,
> nor will summer return though I will it so.
>
> The sea lay below me, white and red,
> white-skinned wave-crest and dark-blue trough,
> receding and nearing,
> joy with its breath held,
> swelling and breaking,
> with healing in its hurting;
> and I grasped a moment
> to think of the mutability
> that lay below me,
> and to think of the constancy
> that I see now I utterly lacked.

The bitter-sweet and intimate relationship between Thomson and his homeland becomes the central theme of *An Rathad Cian / The Far Road* (1970), a collection of fifty-six linked lyrics in free verse. The poet's clear images seem to rise in the most unforced way from the natural landscape or from casual memories, and yet they accumulate to make the book his most sustained statement to date – timeless as Mackay Brown's *Fishermen with Ploughs*, but more in touch with the contemporary world and with his own wry distance from the island he is visiting. Thomson does not make Lewis into Edwin Muir's remembered Eden, but there is a strongly elegiac note in many of his poems; and somewhere between the shafts of his anger and the eloquent music of memory and longing there is an acceptance and a submission to fate which Maclean, for example, resists by turning to the more strenuous tradition of recollection. For Maclean, the evocation of dates, places and names in family or cultural history (as in the lament for his brother, or 'Screapadal') becomes an act of affirmation, with implications for community memory and an understanding of history. Thomson's, by contrast, is a more personal sense of history, with an essentially lyrical and *triste* vision. This seems to lie at the heart of his work even if he has produced topical and satirical verses, or political allegories such as 'The Eagle' ('An Iolaire') or 'The Plough' ('An Crann').

⠀Aspects of Iain Crichton Smith's Gaelic poetry have already been discussed, but the example of his Gaelic short stories and novels should not be underestimated, for this is a small but growing development in Highland publishing, to which John Murray (Iain Moireach) and the Revd Colin Mackenzie (Cailein MacCoinnich) have also contributed.

Donald MacAulay (Domhnall MacAmhlaigh, b. 1930), is yet another Lewis man (it seems to be an island of poets) whose work looks to his origins, critically and otherwise. He is moved by traditional psalm-singing and by the 'liberating, cascading melody' of Gaelic prayer, which is 'my people's access to poetry' ('Gospel 1955': 'Soisgeul 1955'); or he deplores the narrowness of religion, as in 'Self-righteousness' ('Fein-Fhìreantachd'). A spell in Turkey led him to recognise the social intolerance of the small community which is his home ('Amasra, 1957' and 'Holiday': 'Latha Feill'), while his poem 'For Pasternak, for Example . . .' ('Do Phasternak, mar Eiseamplair . . .') reflects on how a poet must sustain his art against the 'contrary wind'. MacAulay is professor of Celtic at Aberdeen, and his work features in an anthology edited by himself, *Nua-bhàrdachd Ghaidlig / Modern Scottish Gaelic Poems* (1976), which contains work by all the above-mentioned writers as well. Among the younger generation notable poetry has been published by Angus Nicolson (Aonghas MacNeacail, b. 1942), Catriona Montgomery (Catriona Nic-Gumaraid, b. 1947) and Fergus MacKinlay (Feargus MacFionnaigh, b. 1948).

Contemporary writing

As a coherent movement the Scottish Renaissance probably ended somewhere in the sixties, although of course the liveliness of the contemporary literary scene cannot be separated from those strong foundations. Some younger writers still see themselves as part of that tradition, while others would deny the fact, or are happily unaware of it. There are older writers, too, such as Muriel Spark and James Kennaway, whose Scottish origins can be discerned in their work, although they have taken little active part in the world of Scottish letters and have spent most of their lives out of the country. Robin Jenkins, on the other hand, has returned to Scotland, and, his Scottish novels, and even his books set in the Far East, show a sensibility deeply affected by the culture and the ethos of his native land. Even more notably, the 'Glasgow novelists' in the sixties and the new dramatists of the seventies have set out to express and to reassess the local and national character of Scottish life, usually in terms which combine a psychological or moral analysis of native inhibitions with a grim urban naturalism. George Douglas Brown's legacy of love and rage is still with us, and, if the house with the green shutters has been sublet and transported to the big cities, there is plenty of desperate life in those rooms yet, as well, perhaps, as a tendency to haunt already familiar ground.

Muriel Spark (b. 1918) spent the first eighteen years of her life in Edinburgh before moving to London and then to Rome. She feels herself to be a 'constitutional exile' in Edinburgh, and yet she recognises that certain habits of mind have survived from her youth. Several critics, too, would claim a distinctively Scottish strain in her work. *The Prime of Miss Jean Brodie* (1961) relates to a clash between different kinds of authority –

indirectly Calvinist and Catholic – as played out between a schoolteacher and the disciple who will eventually betray her. Other readers see a Scottish flavour in Spark's 'mordant irony', and, in either case, the complex moral fate of Jean Brodie, and her confusions between liberal and elitist values, gave Muriel Spark one of her best and best-known novels.

Robin Jenkins (b. 1912) did not identify himself with the Renaissance writers, and having worked as a schoolteacher and travelled widely, he was forty-eight before his first book was published. Nevertheless, most of his novels are set in Scotland (although he has written fiction set around Afghanistan and the Middle East) and they take issue with central problems of morality and the nature of innocence, goodness and maturity in a world seemingly hostile to such qualities. Jenkins sees the urban west of Scotland as a place of crumbling streets or stifling gentility, brutal crowds and lonely individuals, and he sets this against the nearby Highlands as a place of remote beauty, old estates or isolated forests. Of course, good and evil can be found in either scene, but Jenkins's novels gain power from his use of such settings where he finds the symbols which suit the poetic or metaphysical nature of his vision. *The Thistle and the Grail* (1954) describes its Scottish town as a crowded place where all the petty frustrations and hopes of the narrow spirits who live there are given over to football, while *The Cone Gatherers* (1955), has a simpler and more poetic sense of tragic inevitability. It takes place on a country estate during the Second World War, as if a parable of that wider evil were being acted out among the trees and cones, which symbolise both darkness and seed for the future. The action unfolds between a retarded, kindly and hunchbacked forestry worker and the obsessed and unhappy gamekeeper who comes to hate him as he hates his sick wife and his own dire nature. The simpleton's brother and the aristocratic lady owner of the estate are left shaken at the end, after the murder of the poor fellow and the gamekeeper's suicide – as if they had witnessed some cathartic ritual act. Jenkins's predominantly ethical imagination finds one of its best expressions in *A Would-be Saint* (1978), an understated study of the ambiguities of unforced goodness and the problems which it brings to Gavin Hamilton's life as he grows up during the Depression. When war breaks out he becomes a conscientious objector, leaving town to work in the forests, which become the stage for his confrontation with himself and what he owes to a world which cannot understand him. The novelist's most virulent and ambivalent account of cultural life and spiritual failure in Scotland is given in *Fergus Lamont* (1979), the 'autobiography' of a soldier and poet during the 'Renaissance' period. It charts the rise and fall of an egocentric, creative, self-destructive and hypocritical man in a career of repeated petty betrayals and lost love.

It was the failure of another military career through psychological and class conflict which distinguished *Tunes of Glory* (1956), the accomplished first novel by **James Kennaway** (1928–68). The book centres on the characterisation of Colonel Jock Sinclair, a hard-drinking, hard-fighting, vain, coarse, immature, obsolete old soldier, who seems doomed to destroy himself in a clash with the Sandhurst officer who arrives to replace him as acting head of a Highland regiment. In the end it is the new commander who commits suicide and Jock survives to suffer a final breakdown. Kennaway's own restless emotional life was something of a struggle in between bouts of obsessively hard writing. His subsequent novels often deal with destructive marital or emotional conflicts within a family or between lovers, and he gave a specifically Scottish setting to *Household Ghosts* (1961).

By comparison the novels and stories of **Elspeth Davie** (b. 1919) offer a much quieter, but no less sensitive, account of bourgeois life within the daily setting of the city – most usually Edinburgh, where she lives. The stories in *The High Tide Talker* (1976), contain memorable images of the lonely and unique nature of ordinary people conveyed in a clear and subtly polished style. Her novel *Creating a Scene* (1971) deals with the relationship between two art-students and their teacher during a project to help to 'humanise' a housing-scheme. Grimly urban settings in the crowded west of Scotland feature in many novels of the sixties, which set out to explore the nature of 'Scottishness' and the difficulties of achieving any kind of creative life in such an environment.

Alan Sharp (b. 1934) worked in the Clydeside shipyards when he left school before going on to university and eventually to London and America, where he is now a successful screen-writer. *A Green Tree in Gedde* (1965) and *The Wind Shifts* (1976) are the first two volumes of a triology which was never completed. They follow the lives, thoughts and journeys of four characters in search of 'home' in an effort to understand and explore existential questions of sexuality and identity. Sharp set himself a large scale task with these picaresque novels, and under the influence of Henry Miller and Joyce he adopted a highly-wrought and various prose, moving from impersonal narrative to impressionism, terse dialogue and elaborately poetic evocations. It was a brilliant and ambitious debut, but Sharp seems to have left it unfinished with something of an air of relief. **Gordon Williams** (b. 1934) has a clearer and more professionally economical prose style, and a sharper rage at the nature of Scottish failings – especially in matters of drink, sexual guilt and physical violence. *From Scenes Like These* (1968) accumulates these aspects of the national inferiority-complex in the life of young Dunky Logan, to create one of the darkest pictures of Scottish life since *Gillespie. Walk Don't Walk* (1972) is more cheerfully scathing about national limitations, as it tells how a Scots novelist copes with a promotion-tour of America, when all his images of that country have come to him from his boyhood love of Hollywood films. The novels of George Friel (1910–75), on the other hand, have stayed in Glasgow to chronicle the lives of lonely individuals against the pressures of the city – most notably in his grimmest and last novel, *Mr Alfred, MA* (1972).

William McIlvanney (b. 1936) explored the environmental and family tensions of life in the urban west with his first two novels – *Remedy is None* (1966) and *A Gift from Nessus* (1968). His third book, *Docherty* (1975), links the 'hard man' theme to expressive naturalism in order to describe the hardship and courage of his hero's life as a coal-miner, seen from the point of view of his son in the years before and during the Depression. An equally deeply felt and indirectly autobiographical account of working-class aspiration is sustained in *The Dear Green Place* (1964) by Archie Hind (b. 1928), in which its protagonist's unsophisticated commitment to his own talent and his dreams of being a novelist are described against the hardships of his background and social circumstances. The well-written stories of Alan Spence and Carl MacDougall derive from similar roots in colloquial realism, and an equally humorously bizarre development from this mode has appeared in the collection *Not Not While the Giro* (1983) by James Kelman. The most striking and far-reaching achievement in recent fiction has been *Lanark* (1981), the work of many years, written and illustrated by **Alasdair Gray** (b. 1934). It is a large, complex, nightmarish and witty novel, which takes its hero beyond sordid urban realism, and beyond life itself, to explore the author's surreal and anti-utopian vision of modern society. With a very Scottish combination of scholarly weight and flippancy, this extraordinary book follows in the modernist tradition of Kafka, Burroughs and Borges, and yet it belongs equally convincingly to the allegorical visions of *The City of Dreadful Night, A Voyage to Arcturus* or the fantasy-worlds of George MacDonald. Further prose-writers who show a welcome awareness of modern European and American literature would include Giles Gordon, Alan Massie and John Herdman whose *Pagan's Pilgrimage* (1978) explored the pains and perversities of the Scottish Presbyterian sensibility with an acerbically philosophical and satirical style.

These writers bring us to an immediately contemporary generation whose work is still in the process of defining what the map of Scottish literature will look like in the last thirty years of the century. Tom Buchan and Alan Jackson came to prominence in the late sixties as poets who made their muse a medium for popular expression and social comment. The plainer political and personal verses of Alan Bold are equally accessible, as are the poems of Ken Morrice, Robin Bell, Valerie Gillies and the spritely wit with which Liz Lochhead recounts personal relationships and the female condition. Stewart Conn makes a sparer and more reflective verse out of his thoughts on family life, while Alasdair Maclean derives a darker and more personal vision from his west Highland background. Douglas Dunn's poems have been widely published and broadcast, and since his return to Scotland Northern themes – especially in *St Kilda's Parliament* (1981) – have begun to engage him more. Kenneth Whyte and Alastair Reid have lived mostly in France and America, and their poetry, especially Whyte's, has a sparer intellectual focus – reminiscent, perhaps, of the fine poems of Burns Singer (1928–64), and equally notable in the analytical reserve of Robin Fulton, a long-time editor of *Lines Review* who is currently working in Scandinavia. George Macbeth has taken a much more surreal vein, although his recent poetry has abandoned black humour in favour of a gentler response to nature. On the other hand, the finely modulated longer verses of David Black have created a remarkably consistent fantasy-world out of his interest in archetypal images and Grimm-like tales, while the poems of Roderick Watson meditate on how landscapes and objects are marked by the past and permeated by memory. Walter Perrie shows a similar interest in modernist techniques in the linked themes of his longer poems, as do Ron Butlin and Andrew Greig. The story – and the fable too – is still unwinding in all three of Scotland's languages, but let us 'mak up work heirof', as Douglas says, 'and clos our buke'.

Further reading

Literary history

BOLD, ALAN: *Modern Scottish Literature* (London: Longman, 1983).
—— *The Ballad* (London: Methuen, 1979).
BUCHAN, DAVID: *The Ballad and the Folk* (London: Routledge and Kegan Paul, 1972).
CAMPBELL, IAN: *Kailyard: A New Assessment* (Edinburgh: Ramsay Head Press, 1981).
—— (ed.): *Nineteeth Century Scottish Fiction* (Manchester: Carcanet, 1979).
CRAIG, DAVID: *Scottish Literature and the Scottish People, 1680–1830* (London: Chatto and Windus, 1961).
DAICHES, DAVID: *The Paradox of Scottish Culture* (London: Oxford University Press, 1964).
—— (ed.): *A Companion to Scottish Culture* (London: Edward Arnold, 1981).
——: *Literature and Gentility in Scotland* (Edinburgh: Edinburgh University Press, 1982).
FULTON, ROBIN: *Contemporary Scottish Poetry* (Edinburgh: Macdonald, 1974).
GLEN, DUNCAN: *Hugh MacDiarmid and the Scottish Renaissance* (Edinburgh: Chambers, 1964).
HART, FRANCIS: *The Scottish Novel* (London: John Murray, 1978).
HENDERSON, T. F.: *Scottish Vernacular Literature*, 3rd rev. edn (Edinburgh: John Grant, 1910).
HUTCHISON, DAVID: *The Modern Scottish Theatre* (Glasgow: Molendinar Press, 1977).
LINDSAY, MAURICE: *History of Scottish Literature* (London: Robert Hale, 1977).
MACLEAN, MAGNUS: *The Literature of the Highlands* (London and Glasgow: Blackie, 1925).
MILLAR, J. H.: *A Literary History of Scotland* (London: Fisher Unwin, 1903)
ROYLE, TREVOR: *The Macmillan Companion to Scottish Literature* (London: Macmillan, 1983).
SMITH, G. GREGORY: *Scottish Literature, Character and Influence* (London: Macmillan, 1919).
THOMSON, DERICK: *An Introduction to Gaelic Poetry* (London: Gollancz, 1974).
—— (ed.): *A Companion to Gaelic Scotland* (Oxford: Blackwell, 1983).
WITTIG, KURT: *The Scottish Tradition in Literature* (Edinburgh: Oliver and Boyd, 1958).

BIBLIOGRAPHY

AITKEN, WILLIAM R.: *Scottish Literature in English and Scots* (Detroit, Mich.: Gale Research, 1982).

BURGESS, MOIRA: *The Glasgow Novel 1870–1970* (Glasgow: Scottish Library Association, 1972).

History

CAMPBELL, R. H.: *Scotland since 1707* (Oxford: Blackwell, 1965).

—— and SKINNER, A. S.: *The Origins and Nature of the Scottish Enlightenment* (Edinburgh: John Donald, 1982).

CHITNIS, ANAND, C.: *The Scottish Enlightenment: A Social History* (London: Croom Helm, 1976).

DAICHES, DAVID: *Scotland and the Union* (London: John Murray, 1977).

DICKINSON, W. C.: *Scotland from the Earliest Times to 1603* (Edinburgh: Edinburgh University Press, 1965).

FERGUSON, WILLIAM: *Scotland 1689 to the Present* (Edinburgh: Oliver and Boyd, 1968).

HARVIE, CHRISTOPHER: *Scotland and Nationalism* (London: Allen and Unwin, 1977).

KERMACK, W. R.: *The Scottish Highlands: A Short History, 1300–1746* (Edinburgh: Johnston and Bacon, 1957).

LENMAN, BRUCE: *An Economic History of Modern Scotland 1660–1976* (London: Batsford, 1977).

RENDALL, JANE: *The Origins of the Scottish Enlightenment* (London: Macmillan, 1978).

SMOUT, T. C.: *A History of the Scottish People 1560–1830* (London: Collins, 1969).

General

AITKEN, A. J. and McARTHUR, T. (eds): *Languages of Scotland* (Edinburgh: Chambers, 1979).

ASH, MARINELL: *The Strange Death of Scottish History* (Edinburgh: Ramsay Head Press, 1980).

CAMERON, DAVID KERR: *The Ballad and the Plough* (London: Gollancz, 1978).

COLLINSON, F. M.: *The Traditional and National Music of Scotland* (London: Routledge and Kegan Paul, 1966).

CRAWFORD, THOMAS: *Society and the Lyric: A Study of the Song Culture of Eighteenth Century Scotland* (Edinburgh: Scottish Academic Press, 1979).

DAVIE, GEORGE ELDER: *The Democratic Intellect* (Edinburgh: Edinburgh University Press, 1964).

DUNBAR, JOHN TELFER: *Highland Costume* (Edinburgh: William Blackwood, 1977).

FYFE, J. G. (ed.): *Scottish Diaries and Memoirs 1550–1746* (Stirling: Eneas Mackay, 1928).

—— *Scottish Diaries and Memoirs 1746–1843* (Stirling: Eneas Mackay, 1942).

GRAHAM, HENRY G.: *The Social Life of Scotland in the Eighteenth Century* (London: A. and C. Black, 1909).

HAY, GEORGE: *Architecture of Scotland* (Northumberland: Oriel Press, 1977).

MACAULAY, DONALD (ed.): *Modern Scottish Gaelic Poems* (Edinburgh: Southside, 1976).

MACNEILL, SEUMAS: *Piobaireachd* (Edinburgh: BBC, 1968).

McNEILL, F. MARIAN: *The Silver Bough*, 4 vols (Glasgow: William Maclellan, 1957–68).

MILLER, KARL (ed.): *Memoirs of a Modern Scotland* (London: Faber and Faber, 1970).

MILLMAN, R. N.: *The Making of the Scottish Landscape* (London: Batsford, 1975).

MUIR, EDWIN: *Scott and Scotland* (Edinburgh: Polygon Books, 1982).

MURISON, DAVID: *The Guid Scots Tongue* (Edinburgh: William Blackwood, 1977).

ROSS, ANNE: *Folklore of the Scottish Highlands* (London: Batsford, 1976).

SCOTTISH GAELIC TEXTS SOCIETY: The works of almost all the older Gaelic poets, usually with translations and helpful introductions, can be found in the publications of this society in Edinburgh.

SHIRE, HELENA M.: *Song, Dance and Poetry at the Court of Scotland under James VI* (Cambridge: Cambridge University Press, 1969).

THOMPSON, HAROLD W.: *A Scottish Man of Feeling: Some Account of Henry MacKenzie Esq. of Edinburgh and of the Golden Age of Burns and Scott* (London: Oxford University Press, 1931).

WATSON, W. J. (ed.): *Bàrdachd Ghàidhlig: Specimens of Gaelic Poetry 1550–1900* (Glasgow: An Comuun Gaidhealach, 1959).

Chronological table

Abbreviations: *d.* = dies; D = drama; P = prose; *r.* = reigned; V = verse

DATE	AUTHOR	EVENT
500		*Scoti* established in Dalriada
c.600	*Gododdin* (V)	Battle between Welsh and Angles at Catterick
1058		Malcolm III Canmore (*r.* 1058–93)
1093	*Duan Albanach* (V)	
1124		David I (*r.* 1124–53)
1200	Scottish Gaelic bardic poetry well established	
1249	The 'golden age'	Alexander III (*r.* 1249–86)
1286		Disputes over Scottish succession
1297		Wallace; Battle of Stirling Bridge The War of Independence (1296–1328)
1305		Wallace executed in London
1306		Bruce kills Comyn; crowned king (*r.* 1306–29)
1314		Battle of Bannockburn
1320		Declaration of Arbroath
1374–5	Barbour, *The Bruce* (V)	
1394		James I *r.* 1394–1437)
1400		Chaucer *d.*
1406		James I captured by English

DATE	AUTHOR	EVENT
1411	Lachlann MacMhuirich, *Harlaw Brosnachadh* (V)	Battle of Harlaw
1412		University of St Andrews founded
c.1424	James I, *The Kingis Quair* (V)	
1437		James II (r.1437–60)
c. 1450	Holland, *Buke of the Howlat* (V)	
1451	Sir Gilbert Hay, *The Buke of Armys* (P)	University of Glasgow founded
1460	Corcadail, 'O rosary that recalled my tear' (V)	James III (r.1460–88)
c.1460	Henryson, *The Morall Fabillis* and *Testament of Cresseid* (V)	
1470		Malory, *Morte d'Arthur*
c.1477	Blind Harry, *Wallace* (V)	
1478		Caxton prints *Canterbury Tales*
1488		James IV (r.1488–1513)
1495	Dunbar, poems at court	University of Aberdeen founded Erasmus at Oxford W. Indies discovered by Columbus
1509		Henry VIII takes throne of England
1512	Book of the Dean of Lismore (collection of Gaelic verse)	
1513	Gavin Douglas, *Eneados* (V)	Battle of Flodden James V (r.1513–42)
1520		Luther, 'On Christian Freedom'; Papal ban
1533	Bellenden translates Boece's *History and Chronicles of Scotland* (1527) into Scots (P)	
1542		Mary Queen of Scots (r.1542–87) Copernicus, *De Revolutionibus* (1543)
1549	*The Complaynt of Scotland* (P)	

DATE	AUTHOR	EVENT
1552	Sir David Lindsay, full performance of *The Thrie Estaits* (D)	
1557	George Buchanan, *Jephtha* (Latin D)	
1558		Elizabeth I takes throne of England
1560	Knox *et al.*, *First Book of Discipline*	Reformation Parliament
1567	Wedderburn brothers, *Gude and Godlie Ballatis* (V)	James VI (*r.* 1567–1625)
1568	Bannatyne Manuscript (V)	
1570		Donald Mor MacCrimmon born; family piping-dynasty established in Skye
c.1575	Robert Lindsay of Pitscottie, *History and Chronicles of Scotland* (P)	
1580s	James VI and 'Castalian band' at court (V) Poems of Alexander Scott	University of Edinburgh founded (1582) Montaigne, *Essais* Shakespeare, *Love's Labours Lost*
1597	Montgomerie, *The Cherry and the Slae* (V)	
1603		UNION OF CROWNS; James VI goes to London
1605		Bacon, *Advancement of Learning* Shakespeare, *King Lear.*
1611		King James Bible Galileo discovers moons of Jupiter
1614	Drummond, *Poems* (V)	
1620		Mayflower sets sail for America
1623	Drummond, *Flowers of Sion* (V) and *A Cypresse Grove* (P)	
1625		Charles I (*r.* 1625–49)
1637–8		Riot in St Giles'; National Covenant Descartes, *Discourse on Method*
1639		Civil War (1639–49)

DATE	AUTHOR	EVENT
1643		Solemn League and Covenant
1649–51		Charles I executed; Montrose hanged; Commonwealth established Charles II crowned at Scone; Scotland subdued under Monck
c. 1650	Robert Sempill, 'Habbie Simson' (V)	
1653	Urquhart translates Rabelais (P)	
1660	Gaelic poetry on Montrose wars and exhortations to Charles, by Iain Lom	Restoration of Charles II (r. 1660–85) Royal Society established
1666		Covenanters march on Edinburgh; Battle of Rullion Green 'The Killing Times'
1667		Milton, *Paradise Lost*
1679		Covenanters defeated at Battle of Bothwell Brig
1685		James VII and II (r. 1685–1701)
1686		Newton, *Principia*
1688		'The Glorious Revolution'; James dethroned William and Mary (r. 1689–1702)
1690		William defeats James at Battle of the Boyne
1692		Massacre of Glencoe
1698		Darien scheme
1701	Gaelic poems by Niall MacMhuirich and Morison ('An clàrsair dall')	James II dies; his son the 'Old Pretender' recognised by Louis XIV as heir to British throne Queen Anne (r. 1702–14)
1704	Fletcher of Saltoun opposes Union (P)	
1707		UNION OF PARLIAMENTS

DATE	AUTHOR	EVENT
1706–11	Watson (ed.), *Choice Collection* (V)	Pope, *Essay on Criticism* Shaftesbury, *Characteristics of Men, Manners* (1711)
1715		George I (r. 1714–27) Jacobite rising for Old Pretender
1721	Ramsay, *Poems* (V)	
1722		Bach, *Well-tempered Clavier*
1724	Ramsay (ed.), *Tea Table Miscellany* and *The Ever Green* (V)	Swift, *Drapier's Letters*
1725	Ramsay, *The Gentle Shepherd* (D)	
1727		George II (r. 1727–60)
1729		Swift, *A Modest Proposal*
1730	James Thomson, *The Seasons* (V)	
1736		Porteous riots in Edinburgh
1739–40	Hume, *Treatise of Human Nature* (P) 'The Scottish Enlightenment'	Richardson, *Pamela* Handel, *Messiah* (1742)
1745		Jacobite rising for Charles Edward Stuart
1746		Battle of Culloden
1748	Hume, *An Enquiry Concerning Human Understanding* (P)	Smollett, *Adventures of Roderick Random* Richardson, *Clarissa*
1751	Gaelic poems of MacMhaighstir Alasdair published in Edinburgh	
1756	Home, *Douglas* (VD)	
1759	Adam Smith, *Theory of Moral Sentiments* (P)	Voltaire, *Candide* Sterne, *Tristram Shandy*
1760s	'Gaelic vernacular revival' Poetry of Rob Donn	

DATE	AUTHOR	EVENT
1760	James Macpherson, *Fragments of Ancient Poetry* ('Ossian') (V)	George III (*r.* 1760–1820)
1761		Rousseau, *Julie, ou la Nouvelle Héloise*
1764–5		Walpole, *Castle of Otranto*
1767–8	Gaelic poems by Duncan Bàn Macintyre and Duguld Buchanan published in Edinburgh	Percy's *Reliques*
	Gaelic poems of MacCodrum	
1770		Watt's steam condenser; Industrial Revolution
		Rousseau, *Confessions.*
1771	Henry Mackenzie, *The Man of Feeling* (P)	
	Encyclopaedia Britannica published in Edinburgh	
1773	Fergusson, *Poems* (V)	Goethe, *Werther* (1774)
		Priestley discovers oxygen
1766	Adam Smith, *Wealth of Nations* (P)	American War of Independence
1780s	Gaelic poems of Ross	Kant, *Critique of Pure Reason* (1781)
1785	Boswell, *Tour of the Hebrides* (P)	
1786	Burns, *Poems, Chiefly in the Scottish Dialect*, Kilmarnock edn (V)	
1787– 1803	Burns (ed.), *Scots Musical Museum*	Mozart, *Don Giovanni* (1787)
		Charles Edward Stuart dies (1788)
1789		French Revolution
		Blake, *Songs of Innocence*
1790		Paine, *Rights of Man*
1791	Boswell, *Life of Johnson* (P)	Wordsworth and Coleridge, *Lyrical Ballads*
1798		

DATE	AUTHOR	EVENT
1800		Napoleon in power Beethoven, First Symphony
1802	Jeffrey starts *Edinburgh Review* Sir Walter Scott (ed.), *Border Minstrelsy*	
1805	Scott, *Lay of the Last Minstrel* (V)	Battles of Trafalgar and Austerlitz
1810	Scott, *The Lady of the Lake* (V)	
1811		Luddite riots
1812		Byron's *Childe Harold*, I and II Austen, *Pride and Prejudice*
1813	Hogg, *The Queen's Wake* (V)	
1814	Scott, *Waverley* (P)	
1815		Battle of Waterloo
1816	Scott, *The Antiquary* and *Old Mortality* (P)	Beethoven, Fifth Symphony
1817	*Blackwood's Magazine* founded	Keats, *Poems*
1818	Scott, *The Heart of Midlothian* (P)	
1819	Scott, *Ivanhoe* (P)	'Peterloo Massacre' Schopenhauer, *The World as Will and Idea*
1820		George III (*r*.1820–30)
1821	Galt, *The Ayreshire Legatees* and *Annals of the Parish* (P)	Constable, *The Hay Wain* Napoleon *d*.
1823	Galt, *Ringan Gilhaize* (P)	
1824	Hogg, *Confessions of a Justified Sinner* (P)	
1830		William IV (*r*.1830–7) Stendhal, *Le Rouge et le Noir*
1832		First Reform Bill
1836	Carlyle, *Sartor Resartus* (P)	Dickens, *Pickwick Papers*

DATE	AUTHOR	EVENT
1837	Carlyle, *The French Revolution* (P)	Victoria (*r.* 1837–1901)
1841	Carlyle, *On Heroes and Hero Worship* (P)	Edinburgh–Glasgow railway-line opens (1842)
1843		Disruption of the Church of Scotland: United Free Church formed
1840–60	Gaelic poetry of Livingstone *Whistle-Binkie* anthologies (V) and 'Spasmodics' (D, V) Novels of Mrs Oliphant	'Year of Revolutions' in Europe (1848) Marx–Engels, *Communist Manifesto* (1848) Tennyson, *In Memoriam* 1850) Melville, *Moby Dick* (1851) Crimean War (1854–6) Baudelaire, *Les Fleurs du Mal* (1857) Darwin, *Origin of Species* (1859)
1858	George MacDonald, *Phantastes* (P)	
1870s	Gaelic poetry of John Smith	
1879	Stevenson, *Travels with a Donkey* (P)	Ibsen, *A Doll's House* Tay Bridge disaster
1880–1	James Thomson, *City of Dreadful Night* (V)	Dostoevsky, *The Brothers Karamazov*
1882	Gaelic poetry of Mary Macpherson	The 'battle of Braes' on Skye Highland Land League
1883	Stevenson, *Treasure Island* (P)	
1886	Stevenson, *Dr Jekyll and Mr Hyde* and *Kidnapped* (P)	Daimler Benz motor car Seurat, *La Grande Jatte* English translation of *Das Kapital*
1888	Barrie, *Auld Licht Idylls* (P)	Scottish Labour Party formed with Keir Hardie and Cunninghame Graham
1889	Stevenson, *The Master of Ballantrae* (P) Barrie, *A Window in Thrums* (P)	Yeats, *The Wanderings of Oisin*
1890	MacGonagall, *Poetic Gems*	Forth rail bridge completed
1893	Davidson, *Fleet Street Eclogues* (V)	

DATE	AUTHOR	EVENT
	Crockett, *The Stickit Minister* (P)	
1894	Maclaren, *Beside the Bonnie Briar Bush* (P) Sharp, *Pharais* (P)	The Yellow Book Debussy, *L'Apres-midi d'un faune*
1895	George MacDonald, *Lilith* (P)	Trial of Oscar Wilde
1896	Stevenson, *Weir of Hermiston* (P) Munro, *The Last Pibroch* (P)	
1898	Buchan, *John Burnet of Barns* (P)	
1900	Charles Murray, *Hamewith* (V) Cunninghame Graham, *Thirteen Stories* (P)	Freud, *Interpretation of Dreams* Sibelius, *Finlandia* Chekhov, *Uncle Vania*
1901	George Douglas Brown, *The House with the Green Shutters* (P)	Edward VII (r.1901–10)
1904	Barrie, *Peter Pan* (D)	Rennie Mackintosh designs Willow Tea Rooms in Glasgow Synge, *Riders to the Sea*
1907	Davidson, *Testament of John Davidson* (V) John MacDougall Hay, *Gillespie* (P)	Picasso, *Les Demoiselles d'Avignon* Bergson, *Creative Evolution*
1910		George V (r.1910–36) Marsh (ed.), *Georgian Poetry* (1911)
1913	Compton Mackenzie, *Sinister Street* (P)	Stravinsky, *Rite of Spring* Lawrence, *Sons and Lovers*
1914		First World War (1914–18) Yeats, *Responsibilities* Joyce, *Dubliners*
1915	Buchan, *The Thirty-Nine Steps* (P) Norman Douglas, *Old Calabria* (P)	Einstein, General Theory of Relativity

DATE	AUTHOR	EVENT
1916		Easter Rising in Dublin
1917	Norman Douglas, *South Wind* (P)	Russian Revolution Jung, *The Unconscious*
1919		'40 Hour' strike in Glasgow. Troops called out; 'Red Clydeside'
1920	Grieve ('Hugh MacDiarmid') (ed.), *Northern Numbers* (1920–2) David Lindsay, *A Voyage to Arcturus* (P)	Prohibition in America (until 1933)
1922	Grieve (ed.), *Scottish Chapbook*	Eliot, *The Waste Land* Joyce, *Ulysses* Mussolini marches on Rome and forms Fascist government
1923		John Maclean *d.*
1925	MacDiarmid, *Sangschaw* (V) Muir, *First Poems* (V)	
1926	MacDiarmid, *Penny Wheep* and *A Drunk Man Looks at the Thistle* (V) Gunn, *Grey Coast* (P)	General Strike Kafka, *The Castle*
1928		National Party of Scotland formed Women get vote in Britain
1929	Linklater, *White Maas Saga* (P) Grant and Murison, *Scottish National Dictionary* (1929–76)	Trotsky expelled from Russia Wall Street crash Labour government in Britain
1930	Bridie, *The Anatomist* (D)	Gandhi starts civil disobedience in India
1931	Linklater, *Juan in America* (P) MacDiarmid, *First Hymn to Lenin* (V)	Scottish Party formed MacDonald forms National Government to balance budget Riots in Glasgow and London; Naval mutiny at Invergordon
1932	Gibbon, *Sunset Song* (P) MacDiarmid, *Scots Unbound* (V) Muir, *Poor Tom* (P) MacColla, *The Albannach* (P)	Hunger marches in Britain

DATE	AUTHOR	EVENT
1933	Gibbon, *Cloud Howe* (P) Bridie, *A Sleeping Clergyman* (D) MacDiarmid, *Second Hymn to Lenin* (V)	Reichstag fire. Hitler takes power; Jews persecuted in Germany Orwell, *Down and Out in Paris and London*
1934	Gibbon, *Grey Granite* (P) Linklater, *Magnus Merriman* (P) MacDiarmid, *Stony Limits* (V)	Scottish National Party formed
1935	George Blake, *The Shipbuilders* (P) Soutar, *Poems in Scots*	
1936	Muir, *Scott and Scotland* (P) Craigie, Aitken and Stevenson, *Dictionary of the Older Scottish Tongue*	Edward VIII abdicates George VI (r. 1936–52) Spanish Ciivil War (1936–9)
1937	Gunn, *Highland River* (P) Muir, *Journeys and Places* (V) Compton Mackenzie, *The Four Winds of Love* (P) (1937–45) McLellan, *Jamie the Saxt* (D)	Scottish Gaelic Text Society
1939		Second World War (1939–45)
1941	Gunn, *The Silver Darlings* (P)	Battles of El Alamein and Stalingrad Pearl Harbor; America enters war
1943	Sorley Maclean, *Dain do Eimhir* (V) Lindsay (ed.), *Poetry Scotland* (V) (1943–9) MacDiarmid, *Lucky Poet* (P) MacCaig, *A Far Cry* (V)	
1944	Gunn, *The Green Isle of the Great Deep* (P) Bruce, *Sea Talk* (V)	D-Day Normandy landings Construction of atomic bomb Eliot, *Four Quartets*
1946	Linklater, *Private Angelo* (P)	
1948	Goodsir Smith, *Under the Eildon Tree* (V) Henderson, *Elegies for the Dead in Cyrenaica* (V)	Lindsay's *Satire of the Three Estates* performed at second Edinburgh International Festival

DATE	AUTHOR	EVENT
1949	Muir, *The Labyrinth* (V)	Orwell, *1984*
1950		Korean War (1950–3) Pound, *Cantos*
1951	Derick Thomson, *An Dealbh Briste* (V) Gunn, *The Well at the World's End* (P)	School of Scottish Studies founded
1953		Coronation of Elizabeth II Stalin *d.* Beckett, *Waiting for Godot*
1954	Muir, *An Autobiography* (P)	
1955	MacCaig, *Riding Lights* (V) MacDiarmid, *In Memoriam James Joyce* (V) Graham, *The Nightfishing* (V)	
1956	Jenkins, *The Cone Gatherers* (P) Gunn, *Atom of Delight* (P)	Suez crisis Russia invades Hungary
1959	Brown, *Loaves and Fishes* (V) Goodsir Smith, *Figs and Thistles* (V)	
1960	Muir, *Collected Poems* (V)	Oil discovered in North Sea
1961	Crichton Smith, *Thistles and Roses* (V) Jenkins, *Dust on the Paw* (P)	Berlin Wall built Mass CND rally in Trafalgar Square Gagarin in space
1962	MacDiarmid, *Collected Poems* (V)	Cuban missile crisis Solzhenitsyn, *One Day in the Life of Ivan Denisovich*
1963		Assassination of President Kennedy
1965	Crichton Smith, *Biobull is Sanasan Reice* (V) Sharp, *A Green Tree in Gedde* (P)	
1966	McIlvanney, *Remedy is None* (P) Garioch, *Selected Poems* (V)	Rise of SNP popular support

DATE	AUTHOR	EVENT
1967		Scottish Arts Council established
1968	Morgan, *The Second Life* (V) Crichton Smith, *Consider the Lilies* (P) Williams, *From Scenes Like These* (P)	Oil rigs in North Sea Moves towards Devolution proposed Martin Luther King assassinated
1970	Derick Thomson, *An Rathad Cian* (V) Crichton Smith, *Selected Poems* (V)	
1971	Davie, *Creating a Scene* (P) MacCaig, *Selected Poems* (V) George Mackay Brown, *Fishermen with Ploughs* (V)	

Index